(Continued on back endsheets)

Dictionary of Literary Biography®
Yearbook: 1993

Dictionary of Literary Biography®
Yearbook: 1993

Edited by
James W. Hipp

George Garrett, Consulting Editor

A Bruccoli Clark Layman Book
Gale Research Inc.
Detroit, London

Printed in the United States of America

Published simultaneously in the United Kingdom
by Gale Research International Limited
(An affiliated company of Gale Research Inc.)

The paper used in this publication meets the minimum requirements
of American National Standard for Information Sciences–Permanence
Paper for Printed Library Materials, ANSI Z39.48-1984. ∞ ™

Library of Congress Catalog Card Number 94–075218
ISBN 0-8103-5560-4

I(T)P

The trademark ITP is used under license.

10 9 8 7 6 5 4 3 2 1

Contents

Obituaries

Plan of the Series

. . . Almost the most prodigious asset of a country, and perhaps its most precious possession, is its native literary product – when that product is fine and noble and enduring.

Mark Twain*

The advisory board, the editors, and the publisher of the *Dictionary of Literary Biography* are joined in endorsing Mark Twain's declaration. The literature of a nation provides an inexhaustible resource of permanent worth. We intend to make literature and its creators better understood and more accessible to students and the reading public, while satisfying the standards of teachers and scholars.

To meet these requirements, *literary biography* has been construed in terms of the author's achievement. The most important thing about a writer is his writing. Accordingly, the entries in *DLB* are career biographies, tracing the development of the author's canon and the evolution of his reputation.

The purpose of *DLB* is not only to provide reliable information in a convenient format but also to place the figures in the larger perspective of literary history and to offer appraisals of their accomplishments by qualified scholars.

The publication plan for *DLB* resulted from two years of preparation. The project was proposed to Bruccoli Clark by Frederick C. Ruffner, president of the Gale Research Company, in November 1975. After specimen entries were prepared and typeset, an advisory board was formed to refine the entry format and develop the series rationale. In meetings held during 1976, the publisher, series editors, and advisory board approved the scheme for a comprehensive biographical dictionary of persons who contributed to North American literature. Editorial work on the first volume began in January 1977, and it was published in 1978. In order to make *DLB* more than a reference tool and to compile volumes that individually have claim to status as literary history, it was decided to organize volumes by topic, period, or genre. Each of these free-standing volumes provides a biographical-bibliographical guide and overview for a particular area of literature. We are convinced that this organization – as opposed to a single alphabet method – constitutes a valuable innovation in the presentation of reference material. The volume plan necessarily requires many decisions for the placement and treatment of authors who might properly be included in two or three volumes. In some instances a major figure will be included in separate volumes, but with different entries emphasizing the aspect of his career appropriate to each volume. Ernest Hemingway, for example, is represented in *American Writers in Paris, 1920–1939* by an entry focusing on his expatriate apprenticeship; he is also in *American Novelists, 1910–1945* with an entry surveying his entire career. Each volume includes a cumulative index of the subject authors and articles. Comprehensive indexes to the entire series are planned.

With volume ten in 1982 it was decided to enlarge the scope of *DLB*. By the end of 1986 twenty-one volumes treating British literature had been published, and volumes for Commonwealth and Modern European literature were in progress. The series has been further augmented by the *DLB Yearbooks* (since 1981) which update published entries and add new entries to keep the *DLB* current with contemporary activity. There have also been *DLB Documentary Series* volumes which provide biographical and critical source materials for figures whose work is judged to have particular interest for students. One of these companion volumes is entirely devoted to Tennessee Williams.

We define literature as the *intellectual commerce of a nation:* not merely as belles lettres but as that ample and complex process by which ideas are generated, shaped, and transmitted. *DLB* entries are not limited to "creative writers" but extend to other figures who in their time and in their way influenced the mind of a people. Thus the series encompasses historians, journalists, publishers, and screenwriters. By this means readers of *DLB* may be aided to perceive literature not as cult scripture in the keeping of intellectual high priests but firmly positioned at the center of a nation's life.

*From an unpublished section of Mark Twain's autobiography, copyright by the Mark Twain Company

DLB includes the major writers appropriate to each volume and those standing in the ranks immediately behind them. Scholarly and critical counsel has been sought in deciding which minor figures to include and how full their entries should be. Wherever possible, useful references are made to figures who do not warrant separate entries.

Each *DLB* volume has a volume editor responsible for planning the volume, selecting the figures for inclusion, and assigning the entries. Volume editors are also responsible for preparing, where appropriate, appendices surveying the major periodicals and literary and intellectual movements for their volumes, as well as lists of further readings. Work on the series as a whole is coordinated at the Bruccoli Clark Layman editorial center in Columbia, South Carolina, where the editorial staff is responsible for accuracy of the published volumes.

One feature that distinguishes *DLB* is the illustration policy – its concern with the iconography of literature. Just as an author is influenced by his surroundings, so is the reader's understanding of the author enhanced by a knowledge of his environment. Therefore *DLB* volumes include not only drawings, paintings, and photographs of authors, often depicting them at various stages in their careers, but also illustrations of their families and places where they lived. Title pages are regularly reproduced in facsimile along with dust jackets for modern authors. The dust jackets are a special feature of *DLB* because they often document better than anything else the way in which an author's work was perceived in its own time. Specimens of the writers' manuscripts are included when feasible.

Samuel Johnson rightly decreed that "The chief glory of every people arises from its authors." The purpose of the *Dictionary of Literary Biography* is to compile literary history in the surest way available to us – by accurate and comprehensive treatment of the lives and work of those who contributed to it.

The *DLB* Advisory Board

Foreword

The *Dictionary of Literary Biography Yearbook* is guided by the same principles that have provided the basic rationale for the entire *DLB* series: 1) the literature of a nation represents an inexhaustible resource of permanent worth; 2) the surest way to trace the outlines of literary history is by a comprehensive treatment of the lives and works of those who contributed to it; and 3) the greatest service the series can provide is to make literary achievement better understood and more accessible to students and the literate public, while serving the needs of scholars. In keeping with those principles, the *Yearbook* has been planned to augment *DLB* by reflecting the vitality of contemporary literature and summarizing current literary activity. The librarian, scholar, or student attempting to stay informed of literary developments is faced with an endless task. The purpose of *DLB Yearbook* is to serve those readers while at the same time enlarging the scope of *DLB*.

The *Yearbook* is divided into two sections: articles about the past year's literary events or topics; and obituaries and tributes. The updates and new author entries previously included as supplements to published *DLB* volumes have been omitted. (These essays will appear in future *DLB* volumes.) Among the pieces included in the articles section are a list of the archives of publishers, journals, and literary agents in North America, a printing of an unpublished section of H. L. Mencken's *My Life as Author and Editor,* a transcription of the reminiscences of antiquarian bookdealer Walter Goldwater, an account of the American Library in Paris, and extended discussions of the year's work in fiction, drama, literary theory, and literary biography. Due to unforeseen circumstances, the poetry segment has not been included. The *Yearbook* continues two surveys begun in 1987, an overview of new literary journals and an in-depth examination of the practice of book reviewing in America. In addition, the *Yearbook* features the Nobel speeches of the winner of the 1993 Nobel Prize in literature, Toni Morrison.

The death of a literary figure prompts an assessment of his achievements and reputation. The obituaries section marks the passing of Kay Boyle, Albert Erskine, Daniel Fuchs, William Haggard, William Ober, and Wallace Stegner.

Each *Yearbook* includes a list of literary prizes and awards, a necrology, and a checklist of literary histories and biographies published during the year.

This *Yearbook* continues the *Dictionary of Literary Biography Yearbook* Awards for novel, first novel, volume of short stories, and literary biography.

From the outset, the *DLB* series has undertaken to compile literary history as it is revealed in the lives and works of authors. The *Yearbook* supports that commitment, providing a useful and necessary current record.

Acknowledgments

This book was produced by Bruccoli Clark Layman, Inc. Karen L. Rood is senior editor for the *Dictionary of Literary Biography* series. James W. Hipp was the in-house editor.

Production coordinator is George F. Dodge. Photography editors are Edward Scott and Robert S. McConnell. Layout and graphics supervisor is Penney L. Haughton. Copyediting supervisor is Bill Adams. Typesetting supervisor is Kathleen M. Flanagan. Julie E. Frick is editorial associate. The production staff includes Phyllis A. Avant, Joseph Matthew Bruccoli, Ann M. Cheschi, Patricia Coate, Wilma Weant Dague, Brigitte B. de Guzman, Denise W. Edwards, Sarah A. Estes, Joyce Fowler, Laurel M. Gladden, Stephanie C. Hatchell, Jolyon M. Helterman, Rebecca Mayo, Kathy Lawler Merlette, Pamela D. Norton, Patricia F. Salisbury, and William L. Thomas, Jr.

Walter W. Ross and Deborah M. Chasteen did library research. They were assisted by the following librarians at the Thomas Cooper Library of the University of South Carolina: Linda Holderfield and the interlibrary-loan staff; reference librarians Gwen Baxter, Daniel Boice, Faye Chadwell, Cathy Eckman, Gary Geer, Qun "Gerry" Jiao, Jean Rhyne, Carol Tobin, Carolyn Tyler, Virginia Weathers, Elizabeth Whiznant, and Connie Widney; circulation-department head Thomas Marcil; and acquisitions-searching supervisor David Haggard.

The excerpt from *My Life as Author and Editor,* by H. L. Mencken, is published by permission of the Enoch Pratt Free Library of Baltimore in accordance with the terms of the will of H. L. Mencken.

Dictionary of Literary Biography®
Yearbook: 1993

Dictionary of Literary Biography

The 1993 Nobel Prize in Literature
Toni Morrison

(18 February 1931 –   )

See also the Morrison entries in *DLB 6: American Novelists Since World War II; DLB 33: Afro-American Fiction Writers After 1955,* and *DLB Yearbook: 1981.*

BOOKS: *The Bluest Eye* (New York: Holt, Rinehart & Winston, 1970; London: Chatto & Windus, 1979);

Sula (New York: Knopf, 1973; London: Allen Lane, 1974);

Song of Solomon (New York: Knopf, 1977; London: Chatto & Windus, 1978);

Tar Baby (New York: Knopf, 1981; London: Chatto & Windus, 1981);

Beloved (New York: Knopf, 1987; London: Chatto & Windus, 1987);

Jazz (New York: Knopf, 1992; London: Chatto & Windus, 1992);

Playing in the Dark: Whiteness and the Literary Imagination (Cambridge, Mass.: Harvard University Press, 1992).

NOBEL BANQUET STATEMENT

Toni Morrison

Toni Morrison (photograph © The Nobel Foundation)

Your Majesties, Your Highnesses, Ladies and Gentlemen:

I entered this hall pleasantly haunted by those who have entered it before me. That company of laureates is both daunting and welcoming, for among its lists are names of persons whose work has made whole worlds available to me. The sweep and specificity of their art have sometimes broken my heart with the courage and clarity of its vision. The astonishing brilliance with which they practiced their craft has challenged and nurtured my own. My debt to them rivals the profound one I owe to the Swedish Academy for having selected me to join that distinguished alumnae.

Early in October an artist friend left a message which I kept on the answering service for weeks and played back every once in a while just to hear the trembling pleasure in her voice and the faith in her words. "My dear sister," she said, "the prize that is yours is also ours and could not have been placed in better hands." The spirit of her message with its earned optimism and sublime trust marks this day for me.

I will leave this hall, however, with a new and much more delightful haunting than the one I felt

Dust jacket for Morrison's Pulitzer Prize–winning novel about
an escaped slave in post–Civil War Ohio

upon entering: that is the company of laureates yet to come. Those who, even as I speak, are mining, sifting and polishing languages for illuminations none of us has dreamed of. But whether or not any one of them secures a place in this pantheon, the gathering of these writers is unmistakable and mounting. Their voices bespeak civilizations gone and yet to be; the precipice from which their imaginations gaze will rivet us; they do not blink nor turn away.

It is, therefore, mindful of the gifts of my predecessors, the blessing of my sisters, in joyful anticipation of writers to come that I accept the honor the Swedish Academy has done me, and ask you to share what is for me a moment of grace.

NOBEL LECTURE 1993
Toni Morrison

"Once upon a time there was an old woman. Blind but wise." Or was it an old man? A guru, per-

haps. Or a griot soothing restless children. I have heard this story, or one exactly like it, in the lore of several cultures.

"Once upon a time there was an old woman. Blind. Wise."

In the version I know the woman is the daughter of slaves, black, American, and lives alone in a small house outside of town. Her reputation for wisdom is without peer and without question. Among her people she is both the law and its transgression. The honor she is paid and the awe in which she is held reach beyond her neighborhood to places far away; to the city where the intelligence of rural prophets is the source of much amusement.

One day the woman is visited by some young people who seem to be bent on disproving her clairvoyance and showing her up for the fraud they believe she is. Their plan is simple: they enter her house and ask the one question the answer to which rides solely on her difference from them, a difference they regard as a profound disability: her blindness. They stand before her, and one of them says, "Old woman, I hold in my hand a bird. Tell me whether it is living or dead."

She does not answer, and the question is repeated. "Is the bird I am holding living or dead?"

Still she doesn't answer. She is blind and cannot see her visitors, let alone what is in their hands. She does not know their color, gender or homeland. She only knows their motive.

The old woman's silence is so long, the young people have trouble holding their laughter.

Finally she speaks and her voice is soft but stern. "I don't know," she says. "I don't know whether the bird you are holding is dead or alive, but what I do know is that it is in your hands. It is in your hands."

Her answer can be taken to mean: if it is dead, you have either found it that way or you have killed it. If it is alive, you can still kill it. Whether it is to stay alive, it is your decision. Whatever the case, it is your responsibility.

For parading their power and her helplessness, the young visitors are reprimanded, told they are responsible not only for the act of mockery but also for the small bundle of life sacrificed to achieve its aims. The blind woman shifts attention away from assertions of power to the instrument through which that power is exercised.

Speculation on what (other than its own frail body) that bird-in-the-hand might signify has always been attractive to me, but especially so now, thinking as I have been, about the work I do that has brought me to this company. So I choose to read the bird as language and the woman as a practiced writer. She is worried about how the language she dreams in, given to her at birth, is handled, put into service, even withheld from her for certain nefarious purposes. Being a writer she thinks of language partly as a system, partly as a living thing over which one has control, but mostly as agency — as an act with consequences. So the question the children put to her: "Is it living or dead?" is not unreal because she thinks of language as susceptible to death, erasure; certainly imperiled and salvageable only by an effort of the will. She believes that if the bird in the hands of her visitors is dead the custodians are responsible for the corpse. For her a dead language is not only one no longer spoken or written, it is unyielding language content to admire its own paralysis. Like statist language, censored and censoring. Ruthless in its policing duties, it has no desire or purpose other than maintaining the free range of its own narcotic narcissism, its own exclusivity and dominance. However, moribund, it is not without effect for it actively thwarts the intellect, stalls conscience, suppresses human potential. Unreceptive to interrogation, it cannot form or tolerate new ideas, shape other thoughts, tell another story, fill baffling silences. Official language smitheryed to sanction ignorance and preserve privilege is a suit of armor, polished to shocking glitter, a husk from which the knight departed long ago. Yet there it is: dumb, predatory, sentimental. Exciting reverence in schoolchildren, providing shelter for despots, summoning false memories of stability, harmony among the public.

She is convinced that when language dies, out of carelessness, disuse, and absence of esteem, indifference or killed by fiat, not only she herself, but all users and makers are accountable for its demise. In her country children have bitten their tongues off and use bullets instead to iterate the voice of speechlessness, of disabled and disabling language, of language adults have abandoned altogether as a device for grappling with meaning, providing guidance, or expressing love. But she knows tongue-suicide is not only the choice of children. It is common among the infantile heads of state and power merchants whose evacuated language leaves them with no access to what is left of their human instincts for they speak only to those who obey, or in order to force obedience.

The systematic looting of language can be recognized by the tendency of its users to forgo its nuanced, complex, mid-wifery properties for menace and subjugation. Oppressive language does more

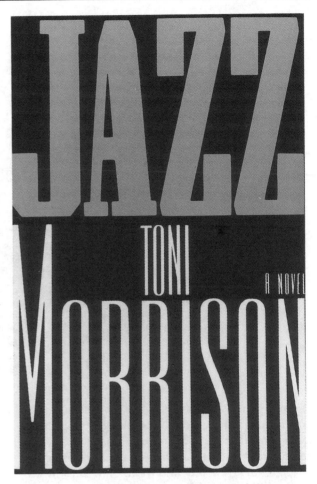

Dust jacket for Morrison's sixth novel, a story of male/female passion set in Harlem during the Jazz Age

than represent violence; it is violence; does more than represent the limits of knowledge; it limits knowledge. Whether it is obscuring state language or the faux-language of mindless media; whether it is the proud but calcified language of the academy or the commodity driven language of science; whether it is the malign language of law-without-ethics, or language designed for the estrangement of minorities, hiding its racist plunder in its literary cheek — it must be rejected, altered and exposed. It is the language that drinks blood, laps vulnerabilities, tucks its fascist boots under crinolines of respectability and patriotism as it moves relentlessly toward the bottom line and the bottomed-out mind. Sexist language, racist language, theistic language — all are typical of the policing languages of mastery, and cannot, do not permit new knowledge or encourage the mutual exchange of ideas.

The old woman is keenly aware that no intellectual mercenary, nor insatiable dictator, no paid-for politician or demagogue; no counterfeit journalist would be persuaded by her thoughts. There is

Toni Morrison (photograph by Brian Lanker)

and will be rousing language to keep citizens armed and arming; slaughtered and slaughtering in the malls, courthouses, post offices, playgrounds, bedrooms and boulevards; stirring, memorializing language to mask the pity and waste of needless death. There will be more diplomatic language to countenance rape, torture, assassination. There is and will be more seductive, mutant language designed to throttle women, to pack their throats like paté-producing geese with their own unsayable, transgressive words; there will be more of the language of surveillance disguised as research; of politics and history calculated to render the suffering of millions mute; language glamorized to thrill the dissatisfied and bereft into assaulting their neighbors; arrogant pseudo-empirical language crafted to lock creative people into cages of inferiority and hopelessness.

Underneath the eloquence, the glamour, the scholarly associations, however, stirring or seductive, the heart of such language is languishing, or perhaps not beating at all – if the bird is already dead.

She has thought about what could have been the intellectual history of any discipline if it had not insisted upon, or been forced into, the waste of time and life that rationalizations for and representations of dominance required – lethal discourses of exclusion blocking access to cognition for both the excluder and the excluded.

The conventional wisdom of the Tower of Babel story is that the collapse was a misfortune. That it was the distraction, or the weight of many languages that precipitated the tower's failed architecture. That one monolithic language would have expedited the building and heaven would have been reached. Whose heaven, she wonders? And what kind? Perhaps the achievement of Paradise was premature, a little hasty if no one could take the time to understand other languages, other views, other narratives. Had they, the heaven they imagined might have been found at their feet. Complicated, demanding yes, but a view of heaven as life; not heaven as post-life.

She would not want to leave her young visitors with the impression that language should be forced to stay alive merely to be. The vitality of language lies in its ability to limn the actual, imagined and possible lives of its speakers, readers, writers. Although its poise is sometimes in displacing experience it is not a substitute for it. It arcs toward the place where meaning may lie. When a President of the United States thought about the graveyard his country had become, and said "The world will little note nor long remember what we say here. But it will never forget what they did here." His simple words are exhilarating in their life-sustaining properties because they refused to encapsulate the reality of 600,000 dead men in a cataclysmic race war.

Refusing to monumentalize, disdaining the "final word," the precise "summing up," acknowledging their "poor power to add or detract," his words signal deference to the uncapturability of the life it mourns. It is the deference that moves her, that recognition that language can never live up to life once and for all. Nor should it. Language can never "pin down" slavery, genocide, war. Nor should it yearn for the arrogance to be able to do so. Its force, its felicity is in its reach toward the ineffable.

Be it grand or slender, burrowing, blasting, or refusing to sanctify; whether it laughs out loud or is a cry without an alphabet, the choice word, the chosen silence, unmolested language surges toward knowledge, not its destruction. But who does not know of literature banned because it is interrogative; discredited because it is critical; erased because alternate? And how many are outraged by the thought of a self-raved tongue?

Word-work is sublime, she thinks, because it is generative; it makes meaning that secures our difference, our human difference – the way in which we are like no other life.

We die. That may be the meaning of life. But we do language. That may be the measure of our lives.

"Once upon a time, . . ." visitors ask an old woman a question. Who are they, these children? What did they make of that encounter? What did they hear in those final words: "The bird is in your hands?" A sentence that gestures toward possibility or one that drops a latch? Perhaps what the children heard was "It's not my problem. I am old, female, black, blind. What wisdom I have now is in knowing I can not help you. The future of language is yours."

They stand there. Suppose nothing was in their hands? Suppose the visit was only a ruse, a trick to get to be spoken to, taken seriously as they have not been before? A chance to interrupt, to violate the adult world, its miasma of discourse about them, for them, but never to them? Urgent questions are at stake, including the one they have asked: "Is the bird we hold living or dead?" Perhaps the question meant: "Could some one tell us what is life? What is death?" No trick at all; no silliness. A straightforward question worthy of the attention of a wise one. An old one. And if the old and wise who have lived life and faced death cannot describe either, who can?

But she does not; she keeps her secret; her good opinion of herself; her gnomic pronouncements; her art without commitment. She keeps her distance, enforces it and retreats into the singularity of isolation, in sophisticated, privileged space.

Nothing, no word follows her declarations of transfer. That silence is deep, deeper than the meaning available in the words she has spoken. It shivers, this silence, and the children, annoyed, fill it with language invented on the spot.

"Is there no speech," they ask her, "no words you can give us that helps us break through your dossier of failures? Through the education you have just given us that is no education at all because we are paying close attention to what you have done as well as to what you have said? To the barrier you have erected between generosity and wisdom?

"We have no bird in our hands, living or dead. We have only you and our important question. Is the nothing in our hands something you could not bear to contemplate, to even guess? Don't you remember being young when language was magic without meaning? When what you could say, could not mean? When the invisible was what imagination strove to see? When questions and demands for answers burned so brightly you trembled with fury at not knowing?

"Do we have to begin consciousness with a battle heroines and heroes like you have already fought and lost leaving us with nothing in our hands except what you have imagined is there? Your answer is artful, but its artiness embarrasses us and ought to embarrass you. Your answer is indecent in its self-congratulation. A made-for-television script that makes no sense if there is nothing in our hands.

"Why didn't you reach out, touch us with your soft fingers, delay the sound bite, the lesson, until you knew who we were? Did you so despise our trick, our modus operandi you could not see that we were baffled about how to get your attention? We are young. Unripe. We have heard all our short lives that we have to be responsible. What could that possibly mean in the catastrophe this word has become; where, as a poet said, "nothing needs to be exposed since it is already barefaced." Our inheritance is an affront. You want us to have your old, blank eyes and see only cruelty and mediocrity. Do you think we are stupid enough to perjure ourselves again and again with the fiction of nationhood? How dare you talk to us of duty when we stand waist deep in the toxin of your past?

"You trivialize us and trivialize the bird that is not in our hands. Is there no context for our lives? No song, no literature, no poem full of vitamins, no history connected to experience that you can pass along to help us start strong? You are an adult. The old one, the wise one. Stop thinking about saving your face. Think of our lives and tell us your particularized world. Make up a story. Narrative is radical, creating us at the very moment it is being created. We will not blame you if your reach exceeds your grasp; if love so ignites your words they go down in flames and nothing is left but their scald. Or if, with the reticence of a surgeon's hands, your words suture only the places where blood might flow. We know you can never do it properly – once and for all. Passion is never enough; neither is skill. But try. For our sake and yours forget your name in the street; tell us what the world has been to you in the dark places and in the light. Don't tell us what to believe, what to fear. Show us belief's wide skirt and the stitch that unravels fear's caul. You, old woman, blessed with blindness, can speak the language that tells us what only language can: how to see without pictures. Language alone protects us from the scariness of things with no names. Language alone is meditation.

"Tell us what it is to be a woman so that we may know what it is to be a man. What moves at the margin. What it is to have no home on this place. To be set adrift from the one you knew. What it is to live at the edge of towns that cannot bear your company.

"Tell us about ships turned away from shorelines at Easter, placenta in a field. Tell us about a wagonload of slaves, how they sang so softly their breath was indistinguishable from the falling snow. How they knew from the hunch of the nearest shoulder that the next stop would be their last. How, with hands prayered in their sex they thought of heat, then suns. Lifting their faces, as though it was there for the taking. Turning as though there for the taking. They stop at an inn. The driver and his mate go in with the lamp leaving them humming in the dark. The horse's void steams into the snow beneath its hooves and its hiss and melt is the envy of the freezing slaves.

"The inn door opens: a girl and a boy step away from its light. They climb into the wagon bed. The boy will have a gun in three years, but now he carries a lamp and a jug of warm cider. They pass it from mouth to mouth. The girl offers bread, pieces of meat and something more: a glance into the eyes of the one she serves. One helping for each man, two for each woman. And a look. They look back. The next stop will be their last. But not this one. This one is warmed."

It's quiet again when the children finish speaking, until the woman breaks into the silence.

"Finally," she says, "I trust you now. I trust you with the bird that is not in your hands because you have truly caught it. Look. How lovely it is, this thing we have done – together."

The Year in the Novel

George Garrett
University of Virginia

and

Kristin van Ogtrop
Vogue Magazine

You could read all day and not come to the end of good fiction published here every year.

— Phyllis Rose, chairman of fiction judges for National Book Award, 17 November

For a few obsessive souls, books are a necessity that ranks up there with food and housing.

— David Streitfeld, "Books: the Hot New Bestseller," *Washington Post,* 29 November

It was supposed to be a slow year for the novel, for fiction in general, especially for literary fiction; and so it seemed to be as nonfiction took over most of the space in the book pages, and, from the year's beginning to the end, some critic or other took the time and found the space to publish a lament for the absence of major works of fiction by major writers. Nevertheless, the usual number — somewhere between two hundred and three hundred titles — of books of fiction were nominated for the National Book Award (NBA), and (from George Garrett's experience as one of the five judges of fiction for 1993) at least 10 percent of them, thirty or so titles, were serious contenders for that prize. This appears to be roughly the same percentage that surfaced in 1990 when Paul West (see "Felipe Alfau and the NBA," *Review of Contemporary Fiction,* Spring 1993) served as a fiction judge and elected to write about the experience. *Publishers Weekly* (1 November) offered a list of 25 books, "PW's Best Books 1993," chosen as favorites by the editors. All of the selections were literary novels, with only one blockbuster, John le Carré's *The Night Manager* (Knopf), in their midst. Of the 14 books selected as "Editor's Choice" of the best books of 1993 by the *New York*

Times Book Review (5 December), 6 were works of fiction, 3 of them short-story collections. In the same issue of the *Times Book Review* under the listing of "Notable Books of the Year," the editors listed some 150 books, only a few of which had appeared briefly on any best-seller list. The one notable exception was Alan Lightman's *Einstein's Dreams* (Pantheon) — which was noted in *Dictionary of Literary Biography Yearbook 1992* — a surprising best-seller, considering the genuinely literary nature of the book. The *Times* accurately describes the book as "spare, poetic fantasies about what Einstein might have dreamed when he was still a 26-year-old patent clerk in Switzerland."

With the distinct advantages of hindsight one can conclude that, in terms of quality at least, it was not a slow year for fiction, that, in fact, a significant number of outstanding novels were published, some of them by writers of firmly established reputation: Frederick Buechner, James Dickey, Harriet Doerr, Samuel Beckett, Bobbie Ann Mason, Sue Miller, Oscar Hijuelos, Joyce Carol Oates, Bharati Mukherjee, Isabel Allende, Ishmael Reed, Ernest J. Gaines, Brian Moore, Philip Roth, George V. Higgins, Alasdair Gray, T. Coraghessan Boyle, Margaret Atwood, Larry McMurtry, Elmore Leonard, Tony Hillerman, and Patrick O'Brian. There was a multitude of books by good writers at mid career and a surprising number of first novels. Yet it is also apparent that these writers, with the odd exception of Lightman — even though some of them have appeared on best-seller lists — are on a different track from the blockbuster types whose names dominate the end-of-the-year hardcover and paperback best-seller lists: Robert James Waller, Stephen King, Tom Clancy, Dean Koontz, Anne Rice, Ken Follett,

Dick Francis, Nick Bantock and Danielle Steele. Two moderately surprising appearances on the "Paperback Best Sellers" list of the *Times* owe their moment of glory to successful movie tie-ins: Kazuo Ishiguro's *Remains of the Day* (Vintage) and Edith Wharton's *The Age of Innocence* (Collier). At the National Book Award dinner at the Plaza Hotel (17 November) King bought a table, just like a publisher, and invited some friends, best-selling authors who agreed to the satiric requirement that they have never and will never win the award themselves for their own work. Among those friends who cheerfully accepted were Donald Westlake and John Grisham. Some sense of the divorce between the commercial and the literary is clearly evident in James Colbert's review of Grisham's *The Client* (Doubleday), 28 February in the *Chicago Tribune*: "But if it is sad that such flawless lack of distinction achieves such success, one still wonders whether that occurs because the market is so good at selling particular pieces of it." Whatever the causes and reasons, the separation of blockbuster and the literary is much the same in all environments. The *Chronicle of Higher Education* ("What They're Reading on College Campuses," 1 September), produced a list based on reports of fifty university and college bookstores nationwide, which was not noticeably different from other lists and featured the usual suspects – Grisham, Waller, Michael Crichton, and so forth.

Lists being in order these days, I am not too shy to produce my own "Honor Roll" of favorites for 1993, the novels of the year that moved and delighted and instructed me most. The reader is to be reminded that not only are all lists, public and private, an inadequate form of representation, but also that, by the luck of the draw, all of the books I encountered (even judging for the NBA) are only a small part of the big picture and only vaguely representative of it. The question is not whether good books escaped my attention or the attention of the book pages. The statistical probability is that many good books are bound to have been lost in the literary shuffle. All that can be claimed for this accounting is that it is representative, a selection of the books that came to my attention in several ways.

HONOR ROLL 1993

Douglas Bauer, *The Very Air* (Morrow). Bauer has tapped into the archetypal American figure of the confidence man with Luther Mathias, rogue and hustler of patent medicines and cures all across the Southwest and Mexico.

Richard Bausch, *Rebel Powers* (Houghton Mifflin). Bausch, who won the *Dictionary of Literary Biography* Award for a Distinguished Novel Published in 1992 for *Violence* (Houghton Mifflin), again explores the resiliency of a loving family when subjected to powerful, unanticipated outside pressure. Told by Thomas Boudreaux in the present, but dealing with the late 1960s when he was seventeen years old, *Rebel Powers* tells what happens when his father is sent to Federal prison in Wilson Creek, Wyoming, for stealing a typewriter. By the end of the book the family (three generations) is partly broken, but healing, and Thomas has learned a kind of bleak wisdom: "It was somehow as though we had been involved in a kind of a game, a playing at life, an acting out. And it had gone its own way in spite of us." With each new novel (five now) Bausch is emerging as a major figure of his generation.

Charles Baxter, *Shadow Play* (Norton). Wyatt Palmer is the assistant city manager of Five Oaks, Michigan (which figures in other fiction by Baxter). To help to save the town he assists in bringing in a chemical plant, WALD/CHEM, which soon enough proves seriously unsafe for everyone. Wyatt's eccentric Aunt Ellen gets to articulate the general "message": "We have to save the world, if we want to live in it, because God won't."

Madison Smartt Bell, *Save Me, Joe Louis* (Harcourt Brace). Bell's seventh novel, and, appropriately for a writer of growing reputation, his best work so far, centers on two violent petty criminals, McCrae and Charlie (later joined by Porter), whose actions take them from Hell's Kitchen to Baltimore to the rural South. Bell's sense of and use of *place* in fiction is exact and evocative, and he can handle violence (and the motives for it) as adroitly as any living writer.

Frederick Buechner, *The Son of Laughter* (Harper San Francisco). This is Buechner's fourteenth novel (and twenty-eighth book) in a long, productive, and distinguished career, beginning with *A Long Day's Dying* (1950). *The Son of Laughter* is the story of Jacob and four generations of his family, from old father Abraham through Joseph, stories which occupy half of the chapters of the book of Genesis, and which are beautifully told here in the first person by Jacob: "It was less a pain I felt than a pain I saw. I saw it as light. I saw the pain as a dazzling bird-shape of light. The pain's beak impaled me with light. It blinded me with the light of its wings. I knew I was crippled and done for . . ." *The Son of Laughter* is my choice for the best novel I encountered in 1993.

George Cuomo, *Trial by Water* (Random House). Cuomo has been a highly regarded writer for many years, and his new novel arrives with much advance praise, including that of *Kirkus Reviews* aptly describing the novel as "a suspense story that adroitly encompasses family solidarity, class tensions, and teenage culture, [written with] exquisite even-handedness." Richard Yates wrote: "Cuomo creates vivid characters, significant action, stories you can't stop reading and can't forget." In the marketplace this fine novel did not receive the attention it deserves.

James Dickey, *To the White Sea* (Houghton Mifflin). Dickey's third novel is told in the first person by an extraordinary man who proves to be a ghost. It is the account of how Muldrow, a B-29 gunner who bails out over Tokyo in March 1945, manages by desperate measures to work his way north more than four hundred miles to the wilderness of Hokkaido. R. V. Cassill accurately describes the novel (on the book jacket) as "a farewell to arms wrought in the vortex of blood, fire, and snow, a myth of return to predatory harmony."

Harriet Doerr, *Consider This, Senora* (Harcourt Brace). Doerr, whose *Stones for Ibarra* won the American Book Award for 1983 (and who is now eighty-three years old herself), places her second novel in the small Mexican town of Amapolas, dealing mainly with the impact of living in Mexico on a group of American expatriates. "Their roots are shallow from frequent transplanting," one of the locals says. Doerr is here, as before, beautifully clear and accessible, an admirable observer.

Roddy Doyle, *Paddy Clarke Ha Ha Ha* (Viking). Like his earlier novels, which included *The Commitments* (1988), this winner of the Booker Prize is set in Barrytown at the edge of Dublin in the 1960s. This one, narrated by ten-year-old Patrick Clarke, won widespread rave reviews, including these words from Gail Caldwell at the *Boston Globe* (19 December): "In his dash-punctuated dialogue and proletarian poetics, he captures a working-class Ireland with a near-boisterous affection for language — as apparent in schoolyard jeers as it is in the implicit laments that warring parents never utter."

Ernest Gaines, *A Lesson Before Dying* (Knopf). Set in 1948 in the Louisiana town of Bayonne, Saint Raphael Parrish, and narrated by Grant Wiggins, an idealistic young black schoolteacher, Gaines's eighth novel (and his first in ten years) is a powerful and moving story of crime and punishment and courage — surely the most compassionate and

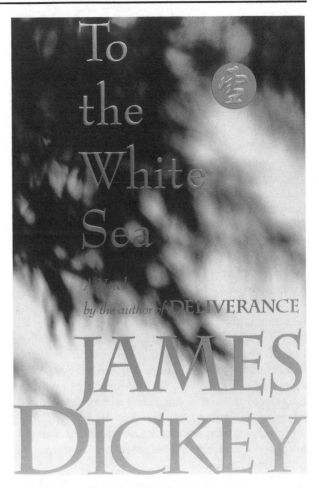

Dust jacket for James Dickey's third novel, a violent story set in Japan during World War II

thoughtful novel written by an African-American writer in a good while.

Kaye Gibbons, *Charms for the Easy Life* (Putnam). In her fourth novel since her debut in 1987, and her first book with a major commercial publisher, Gibbons tells the story of three generations of powerful, independent women — Charlie Kate, grandmother; Sophia, her daughter; and Margaret, the granddaughter. Charlie Kate is a healer and midwife in the county, and the action covers roughly fifty years. These three women are rare beings — readers ("When a good book was in the house, the place fairly vibrated"). Among the judges, *Charms for the Easy Life* was a strong contender for the National Book Award.

Alasdair Gray, *Poor Things* (Harcourt Brace). Winner of the Whitbread Prize for 1992, this is a wonderfully complicated and lively, fully "open" example of postmodern metafiction at its finest. The proposition is that Gray has come into possession of an old book, the memoirs of a nineteenth-century public-health officer in Glasgow ("Episodes from the Early Life of Archibald McCandless, M.D."). The volume gives Gray, regarded now as Scotland's leading living novelist, room to play his games and try to work (as he puts it) "as if we live in the early days of a better nation."

Kathryn Harrison, *Exposure* (Random House). Ann Rogers, thirty-three-year-old daughter of famous photographer Edgar Rogers who committed suicide in 1978, faces huge personal problems as a retrospective show of her father's work (including many photographs of herself as a teenage model) is opening at the Museum of Modern Art. Ann suffers a serious breakdown. Mannered and sophisticated, *Exposure* is, nevertheless, a consummate regional (New York City) novel and a moving study of the effect an artist and his art can have on others.

Ernest Hebert, *Mad Boys* (University Press of New England). Hebert is author of seven novels, all set firmly in New Hampshire. This latest, described by critic Jay Parini as "*Huckleberry Finn* meets *On the Road*," follows the fortunes of thirteen-year-old Web Clements who has lost his memory (among other things) and sets out in our satiric and surreal United States to find out who he is and what he is doing here. Hebert, who teaches at Dartmouth, is a classy novelist who deserves a lot more attention than he has received so far.

George V. Higgins, *Bomber's Law* (Holt). Higgins has long since graduated from genre fiction into the mainstream of contemporary American writing. Higgins's latest plot is, as usual, intricate and credible, and his central character, state trooper Sgt. Harry Dell'Appa, is one of his finest — a hard-edged, tough-minded, free and easy talker. People talk like fallen angels in the world of Higgins. He has produced twenty-five first-class books including *The Friends of Eddie Coyle* (1972). His publisher has some cause for hopeful crankiness: "Perhaps it's time for the bookselling community to consider why this writer . . . is a legend only to an inner circle of thirty-five thousand souls."

Edmund Keeley, *School for Pagan Lovers* (Rutgers University Press). Author of five other novels and several books of nonfiction, as well as a prominent translator of modern Greek poetry and fiction, Keeley tells a love story, involving Hal Gogarty, a young American schoolboy living in Salonika in 1938, and Magda Sevillas of a Greek-Jewish family. They have an idyllic affair on the island of Thassos before the world, their families, and, finally, World War II, tear them apart. The story is told in the first person by Hal, years afterward. Of this fine novel,

Pulitzer Prize–winning poet Carolyn Kizer has written: "The whole novel is suffused with the courage, honor, and decency of its protagonists, all bathed in the incomparable golden light of Greece."

Brett Laidlaw, *Blue Bel Air* (Norton). In this, his second novel, Laidlaw tells a complex love story concerning a reporter, Bryce Fraser, and two women, Carla and Sylvia, all of it suffused by the presence of Sylvia's grandmother's car – a 1962 blue Bel Air. Laidlaw is a greatly gifted, spare, lucid, thoughtful, and thought-provoking writer.

Elmore Leonard, *Pronto* (Delacorte). On certain days, in some years, Elmore Leonard can seem to be the best living American writer and his thirty-one (counting this one) novels national treasures. The thriller is his headquarters, but he will not rest easy in the ghetto of the genre. This one, with, typically, a couple of brand-new wrinkles, is aptly described by the publisher as what happens "when a bookie, a U. S. marshal, and a trio of thugs from Miami's underworld pay a visit to Rapallo." Critics are so used to Leonard's excellence that this one opened to mixed reviews.

Larry McMurtry, *Streets of Laredo* (Simon and Schuster). A sequel set fifteen years after the events of *Lonesome Dove* (1985), this new novel features survivor Woodrow Call, summoned from retirement to mount a deadly search-and-destroy mission seeking a young Mexican train robber and killer. It has narrative richness and complexity and a full cast of wholly memorable characters; but the tone is, as it must be, elegiac. Here the heroic Woodrow Call has a vision of the end of things: "Ben Lily and Goodnight and Roy Bean and, he supposed, himself – for he, too, had become one of the old ones of the West. When Lily fell, and Goodnight, and Bean and himself, there wouldn't even be echoes, just memories."

Brian Moore, *No Other Life* (Doubleday). Moore, author of eighteen novels, here has Canadian Father Paul Michael of the "Albanesian Order," serving on the imaginary island of Ganae (Haiti), writing down a record of the life of his pupil and friend Jean-Paul "Jeanott" Cantave (Bertrand Aristide). Father Paul's overwhelming question is: "What was my duty? Was it, as the Cardinal said, to save these people's immortal souls, or was it to help Jeanott relieve their mortal misery?"

Patrick O'Brian, *The Wine Dark Sea* (Norton). This is the sixteenth in the widely acclaimed series (all in print) of novels about Royal Navy officer Jack Aubrey and Stephen Maturin, scientist and surgeon. In the new novel they are on the *Surprise* in the Pacific headed for Peru. It is, as you might expect, thoroughly satisfactory. O'Brian has been "discovered" and lifted into the category of celebrity. There is a *Patrick O'Brian Calendar* for sale in the bookstores, and his publisher now regularly mails out the *Patrick O'Brian Newsletter*. It is the happy story of an elderly writer of undiminished gifts enjoying the full portion of earned success.

Richard Powers, *Operation Wandering Soul* (Morrow). This is the fourth novel by Powers, whose first novel, *Three Farmers on the Way to a Dance,* was widely praised and admired in 1985. Here, alternating narrative chapters with others about historical events, Powers tells the story of Richard Kraft, a surgical resident in pediatrics in Angel City (Los Angeles), and child therapist Linda Espera. The novel received mixed notices, honoring the powerful subject (terribly sick and wounded children), the extraordinary, sometimes brilliant writing, troubled by the habit of being too clever. Because of the special quality of its writing, it was on the final short list for the National Book Award: "A girl is screaming. Through sheets of graphite, conducting air, annihilating paradise darkness, a scream trickles. Something young, as green as freshly cut grass, panic-whispers over night's dead receiver."

E. Annie Proulx, *The Shipping News* (Scribners). This novel, Proulx's second, was awarded a string of prizes. It is set mostly in a beautifully realized Newfoundland, specifically the village of Killick-Claw. Basically the story follows its protagonist, Quoyle, his daughters, and kinfolk, when, following the death of his wife, he returns to his ancestral home in Newfoundland to work for the weekly paper, *The Gammy Bird*, and somehow get through one terrible winter inwardly and outwardly intact. The energetic prose style is often marked by the staccato of sentence fragments: "Partridge back on the line two days later. Pleased to be fixing Quoyle's life up again. Quoyle made him think of a huge roll of newsprint from the pulp mill. Blank and speckled with imperfections."

Ishmael Reed, *Japanese by Spring* (Atheneum). Satirist Reed takes on the current climate of politically correct multiculturalism in the academy. The central character is "Chappie" Puttbutt, a teacher looking for tenure and more at Jack London University. Jack Byrne, writing for the *Review of Contemporary Fiction* (Fall 1993), argues that "his great skill is to create topical scenes and characters to represent his favorite subjects for ridicule." Byrne calls the satire of this African-American writer "as classical as Rabelais and Swift, and as meaningful."

Roddy Doyle, Irish author of the Booker Prize–winning Paddy Clarke Ha Ha Ha

Richard Russo, *Nobody's Fool* (Random House). The third novel by this teacher at Colby College in Maine is set in the upstate New York town of Bath, a place whose mineral springs ran dry in 1750. Its protagonist, Donald Sullivan (called "Sully"), is middle-aged, out of work, hobbled by a bad knee, and linked to a marvelous cast of characters including his former wife Vera, his mistress Ruth, and his son Peter, who is a college professor. Russo is a past-master of dialogue and of the subtle contradictions that compose the character of even the most ordinary people.

Bob Shacochis, *Swimming in the Volcano* (Scribners). This novel was, effectively, runner-up for the National Book Award. It is a first novel by an award-winning short-story writer. Here Shacochis has created a very large novel, as much about the prototypical Caribbean island of Saint Catherine, its geography and history and politics, as it is about its central character, Mitchell Wilson, an American working for the Ministry of Agriculture. It tells the story of the rise and fall of local factions and governments, complicated by the arrival on the scene of Johanna Woods, a woman Wilson had once loved and lost.

Susan Richards Shreve, *The Train Home* (Doubleday). Will Huston, an Irish actor, goes to Washington, D.C., disguised as a priest in an effort to avenge his brother's murder in Belfast. There he encounters Anne Blakemore, an opera singer; their lives become entangled, and the tale turns into a love story. It is set in the fall of 1991. Shreve is an able, experienced, and productive novelist who has not yet received her proper share of attention.

David R. Slavitt, *Turkish Delights* (Louisiana State University Press). With the publication of this latest novel Slavitt is coming very close to fifty books — novels, stories, poetry, translations, and nonfiction. *Turkish Delights* is an ingenious joining together of three different first-person narratives — Selim, fourth son of a Turkish sultan; Pietro, second son of a nineteenth-century Venetian family; and Asher, only son and a twentieth-century, second-generation American Jew whose life experiences are at least shadows of the author's own. *Turkish Delights* is a cheerful metafiction and has been roundly praised by Herbert Gold: "This is a marvelous entertainment, witty, disabused, and filled with surprising moments of passion."

Charlie Smith, *Chimney Rock* (Holt). Smith's fourth novel and his first set outside of the South, *Chimney Rock* is an apocalyptic Hollywood novel, beginning with a fistfight at the Academy Awards and ending with the 1992 Los Angeles riots. Principal characters are narrator Will Blake, a film actor from a third-generation movie family; his wife Kate, whose screen name is Zebra Dunn; his father, Clement, a movie producer; and the haunting memory of his late brother Bobby, a suicide. The Los Angeles evoked here is the Los Angeles of Nathanael West and, perhaps, Joan Didion — "Everything was dusty and vague." Parini, in the *New York Times Book Review* (9 May), praises it for "breathless energy" and calls the book a "*fin-de-siecle* nightmare." Will Blake has his own description: "So the clock ticks, and every tick speaks disaster. The theme is loss. What we have lost, what we will lose."

Melanie Rae Thon, *Iona Moon* (Poseidon). Reviewing this novel, Thon's second novel and third book, for the *Los Angeles Times Book Review* (25 July), Julia Cameron was not wrong to assert that "Thon is the Diane Arbus of writers." This is a story of death and misery in Idaho. Iona Moon is a potato farmer's daughter who tries her best to escape from the harsh world of White Falls in the 1960s, escap-

ing for a time to Spokane and Seattle where, among other things, she has a love affair with a married, one-legged Indian. What lifts the work to the grace of art is Thon's writing and the simplicity and sincerity of her stated theme: "It is the wounded heart that makes us human in the end."

Richard Watson, *Niagara* (Coffee House). Loosely based on fact, *Niagara* in parallel narratives tells the story of two people who, early in this century, challenged Niagara Falls — Jean Francois Gravelet, a French tightrope walker, and Nebraska schoolteacher Anna Edson Taylor, who went over the falls in a barrel. As Taylor puts it near the end of her story: "Remember me, what I did, on October 4th 1901, Anna Edson Taylor, a widowed schoolteacher, admitted age forty-one, but I was really forty-five. The first person to go over Niagara Falls on purpose, in a barrel, and survive. . . ."

Sylvia Wilkinson, *On the 7th Day God Created the Chevrolet* (Algonquin). Sylvia Wilkinson is author of five earlier novels, two nonfiction books, and several juvenile titles, but it has been a decade since her last book. Here, in a story about the vanished dirt-track, stockcar racing days, Wilkinson for the first time uses her own professional racing experience to tell the story of stockcar drivers Tom Pate and his brother Zack as the world changes around them, and they must decide between racing cars or life on the family farm.

Nancy Willard, *Sister Water* (Knopf). Willard has published several collections of poems and short stories as well as prize-winning children's books and one earlier novel. She has been justly praised for her qualities of imagination and innovation. *Publishers Weekly* is quoted by the publisher in the first review of this novel: "Willard's gift for seamlessly mixing the magical and the mundane puts her in the company of Anne Tyler and Alice Hoffman." *Sister Water* concerns a family in Ann Arbor, Michigan, who are visited by a ghost, a mystic, and several sorts of angels.

Among the other significant literary novels which appeared in 1993, a good number were by writers of prominent and sustained reputation. Philip Roth returned, still teasing the idea of the double self, in *Operation Shylock: A Confession* (Simon and Schuster), in which a famous author named Philip Roth, recovering from the side effects of Halcyon, travels to Israel where he meets (among other unusual characters) a man named Philip Roth who is urging the Jews to return home to Europe. It is Jinx Possesski, Palestinian activist, who reassures the "real" Roth: "I assure you that Arafat can differentiate between Woody Allen and Philip Roth." At the risk, late in a distinguished career, of being named the "Mr. Ed" of American literature, John Hawkes in his fourteenth novel, *Sweet William: A Memoir of Old Horse* (Simon and Schuster), uses his central character, the horse, as the first-person narrator. It is witty, thoroughly imagined, and somewhat Swiftian – and somewhat silly: "It was not a mere coincidence that one of the only horses I ever loved was a pony or that throughout my life I never loved any but the smallest of girls and no woman larger than a small girl." Several older writers were represented by new novels: Morris West, in *The Lovers* (Donald Fine), tells the love story, set in 1952, of sixty-five-year-old Bryan de Courcy Cavanagh, an international lawyer from Australia, and Principessa Giulia Farnese; in *The Hope* (Little, Brown), Herman Wouk, through the vision and memory of Israeli officer Zev Barak, re-creates the first twenty years of the state of Israel; Howard Fast, who over the years has turned out more than eighty books, sets his new novel, *The Trial of Abigail Goodman* (Crown), in a Southern town in the near future where Abigail Goodman is tried for having an abortion (a capital crime) and barely escapes with her life.

Writers of distinction from a somewhat younger set, made 1993 a busy year for the novel. Joyce Carol Oates, in *Foxfire: Confessions of a Girl Gang* (Dutton), writes about a girl gang, one of whose mottoes was "Men Are The Enemy!" It is narrated by Maddy, a middle-aged woman remembering the 1950s in upstate New York. Calling the book "oddly strained and contrived," Michiko Kakutani concludes her review (*New York Times,* 16 July): "*Foxfire* is a dud." Bobbie Ann Mason in her third novel, *Feather Crowns* (HarperCollins), gives her protagonist, Christie Wheeler, the problem and results of giving birth to quintuplets in rural Kentucky during the early 1900s. The book covers from 1900 to 1936 and the year 1963. *The Man Who Was Late* (Knopf), by Louis Begley, author of the much-praised *Wartime Lies* (1991), is the story of Ben, a Jewish refugee from Central Europe who becomes an enormously successful international banker, as told by his friend Jack, a journalist who is also executor of Ben's estate. Ben's inner story is the inability to find happiness; he writes in his diary: "Darkness and loneliness, Mother. I fain would be happy but do not know how." *Eclipse Fever* (Knopf), by Walter Abish, who won a PEN/Faulkner Award for his second novel, *How German Is It* (1980), is set in Mexico, and the main character in a complex cast is Alejandro, a Mexican literary critic. It is less "experimental" than Abish's earlier work, but nevertheless entangles several plot lines and develops the story in a series of short, titled chapters. Patrick McGrath, whose most recent novel was *Spider* (1991), tells of the consequences of an adulterous love affair, as related by a father (Dr. Edward Haggard) to his son in *Dr. Haggard's Disease* (Poseidon). Of this novel Katherine Dunn reported, in *Washington Post Book World* (2 May), that it is "not just readable but engrossing, and as neurotic as a self-devouring snake."

"I wanted to write a book about what it's like to fall in love now," said Sue Miller in the *New York Times Book Review* (11 April), describing the origins of her third novel, *For Love* (HarperCollins). Her protagonist is Lottie Gardner, a freelance magazine writer in her early forties. Over a summer in her hometown, Cambridge, she is forced to reconsider her life, past and future. *For Love* earned mixed reviews. So did Alice Adams's latest, her eighth novel, *Almost Perfect* (Knopf), which is about the love affair of commercial artist Stella Blake and Richard Fallon, "an almost perfect man," in San Francisco. Novelist and screenwriter (she won an Oscar for *A Room With a View* and has written sixteen movies for Merchant-Ivory) Ruth Prawer Jhabvala published *Poet and Dancer* (Doubleday), a slender and evocative novel set in Manhattan involving two families and is chiefly about the intense and subtle lifetime relationship of Angel, a poet, and her cousin Lara, a beautiful dancer. About Angel's gift we are told: "It came very hard. When she was small, words had flown out of her like birds, now they fell back into her like stones." Margaret Atwood's *The Robber Bride* (Doubleday) is a reversal of the fairy tale, "The Robber Bridegroom." Set in Toronto on Tuesday, 23 October 1990, it places three female friends – Tony, a scholar; Charis, a flower child; and Roz, a businesswoman – in a fight for life against Zena, whose power is stealing men from other women and who apparently returns from the dead. She is a two-dimensional force for evil, but the other three are fully dimensional and have complex stories to tell.

T. Coraghessan Boyle, who has been accurately described as creator of "a mix of P. T. Barnum and Franz Kafka," sets his latest novel, *The Road to Wellville* (Viking), in Dr. John Harvey Kellogg's Battle Creek Sanitarium during the winter of 1907. It is a large and satiric novel full of comedy and confidence men. Satiric in a bleaker, different way is Frederick Barthelme, whose fifth novel, *The Brothers* (Viking), is set "in Biloxi, on the dirty, soured, dinky coast of Mississippi." Marked by Barthelme's sharp eye for details, relevant and irrel-

Dust jacket for George V. Higgin's twenty-fifth novel, an
intricately plotted story of the Massachusetts state police

evant, and by his hip, knowing style, it is a record of America the unbeautiful, represented in the story of two moderately worthless brothers, Bud and Del Tribute, Bud's wife Margaret, and his new girlfriend Jen, a counterculture journalist. Jen is full of youthful wisdom: "Screwing kind of sucks, doesn't it? I hate it sometimes. It doesn't matter who you screw anymore." Del, perhaps inadvertently describing the book, has some worldly wisdom of his own: "There isn't any story. It's not the story. It's just this breathtaking world, that's the point." Oscar Hijuelos, whose novel *The Mambo Kings Play Songs of Love* (1989) won the Pulitzer Prize, begins his latest novel, *The Fourteen Sisters of Emilio Montez O'Brien* (Farrar, Straus and Giroux), in 1921 in Cobbleton, Pennsylvania, and covers the lives of the fourteen O'Brien sisters and their brother, Emilio, who becomes a Hollywood star – "Having watched his career slowly dissipate over the past few years, he would go for days without so much as one drink,

trying hard to forget the feelings that plagued him." The family under siege is Frederick Busch's subject in *Long Way From Home* (Ticknor and Fields), his sixteenth book of fiction. Sarah, an interior decorator in Doylestown, Pennsylvania, married and with a son, Stephen, upsets her world as a result of an obsessive and finally successful search to find her birth mother. Adoption figures also in Jonathan Carroll's eighth novel, *After Silence* (Doubleday). Told in first person by cartoonist Max Fischer, it tells how he becomes deeply involved with Lily Aaron and her nine-year-old son, Lincoln, later discovering by accident that her life stories are not true and that Lincoln was, in fact, kidnapped by her as an infant. "California is full of people from the dark side of the moon," he observes. Adoption and kidnapping are part of Barbara Kingsolver's *Pigs in Heaven* (HarperCollins), a sequel to *The Bean Trees* (1988). Taylor Greer is the single mother of an abandoned Cherokee child and comes into a custody conflict with Cherokee lawyer, Annaware Fourkiller. In an interview about this conflict Kingsolver explained: "The media view the basic unit of good as what is best for the child; the tribe sees it as what is best for the group. These are two very different value systems with no point of intersection." The 1993 *Los Angeles Times* Prize for Fiction was awarded to Kingsolver for *Pigs in Heaven*. Another form of "adoption" is the subject of Australian writer David Malouf's highly praised *Remembering Babylon* (Pantheon). Set in a remote part of Queensland in the 1850s, it follows the impact on a small community of settlers of the arrival of Gemmy Fairley, a British cabin boy who had been thrown overboard while sick and then was saved and raised by Aborigines. Abandonment and cultural conflict are important elements also in Susanna Moore's *Sleeping Beauties* (Knopf). Clio, whose great-grandmother was a Hawaiian princess, is raised by an eccentric aunt in her native Hawaii. She escapes for a time by marrying a Hollywood movie star, then finds her way home to her proper heritage through Hollywood and Casablanca. There is an unquestionably splendid evocation of the islands. Fae Myenne Ng's *Bone* (Hyperion) is set in San Francisco's Chinatown and concerns the Long family. Another cross-cultural point of view is revealed in Isabel Allende's first "American" novel, *The Infinite Plan* (HarperCollins), which follows the complicated life and times of California corporate lawyer Gregory Reeves, who chooses to dedicate himself to representing the poor.

There were dozens of other novels published in 1993, adequate, competent or better, which could be listed and briefly described, books which often were reviewed favorably. But with the limited space that this yearly roundup allows, it seems more worthwhile to single out books which stand out as "interesting," different in one way or another from the ordinary, no matter how competent the ordinary may be. These are books by writers who took some chances, tried to create something unusual in form or content or both. Take, for example, William Gibson, who has been called "king of cyberpunk." His *Virtual Light* (Bantam) is set in the year 2005 in California, by then divided into sister states, NoCal and SoCal. Berry Rydell is a security cop. His roommate, Kevin Tarkovsk, wears a bone through his nose and works in a wind-surfing boutique called Just Blow Me. In this wicked, pollution-ridden world of the near future there is still fun, both high and low ("Name 'Pavlov' ring a bell?"). Kathe Koja, described by her publisher (Delacorte) as on the "cutting edge of psychological horror," tells the story of Bibi, a dancer who seriously seeks to explore and exploit the inner and outer limits of her body in *Skin*. *Living in Little Rock With Miss Little Rock* (Knopf) is the sixth novel by Arkansas writer and authentic Friend of Bill, Jack Butler. Described by the publisher as "a rollicking, explosively inventive novel about God, sex, death and politics in Bill Clinton country," the story has a very unusual narrator ("Howdy, I'm the Holy Ghost") and focuses on Charles Morrison, "the Atticus Finch of Arkansas," and his wife, Lianne, formerly Miss Little Rock. Lewis Shiner in his fourth book, *Glimpses* (Morrow), mixes fact and fiction in a complex story about near-mystical hallucinations which become reality. The jacket bears a heartfelt blurb from Dr. Timothy Leary. Set in Vienna at the turn of the century, *Henry James' Midnight Song* (Poseidon), by Carol De Chellis Hill, is essentially a thriller mixing up fictional characters and real people like Henry James, Sigmund Freud, Edith Wharton, Arthur Schnitzler and so forth – not everybody's cup of tea. Writing in the *New Criterion* ("Wharton Redux?," November 1993), James Tuttleton took a negative point of view: "In all of this Miss Hill is merely recycling what has already become a stale postmodernist convention, the degradation of real people because the writer's imagination isn't equal to inventing a fictive life worth the reader's attention." Douglas Hobbie's *The Day* (Holt) is set in a small town in western Massachusetts on Thanksgiving Day, 1991 and carries an extremely rare blurb by Roth. Steve Shagan's *A Cast of Thousands* (Pocket Books) takes a leaf from the film, *The Producers*. Here top motion-picture executives, as part of a

takeover scheme, create the absolutely worst and most expensive movie they can mange. But of course it turns out to be a smash hit. High comedy and satire of the New York City academic scene are to be found and enjoyed in *Rameau's Niece* (Ticknor and Fields) by Cathleen Schine, the flip side of "Rameau's Nephew" by Denis Diderot. John Calvin Batchelor is always up to something new and different. In *Peter Nevsky and the True Story of the Russian Moon Landing* (Holt) he turns back the clock to 1969 and allows Peter Nevsky, cosmonaut, together with a boozy bunch of Russian World War II aces, to beat *Apollo II* to the moon. Equally eccentric is Wilton Barnhardt's *Gospel* (St. Martin's Press), which sends young Lucy Danton and Professor Emeritus Patrick Virgil O'Hanrahan all over the world (Oxford, Ireland, Italy, Greece, Israel, Africa, and New Orleans) looking for a scroll containing the lost gospel of the disciple Matthias. The narrative chapters alternate with excerpts from the Gospel, presented with footnotes and full scholarly apparatus. *Tintin in the New World* (Morrow), by Frederic Tuten, takes Tintin, the twelve-year-old detective and star of the real French comic-book series (1930–1976), to Peru with Captain Haddock, a drunk, and his dog Snowy (who has several monologues), where they meet up and interact with four major characters from Thomas Mann's *The Magic Mountain*. Poet and story writer Janet Kaufman created *The Body in Four Parts* (Graywolf) in a form her publisher calls "a non-linear passion play," and describes as "a strange and dizzying novel about the nature of human nature." Poet, literary novelist, and mystery writer Stephen Dobyns has a huge talent and overwhelming energy. His latest, *The Wrestler's Cruel Study* (Norton), comes with blurbs from (among various worlds) Stuart Dybek, Stephen King, Robert Boswell, and, above all, grandmaster poet Hayden Carruth – "It is the Supreme Fiction toward which the Twentieth century has been steadily advancing from the start." How can this one be described? The publisher does its best on the book jacket: "Part quest (in pattern), part comic book (in tone), and chiefly an exploration of a young man's search for his missing fiancée, it deals with such matters as heroes, good and evil, wrestling, kidnapping, and subplots from the Brothers Grimm. . . ."

In full affirmation of the new and improved in fiction, you open *Zimzum* (Pantheon) at random and begin to read: "So what about alacrity? Did anybody ever hear of alacrity? Was there alacrity? There was no alacrity. I saw no alacrity. I looked and what did I see? I saw not one indication of alacrity." Gordon Lish, a lively master of new twists has written a novel of six sections, each with a different-same narrator, ranging from two to fifty-five pages. That much can be said. Serious critics can say more Brian Evenson in *Review of Contemporary Fiction* (Fall 1993): "*Zimzum* advances through sentential variation and permutation, employing the formal repetition common to musical arrangements to liberate the powers of utterance." Need I say more?

Then there are the books by writers known for things other than writing and/or writers who have achieved some sort of celebrity status – for example, playwright David Rabe, whose 1993 novel, *Recital of the Dog* (Grove), follows a painter into a deep, finally murderous madness. Kate Lehrer, wife of television newsman Jim Lehrer (both of them part-time novelists now), published her second novel, *When They Took Away the Man in the Moon* (Harmony), which is about the life and loves of H. A. Reese, a Washington political consultant from Rollins, Texas. Maureen Earl, wife to Clifford Irving, wrote about the factual story of the Jewish passengers on the SS *Atlantic,* who headed for Palestine in October 1940 but were interned by the British for five years at the Beau Bassin Camp on Mauritius, in *Boat of Stone* (Permanent). Lynn Stegner, daughter-in-law of the late Wallace Stegner, wrote *Undertow* (Baskerville), a love story set in California during the 1980s. Bangor, Maine's, Tabitha King published *One on One* (Dutton), a love story in the unlikely world of high-school basketball. Theatrical director Eric Blau is represented by a serious novel, *The Beggar's Cup* (Knopf), which is the title of a movie script about Theodor Herzl and Israel to be produced by Holocaust survivor Morris Albert Cohen in Hollywood and Israel. John Wayne and other movie people appear "in person" in the novel. Writer Kim Wozencraft became "known" as the author of the autobiographical best-seller *Rush,* which was made into a movie. Here, in *Notes From the Country Club* (Houghton Mifflin), she writes the story of Cynthia Mitchell, inmate of the Fort Worth Correctional Center. Since Wozencraft served jail time, the story, though not strictly autobiographical, is founded upon authenticity. Sometimes when a very popular writer, Jackie Collins for example, gains considerable public visibility becoming a celebrity in her own right, she takes her image seriously and must consider herself as a role model. Consider this note attached to *American Star* (Simon and Schuster): "While *American Star* contains descriptions of unprotected sex appropriate to the period in which the story is set, the author wishes to emphasize the importance of practicing safe sex and the use of condoms in real life."

It was a year marked by a surprising number of new editions, sequels, reissues, and new versions. Thanks to the commercial success of Alexandra Ripley's *Scarlett,* publishers have shown a general interest in sequels. There were two sequels to *Pride and Prejudice,* both receiving mixed reviews: *Presumption* (M. Evans) by Julia Barrett and Emma Tennant's *Pemberley* (St. Martin's Press). Susan Hill produced a sequel to Daphne Du Maurier's *Rebecca*: *Mrs. DeWinter* (Morrow). Perennial interest in Sherlock Holmes, together with *The Oxford Sherlock Holmes* (Oxford University Press) in nine volumes and adding up to 2,873 pages, edited by Owen Dudley Edwards, surely inspired several original Holmes stories. Nicholas Meyer, author of two earlier Holmes novels, *The Seven-Per-Cent Solution* (1974) and *The West End Horror* (1976), returns to Holmes in *The Canary Trainer* (Norton). In this version Homes has miraculously survived his apparent death at Reichenbach Falls and now is discovered playing the violin for the Paris Opera. Sena Jeter Naslund also produced *Sherlock in Love* (Godine). These two taken together were described as "depressing exercises in antiquarianism" by George Grella in the *Washington Post* (21 November).

New editions of popular novels out of the near past included the thirty-fifth-anniversary issue of Pat Frank's apocalyptic novel *Alas, Babylon* (Harper-Collins) and a fortieth-anniversary edition of Ray Bradbury's *Fahrenheit 451* (Simon and Schuster). Two classics of modern fiction, Edith Wharton's *The Age of Innocence* (1920) and Virginia Woolf's *Orlando* (1928), appeared in mass-market paperback format, thanks to 1993 film versions of these stories. Scholar Viola Hopkins Winner edited texts of two novels by Wharton, *Fast and Loose* and *The Buccaneers* (University of Virginia Press), the former a novel Wharton began at age fourteen, the latter the novel she left unfinished at seventy-five. For an excellent survey of the Wharton phenomenon see Andrew Delbanco, "Missed Manners: The strange new life of Edith Wharton," *New Republic* (25 October). The latest volume in *The Cambridge Edition of the Works of F. Scott Fitzgerald,* edited by Matthew J. Bruccoli, *The Love of the Last Tycoon: A Western* (Cambridge University Press), presents a critical edition of Fitzgerald's last and unfinished novel whose history was complicated by Edmund Wilson's earlier edition which, until now, was the only version available. The new version fully restores the text of the novel to its 1940 state and offers complete editorial, scholarly, critical, and textual apparatus. Samuel Beckett's *Dream of Fair to Middling Women* (Arcade), the story of an Irish writer, Belacqua Shuah (its narrator is one "Mr. Beckett"), was originally written in 1932. But Beckett, unable to publish it anywhere at the time, set it aside and cannibalized it for later works. Louise Erdrich's first novel, *Love Medicine,* the 1984 winner of the National Book Critics Circle Award, was brought back by her publisher, Holt, in a newly revised and expanded version, with five new sections added to the original. Cashing in on the current box-office power and glory of Michael Crichton, author of *Jurassic Park* (1990) and other blockbusters, Dutton republished his medical-mystery story, *A Case of Need,* which won an Edgar Award in 1968.

Popular novelist Patrick O'Brian had the pleasure of seeing an early novel first published in 1952 reissued. *Testimonies* (Norton) is a tragic love story centered on Joseph Aubrey Pugh, who leaves Oxford to live in a Welsh village and work on his study of "The Bestiary Before Isidore of Seville." He falls in love with a farmer's wife, Bronwen Vaughn, with disastrous consequences for everyone involved. When the book first appeared in 1952 O'Brian was praised by poet and critic Delmore Schwartz in the *Partisan Review* as a major literary artist: "What O'Brian has accomplished is literally and exactly the equivalent of some of the lyrics in Yeats's *The Tower* and *The Winding Stair* where within the colloquial and formal framework of the folk poem a story of the greatest sophistication, consciousness and meaning becomes articulate!" For an excellent piece on O'Brian, see John Balzar, "Regressive Pleasures," *Los Angeles Times Book Review* (2 January 1994). Published for the first time in the United States was prolific author Paul West's first novel, *Tenement of Clay* (McPherson). Set in the slums of an American city, New Babylon, and told in the first person by midget wrestler Pee Wee Lazarus, its central figure is Papa Nick, "a self-righteous man attempting to provide temporary salvation to a hodgepodge of the homeless." In the afterword critic Bill Marx celebrates West's style: "In this literary revolution, style is a dark sacrament, a heretical sign of authorial grace."

There were new translations of celebrated foreign works during the year. Joachim Neugroschel produced a highly praised translation of Franz Kafka's shorter works – *The Metamorphosis and Other Stories* (Scribners). Knopf published a new translation of Mann's *Buddenbrooks* by John E. Woods. The much praised team of Richard Pevear and Larrissa Volokhonsky brought out the latest in their new translations of Dostoevsky – *Notes From Underground* (Knopf), with a foreword and extensive notes.

Other significant new editions include Marguerite Young's *Miss MacIntosh, My Darling* (1965), republished in two volumes by Dalkey Archive; Elizabeth Crook's *The Raven's Bride: A Novel of Eliza Allen and Sam Houston* (Southern Methodist University Press), originally published by Doubleday and here reappearing in the Southwest Life and Letters Series. Leon Forrest's huge novel, *Divine Days,* originally published in 1992 by Another Chicago Press and ignored by everyone except the Chicago newspapers, the *New Republic,* and the *DLB Yearbook,* was brought out by Norton in a new hardcover edition. Second Chance Press, beginning in February and thereafter releasing one title a month, republished ten erotic novels by Marco Vassi under the general title, "The Vassi Collection." Viking Penguin republished six novels by Henry Green in two volumes – *Loving/Living/Party Going* and *Nothing/Doting/Blindness/.* Gathering up the full text of *The Sheltering Sky* (1949), parts of three other novels, a novella and twelve short stories, together with poems, essays, letters, journals, and an interview, Ecco Press published *Too Far From Home: Selected Writings of Paul Bowles.* Poseidon created *Classic Crews: A Harry Crews Reader* which included two novels, *Car* (1972) and *The Gypsy's Curse* (1974), three essays, and Crews's autobiographical book *A Childhood* (1978). Cult figure Charles Bukowski, usually published by Black Sparrow, was spotlighted by HarperCollins for *Run With the Hunted: A Charles Bukowski Reader.*

The South continues to try to preserve and maintain its modern tradition. J. S. Sanders continued with the development of its Southern Classics Series, adding titles by (among others) Robert Penn Warren, Madison Jones, Carolyn Gordon, Elizabeth Maddox Roberts, Andrew Lytle, and Allen Tate. At year's end (see *The Chronicle of Higher Education,* 4 January 1994) Louisiana State University announced a new series, Voices of the South. The first list, due out in early 1994, includes fiction by Peter Taylor, Fred Chappell, Ellen Douglas, George Garrett, Lee Smith, and Elizabeth Spencer. Rediscovery and reissue are likewise beginning to use audio books to take advantage of current interests. For example, Shelby Foote's *Shiloh* (1952) has been released by Recorded Books. Here Foote reads some of the text himself, and there is a fifteen-minute interview with the author.

Many of the barriers separating genre and mainstream fiction seem to be breaking down. That thrillers are more and more part of the literary mainstream is evident in a *Time* magazine article, "Solve It Again, Sam" (15 November) by John

E. ANNIE PROULX

The SHIP-PING NEWS

A NOVEL

Dust jacket for E. Annie Proulx's Pulitzer Prize-winning novel set in Newfoundland

Skow, devoted to Joseph Wambaugh, Elmore Leonard, George V. Higgins, and Lawrence Block. Two other writers who were widely reviewed and praised in the book's pages were Tony Hillerman and Denmark's Peter Hoeg. Hillerman's *Sacred Clowns* (HarperCollins), following a three-year gap since his last Navajo mystery, is the thirteenth novel about Joe Leaphorn, now a lieutenant of the Navajo tribal police, and his deputy Jim Chee. Peter Hoeg's *Smilla's Sense of Snow* (Farrar, Straus and Giroux) received extraordinary reviews and was selected by the editors of *Publishers Weekly* as one of the "Best Books of 1993" (1 November). Told in the first person by thirty-seven-year-old Smilla Qaavigaaq Jaspersen, the daughter of an Eskimo mother and Danish father, the mystery is triggered at the outset by the death of six-year-old Isaiah Christiansen and leads to icy Greenland and complex chicanery. Wambaugh's *Finnegan's Week* (Morrow), his fifteenth book, is a story of toxic waste set in San Diego, in which detective Finbar Finnegan teams up

with two female cops, Nell Salter and Ann Doggett, against the bad guys. Dick Francis's thirty-second novel *Decider* (Putnam), was a best-seller. Protagonist Lee Morris inherits seven race horses and then has to solve a case of arson. To the animal-rights people Francis explains: "Horses run and jump because they like to."

Other old-timers of solid reputation brought out thrillers this year. Ed McBain's *Mary, Mary* (Warner) returns to Florida and the ongoing character of defense attorney Matthew Hope, here successfully defending Mary Barton. Detective Dave Robicheaux gets tangled up in the business of shooting a Civil War movie in James Lee Burke's *In the Electric Mist with Confederate Dead* (Hyperion). The amazingly productive Donald E. Westlake brought out *Don't Ask* (Mysterious Press), eighth in the series of caper novels featuring the burglar John Archibald Dortmunder (whose motto is *Quid lucrum istic mihi est?* — What's in it for me?) and his well-established buddies — Stan Murch, Kelp, and Tiny Bulcher. This one involves a trip to Eastern Europe in an attempt to steal a holy relic. During 1993 Westlake was elected as a grandmaster by the Mystery Writers of America. James Crumley produced his fourth private-eye novel in a career of eighteen years, his first book in ten years — *The Mexican Tree Duck* (Mysterious Press). C. W. Sughrue, star of Crumley's earlier three thrillers, goes on a road trip searching for the kidnapped mother of a biker. Scott Turow's *Pleading Guilty* (Farrar, Straus and Giroux) is his third "legal" thriller. Mack Malloy, former policeman and now a member of the law firm Gage and Griswell, is sent in search of missing partner Bert Kamin and a large sum of missing money. John le Carré's *The Night Manager* (Knopf) moves from earlier Cold War preoccupations to contemporary drugs and arms dealing. With the Persian Gulf War in the background, Jonathan Pine, who at the outset is night manager of a Zurich hotel, goes up against the bad guys headed by the villainous Richard Onslow Roper. The indefatigable Ruth Rendell published *The Crocodile Bird* (Crown) under her own name and *Anna's Book* (Harmony) as Barbara Vine. In the latter the diaries of Anna Westerdy, a Danish woman living in England deeply concerned with an eighty-year-old mystery, are published and become a best-seller. In the former a wounded mother, Eve, raises her daughter, Liza, in strict seclusion and is willing to go to any length to preserve that privacy. Two thrillers by celebrities were Jim Lehrer's *Blue Hearts* (Random House), an inside-the-beltway thriller (evidently a new subgenre) involving a former secretary of state; and *Murder in the Senate* (Doubleday) by Sen. William S. Cohen and Thomas B. Allen. Here the protagonist is Jeffrey "Fitz" Fitzgerald, fictional chief of the Capitol police. An 18 January review in the *Washington Post* had these kind words: "This is not a memorable book, or an important one . . . but it is very entertaining." Two posthumous novels were Chester Himes's *Plan B* (University of Mississippi Press), last of the Harlem thrillers featuring Coffin Ed Johnson and Grave Digger Jones, still unfinished when Himes died in 1984; and Charles Willeford's *The Shark-Infested Custard: A Novel of Crime, Vice and Sex* (Underwood-Miller). Willeford wrote thrillers for many years and had some popular success in the 1980s with a series of novels featuring Hoke Moseley. This last novel is told in four separate stories linked by point of view.

Other newer voices made a mark during the year. Randall Silvis, who earlier won a Drue Heinz Literature Prize, wrote *An Occasional Hell* (Permanent), concerning Ernest DeWalt, former private investigator and novelist who takes a job at Shenango College in rural Pennsylvania, only to become deeply involved in local complexities of crime and punishment. Kit Craig's *Twice Burned* (Little, Brown), the second novel under this pseudonym by veteran literary novelist Kit Reed, is a story of murder and psychological terror centered around young and mysterious identical twins – Jane ("Jade") and Emily ("Emerald") Archer. Larry Beinhart's *American Hero* (Pantheon) is a bold mix of fact, fiction, and fantasy. Among the real characters included in his design are George Bush, James Baker, and Saddam Hussein. Beinhart is author of three earlier thrillers and has won an Edgar award. *The Man Who Invented Florida* (St. Martin's Press) is the third thriller by former Gulf Coast fishing guide Randy Wayne. Timothy Watts is new to the genre but aroused interest and received praise for his *Cons* (Soho), starring ex-convict "Cully" Cullen and mainly set in and around Beaufort, South Carolina. George Baxt's *The Marlene Dietrich Murder Case* (St. Martin's Press) in which Marlene and Anna Mae Wong get together and catch a killer, is the latest in his ongoing series of celebrity thrillers. *O Little Town of Maggody* (Dutton) by Joan Hess introduces protagonist Arly Hanks, female chief of police of an Ozark hamlet. Martha Grimes, in her twelfth Richard Jury mystery, *The Horse You Came In On* (Knopf), brings English police superintendent Jury and his loyal Sergeant Wiggins across the Atlantic to Baltimore to solve a murder case. Frederick Barton's *With Extreme Prejudice* (Villard) was described by David Nicholson of the *Washington Post* (7 December) as "a mystery concerning alcoholic newspaper movie

critic Mike Barnett's search to discover the truth behind his lawyer-wife's death in a traffic accident." It is set in New Orleans and deals with the subjects of race and racism. Two writers of blockbusters tried their hands at thrillers this year. Dean Koontz's *Mr. Murder* (Putnam), his twenty-third novel, joins together the horror and mystery genres, creating a story in which a kind of Frankenstein monster tries to take the life of look-alike-mystery writer Marty Stillwater. In *A Dangerous Fortune* (Delacorte) Ken Follett develops a mystery set in Victorian England, beginning in 1866 with a drowning at Windfield School. Meanwhile, in *Bodies Electric* (Crown), Colin Harrison, author of an earlier novel and husband of literary novelist Kathryn Harrison, continues the subgenre of the "corporate thriller" with an intense urban love story. Toby Olson, a distinctly literary author, a winner of the PEN/Faulkner Award, published a kind of thriller with *At Sea* (Simon and Schuster). Its protagonist is Peter Blue, a policeman in Provincetown; but Olson uses the plot line and some of the general conventions of the thriller for other philosophical purposes striving, in his own words, for "representation, though of an entirely different order."

One of the most vigorously and successfully promoted books of the year was a thriller – Carl Hiaasen's *Strip Tease* (Knopf). Hiaasen, a topflight investigative journalist for the *Miami Herald,* here turned his attention on a corrupt and troubled Florida congressman, Dave Dilbeck; his fixer, Moldy Moldowsky; and a group of nude dancers in local strip joints, especially Erin Grant. The worlds of the big sugar lobby ("Every few years, the Congress of the United States of America voted generous price supports for a handful of agricultural milllionaires in the great state of Florida"), the local crime scene ("She was also aware that in the Southern District of Florida, the United States attorney spent exactly zero manhours in pursuit of mail thieves, as the government's time was consumed by the prosecution of drug dealers, gunrunners, deposed foreign dictators, savings-and-loans executives, corrupt local politicians and crooked cops of all ranks"), and the outlandish arena of the strip joints ("Erin was constantly reminded of the ridiculous power of sex; routine female nakedness reduced some men to stammering, clammy-fingered fools") come vividly to life. There are even moments of philosophical import – "'Men will try anything,' Monique, Jr., said skeptically. 'Anything for pussy.'" With *Strip Tease* Hiaasen joins the company of the top guns of the thriller. The jacket quotes grandmaster Donald Westlake: "He is so good he ought to be illegal."

For various reasons the genre of the historical novel continues to shrink in importance; but, nevertheless, the imagined past continues to engage some of our best writers and at least some readers. Bharati Mukherjee, now an American citizen, brings together the history of India and America in *The Holder of the World* (Knopf). In this, her sixth work of fiction, Mukherjee tells the story of Hannah Easton, born in the New England colonies in 1670, who follows her husband to India and ultimately becomes Salem Bibi, the prized consort of a Hindu raja. It is a double story from the point of view of Beigh Masters, a contemporary New England woman (married to Venn, an Indian computer scientist) tracing the history of her ancestor, Hannah. Author of seventeen novels and other books, including the critically praised *In a Dark Wood Wandering* (1989), Dutch novelist Hella S. Hasse is represented by *Threshold of Fire* (Academy Chicago), which is concerned with the Roman Empire and the court of the Emperor Honorius during June and July of 414 A.D. Pop writer Colleen McCullough brought out the third volume in her ongoing story of ancient Rome – *Fortune's Favorites* (Morrow), all about Julius Caesar and Pompey the Great. Several novels focused on eighteenth-century France with the Revolution either soon coming or in progress. Delia Sherman's *The Porcelain Dove* (Dutton) is the story told in the first person (ostensibly written with a magic quill) by Berthe Devet, maid to a duchess, involving an urgent quest to find a fabulous porcelain dove. Hilary Mantel's *A Place of Greater Safety* (Atheneum), a mixture of real and imaginary characters and with constantly shifting points of view, concerns the French Revolution and its leading figures. So does *Dr. Guillotine* (Sinclair-Stevenson) by actor Herbert Lom, though the story is centered mainly on Jean-Paul Marat, Charlotte Corday, and, of course, Dr. Joseph Guillotine. Other novels dealt with historical characters. A first novel by Francis Sherwood, *Vindication* (Farrar, Straus and Giroux) is loosely based on the life of Mary Wollstonecraft (1759–1797). This was widely reviewed and praised in spite of some inevitable lapses. For example, while William Blake recites one of his poems: "Mrs. Blake rolled her eyes. 'William, I think you have had a drop too many.'" Swedish novelist Sigrid Combuchen in *Byron* (Heinemann) adds an interesting twist to the biographical novel, putting Byron's poetic theories to work in glossing and explicating his life. Told in multiple points of view, the novel uses real and imaginary characters from the modern Byron Society. *Refinements of Love: A Novel About Clover and Henry*

Adams (Pantheon) by Sarah Booth Conroy is a fictional version of the journals of Marian Clover Adams, wife of Henry, who killed herself in 1885. Max Byrd, in *Jefferson: A Novel* (Bantam), focuses on Jefferson's time in Paris as ambassador as seen through the eyes of his secretary William Short. Though Jefferson in fact destroyed his wife's journals and letters, novelist Roberta Grimes here recreates them in a fictional version, covering the years from 1770 to 1781 in *My Thomas: A Novel of Martha Jefferson's Life* (Doubleday). Moving more toward the strictly fictional we have novels like Newfoundland poet John Steffler's highly praised example of "Canadian magic realism" – *The Afterlife of George Cartwright* (Holt), based on the journal of a mythical character. In *The Life and Times of Captain M.* (Knopf), Douglas Glover tells the story of the American Revolution from the standpoints of three people – Capt. Hendrick Nellis, a Tory officer; his son Oskar, on the other side; and Mary Hunsacker, a German immigrant kidnapped by Indians. Oskar narrates all the stories.

A fine Elizabethan tale Stephanie Cowell's *Nicholas Cooke: Actor, Soldier, Physician, Priest* (Norton), first volume of a planned trilogy, arrives with considerable advance critical praise. Set in the late sixteenth and early seventeenth century, this is the picaresque story of Nicholas Cooke, who does a little bit of everything and somehow comes to know just about everyone including Will Shagspere from Stratford and Kit Morley (Marlowe), poet and pederast. By the end Cooke comes to a kind of wisdom: "Does one find peace irrevocably in this dirty, sweet, tattered world, the mystical and unholy place in which we have woken? Aye, for sweet moments." Dan Jacobson's *The God-Fearer* (Scribners) links history to fable, positing the situation that the Jews overcame the Roman Empire and that the last Christians, "Christers," are a persecuted, ghettoized minority. Alan Decker McNarie's *Yeshua: The Gospel of St. Thomas* (Pushcart) puts the disciple "Doubting Thomas" in prison in India, remembering his life forty years after the crucifixion. How far back can an historical novel go? David Rosenberg's *The Lost Book of Paradise* (Hyperion) tells the story of Adam and Eve as filtered through the mind of Devorah Bat-David, a scholar working in the archives of Solomon.

While somewhat subdued, like the economy, compared to other years the area of translation was nevertheless widespread in its offerings. From younger writers in Japan came *Kitchen* (Grove) by Banana Yoshimoto, the story of Shishosetsu Mikage who loves kitchens of all kinds and likes the company of gay men (this book sold two million copies in Japan); and Ryu Murakami's *Sixty-Nine* (Kodansha), another first-person story, this one told by seventeen-year-old Kenesuke Yazaki, who, among other things, is trying to create a movie with his friends. From China came *Red Sorghum* (Viking) by Mo Yan, a northern Chinese story of bandits and rebels which began with oral accounts of rural life in the sorghum country of Shandong and is announced as having been inspired by the work and example of Gabriel Garcia Marquez. *Black Snow* (Atlantic Monthly) recounts the story of Li Huiquan, a petty criminal and loser (and an orphan) who tries to survive on the social edges of a changing China. Both of these books were originally published in the 1980s. From contemporary Vietnam came *Paradise of the Blind* (Morrow), by Duong Thu Huong. The story of a Vietnamese family badly torn by the events of our era, the narrative is told from the point of view of a young Vietnamese woman, Hang, who works in a Russian factory and remembers her home. Indonesian novelist Pramoedya Ananta Toer is represented by *Child Of All Nations* (Morrow), part of the "Buru Tetralogy." This tells the life story of a young Javanese, Minke, who is the first member of his family to graduate from Dutch Secondary School in the Colonial days. Ben Okri, who earlier won a coveted Booker Prize for his *The Famished Road* (1991), published a sequel to that novel of Yoruba magic realism – *Songs of Enchantment* (Doubleday). Again the narrator is Azaro, the *Abiku,* or spirit child. This novel deals mainly with the time of civil war in Nigeria and was described by K. Anthony Appiah in the *Washington Post* (3 October) as "like a collection of excerpts from the earlier books." Appiah adds that "those who have not read the earlier books will find this one simply unintelligible." In *With Downcast Eyes* (Little, Brown) Moroccan novelist Tahar Ben Jelloun offers a story about, and told by, Fatma, reporting on her life from age ten to adulthood and set in a village of the Atlas Mountains and in Paris. From Egypt and written in English was *In the Eye of the Sun* (Pantheon), by Ahdaf Soueif. This, too, is the life story of a woman, Asya al-Ulma, who is torn between the worlds of England and Egypt and between her Egyptian husband Saif Madi and an English lover, Gerald Stone. *Arabian Jazz* (Harcourt Brace) by Diana Abu-Jaber tells of two sisters, Jemorah and Melvina of Palestinian-American background.

Latin-American authors continued to make a mark in the United States. Widely reviewed was *Before the Night Falls* (Viking), a memoir and/or autobiographical fiction by Reinaldo Arenas, prominent

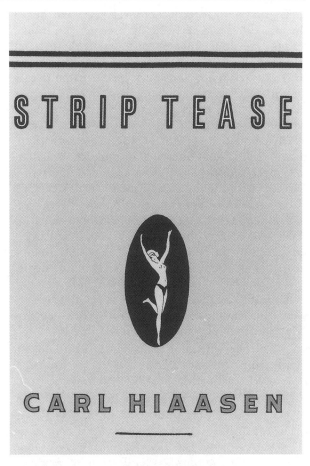

Dust jacket for the novel that places Carl Hiaasen among "the top guns of the thriller"

Cuban writer. Arenas, a homosexual who suffered from AIDS and recently committed suicide, created a poetic form which G. Gabrera Infante described as "a downpour of memories at his open grave." Another blending of fact and fiction is Fernando Alegria's *Allende: A Novel* (Stanford University Press). Alegria, a Chilean, who was the official biographer of Salvador Allende at the time of his death, tells the life of his subject as a kind of fiction: "There are moods I must describe and interpret, words that I can hear which perhaps were not said, rumors, events that I did not witness and yet I feel I know how they happened." Also from Alegria there was a translation of his fourth novel, originally published in Spanish in 1964, *The Maypole Warriors* (Latin American Literary Review). Here Alegria, who has been called a master of "the fiction of displacement," tells the story of a Chilean family in the late 1930s, divided between the politics of the left and rising support for the Nazis. Peruvian novelist Alfredo Bryce Echenique is represented by the first English edition of a much praised novel, *A World for*

Julius, first published twenty-three years ago. Set in the late 1940s and early 1950s, it centers on Julius, youngest of four children, and details the palatial world of the very rich. In *Shadows* (Knopf), Argentinian Osvaldo Soriano spins the surrealist tale of an unnamed narrator looking for a place to cash in his ticket after a railway derailment and who meets with a series of other derailed wanderers. Translated from Brazilian Portuguese, *Turbulence* (Pantheon) by Chico Buarque, a popular Brazilian folksinger, tells the story of an unnamed upperclass narrator without any commitments, who steals his sister's jewels, trades them for dope, and gets himself in deep trouble. The story allows for a sharp clashing contrast between the world of Brazilian affluence and the world of the slums and shanty towns. Jorge Amado, author of twenty-one novels, tells in *The War of the Saints* (Bantam) of forty-eight hours in Bahia where, in his own form of magic realism, the author collaborates with Saint Barbara Yansan to help his central characters find love.

The overwhelming majority of foreign novels published in America during 1993 came from Europe and from English-speaking countries.

Albanian master Ismail Kadare, in the fourth of his novels so far published here, *The Palace of Dreams* (Morrow), creates a mysterious quasi-allegorical story of the *Tabir Sarrail,* a government place for the involuntary collection of dreams. Mark-Alem, a member of the ancient and distinguished Quprili family, works there as a dream collector. Serbian Milorad Pavic tells a complex story-riddled version of the Hero and Leander myth in *The Inner Side of the Wind, Or, the Novel of Hero and Leander* (Knopf). The principals, Heronea Bukur (born 1910) and Leander (Radacha Chihorich), an illiterate seventeenth-century stonecutter and picaro, are separated by a sea of time. Learning to read, Radacha encounters the myth and tells his tutor, "Perhaps Leander swam through time, not through water." Serbo-Croatian novelist Aleksander Tisma, in *Kapo* (Harcourt Brace), tells the story of Flamian, who served as a Kapo at Auschwitz and is still obsessed forty years later with the memory of Helena Lifka, a Jewish woman. In Czech writer Ivan Kilma's *Judge on Trial* (Knopf), Judge Adam Kindl is assigned to a no-win murder case. In this story the present action is told in a third-person narration while the chapters set in the past are developed in first-person monologues. Martin M. Simecka was a young Czechoslovakian novelist when he wrote *The Year of the Frog* (Louisiana State University Press), but by the time it appeared in the United States he was a citizen of the new nation-

state of Slovakia. The story is about a young man, Milan, who is confined to a series of menial jobs — clerk in a hardware store, hospital orderly — because his father is a dissident. This novel won the Pegasus Prize for Literature sponsored by Mobil Oil Corporation, and they sent the author on a cross-country tour of the United States. From Russia there was a first novel, and a big best-seller in Europe, *Russian Beauty* (Viking), the story of beautiful and erotic Irinia Tarakazova about whom John Finder wrote in a *Boston Globe* review (18 April): "Irinia is equal parts Molly Bloom, Emma Bovary, Fanny Hill, and Isadora Wing." This lively and satiric metafiction is set during the Soviet era. A rare translation from Estonian was Jann Kross's *The Czar's Madman* (Pantheon), set in the early nineteenth century and centered on Col. Timotheus von Brock.

Sweden's famous film director Ingmar Bergman wrote a mixed form of novel, memoir, and screenplay about himself and his parents (using slightly changed names) in *The Best of Intentions* (Arcade). This story was produced as a film in 1992. French writer Dan Franck tells the story in *Separation* (Knopf) of a young, unnamed couple, married for seven years and with two children, chiefly narrated by the husband and covering a time span of 135 days in Paris. Wrote Richard Eder about it in the *Los Angeles Times Book Review* (26 December): *Separation* is a very precisely delineated slice not of life but of life's pain." Described by Carlin Romano in the *Philadelphia Inquirer* ("On Books," 25 April) as "an Italian Alison Lurie," Francesca Duranti in *Personal Effects* (Random House) tells a story of the literary world on both sides of the (then) Iron Curtain, featuring biographer and media figure Valentina Barbieri. *Procedura* (Villard) by Salvatore Mannuzzu, winner of the Viareggio Prize for fiction, received considerable attention in the United States. Set in Sardinia and Rome in the late 1970s, it tells of a prominent Italian judge, Valerio Garau, who dies suddenly and mysteriously. The narrator, himself a judge (like the author), is assigned to investigate the death. He discovers a whole hidden and corrupt world of which he had been unaware of and, instead of answers, he comes up with only deep and immutable questions. Among the leading German novels in translation were Michael Kruger's *The Man in the Tower* (Kruger), telling of a high-minded, intellectual German painter who lives in a tower in France and who, in spite of himself, becomes involved with some corrupt and ambiguous people. Patrick McGrath writing about the book in the *New York Times Book Review* (4 April) called it "a picture of a shallow, rubbishly materialistic Europe decaying in all spheres: political, ecological, intellectual and esthetic." In *Silent Close No. 6* (Readers International) by Monika Maron, Rosalind Polkowski works as the personal secretary of a retired Communist party leader, Herbert Beerenbaum. Set in the days shortly before the fall of the German Democratic Republic, this third novel of Maron's is not entirely without hope for the future: "Everything depended on Beerenbaum's death and that of his generation." Gerhard Kopf has an anonymous first-person narrator, a professor of Lusitanics (the science of loss) at the center of his intensely literary novel, *There Is No Borges* (Braziller). This is Kopf's first book to be published in America.

Two novels from Israel attracted attention and earned favorable reviews. In *Bone to the Bone* (Grove/Atlantic) by Nathan Shaham, the narrator and protagonist is Avigdor Berkov, a seventy-year-old Russian emigre who is writing a memoir of his life and of the twentieth-century socialist movement. The distinguished Amos Oz wrote about Efraim ("Fima") Nisan, once a gifted poet, now working as a poet at an abortion clinic, who spends more of his time in imagination and dreams than in the "real" world, in *Fima* (Harcourt Brace). It was a good year for Irish fiction, though the picture of Ireland coming from these novels is a bleak one. Roddy Doyle's latest, *Paddy Clarke Ha Ha Ha* (Viking), winner of the Booker Prize, is treated elsewhere, but there were other strong novels. In his first novel, *The Heather Blazing* (Viking), Irish journalist Colin Toibin follows the lives of one family – High Court Judge Eamon Redmond, his daughter Niamh, and his son Donal (of the Irish Council for Civil Liberties) – which becomes representative of the contemporary national experience. Patrick McCabe's *The Butcher Boy* (Fromm International), his third novel, though not without a share of humor, is a savage story of madness and murder told in perfect pitch and tone by Francie Brady. It is set in the Ireland of the late 1950s and early 1960s. John Banville, literary editor of the *Irish Times* and a highly productive and innovative novelist, has linked his latest novel, *Ghosts* (Knopf) to his earlier *Book of Evidence* (1989). The nameless narrator has just served ten years in jail and now works for an art expert, Silas Kreutznaer, in a rundown mansion on an island off the Irish coast. Complexities arise when a boat runs aground and the passengers come ashore. Writing a front-page review for the *New York Times Book Review*, Wendy Lesser opined: "The achievement of *Ghosts* is to use words as brush-

strokes, to create in language an artwork that has all the appeal of a complex painting."

There is so much exchange these days across the Atlantic that it is tricky, if not difficult, to find works which are inescapably British. In *Now You Know* (Viking) Michael Frayn, author of other novels and the successful play *Noises Off* (1983) has created a farce built on the character of Tony Little, founder of OPEN, who is obsessed with trying to create a world without secrets. In *Hotel Pastis: A Novel of Provence* (Knopf) Peter Mayle, who has made a reputation and a small fortune writing nonfiction about the simple wonders of Provence, tried his hand at a novel about an advertising executive who abandons the London world for Provence. Inescapably British, if opposite sides of the same coin, Fay Weldon and Anita Brookner produced new variations on familiar themes. Miss Brookner's *Fraud* (Random House) is, in the words of the *New York Times,* "a novel that explores relationships between aged parents and adult children"; Fay Weldon's *Trouble* (Viking) is typically bitter and funny in its view of chaotic domestic derring-do. Set mostly (except for sidebars in London and in Nashville, Tennessee) in Swaithey in Suffolk, beginning on 15 February 1952 during the two minutes of silence for the death of King George VI, Rose Tremain's *Sacred Country* (Atheneum) is the story of Mary Ward, who *thinks* a message to her guinea hen in the opening scene, announcing her principal problem (and subject): "I have a secret to tell you dear, and this is it. I am not Mary. That is a mistake. I am not a girl. I am a boy." Jamaican writer Victor Headley's *Yardie* (Atlantic Monthly) is already a kind of cult book in England. It tells the story of D., an illegal immigrant who rises high (in the underclass) through the drug trade. It concerns Jamaican drug gangs in London, and much of the book is in dialect: "If a man grudge you for your car, your girl, any'ting, him will kill you an' take it from you." From New Zealand came first novelist Damien Williams's *The Miserables* (Harcourt Brace), telling the story of Brett Healey, thirty-year-old literary editor of a newspaper. Rodney Hall added to his Australian trilogy with *The Grisly Wife* (Farrar, Straus and Giroux), a story of twenty-two years in the early days of New South Wales, told by a woman missionary who is part of a strange cult. *Loving Daughters* (Norton) was originally published in Australia in 1984 and is described in "Notable Books of the Year" in the *New York Times Book Review* as concerning "a humanly imperfect rural family on whom the outside intrudes in the form of a handsome, single English clergyman." Australian

Thomas Keneally, who won a Booker Prize in 1982 for *Schindler's List,* tells the story in *Woman of the Inner Sea* (Doubleday) of thirty-eight-year-old Kate Gaffney-Kozinski, who flees suburban Sydney for a hard life in the northwest in the old-fashioned town of Myambagh. After a series of adventures and misadventures, she is ready and able to reclaim her life. Finally, several novels from South Africa earned attention: Lynn Freed's *The Bungalow* (Poseidon); *Cape of Storms* (Simon and Schuster) by Andre Brink; and Karel Schoeman's *Take Leave and Go* (Sinclair-Stevenson), a novel about the life of an Afrikaans poet. Lionel Abraham's *The Celibacy of Felix Greenspan* (Academy Chicago) is set in Johannesburg and follows a young man who is a victim of cerebral palsy through seventeen episodes, from his childhood to his late twenties.

The Southern novel, once at least a regional variation if not a distinct genre, is more and more mainstream, and less easily defined. Many writers use the South as a setting and many Southern writers feel free to use other historical or geographic settings. But this year, as in other years, there were a number of outstanding and distinctly Southern novels, teasing along the edges of the regional tradition. Sarah Gilbert's *Summer Gloves* (Warner) is her third novel, this time a first-person story told by the aptly named Pammy Outlaw. Pam Durban's *The Laughing Place* (Scribners) is set in Timmons, South Carolina, and treats the Vesses family while under siege. Louise Shivers enjoyed a considerable success with her earlier novel, *Here to Get My Baby Out of Jail* (1983). Her new book, *A Whistling Woman* (Longstreet), is a post–Civil War story beginning in 1867 and ending in 1910 in Richmond. It is the story of Chaney Weeks and her daughter Georgeanna and builds to an horrific (and satisfactory) scene of pure Southern Gothic: "After I'd chopped him up into as many pieces as I could, I took it all, wrapping it up in two sacks and burying it all in the black mire under the outhouse. . . . Nobody ever came looking for him." David Payne's *Ruin Creek* (Doubleday) offered narratives of three people in a North Carolina family during the 1950s – Jimmy Madden, his wife May, and their eleven-year-old son Joey. By the end Joey has learned that "even if love wasn't strong enough to hold our world together, it still made the broken pieces shine." Mark Childress's fourth novel, a story about Alabama and Hollywood in 1965, *Crazy in Alabama* (Putnam) earned him an audio sale to HarperAudio, translation rights in seven countries, and selection as a Literary Guild Featured Alternate. It tells the story of the coming of age of orphan Peejoe and his Aunt Lucille, dividing the nar-

rative between them. Fannie Flagg is quoted as surmising: "If Flannery O'Connor and Stephen King had written a book together, this would be it." Although it is plotted, more or less, as a crime story, T. R. Pearson's *Cry Me a River* (Henry Holt) has a huge cast of eccentric characters, "a large gallery of complex, driven figures," wrote William T. Vollman in the *New York Times Book Review* (11 April), adding: "I would say that this novel is about two-thirds digressions by weight, and the digressions are delicious." Not everyone agreed. Though *Cry Me a River* opened with starred reviews in *Publishers Weekly* and *Kirkus Reviews,* and it was claimed by its publisher as Pearson's "breakthrough" book, this novel, the author's sixth, opened to a mixed reception. From the outset Pearson has been praised for his highly personal style, described by Michael Upchurch in the *Seattle Times* as "a head-on collision between L'il Abner and Gertrude Stein."

Novels with a minority ethnic background or point of view can be expected to thrive in the climate of multicultural diversity, but, in a relative sense, there were a limited number of such books this year and, within any given grouping, more variety than one might have anticipated. The leading African-American novel of the year, intended to follow *Roots* in true blockbuster manner, Alex Haley's *Queen* (Morrow) turned out to be a commercial and critical disaster. A posthumous book, left unfinished by Haley when he died, the book was edited and ghosted by David Stephens. Where *Roots* dealt with Haley's mother's side of the family, this book is concerned with his father's line. It was greeted by negative reviews, where it was reviewed at all, and is rich in the kind of bad writing that reviewers love to discover: "Sally moved in what she often thought was a hypocritical hemisphere with regard to her son's libido." Say what?

Cyrus Colter's *City of Light* (Thunder Mouth) is set in Paris and centered on Paul Kessey, a light-skinned and privileged black man, hurt by racism and haunted by his heritage. He is killed by the outraged husband of a woman named Cecile Foumier, with whom Paul is having an affair. Albert French's *Billy* (Viking) is set in the 1930s in Mississippi and is the story of a ten-year-old black boy convicted of and subsequently executed for the murder of a white girl. Though the situation is crudely composed and, at best, wildly improbable then or now, the writing in a collective third-person voice is at times exciting. John Edgar Wideman describes that voice as somehow at once traditional and unique: "Rich, uncluttered, containing echoes of Zora Neale Hurston's vernacular lyricism, Richard Wright's stark naturalism, the bardic narrator of Jean Toomer's *Cane, Billy* is the debut of a unique voice." Trey Ellis writes in another kind of voice from another kind of black experience — "Marquita, my mother, was doing her residency at the University of Michigan, and Fletcher, my dad, was finishing his Ph.D. in sociology." His first book, *Platitudes* (Vintage), is sophisticated and satiric. So, in a slightly different way, is *Home Repairs* (Simon and Schuster), this being the diary of a privileged young man, Austin McMillan, from 17 February 1979 to 28 February 1988. Austin devotes himself to the ways and means of making out with women.

African-American women writers produced a number of interesting novels. Dori Sanders, in *Her Own Place* (Algonquin), tells the story of a black farming family in South Carolina and of Mae Lee Barnes, who raises five children as a single parent with some help from others. *Free* (Dutton) by Marsha Hunt is her third book and second novel. Set in Germantown, Pennsylvania, in the early 1900s, it is about the brief love affair between a black stable boy and a visiting young Englishman. The story of a tyrannical mother, Esther Lovejoy, and her three daughters Betty, Emily, and Annie Ruth, who come home to Mulberry, Georgia, for the funeral of the mother is told in *Ugly Ways* (Harcourt Brace) by Tina McElroy. Points of view, including the ghost of the mother, are shifting; but Ernest, her husband, has the last word at the funeral — "Esther Lovejoy's life spoke for itself." Michelle Cliff, in *Free Enterprise* (Dutton), tells of Jamaican Annie Christmas and Mary Ellen Pleasant of New England, who both become involved with John Brown's raid on Harper's Ferry. It begins in 1920, with the aged Annie living on the Mississippi River near the lepers' colony at Carville, and moves back and forth in time from 1858 onward. Like *Billy* this is a wildly improbable story and is crude as history, but it is written in an interesting way. Another novelist from the islands, this one a Trinidadian, Kelvin Christopher James has written *Secrets* (Villard), a gracefully poetic version of the life of a young woman, Uxann, who endures much without breaking. Fluent style and dimensional characters, both sharply evident in *Jumping Ship and Other Stories* (1992), his other book, make *Secrets* a powerful novel.

It was a year when, obviously, publishers were looking for books about the gang experience. Among these were Luis J. Rodriguez's *Always Running* (Curbstone); Bob Sipchen's *Baby Insane and the Buddha* (Doubleday); and Abraham Rodriguez, Jr.'s *Spidertown* (Hyperion). This last book and its author were well

Dust jacket for David Leavitt's novel that was the subject of a lawsuit in Great Britain brought by Sir Stephen Spender

and widely publicized. Set in contemporary South Bronx, it is the story of Miguel, dope runner for Spider, who falls in love with Cristalena, and has as good friends Amelia, Firebug, and a good cop named Sanchez. Jess Mowry, whose earlier *Way Past Cool* (1992) made a mark, brought out *Six Out Seven* (Farrar, Straus and Giroux). Beginning as two stories (that of Corbitt Wainwright, age thirteen, in rural Mississippi, and Lactameon, also thirteen, a 350-pound gang member in West Oakland, California), it comes together when Corbitt flees to California, "where everything be better for everybody."

There were several novels by Native Americans that received some notice and attention. Ron Querry's first novel, *The Death of Bernadette Lefthand* (Red Crane), is set in Dulce, New Mexico, in the Navajo Nation and is told by a choir of separate voices. It deals with magic, witchcraft, and alcoholism, and is partly a murder mystery. Thomas King's *Green Grass, Running Water* (Houghton Mifflin) intercuts the telling of creation myths with contemporary events and stories of the Blackfoot Tribe in alberta, Canada. There are myths, magic realism, and a good deal of rowdy comedy. *Dawnland* (Fulcrum) is by Joseph Bruchac, an Abenaki storyteller. Here he uses the novel form to re-create the time between the end of the Ice Age and the coming of the Europeans. Young Hunter is sent forth on an urgent quest by Bear Talker. It is a picture of tribal life in those early days. Most widely promoted among these was *The Lone Ranger and Tonto Fistfight in Heaven* (Atlantic Monthly) by Sherman Alexie. The author, a Spokane/Coeur d'Alene Indian, tells a sequence of stories of various kinds, all dealing with life on the Spokane Reservation in the 1960s and 1970s.

Representative of the continuing literary creativity of the American Hispanic culture are *La Maravilla* (Dutton) by Alfredo Vea, Jr., *So Far From God* (Norton) by Ana Castillo, and *In Search of Bernabe* (Arte Publico) by Graciela Limon. Limon, who has firsthand knowledge, tells a powerful and complex story of the civil war in El Salvador. Ana Castillo has published two previous novels, one of which, *The Mixquiahuala Letters*, received the American Book Award in 1987. In *So Far From God* (Norton), set in the village of Tome in central New Mexico, she recounts the real and mythical history of the place and of the two decades in the lives of a single Chicana family. Her publisher describes her highly personal manner as "homegrown magic realism." *La Maravilla* (Dutton) is the first novel by Alfredo Vea, Jr., who started as a migrant farm worker and is now an attorney in San Francisco. He sets his story in the unincorporated community of Buckeye, not far from Phoenix. At the heart of the story, set in summer 1958, is the boy Beto, being raised by his grandparents; but there is a very large cast of characters and enough history, myth, and events to fill an eight-foot shelf of novels. It is, at least in part, autobiographical; for the author writes: "The flesh of the book is fiction; the bones are real."

Not surprisingly, in view of the present climate of relative tolerance and the growing awareness of the gay community as a market, publishers are more and more openly appealing to that community with fiction, some of it sexually explicit. One serious literary controversy of the year arose from the publication of *While England Sleeps* (Viking), by the prominent young gay novelist David Leavitt. Leavitt's story, set in Berlin, London, and Spain during the middle and late 1930s, deals with the love affair of Brian Botsford (forty years later a highly successful Hollywood screenwriter as he tells the story) and Edward Phelan, a young working-class Englishman. Leavitt's third novel began its public life smoothly enough as reviewers, by and large, praised Leavitt for his imaginative reconstruction of the places and the period. Soon enough, however, reviewers began to notice astonishing parallels to Stephen Spender's 1948 autobiography *World Within World*. Covering this for the *Washington Post* ("Whose Life Is It Anyhow?" 12 September), David Streitfeld interviewed Leavitt, whose replies were inconsistent; the publisher's attorney; and Stephen Spender, who was outraged: "I am simply amazed how anyone purporting to be a writer of fiction can be so idle, slovenly and dishonest as simply to lift incidents from my autobiography and describe them as having happened to a fictitious narrator in his novel." Spender subsequently sued in Great Britain; in early 1994 Viking agreed to pull the novel from distribution. (See "Poet Sues Novelist for Lifting Part of His Life," by David Streitfeld, *Washington Post*, 26 October.) Leavitt is quoted: "I'm perfectly willing to admit the fact that this novel uses his life as a springboard. I'd never deny it." All this aside, the editors of the *New York Times Book Review* listed *While England Sleeps* as one of the "Notable Books of the Year."

Another prominent and highly regarded young writer of gay/lesbian literature is Britain's Jeanette Winterson. She won a Whitbread Prize with her first book and immediately became something of a cult figure. Writing about this (*New York Review of Books*) Gabriele Annan allowed: "She bounced into the limelight squawking like a literary Donald Duck with Byronic leanings." Her new novel, her fourth so far, *Written on the Body* (Knopf), is a love story told by a narrator of unknown and unstated gender. A careful reader will easily tell, however, that the narrator must be a woman. This emotionally complex story received mixed notices, but Winterson was generally praised for her style.

Other gay/lesbian novels which were well promoted and widely reviewed include Jennifer Levin's *The Sea of Light* (Dutton), the story of Brenna Allen, a college swimming coach; Greg Johnson's *Pagan Babies* (Dutton), set in smalltown Texas in the early 1960s and Atlanta later; James Robert Baker's *Tim and Pete* (Simon and Schuster), exploring the brutal world of "rough trade"; Stuart Edelsom's *Black Glass* (Demi Press), set during the Vietnam War and concerning the love affair of two sailors, Bruce and Ralph; Dale Peck's *Martin and John* (Farrar, Straus and Giroux), a first novel about a Kansas-born New York hustler and his lover, both suffering from AIDS; Geoffrey Rees's *Sex with Strangers* (Farrar, Straus, and Giroux), a first-person story by college student Thomas Hobart, who has a series of love affairs, including one with Dennis, a railway conductor; William Hayward Henderson's *Native* (Dutton), in which a gay cowboy falls for a young runaway; Fenton Johnson's *Scissors, Paper, Rock* (Pocket Books), a series of eleven linked stories concerning Raphael Hardin, gay, thirty-six, and dying of AIDS, coming home to rural life at Strang Knob, Kentucky. Christopher Coe's second novel, *Such Times* (Harcourt Brace), received attention and some acclaim for its picture of gay life in the 1970s and 1980s (" 'So many men, so little time' was a popular T-shirt slogan in the very early eighties"). This is a first-person story told by Timothy, who is slowly dying of AIDS, about his older mentor and lover, Jasper, who is already dead of it. Bernard Cooper, whose earlier *Maps to Anywhere* (1990) won a PEN/Hemingway Award, is more concerned with family life in general than homosexuality in *A Year of Rhymes* (Viking), but this story, set in Southern California in the 1950s, has strong gay elements.

Every year the category of the "experimental" novel seems to shrink a little. Even experimental writers don't like the word or the label. In a sense they are right; for most of the devices and attitudes of the avant-garde have gradually been co-opted, anyway consolidated into mainstream fiction of every kind. Still, there are a few people busily and regularly at work whose efforts can be justly described as at least relatively experimental. There is no question about Kathy Acker, whose latest, *My Mother: Demonology,* comes from a mainstream publisher, Pantheon. Some other experimental fictions which were brought out by commercial publishers include Steve Erickson's *Arc D'X* (Poseidon), which begins with the burning alive of a slave woman, moves on to tell a story about Sally Hemings and Thomas Jefferson, kicks into a violent near-future (they are rebuilding the Berlin Wall), and then allows the author, to show up in Berlin and be murdered. Here the writing is straightforward; it is the substance which is defiantly odd. Erickson, author of four other novels and working as film critic for the *L.A. Weekly,* is something of a cult figure. So is Donald Harington, whose *Ekaterina* (Harcourt Brace) takes place in the town of Stay More, Arkansas, in the Bodarks (Ozarks) and deals with Ekaterina, a Svanetian princess (among other things) and a skillful seducer of twelve-year-old boys in quasi-Nabokovian fashion. The first half of the book is narrated in first person by a ghost, one Daniel Lyam Montross; later the story is told by a cat. Peter Strobe had high praise for the author in the *Washington Post Book World,* 6 June: "Harington is

a true original, and what he accomplishes radiates fascination." Jon Stephen Fink, whose first novel *Further Adventures,* is published by St. Martin's Press, is also the author of a nonfiction, oddball classic – *Cluck! The True Story of Chickens in the Cinema.* The novel is a wild and woolly monologue by Ray Green, also known as Reuven Agronousky, Peter Tremayne, and the Green Ray, a onetime radio superhero now looking for a chance to do good things in real life. He fails. "I am not the man who I was before," he tells us, "and even before I was not him either." Knopf published *Time Remaining,* by James McCourt, a series of interweaving monlogues on the general subject of gay life, at home and abroad, over the past forty years. Small presses remain the principal sources of the experimental – books like Mark Amerika's *The Kafka Chronicles* (Black Ice), described by Martin Schecter in the *Philadelphia Inquirer* (5 September): "His work isn't so much a book as it is a Dadaist demonstration, once again honoring the dictum that it's the artist's sacred duty to destroy what commerce has made common." Note that across the country the major book pages have found (from time to time) space to review these works. Fiction Collective Two nominated its novel *The Alphabet Man,* by Richard Grossman for the National Book Award, and although it was not shortlisted, it was indeed seriously considered. The publisher sums up the book as follows: "Part thriller, part psychological and linguistic masterpiece, Grossman's explosive fiction convinces us that if there is a pure poetry in the modern world, it must be rooted in madness, prophecy, and bloodshed." *The Alphabet Man* was selected for publication in a contest judged by Acker.

Emerging as the leading publisher of the experimental in America, partly on the basis of success and simple survival in an indifferent climate, is Dalkey Archive Press. Their books are regularly (and favorably) reviewed in the leading publications; and in addition to significant translations (Jacques Roubaud's *The Princess Happy,* Piotr Szewc's *Annihilation,* and Raymond Queneau's *Saint Glinglin*) this year their list included new editions of Gilbert Sorrentino's *Aberration of Starlight,* Paul West's *Words for a Deaf Daughter and Gala,* and Joseph McElroy's huge *Women and Men.* Among their outstanding new books were *Ava* by Carole Maso, nominated for the National Book Award; *Century 21* by Ewa Kuryluk; *Sister Carrie* (from the jacket – "*Sister Carrie* reads as if Dreiser said, 'I love you' but didn't mean it, went to bed with Donald Barthelme and William Burroughs, and named the result Lauren Fairbanks") by Lauren Fairbanks; and *Sin-*

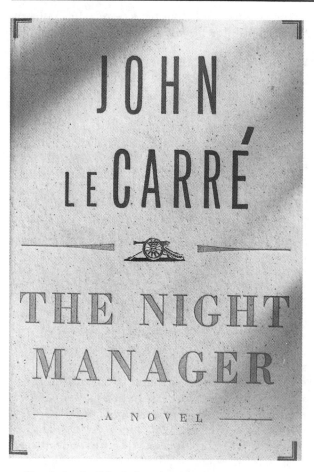

Dust jacket for John le Carré's novel about drug running, government corruption, bureaucratic in-fighting, and spying

gular Pleasures ("The sole subject of this unique book of short fiction is masturbation") by veteran novelist Harry Matthews. Other small presses which actively published experimental fiction in 1993 include: Sun + Moon, Serpent's Tail, Four Walls Eight Windows, Godine, Overlook Press, Asylum Arts, Coffee House, Exact Change, White Pine, Coach House, Five Fingers, Avec Books, Bamberger Books, Story Line, Black Sparrow, Fjord, Marlboro, Plover Press, Garland, Milkweed, and Paragon. If the experimental is a shrinking category, many people seem to be unaware of that fact.

Of course, not all small presses are dedicated to the purely and simply experimental. More and more, literary books which might until recently have been published by commercial houses are showing up on the brief lists of small presses. *The Empty Lot* (Another Chicago Press) by Mary Gray Hughes is set in a Texas college town and depicts an ambitious academic couple fighting each other for possession of their suburban home. Max Childers's *Alpha Omega* (Wyrick) brings Southern

Gothic and country music together in the story of a group of criminals involved in creating a theme park – Graceland-by-the-sea. Jonathan Strong's *An Untold Tale* (Zoland) announces its story line at the outset: "I want to tell what befell us when Sam Lara, the wanderer, finally made his way home." Sibyl James's *The Adventures of Stout Mama* (Papier-Mache) is told briskly in forty-six short takes, but is essentially conventional – "Stout Mama is politically eclectic. She hasn't shaved her legs in years, but she paints her toenails." *The Correspondence* (Fromm International) by Evelin Sullivan is self-reflexive but reasonably straightforward, being told in the form of a biography – and letters and notes – theoretically being written during 1991 and concerning Alex Merry, a movie star and stage actor who committed suicide.

Not properly a part of this report, it nevertheless deserves mention that the year saw a number of outstanding collections of novellas published: A. S. Byatt's *Angels and Insects: Two Novellas* (Random House); Norman Manea's *Compulsory Happiness* (Farrar, Straus and Giroux); *Proofs: And Three Parables* (Granta) by George Steiner; *The Rest of Life: Three Novellas* (Viking) by Mary Gordon; *Van Gogh's Room at Arles: Three Novellas* (Hyperion) by Stanley Elkin; *Little Kingdoms: Three Novellas* (Poseidon) by Steven Millhauser; Tom Pilkington's *Careless Weeds: Six Texas Novellas* (Southern Methodist University Press); *Taratuta and Still Life With Pipe* (Norton) by José Donoso; *The Novellas of Martha Gellhorn* (Knopf); and *The Little Town Where Time Stood Still* (Pantheon) by Czech writer Bohumil Hrabal.

The reader will have noticed that most of the types of novels dealt with in this article have included some first novels. In many cases the fact that a book is the debut publication for an author is irrelevant. But gradually, as much a convenience for promotional purposes and the literary press as anybody else, first books have been marketed as a type. During 1993 there were a large number of identified first novels, that is introductions of new talent with a future. For the most part these books are gently and widely reviewed and their authors welcomed to the literary scene. *Publishers Weekly* (30 August) devoted a major article, "First Fiction: The Winding Road to Readership," dealing with some thirty first novelists of various kinds as representative of the year and the scene.

Few novels of any kind received the attention and scrutiny of Frank Conroy's *Body & Soul* (Houghton Mifflin). Conroy had published a much-praised memoir, *Stop-Time* (1967), and a collection of stories, *Midair* (1985), and is the director of the celebrated Iowa Writers Workshop; so his book, genuinely awaited, was thoroughly reviewed. This story of the life of a musical prodigy, Claude Rawlings, was treated with respect, but earned uniformly mixed reviews. Not even Conroy caught the attention of more reviewers than Scott Smith and his first novel, *A Simple Plan* (Knopf). Three men in the woods – the protagonist Hank Mitchell, his brother Jacob, and a friend stumble onto a crashed airplane where they find a duffel bag containing $4 million. This good luck turns into a kind of curse for them. Something similar seems to have happened to the author, who had earned a couple of million dollars before the book appeared. Reviews were not good, most reviewers not crediting Smith with the construction of a credible plot or with achieving his literary claims. Time will tell for Smith's talent, and meanwhile there is the consolation of the bank.

There were genuinely outstanding first novels during the year, and here is a brief "honor roll" of the best of them in my judgment.

Michael Parker, *Hello Down There* (Scribners). Set in Trent, North Carolina, in the early 1950s, it is a wonderfully lively novel about a web of connection involving a rich young man, Edwin Keane, a morphine addict; a pharmacist; and the Speight family, especially Eureka and her brother Randall, who watch over the town and its people from a tree in the churchyard. In a rave review in the *New York Times Book Review* (21 February) Frederick Busch praised Parker for "his bone-deep affection for his characters; his love of clear, crisp, pungent language; his ability to write about the disgust with oneself and much of creation that may be the mood of our age; and, in spite of this, his confidence in the possibility of redemption."

William Baldwin, *The Hard to Catch Mercy* (Algonquin). This is probably the only first novel of the year that can be called generally superior (it is larger, more ambitious, more risk-taking) to *Hello Down There*. Baldwin spent fifteen years trying to find a publisher for this work, constantly revising and reworking it as he waited. It is accurately described by Robert Gingher in "Passing By the Dragon," *The World & I* (July 1993): "Set in a Carolina fishing village caught between the heritage of the Civil War and the current First World War, *The Hard to Catch Mercy* probes what Faulkner called 'the human heart in conflict with itself' without which art labors in vain." Writing in *Chronicles* (October 1993), Fred Chappell said: "I can't think of another contemporary writer

who has made a more splendid debut than William Baldwin. Here is a writer I intend to keep reading." I can only add that *The Hard to Catch Mercy* is my choice for the best first novel published in 1993.

The Art Seidenbaum Award for First Fiction, given by the *Los Angeles Times,* went to Paul Kafka for *Love (Enter)* (Houghton Mifflin). This is the story of Dan Schoenfeld, a resident in obstetrics in New Orleans, who is remembering the things that happened to him five years earlier in Paris. It is an epistolary novel written on a computer, and "Love" is the code word that unlocks his computer files.

Jesse Lee Kercheval, *The Museum of Happiness* (Faber). The story of Ginny Gillespie and Roland Keppi of Alsace Lorraine; the book begins in 1929 in Florida as Ginny takes Roland's (her dead husband) ashes back to Paris. The book is a recapitulation of their lives and love. Kercheval's collection of short stories, *The Dogeater*, won the Associated Writing Programs Award in 1987.

Amanda Filipacchi, *Nude Men* (Viking). A first-person story told by twenty-nine-year-old Jeremey Acidophilus, who writes for *Screen* magazine, details his involvement with Lady Henrietta, who paints male nudes for *Playgirl;* her daughter Sara; a talking cat; and a dancing magician. A little decadent (it is that time of our own century), it is also lively and sophisticated.

Christina Baker Kline, *Sweet Water* (Harper-Collins). Cassie Simon, a sculptor in New York, inherits her grandfather's house in Sweetwater, Tennessee, and finds herself in the middle of a family mystery involving the death of her mother years before.

Jeffrey Eugenides, *The Virgin Suicides* (Farrar, Straus and Giroux). Not a likely subject – five teenage sisters of the Lisbon family in Grosse Point, Michigan, kill themselves over a twelve-month period – but the book was widely reviewed and highly praised. That it works at all is the result of several things: the book is short, the collective narrator creates a distance and an odd angle on events, and, above all, reviewers were captured by the stylish prose: "What lingered after them was not life, which always overcomes natural death, but the most trivial list of mundane facts: a clock ticking on the wall, a room dim at noon, and the outrageousness of a human body thinking only of herself. Her brain going dim to all else, but flaming up in precise points of pain, personal injury, lost dreams. . . ."

Donald Antrim, *Elect Mr. Robinson for a Better World* (Viking). This first novel received much publicity, in part because of an unusually large advance, but also precisely because the author appeared to resist the spotlight. The book is described by the publisher as "a wickedly funny tale" set in a world "where neighboring families conduct full-scale wars in local parks, and spike-embedded trenches encircle homes and manicured lawns." Schoolteacher Pete Robinson, himself certifiable, wants to lead the people to sanity. It is an excellent example of Swiftian satire for the 1990s.

Kathleen Whitsitt Egbert, *The 23rd Dream* (Southern Methodist University Press). Egbert tells the story of Adam and Marian Stauffer and their three children and gives an account of their year-long ordeal as Adam faces death. It is about the death of a young man, husband and father, and is told with a serene, refined, intense, and deeply moving simplicity.

Other outstanding first novels of the year include: Maria Flook's *Family Night* (Pantheon); Mark Frost's *The List of 7* (Morrow); Annie Dawid's *York Ferry* (Cane Hill); Beverly Coyle's *In Troubled Waters* (Ticknor and Fields); Tommy Hays's *Sam's Crossing* (Atheneum); Robert Ellis Gordon's *When Bobby Kennedy Was a Moving Man* (Black Heron); Anna Monardo's *The Courtyard of Dreams* (Doubleday); Marina Rust's *Gatherings* (Simon and Schuster); Kevin Baker's *Sometimes You See It Coming* (Crown); Jim Lewis's *Sister* (Graywolf); Sherri Szeman's *The Kommandant's Mistress* (HarperCollins); Gary Reiswig's *Water Boy* (Simon and Schuster); T. M. McNally's *Until Your Heart Stops* (Villard); P. H. Liotta's *Diamond's Compass* (Algonquin); Mark Richard's *Fishboy: A Ghost Story* (Doubleday); Shann Nix's *Wildcatting* (Doubleday); and Greg Iles's *Spandau Phoenix* (Dutton).

Oddities: *Fast Sofa* (Morrow) by Bruce Craven (a late volunteer for "The Brat Pack"), comes with a 45-rpm-record soundtrack and the suggestion on the book jacket – "Play this novel loud!" Jacqueline Deval's *Reckless Appetites: a culinary romance* (Ecco) includes roughly one hundred menus and recipes (mostly literary in origin) and an extensive bibliography.

There were surprisingly few war and military first novels this year. World War II is the time frame for retired advertising executive Everard Meade's *The Dignity of Danger* (Burning Gate). Rolando Hinojosa, who in fact is the author of twelve books in the Klail City Death Trip Series, tells in diary form from 25 June 1950 to 1 September 1951 of the early days of the Korean War in *The Useless Servants* (Arte Publico). There were the author says, "No heroes; just men in combat." John

P. McAfee's *Slow Walk in a Sad Rain* (Warner) is a black comedy about a Special Forces unit in Vietnam. Robert O'Connor's *Buffalo Soldiers* (Knopf) is a story about garrison duty and dope dealing in Germany.

A TALK WITH FOUR FIRST NOVELISTS
BY KRISTIN VAN OGTROP

Anyone who reads *Publishers Weekly* on a regular or even infrequent basis knows that the business of buying, publicizing, and reviewing books is often a one-sided deal. In other words, it is easy for consumers to hear editors and publicists crow about their successes (and, not so often, failures). However, the voice of the Single, Lonely, Garret-Dwelling Author is often hard to make out, unless the author is someone of extraordinary esteem or sales. Yet the S.L.G-D. authors, if given the time and space to tell their own publishing tales, have much to say about the struggle of Art versus Life, or Writing versus Publishing. And first novelists in particular (individuals whose illusions about putting out a book, if they ever had any, are most recently shattered) know much about the vicissitudes, cruelties, and unexpected kindnesses of those in charge of the world of books. The sell-and-promote experiences of the following four writers, all of whom published first novels in 1993, are as personal and varied as the subjects of their books.

Take the case of David Bowman. When he finished his novel, *Let the Dog Drive,* he shopped it around, without an agent, to a dozen New York publishing houses. He found no takers, but Barbara Epler at New Directions suggested that he submit it for New York University Press's Bobst Award for first fiction (judged by Amy Hempel and Mark Richard). He won – and that is when his work really began. "NYU didn't have much of a budget to promote the book," Bowman says, "and so they didn't have pre-pubs for reviewers. I xeroxed and bound, then hand-delivered fifty copies of the book, and got reviewed by a number of places that way." He did not get reams of reviews, but he "got some great ones. . . . I got a great review in the Sunday *New York Times,* and was included in the list of the best books of 1993 [on 5 December]." Bowman's success certainly has a serendipitous feel. For example, he read an article in *Poets and Writers* about selling film rights; the article mentioned an agent at Creative Artists Agency, (CAA) which Bowman had never heard of – who had sold the rights to a "difficult" book. He wrote the agency a letter, and is now a CAA client. Voilá. Bowman relays this information as if he were describing a routine trip to the corner delicatessen; however, one is reminded of watching David Copperfield (the magician, not the novel) on television. It cannot possibly be that easy. But Bowman's luck belies the fact that he worked hard to promote himself. When he says "The book got more attention than anybody expected," he quickly adds, "I had no expectations. Just determination." *Let the Dog Drive* will be published in paperback by Penguin in 1994.

When navigating the stormy seas of publishing, determination is one guide any first novelist can scarcely afford to lose. Even those first novelists whose books are published by houses bigger than New York University Press must play some role in the publicizing of their books. Michael Parker, whose novel *Hello Down There* was published in 1993 by Scribners, acknowledges that he had to play an active role in his own promotion – he even arranged some of his readings and book signings. In fact, Parker finds it remarkable that publishers do not promote first books as aggressively as second ones; he is learning this firsthand, because Scribners is publishing his collection of novellas, *The Geographical Curve,* in June 1994 (the same week Penguin will publish his novel in paperback in its Contemporary American series). "I didn't know what to expect," Parker says. "I did know that for first novelists, there isn't a big hubbub. But I didn't concern myself with Scribners' promotion of my book because I didn't know anything about it. I'm not being snotty or arty, I just didn't know anything about publicity." He adds, "It is to the advantage of first novelists to promote themselves. You can't expect a publisher to send you on a thirty-five-city book tour." Now Parker is savvy. "I now know more of what to ask for, and what *not* to ask for," he says, pointing out that he had rather fight over his blurbs and jacket copy than whether or not he is going to be sent to Seattle. In terms of reviews Parker says, "I was really pleased. Most were positive, and there were a few mixed ones I felt I could learn something from." Parker received fifty or sixty notices, mostly on the East Coast, which was "a little disappointing. Everyone wants his work to be promoted nationally."

National reviews – particularly in the *New York Times* or in large-circulation magazines – are the stuff of which first novelists dream. Christina Baker Kline, whose first novel *Sweet Water* was published in 1993 by HarperCollins, says, "I got great reviews; I have, all told, about forty. But none of the national magazines wrote about my book – which was surprising to

me, particularly as it was a 'women's' book." However, Kline has few complaints, as she acknowledges: "I do feel lucky that I got so many reviews." She attributes much of her success to her publicist Ron Longe, who – alas – got a new job based upon the success he had in marketing her book. "A first novelist has to have good publicity," Kline insists. "No one is familiar with your work, and no one will show up for readings unless there has been some publicity beforehand." When she sold *Sweet Water,* Kline had few expectations; in fact, HarperCollins was planning to do a minimal amount of publicity – that is, until the Literary Guild picked up the novel and *Reader's Digest* published over one million copies of a condensed version, with a John Grisham novel. "My expectations were low," Kline states, "but once things start happening, you expect more." And, in many ways, her expectations were met. "We sold all rights except for first serial," she declares. "I've already earned ten times my advance." HarperPerennial will publish *Sweet Water* in paperback in May.

In terms of selling rights – or, more specifically, foreign rights – Amanda Filipacchi triumphed in 1993. Her novel *Nude Men,* published by Viking, was sold to seven countries even before it appeared in the United States. Now the count has grown to nine, and "things keep occuring," Filipacchi says, "even six months after the publication date." "Things" include a large amount of publicity the young novelist is now doing to promote the book overseas. Like Bowman, Filipacchi received her worst review in the *Los Angeles Times;* however, unlike many first novelists, she received a number of notices in national magazines, including *Time, Vanity Fair, Interview, Elle,* and *Vogue.* Still, she was disappointed that her book was not reviewed in the *New York Times.* Unlike the other novelists considered here, Filipacchi did little to promote her book besides show up at the assigned places and times – places and times determined by Giulia Melucci, her publicist at Viking. However, Filipacchi did devise an unorthodox method for gauging her sales firsthand: "The only thing I did," she divulges, "was go to the bookstores and secretly count copies. The bookstores had my book, but I couldn't tell how many were selling. So I started marking them. I turned down the very end of the corner of the last page, and then bought a pair of Rollerblades so I could zoom quickly from one store to the next." By employing this somewhat rudimentary procedure, Filipacchi learned that her books were selling. Call it reinventing the promotional wheel.

Dictionary of Literary Biography Yearbook Awards for Distinguished Novels Published in 1993

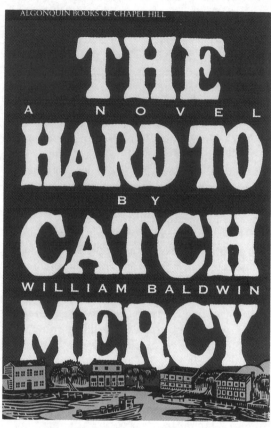

Dust jackets (left) for Frederick Buechner's novel about the biblical generations of Abraham, Isaac, Jacob, Esau, and Joseph and (right) William Baldwin's novel about life in the South Carolina Low Country

NOVEL

In January 1950, with the publication of his first book, *A Long Day's Dying,* Frederick Buechner was at age twenty-four about as famous as a young writer can be in America. Since then he has published twenty-seven books of fiction and nonfiction. *The Son of Laughter* is his finest work to date, a richly poetic and wholly credible first-person account (told by Jacob) of the generations of Abraham and Isaac, Jacob and Essau, and Joseph and his brothers. No word is wasted or redundant; the prose sings and shines. As Annie Dillard wrote in the *Boston Sunday Globe* on 20 May 1993: "He magnifies the comic and tortured human drama by presenting Jacob unforgettably, and his story's power never lets up."

— George Garrett

FIRST NOVEL

Years in the making, and more years spent in finding the right publisher (Algonquin), William Baldwin's *The Hard to Catch Mercy* is a magnificent achievement and is accurately described by Fred Chappell (*Chronicles,* October 1993) as: "an old-fashioned story, unabashedly melodramatic, unashamedly moral in purpose, unblushing in its determination to entertain." This large story of a small place in the South Carolina Low Country has justly captured the attention and enthusiasm of many discerning critics. Robert Gingher speaks for all of them in his praise of the book (*The World & I,* July 1993): "Like any story worth its sweat, it pays homage to the familiar, enabling us to rewitness imaginatively our own pasts, flaming in memory's labyrinth and lighting up that faraway dark side of the moon."

— George Garrett

The Year in the Short Story

David R. Slavitt
University of Pennsylvania

A door closes, but a window opens, or maybe just a transom or trapdoor. Or the flap on a pair of Dr. Denton's. What I want to figure is the further marginalization not just of short stories but of all serious literature – poetry and novels too – all culture for that matter, edged out by the mergers of huge corporations voracious for "software." Viacom, a cable company, and QVC, the home shoppers' channel, bid against each other at astronomical levels for control of Paramount, of which Simon and Schuster (S&S) is a subsidiary, and it hardly even matters that S&S has the two biggest books of the year – Rush Limbaugh's *See, I Told You So* and Howard Stern's *Private Parts*. Those are "books," which is to say that ordinary libroid objects that are not spun off from syndicated radio shows are something else . . . samizdats like those underground Soviet writers used to circulate, but here they do not need to be censored because nobody cares. Nobody has to copy these things out in longhand by the guttering light of a tallow candle because they get printed and distributed (more or less) by . . . Southern Methodist University Press?

What is a Southern Methodist? Is that a sect or a location?

Whatever it is, I'm a believer, willing to join the church and sing in the choir because they are taking up the slack. The University of Very Far Away, but if that's where the game is, that's where you play.

It used to be that the trade presses had become a little bit odd, picky and unpredictable, but you could still find good fiction on the Farrar, Straus and Giroux list, or Knopf's, or Atheneum's. Sometimes it can even still happen, although it seems to be mostly at random (with an emphatically small "r") and because some editor with a little power has a fondness for some writer or other. Reynolds Price is the only quality writer to have maintained a long-term relationship with Atheneum/Macmillan (which became the property of Robert Maxwell, that embarrassingly clownish crook who drowned himself), and he has a new book of stories out this year. But he is like John Updike, another lucky idiot who does not understand that the water in which he is swimming is full of sharks and Portuguese man-of-wars, and who is, for that very reason, left alone. The decisions by the Louisiana State University Press and by the Indiana University Press to get the hell out of the fiction business because they were losing money and it was insane to try to get the scholarly books to make good on the losses of their cultural philanthropies in upper-brow fiction were not easy or pleasant, but they were sane. The economy was sluggish, the market for fiction was depressed, and the universities and public libraries on which university presses depend for a certain degree of support are all in straitened circumstances. And to add insult to injury, the National Endowment for the Arts (NEA) has introduced a giddy uncertainty into the business, which is probably worse than no support at all. They support a few presses here and there, but not reliably and never for long, and the effect is like humanitarian aid to sub-Saharan countries. You dig a few wells, you watch the population double, and then, bored or more concerned by some other international problem, you walk away to leave in your wake a much worse famine than anyone could have imagined in the first place. With the benign looniness of a Renaissance Italian duke, the NEA contrives to drive directors of presses crazy. In the process, what the arts lose, Prozac gains.

In which case, Southern Methodist University (SMU) and these other arrivistes may be commendable but are clearly certifiable. Out of their cotton pickin' minds! (Or is it sorghum down there? Or vetch? Or perhaps graham, from which they make those nice crackers?) There are little enclaves in other presses, endowed programs like the Drue Heinz Prize that the University of Pittsburgh Press operates, or the Flannery O'Connor Prize of the University of Georgia. There are more or less reliable subventions, such as those which the University of Iowa gets from the Iowa Arts Council for its short-story series (the Iowa Short Fiction Award

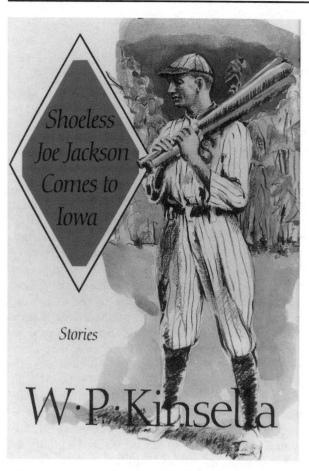

Dust jacket for the collection of W. P. Kinsella stories that was originally published in Canada in 1980

and the John Simmons Short Fiction Award). There are individual fiefdoms of the kind that John Irwin has at Johns Hopkins, where he gets to pick a book of poems or a collection of stories that they will bring out. But SMU now devotes its entire fall list to fiction and does its regular academic publishing in the spring. Keith Gregory, the director, explains this anomaly by giving credit to the SMU administration, which supports the program, and to Kathryn Lang, his senior editor in charge of acquisitions, and he makes it sound almost reasonable. After all, colleges and universities have to compete with one another, and this is a much cheaper and more interesting way for an institution to make a name for itself than with a football program. Whoever heard of Tulane except as the venue of the *Drama Review?* Or Kenyon or Beloit, except as places the magazines came from? Besides, the poor fools who write these stories seem to have no idea what is going on. Like the cows and the chickens in a depression, they keep right on producing. And this means that in the piles of manuscripts that arrive at Texas and Missouri and Arkansas there is much fine work,

an embarrassment of riches from which to pick and choose. From a purely belletrist point of view, the short story is enjoying a flourishing as remarkable as its commercial precariousness. Indeed, these may be different aspects of the same phenomenon. Back in the heyday of the short story in the literary marketplace, the short story was how F. Scott Fitzgerald could hustle up a few dollars, writing something that the editors of the *Saturday Evening Post* might want. There are no such opportunities anymore — and no such temptations. As a demonstration that those times are gone, let me cite a passage from a letter I got this year from a distinguished short-story writer who, in an unbuttoned moment, put it as forcefully and plainly as possible: "There are almost no serious magazines doing short stories anymore. *Mademoiselle* has dropped fiction after fifty distinguished years and has retooled itself for sixteen-year-olds who want to be eighteen, and that's a great loss. *The New Yorker* is *Vanity Fair* is *People* is the *New York Times:* one big self-congratulatory exercise in hip irony. The *Atlantic* thinks a story has to follow guidelines set down by *Writer* magazine: old-fashioned plot, limited idea of character and language. And *Esquire* is for male 44-year-olds who want to be eighteen. This is why only university presses and literary journals are left."

We begin this year's conspectus, then, with the SMU offerings, which include the following, alphabetically:

● Anthony Bukoski's *Children of Strangers* is a collection of stories about Polish-Americans and others in Superior, Wisconsin, where the author lives "in the home where he was reared," as the flap copy tells us. Superior is not what one would call a glamorous place, but it is nonetheless full of memories. As Grandmother Mizinska makes clear in "Tango of the Bearers of the Dead," she has spent much time out in the garden, "which over the years has become a place of memories I wish to forget. In order to destroy them, I will treat the garden with salt, plant it deep. . . . For years I have cut back raspberry bushes, wishing they were memories. Dreams hang like fragile glass in the air of the garden. They grow out of the fertile earth."

Bukoski writes a plain, even gnarled prose, in which the homeliest object or most fleeting gesture can suddenly shimmer with significance. In "Durum Wheat," Andy Borzynski, the guy who sweeps the floor, "drops his broom, makes the Sign of the Cross, and runs into the boiler room. . . . When he's excited his hands fly around. Those are his languages and prayers."

● Lee Merrill Byrd's *My Sister Disappears* is a series of soundings into different kinds of grief, suffering, and loss but with special attention to the absurd adaptations and maladaptations to these terrible trials of which the human spirit is capable. Byrd's poise is wonderful, and she verges on comedy and even farce without ever breaking the mood or losing track of the hard centers of pain with which her men and women are trying, as well as they can, to cope.

● W. P. Kinsella's *Shoeless Joe Jackson Comes to Iowa* is proof positive that the commercial publishing world is broken. The collection was previously published in Canada in 1980, and its title story is the germ of what became the novel *Shoeless Joe* (1989), which became in turn the successful film *Field of Dreams*. In the old days editors would have been sending him letters (or even flowers and candy) in the hope that he might have something in the way of an uncommitted manuscript. Evidently, it is not happening anymore – or else Kinsella has an odd distaste for cash advances, which the commercial houses generally offer and the university presses generally do not. After thirteen years his manuscript makes it at last with a Stateside publisher. These are sturdy, engaging, lively stories, not at all "artsy." If some of them are a little surrealist – like the title piece – others are more naturalistic and even conventional. They are widely and favorably reviewed as they deserved to be.

●Janet Peery's *Alligator Dance* has reminded some critics of the work of Ellen Gilchrist, which is an observation with a certain truth to it, if only because both writers are female and tend to look backward to the formative years of late childhood and adolescence for moments of clarity in a generally muddled and complicated world. Peery is not at all a Gilchrist knockoff, though, and her terrain extends from Wisconsin down through the sunbaked Southwest. She has a fine ear and can suggest the liveliness of spoken regional English without ever seeming to condescend. One story begins: "The man I called my husband had a God who made him do some things I couldn't cotton. For forty years I told him that his hard head was the one true bone of our contention, but he just laughed, and looked at me like I was joking, which I was, but only half."

●Louis Phillips's *A Dream of Countries Where No One Dare Live* is, in some ways, my favorite of this uniformly admirable series of books, not "better" necessarily (whatever that means) but more engaging, weird, willing to take odd chances. Phillips has a linguistic energy that suggests what the flap copy confirms – that he is a poet as well as a playwright and writer of children's books. He's got one story called "In the House of Simple Sentences" in which he begins: "Sentence number one: *We, in spite of nightmares, still fall asleep.* Variations on that sentence include:

    1. In spite of nightmares we fall asleep still.
    2. We fall asleep still in spite of nightmares.
    3. Still we fall asleep in spite of nightmares.
    4. In spite of nightmares, still we fall asleep."

This is up there with Jorge Luis Borges and Italo Calvino, I should think. And it is not even my favorite piece in the collection. For the sheer effrontery of its moves, and the rueful panache of its narrator, the one I adore is "Edna St. Vincent Millay Meets Tarzan." The academic ne'er-do-well who is speaking confides in us: "All afternoon I had confused Dorothy Parker with Edna St. Vincent Millay. I had done worse than that. I had confused Edna St. Vincent Millay with her own goddamn self, by which I mean to say that I kept referring to her as Saint Edna Vincent Millay. In spite of many sins, both of omission and commission, my Catholic boyhood had caught up with me, along with two vodka sours." Just lovely!

● Paul Ruffin's *The Man Who Would Be God* is a collection of shrewd, sidewise looks at simple country people who turn out to be mythic, weird, and altogether hyperbolic. "Jesus, half the people outside the lights of this town would kill you over a glass of iced tea," one character remarks, and he's not just whistling "The Yellow Rose of Texas," either. A lot goes on in Ruffin's stories – honest observation of people and places, and then a series of delicate literary games – as in the title piece with its wink and nod at Rudyard Kipling. He, too, is a poet, and, even though these are not all "poetic" stories one can sense the meticulous care in the crafting of the sentences.

Finally, although it fits imperfectly into the Dictionary of Literary Biography arrangement, there is also a volume called *Careless Weeds: Six Texas Novellas,* edited by Tom Pilkington. Because the editors have not been silly enough to assign "The Year in the Novella," I might as well remark here that this is an impressive collection, and that the press here too is operating in a sensible way, exploiting a regional audience (and market), serving a region's writers, and bringing out work of high quality all at once. The six novellas are by Jane Gilmore Rushing, Margot Frazer, David L. Fleming, Clay Reynolds, Pat Carr, and Thomas Zigal, and these were the successes in a field of twenty-four entries.

SMU is not without competition in the short-fiction business. The University of Missouri Press, which for some years had an interesting series of slender volumes of first collections, has now put out a substantial line of impressive books. Georgia, Iowa, Arkansas, Pittsburgh, and Johns Hopkins are reliable players, and Triquarterly Press and Rutgers have come into the game. Their entries last year were these:

● James Hannah's *Sign Languages* (University of Missouri Press) is an aggressively hard-edged collection of stories about the despised and disaffected, who are of interest because of the way their skewed perceptions can distort but also clarify the world in which the rest of us live. These cranks and losers are difficult to like, but that is what Hannah finds attractive about them. He delights in such details as "the thick strand of saliva connecting the corner of his lip to a liver spot on the back of [Mr. Warrant's] hand the shape of Chile." This is not what anyone would call charming, but Hannah brings to it an impressive conviction that, most of the time, carries us along.

● Gerald Shapiro's *From Hunger* (University of Missouri Press) is a book that made me laugh out loud many times. And for that reason I thought it could not be serious, earnest, or profound. But even during the great orgy of reading I went through for this roundup, I kept remembering lines and moments in Shapiro's stories. He does magic realism, but instead of being a South American exotic, he is a Jew in Nebraska, which is still fairly exotic, I would think. But the passion of these pieces is ecumenical, universal. In "The Community Seder," Rothblatt, a concentration camp alumnus, shows off his tattoo and then delivers what must be one of the great lines of the year: "I used to say, be a good person, be a *mensch,* live the life of a righteous Jew, so you can go to heaven and meet God and stick a knife in His heart and twist it."

● Darrell Spencer's *Our Secret's Out* (University of Missouri Press) is rather old-fashioned in its tone, with the tough-guy pose on the one hand, but then, on the other, the sensitivity of the aperçus. It is a reliable combination, and Spencer uses it efficiently to perform various turns with various loners and losers of the wastelands of Utah and Nevada. These are agreeable and engaging pieces, and Spencer has a fine sense of how the sunlight can glint off driveway gravel to make it shine like precious stones. If, as one of his characters remarks, "a man's true character comes out in a game of high stakes poker," it is sometimes necessary to admit, as this fellow does, "Truth is, I'm not sure anymore I know what game it is we're playing. Or who is in, who's anteed."

● Ruth Ciresi's *Mother Rocket* (University of Georgia Press) is sometimes a bit wifty. When Jude

Silverman, "a Jewish Chicken Little," is asked why she does not get rid of all those superstitious slave chains, she "stomped her foot. The very idea! 'Jingle, ergo sum' she said." A lot of that can go a very long way indeed, but there is, just under the frenetic surface, a slower and stronger current of disappointment, boredom, uncertainty, and chagrin about which Ms. Ciresi is sometimes uncannily accurate. It is a mark of her success that when she has one of her characters consider how the "roar of the vacuum cleaner and the buzz of the lawn mower" are better than the "silence of a solitary life," it is not just a good line but a characteristic one, a strand of the curious but quite palpable fabric of life she has managed to create.

● Judith Oritz Cofer's *The Latin Deli* (University of Georgia Press) is a collection of stories and poems. That the poems are outside my bailiwick is a relief, because I do not think much of the way the lines always end at predictable syntactical places. Indeed, the poems' earnestness and technical artlessness were enough to arouse in me a degree of worry about the stories, which are also earnest but not artless. Cofer writes about the Puerto Rican barrio in New Jersey, where, in El Basement of El Building, the women meet on Saturday mornings to wash their clothes and exchange gossip. There is a wealth of vivid detail as jumbled and redolent and persuasive as the wares of the deli of the title piece, and the level of the work in prose is quite high.

● Dianne Nelson's *A Brief History of Male Nudes in America* (University of Georgia Press) is a fine book, a woman's book, as people would have said before the days of politically correct speech. We get stories of mothers and daughters, either being noble together or else with one of them somewhat less than noble so the other can forgive or accept her. Men are often bums — one is even a kidnapper — but Nelson does not blame them really. They are strange creatures almost as odd as animals, like the elk who "discovered the dryer vent on the back wall of our house and stood there to get warm, basking in the sweet, foreign breeze of fabric softener."

● Elizabeth Searle's *My Body to You* (University of Iowa Press) is another "woman's book," and if one has the feeling of having wandered into the better lingerie section of a department store, there are many worse places to be. What makes Searle's stories work, I think, is her technical adventurousness, the way she puts different colors and textures together in a kind of prose collage. "News," for instance, begins: "Baby disappears, Tornado rips Ohio, Chickens die in piles in the heat. Good evening. Our table tilts toward Dad under a weight of loaded plates: hot corn, warm slaw, sweet or glazed or baked potatoes, fried chicken. Ninety-eight degrees outside, and supper steams away, our three faces flushed. Grease equals love." I cannot imagine anyone not reading on. And few will be disappointed.

● Enid Shomer's *Imaginary Men* (University of Iowa Press) is yet another woman's book, but this one concentrates on relationships, familial mostly. Shomer's work is of a high quality, and she takes the kind of delight in prosiness that only a poet can. (Her books of verse include *Stalking the Florida Panther* and *This Close to the Earth*.) The piling on of wonderful specificities in which she revels is a poet's holiday. An early passage in "Tropical Aunts" is a reasonable example of what I mean: "Debs was the older, a stormy rich blond who had been widowed. She lived a reclusive life in a houseboat on the Miami River. Without a phone, she could only be contacted through her attorney, like a movie star. Ava was a redhead with a reputation for borrowing money. Everyone knew she'd had to get married to her first husband. This was the biggest scandal so far in our family. After she had the baby, she got divorced, lost custody, and married an osteopath who worked nights as a stand-up comic in the hotels of Miami Beach." What zest, what verve, what wonderful *Alltäglichkeit!*

● Joe David Bellamy's *Atomic Love* (University of Arkansas Press) is a series of virtuoso performances, sometimes brilliant and sometimes only willful and mannered. Endings are arbitrary, ambiguous, runic . . . but then, in life, there are not neat peripeteias and elegant ironic conclusions. These are conventions of stories, which Bellamy is engaging bravely, and one must admire him for taking risks, even sometimes at the expense of pieces that would, by conventional methods, succeed — as the title piece, a wonderfully grown-up love story of a woman who remembers her childhood in New Mexico, the atomic testing, and what that testing did to the terrain and, in particular, to the retinas of the rabbits miles away from ground zero. Her "affair" — it is a couple of weekends in New York with a lawyer she met at a tennis resort — is brief, but strenuous enough, both in terms of lust and guilt, to make the whole nineteenth-century tradition resonate. The small details are right (yes, the Stanhope café is where they'd go!), and the sheer excess of the atomic testing seems perfectly natural. But the ending, a conversation with a professional baseball player on the plane home, is truly strange. Still, it is not as if Bellamy is not cagey and shrewd. He

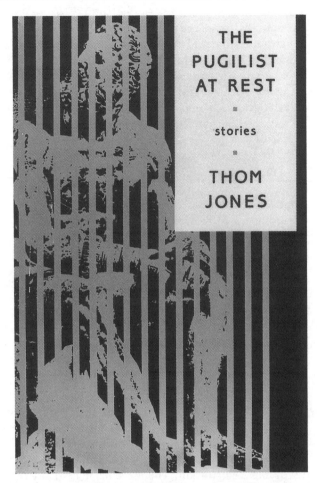

Dust jacket for Thom Jones's collection of short stories about how beleaguered characters bear up under stress

demonstrates in other stories, "Roth's Deadman," for instance, how much he can do with no tricks at all.

● Stewart O'Nan's *In the Walled City* (University of Pittsburgh Press) is the 1993 winner of the Drue Heinz Literature Prize, which means a ten-thousand-dollar cash award, publication by the University of Pittsburgh Press, and, for all I know, a pickle pin. From 326 manuscripts that were submitted, there must have been a winnowing down to ten or twenty, every one of them good, some of them perhaps to be published by other presses next year. From the finalists, a name author picks the winner, this year the chooser being Tobias Wolff — and O'Nan's stories, not surprisingly, turn out to be about guys who drive trucks or operate bulldozers at a dump, who live over McCrory's, and who turn off the lights "to save on the electric." The undershirt and beer-can school of verismo assumes that the simple people have lives that are more directly true and real than the effete types who read *The*

Threepenny Review or *Ascent* (in which O'Nan's work has actually appeared). I confess the small chip on my shoulder only as evidence of the quality of this work, for while I came to it with some suspicion, O'Nan won me over almost immediately and blew me away with several of his pieces. The restraint and the grace of some of his moves have nothing to do with his Carver/Dubus/Wolff settings. The last couple of paragraphs of "Finding Amy" are up there with the best writing I have seen in years.

● Stephen Dixon's *Long Made Short* (Johns Hopkins University Press) is, not surprisingly, a wonderful collection. Dixon's curious knack is for a combination of restraint in the sentences and extravagant, virtuoso display in the structure. In his novels and other collections of stories, he has been refining this mannerism for years now, and he is one of those writers with a small but enthusiastic following — not quite large enough to satisfy a commercial house. His *Frog* was a National Book Award Finalist in 1991 but still did not do quite well enough to be that "break-out book" the hotshot editors are waiting for. The work, nonetheless, continues at a consistently high level, and there is not another writer I can think of who can wring such tension from ordinary conversational exchanges. In "Man, Woman, and Boy," for instance — a story that appeared in the Houghton Mifflin *Best American Stories of 1993* — the unnamed man and his wife are discussing a separation. The piece begins: "They're sitting. 'It's wrong,' she says. 'I know,' he says, 'but what are we going to do about it?' She goes into the kitchen, he follows her. 'It almost couldn't be worse,' she says. 'Between us — how could it be. I don't see how.' 'I agree,' he says, 'and I'd like to change it from bad to better but I don't know what to do.' She pours them coffee. She puts on water for coffee. She fills the kettle with water. She gets the kettle off the stove, shakes it, looks inside and sees there's only a little water in it, turns on the faucet and fills the kettle halfway and then. And then?" This is Harold Pinter, but on the page instead of the stage, which is to say, this is Stephen Dixon, and the opaque surface all but bulges with the emotion that is just behind it. This is an extraordinarily talented man at the very top of his form.

● Jack Matthews's *"Storyhood as We Know It" and Other Tales* (Johns Hopkins University Press) is a little less unconventional than Dixon, but I do not mean that to suggest that he is dull. These are lively, shrewd, often very funny stories — "The King Solomon of the Market District" is hilarious — and their general approach is, actually, classic. As Matthews himself remarks, "I like to think of my characters as accumulations of past moments — forgotten and remembered, adventitious and self-created. If the present moment is the surface, then the past is depth." Like most bits of wisdom that may sound a little too simple, but over the course of the writing of half a dozen novels and as many short story collections, Matthews has shown the rich variety of ways in which the theorem can be applied to most impressive effect.

● Anne Calcagno's *Pray For Yourself* (Triquarterly Press/Northwestern University Press) is a collection of nine fairly unpleasant pieces, mostly having to do with wounds and scabs, literal as well as figurative, and how people recover from them — or do not. She is sometimes funny, and I wish she were even broader in her humor, but mostly she gives us these visions of misery and confinement straight, without condescension or self-congratulation. This is not easy to do, and one admires the skill and the honesty on display, but the book is by no means a fun read.

● Jonathan Gillman's *Grasslands* (Rutgers University Press) is deliberately mythic, which I guess is what happens out there on the South Dakota prairie. The light is different, and there are no mountains or even buildings to put things into any manageable perspective. A pack of coyotes sound off, and the men who have just finished haying stand there and listen: "Calls from a hill to their left answered those from a hill to their right. A chorus of yelps, yowls and whines responded from a hill behind them. All three groups repeated their noises, once, twice, a third time. The men stood like statues on their own hill, listening to the aurora borealis of sound around them. In moments it was over. Silence surrounded them. No one moved. No one spoke." I guess that is how it must be.

● Robert Wexelblatt's *The Decline of Our Neighborhood* (Rutgers University Press) is a wonderful book, a series of takes and gestures that do not betray or distort but somehow emphasize the importance of the most unlikely things, as, for example, the familiar old guy and his arthritic dog who disappear in the very short title story. What has happened to them? It does not really matter, but the world is different now that they are gone. The connections between the people who remain, fragile to begin with, are even more perilously frayed. It is a delicate conceit, but Wexelblatt does not even try to be delicate or artsy. He has the brashness (and good sense) to let us in on what he is doing, to insist that it is not a trick. Which is, of course, exactly what makes it work and gives him his wonderful authority.

Meanwhile, in New York and Boston, from the mainline houses there were still a few books of short stories, as if . . . as if the South Seas islanders in one of those cargo cults had persuaded a few airline pilots that the lines of torches they had set out were actual, operating airfields and every now and then a real plane landed and then took off. Writers who have not yet wised up send in books, and editors, who have managed by whatever series of unimaginable compromises and humiliations to hang on to their jobs, sometimes even contrive to get them through the committee and into print. These are not worse than the university-press books, and not better, just . . . luckier, maybe? They get more attention from the book reviewers, but not a whole lot more. They get a slightly better break for shelf space in stores, but they do not get it for long. These commercial houses let books go out of print quite quickly – often even before the languid quarterlies have got around to noticing them. It is a wash, I would say. Among the most interesting of these relicts:

● Sherman Alexie's *The Lone Ranger and Tonto Fistfight in Heaven* (Atlantic Monthly Press) is about American Indians, although the title, otherwise, is utterly adventitious. Alexie is a Spokane/Coeur d'Alene Indian, and he writes reasonably well about the drunks and wastrels of the Pacific Northwest, particularly the Native Americans. No, I will confess he writes very well, sometimes, and is funny. And he is not responsible for the editors who got such a feeling of overweening virtue from bringing out the work of someone so deserving – as if we are not, all of us, deserving. And Alexie is likable because he knows just how to twit these twits. "Nothing more hopeless than a sober Indian," he writes, and they are shocked, shocked. . . . What candor, what honesty, what . . . excoriating vision. (On the other hand, if one of us non–Native Americans were to say such a thing and omit the verb, he would be challenged as a bigot and a boor.) Still, they are good stories.

● Amy Bloom's *Come to Me* (HarperCollins) is the work of a practicing psychotherapist, which is hardly an instant recommendation. The stories, however, are jargon-free and, on first inspection, most appealing studies of quirks, relationships, and eccentricities. This collection was a National Book Award Finalist, and it is easy to see why. There is an instant intimacy and persuasiveness and then a series of revelations that approximate our notions of what a short story ought to be. The trouble is that too many of the pieces work in similar ways. We get a take on some person – or, more often, a couple of people – and then the revelation of the strange way in which he or she or they have responded to the odd stresses of love and living. Several of John O'Hara's middle-period stories work this way, and while any single one is okay, they diminish in a collection, as do, I think, Bloom's. (The obvious solution to this not-very-serious problem is to let some time elapse between the stories – a luxury no critic can afford himself.)

● Thom Jones's *The Pugilist at Rest* (Little, Brown) is tough-guy fiction, Hemingway resartus, but very well done indeed. Jones gives us grimness – of Vietnam or the less remote but just as physically violent version of any local hospital – and shows how his belabored and beleaguered characters bear up, often with bravery and good humor, which we can admire even as we see how much it costs them. One of Jones's stories has in it a paragraph I found myself remembering through the reading of a lot of the other books in this pile. A sort of thuggish emergency-room doctor (and most ER docs are thuggish, actually, or at least footloose adrenaline freaks) is visiting his elder brother: "Clendon had given me a number of literary magazines to read including stories of his own. I'm a reader, I read them but it was always some boring crap about a forty-five-year-old upper-level executive in boat shoes driving around Cape Cod *in a Volvo*. I mean you actually do finish some of them and admit that 'technically' they were pretty good but I'd rather go to back-to-back *operas* than read another story like that. It was with relief that I returned to the medical journals." Jones is fine, indeed, and a name to look out for in the future.

● Alice Mattison's *The Flight of Andy Burns* (Morrow) offers careful, cautious stories, admirable for the dexterity of their small-finger gestures that throw large shadows on the wall. Frankly, I respect these stories more than I like them – too many of the characters are determined to do good, fix up slums, teach the people in prison how to write poetry, work in soup kitchens, or even just breast-feed in public (as a matter of principle, of course). Their high-mindedness is a bit overbearing, and I am more pleased by their disappointments and reversals than I ought to be. But I am not pretending to be a perfect reader.

● Reynolds Price's *The Collected Stories* (Atheneum) is probably another demonstration of my imperfections and the unreliability of my taste. This volume represents the lifework of a very distinguished writer, a member of the American Academy of Arts and Letters and – perhaps even more rarefied – the Duke University English department.

Dust jacket for the collection of stories Reynolds Price calls "what I've written in adult life by way of fiction shorter than the novel"

These are carefully crafted, meticulous stories, and a few of them are even famous ("The Names and Faces of Heroes," for instance). My cavil – and it is only that – is that they have about them sometimes the air of the study. I am too often reminded of the craftsmanliness or distracted by the artifactual sheen. That famous piece, the title story of an earlier collection, ends as the father, having driven all night with the little boy, "claps his palms one time, and I go on my knees out of dry car heat through momentary snow into arms that circle, enfold me, lift me, bear me these last steps home over ice – my legs hung bare down his cooling side, face to his heart, eyes blind again, mind folding in me for years to come his literal death and my own swelling foes, lips against rough brown wool saying to myself as we rise to the porch, to my waiting mother (silent, in the voice I will have as a man), 'They did not separate us tonight. We finished alive, together, whole. This one more time.'" All those repetitions – circle, enfold, lift, bear; alive, together, whole – are just a

little self-congratulatory, relying on a strange mix of the regional and southern with the high-toned and very literary. (I am probably being unfair, but that is the point of being a critic, is it not? If these judgments were as simple as arithmetic, there would not be criticism but only terse corrections in red pencil.)

● Francine Prose's *The Peaceable Kingdom* (Farrar, Straus and Giroux) addresses many of the same technical problems as Price does, but her touch, especially with children, is so much more delicate. She is a wonderful writer who won me over with an elegant piece called "Ghirlandaio" (to which I was drawn because I remembered the surrealist clerihew: "Ghirlandaio / Was not born in Ohio," but that is neither here nor there). A woman is looking at a book on Renaissance paintings, and it brings back to her a childhood memory of looking at that painting – of an old man and his grandson – with her father, a physician, who pointed out the grandfather's bulbous, grapy nose and diagnosed his condition as lupus erythematosus. "My father walked briskly through the museum, visiting his favorites as if he were making hospital rounds, and in my slippery party shoes I skated after him. The Ghirlandaio double portrait was my father's idea of what art should be, and I was glad that it gave him such pleasure that winter when nothing else did." She remembers that winter clearly, she explains, because, "by the next year my parents would be divorced. It seems incredible now that they never argued in front of me. But it was also the very last year when I chose to take my parents' word for what was real and what wasn't. I believed life was as they told me, as it seemed, and what seemed to be happening on those Sundays was that my father wanted to go to the museum and my mother didn't. . . ." It is a scary world there, for children and for adults too, and images, like those of the painting or like the friezes of an Egyptian tomb later in the same story, can overwhelm the so-called real lives that are swirling about them, informing and reforming them.

● Rafik Schami's *Damascus Nights* (Farrar, Straus and Giroux) is in here as a whimsy, mine, or as I prefer to think, the world's. Schami is a Syrian born in Damascus in 1946 who has lived in Germany since 1963. His book, a series of loosely connected stories by and about Salim the coachman, was published in Germany in 1989 as *Erzähler der Nacht,* which I read more or less as "The Storyteller of the Night." Perhaps at one of those book fairs, a Farrar Straus editor who had had a terrific lunch and was in a good mood made a deal for small change (FS&G does not want to pay a lot for this muffler or anything else, for that matter) and picked up the U.S. rights to what reads more or less like a series of Arabian Nights stories. There is a childlike wonder and intensity to these stories which are exotic and, at the same time, familiar as . . . Aladdin (or Al Al-din). Schami's credo is engaging: "Lies and spices are brothers and sisters. Lies turn any bland fare into a piquant delicacy. The truth and nothing but the truth is something only a judge wants to hear." The stories are engaging too.

● Elizabeth Tallent's *Honey* (Knopf) is a reliable series of adept pieces about relationships, mostly in the pellucid air and under the astonishing skies of New Mexico. There are couples talking or not talking, saying one thing with their words and another with their body language, and working it out together or not. These are such shrewd people that they know how irrelevant their shrewdness is likely to be. "What she hated about starting something new," one woman thinks as she is about to begin a love affair, "is how often you had to wonder if you were wrong. You had to know someone incalculably well before you were sure." People can even divorce and find that the split did not work. This kind of thing takes enormous tact and craft, but Tallent's talents are as abundant as they are eponymous.

● Larry Woiwode's *Silent Passengers* (Atheneum) is the work of a seasoned performer, a craftsman of great restraint and modesty who only now and then allows himself any kind of flamboyant riff – as in the first piece in this volume, a recollection of how it used to be when oranges made it through in late fall or early winter to the bare and frozen prairie he recalls from childhood. At the grocery store, "in the broken-open crates (as if burst by the power of the oranges themselves), one or two of the spheres would be free of the tissue they came wrapped in – always purple tissue, as if that were the only color that could contain their nestled populations. The crates bore paper labels at one end – of an orange against a blue background or a blue goose against an orange background – signifying the colorful otherworld, unlike our wintery one, that these phenomena had risen from." He goes on this way for four pages or so of perfectly remembered, perfectly rendered truth, suggesting how truth of that order is a treasure worth more than anything else in the world. "Oh, oranges, solid *O*s, light from afar in the midst of the freeze, and not unlike that unspherical fruit that first passed from Eve to Adam and from there (to abbreviate matters) to my brother and me. 'Mom, we think we're getting a cold.' 'You mean, you want an orange?' This

is difficult to answer or dispute or even to acknowledge, finally, with the fullness that the subject deserves, a fullness that each orange bears, within its own makeup, into this hard-edged yet insubstantial, incomplete, cold, wintry world." That Woiwode can do this kind of thing is impressive. Even more impressive is how much restraint he shows in only doing it on those rare occasions that really call for it.

Finally, there are the small presses, unaffiliated with universities, that are struggling along somehow and doing interesting and valuable work. They are hanging on or bursting fresh onto the scene, as if another Duesenberg repair shop were just what the country needed for its economic and cultural salvation. Zoland Books, in Cambridge, Massachusetts, is the new house, and while I admire the hell out of them, I would be very cautious about investing money in any of these operations. Among those I noticed – or was able to find out about – this year:

● Jack Agüeros's *Dominoes & Other Stories from the Puerto Rican* (Curbstone Press) is a strong collection of stories about barrio life, rather less sentimental than Cofer's. Their restraint, in fact, is what primarily recommends them, a kind of laconic stoicism that may be the counterweight to Latin extravagance. I think, for example, of the plays of Federico García Lorca, and it seems to me that Agüeros often manages that kind of resonance. His title story, which is in fact about a game of dominoes that turns deadly, is a marvel of apparent effortlessness but nonetheless enormous skill, as if the name of the double blank domino, *la caja de muerta* (the dead man's box), had been waiting forever for just this writer to come along. Agüeros is also a poet, a playwright, and a writer for children and has worked in television. He is, to put it more simply and clearly, a writer of very great gifts.

● Guy Davenport's *A Table of Green Fields* (New Directions, not a small press, really) is aggressively bookish but playfully so, perhaps because that is the only way to trump the cards of players like Harold Bloom or Stanley Fish, reminding the world that there is a degree of gamesmanship in the lit biz that is inevitable and even desirable. These are not conventional stories but jeux d'esprit of a very sophisticated and learned mind that, after drinks time, say, can wonder about the letters that Franz Kafka is said to have written to some little girl to console her for the loss of her doll. Was there ever such a girl and such a doll? Did Kafka write such letters? (Who knows? Who cares?) It is Davenport's delightful idea to imagine the letters, an imaginary world tour that Belinda the doll

Dust jacket for Larry Woiwode's collection of short stories about families living on the Great Plains

makes, a cheerier and briefer kind of cadenza than he did in *Amerika,* but not unimaginably so. The stories work as stories, or entertainments – toys, if you will – and then they work later as legitimate literary criticism, enhancing our understanding and our appreciation of their subjects. It is a weird kind of exercise, but there ought to be room in the literary landscape for at least one Guy Davenport. Otherwise, he would have to invent himself. (Or perhaps he has.)

● Gary Fincke's *For Keepsies* (Coffeehouse Press) worried me a little. The title is perhaps excessively cute? But Fincke ties it down, or at least lets us into the game, which is the skimming of baseball cards against a school wall in blue-collar Pittsburgh, an exercise in which the participants may play "for funsies," or "for keepsies." Most of life, alas, is for keepsies, and Fincke's sense of the grittiness and the energy of Pittsburgh is most impressive. (The only other writer I know who has brought that region to such life is Lester Goran, whose novels are not much read these days but deserve to be.) I won-

dered for a moment whether Fincke had submitted this manuscript for consideration for the Drue Heinz Prize, but . . . maybe not. One of the stories, "Grade Nine," starts out with the protagonist getting fired from the Heinz plant. Literature is perfectly well and good, but it is perhaps indecorous to have a former employee strolling along by the plant and observing: "I walked past vinegar and knew somebody was suffering in there. I passed the warehouse and the research building, the best place I ever worked because you didn't follow a production line. Instead, you waited for some college pro to fool around with the recipe for ketchup. You opened a couple of valves for him whenever he decided it was time, and wondered what difference it would make to anybody's meat loaf if you hesitated five seconds." Indecorous, yes, but great fun.

● Myra Goldberg's *Whistling* (Zoland Books) is a collection of great appeal. Goldberg is technically playful and adventurous, but beneath the agreeable display of literary legerdemain there is a quiet and contemplative spirit gazing at the lives of men and women with intelligence and compassion. One of the pieces, "Hair," seems at first to be just a lot of women telling stories about . . . well, hair. And that is what it is, except that it moves somehow toward the condition of some Greek chorus of women in a tragedy discussing the general grief of things. This is not an easy feat to accomplish, and I kept thinking that it ought to be performed on a stage – actually, as I later discovered, it has been. "Issues and Answers" is a hilarious and devastating description of a dinner party in maybe Georgetown or suburban Virginia, where the savants and experts are so out of touch with the real world in which most of us live that they cannot recognize blatant passion when they see it. Goldberg is a cunning and elegant writer, and her stories are very fine indeed.

● Howard Gordon's *The African in Me* (Braziller) is as ugly a book as I have seen in years – I mean its dust jacket, a garish yellow and black geometrical assault. The stories inside, though, are appealing for their honesty and directness in the representation of the pains of the black experience in America. The location is mostly upstate New York – Gordon is an assistant provost at the State University of New York at Oswego – and the mood is mostly stoic but leavened with a touch of self-mockery. "The Playground of Hostility" begins this way: "In 1954, anytime my friends or family members entered the hospital, they died. I came to believe hospitals were places that summoned death, contagious way stations between wounds and cemeteries. The people that I had known entered the hospital with simple injuries, like bloodied noses and gout, but were discovered to have polio, or sickle-cell anemia, or other life-threatening diseases. People like me died. I came to loathe these places, which masqueraded as institutions of healing. I dreaded the sick quiet, the antiseptic odors. To me, dustless marble floors did not indicate cleanliness; they were reminders that someone's blood had been easily washed away." There are other writers who are more able manipulators of fictional techniques, but Gordon's sheer and unadorned conviction is enough to make these powerful pieces.

● Lloyd E. Hill's *The Village of Bom Jesus* (Algonquin Books of Chapel Hill) is a wild-card sort of book, a series of stories involving a calico cat named Bom Jesus who lives in some remote corner of the Amazon jungle, surrounded by cute Brazilian folkloric creatures and events. Any given story is all right, but together they struck me like a whole series of marzipan candies. There is something a little mannered about the faux naïf tone, but maybe my difficulties have more to do with the fact that I was a difficult kid than they do with Hill's writing. He lived in the Amazon for a while, farming and fishing, and now works as "a fossil preparator," if that is the word for it, reconstructing dinosaurs in Dallas. "The Swamp of Dreams," for instance, begins: "Mankind has its mongers – its fishmongers, tinmongers, warmongers, hatemongers, even its lovemongers. So is it strange that animalkind has its mongers also? Along the upper reaches of the Juruá, the animals who are mongers vastly outnumber folk who are mongers." I have limited patience with this kind of thing, but it is odd enough to be noticed, even by such a grumpmonger as myself.

● David Huddle's *Intimates* (David R. Godine) is a book of extraordinary accomplishment. Even before we got to know each other, I had been a great admirer of Huddle's stories, and, were it not for our friendship and the fact that I write for him regularly (he is editor of the *New England Review*), I might very well have picked *Intimates* as the *Dictionary of Literary Biography Yearbook* Award winner. What I find most impressive about Huddle's work is how he can get tears out of a joke or laughter out of a really painful moment, setting us up for a move in one direction and then, reliably but never predictably, going the other way. He does this with something like spiritual aplomb, and as readers we have the impression we used to have sometimes as children – that we were at last learning secrets about how the grown-ups live. Huddle's subject is mostly men and women, and his epigraph, from James Joyce, is the famous line: "Yes, yes, yes, but what's the He and She of it?" He can write from the woman's point of view as persuasively as from a man's. This is a move that John Updike likes to do sometimes, and is good at, but Huddle is every bit as good and even more surprising. He has an uncannily sure sense of when to be blunt and when to be coy, when to be periphrastic and when to be vulgar, when to say a thing directly or just to hint obliquely at what few other writers can imagine, let alone boast of. And this strategic shrewdness enhances the authority of the stories so that their impact is as great as if we had experienced these things ourselves.

I am sure I have missed some good books. That this is a partial and serendipitous list, I do freely confess. On the other hand, our lives are mostly serendipitous, and we meet this person, or take that job, or settle in that town over there, each encounter and each choice apparently independent and isolated, and then, in late middle age, we look back on a life that seems to have a design, a crafted narrative, as if it were a story some quirky but intelligent author had been putting together. Even a job of work like this, undertaken as randomly as I have done it, looks to have a direction, a tendency – for which, as with my life, I am only in part responsible.

Dictionary of Literary Biography Yearbook Award for a Distinguished Volume of Short Stories Published in 1993

Gerald Shapiro's collection of stories, *From Hunger* (University of Missouri Press), hovers somewhere between South American magic realism and Marc Chagall's flying fiddlers, but Shapiro never seems silly, and he works in a tone and timbre altogether his own. If Isaac Bashevis Singer had been writing in English, and if he had been plucked up out of Manhattan and set down in Nebraska to blink his blue eyes in astonishment under those oppressively wide and matching pale-blue skies, his stories would very likely resemble these. Shapiro takes chances, not to show off, but out of sheer desperation to describe in accurate terms the extravagances of existence.

A typical opening paragraph: "To say that this past year had been a bad one would be to insult all the other bad years of Levidow's long life. As he was apt to tell anyone who would listen, every day fresh misery poured on his head. Fruit spoiled as he carried it home from the market. Cars splashed mud and slush on him, even on the sunniest of afternoons. At the corner of 95th and Amsterdam in broad daylight he was beaten and robbed in full view of scores of passersby, none of whom bore witness to the crime. Levidow's hearing began to short out on him, as though a radio inside his head was on the fritz. His feet ached from morning till night."

There were half a dozen books of stories that I considered, each of them first-rate, good enough to arouse in me not only admiration but envy: the Stephen Dixon, the David Huddle, the Francine Prose, the Janet Peery, and a few others. And there is a kind of justice in the process up to there – the making of the last cut. But the final pick is a matter of taste, of spirit even. As I sit here in Philadelphia and think of this guy out in Lincoln, Nebraska, sending his manuscript down to Columbia, Missouri, with its dreams of Barney Greengrass back on Amsterdam Avenue, my heart melts.

– *David R. Slavitt*

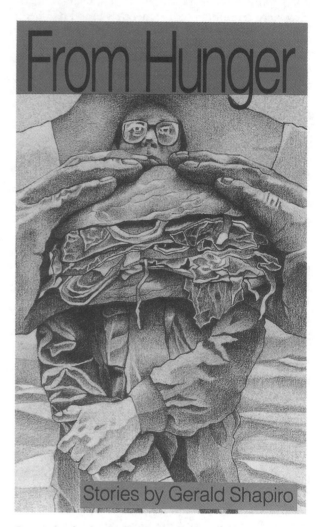

Dust jacket for Gerald Shapiro's collection of short stories in the magic realist tradition

The Year in Drama

Howard Kissel
New York Daily News

On a Monday night in May, *Kiss of the Spider Woman,* a musical version of Manuel Puig's 1976 novel about a gay hairdresser who sacrifices himself for his politically incendiary cellmate in a banana-republic prison, opened on Broadway. The following night was the opening of Tony Kushner's *Angels in America,* subtitled *A Gay Fantasia on National Themes,* which had already won the Pulitzer Prize and later won the Tony for Best Play.

In October was the Broadway opening of *Twilight of the Golds,* a play in which a middle-class, vaguely homophobic young Jewish woman, whose brother is gay, has to decide whether to abort a fetus with a hypothetical "gay" gene.

Off-Off-Broadway, the WPA Theater produced Paul Rudnick's comedy *Jeffrey,* about a young gay man nervous about falling in love in an era when he could lose a lover to AIDS; and Circle Rep mounted Paula Vogel's *And Baby Makes Seven,* about two lesbians who live with a gay man who has fathered a baby with one of them – the title is drawn from the fact that the adults speak to one another not in their own voices but in those of prepubescent children.

It is never possible to characterize a year in drama by finding a dominant theme, but, as this brief sampling of the year in New York theater suggests, the subject matter is increasingly, insistently gay. It has never been a secret that many of those who work in the theater are homosexual, but until quite recently this provided the subtext rather than the text of their material.

Very early in Tennessee Williams's career, for example, *Time* magazine, in a profile, called him a "pervert." Williams was too guileless to conceal his homosexuality. But his plays remain powerful because they are never merely about sex or sexual orientation. Blanche DuBois's discovery of her husband in bed with another man in *A Streetcar Named Desire* (1947) is the turning point in her life; but the play is about the illusions she has created for herself, illusions to sustain herself in an entirely hostile world.

Although only a small percentage of an audience might identify with Blanche's particular predicament – turning on the lights and realizing her worst fears – everyone can understand a woman devising complex, sometimes grotesque, sometimes poetic, strategies to keep harsh reality away; hence the continuing vitality of Williams's play. (Had *Streetcar* been written in the last few years, Blanche might have been a minor, comic character; the play would probably have centered around her husband.)

Williams's career, of course, reached its apex during the 1950s, the age of the man in the gray flannel suit. The point of the 1955 Sloan Wilson novel that gave the period its label is that its hero, despite the blandness of his Madison Avenue uniform, is a complex figure. He had been a genuine hero during World War II, and, although he tries to adhere to the repressive sexual code of the postwar era, he actually has a libido.

Today his concerns would not be concealed under shapeless, colorless, Brooks Brothers attire. He would proclaim his political opinions, his sexual orientation, his comic style, his environmental anxieties through a whole wardrobe of T-shirts. These days subtext is unnecessary.

There is a similar lack of subtlety in much of the dramaturgy of our period. We have come to accept a theater in which characters are types and in which the action illustrates the most commonplace political ideas. Such plays often receive hosannas simply because they echo the critics' own political views, if not those views they know to be fashionable. If some critics' endorsement of *Angels in America,* for example, had an almost hysterical shrillness to it, it may have been because, in the current political climate, to be less than enthusiastic implied homophobia or right-wing hostility.

It seems unmistakable that *Angels in America* is two things, a piece of theater and a political statement. What seems increasingly clear is that the latter has overshadowed the former. (The final confirmation that this is so comes at the very end of the two parts, in the coda, which shall be discussed later.)

Both parts begin with a poignantly comical prologue by an old man. Part 1, *Millennium Ap-*

47

Program covers for the Walter Kerr Theatre production of the two parts of Tony Kusher's Pulitzer Prize–winning play, Angels in America

proaches, opens with an elderly rabbi giving the eulogy for an old woman, whom he did not know except as a member of the remarkable generation who emigrated from the Old World to embark on the great, unpredictable adventure of the New World. " . . . she carried the old world on her back across the ocean, in a boat, and she put it down on Grand Concourse, or in Flatbush, and she worked that earth into your bones," the rabbi says. "You can never make that crossing she made, for such Great Voyages in this world do not any more exist. But every day of your lives the miles that voyage between that place and this one you cross. Every day. You understand me? In you that journey is."

Part 2, *Perestroika,* begins with an aged diehard leftist, Aleksii Antedilluvianovich Prelapsarianov, a member of the Soviet parliament, bemoaning the death of communism, wondering what new system will be able to take its place. He too foresees a great adventure and great pain, as the world

seeks to reorder itself. He asks: "What System of Thought have these Reformers to present to this mad swirling planetary disorganization, to the In-evident Welter of fact, event, phenomenon, calamity? Do they have, as we did, a beautiful Theory, as bold, as Grand, as comprehensive a construct . . . ?"

"You can't imagine, when we first read the Classic Texts, when in the dark vexed night of our ignorance and terror the seed-words sprouted and shoved incomprehension aside, when the incredible bloody vegetable struggle up and through into Red Blooming gave us Praxis, True Praxis, True Theory married to Actual Life . . . You who live in this Sour Little Age cannot imagine the grandeur of the prospect we gazed upon . . ."

Both these prologues have a whimsy, an intellectuality masked in irony and playfulness that seem Kushner's truest, most beguiling voice. Throughout the seven hours of the combined play he hits his mark occasionally, but never as securely as in these openings.

Millennium is, in some ways, a play about denial. Its most interesting character, Roy Cohn (based closely on the historical Roy Cohn, the lawyer and society figure who began his career as an assistant to Sen. Joseph McCarthy), denies that he is a homosexual. By the end of the play he also denies that he has AIDS. As Cohn articulates it, in one of the play's sharpest speeches, to the doctor who diagnoses his terminal condition, "Homosexuals are not men who sleep with other men. Homosexuals are men who in fifteen years of trying cannot get a piss-ant antidiscrimination bill through City Council. Homosexuals are men who know nobody and who nobody knows. Who have zero clout. Does this sound like me, Henry?"

To prove his point Cohn boasts he can pick up a phone, "punch fifteen numbers and you know who will be on the other end in under five minutes?"

His doctor, who gets the point, says, "The President."

"Even better, Henry," Cohn says. "His wife." (The joke refers to the Reagans, since the play is set in the mid 1980s, but it probably works just as well for the current administration.)

Cohn finishes his lecture to his doctor by declaring, "Roy Cohn is not a homosexual. Roy Cohn is a heterosexual man, Henry, who fucks around with guys." As to the diagnosis he declares, "AIDS is what homosexuals have. I have liver cancer."

Kushner's Cohn, like his real-life counterpart, is a wonderfully outrageous character, though by *Perestroika* the shock value has worn off and Cohn's increasingly strident self-assertion and his racist taunting have become repetitive and tiresome, lacking their initial satiric edge.

Throughout *Millennium* Cohn tries to act as a mentor, a latter-day Vautrin, to a handsome, troubled young Mormon lawyer, Joe Pitt, whose religious upbringing has caused him to deny his homosexuality. (Cohn also hopes to place Pitt in the Reagan Justice Department, where he can thwart efforts to indict Cohn. As much as the play is about denial, it is also about the uses of power.)

For all his legal shrewdness, Pitt somehow misses the sexual undercurrents of Cohn's solicitude. He is able to resist Cohn's paternalistic advances, but he finds himself increasingly drawn to an openly gay young legal clerk in his office, Louis Ironson.

Pitt has a wife, Harper, who, at the beginning of *Millennium,* has already lost her grip on reality. Also a Mormon, she has been unhinged by the move from the security of Salt Lake City to the comparatively anarchic climate of New York City. She is also unsettled by the fact that her husband often leaves her to go wandering alone in the city at the oddest hours. Although Pitt has a loyalty to Harper, her erratic, impulsive behavior and her addiction to valium make it easy for him to withdraw from her and succumb to the unmistakable charm of Ironson.

Ironson has abandoned his longtime lover, Prior Walter, because the latter has been diagnosed with AIDS. Ironson is troubled by how readily he drops the man he loves, a man who desperately needs him. It was Ironson's grandmother whom the elderly rabbi eulogized in the prologue of *Millennium.* When Ironson, about to leave his lover, confesses what he is going to do after the funeral, the rabbi is shocked.

He asks the rabbi for some absolution, and the rabbi tells him to find a priest. Louis protests that he is not a Catholic. The rabbi rejoins, "Worse luck for you, bubbulah, Catholics believe in forgiveness. Jews believe in guilt." Ironson manages to assuage his own guilt in flights of glib philosophizing.

It is Ironson, in the midst of one of these Talmudic discourses, who clarifies the play's title. America has no indigenous spirits, he declares, except those of the Native Americans, whose deities have been destroyed. "There are no gods here, no ghosts and spirits in America, there are no angels in America, no spiritual past, no racial past, there's only the political...."

Although the play flirts with conceptions of angels along vaguely Hebraic lines, the actual angels it depicts are considerably less complex. One of the angels makes her entrance shortly after Ironson's speech. It is the ghost of Ethel Rosenberg, come to torment Cohn in what will be his final illness.

Lest there be any mistaking Kushner's desire to beatify her, in *Perestroika* Rosenberg says Kaddish, the Jewish Prayer for the Dead, for Cohn, despite the fact he has boasted of the fact that it was his personal intervention that prompted the vacillating judge in the Rosenberg case to send her to the electric chair. Why Rosenberg, who has returned to earth to observe Cohn's disbarment proceedings, should be so eager to say Kaddish for her nemesis is never made clear. The image requires a kind of faith probably possible only to longtime subscribers to the *Nation.*

The other angel who is a major character in the play makes her first appearance at the end of *Millennium,* when she crashes onto the stage from the wings above and proclaims to the amazed Walter, "The Great Work begins: The Messenger has arrived."

Presumably *Perestroika* will delineate the Great Work to which she alludes. Her major accomplishment, however, is to give Prior sexual solace. Her wonderfully theatrical entrances give him both the erections and orgasms he has been unable to achieve since the onset of his illness. She also gives

Prior a glimpse of heaven, which, he informs us, is very much like San Francisco.

She proclaims Prior as a prophet, which allows him to fly about Manhattan bringing comfort to others. He befriends, for example, both Harper and Pitt's mother, Hannah. Toward the end of *Millennium* Joe calls Salt Lake City in the middle of the night to inform Hannah that he is a homosexual. She immediately sells her house and flies east to counsel him. By the time she arrives in New York her son has succumbed to Louis's advances, and the two are in bed together for most of the early scenes of *Perestroika*.

Hannah gets a job at the Mormon Visitors Center in New York, where she brings Harper to get her out of her depressing apartment. Harper and Prior watch a diorama about Mormon history. One of the figures in the diorama, the stalwart hero leading the Mormons west, looks exactly like Joe (throughout the play the actors take on different roles), and this episode gives Kushner a chance to examine the mythology of Mormonism, a religion whose angels are American-born and -bred.

The plots of both sections are relatively free-floating. In *Millennium,* for example, Prior is visited by ancestors from many centuries ago — an effete seventeenth-century English nobleman and a thirteenth-century English yeoman who was the victim of an earlier plague. In *Perestroika* Roy Cohn's nurse, Belize, a former drag queen, is a previous lover of Prior's. Belize tells Prior, who then tells Louis, that Joe is "Roy's butt-boy," which happens not to be true. Louis, already horrified to learn that he has been fellating a Reagan Republican, knows he must drop Joe.

Louis has an intellectual ambivalence about Joe, despite the fact that Joe uses his cerebral and moral elasticity to provide Louis with a plausible rationale for having abandoned Prior. Louis researches what Joe has written for the judge for whom he clerks. In a novel form of lover's renunciation, Louis rebukes Joe for the conservative slant of his legal briefs, throwing his politically retrograde opinions at him with the rage of Eliza Doolittle flinging her slippers at Henry Higgins.

What is the upshot of all these convoluted proceedings? There is much talk about change, especially in *Perestroika,* the prologue of which ends with Prelapsarianov's declaring, "Yes, we must change, only show me the Theory, and I will be at the barricades, show me the book of the next Beautiful Theory, and I promise these blind eyes will see again, just to read it, to devour that text."

Do any of the characters really change? Joe, of course, accepts his homosexuality. Hannah, his rigid, initially homophobic mother, becomes more accepting of homosexuals. At play's end she has become a gabby New Yorker, sitting on a bench in Central Park theorizing with Louis. It is Hannah who gives the responsa to Prelapsarianov's question at the beginning of the play, declaring, "You can't live in the world without an idea of the world, but it's living that makes the ideas. You can't wait for a theory, but you have to have a theory." (Does the play really illustrate this? Is her formulation all that remarkable?)

Harper leaves Joe, demanding of him only his credit card — when the charges stop piling up, she informs him, he will know she has found herself. Prior, the lucky recipient of Roy Cohn's private stash of AZT, is in remission. Does any of this warrant seven hours of our time?

In fact, the characters, particularly the women, are largely types. At times they even joke about it. When Prior (who sometimes admonishes himself for conforming to "nelly" stereotypes) meets the stern Hannah, learns she is a Mormon, but discovers glints of humor beneath her stolid exterior, he says, "I wish you would be more true to your demographic profile. Life is confusing enough."

The changes the characters undergo are changes of intellectual perception, with little emotional content. Kushner's people constantly verbalize themselves and each other into existence. Sometimes the images are amusing, like most of Cohn's. Sometimes they are tiresomely political, as when Belize describes Cohn as "America — terminal, crazy and mean."

Much of the play already seems a bit dated — there are jokes about the Reagan years and an exceptionally mean-spirited in-joke that plays to gay New Yorkers. (Belize phones Prior with "hot dish": "Get out your oven mitts," he says. "Guess who just checked in with the troubles? The Killer Queen Herself. New York's number one closeted queer." Prior asks, "Koch?")

The final moments of *Perestroika* illustrate what is best and weakest about Kushner's mammoth work. The epilogue takes place at Bethesda Fountain in Central Park. Prior points to the angel atop the fountain and calls her his favorite angel: "I like them best when they're statuary. They commemorate death but they suggest a world without dying. They are made of the heaviest things on earth, stone and iron, they weigh tons but they're winged, they are engines and instruments of flight."

Louis then explains the Biblical significance of Bethesda, an image of healing. Without the self-conscious poetry that often creeps into the play, these lines attain the buoyancy of good verse.

Then Prior brings it all resolutely back to earth. "This disease will be the end of many of us, but not nearly all, and the dead will be commemorated and will struggle on with the living, and we are not going away," he declares. Is this the end of a play or a political rally?

"Bye now," he tells the audience, an unusually coy valedictory. "You are fabulous, each and every one," he says. Is he addressing us all as political adherents? Or is he pleased that we have sat through both parts? Or that we have spent $120? Are we fabulous because he assumes we are all HIV positive?

His final lines are "More life," then, "The Great Work Begins," the words the angel addressed to him toward the end of *Millennium Approaches*. Yes, we know that Prior has become a prophet, but was it necessary to spend another three and a half hours to reach this rhetorical conclusion? The nearly unanimous critical acclaim for *Angels* suggested it was. Among the holdouts were Robert Brustein of the *New Republic*, who noted that Kushner views everything through the "prism of sex"; John Simon of *New York* magazine; Edwin Wilson of the *Wall Street Journal;* and Clive Barnes of the *New York Post*, who likened Kushner to John Dos Passos, an apt comparison for so politically oriented a writer.

Angels in America was the first play to open in New York after receiving the Pulitzer Prize. The second was Robert Schenkkan's *The Kentucky Cycle*, which won the prize in 1992. Like *Angels*, Schenkkan's play, which had been produced in several regional theaters, presented itself as an epic. It, too, came in two parts, totaling six hours. If Kushner's work was characterized by both imaginative and intellectual audacity, Schenkkan's seemed surprisingly square. Its survey of two hundred years of American history in a corner of eastern Kentucky held no surprises, either intellectually or theatrically.

The play begins in 1775 with an Irish settler outwitting a group of American Indians, who, an offstage narrator portentously informs us, were "taught lessons in perfidy by a master of the trade." The settler is the forebear of a succession of thugs whose rapaciousness and bloodthirstiness suggest nineteenth-century melodrama. (Much of the play, in fact, seems pastiche, as Schenkkan models scenes after Clifford Odets, Arthur Miller, and others — one long scene in which a villainous landlord strips a man of all his property and dignity seems exactly like something from melodrama.)

Program cover for the Royale Theatre production of Robert Schenkkan's Pulitzer Prize–winning play

In this vision of American history, fathers are never reluctant to betray or even murder their sons, and vice versa. The dastardliness of the early settlers is literal minded. The later betrayals are subtler though no less destructive. In one sequence, for example, a father who is a labor leader compromises mine safety precautions with shifty management. In doing so he unwittingly sacrifices a son who wanted to follow in his father's footsteps.

In part 1, which takes us to the early Civil War, the play at least offers a bit of exoticism — an American Indian maiden here, some slaves there. By part 2, Schenkkan concentrates on the mining industry, with a lengthy sequence about the growth of unions. This is material we have seen in innumerable films, all of which are far more moving.

For most of its six hours, *Kentucky Cycle* concerns itself with male dastardliness. In its politically correct view of American history, white men are tireless agents of evil, relentless practitioners of sexism, racism, and unimaginable cruelties. Women appear exclusively as victims until the scenes about unionism. Schenkkan has a moment where the beleaguered miners are ready to give up. Somehow they are rallied back to their task by their womenfolk banging on pots and pans. The image has an amateurish, community-theater ring to it. Is Schenkkan's historical vision truthful? To an extent. Is our history more complex and poetic? Yes. Do we need the theater to give us a version of our history simpler and more mean-spirited than its actuality? Probably not.

A far more satisfying historical play is Alan Bennett's *The Madness of George III,* which made a brief tour of the United States in a spectacular production directed by Nicholas Hytner, presented by the Royal National Theater of Great Britain, with Nigel Hawthorne in the title role.

Bennett begins by showing that George was not merely an autocrat but a rigorously conscientious professional. He was, after all, not a native-born monarch. His line had been imported from Germany, and in the early scenes he prides himself on how carefully he has studied his adoptive country. The madness that besets him sets off two crises, both of which Bennett analyses with a wit and humor that belies his more serious intentions. The first question is how George is to be cured. The court physicians all prescribe remedies that strike the modern viewer as primitive and ludicrous, though, as Bernard Shaw observed nearly one hundred years ago, medicine has always been a matter of fashion.

The remedy that eventually restores George to sanity is a radical one, implemented by a rough-spoken country physician. He demands that George undergo the novel treatment of forsaking royal prerogative and being forced to behave like a normal human being. It is an ordeal for George, but it eventually has the desired result. Paradoxically, his return to health is signaled by his sudden resumption of the autocratic airs that come so naturally to him.

Whatever the personal reverberations of George's illness, the graver issue is that of the reins of government. The longer George is unable to govern, the greater the chances that his ne'er-do-well son, George IV, all of whose political ideas are radically different from his father's, will take over. The jockeying for position by the various politicos allied with each man dramatizes the tenuousness of monarchy.

Both crises are resolved happily, though that happiness is provisional. The play ends with a glorious tableau as George III attends a mass celebrating his restoration to health and power. With hindsight we know that George's triumph over his demons is only temporary. Within a few years he will again be mad, and his son will have become regent. If we see George's celebration as ironic and poignant, it nevertheless reinforces our sense that all human victories are provisional – but that does not diminish the cause for jubilation.

It is this larger perspective that makes Bennett's play seem so much more mature than most of what appears on American stages. An interesting exception is *Time on Fire,* a one-man play by the actor Evan Handler about his triumph over leukemia. Often one-person plays seem strained and self-indulgent, but Handler's account of his harrowing struggle with a generally fatal illness seems genuinely heroic. It is also extremely literate, as one can see in a passage where he declares that "No body would allow itself to be punctured and poisoned, to be reduced to a state of heinous malfunction, without an egocentric personality running the show. The body knows that the universe is just as accepting of its death as of its life. Only the frightened person steering the ship believes that the Earth needs him alive. . . . That's what makes chemotherapy possible."

Another one-person show with deep impact is Charlayne Woodard's *Pretty Fire,* her endearing account of what it meant to grow up black in Albany, with occasional excursions to the South, where she visited her grandparents: the title comes from a child's perception of a cross burning on her grandparents' lawn. Even more than Handler's, whose play hinged largely on the grisly events he recounts, Woodard's piece places great demands on her as an actress, since it requires her to play a child, a task that can be wearing for both performer and audience. Woodard does it in a way that stresses the freshness and innocence of a child's vision, which made the things she saw especially painful.

One-person shows have become popular because the economics are ideal, especially since much of the time the performer is also the writer. Over the last few years there has also been a plethora of two-character plays, of which the most interesting this season was Jon Robin Baitz's *Three Hotels.*

The two characters are a husband and a wife. He is a troubleshooter for a company that sells baby formula to mothers in Third World countries. His awareness that his product takes advantage of the women's ignorance and their almost mystical faith in Western technology does not inhibit his salesmanship. The guilt about the product that he blithely, ironically represses, his wife takes to heart. She calls her husband "the Albert Speer of baby food."

Lest the play, however, be taken simply as a statement about First World guilt, the wife is also haunted by the fact that, when they were in Brazil, their only son was murdered by Third World teenagers who coveted his expensive watch. Even this trauma seems not to have affected her emotionally impervious husband.

When she is asked to speak to the wives of other salesmen, to give them tips on what to watch out for in Third World countries, she cannot contain her grief. She voices her resentment of the company. Her husband, one of whose professional specialties has been firing people, is himself fired.

Baitz handles this potentially explosive material as if it were seventeenth-century French tragedy. The play consists of three monologues, two by the husband framing one by the wife. The title is drawn from the fact that each of the monologues takes place in a different hotel in a different country, which accentuates our sense of the dislocation of the characters' lives but also keeps us at an ironic distance from the cruel events, all of which take place offstage.

As is invariably the case with Baitz, still the most gifted of young American playwrights, the language is elegant and ironic. But here the preoccupation with a novel dramatic structure seems to have taken precedence over the theoretically powerful material.

The customarily eloquent Brian Friel sent us a more cerebral play than usual, *Wonderful Tennessee,* which concerns three couples waiting on a beach for a boat to take them to an island off the coast of County Donegal. The boatman they await is called Carlin, a name that echoes Charon, the ferryman who transports souls to the netherworld.

In Friel's 1991 play, *Dancing at Lughnasa,* the narrator speaks of "dancing as if language had surrendered to movement — as if this ritual, this wordless ceremony, was now the way to speak, to whisper private and sacred things, to be in touch with some otherness."

The couples in *Wonderful Tennessee,* whether or not they are waiting for the mythical Charon, are clearly yearning for "otherness." As they wait they sing folk songs, they dance, they chant hymns. They talk about mythology, both Christian and Greek. The island, which they can see in the distance, was once populated by monks "with a rage for the absolute . . . whatever it is we desire but can't express, what is beyond language."

One of the women mentions the Nazareth home where Christ grew up, which, in the year 1294, flew to Italy. Another woman mentions the rituals of Eleusis in ancient Greece. The Christian and the Greek traditions come together in a story someone tells about why the island is now deserted. During the Depression, after returning from a Eucharistic Congress in Dublin, a group of local young people went to the island, became intoxicated, and committed a ritual murder.

The boat they have been waiting for never arrives. Before they return to the workaday world, each member of the party leaves something that matters to him on a post (in the shape of a cross) to which boats might be moored. Unlike *Lughnasa,* which conveyed its primal impulses viscerally and with earthy humor, *Tennessee* deals with transcendence in an intellectual manner, achieving, shortly before it ends, an odd serenity.

At times Friel's elusive style is trying. But this is an Irish play, and so it throbs with music, literal and verbal, and the richness of the actors' voices (all members of Dublin's Abbey Theater) engages the ear even when the play puzzles.

Jonathan Tolins also seems to be aiming for some kind of transcendence in *Twilight of the Golds,* whose title implies a parody of Wagner's *Ring.* Early in the play its young protagonist, a gay man who has been unsuccessful at getting his family to share his love for Wagner, declares, "When art is at its most outrageous, when it cannot be believed, that's when it most resembles life." This is a promising premise for a play that tries to create parallels between Wagner's mythical world and a middle-class Jewish family, both careening toward self-destruction. Tolins, however, rarely follows his own advice.

He begins imaginatively by breaking through the wall of a middle-class New York apartment to reveal a Wagnerian landscape lying just beyond it, but little of what then happens has the scope to make the parallel convincing. The play hinges on a scientific discovery that makes it possible to determine the sexual orientation of a child during early pregnancy. When the young Wagnerite's sister Suzanne and her dull husband discover her unborn son will be gay they contemplate abortion. If there were any real question about their decision, *Twilight* might have been an interesting play. As it is, the outcome is all too predictable.

What makes the play annoying is the fact it does not really play fair with its characters. Certainly the most charming of its characters is the gay son, but when his sister and brother-in-law (and their parents) contemplate the prospect of a gay child, it is as if they have never known anyone gay and have to make their decision merely on stereotypes.

The playwright first belittles them in their inability to embrace the possibility that the unborn child will be as charming and lovable as his uncle.

Program cover for the Plymouth Theatre production of Brian Friel's play mixing images from Christianity and Greek mythology

Then, once Tolins has decided they will make the small-minded decision, he treats them vindictively. In the course of the abortion Suzanne has complications that make it impossible for her ever to be pregnant again.

Is Tolins deliberately imitating Wagner? Is the end of the Golds a conscious parallel of the downfall of the gods? The Golds have unwittingly willed the end of their line. In Wagner's torturous dramaturgy the gods always succumb helplessly to fate. Even the most powerful of them, Wotan, is powerless before ineluctable destiny, a kind of cosmic foreshadowing of the line, "I was only obeying orders."

At least in Wagner there is the music to compensate for the unsatisfying dramaturgy. Tolins offers sharp humor (the hypothetical gay gene absolves the Jewish mother of guilt in having shaped her son — she finds living without guilt a disturbing prospect) and some engaging monologues, in which

the characters address the audience directly. But it is not enough to offset the didactic, irritating plot.

Far more irritating is Paula Vogel's *And Baby Makes Seven,* which begins with childish voices in the dark giving coy, infantile remarks about sex. We learn that the three voices are those of adults, who communicate with one another in the guise of pre-pubescent children. They are awaiting the arrival of an infant. The father is Peter, a gay man. The mother is Anna, his childhood friend, a lesbian. Peter shares a loft with Anna and her lover, Ruth.

The women's relationship consists largely of pretending to be children. Anna is Cecil, a precocious English child. Ruth is both Henri, the little boy from *The Red Balloon,* and Orphan, a stray dog. The arrival of the actual child seems a good reason to abandon these "play" voices, but it turns out to be too difficult. Hence, the title.

Of the plays with gay subject matter, the most entertaining and even moving was Paul Rudnick's *Jeffrey.* In some ways Rudnick's play is a collection of sketches roughly held together by the title character, who fears making an emotional commitment in the age of AIDS. For most of the play Jeffrey tries to escape a handsome young man with whom he has obviously fallen in love at first sight (and who tells Jeffrey right away he is HIV positive.) But the world they inhabit is relatively circumscribed, and they are constantly being thrown together. At the end of the play they finally embrace. The clinch hardly comes as a surprise, but it is touching because it represents, on Jeffrey's part, an embrace of all of life, not just a new sexual partner.

The journey to this embrace is extremely funny. Many of Rudnick's characters are stereotypes (an effete decorator, a chorus boy), but there is invariably something believable, even affecting, underneath the familiar surfaces. The bitchy decorator, for example, counsels Jeffrey, "I said you needed a boyfriend, not a person," a piece of wit heavily marinated in pain. At times the play's juxtaposition of reality and comedy strains credulity (as when Jeffrey is asked by a knife-wielding thug what weapons he carries and he replies, "Adjectives, irony, eyebrows"), but it was acted and directed with such elegance that one regards such overreaching moments as oddities, half-glimpsed out a window on a fast journey through a wildly comic landscape.

A more complicated journey is undertaken by two middle-aged Connecticut women in Terrence McNally's *A Perfect Ganesh.* Both women have lost children. One woman's child died in a freak accident, and the other was the victim of gay bashing.

Both hope to exorcise their grief on an excursion to India. Most of what happens to them there is comic, but the dense religious culture of India invariably reminds them of their losses.

In a peculiar, pivotal scene one of the matrons kneels beside one of India's sacred streams hurling invectives into the air. A curious coincidence is that both tragic incidents involved blacks, and among the ugly words the woman emits are standard invectives against blacks. This is an element of the play that never fits smoothly into an otherwise dexterous, even glib comedy.

After the numerous plays with gay subject matter, the most burgeoning category seems to be plays of urban apocalypse. Given the insanity that characterizes large American cities, particularly New York, where most of these plays are set, it is not hard to write plays about madness and decay. *Marisol* is representative of this genre.

Jose Rivera's grotesque fantasy concerns a middle-class Bronx woman who meets insanity and violence at every turn. The mayhem begins when the woman sitting next to her in the subway is murdered. A close friend becomes a crazed, gun-toting junkie. "This town knows when you're alone," she meditates. "That's when it sends out the goons and death squads." Although much about the play is predictable there are a few unexpected touches, like a scene in which a man gives birth. "Every man should have the experience," he says. "There'd be fewer wars." *Marisol* also offers angel imagery, of a more ferocious sort than Kushner's. Rivera's angels announce they will "kill the King of Heaven and restore the vitality of the universe with His blood."

Marisol and Howard Korder's *The Lights* treat urban madness in a surreal, highly stylized manner. Frank Pugliese's *Aven' U Boys,* a drama about shiftless youths in Bensonhurst, Brooklyn, deals with the subject naturalistically. Pugliese's characters are all cheerfully racist, sexist, and homophobic, although one of them has a yen for transvestites. (He and another of the lads try to sodomize a third with a beer bottle, suggesting, perhaps, some ambiguity in their attitudes toward homosexuality.) All in all, *Aven' U Boys* seems an attempt to bring to the theater the unrelieved brutality of recent movies about urban youth.

Another increasingly popular genre is satire of Hollywood. This is understandable considering that virtually no playwright can make a living in the theater. They tend to support themselves writing screenplays or rewriting the screenplays of others. The best of these screeds against Hollywood is John Patrick Shanley's *Four Dogs and a Bone.* (*The Treatment,* by Martin Crimp, was noteworthy in its ability to combine the clichés of Hollywood satire with those of the drama of urban decay.) Shanley's play is a farce about the movie business written and performed in coarse, staccato rhythms, the language of people who see sentences as jabs and thrusts for power. The play has four characters – an over-the-hill but canny producer, an innocent but ambitious screenwriter, and two clawing actresses. With the mathematical precision farce requires, Shanley sets them sparring at one another two-by-two until the final scene, in which their ambitions and neuroses reach critical mass.

Hollywood bashing has become a genre dear to New Yorkers. (One of the funniest lines is the producer's assault on the writer: "You're from the theater – that's like the Outback of the entertainment business.") But Shanley's play goes beyond the cliches. It is really about the corruption of innocence, a subject of considerably greater appeal than the sins of the movie business.

A. R. Gurney's ongoing survey of mating customs among the WASPs yielded *Later Life,* a study of two middle-aged people who meet at a Boston party and realize they had a brief unconsummated flirtation thirty years earlier. Their nervous, tentative attempts at courtship are interrupted by other guests at the party, giving the play the effect of a divertimento – amusing, touching, not too consequential.

Another divertimento worth noting was Mark St. Germain's *Camping With Henry and Tom,* a play based very roughly on the fact that Henry Ford, Thomas Edison, and Warren G. Harding did go camping together in 1921. In this play their car breaks down, and they are forced to go beyond the charm and bonhomie that characterize their public utterances to one another.

The play turns on Ford's political ambitions, his perception of himself as a great benefactor of humanity who deserves even more wealth and power. Edison is a wry, detached observer of a world from which he seems to be withdrawing. "We're toy makers, Henry, that's all we are," he tells Ford at one point. At another, musing on the popularity of one of his inventions, motion pictures, he imagines they will eventually be adapted for home use, "so we won't even have to get out of our easy chairs to ignore each other." In St. Germain's play the most appealing of the trio is Harding, once considered our most corrupt president. Here (perhaps as an illustration of Sen. Daniel Patrick Moynihan's observation that we are "defining deviancy downward"), he is the most touching.

Among the disappointments of 1993 was *Redwood Curtain,* by Lanford Wilson. The play is set on the edge of a California redwood forest where disoriented Vietnam War veterans wander forlornly. A young woman, part Vietnamese, part American, an acclaimed concert pianist, lives nearby with her dizzy aunt. The young woman seeks out the veterans wandering in the woods, hoping to find her father. The play gains in contrivance as it progresses, its major virtue being the comedy of the airheaded aunt. As an attempt to come to grips with the effect of Vietnam on the American consciousness, *Redwood Curtain* is far less effective than Wilson's 1978 *The 5th of July.*

If the year offered a plethora of plays of despair, none was as literate or as theatrical as Steve Tesich's *On the Open Road,* a cry of anguish camouflaged in sardonic laughter. Set in some nameless country in the midst of a civil war, the play opens with a man perched precariously on a police barricade in a deserted railroad yard. Around his neck is a noose. His slightest movement could knock the barricade over and let the noose do its work.

A well-dressed man enters, pulling a cart full of works of art. He is clearly a looter, but one with great aesthetic sense. The aesthete agrees to save the condemned man, who will lug the cart. They will try to reach the border, where they will barter the art treasures for freedom, since the border guards are "armed connoisseurs." As they trek forward the aesthete teaches the lug about classical music to the point where the latter can identify themes from Wolfgang Amadeus Mozart by Kochel number.

Throughout the play images of high culture provide an ironic counterpoint to the grotesque proceedings as the two journey toward hypothetical freedom. At one point, for example, in order to save their lives, they agree to kill Christ, who has made an unscheduled return to earth. They are persuaded to do so by a smarmy monk who makes a useful analogy. Imagine, he tells them, that they are at a play that seems quite remarkable. Suddenly Euripides or Sophocles appears onstage. They would see that what they thought was a masterpiece was a cheap, banal melodrama. This is roughly the effect on the church of having Christ make a comeback. "If our show is to go on . . . ," the monk declares; he does not need to finish the sentence. The two men understand and undertake the task the monk has proposed. The play is full of scathing wit despite its mood of unrelieved despair.

Curiously, in the midst of all these negative, pessimistic voices, the most hopeful voice raised belongs to Arthur Miller. Despite the fact that his short play *The Last Yankee* is set in a mental institution, it is about renewal, reassessment of values, and belief in the future. In the first scene the husbands of two women suffering from clinical depression are chatting uneasily about the wives they have come to visit. One is a gruff, impatient businessman, the other an easygoing carpenter who happens to be a descendant of Alexander Hamilton. Much is made of the fact that Hamilton, the descendant of one of the intellectual founders of the republic, is a man who works with his hands. But the two agree that what matters today is not status or family or money, but how well one does one's job.

In the second scene we meet the wives. Hamilton's wife is conquering her problems well enough that she attempts to help the businessman's wife, whose depression is clearly more severe. We sense the latter will remain institutionalized, in part because her husband has lost patience with her and is unable to respond in an encouraging way.

Hamilton's wife is Swedish. Her ethnic background comes up in the exchange that gives the play its title. She recalls the harsh prejudices against Swedish immigrants during the nineteenth century. As a representative of the original settlers, her husband says, "I hope I'm the last Yankee, so everyone can start living today instead of 100 years ago."

It is an important statement, considering how much American public discourse that is devoted to reawakening the grievances that underscore its history. The statement works within the personal circumstances of the play, and it is a tribute to Miller's continuing grace as a writer that he can voice larger concerns within the framework of a relatively simple dramatic situation.

Toward the end, for example, there is a beautiful moment where Hamilton's wife asserts that "spiritual is nothing you can see." Hamilton, whose most recent achievement as a carpenter is an altar for a nearby church, responds, "Then why didn't God make everything invisible?"

This is a lyric note we hear too seldom in the theater, and it is especially remarkable from a writer whose voice over the years has sometimes been lugubrious and rhetorical. At a time when most young writers roar with anger and abrasiveness, there is something touching and imposing about the serenity of the lion in winter.

The Year in Children's Books

Caroline Hunt
College of Charleston

Nostalgia and caution ruled the world of children's books throughout 1993. Unlike the previous year, in which juvenile titles appeared with regularity on the *New York Times* best-seller list, 1993 was a year in which no book written primarily for young readers broke into the top ten. Most of the children's books published for the first time in 1993 and widely promoted, reviewed, and sold were sequels, series books, or new titles (often formulaic) from well-established authors. Financial constraints on publishers, booksellers, and libraries contributed to this trend (although nearly a dozen new imprints, several of which brought out some first-rate titles, offered some hope). Meanwhile, the majority of attention given to children's books – both negative and positive – went to older titles. The first half of this year's review examines these trends under several heads: censorship and related issues, the resurgence of old favorites, financial and societal pressures, the conservatism of children's book awards, current books by past award winners, and parallel trends in Britain. The second half of the roundup, necessarily less comprehensive than last year, covers the usual categories: poetry, nonfiction, picture books, books for middle grades, young adult books, and, finally, obituaries. (Alphabet books, counting books, holiday books, and most movie and television tie-ins, are excluded.) All books are 1993 U.S. publications unless otherwise specified.

Individual titles which received wide public notice were, in general, not 1993 books; for instance, Michael Willhoite's *Daddy's Roommate* (1990) and Lesléa Newman's *Heather Has Two Mommies* (1989), both from Alyson Press and both about children of gay parents, continued to attract protests across the country and are now likely to set a record for challenges. The best-publicized clash involving these books began late in 1992 and pitted Joseph Fernandez, chancellor of New York City's schools, against parents and school-board members; the board voted four to three not to renew his contract, and Fernandez left at the end of June. Another dispute, also in June, targeted public libraries: three

Georgia legislators supported the removal of *Heather* from public-library shelves, later modifying their stand to recommend its transfer to the adult section. The controversy drew comments from conservative groups such as Family Concerns, and also resulted in the formation of a gay support group in Hall County, a rural area. In Denver conservative groups objected to the presence of the books in schools, but the Denver Public Library publicly reaffirmed its decision to shelve both books in the children's section. Prince William County, Virginia, took the opposite stand and refused to accept the books as a donation from a parents' group. In Alaska over three hundred children were kept out of school to protest the inclusion of *Daddy's Roommate* in school libraries; the book stayed, on a seven-to-one vote by the Juneau school board. Meanwhile, Willhoite's 1993 title, *Uncle What-Is-It Is Coming to Visit!!* (Alyson Wonderland), potentially at least as controversial, attracted little attention.

Though children's books from the recent past tended to attract negative attention, some from earlier eras renewed their status as favorites. An exhibit which began at the Pierpont Morgan library in September marked the one-hundredth anniversary of Peter Rabbit. Celebrations were held all over the English-speaking world on 4 September, Peter's birthday; both the *Boston Globe* and the *New York Times* published features on Beatrix Potter's Lake District farm as a tourist attraction. Potter's publishers, Frederick Warne and Company, agreed to allow Peter to appear on television in an animated version faithful to Potter's delicate watercolors. The Morgan also mounted an exhibit in honor of the fiftieth anniversary of Antoine de Saint Exupéry's classic *The Little Prince* (with a video narrated by Macaulay Culkin and a commemorative edition from Harcourt Brace Jovanovich), and a sesquicentennial one for Charles Dickens's *A Christmas Carol* (1843). No exhibit marked the sixtieth anniversary of Babar the elephant, but Random House brought out *Babar's Anniversary Album* (half a dozen tales, including three from the 1930s), as well as two new titles: *The Rescue of Babar* and *Babar's Peekaboo Fair* (a pop-up book).

Some less-well-known oldies were also revived. Thomas the Tank Engine, featured in a series (1946–1972) by the Reverend W. Awdry, appeared in assorted formats: large books, small books, cassettes, and toys. *Thomas's Big Railway Pop-Up Book* (Random House) led the nation in sales in its category in June. (Interestingly, the Thomas items did not do well when introduced in 1989, but 1993 was their year. A series on public television, *Shining Time Station*, already incorporates Thomas, and a feature film is planned.) L. M. Boston's *The Children of Green Knowe* and Edgar Eager's *Half Magic,* both fantasies and both still in print, celebrated their fortieth anniversaries; the inside cover of the Viking fall catalogue lauded the thirtieth anniversary of Ezra Jack Keats's *The Snowy Day* (the book was actually published in 1962 and won the Caldecott the next year). Puffin Books revived some older titles, including not only some out-of-print Newbery Honor books but old chestnuts like Albert Payson Terhune's *Lad: A Dog* ("since its original publication over 70 years ago, *Lad: A Dog* has touched countless readers – and it is bound to touch you, too"). Indeed, a surprising number of the authors of "new" releases in this catalogue are dead – not only Terhune, who died in 1941, but John Bellairs, Roald Dahl, Cyrus Fisher, L. Frank Baum, and James Marshall. Even allowing for the fact that these are all paperback reprints, the conservatism of the offerings is notable. Walker Publishing also mined the out-of-print field and announced its reissue of Newbery Honor books ranging from 1946 to 1961. Candlewick issued two posthumous books by Rosemary Sutcliff, who died in 1992: *Chess-Dream in a Garden* and *The Minstrel and the Dragon Pup;* Delacorte published her *Black Ships Before Troy,* adapted from the *Iliad.* There were also well-publicized posthumous publications by Marshall and Robert Westall.

One reason for the conservative nature of many of the 1993 offerings was evidently financial; another was societal. Amid mass layoffs and restructurings in the publishing world as elsewhere, children's book divisions took some hard hits. Little, Brown announced in November substantial cutbacks in its juvenile publishing; unsolicited children's book manuscripts will no longer be accepted, and the total output of juvenile titles is expected to shrink as much as 30 percent. Several long-established bookstores, including at least one children's bookshop, closed in 1993, citing hard times in general and competition from superstores in particular.

(Toys "R" Us, for instance, announced the expansion of its bookselling operation in toy stores.) Libraries, a major market for children's books, were as poor in 1993 as in 1992; branches were closed, hours were shortened, and staff were laid off. Inevitably, this meant fewer specialists ordering fewer children's books with fewer dollars.

In these circumstances it is not surprising that the majority of 1993 offerings from many mainstream publishers were familiar formulae from familiar authors: not only long-term best-sellers like Babar, but clones, prequels, and sequels. Dorothy Kunhardt's *Pat the Puppy* (Golden), on the juvenile best-seller list for August, is an ingenious update of her mother's Golden Book *Pat the Bunny* of twenty years earlier, itself based on an earlier edition of 1940. Tomie de Paola's *Strega Nona Meets Her Match* (Putnam), featuring his lovable witch, sold exceptionally well. So did *Little House on Rocky Ridge,* a fictionalized account of Rose Wilder Lane's girlhood journey to Missouri with her parents, Laura Ingalls Wilder and Almanzo Wilder, written by Lane's adopted grandson, Roger Lea MacBride. (An Indian-education-program employee in Louisiana requested the removal of *Little House on the Prairie* on the grounds that it offended Native Americans, but the Lafourche Parish school board voted to keep the book.) Cary Ryan edited *Louisa May Alcott: Her Girlhood Diary* (BridgeWater), with illustrations by Mark Graham. The American Girls series from Pleasant Company, begun in the mid 1980s, moved into high gear with the introduction of its first African-American, Addy (*Meet Addy: An American Girl,* by Connie R. Porter). Addy, of Civil War vintage, even made the 22 September 1993 cover of *Publishers Weekly.* Each American girl represents a different period in U.S. history (Samantha in the time of suffragettes, Kirsten in pioneer days in Minnesota); all were widely marketed in 1993, with matching dolls and an array of doll accessories.

A parallel reason for the conservatism of so many 1993 titles was societal. Trade books came under closer scrutiny from several groups, thanks to their greater use in many classrooms through the "whole language" approach to reading. Turning away from basal readers, teachers used children's literature integrated into the curriculum; one result was a spate of objections to particular books by concerned parents (and other groups), on grounds ranging from religious fundamentalism to animal rights. Thus, Bruce Coville's *Jeremy Thatcher, Dragon Hatcher,* a 1991 title from Jane Yolen Books which was a favorite with elementary-school readers, was banned in Carroll, Iowa, after complaints from two parents. Though the book was later reinstated, the precedent lingers. William Steig's Caldecott-winning *The Amazing Bone* (1976) withstood a challenge in suburban Seattle; parents objected both to its supposed violence and to the fact that the bone came from a witch.

Indeed, books with dragons, witches, and other potentially magical characters were especially targeted. "Pumsy in Pursuit of Excellence," a program consisting of a dragon puppet, a storybook, and a counseling manual, met stiff opposition in several places and narrowly escaped banning in most of them. A school board member in Charleston County, South Carolina, described Pumsy as "part of text material that is inimical to the Judeo-Christian thought and it's contrary to what most parents want to teach their children." (The Junior Great Books program was under attack for the same reasons in the same county, and elsewhere, in 1993.) Joseph Chambers, whose regional radio ministry is based in North Carolina, denounced Barney, superstar of children's television, as a New Age influence related to demons and devils. Barney Publishing, however, reported an excellent year with nearly a dozen Barney items in print.

Critics and parents alike focused particular attention on horror stories in 1993. Again, this focus was not new but essentially recognized a trend that had been accelerating for several years. An article in *Time* by Paul Gray, "Carnage: An Open Book," quoted some nasty passages as well as remarks by two leading practitioners, Christopher Pike and R. L. Stine. In a piece for the *Washington Post* on 19 July, Jonathan Yardley reacted to a publication from the Institute for Children's Literature: Fear Street, Scream, Goosebumps, Phantom Valley, and Scared to Death are the latest trend, he points out (accurately), "though one not widely known beyond the houses that produce them and the young people who read them." His response is a strong negative. "What is so objectionable about all of this isn't so much the violence per se as the gratuitousness and exploitativeness of it." Judy Druse in *Voice of Youth Advocates* (April) took the opposite position, dealing with the genre as a crowd pleaser and a partial solution to the problem of reluctant readers. Parents and librarians were divided in their feelings about juvenile horror stories, some taking the line that reading (anything) is better than not reading, others perturbed by the genuinely gruesome nature of many horror books. A spirited debate about the value of horror books lasted for weeks on a librarians' electronic discussion group.

Dust jacket for Cynthia Rylant's Newbery Award–winning book about life in rural West Virginia

One change in the horror scene during 1993 involved the extension of the market to younger readers, a trend begun the previous year. Earlier horror books, notably those by Pike, Stine, and Richie Tankersly Cusick, targeted a young adult audience; the newer lines aim at middle-grade readers. As chronicled by M. P. Donleavey in *Publishers Weekly*, Goosebumps (Scholastic), Chiller (HarperTrophy), and Foul Play (Penguin) began this trend in 1992; Shockers (Grosset and Dunlap), Bullseye Chillers (Random House), and Shadow Zone (Random House) extended it further.

Traditionally the children's book year begins with the announcement of the Newbery Award for best children's book and the Caldecott Medal for best picture book. Turning away from risky subjects and risky genres, the American Library Association's award committees gave the nod to two books which exemplified traditional values, traditional literary craftsmanship, and nostalgic subject matter. Like the 1992 Newbery winner, *Shiloh* (Atheneum, 1991), Cynthia Rylant's *Missing May* (Orchard) is set in rural West Virginia. The world of the book – the domain of Aunt May and her grieving widower, Ob – is the imagined world of a simpler way of life, recalling an older America. Nonetheless, it is nicely plotted (with the grieving process transformed into a literal quest), humorous, and cleanly written. The same is true of Emily Arnold McCully's *Mirette on the High Wire* (Putnam), a tale of friendship and courage which won the Caldecott. Here again, though, the dominant impression is that of nostalgia in McCully's wonderful pictures of nineteenth-century Paris.

Both of these award winners attempted to continue their success in 1993. Rylant's *I Had Seen Castles* (Harcourt Brace) was well reviewed but fell short in both plotting and language, particularly in comparison to other recent young adult books reconsidering World War II; she also wrote a creation story loosely adapted from Genesis, *The Dreamer* (Scholastic/Blue Sky), with pictures by Barry Moser. In her seemingly interminable Henry and Mudge series, the thirteenth volume, *Henry and Mudge and the Careful Cousin* (Bradbury), pits Henry and his immense dog against an irritatingly tidy cousin. For the youngest consumers she produced a group of board books: *Everyday Children, Everyday Garden, Everyday Pets, Everyday Town,* and *Everyday House* (Bradbury). "The titles of these books may be unintentionally self-descriptive," noted one reviewer. Unlike Rylant, McCully did not succumb to the temptation to overproduce. *The Amazing Felix* (Putnam) evokes the 1920s imaginatively but lacks the compelling plot of its predecessor; some reviewers were troubled by the weak female characters. McCully also produced a pedestrian entry in the I Can Read series from HarperCollins, *Grandmas at Bat.*

Like Rylant and McCully, some earlier winners of the Newbery and the Caldecott (or their publishers) tried to clone their earlier successes; most fell short. Careful examination of the 1993 titles from this group of authors reveals that many, perhaps the majority, are in fact reissues, some with new illustrations, some abridged, some on cassettes. A sad example is Marguerite Henry, whose great 1949 winner *King of the Wind* was succeeded by a long series of increasingly formulaic books. Her 1992 title, *Misty's Twilight* (Macmillan), chronicling the adventures of Misty's descendant, did not do well with reviewers or readers. For 1993 Henry's reputation rests on *Marguerite Henry's Album of Horses: A Pop-up Book* (Aladdin), adapted from her 1951 favorite, and *Misty of Chincoteague* (Caedmon), a recording of a drastically abridged version of the

1947 classic. Among Newbery winners of the 1960s, E. L. Konigsburg updated and relocated her combination of humor and social criticism in *T-Backs, T-Shirts, Coat, and Suit* (Atheneum), a snappy intergenerational tale of a girl's stay with her eccentric aunt in Florida. Among the 1970s winners, Betsy Byars tapped into the popular grotesque in *McMummy* (Viking), a supernatural tale of a mysterious plant; Paula Fox offered, in *Western Wind* (Orchard/Jackson), another intergenerational tale, this one about a girl who summers with her grandmother on an island off the coast of Maine. Virginia Hamilton's *Plain City* (Scholastic/Blue Sky) features an engaging heroine of mixed race, Buhlaire, and an unusual setting in a riverfront midwestern community, with houses on stilts. Susan Cooper's *Danny and the Kings* (Margaret McElderry Books) was a sentimental Christmas story in which three truck drivers help a small boy. Her other 1993 release from the same publisher, *The Boggart,* adapts the Cooper brand of fantasy to the modern age in a tale of a prankish spirit imported accidentally from Scotland to Canada. Though more than competent, none of these books seemed likely to advance their authors' reputations significantly.

The winners of the Newbery Award in the 1980s fared somewhat better. On the borders of fiction, poetry, and illustration, Nancy Willard's *A Starlit Somersault Downhill*, with illustrations by Jerry Pinkney (Little, Brown), was one of the best contributions by a former Newbery winner; she also collaborated on *The Sorcerer's Apprentice* (Scholastic/Blue Sky, illustrated by Leo and Diane Dillon) and *Telling Time: Angels, Ancestors, and Stories* (Harcourt Brace). Beverly Cleary moved to a picture-book audience with *Petey's Bedtime Story* (Morrow), illustrated by David Small. Cynthia Voigt's 1993 title was *The Wings of a Falcon* (Scholastic), a fantasy adventure in her Kingdom series begun in *Jackaroo* and continued in *On Fortune's Wheel*. The dust jacket shows a typical quest figure in flowing robes, complete with birdlike mask, walking stick, and high boots. Though well reviewed, the book does not meet the standard of the Tillerman books. Robin McKinley's *Deerskin* (Ace) introduces an unlikely (and likable) princess. Moving on to the 1990s, reviews of most of the numerous 1993 books by winners are mixed at best. The prolific Phyllis Reynolds Naylor followed up a recent success, *The Boys Start the War,* with a Halloween sequel, *The Girls Get Even;* the dust jacket promises a third volume, *The Boys Against the Girls* (all from Delacorte). In another series by Naylor, *Alice in April* (Atheneum) shows Alice entering the seventh grade and coping with

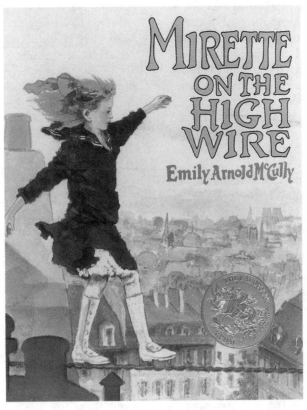

*Dust jacket for Emily Arnold McCully's Caldecott Medal–winning
book about a child's adventures in nineteenth-century Paris*

becoming thirteen (to be continued by *Alice In-Between* in 1994). Her mystery, *The Face in the Bessledorf Funeral Parlor* (Atheneum), is well plotted but negligible; Jerry Spinelli's *Picklemania* (Apple) is another slight comedy.

Among Caldecott winners of earlier years, the 1993 offerings are somewhat more distinguished than for the Newbery authors. Chris Van Allsburg's *The Sweetest Fig* (Houghton Mifflin), pictorially reminiscent of some of his wonderful early work, is more moralistic. Though the nasty Monsieur Bibot and his ironic and patient dog have an undeniable appeal, the subject matter that Van Allsburg has made uniquely his own – the journey of the imagination – has little scope here. Readers and critics alike considered it a major book of the year. Gerald McDermott's *Raven* (Harcourt Brace) retold a Native American trickster story in brilliant colors. De Paola's 1993 Strega Nona book, *Strega Nona Meets Her Match* (Putnam), eclipsed his more original and entertaining *Tom* (Putnam), based on recollections of his own grandfather; he also had two other 1993 books. Ed Young had two distinguished retellings. Indeed,

many of the living Caldecott artists had several books in 1993 – too many to list.

Several award winners did, however, produce important work in 1993 without straying far from the kind of story that made them famous: one in fiction, one in nonfiction, one in pictures. Patricia MacLachlan, whose 1986 Newbery winner *Sarah, Plain and Tall* has achieved genuine classic status, has *Baby* (Delacorte); Maurice Sendak, whose Caldecott winner *Where the Wild Things Are* seems always to have been a part of childhood, has *We Are All in the Dumps with Jack and Guy* (HarperCollins/di Capua); and Russell Freedman, whose biography of Abraham Lincoln was the only nonfiction winner in recent years, offers *Eleanor Roosevelt: A Life of Discovery* (Clarion). *Baby* centers around a foundling and combines surefire plot, appealing characters, and lucid writing in the admirable MacLachlan way. A bookseller in Rockville, Maryland, describes it as "a prime example of a book that the staff loves that's also selling well." She cites the book as her store's leading fall book ("people are snapping it up"). A sequel to *Sarah, Plain and Tall* called *Skylark,* to be released in book form in early 1994, appeared in 1993 on the Hallmark Hall of Fame and is available in video format. Freedman's biography of Eleanor Roosevelt brings out the best of his subject without a trace of mawkishness and blends its lucid text with many stunning photographs, most of them not well known. The Sendak book, as usual, is more problematic. "People either love it or hate it," reports another bookseller, this time in Seattle. *We Are All in the Dumps with Jack and Guy,* comprised of two nursery rhymes spliced together, shows a new complexity of detail that some like and some do not. It is full of allusions to AIDS and various other topics not immediately comprehensible to the average picture-book-age reader (for instance, pictorial tributes to the late James Marshall); the main characters are homeless children. In interviews Sendak has added layers of meaning that no reviewer could have supplied. The question remains whether *Jack and Guy* is in fact a children's book in any ordinary sense, or rather an adult book in picture format. The book is handsomely produced, with thick board covers, textured heavy endpapers (in an unpleasant shade of brown), and beautiful hand lettering by Jeanyee Wong.

Two other Newbery winners who did fine work in 1993 moved away from their award-winning subject matter significantly. Paul Fleischman's *Bull Run* (HarperCollins), an account of the Civil War battle from several points of view, shares with his winning book of poems only the carefulness of the wording and the successful use of different voices; he had written two previous historical novels for young readers, neither of which received the attention it deserved. Lois Lowry's *The Giver* (Houghton Mifflin) aroused more discussion than any other children's book of the year (with the possible exception of the Sendak book). Lowry sets her story in a seemingly ideal society at some unstated future time — unstated because only one person in the community knows the past, the Receiver of Memory. As Jonas studies to become the next Receiver, he learns the cost of his society's stability. Reminiscent of an extended version of Ursula K. LeGuin's story "The Ones Who Walk Away from Omelas," Lowry's novel poses some important questions and leaves the resolution open; the ending has provoked even more disagreement than the rest of this intriguing fable.

The award situation in Great Britain mirrored the trend in the United States. William Mayne won the 1993 Guardian Award for *Low Tide* (Delacorte; British publication 1992); perhaps setting something of a record for longevity as his first major award was the Carnegie Medal over thirty-five

years ago, for *A Grass Rope* (1957). The Carnegie itself went to a previous winner, Anne Fine, for *Flour Babies* (1992), an account of a school assignment — the same assignment used by Eve Bunting in *Our Sixth Grade Sugar Babies* (1990). Fine had another major success in 1993 with the Christmas release of the film *Mrs. Doubtfire,* adapted from her earlier book *Alias Madame Doubtfire* (1988). The Greenaway Prize, for best illustrated book, also went to a previous winner, Anthony Browne, for *Zoo* (Knopf, 1992), a savagely funny account of bestial humans who visit a zoological park.

Although the Mayne book, like all books from this writer, was first-rate, as was *Zoo,* it is troubling that all the major awards should go to long-established figures. Numerous letters to British newspapers, as well as several speeches by authors, complained about what was perceived as the poor state of children's book criticism (or, sometimes, children's books in general). Sales in Britain reflected the same retro quality: three of the top ten juvenile titles reported in the spring (summarizing 1992) were by Roald Dahl, Judy Blume, and Eric Carle (his perennial favorite with the preschool set, *The Very Hungry Caterpillar*), and only two gave representation to important newer voices in British children's books: the Ahlbergs' *The Baby's Catalogue* (over ten years old) at number nine and Terry Pratchett's *The Carpet People* at number ten.

In fact, Dahl was a major focus of discussion on both sides of the Atlantic, thanks to advance comments on a debunking biography by Jeremy Treglown, *Roald Dahl: A Life* (not yet available). Christopher Hitchens stuck up for Dahl in "The Grimmest Tales" in, of all places, *Vanity Fair* (January 1994), praising his subversive qualities and their genuine appeal to children; he does, however, quote some damning remarks from memoirs by Kingsley Amis, whom Dahl urged to write for children because "that's where the money is," adding that no particular sensitivity would be needed because "the little bastards'd swallow it." On the front lines, librarians continued to discuss whether Dahl's juvenile books were too antiadult or were tinged with his (admitted) racism or (presumed) sexism and "ageism"; parents objected to the books' portrayal of the disgusting (one of the major selling points for younger readers). Meanwhile, sales of the books went up and stayed up, as evidenced by the best-seller list cited above.

Collections of poems for young readers were on the whole a distinguished group in 1993; in addition, several of them sold very well. Two leaders in both sales and critical appeal were *From Sea to Shin-*

Dust jacket for Maurice Sendak's book about the homeless

ing Sea: A Treasury of American Folklore and Folk Songs (Scholastic) and *The Dragons Are Singing Tonight* (Greenwillow). The former, edited by Amy L. Cohn, follows the pattern of a previous anthology, *Sing a Song of Popcorn* (1988), and features separate chapters mixing exposition, songs, and stories, each one illustrated by a Caldecott-winning artist (eleven medalists, four Honor Book winners); the effect, which might have been merely miscellaneous, is rich and appealing. Chapters include not only the obligatory Native American myths balanced by pilgrim lore, but a wonderful section on the railroad (with pictures by David Wiesner), and an assortment of twentieth-century lore (including the text of Abbott and Costello's immortal "Who's On First"). Ancillary material in the volume includes biographical information, background, and a bibliography. *From Sea to Shining Sea* deserves every bit of its publishing hype (150,000-copy printing, national publicity tour, and marketing to the tune of a quarter of a million dollars).

The Dragons Are Singing Tonight, written by Jack Prelutsky and illustrated by Peter Sís, offers a collection of verses about – literally – dragons. In a publicity blitz covering more than twenty cities, Prelutsky promoted the book by singing and playing the guitar while Sís drew pictures. (Meanwhile, his earlier volume *Nightmares: Poems to Trouble Your Sleep* [1976], was removed from lower-grade shelves in Berkeley County, South Carolina. "Our kids see enough of this garbage on TV," one school-board member remarked; another board member linked such books to recent expulsions, saying, "we have enough discipline problems in the middle schools." However, the book remained available for intermediate- and

middle-school classrooms.) Another 1993 Prelutsky title, *A. Nonny Mouse Writes Again,* with pictures by Marjorie Priceman (Knopf), escaped notice despite its wryly subversive text.

X. J. Kennedy continued his fine work for children with the humorous collection *Drat These Brats!,* illustrated by James Watts (McElderry). Monica Gunning's collection, *Not a Copper Penny in Me House: Poems from the Caribbean* (Boyds Mills/ Woodsong), was illustrated by Fran Lessac. In a welcome departure from the compulsory read-aloud format of most anthologies, *A Frog Inside My Hat* (BridgeWater) consists of poems that beginners can read on their own.

Again in 1993 the general quality of juvenile nonfiction was high. Reference works continued to proliferate, and 1993 saw the introduction of several new imprints intended for marketing directly to schools; Scholastic Reference, from Scholastic, and U*X*L, from Gale (a series for middle schools), were among the most widely distributed of these. For the individual bookstore customer, Dorling Kindersley (previously distributed in a smaller range of titles in the United States) released numerous well-researched and beautifully produced British books, ranging from children's reference works (Carol Watson, *My First Encyclopedia*) to specialty items (Stephen Biesty, *Cross Sections: Man of War,* with text by Richard Platt). Most were in between, like Elizabeth Waters and Annie Harris's *Royal Academy of Arts: Painting, A Young Artist's Guide,* with practical advice for the budding painter. Oxford University Press, in an unusual departure from its long-standing practice, announced *A History of Us,* by Joy Hakim, a ten-volume series on U.S. history which is the first OUP series to originate in the United States. Rand McNally announced its reentry into the children's trade market with two new series and two revamped ones, all on geography.

Biographies included Andrea Davis Pinkney's *Alvin Ailey,* with illustrations by Brian Pinkney (Hyperion), aimed at younger readers, and Jane Mylum Gardner's *Henry Moore: From Bones and Stones to Sketches and Sculptures* (Four Winds), illustrated with photographs and intended for preschool readers. For the middle grades there were Nancy Loewen's *Poe: A Biography* (Creative Editions) and Barry Denenberg's careful *The True Story of J. Edgar Hoover and the F.B.I.* (Scholastic), the latter striking a balance between the hero-worship of earlier juvenile biographies of Hoover and the more recent sensational disclosures for adult readers. Freedman's biography of Eleanor Roosevelt was discussed earlier.

Two distinguished books showcased a less familiar side of Walter Dean Myers, better known for his gritty fiction. He put together an unusual volume, *Brown Angels: An Album of Pictures and Verse* (HarperCollins), and also contributed a section to Jacob Lawrence's eloquent photo history, *The Great Migration: An American Story* (Museum of Modern Art/HarperCollins), which chronicles the northward shift of African-Americans during the first half of this century. Virginia Hamilton tackled another important era in African-American history in *Many Thousand Gone: African Americans from Slavery to Freedom* (Knopf), about the Underground Railroad.

Several nonfiction books dealt with the arts. Kathleen Krull's *Lives of the Musicians: Good Times, Bad Times (And What the Neighbors Thought)*, illustrated by Kathryn Hewitt (Harcourt Brace Jovanovich), profiles twenty famous musicians, from Antonio Vivaldi to Woody Guthrie. Readers learn not only the basic facts, but also odd tidbits of information: Vivaldi's *The Seasons* was voted "Most Boring Composition" in a survey of New York City radio listeners; Johannes Brahms, creator of the Western world's most famous lullaby, was a notorious snorer; W. S. Gilbert was kidnapped as a child; Igor Stravinsky once wrote something called "Do Not Throw Paper Towels in Toilet," and so on. Philip M. Isaacson's *A Short Walk Around the Pyramids & Through the World of Art* (Knopf) performs a similar service for art history. Opening with a juxtaposition of Egyptian pyramids to I. M. Pei's more controversial pyramid in the Cour Napoleon, Isaacson covers a great deal of ground in a well-informed, stylish, and lucid manner. In architecture, Michael Gaughenbaugh offers *Old House, New House: A Child's Exploration of American Architectural Styles,* illustrated by Herbert Camburn (Preservation Press), less humorous and less widely distributed than the other two but impressive.

Though 1993 brought a welcome end to the tide of books about Columbus and his times, ecology and political revisionism remained alive in a more general sense. Jim Arnosky brought out *Crinkleroot's 25 Fish Every Child Should Know* and *Crinkleroot's 25 Birds Every Child Should Know,* both from Bradbury and both fairly typical of this category. Numerous other offerings dealt with conservation, recycling, water purity, finding nature's wonders in one's own backyard, and the like. (Whales and dolphins remained popular; there were several books dealing with foxes and at least half a dozen on wolves.) A more ambitious undertaking was a collaboration by Ann Durrell, Jean Craighead George, and Katherine Paterson, who edited *The Big Book for Our Planet* (Dutton), an earnest but nicely produced and well-written miscellany. From personal experience Cherie Mason narrated her interaction with a fox named Vicky in *Wild Fox: A True Story*, illustrated by JoEllen McAllister Stammen (DownEast Books).

A major nonfiction book of 1993 was former president Jimmy Carter's *Talking Peace: A Vision for the Next Generation*, from Dutton. Carter is unashamedly idealistic: "As a submarine officer in the U.S. Navy and later as president of the United States, I learned firsthand about the terrible nature of war. This knowledge strengthens my personal commitment to work for the blessings of peace." He describes warlike conditions, both domestic and foreign, including domestic race relations (complete with a poem by Carter on boyhood experiences with segregation), human-rights violations, and more than thirty conflicts around the globe. Said to have written the book out of dissatisfaction with the blandness of current history texts, Carter takes his young readers seriously in his first book for them.

Picture books for the youngest readers were of generally high quality, though this year brought an unusual number of more appeal to adults than to their theoretical audience. Sendak's *We Are All in the Dumps with Jack and Guy* is the most obvious example of this. Jules Feiffer's first book for children, *The Man in the Ceiling* (HarperCollins/di Capua), is another, as are Berkeley Breathed's *Goodnight Opus* and Alan Snow's *How Dogs Really Work,* both from Little, Brown. Jan Marzollo and Walter Wick appealed to all ages with *I Spy Funhouse* and *I Spy Mystery* (both from Cartwheel), the latest in a series of puzzlers with snappy texts and meticulous photographs.

Front cover for the pop-up book based on the Thomas the Tank Engine segments featured on the
PBS show Shining Time Station

Maira Kalman's *Chicken Soup, Boots* (Viking), a favorite with adults, explores careers from short-order cook to therapy dog. Its lively, idiosyncratic text matches the brilliant pictures and fine design; its irony and occasional parody, however, may be lost on its readership. The same is perhaps true of *The Happy Hocky Family* (Viking) by Lane Smith, best known for his joint efforts with Jon Scieszka. Like Kalman, Smith uses the jacket notes to amuse readers: "Lane grew up in the Smith family. There was Mr. Smith and Mrs. Smith and Shane Smith. Shane rhymes with Lane. Ha ha, this is funny." Or is it? "Lane's Caldecott Honor story" follows: "I have a Caldecott Honor. Do you have a Caldecott Honor? I do. Hee hee." The text of the book itself is similarly minimalist and is divided into short chapters ("Coat Story," "Balloon Story," and so on). A few are funny, like "Ant Farm"; one is very unfunny ("The Zoo," in which the family dog disappears inside a crocodile). The book, which is printed on recycled paper (and looks it), has been widely promoted and very favorably reviewed.

Most picture books were less ambitious and more predictable. Denise Fleming followed up her successful *In the Tall, Tall Grass* with *In the Small, Small Pond* (Holt), an appealing volume with minimal text integrated into bright pictures made by putting colored cotton pulp through hand-stenciled patterns. Another sequel was *Carl Goes to Daycare,* by Alexandra Day (Farrar, Straus and Giroux), in which the lovable rottweiler takes charge as usual; this title was heavily promoted, including a tour with a look-alike dog accompanying the author. In *Owen* (Greenwillow), Kevin Henkes returned to the picture-book scene with a deftly told tale of a young mouse and his security blanket. Even the typeface (Goudy modern) is attractive and reassuring.

Some excellent picture books explored the texture of daily life in American minority families. Denys Cazet's *Born in the Gravy* (Orchard) features bilingual dialogue. Kindergartener Margarita reports on her first day in school and on being teased by older children ("Kindergarten babies, born in the gravy!"); no, says Pap, she was born in Guadalajara. This lighthearted, warm picture book may be one of the best multicultural offerings of the year; certainly it is one of the least pretentious. Several of the finest picture books about subcultures were historical. Elisa Bartone's *Peppe the Lamplighter,* with paintings by Ted Lewin (Lothrop, Lee and Shepard), is a simple but satisfying tale of a turn-of-the-century immigrant family in Little Italy. *Sweet Clara and the Freedom Quilt,* by Deborah Hopkinson with paintings by James Ransome (Knopf), tells of a twelve-year-old girl's successful attempts to make a map for other slaves to follow to reach the Underground Railroad. Significantly, these two are not the work of long-established authors; Hopkinson's is her first book for children, Bartone's her second. Chris Raschka followed his 1992 success, *Charlie Parker Played Be Bop,* with an inventive story of a burgeoning friendship in *Yo! Yes?* (Orchard), with one black character, one white one, and a maximum of two words per page. One of the finest picture books of the year, Allen Say's family saga *Grandfather's Journey* (Houghton Mifflin), recounts a Japanese family's move from Japan to the United States, then back to Japan again. A less idyllic period in Japanese-American history is shown in Yoshiko Uchida's *The Bracelet,* illustrated by Joanna Yardley (Philomel), based on the author's own experience in a World War II internment camp.

The most successful picture book from a first-time author was probably *Stellaluna,* by Janell Cannon (Harcourt Brace Jovanovich), an improbable and sentimental story of a young fruit bat brought up by birds. Cannon's haunting pictures, as well as the gentle humor of a bat trying to fly and sleep like a bird, made this a winner in spite of itself. An equally impressive debut was *Mr. Lunch Takes a Plane Ride,* by the husband and wife team of J. Otto Seibold and Vivian Walsh (Viking), a whimsical tale about a dog. Timothy Bush illustrated his own mock-Victorian fantasy, *James in the House of Aunt Prudence* (Crown). Mary GrandPré made her debut as a children's book illustrator for Jennifer Armstrong's *Chin Yu Min and the Ginger Cat* (Crown); a particular favorite with graduate students, Chin Yu Min captured at least one straw poll as the year's best.

The most widely discussed picture-book import of 1993 was a Japanese title from 1977 by Taro Gomi, translated into English by Amanda Mayer Stinchecum as *Everyone Poops* (Kane/Miller). This improbable best-seller consists of brightly colored, primitive-style pictures of animals excreting, accompanied by simple text. ("What does whale poop look like?" asks the centerfold; the picture offers no

answer.) Several booksellers on the West Coast reported runaway sales, though there was a suggestion that some copies were bought as presents for adults. Thanks to the Dewey Decimal System, this title escaped notice by most censors; it can be shelved under Toilet Training.

Though retellings of folktales and other favorite stories were down in number from 1992, they were high in quality. Beginning with creation stories, two outstanding versions (in addition to the Rylant adaptation of Genesis described earlier) were Ed Young's *Moon Mother* (HarperCollins/Perlman), a Native American myth, and a picture-book issue of James Weldon Johnson's poem *The Creation,* with pictures by Carla Golemba (Little, Brown). A West African creation myth was retold by Eric Maddern as *The Fire Children* (Dial), illustrated by Fran Lessac.

Familiar stories included Margaret Hodges's retelling of *Saint Patrick and the Peddler,* illustrated by Paul Brett Johnson (Orchard), and of *The Hero of Bremen,* illustrated by the late Charles Mikolaycak (Holiday House). Robert Bender's *The Three Billy Goats Gruff* (Holt) was one of several, with others coming from Glen Rounds (Holiday House) and Tim Arnold (Margaret McElderry); there were also two British versions not yet published in the United States. Reaching back several decades, the Disney Press brought out a version of *The Grasshopper and the Ants* which Margaret Wise Brown did for the studio early in her career. (Unlike Aesop's original, Brown's has a happy ending.) Among tales by known authors, Hans Christian Andersen's snow queen was presented in two handsome volumes: *The Snow Queen,* translated by Naomi Lewis and illustrated by Angela Barrett (Candlewick); and *Mary Engelbreit's The Snow Queen* (Workman), the popular artist's first book for children. Carlo Collodi's Pinocchio made an appearance in an abridged version told and illustrated by Lorenzo Mattoti (Lothrop), and Washington Irving's story of Rip Van Winkle was retold by Gary Kelley (Creative Editions). Ann Keary Beneduce abridged Jonathan Swift's *Gulliver's Adventures in Lilliput,* turning it into an apolitical adventure story; the book, from Philomel, is remarkable chiefly for the luminous illustrations by Gennady Spirin. Numerous other old favorites were reissued with new illustrations.

Half a dozen retellings involved more drastic adaptations. Arnold Levine's *The Boardwalk Princess,* illustrated by Susan Guevara (Tambourine), adapts the Brothers Grimms' "Brother and Sister" to a turn-of-the-century New York setting (reminiscent of last year's *Beauty and the Beast*). Similarly, David

Delamare moved his *Cinderella* (Green Tiger) to Venice. William Wegman took a different approach in *Cinderella,* casting his weimaraners, appropriately costumed, in the main parts; he did *Little Red Riding Hood* in the same manner (both books from Hyperion). Dav Pilkey's *Dogzilla* and *Kat Kong* are canine and feline parodies, respectively, of the famous films. The Wegman and Pilkey books have been featured in chain bookstores (apparently targeting an adult readership). Finally, a delight for adults and children alike, Eugene Trivizas turned a familiar story around in *The Three Little Wolves and the Big Bad Pig* (McElderry), with hilarious pictures by Helen Oxenbury.

Retellings of less familiar stories, mostly from non-Western traditions, proliferated. Three were of unusual quality: Lawrence Yep's *The Shell Woman and the King* (Dial), with illustrations by Yang Ming-Yi; Tololwa M. Mollel's *The King and the Tortoise* (Clarion), a tale from Cameroon with pictures by Kathy Blankley; and Ed Young's *Red Thread* (Philomel). Young's pastel-and-watercolor illustrations are joined by a continuous red line from beginning to end.

Many of the fictional offerings for middle-grade readers were either series continuations or repetitions of formulae that had worked well for particular authors in earlier years. Horror ruled the sales figures, especially in paperback, and Sweet Valley High, BabySitters Club, and other paperback series continued to sell. With some honorable exceptions, middle-grade fiction was not particularly distinguished.

Best-selling authors tended to revert to formula. Jon Scieszka's *Your Mother Was a Neanderthal,* illustrated by Lane Smith (Viking), carries the popular time-warp trio back to caveman times. Mary James (Mary Jane Meaker, who usually writes for young adults as M. E. Kerr) followed up her well-received *Shoebag,* a realistic tale, with the whimsical fantasy *The Shuteyes* (Scholastic), about a misfit boy's adventures on the planet Alert. Brad Strickland continued his competent work on the late John Bellairs's manuscripts in *The Vengeance of the Witch-Finder* (Dial), with jacket and frontispiece by Edward Gorey; more posthumous Bellairs books will follow. Theodore Taylor's *Timothy of the Cay* (Harcourt Brace), part prequel and part sequel, bracketed the more focused incidents described in *The Cay,* and Cynthia De Felice's *The Light on Hogback Hill* (Macmillan) repeated the brand of deft characterization and scary events used in her earlier books; both lacked the tightness of plot that distinguished their predecessors. *The Mystery of the Cup-*

board (Morrow) continued Lynne Reid Banks's Indian series.

As usual, many titles for this age level centered on family, school, and sports. In *Scooter* (Greenwillow) Vera B. Williams portrays a mother-daughter family adapting to New York City; Elana, the daughter, is one of the year's most appealing characters. Gary Paulsen shows a boy's removal from his dysfunctional family to the country in *Harris and Me* (Harcourt Brace). Another 1993 book by Paulsen, *Dogteam* (Delacorte), covers familiar Paulsen territory but will appeal to readers who have liked his previous books about sled dogs and racing. Gordon Korman's *The Toilet Paper Tigers* (Scholastic) is a competent, formulaic Little League tale. By contrast, Ken Mochizuki's *Baseball Saved Us* (Lee and Low Books), illustrated by Dom Lee, tells of sandlot baseball in an unusual sandlot: a World War II internment camp. Mochizuki draws on his boyhood experiences in just such a camp in Idaho. Lee and Low, a new name in juvenile publishing with a deliberately small number of new releases and a multicultural focus, has made a fine start.

Another newcomer is Ticknor and Fields juveniles, named after the distinguished house whose list was bought out by Houghton Mifflin over a century ago. This new imprint, whose goals are stated in the introductory brochure as "to ignore trends and to identify and nurture gifted writers and artists," offers Garry Disher's *The Bamboo Flute,* one of the outstanding imports for middle-grade readers in 1993. Set in Australia in 1932 (and published there in 1992), this finely written story chronicles an unlikely relationship between a young boy and a disreputable swagman.

Several authors addressed the clash of cultures in fresh and appealing ways. *The Sunita Experiment,* by Mitali Perkins (Joy Street), describes an Indian girl's experiences when her visiting grandmother pressures the family to turn away from American ways; *Sworn Enemies* (Bantam), by Carol Matas, portrays the wartime relationship between two Russian boys, one of whom is Jewish. This was a category in which a few new authors excelled. Carol Lynch Williams developed a plausible relationship between two antiadult eleven-year-olds in *Kelly & Me* (Delacorte), a tale of death and loss. Cara De Vito's *Where I Want to Be,* another first novel, combined the seriousness of a potentially dysfunctional family with a fresh and often humorous prose style. *Dither Farm,* by Sid Hite (Holt), another first novel, approaches family through fantasy. And Rita Dove's first juvenile, *Through the Ivory Gate,* shows a young adult reassessing her childhood.

The most significant books for middle grades in 1993 stretched the limits of the category. As a result, most were shelved in young-adult collections in libraries and stores. Leading titles of this kind were MacLachlan's *Baby* and Lowry's *The Giver,* discussed earlier under Newbery winners; both raise issues more common to young-adult fiction but are written at a level comprehensible to many middle-grade readers and have twelve-year-old protagonists (borderline for young adult).

Donna Jo Napoli's *The Magic Circle* (Dutton), Gary Paulsen's *Nightjohn* (Delacorte), and Nina Bawden's *The Real Plato Jones* (Clarion) also straddle the line. A revisionist tale of Hansel and Gretel, *The Magic Circle* does for the evil witch what Jean Rhys did for Mr. Rochester's first wife; the book, told from the witch's point of view, is a psychological horror story whose protagonist, known only as Ugly One, is doomed to descend gradually into the creature normally associated with the story. Napoli's two earlier books, while competent and entertaining, gave little hint of the talent displayed in this one. Bawden's book depicts a thirteen-year-old boy of mixed Greek and Welsh ancestry who searches for answers about his family and his own identity when his Greek grandfather dies. Many professionals considered the fiction title of the year to be Paulsen's *Nightjohn* (Delacorte), a grim story about a twelve-year-old slave girl who, at great risk to herself and her fugitive teacher, learns to read. Its graphic descriptions of torture and punishment have caused it to be shelved with young-adult titles though its heroine is young and its reading level not particularly difficult.

Change and shock are normal in the young-adult market, so here it was somewhat more surprising to see so many formulaic works. Judy Blume's *Here's to You, Rachel Robinson* (Orchard) continues the family saga begun in *Just As Long As We're Together* (1988). Despite Blume's usual skilled dialogue and plausible family problems, the dénouement, a touching scene on Ellis Island, is simply too pat. Paul Zindel stuck to the successful dual-protagonist plan of several previous books in *David and Della* (HarperCollins).

Two writers with instantly identifiable subjects and styles produced new books in 1993. Francesca Lia Block followed three previous successes with *Missing Angel Juan* (HarperCollins), in which the purple-eyed Witch Baby follows Angel Juan to New York, finds him and herself, and frees the ghost of Charlie Bat; the fourth time around, the magic is gone. One Weetzie Bat book was a wonder, but four are too many. On the other hand,

Robert Lipsyte's *The Chief* (HarperCollins), a sequel to *The Brave* (1991), lives up to its predecessor; more than a boxing novel, more than a Native American novel, the book continues Lipsyte's fast-paced, economical writing and depth of characterization.

Like middle-school stories, many young-adult books center around school, family, and friendship. Norma Fox Mazer takes on a topical subject, sexual harassment, in *Out of Control* (Morrow), a careful and competent book. Harry Mazer's *Who Is Eddie Leonard?* (Delacorte) starts from another topical idea, missing children, and explores the aftermath for the child. Julian F. Thompson's *Shepherd* (Holt) focuses on deception and delusion in relationships, as does Sue Ellen Bridgers's *Keeping Christina* (HarperCollins). All are pedestrian. At the other end of the spectrum, Chris Crutcher's *Staying Fat for Sarah Byrnes* (Greenwillow) has a fast-moving double plot, two memorable characters (one fat, one scarred for life), a scary villain, and a lot of humor. In between, Liza Ketchum Murrow's *Twelve Days in August* (Holiday House), a sequel to *Fire in the Heart* (1989), is a skillful variant on the gay-teammate theme.

More unusual was the 1993 U.S. publication of Maurice Gee's *The Champion* (Simon and Schuster), originally published in New Zealand in 1989 and since made into a successful miniseries. A distinguished contribution to realistic World War II literature, the book describes two weeks in 1943 when a black GI, Jackson Coop, came to stay with the Pascoe family in Kettle Creek, New Zealand. Other distinguished imports were British. Philip Pullman's *The White Mercedes* (Knopf) is a sometimes-graphic tale of deception and revenge set in Oxford, and Farrukh Dhondy's *The Black Swan* (Houghton Mifflin) cleverly meshes a contemporary plot with a sixteenth-century mystery. Turning to fantasy imports, Joan Aiken's *Is Underground* (Delacorte) is a quest story in the Wolves Chronicles series, and Ade Geras's *Pictures of the Night* (Harcourt Brace), third in her Egerton Hall trilogy, adapts the Snow White story.

Another strong contender in the young-adult area was a first novel by Angela Johnson, *Toning the Sweep* (Orchard); Johnson has produced half a dozen books for younger readers, but this sensitive story of loss and identity is her first for young adults. Though the heroine and her family live in Cleveland and the pivotal death of her grandfather took place in Alabama in 1964, most of the book takes place in the California desert, a beautifully realized milieu.

Two fine young-adult novels focus on a daughter's life after her mother's suicide. *Shizuko's Daughter,* by Kyoko Mori (Holt), takes place in Kobe, Himechi, and Nagasaki over the course of seven years. Its carefully detailed setting and its formal, spare prose highlight the experiences of Yuki with her repressed father, obsessively neat stepmother, and faraway grandparents; the impact of the mother/daughter relationship unfolds gradually and convincingly. The same is true of Julie Reece Deaver's *You Bet Your Life* (HarperCollins/Zolotow), though the milieu differs sharply; this one is set in the television and theater world like the author's earlier *Say Goodnight, Gracie* (1988).

War, not much seen in young-adult novels since Walter Dean Myers's outstanding *Fallen Angels,* made a comeback. In addition to Rylant's *I Had Seen Castles* (Harcourt Brace), various others were set during World War II; most of them cover familiar ground done much better years ago by Robert Westall. A fine book by Malcolm Bosse, *Deep Dream of the Rain Forest* (Farrar, Straus and Giroux), uses World War I as a metaphor: its hero, a war orphan, seeks his identity in the jungle where, of course, the kind of "civilization" for which he assumed the war was fought is of little use to him. More contemporary is Kerr's *Linger* (HarperCollins), in which the Gulf War also serves as a kind of metaphor; the action centers on a restaurant, a restriction of setting which gives Kerr's novel more focus than in some of her recent books.

Two young-adult entries resist categorization. Lawrence Yep's *American Dragons* (HarperCollins), an anthology, presents young Asian-Americans; some chapters are essays, some poems, and some fiction, but all concern the special problems of identity within this minority group. Avi's *City of Light, City of Dark* (Orchard) is unusual in another way: its comic-book format, illustrated by newcomer Brian Floca. Though comic books (or "graphic novels," as professionals call them) have become common in science fiction, this is a first by a mainstream writer.

Every writer must also come to the last book, and 1993 saw the deaths of several children's writers and illustrators. Robert Westall, whose Carnegie Medal winner *The Machine Gunners* changed juvenile war books profoundly, died in April. A posthumous volume of short stories, *In Camera,* was published for young adults. In the United States, Ruth Krauss, author of *A Hole Is To Dig* and many other picture books, died in her eighties. Illustrator Charles Mikolaycak died of cancer. Fred Gwynne, known as an actor in Disney films and on *The Munsters,* wrote children's books, one of which, *Easy to See Why* (Simon and Schuster), appeared posthumously.

The Year in Literary Theory

Barry Faulk
University of Illinois – Urbana

and

Amy Farmer
University of Illinois – Urbana

The year in literary theory brought few genuine harbingers of change but did bring a further consolidation of the tendencies that have recently dominated literary study. In American literary study a scrupulous examination of the relations between literary genre and social determinants remains central: the challenge of contextual analysis early offered by "American studies" and evidenced in work such as Leo Marx's *The Machine in the Garden* has been taken up and augmented by recent Americanists. Cultural Studies work, explicitly work indebted to the Birmingham Centre for Cultural Studies, continues to be a growth industry and to influence further literary study and theoretical endeavors. In 1993 Cultural Studies continued to push theoretical analysis beyond literary texts as they have been traditionally defined.

An example of the ambitions of the new cultural study can be seen in Adrian Rifkin's *Street Noises* (University of Manchester Press), a fascinating excursion into the topic of the pleasures of Paris. Rifkin's sources are diverse and not exclusively literary: he reads the Archives Nationales and back issues of *Detective* magazine, as well as the work of Jean Genet and Colette, in order to understand the political use of images of the city. In general *Street Noises* is a persuasive argument for the necessity of reading culture itself as a broader unity even when discrete cultural events, such as the images of the city or "the People" that Rifkin studies, are in constant flux.

Rifkin's book attempts to "unravel some of the senses and nonsenses of [the] timeless popular" representation of Paris and the ideal of Parisian pleasure. Like Judith Walkowitz's *City of Dreadful Delight* (1992), *Street Noises* examines how the consciousness and space of a large urban area is cognitively used and organized by social groups. Like Walkowitz,

Rifkin is interested in how such uses of the city allow the construction of certain types: in Rifkin's case the figures that haunt literature on Paris, such as the ragpicker and the flaneur.

As the last term suggests, Rifkin's analysis supplements Walter Benjamin's original critical project during the 1930s to read "the Paris of the Nineteenth Century." Most surprisingly, Rifkin reads both Benjamin's "Paris" and the Paris of Marcel Carne's classic film *Les Enfants du Paradis* against contemporary images of Vichy Paris. Rifkin's study maps relations between intellectuals and the popular imagination of the city, detailing how both Benjamin and Carne used urban types such as the ragpicker or the provocateur to elaborate allegories about the function of the critical intellectual. Rifkin's reading of Maurice Chevalier's voluminous memoirs in order to delineate how urban entertainment shifted from populist culture to a commodified, global entertainment is further evidence of the ambitions of *Street Noises*.

Neil Nehring's *Flowers in the Dustbin* (University of Michigan Press) also attempts to make sense of London and the history of its postwar subcultures. Like Greil Marcus's *Lipstick Traces* (1989), Nehring's book is an attempt to take U.K. punk circa 1977 seriously; the result is an intriguing and thorough remapping of post–World War II British literature. Nehring goes over territory recently surveyed by Alan Sinfield's *Literature, Politics, and Culture in Postwar England* (1989), but he gives U.K. subcultures their explicit due in literary history. Recent works such as *Lipstick Traces* and Jon Savage's *England's Dreaming* (1991) both insist on the importance of U.K. punk as the crucial moment when the critique of everyday life made by the artistic avant-garde became irrevocably public, a part of "mass culture." Like Marcus and Savage, Nehring assumes that punk's failure suggested complex problems that demanded theoretical understanding.

Flowers in the Dustbin is a meditation on the power of "negativity" and is intended to provoke "cultural dissidence among artists, audiences, critics, teachers, and students – whose function, it will be argued, should overlap considerably." It is also an effort to redefine and expand the scope of the avant-garde as normally understood. Nehring constructs contemporary Cultural Studies as an academic effort to understand how both high and low culture share in "material social experience." Nehring's work elaborates a history of the avant-garde (not to be confused, Nehring details, with high modernism) which stresses their attempts to integrate aesthetic experience into everyday life. The book accordingly takes its place with recent revisionary histories of aesthetics, including Peter Burger's *Theory of the Avant-Garde* (1984) and Martha Woodmansee's *The Author, Art and the Market* (Columbia University Press, 1994).

Flowers in the Dustbin examines "a few provocative moments at which literary texts have been mixed up with popular cultural forms in everyday life." Perhaps the highlight of the book is Nehring's reading of how the antisocial Pinkie of Graham Greene's novel *Brighton Rock* (1938) is taken in by Fred and Judy Vermorel's biography of the Sex Pistols. Nehring argues this appropriation of Greene not only "reinserted the novel into the whole field of cultural practices and social activities" but "corrected, in Greene's case, received judgments about his literary status as well." Nehring's extended discussion of *Brighton Rock* and Greene's anarchist politics is worth the price of the book, but his study of the gender politics behind the angry-young-men movement in the 1950s and of the interactions between Anthony Burgess's *A Clockwork Orange* (1962) and the promotion strategies employed by producer/entrepreneur/Svengali Andrew Loog Oldham to market the Rolling Stones are also engrossing readings of key cultural moments in postwar Great Britain.

Allon White's *Carnival, Hysteria, and Writing* (Clarendon Press) brings together assorted uncollected work from a writer who took a degree from Birmingham Centre for Cultural Studies and whose work *The Politics and Poetics of Transgression* (1986), cowritten with Peter Stallybrass, marks a foundational moment for the Cultural Studies movement. Stuart Hall, one of the founding figures of the Birmingham Centre, provides an excellent introduction to the collection. Hall helpfully contextualizes the importance of White's work and details how it

clarified key debates in Cultural Studies during the 1980s.

Like Nehring's book Stallybrass and White's book (and indeed the collected essays in *Carnival, Hysteria, and Writing*) rethinks the high/low culture divide: they all insist on the relational nature of this polarized opposition. The criticism of White works to destabilize the great divide between high and mass culture by a thorough rethinking of literary history from the Renaissance to John Rechy. White's critical career was dedicated to the argument that "the emergence of a distinctively bourgeois, sanitized conception of the self in post-Renaissance European culture" depended on depicting "various social domains . . . as 'low' and 'disgusting.' " Even more important, White's work went beyond a simple argument about the inescapability of cultural conflict: he argued that both sides of the culture divide needed the other. Presentations of the "People" are not static; rather, they reflect complex cultural processes: middle-class tastemakers feel both attraction and repulsion toward mass culture.

This collection of White's writings includes painful autobiographical forays, which suggest White's personal investment with the metaphors of psychic and physical disintegration he investigated as a scholar. There are also sophisticated historical case studies which demonstrate how serious, "high" discourses are structured by their resistance to "popular" images, dialects, and cultural forms. An essay on academic language, " 'The Dismal, Sacred Word,' " notes the class biases and prejudices behind the creation of academic discourse and Standard English. White observes how glossaries of "cant" terms, such as Thomas Harman's glossary *Caveat or Warening, for Common Cursetors Vulgarely Called Vagabondes* (1567), safeguarded official language from "common" words. The writing of glossaries of slang demonstrates how official languages are used in attempts to sanction what can and cannot be said seriously. White's critical project fixed on examples where the gap between high and low culture was ignored or flaunted, and he acutely analyzed the feelings of vertigo or "hysteria" that could result from this blurring of boundaries. White expertly reads artifacts as various as Francis Bacon's paintings and Charles Dickens's *Bleak House* (1853) in order to clarify what happens when the symbolic order collapses and hysteria ensues.

Just how far theoretical concerns can travel is demonstrated by the fact that the methods White uses to analyze art are also used by Houston Baker in relating the history of an academic discipline. In a collection of Princeton lectures titled *Black Studies, Rap, and the Academy* (University of Chicago Press), the celebrated African-American scholar takes as his starting point how metaphors of Inside/Outside structure how one talks about the academy. Baker utilizes this binary in order to retell the often volatile history of Black Studies in the American university. Baker offers both the method and history of the Black Studies department as a challenge to disciplinary "business as usual" and to essentialist notions of academic work. Because Black Studies retained clear ties to concerns in the public sphere, to nonacademic constituencies and to artistic activity, Baker argues that it challenges static disciplinary labor.

Baker constructs a history of black studies that sets an academic margin in relation to cultural centers in black urban culture; however, the book is also a call for academics to open up and reexamine their relations to broader sections of the public.

Recent controversies over rap music, particularly the celebrity trial of 2 Live Crew for obscenity, are used by Baker as a test case to observe how academic "experts" relate and represent mass culture. Baker uses disputes over rap in order to illustrate how Cultural Studies methods might be utilized to analyze popular media. However, while Baker has intriguing things to say about rap, the Central Park jogging case, and 2 Live Crew's Luther Campbell as "Black Entrepreneur," too many of his arguments simply take other celebrated scholars – mostly Henry Louis Gates and Kimberle Crenshaw – to task for being uninformed about rap and the complexities of popular culture. While Baker calls for scholars to know something about the culture they analyze and occasionally represent in legal controversies, he offers few clear examples of how academics might more profitably use their authority as experts outside the academy.

In many ways a book from the Black Literature and Culture series edited by Baker, Kenneth W. Warren's *Black and White Strangers: Race and Literary Realism* (University of Chicago Press), offers a more thorough interrogation of the relations of race, politics, and art. An analysis of the effects of literary work, Warren's book opens with a salutary reevaluation of claims that are routinely made about the politics of literature. Taking issue with those who claim that literature has direct social effects (including Abraham Lincoln, who greeted Harriet Beecher Stowe with the statement, "So this is the little lady who made this big war") and those who assert, as theorist Walter Benn Michaels has, that "the only relation literature as such has to cul-

ture as such is that is part of it," Warren's book reconceives the political valences of American literature, especially the literature of realism.

Warren's study is also concerned about the construction of national identity: he scrutinizes how stories about black Americans from emancipation to the fin de siècle period interacted with the genre of American realism. Warren's method assumes that race is a deeply heterogeneous reality, difficult to capture or encapsulate. Books as diverse as Henry James's *The American Scene* (1907), Francis E. W. Harper's *Iola Le Roy* (1892), and W. E. B. Du Bois's *The Souls of Black Folk* (1903) are juxtaposed in order to illustrate how ideas about racial identity worked in literary critiques of the Gilded Age. Warren also constructively reads debates about literature's function that were made during the Reconstruction effort and aired in the *Nation* and the *Century* (the latter serialized George Washington Cable, James, and William Dean Howells). He argues that these debates are crucial in demonstrating theories about the political effects and intents of literary realism. In the breadth of texts and the critical rigor he brings to contemporary debates about the politics of literature, Warren's study is in every way exemplary; his study is proof that race is a useful tool for literary inquiry, even in texts that do not explicitly take race as a theme.

David Simpson's *Romanticism, Nationalism and the Revolt Against Theory* (University of Chicago Press) is an intelligent and well-researched intervention in debates about the uses of literary theory. Simpson places current debates about the efficacy of theory that continue to rage over contemporary literary scholarship in the context of debates about the efficacy of method that circulated in England during the French Revolution. Simpson finds a curious genealogy for current disavowals of theory in the academy in the "antirhetoric" rhetoric that circulated in the seventeenth century against Peter Ramus's education reforms. He finds a similar rhetoric in debates about French "theory" and British legal "practice" prominent during the Revolution in France. Simpson details the English reception to Ramism, and later philosophical developments such as utilitarianism, in order to frame more accurately debates about theory and the function of criticism; he uses the history of English resistance to rationalist claims about method in order to give a history to contemporary objections to literary theory. The rewards for Simpson's method are palpable. He convincingly connects the claims of British Common Sense philosophers, the reception to German sensational drama, and arguments over women's role in political critique, to issues at stake in contemporary theoretical debates. The bravura close to his book, "Thoughts on the Present Discontents" – which surveys current academic claims about the nature of literature, the status of theory, and the function of the university as the legacy of debates that raged over the British constitution in the 1790s – demonstrates how dazzling Simpson's comparisons can be. His work presents a forceful argument that "the French Revolution is not 'finished,' and that its legacies, ideological and institutional, cannot be sensibly dismissed as no longer relevant to our arguments about ourselves and our opportunities."

Jeffrey Skoblow's *Paradise Dislocated* (University Press of Virginia) is a demanding study of William Morris's long poem *The Earthly Paradise* (serialized 1867–1870): it is fascinating for its ambitious effort to reclaim Morris's seldom-read poem and for the frame of reference in which he situates Morris's poetry. Skoblow reads Morris against a context of post-Marxist social thought ranging from the Frankfurt school to L=A=N=G=U=A=G=E poets such as Ron Silliman. Skoblow argues that Morris's poem refuses to work as a "commodity" and draws attention to Morris's attempt to "embody" a text that would be mass-produced and circulated. Skoblow claims that Morris established in the poem "a sanctuary from administration," an effort to resist the commodification of the book begun in the nineteenth century through a belated effort to materialize "a world ... drawn from the body and brought into the world as a body." Skoblow's study of Morris sometimes runs aground in abstraction, but it is a fascinating effort to "recover" a neglected poet and reconstruct an oppositional poetic that failed.

The theme of *Paradise Dislocated* is the difficulty and, in a sense, the failure of Morris to resolve his poem; Skoblow offers an analysis of how the reception of poetry has changed in ways that make reading the serialized poem steadily more difficult. None of the limits of Morris's poem is read as a failure. Instead, they are seen as part of Morris's resistance to the culture: to its tendency to forget, to resist privacy, and to prohibit images of plenitude. Skoblow's study compels a reader to believe that the impossibility of reading a certain poem might speak to the broader conditions in which poetry is read. It is an extremely sophisticated attempt to rethink the purpose of art in the "administered" world of advanced capitalism.

Amanda Anderson's *Tainted Souls and Painted Faces* (Cornell University Press) is another study of nineteenth-century British literature that seeks to in-

tervene in current theoretical debates. Anderson's study of the "fallen women" in Victorian literature is broad in scope: besides strong readings of Dante Gabriel Rossetti's "Jenny" (1870) and Dickens's *David Copperfield* (1850), Anderson examines texts conventionally considered "extra-literary," primarily John Stuart Mill's *The System of Logic* (1843). Anderson's book takes seriously W. R. Greg's comment about prostitution in the *Westminster Review* (1850) that "Of all the social problems which philosophy has to deal with, this is we believe, the darkest, the knottiest, and the saddest." She examines the category of the prostitute in order to enter into a philosophically complex and "knotty" debate in Victorian culture; Anderson elaborates how thinking about the fallen women touched problems of volition, agency, and rational autonomy. Her book describes a "pervasive rhetoric of fallenness in mid-Victorian culture" which presents the prostitute as disturbing the self-understanding of the "normative masculine subject." Debates over the fallen woman, Anderson argues, were a deeply divided and contested terrain for the Victorian: a subject area where questions of social reform and philosophical debates about idealism and materialism clashed in discussing sexuality. Fallenness was not simply a reaction toward feminine sexuality, Anderson argues, but an entry way into a culture's most complex understanding of human behavior.

As well as reconstituting Victorian concepts of human agency, *Tainted Souls and Painted Faces* intervenes in contemporary theoretical debates. Where Victorian explanations of the fallen woman often relied on deterministic modes of understanding, Anderson also examines examples where "intersubjective practices" are used to explain the prostitute, particularly in the poetry of Elizabeth Barrett Browning. In Browning's *Aurora Leigh* (1856), "a developed notion of reciprocal recognition" challenges systematic evaluation of the prostitute. Anderson finds in the novel-length poem representations of the prostitute that anticipate Jurgen Habermas's notions of communicative action. Her sophisticated closing chapter challenges poststructuralist notions of the subject and agency from the vantage point offered by Habermas and recent Habermas-influenced critical approaches.

In 1993 performance and drama criticism continued to be invigorated by theoretical methodology. Matthew C. Roudane's collection *Public Issues, Private Tensions: Contemporary American Drama* (AMS Press) contains seventeen essays on a wide variety of topics concerning contemporary drama. In the introduction Roudane argues that postwar American drama demands a criticism that can encompass the "evolving cultural poetics" and the criticism of civic action increasingly evident in American drama. The essays demonstrate the diversity of the American theater and indicate the range of postwar drama's presentation of private mores and public spaces. The book features an attempt to redefine the "historical American drama," an inquiry into the motives behind the representations of violence in the plays of Israel Horovitz, a study of the function of domestic humor in Lanford Wilson, and a debate over sexuality and the pornographic in Sam Shepard's drama. The collection also redefines how domestic tensions are portrayed in the "classic" American drama of Eugene O'Neill, Arthur Miller, and Tennessee Williams and explores continuities in the portrayal of the American family in plays by Shepard, David Mamet, Wilson, Arthur Kopit, Emily Mann, and Megan Terry. Utilizing discourse from women's studies, sociology, anthropology, and literary studies, *Public Issues, Private Tensions* is an important contribution for students of the drama.

Perhaps the most ambitious theoretical essay in Roudane's collection is "Hysteria, Crabs, Gospel, and Random Access: Ring around the Audience," by performance and audience theorist Herbert Blau. Blau's essay surveys a history of postmodern performance looking to theatrical innovations including the Actor's Workshop of San Francisco in the 1950s and 1960s, the theater of Bertolt Brecht, and the plays of Genet and Samuel Beckett. Blau reads the history of the relationship between the spectator and the spectacle as part of the performance itself; for Blau, "if the audience remains a problem it is because, in the construction of meaning, it is always **in question**. The audience is what happens when, performing the signs and passwords of a play, something postulates itself and unfolds in response." Blau's essay complicates the notion of the audience's relationship with the performance and provides a useful opening to a collection focused primarily on dramatic texts as printed texts rather than performance.

Mark Fronko's *Drama as Text* (Cambridge University Press) is a detailed excursus into performance theory, with explicit implications for literary theory. Fronko's concern is with the short-lived phenomena of burlesque ballet in the seventeenth-century French court. Fronko's analysis of a marginal phenomenon is made to seem central to several areas of study: primarily, to the problem of reconstructing theoretical performance and to the "history of the body" offered by the work of Mi-

khail Bakhtin. Fronko also finds startling anticipations of performance art in these court entertainments of the baroque era.

Drama as Text details the baroque ballet, which Fronko reads as a scene of power struggle. Unlike earlier text-centered court ballet, the baroque ballet was nondramatic, disruptive, digressive, and separate from narrative action. Baroque ballet often focused less on verbal theater but more on "elaborately costumed dancing figures, whose physical body is often concealed with deforming constructed shapes"; the dancer was elevated while text was minimized. Often erotic, scurrilous, bodily imagery was a large part of its appeal and humor; politically corrosive, allegorical scenes were presented and often tied to present-day court events.

Attempting to innovate recent theories of performance reconstruction, Fronko works to rethink the "historical event" of performance "through the theory of its effects." Rather than view dance as a performance to be pieced together through stylistic attention and positivist method, Fronko foregrounds the importance of the historically situated spectator in interpreting performance. The autonomy of the body in ballet is geared to the noble spectator in a spirit "betokening criticism and political resistance"; Fronko's study "rehistoricizes burlesque ballet as politicized game playing." To that end he offers an innovative reading of Molière's court ballet *Les Facheux* (1661) as the end of this game playing and "the beginning of a studied transformation of the potentially autonomous noble into an impotent courtier."

Elisa New's *The Regenerate Lyric: Theology and Innovation in American Poetry* (Cambridge University Press) is a revisionary account of an often-contested theme in American poetry: the relation between Ralph Waldo Emerson and the commencement of a uniquely American poetry. Her thesis is a provocation to the critical work of Harold Bloom: where Bloom has argued that Emerson's criticism and practice inaugurated a new American poetic, New writes that American poets Emily Dickinson, Walt Whitman, Hart Crane, Robert Lowell, and Robert Frost all explored theological themes in their poetry to counter Emerson's critique of orthodox theology. The thesis is slightly tortured, since New also claims that Emerson himself was unable to maintain the claims behind his antireligious position and that his own poetry fails as poetry while succeeding as philosophy.

The first of the two parts of *The Regenerate Lyric* reexamines ways in which Emerson's poetics are borne out of his reaction to the Puritan poetry of New England, namely Edward Taylor. New spends the first part reexamining the historical context of Emerson's work and rereads the "The Divinity School Address" in order to disclose two different Emersons: the official antitheological Emerson and the theologically motivated Emerson. These two Emersons challenge the traditional reading of the influential writer but, as New herself points out, make for disjointed poetry. There is an effort at canon revision here in New's work: she plainly labels Emerson's poetry to be "unnervingly undistinguished." However, the poets Emerson inspired, according to New, created the superior "American poem" – a conclusion that suggests more continuity with Bloom's thesis, and a long tradition of American scholarship, than New sometimes suggests.

The second part of the book offers readings on the theological moments in the poetry of Whitman, Dickinson, Stephen Crane, Lowell, and Frost. New's readings suggest that these poets based much of their best poems on their understanding of religion and Emerson. Though she does not limit her readings to source-based criticism, it is the focus of her "theological" criticism of these canonical poets.

A broader approach to literary genres, unified by the theme of national identity, might be found in Peter A. Dorsey's *Sacred Estrangement: The Rhetoric of Conversion in Modern American Autobiography* (Penn State University Press). A thematic study that touches on a variety of American literary works, Dorsey surveys several different kinds of "conversion" experiences, or conversion narratives, in American literature. Utilizing a variety of theoretical approaches to the study of autobiography, including psychological criticism and Hayden White's *Tropics of Discourse* (1985), Dorsey sets up a helpful rhetorical guide to the major features of what he describes as "the Christian conversion pattern." Dorsey notes the tradition of secular conversion narratives from Britain – including Thomas DeQuincey and Thomas Carlyle – which would have touched American autobiography in the early part of the twentieth century.

Working his way chronologically through American literature, Dorsey analyzes Edith Wharton's *A Backward Glance* (1934) and Ellen Glasgow's *The Woman Within* (1954) for an analysis of how these woman writers create a rhetorical space and identity for themselves. In a chapter on "The Varieties of Black Experience: Zora Neale Hurston's *Dust Tracks on a Road* and the Autobiography of Richard Wright," Dorsey reads the autobiography and the conversion narrative as a way of coming to terms with racial marginality. Most interestingly, Dorsey

feels the genre of autobiography works to define and explore a highly unstable notion of a cultural center. Dorsey explains:

> That writers such as Hurston, Wright, Glasgow, and Wharton would see themselves in this way might be expected; and one is more likely to be sympathetic to their feelings of alienation than those of the two Jameses – or least of all – to Henry Adams, the grandson of an American president. Yet all of these figures felt excluded from a mainstream culture they do not take great pains to identify. The America they feel separated from is almost without a center.

Sacred Estrangement concludes by pointing to deficiencies of current literary theory in grappling with the powerful discourse of conversion in both marginal and canonical American texts. Dorsey does not offer firm solutions to this challenge but ends his work with a gauntlet on the ground.

The kind of historical sensitivity evident in the discussion of genre in *Sacred Estrangement* is present in an excellent survey of new historical approaches to nineteenth-century art and literature edited by David L. Miller and titled *American Iconology* (Yale University Press). Taking its title and the ambitious breadth of its study from Erwin Panofsky's groundbreaking work in the theory of "iconology," these essays explore how visible events and icons can be studied, in Panofsky's words, to ascertain "those underlying principles which reveal the basic attitude of a nation, a period, a class, a religious or philosophical persuasion." The essays all endeavor to make sense of how the discourse of art meshed with competing discourses of nationalism, as of religious or political identity. Ambitiously, the book attempts to essay "the social construction of the national subjectivity" in the nineteenth century, a "subjectivity" in the process of transformation as writers and painters increasingly responded to the growth of market forces.

Some of the most fascinating essays in the book address the role of the painter or writer in the expanding marketplace for art; a variety of them follow Panofsky's work in elaborating the particular significations of painting. Sarah Burns's essay, titled "The Price of Beauty: Art, Commerce and the Late-Nineteenth Century American Studio Interior," examines the commodification of fin de siècle American painting by re-creating William Merritt Chase's work and the layout of his studio. Burns makes a fascinating comparison between the new space of the progressive artist's studio and the display space of the new department store; she also analyzes the anxieties over the commercialization of art implied by the contiguity of such spaces.

Robert H. Byer's "Words, Monuments, Beholders: The Visual Arts in Hawthorne's *The Marble Faun*" details how Nathaniel Hawthorne took issue with what Byer categorizes "monumental beholding," a process typified by oration such as Daniel Webster's Bunker Hill speech of 1843. In contrast to forms of oratory that privileged written forms and assumed a shared experience of a heroic past, Hawthorne represents individual encounters with Italian monuments in his romance. Hawthorne's spectators demonstrate a shift to a more fluid, private space of intimacy toward "monuments"; *The Marble Faun* (1860) suggests a new American way of seeing.

For those interested in the changing relations between painting and literature, Miller's collection of historicist essays is impressive and provocative. *American Iconology* provides a sophisticated perspective on the challenges commercial values and mass reproduction offered artistic imagery and the interactions between ways of reading images and ways of making sense of texts. Finally, for scholars interested in the historical question of how American national identity was fostered, Miller's collection is also invaluable.

The convergence of literary theorists, especially from feminist theory and deconstruction, on the Bible as literature and narrative continues to flourish. Virginia Ramsey Mollenkott's *Sensuous Spirituality: Out from Fundamentalism* (Crossroad) and Alicia Suskin Ostriker's *Feminist Revision and the Bible* (Blackwell) both offer interesting historicist strategies for reading biblical texts. Utilizing methods from contemporary Cultural Studies, Mollenkott's work is a challenging look at the relationship between biblical texts and the uses American churches make of them. Mollenkott explores the connections between communities of readers and the interpretive strategies they use when they read as "people of the book." More specifically, Mollenkott examines the multiple uses of "God-language" in the church and the influence of that language on American culture. She offers some fresh readings for familiar biblical texts, texts often decontextualized in their uses in American mainline denominations.

Approaching biblical studies from a more historicist point of view, Ostriker's *Feminist Revision and the Bible* is an eccentric rereading of the literary connections between biblical texts, Greek mythology, Sigmund Freud, and women's poetry. In her chapter (taken from a lecture) on Freud, Greek mythology, and the image of the "mother/goddess," Ostriker recounts a familiar rendering of monotheism and the problem of patriarchy in Genesis, Exodus, and Freud's *Moses and Monotheism*. Following Gerda Lerner's work, *The Creation of Patriarchy* (1986), Ostriker highlights the liminal figure of the mother in the creation story and the stories of Abraham and Sarah and of Miriam the prophetess. Ostriker asserts that while these women are initially strong figures in the narrative, they are subsumed and displaced either by the offspring they produce or the men they assist. Ostriker's second chapter illuminates the influences of Hebrew and Christian texts on poets as various as Dickenson, Elizabeth Barrett Browning, Christina Rossetti and Hilda Doolittle and the narrative modes these poets adopt or resist. In so doing, Ostriker examines the multiple ways these women carry on biblical paradigms or resist images of women that dominated the culture they inhabited.

It is impossible to give anything but a misleadingly broad summation of such diverse scholarship, but all these studies evidence an increasingly subtle reevaluation of the uses of literature. Especially in the work of Anderson, Simpson, and Warren, there is a new and subtle attention toward the social and political valences of literary texts that resists any fixed orthodoxy. The politics of literature in these studies is not simply subversive, nor is it always read off as inferior to more-polemical rhetorics. Rather, in Anderson's inquiry about the "philosophy" of poetry on the subject of the Victorian prostitute, in Warren's reconsideration of the social agenda implicated in the project of literary realism, and in Simpson's history of English resistances to method, there is evidenced an increasingly flexible notion of the use of literature. Such studies move to historicize reading and writing in a manner that avoids the more schematic New Historicism and yet remains historically sensitive and fair-minded. It is to be hoped that new developments in literary theory will take the complex notions about the function of literature developed in these studies as a standard for further critical endeavor.

The Year in Literary Biography

William Foltz
University of Hawaii

The year 1993 brought literary biographies on a variety of subjects: five poets, Alfred Tennyson, Edgar Allan Poe, John Gray, Delamore Schwartz, John Heath-Stubbs; a dozen novelists, Charlotte Brontë, Robert Louis Stevenson, James Joyce, Richard Aldington, Jean Genet, Anaïs Nin, Ernest Hemingway, Stephen Crane, Antoine de Saint-Exupéry, H. Rider Haggard, Anthony Trollope, William Burroughs; three books of letters, one of Schwartz's and two of Aldington's; and two memoirs, by Heath-Stubbs and by Ved Mehta. Then the books themselves can be ill documented or overdocumented, well or sloppily printed, comprehensive or specialized. Six subjects are Americans, one a Scot, another Irish, the rest English. What have they in common? They were all born after 1800, a merely statistical fact. But many of this year's group have emotional lives that are statistically anomalous, an anomaly they treat with exuberance, denial, or just plain other.

Peter Levi's *Tennyson* (Macmillan), while clearly indebted to the fourteen earlier biographers featured in Levi's four-page "Essential Bibliography," reads smoothly, a smoothness easily achieved by avoiding most essential documentation. After ten pages the reader rarely feels compelled to check the few references there are. But should he indulge his compulsion, he will note the running head to the notes on page 343 drops twelve pages of text; Arthur Hallam's widowed sister becomes the mistress of William Makepeace Thackeray on page 290 but not in the index; and if 1842 was "one of the great moments in the history of English poetry" because Tennyson revised his 1832 volume, where can we locate George Eliot's criticism of these revisions to which Levi refers?

The problem with this opinionated biography is determining its readership; the biographer appears unsure. In the United States one in every ten thousand B.A. degrees is awarded in classics (things are not so desperate in Professor Levi's Oxford). Consequently, when Levi does "suspect the influence of Potter's verse translation of Aeschylus" on Tennyson's juvenile "A thousand brazen chariots rolled over a bridge of brass," the barbarian may miss what I assume is a reference to the chorus of the *Septem* and to Robert Potter's 1777 translation. Then there is the odd bit of overkill. Levi traces the origin of "balm-cricket" ("A Dirge," 1830) from a Scotsman's jumbling of entomology, Homer's *Iliad,* and an oddly paginated school text in his own possession. Though Levi's page reads like a dense reply in *Notes & Queries,* never once does he specify which of the eight occurrences of *tettix* (cicada) in Theocritus's *Idylls* he thinks Tennyson adopted. This sort of seeming but slovenly thoroughness is as out of place in a biography as it is in a review. I have the impression that if the source is within reach, someplace in his rooms or across the hall, Levi will provide it; if not, well. . . .

Fortunately, we now have and Levi has made use of Christopher Ricks's expanded three-volume 1987 edition of Tennyson's poetry, so Levi can rely more fully on the Trinity College manuscripts of *In Memoriam* (1850) and juvenilia; further, the third and final volume of Tennyson's letters appeared in 1990: this too has assisted Levi, but not – I think – radically. Readers are still better off with Robert Bernard Martin's *Tennyson, the Unquiet Heart* (1980), a work Levi praises highly.

But, if Levi's is not a new Tennyson psychologically, perhaps then physiologically. Levi vigorously rejects any suggestion of epilepsy, whether inherited or as the result of masturbation; William James's *Varieties of Religious Experience* (1902) settles the case for Levi. But could James's explanation settle it for Tennyson? Whatever it was that ailed Tennyson, Levi implies that the only writers really taken in by the "philistine quacks" of hydropathy (water treatment) were Tennyson and Thackeray. Hydropathy's severity prevented, Levi argues, the Tennyson of 1844 from writing poetry for the first time in his life. But Edward Bulwer-Lytton wrote the first English testimonial, and Tennyson and Thackeray were joined in hydropathy by George Eliot and G. H. Lewes, Thomas and Jane Carlyle,

Dust jacket for Peter Levi's biography of the Victorian poet who served as England's poet laureate from 1850 until his death in 1892

Thomas Huxley and Charles Darwin. Perhaps something else prevented the thirty-three-year-old from poetry. Bruce Hayley, in *The Healthy Body and Victorian Culture* (1978), argues that the total regimen of hydrotherapy was, in fact, efficacious.

Where Levi's Tennyson differs most from that of earlier and recent scholars concerns that banker's daughter, Rosa Baring. She is read out of his life and his poetry, especially *Maud* (1855), in two of the biographer's most angry pages. In fact, Levi's remarks on *Maud* are the best of his criticism of the poet's longer works. Those on *In Memoriam,* little more than a total of twelve pages, are bettered by his argument (though not a new one) that Tennyson's grief began with the deaths of his father and the brother of James Spedding and his brother Edward's incurable madness and only culminated with Arthur Hallam's death. One chapter reduces the "huge botch" of *The Idylls of the King* (1844–1885) to clever plot summaries interrupted with asides.

Levi prefers the poet's shorter works: juvenilia (good and bad), the locodescriptive, and the topical poem. Levi argues that it is in the "personal poem" such as "In the Garden at Swainton" that Tennyson "labours at his true vocation, and reappears as the kind of poet he most truly was." These three stanzas commemorate the deaths of Hallam, Henry Lushington (his sister Cecilia's husband), and Sir John Simeon. Of the last we learn he was a neighbor, a Catholic convert, an M.P., a liberal, and a gentleman: Levi adds "but for whatever reasons he struck a deep note from the poet" – and stops. Biographers owe us more.

What then does this biography offer? For Tennyson's life we have a good treatment of three decades (the 1840s, 1860s, and 1870s). The density of the poet's literary life and acquaintances in the 1840s helps to establish Levi's picture of a writer not struck dumb by grief; the 1860s and 1870s show us the intellectually active poet and member of the Metaphysical Society, a society that represents "Alfred's greatest contribution to public life." Less successful is Levi's treatment of the aging lion: we are told that "somewhere something broke in him." The last twenty pages of this biography are curiously flat. Levi presents a narrative list of obscure late poems from which he selects the memorable line and provides a brief context.

In addition to being a classicist and preferring the more difficult reading, Levi organizes the poet's life around three adjectives. By the time we get to *In Memoriam,* Ovidian (a dozen references) has been replaced by Virgilian (a dozen and a half) to be succeeded by Horatian (another dozen): three stages of Victorian life. And perhaps it is from Juvenal that the biographer has acquired a fine sense of passionate invective: Christopher Wordsworth, "without charm or talent or learning"; Bulwer-Lytton, a "pretentious charlatan who wrote nothing of merit"; Hallam, whose criticism "reads like a more coherent Leigh Hunt" and whose poetry is "about as good as Moore's, intellectually stronger than Campbell's, and [recalling 'Greenland's icy mountains and Africa's golden shores'] technically at least as able as Bishop Heber's"; John Wilson (Christopher North), the "blackguarding, sneering, and malignant critic" and "true patron on much modern academic criticism" whom even "the scum [Francis] Jeffrey" avoided. All this is refreshingly blunt, but not all is deserved.

But the professor Levi is also a poet – and has a better ear than some biographers. He hears the origins of Tennyson in James Thomson's *The Seasons* (1730), in James Beattie, and echoes in his brother

Charles Tennyson's poetry. He also hears Tennyson's faults: "Ida" and "I die" in "The Death of Demone" do clash, and "hearken ere" is translatorese. The ultimate value of this biography lies more in the author's ability to select, analyze, and praise the older poet's sounds than in relating his life.

Barbara Whitehead, author of *The York Cycle of Mysteries,* historical novelist, and Yorkshire antiquary, has written an interesting study: *Charlotte Brontë and Her 'dearest Nell': The Story of a Friendship* (Smith Settle). The Nell is Ellen Nussey, whose great-grandnephew and dedicatee, John T. M. Nussey, provided Whitehead with masses of family material. Nell (1817–1897) survived Brontë (1816–1855) by more than thirty years, guarded Brontë's letters, and recommended that Elizabeth Gaskell write the famous 1858 biography of Brontë, a biography consulted but not listed in the ill-managed bibliography. The letters which Nussey claimed she entrusted to Thomas J. Wise were sold by that infamous literary forger. He went on to call the by-then-seventy-eight-year-old a mercenary haggler. Whitehead is out to restore Nussey's reputation (though she is not the first) and illumine her friendship with the author of *Shirley* (1849), a novel that changed the gender of a Christian name and whose character Caroline Helstone is modeled by Nussey's claim.

The friendship began in 1831 as the thirteen-year-old Nussey discovers a weeping and prone fourteen-year-old Brontë on the floor of Miss Woolner's school at Roe Head. The future novelist smiles through her tears; the two embrace – at least, as Whitehead points out in a footnote, this reconstruction is more likely than the account Nussey gave forty years later for *Scribner's Monthly* in her "Reminiscences" (but in which issue or on what page of the Brontë Society reprint?). Brontë and Nussey visit back and forth in the 1830s: Nussey's home, Rydings, could well be a model for Jane Eyre's Thornfield; in *Jane Eyre* (1847) the month-long visit of Nussey to Haworth in 1833 is interesting, but it is mostly taken from her "Reminiscences," written thirty-eight years later. I grant Yorkshire is a bit grim, but would Ellen have described the miles of scenery near Haworth as "wild and uncultivated" with "steep declivities" and "terrific hills" if she had not read *Wuthering Heights* (1847)? This is not the sort of question Whitehead asks.

Brontë's letters to Nussey formed the basis of Gaskell's famous biography, and Whitehead quotes copiously from them and goes on to wonder if the relationship was erotic. Citing the hardly disinterested Vita Sackville-West and Virginia Woolf for

the affirmative, the biographer finds no lesbianism in today's terms. But two hundred pages later she claims some unspecified commentators were aware of unacceptable lesbian overtones.

Whatever the basis of the relationship, it was not literary. Nor is this biography. We have excerpts of a letter Nussey wrote to Mary Gorham, their friend from Miss Wooler's school. These excerpts speak about Charlotte's visit to Hathersage, a visit which was to be of "vital importance to in the creation of *Jane Eyre*." But having said this, Whitehead fails to document or date the letter. Is it from the collection at the Brontë Parsonage Museum? I suspect it is from "Reminiscences," but could we not have the page number? Too often too much is undocumented.

Nussey did not know until after Emily Brontë's death that all three sisters had published novels. The quality of friendship then was based on a shared past – their early school years. It had its ups and downs: at times Nussey was "an acceptable companion" (the phrase is Charlotte Brontë's in an undocumented letter of 1847); in 1850, after the deaths of her sisters, Brontë seems to use her as a emotional sounding board, and they visit back and forth. But three years later the novelist changes her focus to her future husband. When Brontë dies in March 1855, Nussey's life changes – and so does this biography. Whitehead's focus is now hers: how to preserve Brontë's memory for the next forty-two years. It was Nussey who encouraged Gaskell and lent her many letters. Since Gaskell, as Whitehead points out, had spent only seventeen days with Brontë in her lifetime, we should consult the biography carefully. But whether we should infer that the Brontë family was normally "deeply happy, even joyful" and that Gaskell's gloomy picture was based on the one visit when, for the first and only time in their marriage, the Rev. and Mrs. Brontë were seriously at odds is at least questionable.

Ten years of Nussey's life after the death of Gaskell in 1861 are compressed into three pages. Whitehead brings her back when Nussey publishes her "Reminiscences" and some of Brontë's letters in *Scribners Magazine* in 1871. She spends much of the rest of her life answering queries about the Brontë country from interested publishers, providing biographical keys to the novels, and planning and then burning the sheets to a private edition of the letters in 1887. Her editor and agent was a local antiquary with the probable name of J. Horsfall Turner: the correspondence between them is controlled by the Brontë Society, but the full correspondence "is not available to the public." Though she may have misunderstood Turner's intent, there is little doubt that Thomas J. Wise cheated her; Whitehead argues convincingly that Nussey thought the £125 he gave her was a thank-you from the nation and continued to view the sum this way up to her death in 1895. It is some consolation that Wise's partner cheated Brontë's husband out of even more documents.

Nussey's brother also figures in many biographies of Brontë. On 5 March 1839 she refused the Reverend Mr. Henry's offer of marriage with a — and these are her italics — *decided negative* — but these words are not cited. Whitehead cites instead her admission that she had "no personal repugnance to the idea of a union with you [Henry]" and then informs us that this means that Brontë "liked him physically well enough to be willing to go to bed with him." Henry had also proposed and been refused twice by Lewis Carroll's aunt four days earlier; the second refusal hit him hard, we are told. His precipitancy in asking was due to the Moravian custom of putting decisions to lot. The traditional identification, first made by Nussey, of Henry with St. John Rivers in *Jane Eyre* is rejected: Brontë, we are told, "no doubt . . . met or heard someone, a clergyman or lecturer, whose character had impressed her — and the memory was at hand when she needed such a person as St. John Rivers." This is special pleading. And we should be glad of her decided negative: Henry married well, his bride objected to Nussey and her dog Flossy, and in two years he resigned his occupation and lived off his wife's fortune for the next thirty. Do we need the details about Nussey's sister-in-law's objection to Flossy?

Often this biography is Nussey family history. And which members of her family does this biography consider? Her grandmother, her grandfather, her mother, her father, her three sisters, her two nephews, her three nieces, her seven brothers, her four sisters-in-law, her cousin, her great-niece, and a distant cousin. Some of the pages of Nussey background are useful, for example, material on the local Moravian churches; other times we get a factoid: her brother, a royal apothecary, helped embalm George IV.

A short title list in Brontë's own handwriting of the books the Brontë sisters owned will be of use to scholars but not some of Whitehead's identification: especially Thomson's *The Seasons*. I have yet to see a school edition of *Wuthering Heights* without a map; Whitehead's colleague J. T. M. Hussey has provided a splendid one for *Shirley*. In fact the maps and the seventy-three illustrations will interest any reader of the Brontës' novels.

Like Brontë, Edgar Allan Poe demands psychological analysis; given the turmoil of his life, few critics can resist the temptation to find psychic trauma in his fiction and then read it back into life. Jeffrey Meyers's *Edgar Allan Poe: His Life and Legacy* (Scribners) is a case in point. The dangers can be seen when we consider the literary gothic. If Poe's fiction reflects the gothicness of his life, what about that of his predecessor Horace Walpole or his successor Flannery O'Connor? Analogies, physical or psychological, are slippery things.

Meyers's analogies are mixed: some work, others wander. To establish Poe's desire for revenge on his literary enemies, he posits that there are five sorts of sherry and that the dryness of amontillado was selected to contrast with Montresor's damp catacombs. This is a peculiarly dense reading. Better, if more obvious, is his analogy that both Fortunato and sherry are "sealed up in a deep cave." That both Fortunato and Virginia Poe cough is probably a coincidence, but that the Freemasons have as many ranks (eleven, Meyers claims) as the first number of brick tiers is interesting but deflates Montresor's joke with his trowel. Montresor's revenge fails. Where then is Poe's?

And when we move to a primarily nonbiographical literary criticism, problems of focus still remain. Meyer's reading of "The Fall of the House of Usher" provides us with Meyers's checklist of Poe's "quintessential elements: gloomy landscape, crumbling mansion, somber interior, sorrowful atmosphere, terrified narrator, neurasthenic hero, tubercular heroine, opium dreams, arcane books, premature burial, oppressive secrets, tempestuous weather, supernatural elements, return from the grave and apocalyptic conclusion." Though some have biographical resonances — Poe's opium and neurasthenia — and another might — his wife's tuberculosis — the rest can be located in the gothic of a novelist such as Ann Radcliffe. Usher did not simply "regretfully exclaim: 'We have put her living in the tomb!,' " he went on and "shrieked . . . 'Madman, I tell you that she now stands without the door!' " The narrator is not merely terrified, he lacks all intuitive truth, a theme as characteristic of Poe as the above fifteen.

Then there are missed opportunities. This is especially and unfortunately true of "Murders in the Rue Morgue" and "The Purloined Letter." The parallels to Poe's life are there: love of books, lack of money, and a fall from gentility. Turning to Poe's essays, and this study consistently makes fine use of the unfamiliar ones, Meyers points to Poe's special fondness for puzzles and enigmas in *Gra-*

ham's Magazine. But if we wish to explore Poe and these stories, a recent critic (Judith Fetterley in *Gender and Reading* [1986]) has suggested that if Dupin has thought like a criminal to find the letter, he has felt like a rapist entering the isolated and virgin house on the Rue Morgue, events which illumine Poe's damaged male psyche. Poe's longest work, *The Narrative of Arthur Gordon Pym* (1838) also needs more thorough treatment.

The notes are clear and often copious: for "The Man That Was Used Up: A Tale of the Late Bugaboo and Kickapoo Campaign" we get the text of Jonathan Swift's "A Beautiful Young Nymph Going to Bed" (but not the promised reference to Juvenal's Sixth Satire) to establish how Swift satirizes women's vanity, but Poe attacks man's barbarity. He then ties the genre to Poe's life. His initial reading of it as an attack on the wounded Gen. Winfield Scott, a relation of his disliked stepfather's second wife, is persuasive. My favorite note is the one which explains the workings of a coffin with a speaking tube and electrical alarm, a coffin which released a flag, and one with an explosive device (to deter grave robbers). But since all were invented thirty years after Poe's death and forty years after "The Premature Burial," they would seem to establish our fear of burial rather than Poe's.

In addition to extra information, Meyers often jogs our memory of Poe's stories (not plots): often we may need it, as in, "Berenice" or "The Man That Was Used Up," but is there any high-school graduate who has not read "The Cask of Amontillado?"

Poe's travels and his search for employment are clearly laid out: Meyers moves him easily from city to city, from the *Southern Literary Messenger* to *Burton's Magazine* to *Graham's Magazine* to the *Broadway Journal* and from drink to binge to poison. Meyers's conclusion is a convincing and terrifying understatement: "Drinking, especially before breakfast, was the principal cause of all Poe's difficulties with his employers." Even the sober Poe ruined himself; his Boston debut was literary suicide. Like Poe, Meyers is good with death: Virginia's makes sad reading; Poe's is that of the "saddest and strangest figure in American literature."

Though Kenneth Silverman's *Edgar A. Poe: Mournful and Never-Ending Remembrance* (1992) remains the standard life, Meyers has usefully examined the less familiar tales. In some ways this work is best on legacy. This is true of the last two chapters, "Reputation" and "Influence," almost fifty carefully informed pages. The extensive bibliography on Poe's influence in literature, art, and music

covers thirty years. Nor should the notes be neglected: for example, the twins Roderick and Madeline Usher are types of the pair in Thomas Mann's "The Blood of the Walsungs" (1905). This biography has value in its compassionate rehearsal of the life, more in its literary criticism – for disagreement sharpens our appreciation – but mostly in its treatment of the afterlife of Poe's works.

There is much to be said for novelists writing biographies: Philip Callow's *From Noon to Starry Night: A Life of Walt Whitman* (Ivan Dee) is another statement in favor of it. In addition to his earlier biographies of the young D. H. Lawrence and Vincent Van Gogh, Callow has published nearly a dozen novels in addition to books of poetry. We get, then, a readable biography in which the poetry illumines the life and the life the poetry. This does not mean Callow neglects earlier studies – though his documentation is rather cavalier: the sparing use of Gay Wilson Allen's *The Solitary Singer* (1967) and Justin Kaplan's more recent *Walt Whitman* (1980) supplements Callow's judicious psychological contentions. D. H. Lawrence's reactions of ninety years ago and Paul Zweig's study from 1984 (*Walt Whitman: The Making of a Poet*) extend but do not dominate this biography's literary criticism. Callow, when necessary, has examined the originals of Mrs. Whitman's correspondence at Duke University and the poet's notebook and other manuscripts at the Library of Congress; but most material, as we might expect, has already been published. Though the biography neither reveals nor argues for any radical interpretation of the poet, his times, or his writing, this biography's literary competence will recommend it to all readers.

The crux of Whitman's life remains, as Callow reminds us, that half decade before the first publication of *Leaves of Grass* in 1855, a period of a "maddening retreat into himself." What he was earlier, the schoolboy embraced by Marquis de Lafayette who became an editor or contributor to nine different newspapers, changed to "the first genuine voice of a nation-to-be," from inchoate fop to open collar, from Brooklynite to American, from the Democratic Tammany hack to democrat, in politics, in diction, in enthusiasm. The too-brief seventh chapter explains this transformation, as much as it can, for, as Callow admits in his foreword, "some essential darkness is missing," an admission which defines without limiting this biography.

Whitman's sexual tension, one of chaste and delicate torment, is explored in the "Calamus Poems," but Callow shies away from an excessively autobiographical reading to consider the poems as

Anthony Trollope

Victoria Glendinning

Dust jacket for Victoria Glendinning's study of the Victorian novelist and the effects of his family on his work

fleshy and mystical" and more astutely "buffalo and hermit thrush, man and woman."

Victoria Glendinning's *Anthony Trollope* (Knopf) is not a life and intellectual times, the focus of Prof. N. John Hall's splendid *Trollope* (1992), but a life and family. This work immediately replaces *The Trollopes: The Chronicle of a Writing Family,* by L. P. and R. P. Stebbins (1946). The last fifteen years have seen not only two biographies of Fanny Trollope, the novelist's mother, but two ably edited volumes of her son's letters. Consequently, though this work does draw from some additional private letters, perhaps 90 percent of Glendinning's biography comes from printed sources. The avoidance of the intellectual milieu usually works to this biography's advantage; specialized knowledge is kept to notes, placed where they belong: at the bottom of the page. Citations are generally by title alone.

The writer's residence in Ireland and her earlier biography *Elizabeth Bowen: Portrait of a Writer* (1978) have provided her with considerable information about Trollope in Ireland – but so did James Pope Hennessy's *Anthony Trollope* (1971). At times the Irish information is as simple as that. But more often she includes information one can acquire only through residence or connections, those gossipy bits that illumine, such as, if Trollope's neighbor was the elder sister of Kitty O'Shea, would he then object to his brother's marriage to Frances Ternan, the sister of Dickens's mistress? and Alfred Austin, who befriended Thomas Trollope's stepdaughter, probably knew of Anthony's obscurity in Ireland because Austin's wife's family home was only fifteen miles from Banagher, where Trollope lived.

Glendinning's general plan is to begin with Anthony's mother's *Domestic Manners of the Americans* (1832) and the memoirs of his eldest brother, Thomas Adolphus, *What I Remember* (1887), and fit Anthony in. When she runs out of material from Mrs. Trollope and Adolphus, she takes up Anthony's posthumously published *Autobiography* as a guide, moves back to his earlier travel writings, and when those will not fill in her subject's emotional or psychological interior (for neither was designed to), she has recourse to his novels. Glendinning's use of the novels is perceptive. She hints at her method in a slightly opaque discussion of Marcel Proust two-thirds through her book. Trollope, she argues, the unhappy, insecure, and financially impoverished child, lived on in his works, but as a man he also worked in the post office. Often this works well: especially if we assume, as the biographer invariably does, that narrator and author are the same. So to establish his views on false hair, we have his letters,

poems. Whitman's love for Peter Doyle, a young streetcar conductor whose coded name figures in the notebook, was more likely paternal affection than pederastic. And Callow's subject, as the title of this biography hints, is not Whitman in the glare of the sun, but illuminated by the starry night.

If Callow cannot clear the poets's dark silence, his readings of the poems make much gracefully clear. Much poetry is cited, but never gratuitously. The Manhattan of the poetry is imaginatively explained by Charles Dickens's *Martin Chuzzlewit* (1844); Whitman's "When Lilacs Last in the Dooryard Bloom'd"; by D. H. Lawrence; by the ornithological interests of John Burroughs; and by *Leaves of Grass,* the poem which reconciles Whitman's two great obsessions, doubleness and death. Whitman saw himself as containing multitudes, multitudes this biographer defines as "coarse and delicate, solitary and democratic, radical and conservative, citations to seven novels, a plate from a fashion book, and her analysis of the chignon as hallucinatory incubus. Beginning with the drains of his father-in-law's house, Glendinning uses five novels over a fifteen-year period to establish the novelist's judgment on female cleanliness. There are another 107 "Interests and Opinions" listed in the index. Yet the overlap of narrator and author is not always that clear. If in 1878 Trollope broods about his own death and inheritance in *Cousin Henry*, what was he brooding about when he wrote of codicils in his 1866 *The Belton Estate* or seven years later when he took legal council about heirlooms for *The Eustace Diamonds*?

It is not until two hundred pages of the five hundred are past that Glendinning begins to separate Trollope from his family: the events are his marriage and his first successful novel, *The Warden* (1855). But even so, we are never far from the Villino Trollope, where Thomas Adolphus and his mother entertain every literate Anglophone who passed through Florence for thirty years.

In many ways this is really a family biography: both Anthony's mother, Frances, and his wife, Rose, get a full column in the index, though his mother receives more pages. Even his brother Thomas Adolphus gets equal treatment with Rose. Glendinning, as all earlier biographers, is at a loss with Rose: she was not a novelist and her surviving letters are business-like. What happens then is the introduction of supplementary material: three pages on her father's bank defalcations marginally linked to two speculators, Lopez in *The Prime Minister* (1876) and Melmotte in *The Way We Live Now* (1875), and then to unhinged older men in three other novels. That Rose did not visit the irregular household of George Eliot and G. H. Lewes does not make her a member of "the moral majority"; true, Thomas Trollope and his wife Theodosia received them in Florence, but Theodosia was Anglo-Indian, Jewish, and probably illegitimate. We read that Rose "was upset, and had her ample say about it [Anthony's infatuation with the young American Kate Field] in the privacy of the bedroom, in her deflationary north-county way," only to be told at the bottom of the page, "I cannot prove that he told her, nor that she reacted as I say, but I am sure of it." The biographical has become the novelistic. Worse, a photograph of Rose shows a strong jaw but reminds the biographer of "a nice heifer." In any event, "whatever the strains, Rose was lucky" even though the biographer intimates that so much of her husband's energy (including sexual energy) was "expended in writing fiction that there had never

been enough left over for Rose." Perhaps if Rose had been a novelist she would be accorded more sympathy.

The subject of this book also receives some unfounded speculations which are then qualified in a footnote: Trollope's fantasy is that passionate women such as Lady Laura Kennedy would prefer being beaten to no sex or bad sex but "One could make too much of this." In Trollope's "A Ride Across Palestine" the narrator denies his marriage and "(Did Anthony sometimes do that too? Probably.)". If Trollope's friend Thackeray did rhyme "boobies" with "pubis," it does not imply that Trollope lived somehow in the "lust and risk of the night streets." Worse, for Trollope to write is to masturbate (in this the biographer coyly follows the lead of a Derrida clone in a footnote). Later, having suggested that a few novels depict incest, Glendinning stops short and suggests we "take note, and wonder." She also speculates that Trollope's constant separation from his wife was a reenaction of the separation patterns of his youth – perhaps. But Trollope was a postal inspector, and postal inspectors will travel. If we must read all this, why can we not learn with whom Kate Field, his brother's friend, had a long, unsatisfactory love affair in Florence?

The book has an admirable index not only of topics and novels, but of more than two hundred characters: this allows to reader to locate Bishop Proudie's possible originals even though the title of the novels in which he appears may not be in the text. The few typos, a "forebear" of Thackeray and the loss of a Roman capital turning the reactionary Louis XVIII into his melancholy ancestor, are compensated by more than fifty illustrations. R. H. Super's *Trollope in the Post Office* (1981) and Hall's recent biography have given us much of the vocational, social, and intellectual background of the novelist. Glendinning has filled in much of her subject's interior life, perhaps too much.

The pattern that Ian Bell has produced for Robert Louis Stevenson in *Dreams of Exile* (Holt) is melodramatic: success followed by disaster. Bell's announced focus is on his illness, his Scotland, and his travels, the three factors that formed Stevenson, or Louis, as Bell calls him – and once Louise. The largest topic in the index can be formed by combining "ill health" with "as invalid"; in fact, much of the second half of this biography is the dying Stevenson. It comes as a surprise that Stevenson composed his epithet, "Home is the sailor, home from the sea, / And the hunter home from the hill," not as he died in Samoa in 1894, but on Hyères off the

Riviera coast ten years earlier. The final disposition of his body is ironic. Stevenson, whose announced agnosticism and irregular marriage affronted his tolerant parents, may have his burial site turned into a Mormon tourist attraction.

And for a biography so concerned – and rightly so – with the body of the writer, where are the photographs? Where is one of the two Sargeant portraits of 1884 and 1885, when the writer was thirty-five. Are no pictures of his wife capable of being reproduced?

Bell's regard for Stevenson's body extends to his sex life but not his wife, Fanny. Following the lead of J. C. Furnas' *Voyage to Windward* (1952), Bell shows us that the young Stevenson, though a lazy student in college, was no fornicating Bobby Burns. (In fact, Stevenson condemned the poet in 1879.) There may have been an "enterprising whore" who attempted blackmail, but at most he was "debauched on a part-time basis," a phrase more amusing than actually revealing. The key to Stevenson's sexuality was his deep and basic response to older women, love, or – when that was impossible – adoration. Though this seems to start with his horrid and horrifying nurse, it first approaches passion with Mrs. Sitwell, the intelligent friend of Sidney Colvin, the Slade Professor at Cambridge: Mrs. Sitwell was sympathetic; Stevenson was twenty-two. A near consummation with the sister of a Georgian princess in France was as confused as "The Eastern Question," Stevenson's phrase for the relationship. Bell's reading of this character trait of Stevenson is fair, sympathetic, and succinctly perceptive. But as to his wife, though she loved him as Bell admits some pages after she entered the text, she is the "most difficult of women to explain." Bell's explanations may not convince all, though a marriage between a forty-year-old and a thirty-year-old is anomalous.

Bell argues and establishes that the events of her busy life (a disastrous early marriage, a vile husband, the death of one child, financial worries) made her impressionable and overwrought. But his speculation that she felt that her flight to Europe resulted in that child's death is unsupported by any evidence. When Stevenson first met her, she was "free (up to a point), pretty, exotic, and American to boot." It is easy to dislike Fanny Stevenson for her later actions, and Bell's lengthy exposure of her vanity and selfishness is tempered with remarks on her suffering. But Stevenson must have seen more, a more which may be unrecoverable now; she was not what Henry Adams called her in Samoa, an "Apache squaw."

Though Bell may not like the other side of the Atlantic, he has Scotland and the South Pacific down cold. Bell is a Scot, not fanatically so – like those who, recently remembering that the Tudor monarch was not theirs, sued to remove II from the present queen's coins – but he is enough of one to keep King James a VI not a I. This interest pays off well in those sections, a good fifty pages, which place Stevenson in Edinburgh's New Town, whose brand of Presbyterianism, politics, intellectual life, and even vile climate differs from the Old Town. Useful as it is to learn that Edinburgh is at 55° 57' 23", a city map would be better. Bell, like Stevenson, takes us through the now sadly altered French countryside of Cévennes in *Travels with a Donkey* (1878).

It is in the South Pacific that this biography comes alive again – as Stevenson thought he would. His defense of Father Damien's work at the leper colony at Kaulapapa (not Kaulapepa) on Molokai led to one of the most "delicate, penetrating, and vicious pieces of invective in the language" against a Protestant missionary. Equally acute is Stevenson's picture of Samoa: westernized high chiefs drunk in paradise. It may be special pleading, and there would be lots of blanks spaces, but few readers can locate Apia: we could use a map of the South Pacific.

Bell's defense of Stevenson's hatred of colonialism, should it need one, extends to his subject's fiction. The autobiographical resonances of *Treasure Island* (1883) and *The Master of Ballantrae* (1889) are clarified. Bell shows us a critic superior to Walter Besant, but to argue he was the equal of Henry James is overconfident. Bell's literary approach to Stevenson's fellow writers Edmund Gosse, W. E. Henley, and George Meredith is breezy, passionate, and provoking. But I am not sure why a prideful admission to being a journalist should be heard as exculpation for providing little documentation: Bell's citations are to title only; further, his sources are not immediately qualified: after two important citations from Stevenson's sister-in-law, we learn twenty pages later that she was an "adoring biographer." But this is a sympathetic biography whose quickness and narrative ease more than balance the occasional hurried judgment.

Jerusha Hull McCormack's *John Gray: Poet, Dandy, and Priest* (Brandeis University Press) fully investigates John Gray (1866–1934), a minor poet of the decadent movement. Gray's fame can be dated from October 1890, when he became a Roman Catholic, to the end of May 1895, when he waited in Brussels to learn whether Oscar Wilde, his recent lover (or was he?), was about to be found guilty. Their mutual hairdresser wires the verdict. This brief span is admittedly longer than our century's fifteen minutes, but can 250 pages cover it? Yes, as McCormack demonstrates, but only by including extensive literary analysis. In fact, her chapter on Gray's *Silverpoints* (1893) illustrates that decade better than many standard literary histories. She also includes rather torturous psychological analysis.

McCormack builds on her 1973 dissertation, and, despite some repetition, this most thorough study reads well: the bibliographies of Gray's works and works about him are meticulous, her notes clear. There are two things it lacks: some reproductions of *Silverpoints* and, since her title promises a dandy, his clothes. Gray asks in a letter if a top hat is worn to a duel in France, but we never learn if he wore the notorious green carnation. But McCormack has interviewed the survivors and located the letters from Texas to London to France. Her investigation of the inchoate Gray Archives of the Dominican Chaplaincy in Edinburgh, where the poet died a canon of the Diocese of Saint Andrews, was especially valuable.

The poet's life in brief: born into the working class, a self-educated minor civil servant, the beautiful John Gray falls into a "hyperthyroid" Arts and Crafts community, becomes a Roman Catholic, and falls into a "course of sin"; meets Wilde in 1888 and posed as or was the model for Dorian Gray, lectures on art, and publishes poetry in 1893; breaks from Wilde, takes up with André Raffalovich, a Jewish Ukranian who becomes a Roman Catholic around Aubrey Beardsley's deathbed on 11 March 1898; the death of the illustrator and conversion of the Uranian pushes Gray to Rome that same year, where on 28 October he enters the Scots College. Two years later he emerges, priested, and is assigned to Edinburgh, where Raffalovich, now a spiritual colleague, joins him. Father Gray dies in 1934 austere, sedate, and formal.

McCormack argues that "the tragedy of Gray's early manhood" was his adopting the persona of *Dorian Gray,* that is, by sexual posing this working-class boy gained entrée to literary and social circles such as the Rhymers' Club of William Butler Yeats, Ernest Dowson, Walter Pater, Arthur Symons, and Lionel Johnson and the Independent Theatre of Jack Grein, which produced Henrik Ibsen's *A Doll's House* in 1892, attracted Bernard Shaw, and staged Gray's translation of Théodore de Banville's *Le Baiser.* When it comes to the author of *The Picture of Dorian Gray,* the dates and texts Mc-

Cormack supplies would seem to go against her argument that whether Gray was Wilde's lover is less important and cannot really be determined. Her argument that there was nothing between Gray and Pierre Louÿs is more convincing. But surely the initial toilette scene in Louÿs's *Aphrodite* (1898) between Djala and Crysis owes something to Gray's 1892 "The Barber," the most notorious poem of *Silverpoints.* Even the shape of *Silverpoints* is weird: about 4 inches by 8 1/2 inches, it is odd to the hand, the thin column of italics odd to the eye, and when "breasts rose up and offered each a mouth, / And on the belly pallid blushes crept," the modern reader may laugh and weep as the poem's persona did, though perhaps for different reasons. Though Gray's own poetry may be an acquired taste ("pastiche as a literary form" is the author's severest judgment) McCormack's argument that Gray's translations of Baudelaire, Verlaine, Mallarmé, and Rimbaud helped Pound and Eliot "make it new" is impressive. Almost as convincing is her use of Gray's recently published (1958) short story "The Person in Question" to illustrate how the potential schizophrenia of John Gray posing as *Dorian Gray* resolved itself as Gray separated from the increasingly flamboyant Wilde and joined Raffalovich. By 1894 Gray is a new man – but a worse poet. McCormack provides us with useful extracts of the poet's later etiolated trash.

The last hundred pages or so of this biography treat "The Poet as Priest" and then "The Priest as Poet" (the biographer's chapter titles). With Raffalovich's money he builds Saint Peter's church, still a most fashionable parish in Edinburgh, and offers prayers every January for the soul of Verlaine. But he kept in touch with the London literary world of the next generation: John Masefield and A. J. A. Symonds (both of whom wished to republish poems from *Silverpoints*), Laurence Housman, Lady Gregory, T. Sturge Moore, Roger Fry, Herbert Read, and Graham Greene, who put Raffalovich into *Stamboul Train* (1932). Gray also seems to be responsible for Katherine Bradley ("Michael") turning to God and the Roman Catholic church. Katherine Bradley was the aunt of Edith Cooper ("Field"): they wrote jointly as "Michael Field," and they were famous (Robert Browning praised their works). "Michael" relates in a letter to Gray the sacrificial death of her beloved chow (of which we have a picture); unless I misread her letter, it looks like she thinks the dog becomes apotheosized. That Father Gray restored her to sanity was no mean feat. The eighteen illustrations

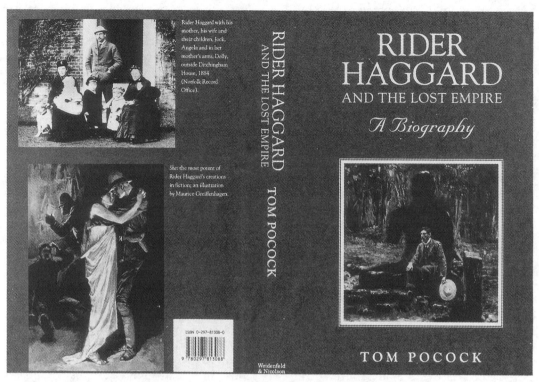

Dust jacket for Tom Pocock's biography of the late-nineteenth-century adventure and romance novelist who was a defender of what he saw as Great Britain's imperial responsibilities

show us the chow, the church Gray erected, and his change from Dorian to a balding yet handsome Dominican.

Tom Pocock, a retired war correspondent and biographer of early-nineteenth-century figures such as Horatio Nelson and William IV, has written a serviceable life which is fairly light on literary analysis in *Rider Haggard and the Lost Empire* (Weidenfeld and Nicolson). Pocock sticks closely to his original and primary sources: H. Rider Haggard's autobiography, *The Days of My Life* (1926), which goes as far as 1912; his written-for-the-public diary, published in 1980, which goes to the year before his death; letters still in private hands; and the Theodore Roosevelt material in the Library of Congress. Since 1960 there have been six biographies or studies of Haggard; Pocock cites them to supplement his material and to provide an occasional literary comment. This is a wise course for a writer whose infamous *She* (1887) is not only the bane of Horace Rumpole but drove V. S. Pritchett to conclude when he reviewed Morton Cohen's 1960 biography that "the author of *She* sent a suction pump" into the unconscious "and drained the whole reservoir of the public's secret desires."

Ten years earlier than John Gray but a half century earlier in manners, Haggard (1856–1925) was born in Norfolk, not a dandy but a squire. One photograph shows him in front of his Norfolk estate, Ditchingham Hall, and actually wearing a Norfolk jacket. Haggard wrote almost sixty novels, but only his early stuff is still in print and read: *King Solomon's Mines* (1885), *She,* and *Alan Quartermain* (both 1887). The other novels, which Pocock justifiably slights, run from Pharaonic Egypt to berserker Iceland. Haggard had twenty-eight films to his credit – but died worth only about $2.8 million in today's money; Indiana Jones, Alan Quartermain's successor, has beat that figure.

Haggard's life and opinions are not as exceptional as his fiction. He is extraordinarily more representative of the last twenty-five years of the nineteenth century than Gray. The younger son of a settled Norfolk family, a heartbroken Haggard begins a four-year appointment as a civil servant in the Transvaal in 1875; the next year he begins his writing career with articles on the dance of the Zulu warrior and the stink of the Boer farmer. He returns to England and makes a satisfactory marriage to a neighboring landed heiress who was also a ward in Chancery. But all the while he remembers his first love, Lily. Twenty years later, after her husband had absconded to Africa with her money, Rider found a house on the coast of Suffolk for her, her children, and even her sisters. Lily then rejoined her husband. Ten years later she returned to the same Suffolk house a dying widow; Haggard "came to her aid, but it could only be financial for her condition was incurable": her husband had given her syphilis. Pocock has found a picture of Lily, but neither the picture of this middle-aged woman nor Pocock's sympathy for Rider's belief in immortal love can quite explain his actions – or even his wife's understanding. It is as though Haggard had lived one of his own novels (suitably sanitized) before he wrote it.

After a trip back to Africa with his bride, Haggard returns to London in 1881, writes his first book on the Zulu king, *Cetewayo and his White Neighbors* (1882), writes two financially unsuccessful novels, despairs, and becomes a lawyer. Then, having bet his brother he could write a better novel than the current best-seller, *Treasure Island,* he began to write. Six weeks later, in September of 1885, the Conference of Berlin ended: Leopold had won the Congo – and Haggard his fame with *King Solomon's Mines.* Ten weeks later he finished *Alan Quartermain* (which he profitably serialized) gave up the law, took the name of the doll with which a nursemaid threatened him, and finished *She* in 1887. Though Pocock argues that it is not until 1909, when his beloved Lily died, that Haggard's fiction began to suffer, most date his decline from 1887, the year of *She* and $150,000 in royalties. After the three novels, it is all downhill; the best we can hope for is what Pocock calls the "lightly draped eroticism" of the sleeping queen in *Cleopatra,* which judging from the paragraph he quotes sounds like a tasteful write-up of a wet-T-shirt contest.

But Haggard continues, as does the concluding two-thirds of this biography. He takes three visits to Egypt; on the last he renews his acquaintance with Howard Carter, whom he met twenty years earlier and who just had discovered King Tutankhamen's tomb; there is a splendid picture of Haggard at rest in the Hall of Osiris. He enters London's literary life; joining the Savile Club, he meets Henry James, H. G. Wells, Max Beerbohm, and Thomas Hardy. Not surprisingly, Kipling remains a lifelong friend: they even share the same study, plots, and, tragically, the deaths of their only sons. Kipling supplied the names for *Red Eve,* a novel of the black plague set on the same coast where Lily died of syphilis two years earlier. Haggard's entry into politics was unsuccessful. He had more success recommending marram grass as a member of the Royal Commission on Coast Erosion than recommending immigration as a member of a Royal Commission on the Colonies. In America in 1905, on a tour of inspection of Salvation Army work camps, he describes "nightfall on the Texas veldt" and dines with Theodore Roosevelt at the White House. He was knighted in 1911 (Kipling said he should accept the honor). After the U.S. entry in World War I Haggard was asked to open a secret correspondence with Roosevelt on America's plans. At the war's end he proposed settling the British veterans in the colonies, especially in Australia to counteract "fifty years hence the countless yellow races, armed to the teeth" (he had also warned of German invasions). He died a late Victorian in 1925.

Given the variety – and inconsistency – of Haggard's views, the index could have used a list of topics. Punctuation is mysterious, and documentation a bit shaky. This is a minor matter when Pocock cites Morton Cohen's *Rider Haggard: His Life and Works* (1960) on Haggard's sympathy for the oppressed Zulus, but Pocock could better defend his subject from those florid accusations of anti-Semitism which Wendy R. Katz makes in her 1987 *Rider Haggard and the Fiction of Empire* if he had told us exactly what Katz was citing. Also, most of the favorable reviews Pocock cites are taken from Haggard's autobiography; the small selections we get of the unfavorable reviews are not from the journals but from D. S. Higgins's *Rider Haggard: The Great Storyteller* (1981). Pocock has written a thoughtful and tempered biography.

If Haggard's travels inform his fiction, the reverse is true of Stephen Crane, who lives in high-school anthologies – at least *The Red Badge of Courage* (1895) does. But the author himself died terribly young – not quite twenty-nine in June of 1900 – trying to repeat his fame. This is not a long life, but Christopher Benfey's *The Double Life of Stephen Crane* (Knopf) provides the first major look at Crane since R. W. Stallman's *Stephen Crane: A Biography* (1968). The problems of a biography of Crane are manifold. First, Thomas Beer's *Stephen Crane* (1923) is a fraud. And since material on Crane's early life is more than sparse, Benfey is forced to take the little he can. At once point he is forced to reading squiggles in Crane's sister's laconic diary. The recent two-volume edition of the Correspondence, family papers at Syracuse University, his companion's notebook at Columbia University, and material from Stallman's biography provide most of Benfey's sources.

But often Benfey questions his sources: Willa Cather's memoir was occasioned by Crane's death and her Poe fixation; the "euphemistic haze" surrounding his early death clouds the memories of

Dust jacket for Chrisopher Benfey's biography that chronicles the attempts of the novelist and short-story writer to live the experiences contained in his fiction

Joseph Conrad, H. G. Wells, and even Henry James. Benfey, in his pursuit for the untainted source, also excludes much. And this leaves the works. This biography's simultaneous assumption and conclusion is that "Crane lived his life backwards, or rather he wrote it forward" or, if this is cryptic, Crane "tried to live what he had already written." Having written *Maggie: A Girl of the Streets* (1893), he fell in love and lived with a whore; having written *The Red Badge of Courage,* off he went to Greece and Cuba; about to write "The Open Boat," "he managed to find himself aboard a foundering steamer." The first two would seem to involve his will, the last, chance ("managed to find himself"). And this is the problem and the interest of this biography. How much did Crane actually will; what could he choose? As professors of economics are appointed to government posts, why should not a William Randolph Hearst impressed by a war book send the writer to cover a war? What Benfey sees as choice may in this case be the market at work. And the market worked well for Richard Harding Davis in the two wars both he and Crane covered. Davis made one thousand dollars a week. But we never learn what Hearst's *Journal* paid Crane. Benfey wishes to see how the "work of art shaped the writer's life," for

"what solidity, and givenness, there is in a writer's life exists first in the writings." There is probably something in this, but Benfey is more clever than convincing. Would Homer have enlisted? And on which side?

This biography has much that is new and moves us toward an clearer understanding of Crane. His father, a Methodist minister, was also a rebel; he fought the Holiness movement, lost, and lost his position in his church. His mother died mentally ill. Crane's usually neglected stories about babies may serve to link *Maggie* with *The Red Badge of Courage.* But the chronology is obscure: Crane published *Maggie* in January 1893, in the spring of which year, Benfey tells us, he started writing the baby stories. Benfey's argument that Crane's awareness of the human body's mortality invests all his works is convincing – and leads to a rereading of Henry Fleming's coming-of-age in *The Red Badge of Courage.* His connecting the Arts and Crafts movement with Crane's poetry is persuasive – more persuasive, since he speaks of Crane's typography – would be one of twenty-six illustrations devoted to the printed page: *The Black Rider* (1895) in Benfey's text looks like a caps lock.

Benfey sees the "halting and elliptical" conversations of the characters in Crane's still-obscure *The*

Third Violet (1897) as establishing and predicting "the terms of Crane's own sexual proclivities and activities": that Crane, having written the novel, was about to be torn between the ideal and the sexual, the upper-class Nellie Crouse of Akron and Dora Clark of street fame. The tenuousness of this argument is atoned for by Benfey's admission that Crane, if he could not report the news, went out to make it: Crane's "gallantry" in defending this hooker was a setup from the beginning. Having gone for the sexual for copy, Crane went for his final companion, the keeper of the Hotel de Dream in Jacksonville. But we learn little about her, aside from her ancestry (not quite Mayflower though John Greenleaf Whittier was some connection), her extravagance (which Crane shared), and that she was "a woman at home in her skin, as the French say." Richard Harding Davis's comment on her during the Greek war, which Benfey quotes, emphasizes her Maggieness: a "bi-roxide blond" in charge of his luggage.

The biographer's selections of Crane's war dispatches from Greece and later Cuba convinces us that Crane wrote well and wrote compassionately. The same is true of the selections from "The Open Boat." Less convincing is the assumption that Crane actually trained for shipwreck.

The year 1992 marked the one hundredth anniversary of another traveler's birth, that of Richard Aldington, who with his wife Hilda Doolittle (H. D.) and Ezra Pound began the imagist movement shortly before World War I. For the next half century he wrote essays and novels; translated Greek, Latin, and French; reviewed French literature for the *Times Literary Supplement* (*TLS*); and knew everybody. Perhaps the closest most readers have been with him was in *The Viking Book of Poetry of the English-Speaking World* (1941) and in his translation (1956) of the *Larousse Encyclopedia of Mythology*. More recently he lives in his former wife's reflected glory.

In 1993 two selections of Aldington's letters appeared. Norman T. Gates's *Richard Aldington: An Autobiography in Letter* (Pennsylvania State University Press) and Caroline Zilboorg's *Richard Aldington and H. D.: The Early Years in Letters* (Indiana University Press). Gates, whose previous scholarship includes the major study of Aldington's poetry and a checklist of his letters, presents a series of three-page introductions to letters he groups chronologically and thematically; for example, "Screenwriter-Biographer: 1939–1946" contains twenty-five letters as do the other four groups with the exception of the last from 1947 to 1962, which has fifty. Given the immense amount of surviving letters, perhaps ten thousand, this is the most effective way to introduce the 154 he chose. Among the nineteen more memorable addressees are Ezra Pound, T. S. Eliot, James Joyce, Amy Lowell, and Harold Munro. Gates's enlarged selection presents the man of letters of the *Egoist* and *Criterion,* the commentator on America (especially Hollywood), and a garrulous, emotionally confused, but honest man.

Zilboorg, the author of numerous articles on the poetry of H. D. and Aldington and on imagism, offers a close and at times myopic view. Her task was both easier and more complex. Easier, since Aldington destroyed both his and H. D.'s letters from 1916 and 1917, Zilboorg has only 92 letters, all the surviving letters of Aldington to H. D. from 19 April 1918 to 17 April 1919. We expect – and get – a thorough fifty-page analysis and commentary. This commentary focuses as much on H. D. as Aldington. H. D.'s sexual initiation and sexual preferences are treated fairly. (Aldington once dispassionately observed that both his wives went to be with other women; he also dispassionately analyzed sexuality in general and for paragraph after paragraph.) Gates has added 14 more letters to H. D. after 1919: 5 from the 1930s, 7 from the 1940s, and 2 from the 1950s. Of the surviving 1200 to H. D., we have then a total of 105 between Zilboorg and Gates.

Born of a lawyer and a novel-writing mother, Aldington grew up in outer London, lost his place at University College when his father's practice failed, moved down Gower to Bloomsbury, sold several poems, and by twenty had begun his literary career. In the same year, 1912, at the home of Coventry Patmore's grandson with whose wife he had a brief affair, he met Ford Madox Ford, Harold Munro, Yeats, H. D., and Pound. H. D., who had come close to being Pound's mistress, became his wife in 1913. They separated after the war (1919) after he had taken up with their mutual friend, "Arabella" Yorke, with whom he generally lived until 1928. He then took up with Bridgit Patmore (the wife of the grandson above), left her for her son's wife Netta in 1937, and eventually married her. The confusing summary of his interior life includes a wife, a mistress, another mistress, and a mistress he married.

It is when Aldington separates from H. D. that Zilboorg's account closes. Zilboorg ends her selection with two appendixes, one biographical (twenty-three people who figure heavily in the letters) and the other periodical (five which published Aldington and H. D.). And each letter ends with thorough, perhaps overly thorough, annotation: two inches of comment for every three of text (Gates's proportion is one to six). What causes this inflation? Some is due to helping the Frenchless reader (though I do not believe "to crush the infamous" is the best translation of *pour écraser l'infâme*), some to linking the authors' experience to their fiction. Some is due to identifying anyone who is glanced at (living or dead or literary); these notes are accurate if not concise. Her annotations to Aldington's scheme for a Poets' Translation Series are admirable, her understanding of the military folly of World War I is balanced. (But Wellington defeats Napoleon ten years too early in her allusion to the Napoleonic Wars.) Much inflation is due to an acute if labored analysis of their troubled relationship. Zilboorg makes cogent use of their fiction and H. D.'s unpublished diaries and letters (especially those to Amy Lowell) but feels obligated to include copious excerpts from Aldington's poetry. This makes his poetry more available. But it is terrible stuff: slippery Hellenism and bad D. H. Lawrence. The later and resumed correspondence between H. D. and Aldington (by the late 1930s they wrote twice a week) is ignored.

From almost the same period (1912–1918) Gates has selected twenty-four letters to four other correspondents. From the war's end we must rely on Gates's selection. Trench warfare does little for a marriage, so his separation from H. D. was expected, but 1915–1917 saw further poems of Aldington along with his colleagues Amy Lowell and Lawrence. The novels he later wrote from his war experiences, *Death of a Hero* (1929) and *All Men Are Enemies* (1930) are sometimes reprinted. In 1919 Aldington places poems and articles in many journals: more importantly he becomes the main reviewer of French literature for the *TLS*, publishes more studies, starts a translation series, meets T. S. Eliot, revisits Italy and D. H. Lawrence, suggests that one way to end the Freida Lawrence imbroglio is to throw her in the Arno, leaves England in 1928, and takes up with Brigit Patmore for the next eight years or so.

Now living in France, by 1934 he has written four novels, a translation of Euripides' *Alcestis,* more articles, and a long poem before he leaves to spend three months in Tobago. He returns to Europe in 1937, separates from Brigit, and takes up with her daughter-in-law, whom he marries eleven days before she gives birth to their daughter Catherine in 1938. And somehow the thirty letters Gates presents cover all this travel and turmoil.

The next selection of more than twenty letters covers the war years. He and his new family leave for New York, where he publishes his memories (*Life for Life's Sake,* 1941), the Viking anthology, and a biography of Voltaire. He serves as a coast watcher in Florida, where he writes biographies, and moves to Hollywood in September of 1942. After three and one-half years, he had no luck with any script but wrote and translated.

In 1947 he is back in Paris working on a biography still important for its honesty, *D. H. Lawrence: Portrait of a Genius, But* . . . (1950); edits an edition of Jane Austen; and publishes his *Collected Poems* in 1948. By 1950 his wife removes permanently to England, leaving him to raise their daughter. Aldington's letters express neither grief nor anger, but an almost querulous bewilderment. He is more put out by the public's reaction to his two biographies: *Pinorman* (1952), his biography of Norman Douglas ("I admire a great artist more than a great bugger"), and his *Lawrence of Arabia* (1955). The cult of T. E. Lawrence protested so vigorously that publishers became wary of republishing Aldington's earlier books. Many of the fifty letters in this concluding sections of Gates's book deal with financial problems: royalties for the D. H. Lawrence book are put in trust for his daughter; the Patmores, mother and son-in-law, want money. He is befriended and supported by the Australian poet Alistair Kershaw, his secretary and literary executor. Gates prints Kershaw's 1987 tribute to Aldington, a man dead twenty-five years who still can "infuriate literary 'schools.'" The royalties from his 1930 novel, *All Men Are Enemies,* in an edition of 225,000 in the Soviet Union, helped him celebrate his seventieth birthday in Moscow. He died back in France on 27 July 1962, three months after the death of H. D.

Gates has given us a larger Aldington and a larger book. His publishers have supplied an errata slip which, though it lists eight glitches, missed the big one: page 60 with twenty-four footnotes has vanished. The author's seventy-page annotated index provides succinct biographies. But, with the exception of the person addressed, no one after page 153 or so seems to be in the index. This valuable book needs a corrected impression.

James Joyce has found another Bolandist, not a Jesuit and not in Belgium, but in Dublin. Peter Costello's *James Joyce: The Years of Growth* (Pantheon) profiles not only the novelist but also his often unholy family. In fact, there are more than 150 index entries for Joyces, with James getting almost sixty, his father thirty-eight, his brother almost thirty; the family household and his wife both get about twenty. This gives a good idea of the focus of the biography, which though it treats Joyce in Paris, Trieste, and Rome, is best with Dublin, a Dublin from the middle to the end of the nineteenth century. Special pleading is rare; the best — or worst — example may be his insistence that Joyce's wildly sexual letters of 1909 are not typical but merely the unhappiness of an ill, undernourished, and impoverished man. Or perhaps it is that "But for Nora, Joyce would have become just another drunken failed poet, of which Dublin at any time has an abundant supply." Readers may shy from some assertions, for example, that the hinted incest of *Finnegans Wake* (1939) reflects John Joyce's household after the death of his wife. Why? Because incest was often the case in "rural Ireland and the poorer quarters of the city."

Costello comes to his study well prepared from previous works, including an earlier (1980) short life of Joyce and a history of the Irish revolution(s) from the death of Charles Parnell to that of Yeats. We have then a study of Irish times as much as an Irish writer. Costello almost too seamlessly links Joyce's texts, especially *Stephen Hero, Exiles* (1918), and *Finnegans Wake,* with biography. But what about Richard Ellman's majestic biography of 1959 and its new (not second) edition of 1982? Though Costello often retells the life from the *Letters,* Stanislaus Joyce's recollections, and Gorman's authorized biography of 1941, his focus on Dublin is sharper than Ellman's and, at times, his material new. Costello makes it clear when he disagrees with Ellman and Stanislaus. In addition he has assimilated much earlier scholarship, as his 350-item bibliography makes clear. (What is less clear is his maddeningly succinct documentation: the direct quotation is documented; for other material we are only given the name of an author.)

What is most new or notable in this biography? There are some minor matters: Joyce's health and treatment at Clongowes, the elementary school of which Costello has written a history is discussed; Dublin addresses are corrected; a sister's godfather is identified; another model for Bloom (complete with and unfaithful Molly) is found; and the University College Dublin professor, whose enthusiasm for the Semitic origins of the *Odyssey* influenced *Ulysses,* is praised. Major and notable contributions are a convincing argument that it was the dismal death of his young brother George that finally drove Joyce from the Catholic church, a possible original for the dead lover of "The Dead" (and Joyce's wife's), and the original of *Stephen Hero's* Emma Cleary (the E. C. of *A Portrait of an Artist as a Young Man,* 1916), a clever and attractive fellow student whom Joyce once propositioned. That Joyce was obsessed with

sex is not news: what is news is Costello's proof that, despite the epiphany in *A Portrait,* Joyce lost his virginity at sixteen and not at fourteen years of age.

The biography proceeds leisurely. After fifty pages of family history, Joyce is born; in forty pages he is fourteen. The next forty pages carry him from schoolboy to young adult of nineteen. Given the emotional storms of adolescence, the financial chaos of his family, and the reader's familiarity with *A Portrait,* this section will be consulted most closely. Costello provides more economic information than any earlier biographer: deeds, bankruptcies, transfers of property, and probate costs are all explained. The last third of Costello's detailed biography covers Joyce's intermittent exile in Europe and his final flight to neutral Switzerland. By the time Joyce and his family arrive in Zurich, *Dubliners* (1914) has been published, *A Portrait* is being serialized, *Ulysses* is being planned, and the war has begun.

There are some mechanical matters: some of the thirty-nine photographs are not where they should be, improper hyphenation is evident, E. F. Benson of the bibliography becomes F. C. in the notes. Joyce's mother changes her name from one of the five genealogies to another. Genealogy is interesting. The chart of the O'Connell family, that of his paternal grandmother, reveals a distant cousinship with Daniel O'Connell, "the Liberator" (1775–1847). For Costello, such information matters, since Joyce is the creature of his DNA and his times. Hence he presents a chart of "genetic characteristics" wherein we can trace Joyce's fecklessness, nerves, musical ability, drinking, and sexuality back to his progenitors. But, since nine great-great-grandparents are missing, "the full picture is not clear," Costello admits. Perhaps less useful is the four-page horoscope prepared with the assistance of a member of the Irish Astrological Society. We have an Irish biography.

It is ironic that the most terse of American writers should get the longest biographies and the most biographies: twenty biographies or biographical studies of Ernest Hemingway have appeared. This year we have slightly more than seven hundred pages of James R. Mellow's *Hemingway: A Life With Consequences* (Houghton Mifflin). What causes such length? Answers must include the sheer mass of two world wars and a revolution; the restless movement with residence in Canada, the United States, and Cuba; the literary friendships and bitter quarrels of novelists, poets, publishers, and editors; the erotic alliances of wives, companions, and teenagers. Then there is the biographer's compulsion to recreate the historic, the modern milieu. Mellow, who ten years ago won the National Book Award for his *Nathaniel Hawthorne in His Times,* has done it again in this biography. Or rather he has done it for a third time; this is the last of an apparent trilogy to define, once again, the same setting. The two earlier volumes, *Charmed Circle: Gertrude Stein & Company* (1974) and *Invented Lives: F. Scott and Zelda Fitzgerald* (1984) gave us Europe and the United States; this volume gives us both — and also Cuba and Africa. A more massive treatment of some of Hemingway's years can be seen in Michael Reynolds's *Hemingway: the American Homecoming* (1992), another third volume. Mellow's also gives us Hemingway and cats and throat problems and piles and dysentery and "sensitivity over head." Do we need such length?

No — do we not know and must it be written this way: "the rubble-strewn Führerbunker, where Hitler suicided at the end of all the misery, disappeared like a nightmare, taking with him his bride of a night and a day: the stacks of corpses, rictus grins, knobby arms and legs piles like bundles of stacked wood?" I quote at length because Mellow writes at length and often. Then the literary flourish: "nothing seemed to improve Hemingway's relationship with a wife like the leaving of her." The mawkish (Hemingway as the Man of Sorrows): "He was a man well acquainted with death." The next sentence affords, depending on one's taste for syntax, an example of fine writing: "Yeats, spending his mornings working in a hotel on the Côte d'Azur, his afternoons in a lawn chair gazing out on forever, died." Yeats died in 1939. He was seventy-four. He was tired. But when Mellow writes well, he is good: the postwar Pound was "more and more the relic of that passing order of modernists who had created an age."

We also have the detailed event. Mellow takes five dense paragraphs to determine if and when Benito Mussolini told Hemingway, as the novelist wrote Pound in January of 1923, the "I couldn't ever live in Italy again." The violence of fascism, the dates on his passport, and the arrival of the dictator at the Lausanne Conference all move toward an equally leisurely conclusion: "The probability is that the confrontation never took place."

Much better, and almost worth the expanded treatment, is Mellow's examination of manuscripts which he ties to Hemingway's life and publishers' reticence. The evolution of the seven-paragraph vignette of a failed affair between a major and a nurse in *In Our Time* (1925) to "A Very Short Story" (1925) and finally to *A Farewell To Arms* (1929) is explained thoroughly. Mellow has examined the

manuscript in the Hemingway Collection at John Fitzgerald Kennedy Library. The change from the narrator getting first "a dose of the clap" to "gotten sick" to the major who "contracted gonorrhea" (the published version) is, as Mellow shows, a "case history of the transaction between life and fiction, and the personal rationalizations deployed in both." Further, Mellow has carefully read some letters of Agnes von Kurowsky held by an anonymous collector. Kurowsky was the original of the nurse and of the future Catherine Barkley of *A Farewell to Arms* and also Hemingway's probable lover. We now have a new and significant date for their final parting. It takes Mellow thirty pages back and forth to make his point (we even get the real train ride twice, separated by twenty pages). This is hard going but worth it.

Mellow also excels in analyzing how the male bonding in Hemingway's fiction reflects the writer's constant need for male approval whether as a hunter, a fisherman, or especially as a man about to begin or leave erotic relationships. Passages from the novels, short stories, letters, and a manuscript at Yale by a childhood friend demonstrate Hemingway the social animal. What, in one of the twenty-six photographs, is that unidentified bullfighter, one of six partially clad men including Hemingway, wearing over his penis?

Also commendable are the author's extensive appraisal of reception criticism and Hemingway's reception of it. We are supplied with parts of nine reviews of *In Our Time* (1925) and hear Hemingway's violent reactions to other writers: he wants James Jones to "suck the puss [*sic*] out of a dead nigger's ear." Yet despite much direct quotation of sent and unsent letters, we do not hear the authentic voice as often as we might like. Mellow suggests that the biographer is a student of avalanches: many readers will be buried by facts and at times otiose commentary.

The same richness, or overload, of material marks Edmund White's *Genet: A Biography* (Knopf), a curious, almost Victorian biography, not because its subject meets the social or moral ideals of the nineteenth century — after all, a writer "who spent many years of his life as a prostitute, a client, or a familiar of the world of sex for sale" hardly qualifies — but because of its bulk. A hundred years ago two volumes would contain these 728 pages. Like its predecessors it is crammed, even stuffed, with excerpts, letters, extracts, and plot summaries. In effect, what White has assembled is more sourcebook for a life of Jean Genet (1910–1986), raw materials along with a chronicle, than a standard life. For instance, we get almost all (two thousand words) of a psychiatrist's report on Genet, the thief of a fine edition of Paul Verlaine's *Fête galantes* in 1943, the year and the occasion he first called himself a writer. We can cull perhaps twenty-five words from the report: a "subject with a frustrated intelligence" who "places freedom of thought and expressing his thought – so long as they seem beautiful to him – above everything else." But should readers have to edit and select? The text of interviews is cited extensively, letters fill the half and the full page, eleven paragraphs from Jean-Paul Sartre's *Saint Genet* (1952) run onto a third page, two accounts (never reconciled) are presented of Genet's introduction to Jean Cocteau. But, in addition to the masses of documents, White has a fine critical sense and distinguishes the essential differences of an André Gide, a Cocteau, a Jean Giraudoux, a Marcel Proust, and a Genet.

Granting that a man who was an abandoned orphan, teenage runaway, often-imprisoned thief, army deserter, political radical, columnist for *Esquire,* and winner of the Gallimard Le Prix de la Pléïades did differ from most, it was his sexuality in his life and writings that most distinguished Genet. White, the author of *States of Desire: Travels in Gay America* (1980), brings to his subject and his sexual milieu a finely tempered dispassion.

White's initial defense of *Our Lady of the Flowers* (1943) – "no purely onanistic work resorts to literary language" – is not that convincing (for half the charm of *Fanny Hill* and most of the shock of A. C. Swinburne comes from that language). Better is the distinction he draws between Genet and other homosexual writers. They resort to an etiology to plea for understanding; Genet presents characters without psychoanalytic history. The others' protagonists feel accursed; Genet's feel self-confident. A strong point of White's confident literary criticism is its refusal to examine only the erotic. However "semantically undetermined" his novels may be, some meaning remains.

The picture White presents us of wartime and postwar Paris is an assembly of the "frivolous, the fashionable, and the capricious," of writers, bankers, artists, cabinet ministers, and singers. Only the clergy were marginalized. These chapters, 8–12, from 1942 to 1954, make the best, though densest, reading in this biography. White proceeds slowly from patron to patronage, from Cocteau to Sartre, from bedmate to bedmate. And given the above picture of Parisian society we begin to understand how Genet might be a stylistic and moral relief. For many Americans the most amazing chapters, about

Dust jacket for Edmund White's study of the French writer and his experiences as a criminal, a prostitute, and a public figure

fifty pages, are those of Genet in Chicago and Hollywood. Genet covered the 1968 Democratic convention for *Esquire;* I can not imagine anyone whom the first Mayor Richard Dailey could dislike more except perhaps Alan Ginsberg and William Burroughs, who also joined Genet in Chicago. He also met the Black Panthers. At first he admired them, and they, on his return to Paris, invited him back in early 1971. He spoke in New York, in Cambridge, and at Yale, and he spoke of the blacks' "poetic vision" of revolution. Huey Newton, from prison, then asked that *faggot* be removed from black political vocabulary. White's deadpan presentation of these surreal years makes them even more so. When, high on Nembutals, Genet danced in a pink negligee for some Black Panthers, Angela Davis's comment that he was "communicating something serious and its flexibility" is enough. In Hollywood he awakes early in a purely anglophone house and calls Jane Fonda to find out where he is. The former wife of Roger Vadim tells him to describe the swimming pool: it was Donald Sutherland's. The (unannounced) twenty-five photos of Genet, his friends, his lovers, and his plays move him from childhood to his defaced gravestone.

White has researched much and quoted much; documentation is scrupulous, and judgment is balanced. The final picture we have of Genet, that of a fashionable outcast and a radical favorite, would please him best.

Noël Riley Fitch's *The Erotic Life of Anaïs Nin* (Little, Brown) gives us a more fashionable favorite. Fitch presents a running commentary on Nin's diaries that corrects facts, offers psychological analysis, and then moves to investigate the transformation of the diary into literature, a literature that included the diaries themselves. Fitch's task then was a difficult one, but she succeeds. Many readers will now have to face the fact that Nin published a fabricated self: to use the author's italics — *"her diary is itself a work of fiction, an act of self-invention. Untrue confessions."* To accept her diaries as true is like assuming that her admitted successor Madonna's *Sex* (1992) is sincere.

There are other difficulties. The diaries consist of 150 or so volumes, or thirty five thousand pages. Those from 1914 to 1934 have been available for the last ten years, but Nin had rewritten much and excluded about 50 percent. Recently two unexpurgated volumes of the childhood diaries have appeared. Even so, Fitch has had to consult the manuscripts at the University of California, Los Angeles. Those from 1935 to 1939 are closed until further unexpurgated editions can appear. Fitch's contention that Nin as a writer was most interesting from 1914 to 1939 might cause her treatment of the last four years of Nin's floruit to be skimpy. Such, fortunately, is not the case. The author has interviewed those who read the 1935–1939 diaries before they were sequestered. We are also fortunate that Fitch's earlier works on the Paris of Sylvia Beech and Hemingway have prepared her so well.

Information about Nin in the 1940s is supplemented by her erotica at UCLA and the Kinsey Institute. After this date Nin censored less, but we can see the biographer's increasing reliance on interviews, for example, almost 150 for 1946–1955. Fitch has also closely studied the manuscripts of Nin's early fiction at Northwestern University, read innumerable private letters, and conducted probably hundreds of interviews. And since anything one writes about Nin, or even sex, is controversial, Fitch's thoroughness is admirable, her arguments convincing, her conclusions compelling.

Equally compelling, because it does not give us rhetorical time to stop, is the use of the historical present; both the subject matter and the method of narration leave the reader slightly out of breath: "She lifts her satin negligee and sits on his swollen sex." This was Anaïs Nin's father. Fitch is the first to treat this recent (1992) revelation of incest at length. In fact, Fitch argues it provides the clue to her erotic existence, for, having slept with her father, she can break with him and the father figures she has slept with, such as Henry Miller and her psychiatrist. The event will also enable her to break with those father figures she will sleep with in the near future, including Sigmund Freud's disciple Otto Rank. Finally she will settle on young men. The complete sequence that Fitch suggests is a movement from sexually abused young girl to courtesan in Paris to goddess among the New York gays to guru of the women of Los Angeles.

But why does she have sex with her father? Fitch finds one major cause: Freud, who in 1905 rejected his earlier seduction theory only to replace it with a theory which would "hide the reality of child abuse for almost ninety years," the Oedipal theory. Her psychiatrist, with whom she had sex, is a pre-1905 Freudian. He warns her that her father wants to sleep with her. Nin, who has read the post-1905 Freud, ignores his advice and travels to see her father in the south of France. This would seem convincing since Fitch argues from the unexpurgated diaries, Nin's novel *The Winter of Artifice* (1939), and the manuscript drafts which preceded it. Such a reading will remain contentious: some diarists edit before they even write. And the equation of any older man with a father figure is a bit pat.

The event, as Fitch records it, took place while "the hot mistral blows outside" in 1933, when Nin was thirty. The earliest years go quickly. By page 58 Nin returns to France, which she left without her father in 1914. She arrives in 1924 married a year but still a virgin; her husband, a sexually inept but tolerant banker, encourages her reading. In five years, having briefly tussled with an older professor from her Columbia days, she is reading Lawrence, Carl Jung, and Freud and talking about sex. A short, balding Brooklynite shows up with his companion: Henry Miller and June Masefield are in town.

Though attracted to Masefield, Nin and Miller both write themselves into bed (she and her father talked themselves into bed). The joining of Miller and Nin had extraordinary consequences: both were enriched intellectually, artistically, and sexually. Her diaries reflect the immediate consequence: the sloppy romanticism of the nineteenth century and "Lawrentian mystic phrases and verbal excess" start to vanish. Coition, as a word, disappears. Her diaries for this period become *The Winter of Artifice, The House of Incest* (1936), and *Ladders to Fire* (1946). Henry Miller's letters to her become first drafts of *The Tropic of Cancer* (1934). Nin aborts their other joint creation.

After the nine-day coupling with her father, a five-month stay in New York, and a break with Otto Rank, Nin returns to Paris, begins a nine-year off-and-on affair with Ganzalo More, moves into a houseboat, and meets the first of a series of her literary children, Lawrence Durrell. Others in America, to which she returns as the war begins, will be Robert Duncan and Gore Vidal. The denseness of her New York life is the crowd; in 1940 her expenses force her to write, for an Oklahoman, erotica on command, an erotica which, after twenty-five years of editing, will put her on the best-seller list (posthumously): *Little Birds* (1976) and *Delta of Venus* (1977). Neither, as Fitch insists, has literary merit. Of course, this was not true at the time. Among the embarrassing praise Fitch has recalled is Kate Millet in 1970: "She is the mother of us all as well as goddess and elder sister." The Modern Language Association held a special session in 1975.

Nor is Nin honest about her desires. Her diary says that it is the spontaneity of the young that attracts her; Fitch says that it is their innocence, which she delights in corrupting. Perhaps Edmund Wilson, with whom she briefly has an affair in 1945, could not be corrupted sexually or intellectually (his reviews are sober). In 1947 she meets the nontraditional student Robert Poole, age twenty-eight to her forty-four. Now begins her bifurcated existence: on the East Coast her banker husband and finances, on the West Coast, her Robert Poole as well as Aldous Huxley, Christopher Isherwood, Timothy Leary, Alan Watts, and the Beats (she is there when Ginsberg strips to demonstrate the nakedness of "Howl"). Nin hails "the new surrealism" born of Ginsberg's Brooklyn (the other Brooklynite, Miller, has retired to Big Sur). By the 1970s, after her edited diaries begin to appear, Fitch presents us with a Nin that is once again a generation behind: her liberation is psychological, not political. She dies editing further diaries; UCLA buys the manuscript diaries in 1977 for one hundred thousand dollars.

Paul Webster, the Paris correspondent of the *Guardian,* has written a tribute to his hero in *Antoine de Saint-Exupéry: The Life and Death of the Little Prince,* (Macmillian). Never has a mailman looked so good. Or written so well. Webster tells us that the three books, *Le Petit Prince* (1943), *Night Flight* (1932), and the essays of *Wind, Sand and Stars* (1939, an early

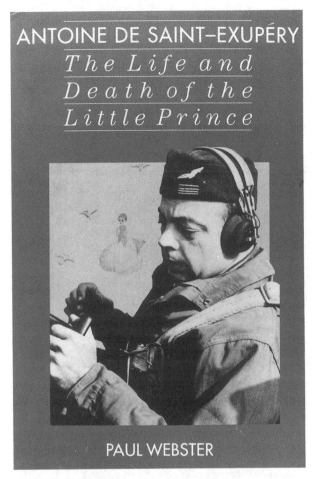

Dust jacket for Paul Webster's biography of the twentieth-century French writer, three of whose books rank among the ten best-selling this century in France

Book-of-the-Month Club selection), are among the ten best-sellers this century in France. That one title is a national school text rather deflates this number, however.

This difference between the life of Anaïs Nin and that of Antoine de Saint-Exupéry, a man only three years her elder, Antoine de can be seen in the index to Nin's life: he never appears (nor does she appear in this indexless biography). The difference is not one of time or place, but of moral setting. The heroic and the erotic rarely overlap. And though Webster, the author of *Pétain's Crime* (1991), tries, he is ambivalent toward his subject's heroism during the early years of Philippe Pétain's collaborationist government: André Gide, whose judgment Webster quotes, saw *Night Flight* as praise of duty, not freedom. Vichy would go for duty.

Relying on earlier biographies, memoirs, and published interviews, none of which is ever documented, Webster begins his life with the unpublished memoirs of Saint-Exupéry's sister which were based on her childhood diary. With a family going back to 1235, growing up in a fatherless château under the gaze of a grandmother who still thought the French Revolution "was a mood rather than a sea-change" primed him for "compulsive nostalgia." (In fact, are his books not about the pain of return?) We see a young man who, though he had an early interests in engines and was part of the airplane mania immediately preceding World War I, came into his own when he came down – and wrote about it. But before that Saint-Exupéry was little: a dull student, a timid fiancé, and a truck salesman who missed the war. His connections recommend his first story to Jean Prévost, who takes the salesman to another territory: the bookstores of Sylvia Beach and Andrienne Monnier, the friend of Gide, André Breton, Guillaume Apollinaire, Louis Aragon, Paul Valery, and, fortunately for Saint-Exupéry, Gide.

This biography gathers interest when in 1926 the amateur aviator gets a job flying the mails to Africa. Webster's treatment of the originals and the events of *Southern Mail* (1929), *Wind, Sand and Stars,* and *Night Flight* are competent summaries of earlier writers. Better is Webster's narrative of his hero's dealings with Bedouin tribes whom he fought while saving downed pilots. Transferred to Buenos Aires in 1928, he meets his future wife, the twice-widowed Consuelo, whose disillusioned memoirs inform and provide Webster with some of the data for an unhappy marriage. The short stories of his sister Simone balance Consuelo's account.

Too often the closest this biography moves us to the interior of Saint-Exupéry is his favorite foods culled from earlier accounts. Even the extracts from Léon Worth's recollections are not helpful. His life as a war correspondent in Spain (as a warrior at his war's beginning) as an exile in New York (where he wrote *Le Petit Prince*) is treated too quickly rather than succinctly.

What would assist this tribute? An explanation of exactly why Saint-Exupéry's *Wind, Sand and Stars* "illuminated France like a beacon" after the Germans defeated her, for other stories tell of a triumph over adversity, a rescue from the elements, or, as in *Night Flight,* from an alien culture. Is the writer's moral philosophy so embedded in his style that he cannot be discussed? The biographer does like Saint-Exupéry and Saint-Exupéry's lucid style, but his occasionally revealing terse phrases leave us wanting more. The continued success of *Le Petit Prince* seems assured, but we are not sure why. Saint-Exupéry died in 1944 having crashed off Nice on a photographic mission. But who died? An au-

thor or a pilot whose political beliefs were of a time before Pétain?

Steel has given readers two things of literary merit: the Free Libraries of Andrew Carnegie and the New Directions publishing house of James Laughlin. Robert Phillips, his subject's literary executor, has given us, with the assistance of Norton, the superbly edited *Delmore Schwartz and James Laughlin: Selected Letters.* I add Norton, for the book is a pleasure to read and hold: a real quarto clearly printed, free of disfiguring superscripts. Granted the volume follows the editing guidelines of Hugh Witemeyer's *William Carlos Williams and James Laughlin: Selected Letters* and Lee Bartlett's *Kenneth Rexroth and James Laughlin* (1991), but Norton did not have to keep up the good work.

These letters comment on two people, a writer and his publisher. In many ways they differed. One is the son of Romanian immigrants, the other an heir to Pittsburgh's Jones and Laughlin Steel Corporation: their temperaments differed (tragically in the case of Schwartz). But both are united by a love of literature and a common undergraduate education: Harvard – or almost, as Schwartz dropped out.

The slightly more than 150 letters from Schwartz, 50 from Laughlin with a few from the staff of New Directions, cover almost a quarter century. Almost all are new – as is a lengthy ode – and almost all entire: the dull is excluded, privacies respected, the annotation thorough. But since the annotations explain everything, including who Adolf Hitler was, the note to the *Palatine Anthology* (1941) mangles syntax and confuses its source; Benjamin Disraeli's response to Irish anti-Semitic taunts lurks beneath the text of letter 88.

We read of constant publication problems, both of production and pay. Laughlin often has to take a firm stand: Schwartz, "totally innocent of any understanding of the technical problems of printing," will not be charged for changes in his book's format, because there will not be any. Laughlin, fortunately, has a small trust: "the minute I began to count on making money, I would drift into printing crap." He rarely did. (Schwartz also took firm stands: no, he cannot install a woman in his Cambridge house and pass her off as Schwartz's sister – cousin, maybe.) Schwartz never returns proofs on time, he accepts advances for work he never wrote, and then he accuses Laughlin of moving him out of a hotel room to make way for his "baggage and a whore." Then, in a succeeding paragraph, Schwartz reviews the fortunes of the *Partisan Review*.

These letters mix business, displeasure, and literary commentary. The last create great one-liners: Pound "really made decent writing possible by yelling all the time"; Eliot, Vladimir Nabakov, Kenneth Patchen, Wallace Stevens, and Williams are illuminated or stripped by Schwartz's wit. He intends to supplement his English composition class at Princeton by studying "the strange English of Dwight D. Eisenhower," advancing hypotheses to explain why his pronunciation of Korea as "career" and "his virtual unfailing inaccuracy in the use of demonstrative pronouns."

Despite the early success of *In Dreams Begin Responsibilities* (1939), we can witness the writer's collapse: the techiness of his second letter to Laughlin in 1937 moves in two years to touchiness over money to dark suspicions in 1940 (Patchen is accused of steaming open a letter from Eliot and then resealing it). In 1943 he begins the year accusing Laughlin of drinking and phalloscoptic behavior in the men's room. At the year's end he asks for a 50 percent interest in New Directions or a retainer of two-thousand dollars a year or that he receive an accurate statement of his royalties. Intermittent paranoia had set in: the locks on the New Directions offices had to be changed. Laughlin, it becomes clear, did all he could and hardly even expected gratitude. The letters offer an intense view into New York, New Yorkers, and New Yorkers who read literature.

Barry Miles's *William Burroughs: El Hombre Invisible* (Hyperion) is a brief, ill-indexed, but not succinct biography of William Burroughs (1914–   ), who acquired the sobriquet of "invisible man" as he pursued young boys through the Casbah in Tangier in the 1950s. Little of this is documented, and much appears hasty. The author's earlier *Allen Ginsberg: A Biography* (1989) was more thorough. Abundant extracts from his subject's works and elaborate and uncritical defenses of the same works extend the work's length. Some extracts, especially from interviews, are often clever and outrageous, what we have come to expect from Burroughs since *The Naked Lunch* was published in 1959 in Paris. (Three years later it lost the article in America; a decade later it became a casebook with the "Ugh!" correspondence from the *TLS*): from the (London) *Guardian* in the 1965: sex, like alcohol "is the other accepted narcotic since it also induces sleep"; and "The only way I'd like to see cops given flowers is in a flower pot from a high window." Burroughs says it again in 1984, and Miles quotes it again. The most useful section of the biography is the twenty-page introduction. This is actually an essay on his influence on writers of his generation (but the promise of more on Ginsberg, Jack Kerouac, and Greg-

ory Corso is not fulfilled) and moves to his influence on present writers (though curiously enough Kathy Acker's tribute is left out). Then on to rock and roll: in 1972 Donald Fagen and Walter Becker took the name of their band, Steely Dan, from a dildo in *Naked Lunch*. Miles's assertion that the term *heavy metal* is from the same novel is not proven. In film we find the Space Bar of *Stars Wars* is from *Naked Lunch,* as is the physician paged in *Repo Man*. Burroughs has also had cameo roles in various more or less obscure cult films. Enough.

After this the uncritical and undocumented life of a man born not to be wild begins. Miles's method is to paint the scene from somewhere and then add the reminiscences of Burroughs from half a century later. That the two might not be the same has not occurred to this friend of Burroughs. It also has not occurred to him to document any letter, to provide any page reference to anything, and, if he has done any research, to provide a note. This lack of attribution, documentation, and research reduces the sixty pages of those two chapters centered about Burroughs's major novel to hearsay. Michelle Greens's *The Dream at the End of the World: Paul Bowles and the Literary Renegades in Tangier* (1991) is better with the city and with Burroughs. Miles gives us kef and catamites. And this is too bad, for Miles has read, if uncritically, a great deal of Burroughs. Oliver Harris's selection of the correspondence published this year as *The Letters of William Burroughs, 1945–1959* (Hyperion) should also be consulted.

Burroughs's Saint Louis childhood and college years are generally unexceptional. That Burroughs kept guns and a ferret at Harvard simply meant his house master failed to recommend him to Bill Donovan of the Office of Strategic Services. That Burroughs avoided the war is not worthy of Miles's comment, but presenting violence is. First, the seventeen-year-old Ginsberg is impressed when Burroughs quotes William Shakespeare when he learns a friend has bitten off part of someone's ear in a bar fight. Second, the same friend a page later kills his former lover: he "stabbed him twice through the heart," and then Miles adds "killing him." But the most outrageous event and outrageous treatment is a drunken Burroughs who fails to shoot a water glass off his wife's head. The glass survives; the wife dies. Then the biographer gives us Burroughs on how this event inspired him to write. That Burroughs came to this conclusion in 1981, thirty years after he killed his wife, would seem to call for comment – but gets none. Nor do we find out if Burroughs was ever sentenced and what this sentence was. And, of course, Burroughs's drug usage is treated sympathetically.

After the Tangier years the biographer follows Burroughs from Paris in 1958, where he briefly joins Ginsberg (by now his editor) and Corso, to an eight-year residence in London. As these travels proceed, so does Miles with those works of his subject most of us will never read, especially *The Soft Machine* (1961), *Nova Express* (1964), and *The Wild Boys* (1971). But since Burroughs has not written that much of merit since the mid 1960s, the biographer must tell us about the Dream Calendar in which, though Burroughs based it on the Mayan, "the days somehow got miscounted" and that Arabs, Indian, and Turks lack an unconscious because they failed to retreat to caves after the nuclear explosion of thirty thousand years ago in the Gobi. Burroughs has returned to America, been hailed as the Grandfather of punk, been featured in *People,* and, as a prepostmodern ecologically aware seer, been interviewed by Barry Miles.

The now totally blind poet and critic John Heath-Stubbs has summed up the first seventy-five years of his life in *Hindsights: An Autobiography* (Hodder and Stoughton) in almost three hundred dense pages. Perhaps they are too dense: there are more than three hundred people in the generally inclusive index, many of whom put in only cameo appearances, for example, Rose Macaulay, Donald Hall, Richard Wilbur, Henry Kissinger (the Summer School Dean), with distinctly minor anecdotes. His method is to introduce a person from the 1940s and 1950s and then jump either to him twenty years later or to his death — whichever comes first.

Heath-Stubbs is a modest man, so the editors should have listed his major publications with dates and should have shifted some paragraphs around: a person introduced simply as "the infamous Tambimuttu" appears six times in the text (once to lose a manuscript of William Empson's) before we learn he was the editor of *Poetry London* during and after the war and later in charge of his own poetry house.

Readers of autobiography anticipate acidulous judgments, and Heath-Stubbs does not disappoint us. The hero in *Lucky Jim* (1954) is a tiresome young man, and its author misunderstands madrigals. Larkin's poetry is "limited both technically and in its range of ideas," and the poet himself was "unnecessarily foul-mouthed" (a nice distinction); John Asbury's verse is "unending verbal drivel"; American bars are uncivilized with chrome plating or uncivilized with common troughs for communal micturition. The worst line given in English poetry is "Darling, I still remember the warmth of your legs" (Nicholas Moore) and in American is "Hey

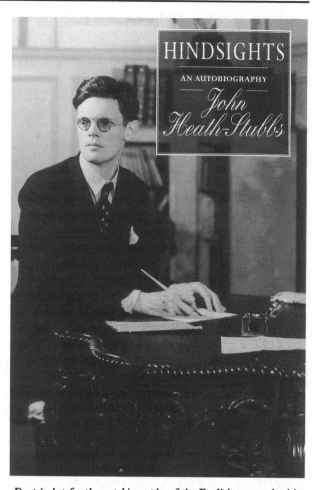

Dust jacket for the autobiography of the English poet and critic that also passes judgment on post–World War II British culture

Hart, don't jump!" (Peter Viereck in a poem addressed to Hart Crane).

In boarding school, which he hated, he fostered those interests which inform not only his poetry but his reviews. As an amateur biologist he tells us how to feed a pond full of medicinal leeches and that "The wasp is a friend of man," a sentence he made misbehaving students — those he could see — copy again and again. And it was this sort of knowledge rather than an honors degree in English (Oxon) that got him a job writing encyclopedia articles. When we join his childhood reading in mythology and folklore, Henry Wadsworth Longfellow's *The Song of Hiawatha* (1855), Nathaniel Hawthorne's *Tanglewood Tales* (1853), and Charles Kingsley's *The Heroes* (1856) to his college reading of Sir James Frazer, it is no wonder his first book of poems was *Wounded Thammuz* (1942), the manuscript of which Herbert Read recommended to George Routledge when the poet was twenty-four.

*Dust jacket for the Indian writer's memoir of his university
education in England*

Barton-on-Sea, where he spent his childhood, was close to Bournemouth: he heard Sir Edward Elgar conduct, saw Anna Pavlova dance, and witnessed Vladimir Horowitz spit at an audience; he also decided Giacomo Puccini has no tunes and that Modest Mussorgsky's *Boris Godunov* explains Russia. After sixty pages he is off to Queen's College on a scholarship for the blind. The two chapters on Oxford are crowded. Oxford just before the war was poetically anti–W. H. Auden and pro–Edith Sitwell. Intellectually it was the university of C. S. Lewis (who stopped English literature in 1830), J. R. R. Tolkien, and especially Charles Williams: Williams was valuable as the poetic mentor who introduced him to Dante and Eliot. Perhaps it is because the academic study of English literature stopped with 1830 that makes Heath-Stubbs's 1950 critical study, *The Darkling Plain,* which covers from then to the end of the century, still so valuable, a book which he himself reviews in this autobiography. From Tolkien's group he learned to appreciate Anglo-Saxon and is almost tempted to say that En-

glish literature since *Beowulf* is a history of steady decline. At Oxford he did attend a variety of séances, did *not* meet Kingsley Amis, but did meet Philip Larkin. He also began his editorial work with the anthology *Eight Oxford Poets* (1941).

The autobiography gathers interest when Heath-Stubbs begins his reviewing career shortly after the war for the *New English Review*; he has not stopped yet. He is also good on postwar readings and the pubs of Soho at the same time. But the names of the pubs and the poets read like a commemorative litany of the vanished and the now obscure. It is to be hoped that those this poet sees as especially valuable, for example, George Barker, will be reread.

In the 1950s is his poetry fellowship to the University of Leeds, a uncongenial city but with a splendid English department, where he avoids both urban damp and, more luckily, creative-writing classes. Until the Suez Crisis his account of his succeeding three-year appointment in Alexandria is some thirty pages of introductory remarks on Alexandria and Coptic theology and liturgy. His later lectures on pre-Colombian Mexico keep our attention. In between these lectures is his recollection of Ann Arbor in 1961, where he brought eighteenth-century verse to life for this freshman. The remainder of the 1960s were for him generally disastrous. But eventually he finishes what John Milton once contemplated, a long poem on Arthur, and receives what the earlier poet would avoid: the monarch's Gold Medal for Poetry.

A lying nanny when he was two caused his lifelong skepticism, though he retains a faith about which he is quietly and honestly reticent. He ends quoting Vaughan Williams: "It is permitted to hope." Heath-Stubbs is equally reticent about sex, and readers may be relieved to read an autobiography in which neither souls nor genitals are laid bare. The poet concludes his life with a chapter on the inconvenience rather than the tragedy of blindness, whether Homer's, Milton's, or his own.

Like Heath-Stubbs, Ved Mehta is blind, but blind at an earlier age (four). His most recent of his nearly twenty books begins as he is graduated from Pomona College in California. We have in *Up at Oxford* (Norton) the recollections of his time at Balliol, which he enter in 1956: he was already an author. In fact, this is the seventh in an autobiographical series, Continents of Exile. Parts of this book may already be familiar to readers of the *New Yorker* and the *American Scholar;* the former accounts for this volume's curiously flat well-mannered prose.

Almost half of this book is devoted to his first year, preceded by a reunion with his family in Paris. Mehta's point of view is that of an Americanized Indian. The American deplores English plumbing; the Indian shudders at haggis. What an American undergraduate might see as a curious ceremony to be performed (the loving cup) or abstruse ritual to follow (U and non-U speech) Mehta expected himself to know even before he arrived at Oxford: he was a son of the Raj. And since he did not, his view, at a third remove, allows the reader to review Oxford and sympathize with the viewer. We also sympathize with administrators who wonder, as this student changes from reading law, then economics, then English, and finally history, in which he takes a second. The college life he presents is oddly innocent, and Mehta knows it: high thinking and high drinking; one experiment with drugs (mescaline), but none with sex. Since the arrival of the New Dark Age of mass culture, Oxford has changed, but Mehta understands the change.

A year as a visiting fellow at Balliol in 1988–1989 allowed Mehta to renew acquaintances and memories

and check his facts: of undergraduates' pastimes he admits that "writing about these goings on from this distance is disconcerting, because they seem childish and silly, yet at the time they were enthralling, and not just to me but to my most sophisticated English contemporaries." We often need to remind ourselves that this man was blind, that he needed readers, and that he was asked on his final examination to compare Offa of Mercia with Edwin of Northumbria – and draw a map. We must admire his surefootedness when he walks among the after-dinner glasses and decanters on a tabletop and praise his confidence as he harangues his listeners on the inadequacy of English male society: in America "ditches are used for trysts rather than for men in a drunken stupor to fall into, as here in England."

These memoirs do not make much intellectual demand on their readers. We are treated to potted lectures: the history of Balliol College reads like a footnote to G. M. Hopkins. Better is his scout's reaction when Mehta told him that the year before he had lived in the poet's sitting room: "Was he in the Parliament?"

The best feature of this memoir is the treatment of the unsuccessful graduate. We do not get the antics of "Fignose" followed by a footnote to "now Sir Ralph Feretory" followed then by a typesetter's or spell checker's nightmare of half the alphabet in caps. We have, instead, three with "troubled lives," all of whom are introduced on the same page. One leaves Oxford a year (three pages) later; the second was a favorite of Winchester's headmaster, took a special First, wrote for the BBC, and committed suicide just before his Emmy-winning show, "The Heart of the Dragon," went on the air (twenty-two pages). (In fact, there are five suicides in this book.) The third took a Third, later joined IBM, and, after he took an axe twice to his father's skull, was locked up and remains so (ten pages). All three excelled at Winchester; their troubles may have been caused, Mehta suggests, by an "overbred intelligence" and a "fast-lane education." Mehta's account, coolly sympathetic and coolly self-critical, creates a proper nostalgia: returns and memories are painful. Readers are probably more sensitive to oral pastiche than they were ten years ago. Consequently, the re-creation of one troubled life by extensive quotations from his former wife is not as convincing as Mehta intends. It is not as bad as "Words We Doubt were Ever Spoken in Anger," but the seams show.

In addition to the unhappy three, Mehta spends eighty pages on his roommate, Jasper Griffin, and other classicists. And this is where the author's modesty gets in the way. Many of us have read Mehta's books, stories, and articles, but we may be unfamiliar with the accomplishments of others. So we might like to know that Martin West's undergraduate ability to apply himself to a text with "limitless energy" and his many prizes have resulted in West's *Greek Elegy and Iamb,* a book one buys rather than consults or takes out. Griffin himself is used to explaining the English school system to American readers. Mehta expands his friend's account of his school days at Christ's Hospital with those of Charles Lamb and Samuel Taylor Coleridge. As Griffin explains the advantages of a classical education, we review the life of Eduard Fraenkel, his seminars, his terrorizing of Harvard scholars, and his *Agamemnon.* But Griffin's speech also sounds like a pastiche or even a lecture on haplography and dittography dumbed down for magazine readers.

What is maddening – and must be deliberate on the part of the publisher – is the lack of an index. Half the pleasure of someone's memoirs is looking up stories about the famous and notorious. My favorite is on page 219: Ginsberg chews on the tie of the professor of poetry while Corso embraces his knees. Both then exclaim "Maestro, maestro, don't leave us!" Auden was the Maestro. There is one (generic) photo: croquet in Balliol's courtyard. There is also arithmetic confusion: Peter Levi, whose *Tennyson* begins these reviews, has joined the Jesuit order at seventeen. We can expect the next of Mehta's series to begin as Kennedy becomes president and the author a fellow at Harvard.

These are not the only noteworthy biographies of this year. Peter Whitebrook's *William Archer: A Biography* (Methuen) gives us the man of letters who translated Ibsen and befriended Joyce. And perhaps E. Jean Carroll's *Hunter: The Strange and Savage Life of Hunter Thompson* (Dutton) belongs here. Among the lives of British poets are a biography by James McKay, [Robert] *Burns* [also: *RB: A Biography*] (Edinburgh: Mainstream), and Tom Leonard's *Places of the Mind: The Life and Work of James Thomson* (BV) (Jonathan Cape). Thomson, a slightly earlier and radically different poet than John Gray. Among American poets we have two biographies: Scott Donaldson and R. H. Winnick's *Archibald MacLeish: An American Life* (Houghton Mifflin) and Andrew Motion's *Philip Larkin: A Writer's Life* (Farrar, Straus, and Giroux).

Novelists still outnumber poets. David Sweetman's *Mary Renault: A Biography* (Chatto and Windus) treats the same sexual concerns as Margaret Foster's *Daphne du Maurier: The Secret Life of the Renowned Storyteller* (Doubleday). Erotic concerns are found in Nicola Beauman's *Morgan: A Biography of E. M. Forster* (Hodder and Stoughton), but more so in Elaine Feinstein's *Lawrence's Women: The Intimate Life of D. H. Lawrence* (HarperCollins). Lawrence's near contemporary gets a brief treatment in Michael Coren's *The Invisible Man: The Life and Liberties of H. G. Wells* (Antheneum). Jenny Uglow's biography expands another novelist's background in *Elizabeth Gaskell: A Habit of Stories* (Farrar, Straus, and Giroux). In America, Carol Gelderman has written a major life of a not-so-major American novelist: *Louis Auchincloss: A Writer's Life* (University of Michigan Press).

Dictionary of Literary Biography Yearbook Award for a Distinguished Literary Biography Published in 1993

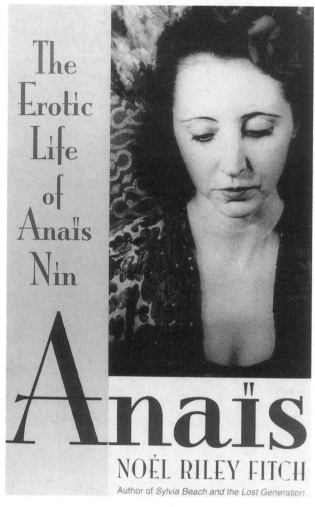

Dust jacket for Noël Riley Fitch's biography of the American writer whose sexually explicit diaries and novels generated notoriety in the United States during the 1960s and 1970s

Noël Riley Fitch's *The Erotic Life of Anaïs Nin* (Little, Brown) goes much beyond Nin's twenty-five or so named companions. Her numerous relationships, especially the one with Henry Miller, have been treated in earlier biographies: here they receive more acute and thorough documentation. This is particularly true of her early years in the Paris of the 1920s and the Los Angeles of the 1960s. Fitch, in relating the actual events of her subject's life – and in an often-rapid historical present – provides a convincing psychological explanation (paternal incest) for her behavior and demonstrates how her life, whether recorded in her diaries or not, became her art. Fitch's task was difficult: from the thirty-five thousand pages of the diaries, more than one hundred interviews, and a close reading of fiction (Nin's, Miller's, even Gore Vidal's), she constructs an erotic life, but not the self-edited erotic life Nin created in her published diaries. A sympathetic distance not devoid of moral judgment and meticulous research has created what Nin never wrote: her life.

– *William Foltz*

Book Reviewing in America VII

George Garrett
University of Virginia

and

Kristin van Ogtrop
Vogue Magazine

I feel that reviewing as it's practiced today – in newspapers, magazines, and Sunday supplements – is contributing to a national perception that books are marginal in our culture . . . that reading is a boring, time-consuming activity.

> – Nan Talese, as quoted in *The National Book Critics Journal* (June).

Other newspapers and the weekly magazines have excellent staff reviewers and smartly edited book sections. Only the Times *has the* Book Review *with its circulation of 1.8 million.*

> – Edwin Diamond, "The Last Word," *New York,* 10 January 1994.

What follows is, first, a general examination by George Garrett of book reviewing and literary journalism in a variety of newspapers and literary magazines and quarterlies. Secondly, Kristin van Ogtrop reports on the reviewing and literary journalism of fashion magazines, which, for a variety of reasons, have become serious, sometimes major, players in the literary arena. Finally, as a conclusion, there are two interviews by van Ogtrop, first a general picture of the year as viewed by editors Nan Talese, Carol Houck Smith, Matthew Carnicelli, and Shannon Ravenel, ending with a more detailed picture of the year in publishing given by a conversation with Jane Gelfman, a prominent and successful literary agent.

BOOK REVIEWING AND LITERARY JOURNALISM IN THE PAPERS

Literary journalism, including book reviewing, takes place in the context of the publishing business, which is about money and people even before it is about books. For many people in the business (see the interview with agent Jane Gelfman) the big-

gest single event in the publishing business during 1993 was the acquisition of Macmillan, itself a merger of several publishing houses, by Paramount, even as other larger units were moving to acquire Paramount. The money involved in the Macmillan acquisition was a cool $553 million. But there was other important news about the money in publishing, money coming in and going out, money bet on the future. Keeping up with the events, the trends, the comings and goings of the literary scene, whether from the angle of the region of New York or nationwide, is made easier by a variety of literary journalism. *Publishers Weekly* is the bible of the business, but the "Along Publishers Row" section of the *Author's Guild Bulletin* regularly offers a brief but accurate account of publishing affairs. Meg Cox of the *Wall Street Journal* regularly publishes pieces concerned with the business aspects of publishing, as does the "Book Notes" column of the *New York Times.* David Streitfeld of the *Washington Post* remains the preeminent all-around literary journalist who, through his column in the Sunday *Washington Post Book World* and in articles and interviews in the "Style" section of the daily *Washington Post,* manages to report on both the business news and on the people who make that news. Other magazines and papers cover particular events or an overview of the publishing scene. Daniel Max of the *New York Observer* is proving to be a strong competitor for Streitfeld. And one of the best overview pieces covering 1993 was "High Fliers and Bumpy Landings," by David Mehegan (*Boston Sunday Globe,* 2 January 1994).

Popular writers and public figures, whose bestsellers and blockbusters, when they in fact work out, fuel the publishing industry, made news as they were kept or seduced by publishers. Anne Rivers Siddons signed on for her next four books with

103

HarperCollins for an advance in excess of $10 million. Contracting with Knopf for three future vampire novels, Anne Rice took home $17 million plus $1.5 million for paperback renewal rights. Michael Crichton got $3.5 million from Warner for his next book, slightly edged out by John Grisham, who received $3.7 million for his. General Colin Powell outdid them both with the $6.5 million he received as an advance for his memoirs from Random House. Other public figures took a turn at the trough. Country singer Dolly Parton agreed to do a book about herself for HarperCollins for an advance, described by *Publishers Weekly* (10 May) as "well into the seven-figure range." Meanwhile Anita Hill (see "Anita Hill to Write Two Books," by David Streitfeld, *Washington Post,* 17 December) took advantage of a deal negotiated by federal appeals judge A. Leon Higginbotham, signing on with Doubleday for an estimated sum of "well over $1 million." Michael Milken signed with Hyperion (owned by Disney) to write his memoirs for an undisclosed amount. Even some first novelists hit the jackpot. Carol O'Connell earned an advance of $800,000 from Putnam for *Mallory's Oracle.* Television writer Allan Folsom captured $2 million from Warner for *The Day After Tomorrow,* a first novel all about a neo-Nazi conspiracy.

None of which means much, of course, unless the big publishers are earning big bucks. Because of the special nature of the book business characterized by delayed and deferred payments and erratic cash flow, accurate figures are slow in coming forward. The figures for 1993 are a long way away, but according to *Publishers Weekly* (13 December), although profit margins dropped in many areas of publishing in 1992, trade books held their own, earning 8.6 percent compared to 8.4 percent in 1991. And margins on trade in paperbacks rose by a full point from 12.7 percent to 13.7 percent. Particularly successful was Harcourt Brace (now Harcourt General) with revenues up 9 percent from the year before and with earnings up some 13.5 percent, or $142 million. During 1993, for example, one learned that in 1991 Random House became the first American publisher to achieve over $1 billion in sales. Bantam Doubleday Dell announced total sales of $650 million in fiscal 1993. Meantime the small presses, growing in activity and importance as mainstream publishers dispense with the midlist books, got a shot in the arm (sometimes) from foundation support. The Lila Wallace Reader's Digest Fund awarded $1.4 million to eighteen small publishers for marketing their product. Graywolf Press

was awarded a grant of $265,000 by the Andrew W. Mellon Foundation.

Throughout the year there were bitter battles between the independent bookstores and the large chains (Walden, Barnes and Noble, B. Dalton, and so forth) and especially the new superstores which have been growing steadily in number since the 1970s. Superstores are characterized by huge inventory of books offered at substantial discounts in a large, spacious environment, sometimes with two or more stories. Walden, with twelve hundred regular bookstores in its chain, is creating superstores under the title Basset Book Shops. There are fifty open already, and more are coming. Barnes and Noble has plans to open one hundred superstores. But even the superstores have encountered threatening competition now that QVC, the home-shopping television network, has begun selling books on the air. Independents are fighting back as best they can. One way is by plugging into published catalogues and book-review magazines created especially for them and emphasizing midlist books, publications like *Review, Hungry Mind Review,* and *Plant's Review of Books.* Another is to work with publishers. (See Meg Cox, "Crown Tries Hand Sell for a Hard Sell," *Wall Street Journal,* 5 May). "Hand sell" is defined by Cox as "personal pitches to bookstores, especially established independents to get them to actively recommend a book to their customers." Some of this is based on the model of the best-selling *Bridges of Madison County* (Warner), but even more it applies to the developing means of promoting "literary" and midlist books. Readings and signings in bookstores, particularly the independents, are more and more encouraged by publishers, as are appearances before local and regional book clubs. These means of promotion also allow for authors to work on their own, creating or simply taking advantage of local contacts. Of course, the superstars are capable of large-scale literary events, as witness Waldenbooks in Fayetteville, Arkansas, which put together what is believed to be the largest autograph session in history – eighty-eight writers of Western novels all signing at the same time.

Other brief bits from 1993: *The Diary of Jack the Ripper,* not surprisingly, proved to be a hoax and was pulled by Warner Books in early September. Academy Chicago, which had planned to publish a book of John Cheever's uncollected stories in 1988 and had been resisted, in court and in the press, by the Cheever family, finally settled on a gathering of stories now in the public domain, first published between 1931 and 1948. Chelsea House announced plans for a new thirty-volume series – "Lives of Notable Gay Men and Lesbians." Penguin, aiming for the same market, brought out at year's end *The Penguin Book of Gay Short Stories* and *Lesbian Short Stories.* Birch Lane Press announced that its novel, *Just This Once,* is the first novel ever to be completely written by a computer. The computer was programmed to think and to write like the late Jacqueline Susann.

If money, getting and spending, is the bread and butter of the publishing world, then people, coming and going and always gossiping, are the spirit of it. There was plenty of large news and small news in the year. Novelist John Irving rated a headline – "A Blow to Morrow" (*Publishers Weekly,* 29 November) – when it was announced that for his forthcoming novel, *A Son of the Circus,* he was leaving Morrow for Random House. This was taken as especially bad news for Morrow, which is for sale. Saul Bellow left his native Chicago to live and to teach in Boston at Boston University. The good news for Toni Morrison was the winning of the Nobel Prize. The beginning of the bad news was the public reaction of several columnists. The *Washington Post's* syndicated columnist Edwin M. Yoder ("Why Toni Morrison?," Chattanooga *Times,* 14 October) was not overjoyed by the selection: "The old fashioned idea that race is irrelevant to judgments of literary value is now obviously passe. When you combine the urge to patronize by race to the perennial weakness of the Swedish Academy for gestures of social significance, what you get is eccentric choices like this one." Also on 14 October appeared "The Other Toni Morrison," by Heather MacDonald (*Wall Street Journal*), which focused on flaws in Morrison's criticism, including, inferentially, the flaw of inverse racism according to party lines. This piece stirred up a hornet's nest of response, pro and con, in "The Real Toni Morrison" (*Wall Street Journal,* 5 November). On Christmas Day a fire destroyed Morrison's country home in Grand View, New York, and seems to have destroyed some of her manuscripts as well. Louis Begley, newly elected president of P.E.N., was accused of using his office to settle scores with enemies and with reviewers who did not praise his work – "Begley's Pen Explodes in His Pocket," by Jeanette Wells (*New York,* 30 August). Stephen King attacked in *Time* (27 September) negative critics not of his own work but of Scott Smith's first novel, *A Simple Plan* (Knopf). Robert MacNamara, although he had legally deposed otherwise in 1984 ("I do not wish to engage in a discussion of my views or anybody else's of the Vietnam War"), signed a contract with Times Books to write a book, tentatively titled *In Retrospect,* to do just that (*Washington Post,* 8 Sep-

tember). Two writers, Norman Mailer and John Richardson, both writing biographical books about Picasso and both edited by Random House's Jason Epstein, quarreled, and as a result Mailer took his book to Nan Talese at Doubleday (see Sarah Lyall, "One Picasso, Two Writers and an Editor on the Spot," *New York Times,* 7 July).

People working within the publishing establishment made large and small news stories also. Tom Phillips of Phillips Publishing International bought conservative publisher Regnery Gateway. Roger Straus III, managing director and heir apparent at Farrar, Straus, and Giroux, resigned from that firm. Brigitte Weeks was replaced as editor in chief of the Book-of-the-Month Club by Tracy Brown of Little, Brown. Hearst Corporation replaced Terry McDonnell, the editor of *Esquire* since 1990, with Edward Kostner of *New York* magazine. McDonnell was assigned as editor to Hearst's *Sports Afield,* perhaps appropriately for this city-bred editor "who likes to think of himself as this rugged Montana guy" (Howard Kurtz, "*Esquire* Nabs New York's Top Editor," *Washington Post,* 22 September). Joni Evans, whose public and private life has attracted media attention in the past, was back in the papers and the magazines when, after five years, Random House closed down her Turtle Bay imprint. "I am very disappointed in what I think is an abrupt and premature decision," Evans was quoted as saying (Esther B. Fein in "Random House Shuts Turtle Bay Books," *New York Times,* 11 February). *Mirabella* quoted Evans as saying, "I went through disbelief, anger, denial – all five stages of grief in five minutes. But then I just let go" (June). Evans resurfaced as a literary agent for the William Morris Agency.

Confession and controversy are always good copy. Harold Brodkey announced, in "To My Readers" (*New Yorker,* 2 June), that "I have AIDS." "I am sixty-two," he wrote, "and it's ecological to die while you're still productive, die and clear a space for others, old and young." This *New Yorker* piece was followed by an interview in the *New York Times* – "Of Brodkey and AIDS: Laugh a Bit, Cry a Bit," by Jeffrey Schmalz (7 June). Wrote Schmalz: "In both the article and the interview, Mr. Brodkey was quite clear about how he had contracted AIDS: through homosexual sex." Schmalz quoted Brodkey as saying "I'd like to give an enormous party in Central Park and invite everybody with AIDS."

A good deal of literary May 1993 was preoccupied with the litigation of the libel suit by psychoanalyst Jeffrey M. Masson against writer Janet Malcolm and the *New Yorker.* This suit for $10 million had been quietly cooking for almost a decade and was the source of a string of articles about the trial in the major papers and magazines, most of them eagerly interested in the revelations of the inner workings of the *New Yorker*. The jury brought in what amounted to a mixed verdict. They found that Masson had indeed been libeled but were unable to arrive at any agreement on damages. The case therefore remains unsettled and is in appeal. Malcolm made news again when she published a three-part essay, "The Silent Woman," about Sylvia Plath and her biographers, together with severe questions about the art of biography in general, in a special double issue (23/30 August) of the *New Yorker*. At year's end a battle outside the law, but involving Michigan law professor and dedicated feminist Catherine MacKinnon, erupted when *Philadelphia Inquirer* book critic Carlin Romano, writing for the "Fall Books" issue of the *Nation* (15 November) wrote a strongly negative review of MacKinnon's *Only Words* (Harvard University Press). MacKinnon argued: "This was a public rape. What Romano did was place me in the position of a raped woman so that he had me where he wanted me. . . ." Romano responded: "Now she's gone from saying pornography is rape to saying book reviewing is rape. Catherine MacKinnon's mind is one long slippery slope." (see David Streitfeld, "Rape by the Written Word," *Washington Post,* 4 January 1994.) The results of all this and the attendant national publicity were about fifty letters and five subscription cancellations to the *Nation*. One letter, bringing together several strands of the year in literary journalism, came from Jeffrey Masson to Romano in defense of the honor of MacKinnon. "If there is anything I can do to hurt your career," he wrote, "I will do it." Within a few weeks the story of MacKinnon and friends versus Romano had even earned pages in *Time* and *Newsweek* (17 January 1994).

None of the above, however, aroused as much media interest as some old-timers whose stories carried over into 1993. One of these was the story of earlier days in the business recollected not so much in tranquillity as from the point of view or hindsight of a century past. Willie Morris's *New York Days* (Little, Brown), a memoir of his days as editor of *Harper's* during the late 1960s and early 1970s, was certainly as widely and fully reviewed as any other book published during the year. Though generally favorable, reviews were mixed. A review in the *New Yorker* (20 September), "Willie's Version," by Louis Menand, judiciously praised and damned the book in the same context: "The memoirs of literary people are traditionally so unreliable that to call them

'self-serving' is nearly a redundancy. Just as long as nobody mistakes them for history. Morris's *Harper's,* though, is history, and when he leaves off reminiscing about the lunches at the Century and the parties at George Plimpton's he does manage to give us some idea of what being an editor was like back in the days when journalism was new." The publication of *New York Days,* together with widespread publicity, led to a public quarrel – on television and in publications including the *New York Times Book Review* – between Morris and the present editor of *Harper's,* Lewis Lapham, whose version of events is somewhat different from Morris's.

Already into his fifth year as the target of a *fatwa,* Salman Rushdie continued to fight for his life and his liberty in the one way open to him – high visibility in the press. Near the end of the year he achieved one stated goal and met briefly with President Clinton at the White House; and, at the same time, he became affiliated with Massachusetts Institute of Technology as a visiting professor. Earlier in the year he had finally met with British Prime Minister John Major. The *Publishers Weekly* coverage of that event ("Major, Rushdie Meet; P.M. Gives Support," 17 May) contained a summary of his efforts so far in the year: "Rushdie himself has visited 10 countries over the past year in order to raise the profile of the campaign." Headlines traced his movements and efforts: "Rushdie Pops Up In Paris"; "Rushdie Optimistic That Death Threat Will Be Lifted"; "Rushdie Awarded Top Booker Prize" (his earlier novel, *Midnight's Children* [1981], was chosen as the best of all twenty-four previous Booker Prize winners); "Muslim Thinkers Rally For Rushdie"; "Rushdie Surfaces To Claim Prize For The Best British Novel In 25 Years" ("I walked into London as a stranger and I ran off with a check, which feels OK"); "Rushdie In Germany For Rapprochement." This latter (*Boston Globe,* 21 August) told of his meeting near Cologne, by private plane, police helicopters, and a convoy of cars, with his Turkish publisher Aziz Nesin, with whom he had quarreled earlier. Nesin had escaped from a fire apparently intended to kill him but which killed thirty-seven others. In October William Nygaard, Rushdie's Norwegian publisher, was shot and seriously wounded. Two books supported Rushdie. In America there was *The Rushdie Letters: Freedom to Speak, Freedom to Write* (University of Nebraska, edited by Steve MacDonough), consisting of a piece by Rushdie, "One Thousand Days in a Balloon"; "Letters to Salman Rushdie," by twenty-five writers including William Styron, Norman Mailer, Günter Grass, and others of like minds; an essay by Tom

Stoppard, "On the Third Anniversary of the Fatwa"; and, by Carmel Bedford, "Fiction, Fact and the Fatwa," a chronology of events concerning Rushdie. Not yet published in the United States, but soon to appear from Braziller, is *For Rushdie,* a collection of essays in support of Rushdie by one hundred Arab and Muslim artists and intellectuals. The first *New York Times Magazine* of 1994 (2 January) presented "Still Writing After All These Years," a brief account of the author describing him as "back in circulation of a sort, visiting presidents, making speeches, and, whether he chooses or not, serving as a kind of literary Zelig, a vessel for meaning, an occasion for other people's ideas." Months earlier John Banville, novelist and literary editor of the *Irish Times,* had published "An Interview with Salman Rushdie" (*New York Review of Books,* 4 March), in which he managed to evoke some weary worldly wisdom from the beleaguered Rushdie: "We are all in some manner alone on the planet, beyond the community of language or whatever; we are poor, bare creatures; it's no bad thing to be forced to recognize these things." Finally, in late December, the Modern Language Association (MLA), at its annual convention in Toronto, held three sessions devoted exclusively to Rushdie and his plight. Rushdie did not attend but sent a letter to be read. The cost to the MLA for extra security (see the *Chronicle of Higher Education,* 12 January) was roughly $13,000.

Another much-publicized writer, Joe McGinniss, may well have wished for the blessings of anonymity and at least some invisibility while his book, *The Last Brother* (Simon and Schuster), a highly speculative and unauthorized biography of Sen. Edward Kennedy, was in the pitiless critical spotlight. For the two months of July and August he was tested to the quick by attacks of the press on his book and on himself. McGinniss's troubles began in early May when, timed to coincide with the annual convention of the American Booksellers Association, Simon and Schuster produced a bound 123-page excerpt openly and casually allowing that some of the thoughts and dialogue had been "created" by the author. Even before the advance reviews and well before the appearance of the book, the press had focused on the story. July was a firestorm. In "Clip Job" (*New York,* 12 July) John Taylor added to the charge of speculative, nonfactual creativity with the additional allegation that McGinniss had depended too much and too closely on the work of others, especially on William Manchester's *The Death of a President* (1967): "McGinniss set out to enrich him-

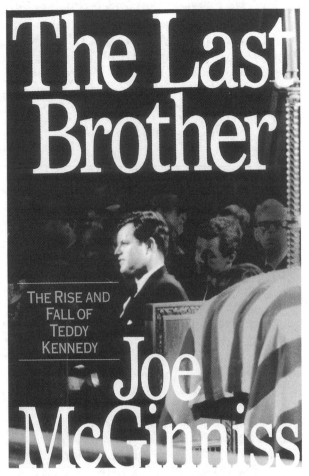

Dust jacket for Joe McGinniss's biography of Ted Kennedy. Lambasted in the press for containing the unacknowledged work of other authors and imagined scenes, the book was a financial and critical failure.

self by exploiting the national fixation with the Kennedy saga, recycling old material . . . circumventing journalistic standards and the conventions of scholarship by claiming the privileges of the non-fiction novelist." Within days the charges had stuck. *Kirkus Reviews* (15 July) argued that it was "difficult, actually, to sympathize with the rich, powerful, aging bestseller of a writer — who, even if half the accusations are true, not only created scenes for this book out of whole cloth but plagiarized William Manchester's *The Death of a President* (1967)." By 21 July Manchester had produced a 35-page memorandum citing more than 100 "similarities." The next day the *New York Times* revealed that McGinniss had rewritten his authorial note for the book — "McGinniss Adds Explanation to His Book." McGinniss was quoted as saying: "I have tried to convey what it might have been like to be Teddy Kennedy." On 27 July Michiko Kakutani, critic for the *Times,* also quoted McGinniss ("Different subjects call for different techniques") in her article "Is It Fiction? Is It Nonfiction? And Why Doesn't Anyone Care?" Kakutani's colleague, Christopher Lehmann-Haupt, reviewed the book for the *Times* on 29 July – "The Minds of the Kennedys as Imagined by McGinniss." Lehmann-Haupt takes the stance of judicious irony ("Writing classes of the future will be richly rewarded by studying the art of inferred hypotheses as wielded in *The Last Brother*") and adds several other books to the list of McGinniss's sources. Cox's piece in the *Wall Street Journal,* 30 July ("Publisher Faulted in Kennedy Book Flap") added what must have been more seriously disappointing news to author and publisher: "Despite conventional wisdom that controversy sells books, there are early signs that *The Last Brother* has been tarnished by a wave of negative publicity." On 2 August *Time* ("Teddy, We Hardly Know Ye," by Priscilla Painton) and *Newsweek* ("Trashing Teddy Kennedy," by Larry Martz) panned the book; as Martz wrote: "But it's simply a bad book, a stale farrago of scandal and pop psychology that begins and ends by trashing its subject." An especially bad day for the book was 4 August. In the *Times* ("Book Notes") Sarah Lyall's column was headlined "265,000 Printed, Very Few Sold." Columnist Richard Cohen of the *Washington Post* castigated McGinniss for "dishonesty" ("Bad Book, Good Senator"). James M. Perry, reviewing the book for the *Wall Street Journal* ("Wild Tales: Retreading the Teddy Saga") wrote: "Over the years, I have wallowed in Kennedy books, and this hulking volume reminds me of a family reunion of all the writers." Other major newspaper reviews prominently trashed the book and its author: *Chicago Tribune,* "The Last and the Lost," by Jon Margolis (1 August); *Los Angeles Times,* "Cast Out of Camelot," by Robert Scheer (8 August); *Boston Globe,* "Virtual Biography," by Gail Caldwell (8 August). Caldwell had this accurate comment to make: "Joe McGinniss's *The Last Brother* is an embarrassingly bad book, but it's made terrific copy for the news industry." By 31 August it was high time for a summary. In "The McGinniss Massacre" (*Washington Post,* 31 August), David Streitfeld was not overstating the case in his description of the author's critical reception: "He's been called a worthless, money-grubbing, no-talent, fraudulent, lying, cheating, sickening disingenuous sleaze in every major newspaper and magazine in America . . ." Before Christmas McGinniss found himself on various lists of the year's worst books.

REVIEWING IN THE PAPERS AND MISCELLANEOUS MAGAZINES

For my examination of the present state of book reviewing I regularly read the *New York Times,* the *Washington Post,* and the *Wall Street Journal.* The Sunday book pages I regularly examined were as follows: *New York Times Book Review, Washington Post Book World, Washington Times, Baltimore Sun,* "Tribune Books" of the *Chicago Tribune, Philadelphia Inquirer, Boston Globe, Los Angeles Times Book Review.* Other Sunday papers to which I had occasional access included the *Atlanta Journal-Constitution, Seattle Times-Post Intelligencer, Miami Herald, Tampa Tribune, Houston Chronicle, Charlotte Observer, New York Observer, Nashville Tennessean,* and *Fort Worth Star Telegram.* To be sure, there is something of an accidental geographical bias in my selections. There are any number of good papers I missed entirely. Three that I know possess outstanding book pages and which I would like to have seen are *Newsday, San Francisco Chronicle,* and the *Raleigh News & Observer,* especially the last, which, with its new editor, David Perkins, has been recently described by man-of-letters Fred Chappell as offering "the best book pages in the South." I should add that, though it is more or less irrelevant to the topic of American book reviewing, I regularly receive and read the *Times Literary Supplement* (*TLS*). It is perhaps significant that it is easy to subscribe to, that the *TLS* is readily accessible on good newsstands all over the country, and that it now has an American editor, James Bowman, who from time to time offers a column called "American Notes."

In general, all these papers are doing surprisingly well with their book reviews and coverage, even the *Baltimore Sun,* still clinging to its single page in the "Perspective" section, still using some syndicated reviews from other papers. The *Sun* has some regular, first-rate reviewers of its own, especially Stephen Marguiles and Anne Whitehouse, who are as full of insight as any in the business. All of these papers, one way and another, have listings and calendars of upcoming literary events and author readings and signings, proving at the least that these means of promoting books have taken root across the nation. The *Washington Times,* ably edited by critic Colin Walters, has the best review coverage of poetry, thanks to the regular contributions of people like Anthony Hecht, Henry Taylor, and Edward Kessler. Walters has kept alive the occasional column, "The Lost Word," devoted to "lost" or forgotten books and written by a variety of writers and critics. Best coverage of audio cassettes (a growing market) is to be found in the "Audio Books" column of the *Philadelphia Inquirer*. Mike Schaffer is the new editor of the book pages at the *Inquirer*. Best coverage of science fiction and fantasy is in the *Washington Post Book World*. Outside of the major national papers, the *Atlanta Journal-Constitution,* working with at least three full pages, now has a section for letters, and there are regularly readers who write in with responses to reviews and especially to the challenges of the often-provocative columns written by book editor Michael Skube. Skube, formerly of the *Raleigh News & Observer,* took over the Atlanta book pages this year. Also new on the beat this year is Larry Kart of the *Chicago Tribune,* who took over in July after longtime editor Dianne Donovan, was promoted to editorial pages. Kart worked for Donovan, and so the changes he has made, other than some new names among the stable of reviewers, are not noticeable. One unusual wrinkle in the *Tribune* scheme is the bringing together of popular fiction as a genre in itself like fantasy or mystery. Thus, without interfering with their excellent coverage of "literary" books, they manage to review more best-sellers (if briefly) than most other papers. *Washington Post Book World,* almost unique in its inside-the-beltway concerns and interests, this year added a new twist to its format, introducing "an occasional series of essays by authors on subjects that concern them in their creative lives." Titled "The Writing Life," this series has included essays by (among others) writers as diverse as James Michener, Craig Nova, David Halberstam, Tracy Kidder, Dominick Dunne, and Umberto Eco. Former editor of the *Los Angeles Times Book Review* Jack Miles continues to write an interesting and provocative column ("Endpapers") for that paper. D. T. Max of the *New York Observer* regularly writes or runs a variety of hip and sophisticated inside pieces on the publishing business and the literary scene. A first-rate example: "Memo to Agents: St. Martin's Plays for High Stakes, Too" (16–23 August). Still the unquestioned leader of the pack, the *New York Times Book Review* does, more or less, what it pleases and during the course of the year published seven original essays on "The Seven Deadly Sins," assigning prominent writers to appropriate subjects, among them John Updike on lust, Gore Vidal on pride, Richard Howard on avarice, and Joyce Carol Oates on despair.

The power of the *New York Times Book Review* derives from several sources, not least being location and tradition, but more importantly size and weight and (thus) influence. Edwin Diamond, in a recent excerpt from a forthcoming book, "The Last Word: Behind the Mystique of The New York Times Book Review" (*New York,* 10 January 1994),

reports that the *Times* manages to review or mention between forty-five and fifty books per issue, which adds up to roughly twenty-five hundred of the seventy-eighty thousand titles published annually. "By restricting the world of the *Book Review* to mainstream titles, [editor Rebecca] Sinkler estimated, the actual selection process came down to choosing from a pool of about 7,000 books a year." Dealing with twenty-five hundred books a year puts the *Review* far ahead of any of the other newspaper book reviews or various combinations thereof. No question. Yet, in terms of the leading books of the year, it appeared that the other major players did not miss much. Nor did the others seem to hang back, as one might expect, and wait to see what the *Review* did. By and large, the other papers were prompt in their choices and reviews. It is also true that the *Review* has access to the largest number of reviewers in the country. What working writer can really afford to tell the editors of the *Review* that he or she is too busy to review a book for them? Nevertheless, by alertly keeping up with the literary scene, the other papers have been able to land excellent and reliable reviewers. Their focus may sometimes have to be local or regional, but their reviewers come from all over the country. The current quality of the book reviews, allowing for all the inherent limitations, is very high. What is evident is that in spite of the domination of the *New York Times Book Review,* or perhaps precisely because of it, these papers all over the country are holding their own (even against their own owners and bookkeepers) and make a real contribution. It may also be the case that the new ways and means of promoting and supporting books by sending out authors on tours for signings and readings have inevitably brought cities and regions into the network. It can matter a good deal what reviews in Richmond or Raleigh, in Seattle or Tampa, say about a book. The choices of books to be reviewed and the assignment of reviews by book editors like Fritz Lanham of the *Houston Chronicle,* Margaria Fichtner of the *Miami Herald,* James H. Bready of the *Baltimore Sun,* Larry Swindell of the *Fort Worth Star Telegram,* David Badger of the *Nashville Tennessean,* or Polly Paddock of the *Charlotte Observer,* and any number of others, matter more than ever; and at times any of these people can be major players. And they know it. This is a slight and subtle change, but it is real, if fragile.

As for the quarterlies and literary and miscellaneous magazines, things seem to be more the same than changing. By and large most of the quarterlies and the literary magazines are, at least as far as book reviews are concerned, too late, too uneven, and too erratic to matter. They may or may not be busily creating the poetry and fiction and literary nonfiction of the present and even the future, but in general they do not take their critical duties as seriously as they might. Many offer reviews, sometimes good ones, but there is neither internal continuity nor timely influence.

The exceptions are significant. The *Sewanee Review,* the *Virginia Quarterly Review,* and the *Hudson Review* are top of the line. Managed and directed by editors who have a record of taking book reviewing seriously, at least as much so as the first-class poetry and fiction they publish, they have developed the means, by a nice combination of short reviews, chronicle reviews, and essay reviews, to deal with an impressive number of books in a timely and influential manner. Although their competition (*Kenyon Review, Georgia Review, Southern Review,* and so forth) over the past year have done less and less of what might be classified as active literary criticism, the *Sewanee, Virginia,* and *Hudson* are doing more than ever. *The Georgia Review* almost joins these others at times, and once in a while publishes something genuinely significant like, for example, Chappell's chronicle review of a clutch of contemporary poets, "Figured Carpets: The Collected and Selected" (Summer 1993). But the *Georgia Review* is tentative in its role as a reviewer of record. So are most of the others. The *Review of Contemporary Fiction* is an outstanding exception. Now at a new address in Normal, Illinois, and produced by the surprisingly successful literary press, Dalkey Archive, the *Review* combines a sequence of critical essays about one or two contemporary writers with roughly fifty short reviews of recent books, both mainstream and small press. The *Review* is one of the very few places where "experimental" literature is seriously noticed. The *Review of Contemporary Fiction* is steadily becoming more and more influential. In 1993 an unusual number of small-press books began to be reviewed in the better book pages of the papers. And books from Dalkey Archive are now regularly reviewed in all the major papers.

Four nonweeklies have become important factors in book reviewing. They are the *New York Review of Books,* the *New Criterion, Chronicles,* and the *World and I,* all celebrated in earlier accounts of "Book Reviewing in America." They remain to be celebrated, having fallen off not at all in their reviewing function.

Once upon a time new and more or less rebellious, the *New York Review of Books* (*NYRB*) has become an honored part of the literary establishment, consistent, if not entirely predictable in its form and content. The quality of *NYRB* reviews is high, and the pieces are long enough and leisurely enough to be satisfyingly thorough. But fiction is not a high-priority item either in space or in timing. There are one or two fiction reviews at most per issue, and often they come along well after the actual marketplace for them has closed. Still there are first-rate fiction reviews by any standard, pieces like Denis Donoghue's "Dream Work" on Cormac McCarthy's *All the Pretty Horses* (24 June). And occasionally there is the rare perfect match of book and reviewer, a superior example of which is William Trevor's "Lives of the Saints" (21 October), an essay-review of *No Other Life* (Doubleday), by Brian Moore. Skube devoted his column in the *Atlanta Journal-Constitution* to this famous magazine – "New York Review at 30: Still Brilliant, but Boring," – arguing that fixed political stances were sometimes inhibitions to influential criticism: "There was no literature apart from politics, which is one reason a writer like, say, Anne Tyler could produce novel after novel before being noticed in the *NYRB.*"

The other three, conservative in orientation and no less political in point of view, have somehow managed to keep political ideology to a minimum force when it comes to book reviewing. *Chronicles,* continuing in the same hands of senior book editor Chilton Williamson, Jr., publishes perhaps a dozen reviews a month of varying lengths. All are good; some are outstanding. The *World and I,* facing the same economy as the rest of us, has shrunk itself a little. "Book World" now offers about a dozen essay-reviews in about one hundred pages once a month. Alert, but, it seems, entirely independent of mind, editors Douglas Burton, Wendy Herstein, Clark Munsell, and others give the books they select and assign to reviewers more sustained and thorough coverage than any other reviews these books may earn. Finally, the *New Criterion.* With literary essays usually present in the main part of the magazine, plus half a dozen essay-reviews of recent books in the back of the book, this monthly has some meaningful impact. No other general magazine does as much with themes and subjects from Greek and Roman classical literature. And the literary essays are solid and valuable. Two superior examples from 1993 are Richard Tillinghast's "They Were as Good as We Were: The Stories of William Trevor" (February) and "Why Should We Read Joyce Cary?" (May), by Bruce Bawer.

Among the other category of miscellaneous magazines (not counting the fashion magazines, which are dealt with separately, below), *Time* and *Newsweek* have, for the time being at least, greatly reduced their book coverage. They still have the same influence when they elect to exercise it, but for the most part they were minor players in 1993. Similarly, *People* magazine has all but forsaken the printed book (without pictures), though they still have "Pages" in their upfront section of "Picks and Pans." And once in a great while they will review a literary novel. At the other end of the spectrum are the crowd of scholarly publications which, though much preoccupied these days with other things than traditional literary criticism or literary scholarship, from time to time enter the literary scene. Dated October 1992, but in fact published in March 1993, *American Notes & Queries* (*ANQ*) presented a lively special issue, edited by Lance Olsen, of contributions by thirty fiction writers on the subject of "The Future of American Fiction." The picture of the future of fiction was generally depressing, but there were positive moments like this one by Joyce Thompson: "Fiction retains its power to access, invoke, evoke, provoke, enrage and engage in ways no other medium yet invented can match."

Somewhere in between *People* and *ANQ*, though under new management inching ever closer to the former, the *New Yorker* has considerably reduced its book reviewing activity. But it is still the *New Yorker* and as such remains important and influential even though its book reviewing – usually one essay-review and a handful of "Books Briefly Noted" – has been scaled down to fit the new format. The new format and its advocate, editor Tina Brown, have been the subject of some serious evaluation. Deirdre Carmody of the *New York Times* ("Tina Brown's Progress at The New Yorker," 12 April) found good reasons to praise Brown and the changes she has made. Citing the fact that Joseph Epstein (as "Aristides") has been intensely critical in the *American Scholar,* Carmody quotes Brown's answer to her critics: " 'Good taste in the prissy sense has never been of interest to me.' " A little later (25 April) Jack Miles, writing in the *Los Angeles Times Book Review* – "What Has Happened to The New Yorker" – was concerned about more serious matters than simply good taste. "The New Yorker," he wrote, "under its new editor, has ceased to be a calm magazine, reflecting and shaping a broadly American and democratic culture, and has become an increasingly anxious magazine, buying and selling the buzz." Probably the best critical look at the new directions at the *New Yorker* is an essay by D. W. Faulkner in the summer issue of the *Sewanee Review* – "Mrs. Brown Meets Mr. Ross." Faulkner concludes: "Even reviews in the current *New Yorker* seem dominated by a cult of personality." Some-

times that habit can be a strength as, for example, the "Critic at Large" essay by Martin Amis on the late Philip Larkin. This piece, "Don Juan in Hull" (12 July), is in fact an essay-review of two books, Larkin's *Selected Letters* and Andrew Motion's biography, *Philip Larkin: A Writer's Life,* neither at the time published or available in the United States, both subsequently published by Farrar, Straus, and Giroux. However, both books had already been published in Britain and had been the occasion for major controversy there. Deftly disposing of criticism that Larkin was a racist and a misogynist, Amis adds personal recollection (Larkin was his father's friend and his brother's godfather) to outline a portrait of Larkin the man and poet, celebrating "the comedy of candor": "Here melancholy still hurts, but it embodies its own comic relief; and dignity is not needed." A superb piece of new *New Yorker* literary journalism.

More and more, popular literary journalism has become allied with book reviewing. With authors in motion, on book tours, giving readings and signings, there is the news factor, resulting in a steady output of articles, profiles, and interviews, all deemed as important as book reviews by the publishers. These pieces show up in all kinds of places as well as the newspapers and magazines. They are certainly to be found in a wide variety of literary publications aimed at general groups: *AWP Chronicle, Authors Guild Bulletin, PSA Journal* (Poetry Society of America), *Poets and Writers,* and others. And they are frequently found in alumni magazines. The downside of this gradual development is the raising of publicity, in and of itself, as a desirable goal for writers. Writing about his fellow novelist William Gaddis ("The Author in Hiding," *Los Angeles Times Book Review,* 28 March), William Gass painted a grim picture for the contemporary writer: "If you are to remain known while writing books (for the books themselves are likely to have a mayfly's life), you must either court the media and let publicity be your pimp like Truman Capote, or cling like old ivy to the walls of the Academy, passing your person around from campus to campus like a canape on a party tray."

The interview of the visiting writer is the most familiar form. Of course, it helps to have a colorful subject. Which may explain why some of the better interview examples of the year deal with poet and novelist James Dickey. In "James Dickey at 70" (*Atlanta Journal-Constitution,* 26 September), Skube managed to elicit some lively comment on Dickey's long-term adversary – poet and cult figure Robert Bly. "Bly is the funniest and most pathetic thing I ever heard of," Dickey is quoted as saying. "He lectures and reads in some long costume made in the Peruvian Andes. I don't know what it is, but I say this. If you can write poetry, you don't have to dress funny – and he can't write. He's never written a memorable line in his life." Margaria Fichtner's *Miami Herald* (14 November) interview with Dickey, "The Poet Survivor," focused self-reflexively on the impact of the subject on the reporter: "This is not an interview: it is an immersion course, a daredevil swerve along the crests and ebbs of James Dickey's mind." David Streitfeld of the *Washington Post,* probably the best all-around literary journalist in the country, can often get good copy from unlikely subjects. One of his best interviews of 1993 (12 August) was "Muriel Spark, Fired Up: Don't Ask the Novelist What's on Her Mind – She May Tell You." As here, for example, when Spark speaks of a former friend and collaborator: "I try not to be too subjective about this, because I hate the man's guts."

The closely related profile, or personality piece, often has an interview as its occasion but moves beyond that to a general appraisal of the subject's work and career. Some of the better profiles I encountered during the year were as follows: "A Southern Road to Freedom," by Ken Ringle, *Washington Post* (20 July), a profile of African-American novelist Ernest Gaines; "The Volcano Lover: Sontag in Sarajevo," by Janine De Diovanna, *New York Observer* (30 August–6 September), a profile of Susan Sontag; "Lets's Do Naked Lunch," by David Gates, *Newsweek* (6 September), a profile of William Burroughs; "Making Monster Huge," by Amy Wallace, *Los Angeles Times Magazine* (4 April), a profile of literary convict Kody Scott, also known as "Monster"; "Surprised by Happiness," by Lorrie Moore, *Elle* (November), a profile of first-novelist Lee Kercheval; "The Ghost Writer at Home on the Range," by Malcolm Jones, a profile of Larry McMurtry *Newsweek* (2 August); "Iconoclastic Writer's Wrongs Make Right," by Brenda L. Fulton, *Erie Times-News* (4 April), a profile of novelist Randall Silvis; "Capturing a Life: Arnold Rampersad's New Directions in Literary Biography and Autobiography," by Jennifer Howard, *Princeton Alumni Weekly* (24 November); and "Woman With a View: Novelist Susanna Moore on Life, Liberty and the Pursuit of Status," by David Colman, *W* magazine (August).

Gold stars for the best and the brightest literary profiles go to the following:

(a) Eileen McNamara, "Papa Waller," *Boston Globe Magazine* (27 June): " 'People tell me I have written *The Sun Also Rises,* that this is a new version

of *The Old Man and the Sea,*' says Robert Waller, author of *The Bridges of Madison County.* No one may be more moved by the force of his creation than Waller himself."

(b) Harold Brodkey, "Conscientious Objections to Gordon Lish and His Army," *New York Observer* (8 March): "Women at the trial or reading about it have said to me they were stirred by Gordon's obsessiveness, and touched by his pathos, his pitiability – by *his dreams,* silly or not."

(c) John Meroney, "The Real Maya Angelou," *American Spectator* (March): "Where JFK offered us genius, Clinton gave us a phantom professor with a broom-closet office and an assumed name."

(d) Georgann Eubanks, "Fred Chappell: The Bard of Canton," *Duke Magazine* (November–December 1993): "His dazzling mastery of craft enables him to take risks in his work, to break the rules, and often to stretch readers to the limits of their suspended disbelief."

(e) "In Full Spate: The Fertility and Generosity of Anthony Burgess," *TLS* (17 December): "Burgess was all for crossing frontiers and cross-breeding cultures, an esperantist of the spirit."

The article in literary journalism may be critical in a popular sense, that is, concerned with the most recent trends and developments, an excellent example being Michael Silverblatt, "The New Fiction of Transgression," *Los Angeles Times Book Review* (1 August). Articles are often generalized views of a particular genre from a particular point of view: Lawrence Block, "My Life in Crime: A Personal Overview of American Mystery Fiction," *American Heritage* (August). Articles are sometimes devoted to a local or regional scene, like this broad treatment of thirty-five contemporary southern Californian writers: Nina J. Gaston, "L. A. and Other Fictions," *Los Angeles Times Magazine* (5 September). Occasionally the article appears as "news," reporting controversy or discovery. For example, there was Cox's "Classic Clash Is Talk of Random House" (*Wall Street Journal,* 30 October), dealing with the internal competition between the Modern Library and Everyman's Library, both under the Random House corporate umbrella. There are those pieces with a literary basis which are presented as straightforward news: Liz McMillen, "New Theory About Mark Twain's Sexuality Brings Strong Reactions from Experts," *Chronicle of Higher Education* (8 September), regarding how the scholarly world, already troubled by Shelley Fisher Fishkin's assertion that Mark Twain based much of the character of Huck Finn on an African-American boy, must contend with the arguments of Andy Hoffman of

Brown University that Twain was gay. Or Philip Nobile's "Uncovering Roots," *Village Voice* (23 February), is a series of accusations concerning the late Alex Haley: "But beyond the plagiarism, and the massive perjury required to cover it up, *Roots,* as Haley well knew, was a hoax, a literary painted mouse, a piltdown of genealogy, a pyramid of bogus research." With the breakdown of the Berlin Wall and the end of the Cold War, various kinds of information concerning literary figures and matters is becoming available and finding its way into print. In Todd Gitlin's "I Did Not Imagine That I Lived In Truth," *New York Times Book Review* (4 April), we learned that prominent East German writer Christa Wolf had served STASI (the secret police) as "an informal collaborator" (*inoffizielle mitarbeiter*) whose code name was "Marguerite." (Wolf's code name for STASI was "Forked Tongue.") We also discovered that Wolf is now living in Santa Monica on a fellowship from the Getty Center for the History of Art and Humanities to rewrite the story of Medea in feminist terms. In a major article in *Washington Post Book World* (7 March), "Better Read Than Red," Vladimir Voinovich offered for the first time a basic account of the ways and means of the Writers Union during Soviet days. Visited by any number of prominent American and European writers over the years, the Writers Union somehow escaped accurate scrutiny and exposure until now: "The bosses managed everything that had to do with literature and got everything the Soviet state had to give. By edict the nation's outstanding writers, they were paid big salaries, granted lavish apartments, dachas, and chauffeured cars. Their books – read by no one – were printed and endlessly reprinted in any case, generating royalties and winning their authors the highest decorations and the state's most prestigious literary prizes. They traveled first class and stayed in the best hotels. Critics were only allowed to compose panegyrics about them. The Union secretaries in the highest positions were likened to Shakespeare, Tolstoy and Dostoyevsky."

Then there are the undeniable oddities, those articles where literature and literary things are arranged to suit nonliterary purposes. Item. In *New Woman* (December) Dr. Ruth Westheimer offered a list of her top ten erotic novels ("For Your Bedroom Bookshelf"). None was from 1993, but *Suicide Blonde* (1992), by Darcey Steinke, made the list. Arguing that "the loosening of sexual roles and the shattering of false machismo with all its limitations has helped alter and broaden the erotic terrain for the 90s," Owen Keehnen, in "Tell Me the Good Parts," *Penthouse Forum* (December), seriously discussed four 1993 literary authors and offered erotic excerpts from their work – Scott Turow, Victor Erofeyev, Trey Ellis, and Harry Matthews.

Not an oddity, but nevertheless remarkable in any season was an article by Paul West, "Felipe Alfau and the NBA" (*Review of Contemporary Fiction,* Spring 1993). Here West gives a rare accounting of how he and his fellow judges for the National Book Award evaluated the more than two hundred books nominated by their publishers in 1990 and came, finally, to bestow the award on Charles Johnson's *The Middle Passage,* described by West as "an inferior, nervously didactic novel," adding later the wistful might-have-been: "If only there had been enough taste in the judges to discern excellence where it showed." To someone like myself who served as a 1993 judge for the National Book Award in fiction, the faults and flaws of the system, as described by Paul West, are real and probably inherent. In the end the winner is bound to be (almost always) a compromise candidate, worthy enough most of the time, to be sure, but not necessarily superior to any number of other excellent books that fall through the gaping cracks of the judging process. As for the weeding-out from the initial nominations, I must endorse West's judgment also: "In about 170 out of some two hundred, I had been unable to find a superb sentence, an unforgettable phrase, a scene that burned home."

Finally, following the example of last year's *Dictionary of Literary Biography Yearbook,* I offer my choices of the best book reviews – gold stars (favorable) and tomahawk chops (negative) for 1993.

Best piece on book reviewing: Edward Hirsch, "Reviewing Poetry," *AWP Chronicle* (October/November): "Writing reviews should be more than offering opinions, more than dismissals and raves. Backslapping is unbecoming and clubbishness should be scorned, but internecine rivalries played out in print are even more depressing. Generosity of spirit is badly in want."

Bruce Allen, "Recreating Haiti," *Boston Sunday Globe* (22 August). Review of *No Other Life* (Doubleday), by Brian Moore. Allen calls this book "not only Brian Moore's best yet but one of the finest political novels – perhaps one of the finest novels – of recent years."

Madison Smartt Bell, "The Return of the Green Ray," *New York Times Book Review* (11 April). Review of *Further Adventures* (St. Martin's Press), by Jon Stephen Fink: "The craziness comes through loud and clear. Mr. Fink has brought off the inter-

Dust jacket for Willie Morris's memoir of his tenure in the late 1960s and early 1970s as the editor of Harper's

esting trick of presenting what often looks like an authentically psychotic monologue in a form sufficiently coherent to be understood."

Madison Smartt Bell, "With 'Oracle' Stories, Peter Taylor Monitors Decline with Careful, Sidelong Looks," *Baltimore Sun* (14 February). Review of *The Oracle at Stoneleigh Court* (Knopf), by Peter Taylor: "Peter Taylor's stories are most immediately striking, and in the end most memorable, for their quality of voice. It's a voice that buttonholes you, insinuates itself into your ear, so that the story experience is more like listening than reading."

Fred Chappell, "Beautiful Excess," *Chronicles* (October). Review of *The Hard to Catch Mercy* (Algonquin), by William Baldwin: "It fills and overfills that neatest definition of a good novel: it is both serious in its intentions and great fun to read. I can't think of another contemporary writer who has made a more splendid debut than William Baldwin."

Annie Dillard, "The Ancient Story of Jacob, Retold in a Passionate, Exalted Pitch," *Boston Globe* (30 May). Review of *Son of Laughter* (Harper San Francisco), by Frederick Buechner: "He magnifies the comic and tortured human drama by presenting

Jacob unforgettably, and his story's power never lets up."

R. H. W. Dillard, "The Best Woman a Man Could Make," *The World and I* (May). Review of *Poor Things* (Harcourt Brace), by Alasdair Gray: "If we are to work as if we live in the early days of a better nation (one that has never existed), both Alasdair Gray and Umberto Eco would agree, we must produce open work. In literary terms this means a work that actively engages the reader in its production, in constructing its story and that story's meaning."

Robert Gingher, "Passing by the Dragon," *The World and I* (July). Review of *The Hard to Catch Mercy*, by Baldwin: "Were it not for Algonquin's exceptional practice of investing in first-time writers, Baldwin's unsolicited, unrepresented manuscript would likely never have seen the light of day. A novel of this magnitude, one that paints a comprehensive world with such impersonal vision and humility, is hard to catch."

James W. Hall, "The Good Killer," *Washington Post Book World*. Review of *Shella* (Knopf), by Andrew Vachss. Hall writes of Vachss's power in language: "It comes from the hypnotic cadences of John's speech, from the Diane Arbus flashbulb-in-your-face realism, and from the elliptical yet pungent string of simple declarative sentences. The eye speeds through the pages, dragged ahead by a fascination for this sleazy yet morally tricky universe."

Marcie Hershman, "A Chronicle of Violence and Numbed Emotions," *Boston Globe* (23 May). Review of *Save Me, Joe Louis* (Harcourt Brace), by Bell: "Bell, the author of six other novels, is a wonderful writer. He knows how to authenticate worlds which in less deeply drawn books more often appear as romanticized and exotic. Simply, he takes the time to pay attention."

Irving Malin, "Unresolved Mysteries," *Michigan Quarterly Review* (Summer). Review of *A Friendly Deceit* (Johns Hopkins), by Greg Johnson, and *Skin* (Ontario Review), by C. E. Poverman: "The stories suggest that although we seem to be secure and normal, we are, nevertheless, haunted by the fact that we are on the edge — we can hardly contain hidden motives; we lie to ourselves, our friends and relatives."

Thomas McGonigle, "Delmore Schwartz Was a Fan," *Los Angeles Times Book Review* (2 January 1994). Review of *Testimonies* (Norton), by Patrick O'Brian: "There is a sort of desperate giving in to the fantasy that people who speak an obscure language, have bad plumbing and sleep in close proximity to their farm animals are somehow both more compassionate and closer to nature."

Kit Reed, "Wherein Not Much Happens, But, oh, Those Characters," *Philadelphia Inquirer* (11 July). Review of *Nobody's Fool* (Random), by Richard Russo: "Russo's people are eccentric and sometimes look funny or smell bad, but whether or not you'd want them in your living room, they're completely likable."

Andy Solomon, " '68: Heroes Fall and a Family Falls Apart," *Miami Herald* (8 August). Review of *Rebel Powers* (Houghton Mifflin), by Richard Bausch: "Over the past decade, Bausch has created a body of fiction that places him in the top echelon of contemporary writers. *Rebel Powers* may be the most authoritative expression yet of the extraordinary insight and compassion he brings to his characters."

Jon Manchip White, "A Politician-Priest, Haitian Style, Is Brought to Life by Brian Moore," *Chicago Tribune* (19 September). Review of *No Other Life,* by Moore: "*No Other Life* demonstrates the skills we have come to associate with Brian Moore's fiction. There is the assured touch with a scene, the business-like unfolding of the narrative, the muscular yet elegant style."

Anne Whitehouse, "Two Violent Drifters Stumble Through Baltimore On The Way To Catastrophe," *Baltimore Sun* (23 May). Review of *Save Me, Joe Louis,* by Bell: "While the violence that Mr. Bell describes may be – and often is – gratuitous, his writing is economical, poetic, dramatic and powerful."

One of the standard tropes in most articles about book reviewing is the wistful complaint that there is so little real criticism in the book pages, that, with the exception of cases of feeding frenzy, like the McGinniss episode if 1993, there are so few negative reviews. In part this complaint is justified; because to many editors, reviewers as well, it seems a waste of precious space. For every negative review there is a good or worthwhile book that must be ignored. Still, negative reviews find a place in the book pages; and it seemed to me that 1993 offered a full share. There was no difficulty in finding them, and there was a serious problem in selecting the best among them. Here are the best (in this observer's opinion) of the Tomahawk Chops of 1993.

Bruce Bawer, "Beautiful Dreamers," *Washington Post* (13 June). Review of *Operation Wandering Soul* (Morrow), by Richard Powers: "For all the brilliance of his prose, his reflections about man and so-

ciety barely surpass the intellectual level of 'We Are the World.' "

Madison Smartt Bell, "From T. R. Pearson, a Police Procedural Set in South," *Philadelphia Inquirer* (10 January). Review of *Cry Me A River* (Holt), by T. R. Pearson: "The cast of characters is more or less the usual: nutty old ladies, slutty young ladies, vomiting drunks, a truck-driving poet, a fey homosexual, cops shooting themselves in the foot and so forth – familiar stereotypes one and all. They appear in episodes that have all the subtlety, sophistication and resemblance to real life of an installment of *Hee-Haw* or *The Three Stooges*."

Don Belton, "From Hunt, a Tale of Taboos Set in Early-1900s Germantown," *Philadelphia Inquirer* (11 February). Review of *Free* (Dutton), by Marsha Hunt: "*Free* suffers from lack of nerve, as if Cinderella, all tricked out in her charmed finery, had stayed fretting with her powder and curls in her carriage, until the carriage turned back into a pumpkin and her shimmery frock, a rag."

Nicholas Delbanco, "Cyrus Colter's Tale of Virulent Racism and Parisian Passion," *Chicago Tribune* (15 August). Review of *City of Light* (Thunder Mouth), by Cyrus Colter: "At spotlit intervals *City of Light* attains a vivid immediacy; all too often, though, its characterization is caricature and its power dim."

David Gates, "Great Expectations, No Satisfaction," *Newsweek* (27 September). Review of *Body & Soul* (Houghton Mifflin), by Frank Conroy: "*Body & Soul* has both the improbability and the predictability of a pop best seller; from Conroy that's the last thing we would have predicted."

Paul Gray, "Words Without Music, for Sure," *Time* (27 September). Review of *Body & Soul,* by Conroy: "It's plodding, chronological course never swerves or jolts; it sadly lacks the sound track it cannot have."

Winston Groom, "Marching to a Different Humdrum," *Los Angeles Times Book Review* (21 March). Review of *Shadow Play* (Norton), by Charles Baxter. "Baxter has created a scenario in which alienation and anxiety are the norm, a kind of dubious universe where people are neither good nor evil but instead are driven by 20th Century pragmatism into a twilight zone of utter practicality."

Bernard Knox, "War Within and Without," *Washington Post* (12 September). Review of *While England Sleeps* (Viking), by David Leavitt: "The long arm of coincidence is so hard at work in his adaptation of Spender's sober account that the reader begins to wonder whether perhaps Leavitt is playing post-modernist games – self-parody? magic realism?"

Peter Kurth, "Oates' Latest Is Thelma and Louise for the Headachy Set," *New York Observer* (16–23 August). Review of *Foxfire* (Dutton), by Joyce Carol Oates: "I'm tired of victims in all their guises, and I might have taken more kindly to *Foxfire's* assortment of battered little hoodlums if Ms. Oates had shown the slightest sign of distance, some redeeming new perspective, regarding their distress."

Gene Lyons, *Entertainment Weekly* (10 September). Review of *No Other Life*, by Moore: "But when the prolific Irish-born author allows theological preoccupations to overwhelm his plot and characters, the result resembles less a novel than a case study concocted out of the Baltimore Chatechism."

Francine Prose, "She Got What She Deserved," *Washington Post* (4 April). Review of *For Love* (HarperCollins), by Sue Miller: "*For Love* is the sort of novel in which we get to know the heroine so intimately that we repeatedly follow her into the bathroom to watch her brush her teeth – an act that reveals little about character."

Joe Queenan, "Twilight of the Today," *Wall Street Journal* (29 January). Review of *Making the Mummies Dance* (Simon and Schuster), by Thomas Hoving: "By the end of *Making the Mummies Dance*, one feels a certain pity for a man whose contributions to the cultural history of this nation have been largely overshadowed by his incessant grandstanding. . . . In this sense, he embodies everything that New York stands for: cupidity, extravagance, lack of respect for tradition, an insatiable need to be amused, and a vulgarity that would make a Philistine gasp."

Donna Rifkind, "Pall in the Family," *Washington Post* (27 May). Review of *Long Way From Home* (Ticknor & Fields), by Frederick Busch: "In its artificiality, tedious zigzagging narrative and meretriciously violent ending, *Long Way From Home* is a long way from either serious fiction or genuine entertainment."

Alexander Theroux, "Portrait of Laure: Life and Hard Times of a Novel's Narrator," *Philadelphia Inquirer* (5 September). Review of *My Mother: Demonology* (Pantheon), by Kathy Acker: "Art, Acker assumes, is page after tedious page of masturbatory fantasies, oafish copulations, and hateful disclosures of the crudest kind imaginable. Nothing is too low for comment, no vile word too disgusting to repeat . . . The language is the tired and shopworn language of the streets. There is no candor, only vulgarity; no confession, only cliche."

As in years gone by, many reviews by the professionally curmudgeonly Jonathan Yardley could easily qualify as Tomahawk Chops or even a Golden Hatchet Award. My favorite in 1993 is "Sticks and Stones," *Washington Post* (19 September). Review of *Only Words* (Harvard), by Catherine A. MacKinnon: "*Only Words* is a dangerous, paranoid book. Its prose may be muddy and humorless, and its fuzzy thought may masquerade as dense legalese, but about one thing it is absolutely clear: Individual rights must be subordinated to the larger interests of society as defined by Catherine MacKinnon and others of her persuasion."

To end this section on a more affirmative note I hereby select poet and novelist Fred Chappell as the best all-around book reviewer for 1993. Chappell is extraordinary not only in the number of high-quality book reviews he wrote during the year, but also for the variety of places – newspapers, quarterlies, literary magazines – his work appeared. Chappell published outstanding reviews in the *Atlanta Journal-Constitution, Charlotte Observer, Fayetteville Observer-Times, Greensboro News and Record, Newsday, Raleigh News & Observer, Washington Post Book World, Chronicles, Georgia Review, Greensboro Review, Louisiana Literature, Mid-American Review, Southern Humanities Review, The Southern Review,* and others. During the year Chappell also brought out a critical book – *Plow Naked: Selected Writings on Poetry* (University of Michigan Press), part of the Poets on Poetry series.

THE LITERARY YEAR IN THE FASHION MAGAZINES

Kristin Van Ogtrop

Magazine readers, apparently, are not book readers. It is a brutal truth: the longer one remains in magazines, the more one realizes how relatively unimportant books have become. Often, when page budgets are tight, book coverage is the first thing to be dropped. Despite the grim climate, however, some magazine editors managed to present interesting, vital (and only occasionally repetitive) articles about the world of literature and letters in 1993.

First, the relevant shakedowns:

In the spring it was announced that Amy Gross, then editor of *Mirabella,* was moving to *Elle* to serve as editorial director. Rumors flew in the weeks that followed as to which staff members would defect. One by one, key editors jumped ship, among them the respected literary editor Pat Towers. Because of such changeovers and Gross's strong reputation as an editor, the premier September issue of *Elle* was eagerly awaited.

The second shoe dropped at the end of September, when the staff at *New York* magazine assembled at 11 A.M. one morning to learn that Ed Kosner, editor in chief for the last thirteen years, would be leaving to take over *Esquire*. Terry McDonnell, who had worked as editor in chief of *Esquire* for three years, was to take over another Hearst property, *Sports Afield* – not, it was clear, a promotion. Kosner had been negotiating with *Esquire* since the spring, and for talks to occur at that level – and involving two monolithic publishing companies, K-III and Hearst – without word leaking was nothing short of miraculous. (At this writing, over two months after Kosner dropped the bomb, K-III still has not found an editor to replace him. The corporation has hired a head-hunting firm, with managing editor Peter Herbst as acting editor in chief in the meantime.)

These editorial coups and crossovers suggest that some interesting changes are afoot in the land of women's and men's fashion magazines. The coverage of books may change commensurately. Great improvements have already been made with the new *Elle*.

The men's magazines in 1993, for their part, showed both improvement and decline. After a disappointing showing in 1992, McDonnell's *Esquire* had a mixed year. *Esquire* devotes a healthy amount of its page space to book reviews, book excerpts, and fiction. Unfortunately, the magazine does not do any of the above as well as *GQ* does. Book coverage in *Esquire* ("The Magazine for Men") seems, for lack of a better word, predictable. There are, one senses, such things as "*Esquire*" books, and there are certain men who set out to write them. Two authors, both featured in the May "Man at His Best" section, are sure examples. Their book titles alone give them away: *Cock and Bull* (by Will Self, Atlantic Monthly), and *The Virgin Suicides* (by Jeffrey Eugenides, Farrar, Straus, and Giroux). Thom Jones – ex-Marine, ex-janitor and rumored tough guy – whose book *The Pugilist at Rest* was covered in June, is also representative of the *Esquire* penchant for machismo.

There were, however, some flashes of originality in 1993 coverage in *Esquire*, beginning with Philip Weiss's January piece on the current life of Salman Rushdie, five years into his *fatwa*. And in April, Jennet Conant wrote a lengthy article on Knopf head Sonny Mehta. While it is undisputed that Mehta *publishes* a lot of books, he has not yet written a book on which his name is listed as author, so Conant's piece cannot technically be called a book review. September brought a long piece on *Short Cuts*, the Robert Altman movie, and, although the movie is based on Raymond Carver's stories and Carver does figure in the piece, it cannot be counted, either. Too much Hollywood lingo. Too many cartoon drawings of actors.

The fiction in *Esquire*, however, made up for its B-minus book reviews in 1993. Most notable was the July "Summer Fiction Special," with stories by James Salter, Ann Beattie, Peter Matthiessen, Jayne Anne Phillips, Richard Ford, and Cormac McCarthy. In a time when fiction appearing in the slick magazines is becoming an exception, *Esquire* persists, all the while giving *Harper's*, the *New Yorker*, and the *Atlantic* a run for their money.

Details, however, did not prove itself as able a competitor in 1993 – in terms of books, at least. While covering better-known authors such as T. C. Boyle (*The Road to Wellville*, Viking) and Thom Jones (*The Pugilist at Rest*, Little, Brown) the editors at *Details* reached far afield for more unusual books. So far afield, in fact, that the magazine's book coverage took on a decidedly New Age tone, filled with people who make a living by predicting the day the world will end. In January Michael Krantz described *Mondo 2000: A User's Guide to the New Edge* as "a technicolor introduction to the oncoming Digital Millenium." In April the magazine published a profile of Terence McKenna ("cosmic explorer") to coincide with the arrival of his book *True Hallucinations*. One wonders how writers like David Halberstam (*The Fifties*, Villard) manage to get their books covered in *Details*, as Halberstam did in June; the venerated journalist signified a brief, lucid landing in an otherwise spacey year.

Most *Details* coverage consists of short, back-of-book pieces and minireviews, although February featured a long article on Hunter S. Thompson. *Details* is not yet a bookseller's nirvana; in three months of 1993 (February, March, and July) the magazine had no book coverage at all. Readers, however, didn't complain. *Details* ad pages skyrocketed this year, making it one of the hottest magazines of 1993.

Still, none of the men's magazines came close to *GQ* in terms of number of books covered, topics considered, and well-known writers employed. In preparation for this study, the stack of clips from *GQ* was substantially thicker than that of any other magazine. *GQ* book coverage ran the gamut from an excerpt from Edmund Wilson's *The Sixties* (Farrar, Straus, and Giroux) in February to an April essay by James Atlas on Philip Roth, Gore Vidal, and John Updike to Joseph Nocera on Peter Lynch (*Beating the Street,* Simon and Schuster) in June. Despite a startling omission of book coverage in the July issue, literary editor Tom Mallon returned in August with his standard, generous formula: one short review in "GQ Critiques," one longer book review (this time Paul West on new editions of Proust), and one piece of fiction ("Going Home With Uccello," by Ann Beattie). There were still several of Mordecai Richler's "Books and Things" columns peppered throughout the year, although not as many as in 1992. In September *GQ* published this critic's personal favorite of all the articles on Joe McGinniss's *The Last Brother* (Simon and Schuster), written by Michael Kelly, Washington correspondent for the *New York Times.*

Not only does *GQ* regularly publish fiction, but this year they started a fiction contest (picking up where *Mademoiselle* left off), named for Frederick Exley and won by a yearbook publisher by the name of Talton Weber, who sent a load of Amish cheese to the *GQ* editorial staff after he cinched the prize.

Last year *Mirabella* easily won the book race (thanks, most likely, to the efforts of book editor Towers). This year, while overall pages continued to decline, the features editors made it quite clear that they were not going down without a fight. In the September issue of *Mirabella,* which numbered a paltry 194 pages, there were eight pages of book coverage, including an excerpt from Susan Swan's *The Wives of Bath* (Knopf), with an accompanying interview of Swan. In contrast, *Vogue* had five pages of books in an issue that was 604 pages long, and *Harper's Bazaar,* at 454 pages, gave books only one page.

Book coverage of *Mirabella* has a free-for-all feel. Take, for example, Vince Passaro's February article on Lorrie Moore, who did not publish a book in all of 1993. The magazine covers books in as many formats as possible, including question and answer (Clarissa Pinkola Estes – *Women Who Run With the Wolves* [1992] – in July; David Rieff – *The Exile* [Simon and Schuster] – in August), excerpts (Susan Swan in September; Meredith Etherington-Smith's *Dali* [Random House] in October), fiction (by Amy Bloom, July), and "Short List," Vince Passaro's brief recommendations/reviews that appear nearly every month.

The editors who left *Mirabella* for *Elle* in 1993 brought their commitment to literary coverage with them. Book coverage in *Elle* in the past few years has been embarrassing. February and March issues were devoid of any book reviews. In April the mag-

azine published a piece on fashion designers and their comic book inspirations (perhaps that's a book story?); in April and July there were short pieces on Eugenides as well as Amanda Filipacchi (*Nude Men,* Viking). In August *Elle* published a strange piece on Sally Quinn that had nothing to do with the publication of a book.

Then came September, and new editorial director Amy Gross's debut. Gross published several short pieces, as well as a long, informative article by *New York Observer* literary editor D. T. Max on what makes books hot in Hollywood. With the arrival of the October issue it was plain that September's book coverage was not just beginner's fervor. Although most of it was presented in a short format, the book reviews in October were varied and plentiful. And the October issue brought a Lorrie Moore short story, "Agnes of Iowa." In November came more of the same, with a long piece on Naomi Wolf (*Fire with Fire,* Random House) containing the funniest quote of 1993, highlighted and enlarged for those fanning through the magazine's pages: "Yes! You can have breasts and use footnotes!" Also in November Lorrie Moore interviewed Jesse Lee Kercheval (*The Museum of Happiness,* Faber and Faber); in addition, the magazine published two short pieces by Walter Kirn – *The Illustrated Woody Allen Reader* (Knopf) – and Mary Cantwell – on Diana Trilling's *The Beginning of the Journey* (Harcourt Brace).

So, compared to last year, the literate female populace has gained a magazine with the improvement of *Elle* without, apparently, losing much from *Mirabella* but ad pages.

Even *Harper's Bazaar,* under the still relatively new direction of Liz Tilberis, is on the up-and-up. Their coverage of international writers in 1993 was unparalleled. In March *Harper's Bazaar* published a profile of Japanese writer Haruki Murakami (*The Elephant Vanishes,* Knopf); in April, the magazine continued this course by profiling Vietnamese novelist Duong Thu Huong (*Paradise of the Blind,* Morrow). One does not have to look closely to realize that Asian writers are terribly neglected both in the U.S. book market and the U.S. mass-market magazines. *Harper's Bazaar* should be commended for bucking this tendency.

Nonetheless, the book coverage in *Harper's Bazaar* is currently the weakest of the women's magazines. Despite the Asian interest, much of the book material is predictable: an excerpt from Susanna Kaysen's *Girl, Interrupted* (Turtle Bay) in May, a short story by Jay McInerney in July, an interview with Linda Fairstein – *Sexual Violence* (Morrow) –

and Katie Roiphe – *The Morning After* (Little, Brown) – in September, a review of Frank Conroy's *Body and Soul* (Houghton Mifflin/Seymour Lawrence) in October, a profile of Naomi Wolf in November. There was a curious Q&A with Susan Sarandon and Gore Vidal in January, but one would be hard-pressed to consider this a book piece. One thing *Harper's Bazaar* could use is a section that would cover several books in a short space, like "Short List" in *Mirabella* or "Arts in Brief" in *Vogue*

Which brings us to *Vogue*. The frequency and nature of book reviews in Anna Wintour's magazine was consistent in 1993 with the previous year. Unlike *Harper's Bazaar* or *Elle, Vogue* ran at least one book feature every month. One quirky new addition to the magazine's book coverage in 1993 came with the overhauled "People Are Talking About" section. "People Are Talking About" has endured a mishmash of different incarnations over the years, but now, as written by Charles Gandee, it is a monthly study of timely happenings, including books. The section also allows *Vogue* to mention books it would not necessarily pick for a long review – for example, children's books by famous people in April and *The World Guide to Nude Beaches & Recreation* (Naturist Editions) in July.

In its traditional book coverage, the magazine sticks mainly to straightforward book reviews (which are inherently positive, as nearly all book criticism to be found in the fashion magazines is) although there were, sprinkled throughout the year, several "theme pieces." In January, for instance, James Atlas wrote an article on three books celebrating romantic unions; Rick Marin (or UbiquiRick – the most published freelancer in New York) studied new editions of classic books in April; in June Edmund White covered four books about the 1950s; and in October Edward Jay Epstein covered three new books on the Kennedys. Although *Vogue* did break from the predictable path occasionally in 1993 (Karen Grigsby Bates on Karen Hudson's book *Paul R. Williams, Architect: A Legacy of Style,* from Rizzoli, in November), for the most part the books reviewed in its pages were books that received notice elsewhere, if not from *Vogue* competitors: popular picks included Jeanette Winterson's *Written on the Body* (Knopf), Thomas Keneally's *Woman of the Inner Sea* (Nan A. Talese/Doubleday), Philip Roth's *Operation Shylock* (Simon and Schuster), Susanna Moore's *Sleeping Beauties* (Knopf), and Margaret Atwood's *The Robber Bride* (Nan A. Talese/Doubleday). There is little evidence, in reading any of the fashion magazines studied here, that small publishers have a chance of getting their lists

publicized in the likes of *Vogue* and its competitors. However, in the case of *Vogue,* the new "People Are Talking About" is a good place for smaller publishers with more unorthodox titles to look.

One small disappointment about *Vogue* in 1993: the lack of the "Arts in Brief" sections that have served – like "In Short" of *Mirabella* – to showcase books devoting substantial space to any one.

Finally, in a class all by itself, *Vanity Fair.* Last year, many people read Graydon Carter's first issue with caution, not wanting to admit that he could possibly do as fine a job as the inimitable Tina Brown. The truth is – rumors of Carter's demise notwithstanding – the magazine has not changed terribly much. It still has the same kind of writers, the same kind of stories, the same Demi Moore on the cover. In terms of books, *Vanity Fair* seems to have improved over the last year. The magazine featured long author profiles (the closest fashion magazines come to "long" reviews), including P. D. James (*The Children of Men,* Knopf, in March, David McClintick (*Swordfish,* Pantheon, in May, and Carl Hiaasen (*Strip Tease,* Knopf, in September. In terms of sheer length, the bookish articles in *Vanity Fair* win by a substantial margin; even *GQ* is a not-terribly-close second. One supposes the articles' extraordinary length is caused by the all-inclusive, personal detailing: that P. D. James's husband threw himself out of a window, that David McClintick wept in Binky Urban's office when she promised to take him on as a client.

Once again, many books in *Vanity Fair* are covered in the "Hot Type" section of "Vanities," in which the enormously talented (and, in the case of "Hot Type," underutilized) Henry Alford lists approximately a dozen new books. "Vanities" is also a good forum for shorter author profiles, including some literary heavyweights: Josephine Hart on Ruth Prawer Jhabvala (*Poet and Dancer,* Doubleday) in March; Jay McInerney on Robert Olmstead (*America by Land,* Random House) in May; David Halberstam on Frank Conroy (*Body and Soul,* Houghton Mifflin) in September.

There were two notable *Vanity Fair* book treatments in 1993, both controversial. First, in September, the magazine published an interminable excerpt, "The End of Camelot," from the Joe McGinnis book – an editorial decision most certainly made before McGinnis's name became publishing mud. Unfortunately for *Vanity Fair,* by the time the issue came out, Simon and Schuster had moved up the book's publishing date and McGinnis's name had been so long commented upon in the newspapers and elsewhere that readers were tired of seeing it. The second controversial article of the year was ahead of the curve; in fact, it helped create the curve. In October Michael Shnayerson, son of Robert Shnayerson – who was briefly the editor of *Harper's* – wrote an adoring piece on Willie Morris, who was also briefly the editor of *Harper's,* on the occasion of the publication of his second autobiography, *New York Days* (Little, Brown). Rarely has such a flurry of impassioned letters to the editor been undertaken as after the Morris book was reviewed in *Vanity Fair* and the *New York Times Book Review.* Lewis Lapham – who disagrees with important details regarding Morris's editorial demise – was busy for weeks; pro-Lapham, pro-Morris camps figuratively duked it out in offices and restaurants all over town. We, as readers, were left with the feeling that we will never know the truth.

IN THE BELLY OF THE BEAST: THE YEAR IN PUBLISHING FROM THE INSIDE

To examine the point of view of people within the publishing establishment, van Ogtrop of *Vogue,* representing the *DLB Yearbook,* interviewed several prominent editors, staff writer David Streitfeld of the *Washington Post;* and, in an extended question-and-answer session, she talked about the past year and the future with highly regarded agent Jane Gelfman of the Gelfman Schneider Agency. Events early in 1994 – the end of the line for Atheneum and Ticknor and Fields, and the sudden and severe cutbacks at the trade division of Harcourt Brace (in spite of a highly successful 1993) give Gelfman's bleak view of the future some of the weight of fulfilled prophecy.

When asked to reflect on 1993, one may remember the more dramatic moments. The World Trade Center bombing. The flood in the Midwest. The Rabin/Arafat handshake.

In the world of book publishing, there were comparable shakedowns and emerging new trends. While they did not necessarily make the pages of the *New York Times,* they kept phone lines and fax machines busy among the creative and stalwart few who choose to concern themselves with the business of books. We asked five publishing veterans to describe what occupied their minds over the past year.

Carol Houck Smith, an editor and vice-president at Norton, points to "the loss, or selling, of certain companies and the further evolution of the conglomerate world," as a significant trend that marks 1993. Accompanying this development was

"the lessening of individual imprints and the expansion of the superstores." "This," she adds, "is a problem from the point of view of midlist books and literary fiction – things that I like." Smith praises independent bookstore staff members who know their customers not only by sight but also by literary tastes, "and can give them personal attention" – attention superstores have not yet proven they can offer.

Nan Talese, president, publisher, and editorial director of Nan A. Talese books, and senior vice-president of Doubleday, also saw 1993 as the year of the superstore. She too cites the lack of personal attention as a major drawback of these behemoth bookstores. "Independents are run by people who really read and discover any number of authors. Superstores are fine if you know what you want, but if you need help, you're out of luck. Unless they start to train staff to read. . . . " The failure of the independents affects Talese on a more personal level. "If the independents close, who will discover new writers? Between superstores and price clubs, the established writers, or those with film deals, will sell four hundred thousand, five hundred thousand, a million copies in hardcover – but everyone else will be squeezed out. I publish a lot of first novels, writers who aren't selling a great many copies. I send my galleys to independents, and that's how a number of my writers – Margaret Atwood, Pat Conroy, Ian McKewan – got launched. Independent bookstore owners know their customers individually, and know their customer's tastes." But Talese is also sanguine about the superstores' influence. "They bring books to people who might not ordinarily think of reading in their free time."

The fall of the independents is noticed and discussed even beyond book publishing's hallowed halls. David Streitfeld, a staff writer at the *Washington Post,* points to "the rise of the superstores and the concurrent decimation of major publishers" as the biggest publishing news of 1993. However, he's puzzled by one thing. "You'd think," he remarks, "that with more and bigger bookstores, more publishers would be able to make material available. But if this trend continues this way, we're going to have one publisher furnishing the books at *all* of these stores. Soon we will be down to nine major publishing companies, yet in some cities – Chicago, for one – the amount of floor space in bookstores has doubled in the last year and a half."

If the market does indeed dwindle to nine houses, they will be – according to Matthew Carnicelli, a Dutton editor – nine houses that can publish works extremely quickly. "Even though publishing is essentially a dinosaur," Carnicelli states, "it is in an odd position right now. It is beginning to compete with magazine publishing." He cites as examples the several "quickie" books published in 1993: *Creating A Government That Works Better And Costs Less,* which was first self-published by the government, then picked up by both Dutton and Times Books; a Dutton "instant biography" of Hillary Clinton; and another Times book on the new health-care plan. Politics obviously lends itself to quickie coverage. "Every time Ross Perot had something to say," Carnicelli laughs, "he published a book. He even had a quickie book on NAFTA!" Thus publishers are picking up the pace. Carnicelli points out that "this year has made it more clear that publishers will have to adapt technologically to compete with electronic media. Say I have a biography of Boris Yeltsin, which an author has written and I'm editing. Usually it takes nine months to get out a hardcover book. But if a coup happens – then we have to get the books out in one month." Unfortunately, "quiet, profound" books do not get much attention in such a publishing climate. "As publishing gets more commercial, we have to reduce our books to one pitch line – in the same way that politicians rely on sound bites."

And speaking of quickie books, a book that took fourteen days to write is the book that took the 1993 best-seller lists by a storm. Shannon Ravenel, editorial director of Algonquin Books, believes the success of Robert James Waller's *The Bridges of Madison County* was the most important publishing development of 1993, as well as "a phenomenon that is hard to explain." Ravenel continues, "A lot of us in literary publishing are trying to explain it to ourselves. Warner made it look like a sweet little literary book; the bookstores picked it up and made it a bestseller." Ravenel compares the marketing of *Bridges* to that of Stephen Hawking's *A Brief History of Time* (1988) or Josephine Hart's *Damage* (1991): "People want to be reading literature but they aren't really up to it – they are thrilled when they find a book that looks like literature but is really accessible. The campaign was definitely run to make the book look serious." According to Ravenel, smart marketing was the all-important consideration for 1993. It is no accident that *Bridges* was published in the smaller, five-by-seven inch format – a format Ravenel has long been calling "the Algonquin size." The "little" book is now a very big idea – and one that Algonquin Books of Chapel Hill, North Carolina, discovered years ago.

Dust jacket for Robert James Waller's first novel, the success of which inspired debate and discussion about literary quality and marketing strategy

INTERVIEW WITH AN AGENT

On 11 November 1993, Kristin van Ogtrop interviewed literary agent Jane Gelfman, of Gelfman Schneider Literary Agents, about the most notable events in publishing of the past year. Over lunch at New York's Symphony Cafe, here is what Gelfman had to say:

VAN OGTROP: So do you thing it's been a tough year for everyone in publishing?

GELFMAN: Yes. I think that, as the publishing companies merge, what is published also contracts. It's harder and harder to sell literary fiction, and it's harder to sell to publishers who are cutting their lists, and who have to justify their bottom line on the basis of fewer and fewer books – to editors who are more pressed to *acquire* than to *edit,* and who have to justify their jobs every single year. Of course, if you're asking me what the significant things in 1993 are, you could certainly put right at the top of the list the mergers of the publishing companies, including the acquisition of Macmillan *today*, by Paramount, for $553 million. Charles Scribner must be turning over in his grave; Scribners, Atheneum, Macmillan, are now part of greater Paramount Publishing, which previously absorbed Prentice-Hall. I think it's clear that a lot of functions of Macmillan will be merged into Paramount Publishing. It also seems clear that part of the reason for Paramount's eagerness to absorb Macmillan was to get rid of the cash that it had that made it more attractive to QVC for a takeover. If QVC is ultimately the successful bidder for Paramount, then Si Newhouse will be sitting on the board of Paramount Publishing. The whole thing is bad for the world of literature and letters.

VAN OGTROP: Looking down the road, do you see this trend backfiring later on – there's going to be a revolt, and everyone's going to see that publishing has got to go back to the way it used to be?

GELFMAN: No. I don't. It's like the second law of thermodynamics: everything dissipates and becomes more diluted. I don't see publishing becoming a nineteenth-century form again. I see the mass marketization of publishing as well as of the movies and television.

Recently the ballet of *The Nutcracker* was made into a film by the New York City Ballet; when it was screened in California, some of the audience said they didn't understand the plot, and so the distribution company decided they should have a voice-over narrative. You would think that a ballet that has been seen by generations – by hundreds of thousands of five-year-olds who didn't have any trouble understanding the plot – would not need to be explained in a voice-over narrative in a movie. But it's an example of how the media are so over-simplified that people no longer work for any kind of understanding (of literature or anything else); if they can't understand a simple *Nutcracker* ballet, how can they be expected to read a novel?

VAN OGTROP: Which is why I was thinking earlier of *The Bridges of Madison County.* I think it's fitting that it's a book that took fourteen days to write –

GELFMAN: And takes about fourteen minutes to read –

VAN OGTROP: – is what's dominated the 1993 publishing scene.

GELFMAN: I don't really mean to denigrate *The Bridges of Madison County.* If people will read a book, any book, I'm happy. I don't care if it's a comic book or a good book or a mass-market book – if they will *read* something rather than watching television, that's okay with me, and I want to encourage that.

VAN OGTROP: Well, that's thinking positively.

GELFMAN: I do think positively. Or I wouldn't be in the book publishing business. You have to be an insane optimist.

Anyway, that's one of the things that certainly stands out in 1993: the merger of the large publishing companies, the contraction of their lists, and the demand for books that are more accessible to wider, more general audiences, rather than the traditional literary fiction which stretches the world.

VAN OGTROP: Do you think the triumph of the superstores plays into that? That these publishers are publishing for stores like that?

GELFMAN: Certainly the chain stores, and the mall stores, to a great degree do reflect a mass market audience. But in the Barnes and Noble store on 83rd and Broadway, they have a huge back list – they have *every* author's back list, including contemporary literary writers. When the store first opened, they had a very knowledgeable staff: all the staff knew where everything was, and what everything was. They could advise you and show you where things were. I understand that now the staff is less knowledgeable, and I have the feeling that maybe they have an expert traveling staff that opens new stores.

VAN OGTROP: Like a circus.

GELFMAN: Exactly. I think that if the new megabookstores are going to have that kind of space, then they will stock the back list books, and that's a positive thing. On the other hand, they may all go out of business if all they can sell is one hundred thousand copies each of Stephen King and *The Bridges of Madison County.* Then they won't need that space. Traditionally, it's not so easy to sell books. If they can do it, more power to them. I was excited when I walked into the Barnes and Noble and saw all those books and all those people and all those children.

VAN OGTROP: Is that the one with the café?

GELFMAN: Yes. It has a café, it has readings all the time – it's a neighborhood place. They have comfortable chairs with lights, where you can sit and read books. It has a welcoming atmosphere, as opposed to *some* of the independent bookstores, which people are moaning about being threatened. Shakespeare and Company, on 80th Street and Broadway, has always stocked huge quantities of backlist books, but the staff was sometimes surly, and the aisles so cramped you had to walk sideways.

I don't really know how the megabookstores will fare – maybe in ten years they'll be selling T-shirts instead of books. But at the moment, the more books that are sold, the happier I am. If somebody's going to read one book, he or she just might enjoy the experience enough to read another.

The other thing that's new in publishing this year is the increasing attention to and development of electronic rights.

VAN OGTROP: That's something I don't understand very well.

GELFMAN: It's very interesting. We're all grappling with it. Publishers are rewriting their boilerplate as fast as they can. This is a kind of shakedown period, in which there is an ongoing discourse between publishers and authors, including agents, about what electronic book rights really are: whether they are in fact a publishing right for the publisher or an ancillary or subsidiary right; whether publishers should have the automatic right to publish in electronic formats as well as on paper; whether they should have the right to license those rights as they license book club rights and paperback rights, or whether those rights actually belong to the author. There is controversy as to whether some of the electronic rights that are being sought by publishers conflict with film rights. And so, in this period, there is a lot of controversy and argumentation about who really has the right to control and license and publish those electronic versions. Naturally, we agents believe these rights should be controlled by the author, but publishers don't always agree.

VAN OGTROP: Are different people doing all different kinds of things?

GELFMAN: Yes.

VAN OGTROP: So it's total mayhem.

GELFMAN: Well, there are what they call "expanded books," which are for reading only – the verbatim text with nothing added. Those are the rights that publishers feel most justified in asking for, and authors and agents feel most sympathetic toward letting them have – at least for an initial period in which they either acquire and exercise them, or don't. They should have a limited period to decide whether or not they want to exploit these rights. What they're asking for is that that right be part of their publication rights for the term of copyright. There is also controversy about what are called CD-ROM rights, or licensing of other electronic rights in more expanded versions, which include music, sound and background information, and other materials that are adaptations, and other video increments.

I'm in the middle of negotiating a contract right now where a publisher has just added an entire page of tiny print to its boilerplate contract, asking for the right to publish in CD-ROM the right to license, and setting out royalties now, which is premature, I think. But certainly everyone is really addressing the subject this year for the first time. You can't just ignore it and say, "Take out the electronic rights clause."

VAN OGTROP: What is the thing in the recent past that most resembles this, as far as such a huge change?

GELFMAN: Well, it's not the same degree, but when audiocassettes started to be big business, publishers initially argued that that was their right to exploit – like book-club rights. But agents and authors argued successfully in most cases that it was not. I never give audio rights to publishers unless they pay for it. We have been very successful in licensing audio rights ourselves, and we believe that those rights belong to an author. You know, first serial is something that's always subject to negotiation, but book club is something that publishers have traditionally had the rights to license, and still do. That was a game that was lost a long time ago, book club licensing.

The other thing about 1993, which we were talking about before, is the contraction of the publishers' lists. This means that it's harder than ever to publish literary fiction. The result it that literary fiction that's based on wonderful observation and character exploration is the hardest to sell now. Novels that are currently selling best are the novels with strong plots and subjects. You can sell a wonderful first novel that's a plot novel, but it's almost impossible to sell one that's a coming-of-age or a character novel, unless you sell the movie rights in advance. I'm only being a *little* cynical here.

VAN OGTROP: Give me an example of a plot novel and a coming-of-age novel.

GELFMAN: The Donna Tartt novel is a plot novel. High concept, besides. A character novel. . . .

VAN OGTROP: Something like Mona Simpson's first novel?

GELFMAN: Or Bobbie Ann Mason. An example of a coming-of-age novel which was successful was *Bastard out of Carolina* (1992), by Dorothy Allison. But that novel had a lot of impetus from the fact that the author is a well-known lesbian, and there was a lot of controversy which got attention for the book, and then there was a wonderful review in the *New York Times* after the book was published –

VAN OGTROP: By George Garrett –

GELFMAN: Right. But in the past year I have had to turn down so many beautifully written novels because I knew I wouldn't be able to sell them, and I didn't want to break my heart. What I write to people – and it's absolutely true – is that it's much harder to represent well the people whose work I am already committed to, and I have to concentrate my efforts on them. I only take on a client if I absolutely cannot say no.

VAN OGTROP: That must not happen very often.

GELFMAN: It doesn't happen very often. What you don't say no to is the thing that you like – maybe nonfiction, a biography of somebody interesting – that you know you can sell.

VAN OGTROP: A timely book, about an issue that's hot in the press –

GELFMAN: Right, with a political or a social issue: the spate of incest books a couple of years ago, or books about feminist subjects. What hap-

pens is that fiction sales revert to genre. You can say a novel is a "hot new thriller," or you can say it's a "murder mystery," or you can say that it's "a love story like *Dr. Zhivago* or *Gone with the Wind*." We do everything we can to identify our literary fiction. Publishers send authors out to read, hoping that they will build up some kind of readership, some kind of audience, some kind of recognition. I consider that my job is not only to sell the book to the publisher but also to help the publisher sell the book and help the publisher to find ways to promote the author, ways to promote the book, people to give quotes. Getting quotes is very important. When people go into a bookstore, look on the back of the book and see a quote from someone whose book they've read – you know, it's like a friend tells you that a movie is great: it's in your mind, you have an association, someone has recommended it to you, someone whom you trust.

VAN OGTROP: Going back to *The Bridges of Madison County* again, was that all word of mouth?

GELFMAN: That was certainly a large part of it, but wasn't it also sold to the movies before? You should call up Molly Friedrich, the agent, and ask her.

VAN OGTROP: Earlier this year Joni Evans gave a talk about how to get into publishing, and I went with my friend Dan Max, who is the literary editor of the *New York Observer,* because he wanted to cover it for the paper. Daniel knows Larry Kirshbaum, so we sat next to him, and Joni Evans kept going back to *The Bridges of Madison County* in her talk, and then she noticed the editor of the book in the audience. She made him stand up – and this was in June or July – and tell the audience that the first printing of the novel was twenty-nine thousand, and they were up to something like 1.2 million at that point. When something like that is sold to the movies, does it make a lot of papers?

GELFMAN: Absolutely. They also have a Rights column in *Publishers Weekly* – all the bookstore people read that. If you announce a million-dollar sale of a book to the movies, and it's going to star Paul Newman or Robert Redford, that absolutely enhances the sale of the book, and it makes the publisher spend more money on the book because they're going to sell more copies and make more money on paperback, whether they're publishing it themselves or licensing it. They're going to get more money for the paperback, because the paperback will be published at the same time that the movie is released, and they'll have a movie tie-in, if it's a big movie. If you looked at the best-seller list last summer, the fiction paperback best-seller list was almost all movie tie-ins. Not necessarily books that were novelizations of movies, but books that had been made into movies and were now back in print, or —

VAN OGTROP: Like Michael Crichton.

GELFMAN: Michael Crichton's books. *The Age of Innocence.*

VAN OGTROP: John Grisham.

GELFMAN: A River Runs Through It. Of the fifteen books, ten of them were related to movies.

VAN OGTROP: Going back to something you were talking about before, in terms of publishing houses contracting their lists, and all of these mergers, do you feel that publishing has snapped back from the recession at all? I know that magazine publishing hasn't.

GELFMAN: I do not. Bob Miller of Hyperion told me the other day that sales volume was actually up in 1993. Usually, in any given year sales *revenues* are up, but it frequently turns out, if you read closely, that the increase in revenue is a function of the increase in prices of books, and that the actual quantity of books sold is either the same or lower than the year before. Bob said to me that the actual numbers of books sold were up this year. I asked what those books were, were they hundreds of thousands of copies of *The Bridges of Madison County* and Michael Crichton and Grisham? Probably, is the answer. Still, my answer to your question is no. Publishing has not bounced back in the sense that they're selling all of the books that they buy better. They're selling some of the books that they buy *much* better: the top of their list, the brandname best-sellers. And they're selling the other books less well, and that's why it's harder and harder to sell literary fiction, or books with a limited market. We see royalty statements that are heartbreaking.

VAN OGTROP: Were there good things in 1993?

GELFMAN: What is great every year is that the odd, unusual book that is truly wonderful can find its way. We had a very big success this year with Alan Lightman's book, *Einstein's Dreams,* which is a lovely, imaginative work of fiction. Pantheon did a beautiful job of producing and designing the book, of backing it and promoting it, and that book was on the best-seller list for over twenty weeks. The book had a huge paperback sale; we sold it in twenty-one foreign countries, and we're not finished yet; it had an audio sale, it had a book-club sale; and I'm now in the process of selling the movie, record album, and CD interactive rights for the book.

VAN OGTROP: Record album?

GELFMAN: Yes. A record producer wanted to commission a number of contemporary composers to compose pieces on the themes of the different dreams. What's great about publishing is that a wonderful, inventive, imaginative work can triumph, or that a wonderful novel can succeed. This is what keeps us all going. There is always hope. To get a book published, to have it be part of the real world, even if you have to take a small advance, and even if it sells a modest number of copies — it's *there:* somebody can find it. *The Beans of Egypt, Maine* was a little regional novel that was fresh and new. That book was published in 1985 and was a surprising success. A movie is now being made of *The Beans of Egypt, Maine,* and Carolyn Chute's new novel is about to be published. I have high hopes for her new novel, *Merry Men,* which is one of the finest, most extraordinary novels that I have read in many years. It's very complex and a different kind of novel from her first one, and requires a lot more from the reader. Madison Bell has a new novel almost finished, too.

VAN OGTROP: So what would you say keeps you going, when you're feeling depressed about the industry?

GELFMAN: What keeps me going is that I really love what I do; I feel it's useful and important. I feel that there is always hope for talent, and it excites me to be a participant in the publishing of good books. That's what I care about, and I feel privileged to be able to do it, really.

The Shakespeare Globe Trust

Pip Plummer
Shakespeare's Globe

Just over forty years ago a young American actor and director, Sam Wanamaker, came to Britain – and decided to remain. In doing so he furthered his deep-felt regard for and love of the works of William Shakespeare and laid the foundations of his magnum opus – the faithful reconstruction of Shakespeare's Globe on London's Bankside, close to the site of the original theater. The dream that forty years ago seemed so fanciful has today been transformed into a burgeoning reality with the Globe rising on its Bankside location, opposite Saint Paul's Cathedral across the river Thames, in what is now known as "Shakespeare's London."

The Shakespeare Globe Trust was established in 1970 as an educational charity and is dedicated to the study, appreciation, and excellence in performance of Shakespeare's plays as part of an international educational and cultural resource for people everywhere. While the trust is a charity, its sister organization, the International Shakespeare Globe Centre, is the operational arm of the trust which commissions all the building works for the new center; all donations to the trust are transferred to the center to fund the building program and administration management.

Sam Wanamaker's dream became a compelling vision when he realized that the strategically placed, one-acre-sized waterfront location could not only be the home of the "jewel in the crown" – the Globe – but also a worldwide resource combining education and learning with entertainment, culture, and the heritage of spoken English. When completed the International Shakespeare Globe Centre will incorporate:

the Shakespeare Globe Museum and Exhibition – a theatrical experience revealing Shakespeare's contribution to the development of the Elizabethan and Jacobean stage, the golden age of the English language and the social forces which created it;

the Globe Education Centre – an international facility for the study, enjoyment, and appreciation of Shakespeare in performance;

Sam Wanamaker, founder of the Shakespeare Globe Trust (courtesy of Shakespeare's Globe)

an audio-visual archive and library providing a resource of Shakespeare in performance in the various media of theater, film, television, and radio;

the Inigo Jones – an elegant "private" theater of the period, built to the great architect's surviving design and used for concerts, poetry readings, plays of the seventeenth century, lectures, and recitals;

a small cinema and lecture hall running regular film and television programs;

a grand piazza, surrounded by shops, apartments, and restaurants.

126

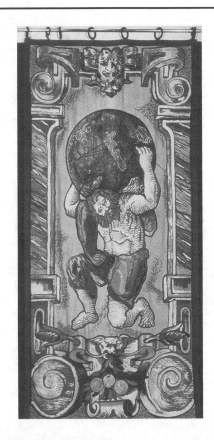

The four New Zealand hangings to be placed above the stage of the rebuilt Globe; clockwise, from top left: Atlas, Hercules, Adonis, and Venus (courtesy of Shakespeare's Globe)

Construction of the Globe in September 1993 (courtesy of Shakespeare's Globe)

To achieve full authenticity in rebuilding the Globe, Wanamaker approached Peter McCurdy, a world-renowned specialist in the restoration of historic timber-framed buildings and one of the few people in Britain well versed in the joinery techniques of the sixteenth and seventeenth centuries. Two of the Globe's twenty all-oak frames were raised on the site and officially unveiled by Prince Edward in June 1992. This was the culmination of some three months' skilled work by timber-frame craftsmen, who converted freshly hewn English oaks into a series of vertical and horizontal beams using traditional techniques. A few months later thatch was added to the roofs of the two bays, making it the first building in central London to have a thatched roof since the Great Fire of 1666, another development unique to the Globe project.

All this has been and will be achieved without – so far – any fiscal contribution from the British government or from the European Community, despite the fact that the center will be a celebration of the Western world's leading classical playwright. As a registered charity the Shakespeare Globe Trust is almost entirely reliant on gifts and donations from both concerned individuals and businesses and organizations of all sizes, pursuits, and interests.

Support for the project takes many forms, such as the sponsoring of one or more of the flagstones which will cover the piazza, while the trust also seeks to involve schools and colleges in the task of rebuilding the Globe; this is done through its Globelink. Schools in the Globelink scheme are asked to raise two hundred pounds or more toward building "the Heavens" – the roof over the Globe stage. Successful schools are given a time capsule to fill with whatever they choose; all these capsules will be buried in a specially created vault directly under the center most point of the Globe theater.

Friends of the Globe exist not only in the United Kingdom but also across the world, giving their time and expertise as well as their money toward the essential funding. One of the most exciting of the Friends' undertakings recently has been the international tour of the four superb hangings made by the ladies of the Wellington Shakespeare Society. The intention is that these should be used as arras hangings on the stage of the Globe theater when ready. They depict Atlas, Hercules, Adonis, and Venus, the former two being the smaller, while the larger are of course the eponymous hero and heroine of Shakespeare's most famous poem.

When the designs of Raymond Boyce were approved by the International Shakespeare Globe Centre Academic Committee, various embroiderers' guilds across New Zealand sent delegates to seminars which were organized by the creative designer. Each city or district was given a particular slip on which their members would work – an enormous task involving over five hundred people. The hangings were officially unveiled in 1991 by the governor-general of New Zealand and commenced the tour in the spring of 1993, with plans to have them in London and in their rightful place the following year.

The Shakespeare Globe Museum – still in Bear Gardens until its new home is ready – helps its visitors to learn more of the project itself and the work of the trust in general. It is open seven days a week all year round and houses the only exhibition in the world dedicated to Shakespeare and the Elizabethan theater.

The year 1993 was most significant in the development of the Globe's plans, and it was on that important date – 23 April – in that year that a most moving moment of history occurred. Sir John Gielgud, the greatest Shakespearian actor of modern times, spoke on the site the first words of Shakespeare to be heard from this part of Bankside since the original Globe was destroyed in 1644. This was on the occasion of the Globe site's dedication ceremony, when Sir John led a distinguished company of players in formally marking the playhouse's rebirth.

Gielgud, who was honorary president of the Shakespeare Globe Trust, was honored at the beginning of 1993 by receiving the first Shakespeare Globe Award for his lifelong contribution to Shakespeare productions and to the classical theater. This award is now established as an annual ceremony, with six major categories. The first of these, of course, is the International Shakespeare Globe Award, which is to be presented to the person or organization whose contribution to the understanding and appreciation of Shakespeare's work was on a universal scale. The other five awards are: the Sir John Gielgud Award for Best Actor; the Dame Peggy Ashcroft Award for Best Actress; the Peter Brook Award for Best Director; the Sir Tyrone Guthrie Award for Best Producer; and the Richard Burton Award for Best New Actor. But while the professional experts are thus honored, the educational aspects of the Globe's activities also continue apace.

A highly significant and ambitious project – the Hamlet Project – has been initiated, with the involvement of over fifteen hundred students. Theater, film, illustration, music, ballet, and dance are all included in this international schools' project which will be launched and operated by Globe Education. More than sixty schools from Great Britain, Denmark, and Germany will take part, and there will be Project Centres in Great Britain at Chester, Cheltenham, Stratford-on-Avon, Guildford, and London, as well as Arhus, Odense, and Copenhagen in Denmark, and Bremen and Hanover in Germany.

Workshops on the play, given at each center, will trigger practical work in the classroom, and when the program is complete, the schools will present their work to each other. In addition to looking into the ways in which the play has been translated into various media and language, and having the opportunity of seeing on video contrasting film versions, those taking part will also be introduced to Hamlet choreography, with John Neumeier working with Hamburg Ballet students. Kim Brandstrup's modern dance "Hamlet-Antic" will tour England and Denmark with accompanying workshops. This particular project will culminate in the spring of 1994 with two international events. Representative schools from each country will be invited to Bremen, as guests of the Bremen Shakespeare Company, for a weekend workshop, and plans are afoot to celebrate the project's success suitably in London.

A radical aspect of the Globe project is what might be termed its internationality. It may center itself in the heart of London, but all over the world there are linked organizations working to the common end. In the United States the mid-America and western regions of the Shakespeare Globe Centre work tirelessly to raise funds by putting on various events; the Annual Shakespeare Globe Day at the races at Arlington is one such, made possible by generous sponsorship from Reuters. Also a new midwestern project – the Shakespeare Enterprise – has been initiated and consists of an auction of Shakespearean roles for scenes to be performed at the region's annual meeting. The western region's educational program operates out of Los Angeles and is in the capably protean hands of education director Louis Fantasia; it includes various events such as a "Reading and Performance" series, which enjoys the backing of numerous downtown businesses. Similarly, all manner of activities go forward throughout the year in Denmark, New Zealand, Australia, and Japan, with their progress being recorded in the *Globe,* the quarterly newsletter published in Bankside. Thus a dream which started four decades ago is starting to become tangible reality, and this is an exciting time. But there is still a long way to go.

Julian Barnes

(19 January 1946 –   )

Merritt Moseley
University of North Carolina at Asheville

BOOKS: *Metroland* (London: Cape, 1980; New York: St. Martin's Press, 1981);

Duffy, as Dan Kavanagh (London: Cape, 1980; New York: Pantheon, 1986);

Fiddle City, as Kavanagh (London: Cape, 1981; New York: Pantheon, 1986);

Before She Met Me (London: Cape, 1982; New York: McGraw-Hill, 1986);

Flaubert's Parrot (London: Cape, 1984; New York: Knopf, 1985);

Putting the Boot In, as Kavanagh (London: Cape, 1985);

Staring at the Sun (London: Cape, 1986; New York: Knopf, 1987);

Going to the Dogs, as Kavanagh (New York: Pantheon, 1987; London: Viking, 1987);

A History of the World in 10 1/2 Chapters (New York: Knopf, 1989; London: Cape, 1989);

Talking It Over (New York: Knopf, 1991; London: Cape, 1991);

The Porcupine (New York: Knopf, 1992; London: Cape, 1992).

SELECTED PERIODICAL PUBLICATIONS –
UNCOLLECTED: "Letter from London," *New Yorker* (5 March 1990; 11 June 1990; 7 January 1991; 30 September 1991; 6 January 1992; 4 May 1992; 20 July 1992; 28 December 1992; 30 September 1993).

Julian Barnes (photograph by Miriam Berkley)

Julian Barnes is one of the most celebrated, and one of the most variously rewarding, of Britain's younger novelists. The author of seven novels published since 1980 – *Flaubert's Parrot* (1984) and *A History of the World in 10 1/2 Chapters* (1989) are probably the books best known in America – he has also written four exceptional detective novels and is a busy journalist. Since 1990 he has been the London correspondent of the *New Yorker* magazine, contributing "Letters from London" every few months on subjects such as the royal family and the quirkier side of British politics.

Barnes's fiction has been acclaimed by readers as different as Carlos Fuentes and Philip Larkin; reviewers and interviewers sum him up with praise such as Mark Lawson's claim that he "writes like the teacher of your dreams: jokey, metaphorical across both popular and unpopular culture, epigrammatic." Though he is regularly called erudite and philosophical, he is also witty and humane; as David Coward explains: "The modern British novel finds it easy to be clever and comic. Barnes also manages that much harder thing: he succeeds in communicating genuine emotion without affectation or embarrassment."

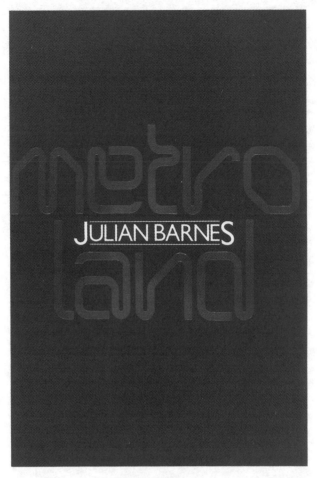

Dust jacket for Barnes's first novel, a story of adolescence and coming-of-age

Partly because of his friendship and alliance with Martin Amis, a famously precocious author, Barnes seems to see himself as a late starter. His first novel was published in 1980, when he was thirty-four; since then his output has been impressive in quantity as well as quality.

Julian Patrick Barnes was born in Leicester on 19 January 1946; his parents, Albert Leonard and Kaye Barnes, were middle-class northerners, both French teachers. The family moved to the London suburbs while Barnes was a small boy; he attended the City of London School on a scholarship, followed by Magdalen College, Oxford, where he studied languages, receiving a B.A. in 1968. He took a job as editorial assistant on the *Oxford English Dictionary;* after four years there he moved to London to study law but became involved instead in journalism, reviewing novels, then serving as assistant literary editor and television critic of the *New Statesman,* contributing editor to the *New Review* (where he published under the name Edward Pygge), deputy literary editor on the London *Sunday Times,* and television critic for the London *Observer.* He has been a full-time writer rather than an employee of a periodical since leaving the *Observer* in 1986, but he still reviews and comments regularly for journals including the *Times Literary Supplement* and the *New York Review of Books.* In 1987 he married Pat Kavanagh, a prominent literary agent.

Though his novels have never won Britain's prestigious Booker Prize (*Flaubert's Parrot* was one of the six finalists), his first novel, *Metroland* (1980), won the Somerset Maugham Prize; he has won other English awards, and (oddly) his novel *Flaubert's Parrot* was given the Prix Medicis, a French recognition for the year's best book of essays; he is also a Chevalier de l'Order des Arts et des Lettres, a distinction undoubtedly gratifying to a lover of France and French literature.

Barnes has been called by Mira Stout "the chameleon of British letters," and it is certainly true that each of his books – at least his novels published

Dust jacket for the experimental novel about the relationship between life and art that was an international best-seller

under his own name – is distinctive. He is careful not to repeat himself and speaks contemptuously of the expectations of some reviewers that after *Flaubert's Parrot* he should have written, in the words of Amanda Smith, "*Victor Hugo's Dachshund.*"

His first novel, which took him eight years to write, is the deceptively calm *Metroland*. Like many another first novel, it is a story of adolescence and coming-of-age. It demonstrates certain features which are constants in Barnes's fiction: wit, familiarity with French culture, shapeliness and high finish, and a delicate concern with love and jealousy.

The story is of a young Londoner, living in the suburbs served by the Metropolitan railway line (hence "Metroland"), and his friend Toni. They are sardonic about school and sports and particularly about English middle-class culture as represented by their parents. Their rebellion is mostly verbal but funny. In part 2 Christopher is in France for the events of May 1968; he misses these but achieves a

sexual initiation with a French girl. In the third part the adult and settled Christopher, back in "Metroland," is married and a solid bourgeois. The ironies of his failed rebellion are complicated by arguments with Toni, who is nowhere near so assimilated to middle-class "adulthood," and by stresses in his (mainly happy) marriage. The novel ends with something of a dying fall; it is a short, not exciting, but highly accomplished study of adolescence, seen not just as being young but (with etymological accuracy) as *becoming adult* – with all that implies about narrowing horizons, settling down, and accepting one's own ordinariness.

Duffy was published in the same year as *Metroland;* a tense thriller set in London's sleazy Soho and featuring a bisexual detective no longer with the police because of blackmail by (more) crooked cops, it is obviously quite different. Barnes went on to write three more novels about Duffy, all published under the pseudonym of Dan Kavanagh; there is something schizoid about this procedure – he writes the Kavanagh books in a different place and on a different typewriter from his Barnes books and obviously calls on different aspects of his own mind. The thrillers are active, louche, violent, thoroughly plotted. Perhaps the plot making which critics miss in *Metroland* and *Flaubert's Parrot* is held over for the Duffy books. Duffy is a complicated character, rather tormented in his bisexuality. *Duffy* shows the result of serious research into the seamy world of London's sex industry; in *Duffy,* as in its successors, the crime tends to be theft or fraud rather than murder, though Barnes successfully imbues the book with a feeling of menace.

The next installment of Duffy's adventures followed the next year and was set at Heathrow airport, called "Fiddle City" because of the enormous opportunities for crime and deception there. Duffy goes underground in a shipping concern to solve a complicated case involving contraband and drugs.

Before She Met Me (1982) – like each of Barnes's mainstream novels – is quite different from the one which preceded it, in this case *Metroland.* The story of Graham Kendrick, a mild academic who first falls in love with a beautiful actress and leaves his family for her, then becomes progressively more obsessive about his wife's sex life before they met, the novel is gripping, disturbing, and moving. A relatively understated, tender, but penetrating treatment of infidelity and jealousy appears in the last section of *Metroland,* and almost all of Barnes's novels, whatever else their subject, are partly about love and jealousy. *Before She Met Me* displays the strongest, grimmest kind of jealousy.

Told from an omniscient point of view, the novel examines the reactions of Graham and his wife Ann to his growing mania, as well as that of his friend-confidant Jack and former wife Barbara. The novel is intermittently funny, in a way which survives even the growing horror. Treating the Duffy series as a separate oeuvre, *Before She Met Me* is a remarkable second novel.

In 1984 Barnes published his breakthrough, *Flaubert's Parrot.* In a 1989 interview with Smith, Barnes said that he feels "enormous affection" for it "because it's the book that launched me." Experimental in both form and content, *Flaubert's Parrot* presents itself as a nonfiction book about Gustave Flaubert by a widowed English doctor, Geoffrey Braithwaite, which grows out of the discovery that there is more than one stuffed parrot in Normandy identified as the parrot Flaubert borrowed while he was writing "Un Cour Simple." From here the book develops into a subtle, witty speculation on the rela-

Dust jacket for the British edition of Barnes's 1993 novel that examines the fall of a Communist leader

tionship between life and art, the knowability of the human personality, the nature of fame, and many other topics; there is also a sly but increasing strain of the autobiography of Braithwaite and (as usual with Barnes) serious matter on the nature and meaning of married love.

In form the book is eclectic; it contains alternative chronologies of Flaubert's life, a dictionary of received ideas about the author, an examination paper, and a portrait of Flaubert as he might be explained by his mistress Louise Colet. It is erudite, playful: as Coward writes, the book is "an extraorinarily artful mix of literary tomfoolery and high seriousness." This is the first of Barnes's novels to be thought of as postmodern.

Barnes's next book was another "Dan Kavanagh" Duffy book, *Putting the Boot In* (1985), this one set in the world of minor professional soccer. Like his first two detective books, it shows a command of the conventions of the genre and the kind of authority which comes from getting the information right. The feel of the football scenes is well done; this may in fact explain why this book has never been published in the United States, where its football world might be untranslatable. In all his books Barnes is careful to make the details accurate – as *Flaubert's Parrot* is, among other things, a treasury of real information about Flaubert, so the Duffy novels are full of information about Soho's sex industry, Heathrow airport, football, and dog racing.

Though his authorship of the "Dan Kavanagh" novels was not a complete secret in literary London, the world judges Julian Barnes on the novels published under his real name. The one which followed *Flaubert's Parrot* is *Staring at the Sun* (1986). A different book, it is an understated study of a woman named Jean Serjeant, from her childhood during World War II to her life in the twenty-first century. It is not funny; it is not particularly experimental, except for the mild futuristic quality of the third section, set in the 2020s; the main character, though quietly strong, enduring, and heroic, is an "ordinary," "private" woman. The central image of the novel is that of a flier who, by dropping his plane dramatically at dawn, can see the sun come up twice: this is described as an "ordinary miracle."

Jean Serjeant's life is meant to be that same sort of ordinary miracle. In this book more than any before it Barnes delves into ultimate questions about death, the afterlife, and religion. Reared without religion and never having been to a church, he describes, in an interview with Kate Saunders, the contents of *Staring at the Sun* as "DIY theology."

Though it received many good reviews, *Staring at the Sun* disappointed many readers. After the tour de force of *Flaubert's Parrot,* it seems tame, perhaps a bit *brown.* Barnes has clearly been nettled by this reaction. He has derided the expectation that his follow-up book should have been *Tolstoy's Dachshund,* and he sums up his attitude toward the book in an interview with Andrew Billen: "As soon as you say you were disappointed, I get deeply protective about the novel. I say: Carlos Fuentes [who reviewed it in the *New York Times*] liked it – so sod you. This is the writer's response. It's like criticising your fourth child."

In 1987 Barnes published what seems to be his last Duffy book, *Going to the Dogs,* set in the south London world of greyhound racing. Perhaps so well-established as a "serious" novelist and in-demand journalist that he no longer has time for his alter ego, perhaps running out of inspiration (this Duffy novel is weaker than its predecessors), he also tells Lawson that a "recyclable hero" has been "more tiresome than he expected."

In 1989 came the novel which, in ambition, complexity, and experimental quality, seemed the real successor to *Flaubert's Parrot – A History of the World in 10 1/2 Chapters.* It really is a history of the world; the first chapter is about Noah's ark, the last one about Heaven. In between are chapters on a medieval church prosecution of termites, an American astronaut's quest for the remnants of Noah's ark, the making of a movie in the South American jungle, and Théodore Géricault's painting *The Raft of the Medusa.* The ten chapters are as variable in style as in content, including not only art criticism but letters, a journal, the records of a trial, and a dream (of heaven).

Like *Flaubert's Parrot, A History* challenges conventional definitions of the novel. It certainly lacks a unified plot, developing characters, consistent fictionality, and consistent verisimilitude. It is a novel of ideas, certainly, unless it is not a novel. In an interview with Lawson, Barnes responds to his critics who say that he is really an essayist who disguises his essays as fiction for commercial reasons: "My line now is I'm a novelist and if I say it's a novel, it is. . . . And it's not terribly interesting to me, casting people out of the realm of fiction."

One of the characters announces that "Everything *is* connected, even the parts we don't like, especially the parts we don't like." Even though she may be delusional, this is true nonetheless, at least of the novel. It is connected by a virtuoso network of motifs – the obvious one being water voyages of salvation, Noah and his ark recurring in most of the chapters. Another striking motif is (surprisingly) woodworms; a slighly less important one is reindeer, and there are others.

Like most of Barnes's books, this one is philosophically rich. There is meditation on the meaning of human life, on religion and the afterlife, on the nature of history – is there history or only various "histories" – and, most prominently, on love. The half chapter is about love, and its message is that, in a universe where history is an unreliable set of stories of disasters, our salvation is love: "We must believe in it, or we're lost." Perhaps the voice that speaks these words is (like the other voices), wrong; perhaps this chapter is ironic; it does not seem that way.

Typically, Barnes's next two books were almost as different from *A History,* and from each other, as could be imagined. *Talking It Over* (1991) returned, in a way, to the territory of *Metroland;* a story of contemporary London life, it is a study of love, sex, and marriage. The characters are three: Stuart, Oliver, and Gillian. Stuart is the rather dull but worthy man who feels, and is treated as, an inferior to his witty and flashy friend Oliver. Gillian is

Stuart's wife. Soon after Stuart and Gillian marry, Oliver decides that he loves Gillian, and he dedicates his life to making her fall in love with him — with eventual success. *Talking It Over* is a story of how love works, how infidelity happens despite good intentions, and how jealousy feels.

Barnes likes three-part structures (*Metroland* and *Staring at the Sun* are both three-parters), and this is a triple presentation, or series of statements, by the three parties to its central triangle. They give different versions of the story, or "history," of course, and in their own domestic way illustrate the same point as *A History:* history is just a series of competing, perhaps overlapping, stories.

In *The Porcupine* (1992) he turns his attention to contemporary history, specifically the fall of communism. Set in a place not called, but clearly based on, Bulgaria (and first published there, in Bulgarian), *The Porcupine* is Barnes's most political book. In it an overthrown dictator, Stoyo Petkanov, justifies himself, resists the attempts of his accusers (many of them formerly his supporters) to change the rules by which Stalinist societies measure successful government, and tweaks his prosecutor, an anguished former Communist named Peter Solinsky.

This is a muted book, one which relies on the recent history of Eastern Europe but continues to question the meaning of history. Though Petkanov is a monster, he is given arguments that are by no means easy to dismiss; in their disputes he often seems to get the better of Solinsky. There is a love complication here, too; as Solinsky's obsession with convicting Petkanov (on charges other than the ones of which he is really guilty) grows, his own self-doubts strengthening his determination, his wife loses her respect for him and leaves. Solinsky gives himself to evil means for a good end; were Petkanov's crimes any different?

The Porcupine, which at one point reached near the top of the best-seller list in Bulgaria, has had generally good reviews in England and the United States. By now Barnes's readers and reviewers will have learned to expect something different from each new book. Though the constants of his fiction remain — high craft, verbal brilliance, a determination to deal in ideas without giving way to didacticism, frequent experimentation in either subject or form or both — the other constant is variation. Lawson, challenging himself to encapsulate Barnes's style, offers the phrase "alternative versions." This is true on many levels: on that where Stuart and Oliver offer alternative versions of how Oliver ended up with Stuart's wife (*Talking It Over*); on that where ironic domesticity (*Metroland*) and desparate and squalid vice (*Duffy*) come from the same writer in the same year; and on that where each new Barnes book offers an alternative version, a different approach, even a new and distinctive voice. Whatever his next book is, it will not be *The Hedgehog,* and it will not be *Zola's Dachshund;* it will be something different, novel, and surprising.

Interviews:

Kate Saunders, "From Flaubert's Parrot to Noah's Woodworm," *Sunday Times* (London), 18 June 1989, p. G9;

Amanda Smith, "Julian Barnes," *Publishers Weekly,* 236 (3 November 1989): 73–74;

Andrew Billen, "Two Aspects of a Writer," *Observer Colour Magazine* (London) (7 July 1991): 25–26;

Mark Lawson, "A Short History of Julian Barnes," *Independent Magazine* (13 July 1991): 34–36;

Mira Stout, "Chameleon Novelist," *New York Times Magazine,* 22 November 1992, pp. 29, 68–72, 80.

References:

David Coward, "The Rare Creature's Human Sounds," *Times Literary Supplement,* 5 October 1984, p. 1117;

Michiko Kakutani, "Britain's Writers Embrace the Offbeat," *New York Times,* 5 July 1990, pp. C11, C15;

Paul Levy, "British Author, French Flair," *Wall Street Journal,* 11 December 1992, p. A10;

Gregory Salyer, "One Good Story Leads to Another: Julian Barnes' *A History of the World in 10 1/2 Chapters,*" *Journal of Literature & Theology,* 5 (June 1991): 220–232.

James Dickey at Seventy – a Tribute

Ernest Suarez
The Catholic University of America

On 17–18 September 1993 the University of South Carolina hosted an elegant and multifaceted celebration of James Dickey's literary achievements. The conference, organized by the Thomas Cooper Society, a university libraries support group, featured Pulitzer Prize winners R. W. B. Lewis and Richard Howard, the distinguished critic Monroe Spears, the editor of the *Paris Review* George Plimpton, and several other writers. A diverse audience of academics, students, and readers attended events ranging from the presentation of papers evaluating Dickey's creative practice to a Critic's Roundtable to a fifty-dollar-per-plate banquet including a multimedia tribute to Dickey that Plimpton emceed.

Richard Howard, professor of English and creative writing at the University of Houston and the author of many books, including a Pulitzer Prize–winning collection of poetry, *Untitled Subjects* (1970), began the afternoon's first session, "James Dickey as Critic," with a lecture titled "Dickey, Poet and Critic *ergo* Poet." Howard focused on the tradition of the "poet-Critic," particularly Dickey's relation to other American poet-critics, pointing to "an old and tenacious prejudice against criticism-as-practiced-by-poets." Howard asserted that, "with the exception of Emerson," the poet-critic does not appear in American letters until after World War I, with the emergence of the New Critics, and claimed that "in Dickey's case we have been so enlivened and enhanced by the poetry that I think it has been, or has become, difficult to perceive the order of excellence in the criticism, and to realize that it was the production of this criticism, during the very years when Dickey was also producing his most remarkable work in verse, which *enables* that very poetry to constitute one of the strongest and most powerfully wrought expressions of human aspiration in the realms of both body and spirit that our country and our moment has to show." Howard went on to discuss several instances from *Babel to Byzantium* (1968) that reveal Dickey's criticism at "its most judicious, most delicate, most responsive" moment.

James Dickey

Joyce Pair, professor of English at Dekalb College and the editor of the *James Dickey Newsletter,* followed Howard with an essay titled "Blueberry Pancakes and Pound," which addressed how Dickey's conception of the image has contributed to his success as a critic and a teacher. Drawing on Dickey's published lectures "The Water-Bug's Mittens: Ezra Pound, What We Can Use" (1979) and "LIGHTNINGS or Visuals" (1991), Pair discussed how Dickey's critical acumen concerning Pound's use of the image has contributed to Dickey's own poetic method, as well as to his ability to convey to students the image's creative possibilities.

The final presentation of the first section was delivered by Gordon Van Ness, associate professor of English at Longwood College and the editor of

Dickey's early notebooks. Van Ness's lecture, "The Synthetic Apple, The Old Crystal Radio Set, and The Flock of Fish: James Dickey's Literary Criticism," surveyed Dickey's critical output by dividing it into three phases. Dickey's "early critical reviews and essays . . . constitute general attempts to characterize poets and poetry," while the middle phase represents "detailed efforts to present himself both as a poet and man." Most recently Dickey "has sought to search out and reveal more thoroughly the nature of emotionally vital poetry," a process which Van Ness feels establishes "a new direction by which [Dickey's] own poems might expose previously undiscovered truths."

Lewis, professor emeritus of English and American studies at Yale University and author of *The American Adam* (1955) and a Pulitzer Prize-winning biography of Edith Wharton, chaired the afternoon's second session, "James Dickey as Novelist." His address, "James Dickey's Fiction: the Literary Kinship," linked Dickey's work to that of William James, Robert Penn Warren, Fyodor Dostoyevsky, Herman Melville, and Walt Whitman. Among the associations Lewis detailed were Dickey's affinities with James's emphasis on "life at the edge and the heroic life," qualities reflected by both men's propensity to "stretch the word *action* as far as it will go," and parallels between the "mysterious secret networks" in Dickey's *Alnilam* (1987) and in Dostoyevsky's *The Possessed* (1871). Dickey's most recent novel, *To the White Sea* (1993), was compared to Whitman's "Song of Myself" and to Melville's use of "whiteness" in several works. Lewis illustrated how the conclusion of *To the White Sea* resembles "Song of Myself," as each work's narrator claims a pantheistic absorption with his surroundings that allows his presence to be felt continually.

Richard Calhoun, professor of English at Clemson University, editor of the *South Carolina Review* and co-author of *James Dickey* (1983), presented a lecture titled "James Dickey's Fictional Moves." Calhoun, a pioneer in Dickey scholarship, surveyed his relationship with Dickey's work "for more than twenty-five years," recalling a poetry reading Dickey gave at Clemson immediately after the release of *Buckdancer's Choice* (1965) that helped inspire his interest in the poet. Calhoun commented that his long involvement in Dickey scholarship has shown him how Dickey's "work – poems, novels, criticism, interviews, self-interviews, and all miscellaneous prose – is of a piece in that" Dickey is "concerned in all genres with the same or similar themes." Calhoun proceeded to compare *Deliverance*

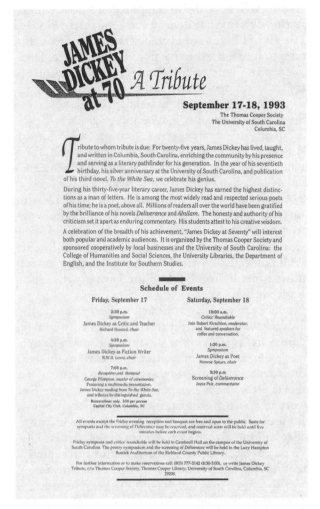

Poster of events for the celebration and tribute held in honor of poet, novelist, and critic James Dickey

(1970), which has illicited "valid readings from every major critical perspective," with *Alnilam* (1987), which "has puzzled critics into silence," a situation that he attributed to the fact that *Alnilam* is "too ambitious," technically and thematically. Commenting on *To the White Sea,* Calhoun claimed that "there is no comparable account of the Asian raid that may have inflicted more casualties and damage than any other air raid in WW II . . . It is a WW II remembrance, written in the aftermath of the horrors and cruelties of Vietnam."

Ernest Suarez, assistant professor of English at the Catholic University of America and author of *James Dickey and the Politics of Canon: Assessing the Savage Ideal* (1993), presented the afternoon's final paper, "Covert Narrative Strategies in *To the White Sea*." Suarez analyzed Dickey's exploration of the relationship between romanticism and hedonism in the novel. According to Suarez, in the novel Dickey investigates how the protagonist's romantic imagination is a tremendous, even enviable, resource that allows him to survive, as well as a cause and symptom of a destructive psychic imbalance. Dickey creates a tension between the work's ostensibly desperate dramatic situation, a soldier struggling for his life in enemy territory, and the atavistic pleasure in which the character indulges during that struggle. In order to achieve this tension and set up Muldrow's self-reliant brand of transcendental romanticism, Dickey creates a "covert" narrative that makes Muldrow's sociopathic tendencies, which in retrospect are evident, "invisible" to the reader for the first third of the novel. However, as the work progresses and Muldrow's desire for invisibility – he wants to blend into the landscape so that he cannot be detected – increases, the destructive aspects of his romanticism become increasingly visible to the reader.

On the evening of 17 September, a banquet in Dickey's honor was held at the Capitol City Club in Columbia. A slide show, featuring Ronald Baughman's narration accompanied by Gene Crediford's photography, displayed images – literal and metaphoric – that have comprised Dickey's twenty-five years in South Carolina, including Dickey's home, the university campus, the surrounding countryside, and the night sky – Dickey's "starry place between the antlers." George Plimpton presented a lighthearted address on the "dangers" of associating with Dickey. Plimpton drew on Dickey's writing – *Deliverance,* "Falling," and many other works – to point out the things which occur in "this dangerous man's life." After Plimpton's address, Dickey read excerpts from *To the White Sea* and from a long poem in progress, and then Theron Raines (Dickey's agent), Marc Jaffe (his editor), Richard Howard, and others gave testimonials in Dickey's honor.

The Critic's Roundtable, moderated by Robert Kirschten, author of *James Dickey and the Gentle Ecstasy of Earth* (1988), gathered on the morning of 18 September for a freewheeling two-hour session. Kirschten presented the panelists – Calhoun, Howard, Lewis, Susan Ludvingson, Pair, Suarez, and Van Ness – with several topics for discussion: "What does Dickey do best, and what about his work do you think will last?"; "What are his two most important poems and why?"; "Given your geographic and cultural/critical location, what has been the response to Dickey's work in your area, especially in regard to the early, middle, and later periods?"; "How much of the negative criticism against Dickey has been personal and 'political' rather than poetic?"; "Has there really been a literary Civil War regarding Dickey? If so, who is on which side?"

During the conference's final session, "James Dickey as Poet," disaster ensued as Monroe Spears, the day's featured speaker, was struck by a heart attack. Spears, professor emeritus of English at Rice University and the author of many books, delivered an essay detailing the various phases of Dickey's career. Spears described the young Dickey who took several classes from Spears at Vanderbilt University, recounting the fledgling poet's intellectual acuity and curiosity. He detailed Dickey's struggles to become a poet and his work as a poetry reviewer during the 1950s, as well as his rise to prominence in the 1960s, and went on to analyze Dickey's poetic experiments of the last two decades. However, as Ludvingson, professor of English at Winthrop College and the author of several books of poetry, began her lecture on the relationship between *To the White Sea* and the poems "Sled Burial, Dream Ceremony" and "A View of Fujiyama After the War," Spears, seated in the auditorium's first row, suffered the heart attack, resulting in the cancellation of the remainder of the events, including Elizabeth Adams's lecture and a dramatic rendition of Dickey's "May Day Sermon," directed by John Gallogly and featuring actress Bridget Hanley. Professor Spears is currently recovering at his home in Sewanee, Tennessee.

New York City Bookshops in the 1930s and 1940s: The Recollections of Walter Goldwater

Walter Goldwater was a veteran antiquarian book dealer who owned and operated the University Place Bookshop at various locations in New York City from 1932 until his death in 1985. During his career in the book business, Goldwater specialized in books relating to black studies, Africa, the Caribbean, chess, radical literature, and incunabula. These recollections were transcribed and edited from tape recordings Goldwater made on an unknown date, probably in the early 1980s. The unidentified interviewer functions more as a prompt and audience than an interviewer. This is not a strict transcription, as the recollections were edited for readability. The recordings were made available to the *DLB Yearbook* through the help and permission of Walter Goldwater's daughter, Dr. Linda Gochfield, and antiquarian book dealer Joseph Felcone of Princeton, New Jersey. Information about names of book dealers and the location of bookshops was provided by Marvin Mondlin of the Strand Book Store in New York City. His information is initialled M. M. within brackets. Names that remain unclear are also bracketed.

GOLDWATER: I've made a list, which I sometimes do when I can't sleep at night, of people who were in the book business when I started and who died. Each one of these, I think, had some interest. I've put them down quite at random; therefore, there is no order. I'll say a few words about each. If I say more than a few words, it will go on forever.

Rabbi Heller, as we called him, was a man who was very literate and very interested in Judaica, and so on. He went into partnership on Fourth Avenue with a man named Mankoff who was interested only in D. H. Lawrence. The two of them thought they might make a go of it. This was in the middle 1930s. The shop was at 110 Fourth Avenue.

They thought they might get along very well, because they were both intellectuals. But Mr. Heller was not able to stand the way Mankoff did things. I remember that one day he came to me and said, "You know what that man said? He came in in the morning and he said to me, 'Lawrence has conquered death.' How can you work with a fellow like that?" The shop broke up. Mankoff went to work for Concord Book Shop, which was one of the shops on Forty-second Street which handled new books, mainly semierotica. Later on Heller went into business for himself a little further down Fourth Avenue at number 84 and was there for a number of years, then went to New Rochelle, where he was for a long time. He finally died. He was one of the more amusing people in the book business.

Peter Stammer was one of the oldest on Fourth Avenue and was famous for being anticustomer. He is the one about whom the stories are told, about how he said, "I will charge you five dollars for this," and, if the person demurred, he said, "If you come back, it will be ten dollars." And if the person demurred again, he simply tore up the pamphlet and threw it away. The general lot of these stories is apocryphal. Probably in each case, it happened once, or something like that.

INTERVIEWER: Is he the one who used to tear up presentation copies?

GOLDWATER: I don't believe he actually did. He much more likely pretended to. However, my experience with him, which was quite extensive, led me to believe that, although some people looking at him from the outside might think he was an affable old codger, actually he was a scoundrel from the very beginning. If he did anything like this, it was most unusual. He might even have three or more copies of the same item still available. However, this has never been established.

INTERVIEWER: Did he start on Fourth Avenue?

GOLDWATER: There was some question as to whether he did. He and Schulte were the earliest on Fourth Avenue, as far as we knew.

Walter Goldwater and Eleanor (Lowenstein) Goldwater

INTERVIEWER: It was a general bookshop?

GOLDWATER: Yes. All shops that I have anything to do with, unless I mention it, are general secondhand and out-of-print bookshops. And they made their living by people coming in from the street and buying books at a price which was generally low, but which represented a very, very substantial profit. The question of the rare book as a specialized business did not come in until much later, and I was partly responsible for that. I said yes, I have a general bookshop, but I specialize in Africa or the Negro, whereas most people on Fourth Avenue said, "We have a general bookshop," and did not add anything. Later on, one would say that such and such a shop specialized in fiction, such and such a shop in Americana, and so on. But when I first started in this business, there was no such thing. Everybody was a general bookshop.

INTERVIEWER: Was Stammer's a big shop?

GOLDWATER: Stammer's was very, very big, from floor to ceiling, and cellar, and upstairs. It was absolutely tremendous. It was probably one of the largest stocks in the country.

INTERVIEWER: When did he die?

GOLDWATER: Probably in the mid forties or so. And then the shop was taken over by his son-in-law and by Noy Berenson, who was his employee. Noy was dishonest and was known throughout the trade for being dishonest. Since it was known, the probability is that Stammer knew it, because Stammer was not a person who was anybody's fool. However, again, he may have figured it was worth the trouble and it was a small matter and that, considering the amount of books he had, and so on, and the amount of dishonesty, it probably was just a question of some books being sold without being paid for. Later on, after his death, Noy and the son-in-law became what we thought was partners but probably was not. It was probably that the son-in-law owned the shop that employed Noy.

INTERVIEWER: So, what finally happened to the shop?

GOLDWATER: Just a year ago he sold it out to an antiques place. He owns the building. He had been running the shop in a very old-fashioned and tired way for twenty years since Stammer died, or the fifteen since Noy left him. Noy went to work first to The Seven Bookhunters and then, being found dishonest there, went to AMS, Abraham's Magazine Service. He's a very nice fellow, and we've always been good friends. But I wouldn't want him to work for me, although at a certain point it looked as though I was going to have to employ him, because nobody else was going to. But, fortunately, I got out of that. In the case of his being fired from The Seven Bookhunters, it was a case of where Louis Scher, who just recently died, found out he was dishonest and made sure that he left, not at the end of the week, but at that very moment, giving him pay till the end of the week and a few more weeks, just to make sure he got out.

Next to Stammer's was one of the other two big shops on the avenue, run by Abe Geffen. This was as big as Stammer's but didn't have the space in the cellar and the upstairs. It was, however, also absolutely tremendous. Mr. Geffen was a little man who was also quite unpleasant and generally wasn't known around the avenue. People didn't go in there much. He had two employees, however, Sy Silverman and Milton Applebaum, who took over the shop after he died, very early in the 1940s, I believe that was, and kept it up for quite a while. I think that it must have been early in the forties because I think both the boys went to the army. I know that Sy did and, later on, Sy went into business for himself, became Humanities Press, Hillary House, and a great many other names, and is very successful now as a publisher as well as a bookseller. Milton Applebaum continued the shop on Fourth Avenue for as long as he could legally keep it open when the building was supposed to be torn down. He fought them tooth and nail for several years after it was supposed to go, but eventually had to leave and took a shop on Broadway, where he now is. He calls himself the Arcadia Bookshop. He and Sy were always, however, called the "Geffen boys." Nobody ever called them anything else except the "Geffen boys."

On Fourth Avenue, just below here, between here and Schulte's, was a place which is now part of the Grace Church, which owns the whole thing and at that time also did but kept that as a shop, was Frank Bender, who specialized in art books. He was one of the few specialist shops. He also had a general shop, but he was interested in art books. Our old friend Leonard Sachs, that I mentioned previously was one of the first persons I met in the book business, was working for him. He thought Leonard Sachs was dishonest. We don't believe he was. Eventually, however, he did get rid of Leon-

ard, and Leonard worked for a man on the opposite side of Fourth Avenue, whose name was [Schoenberg], I believe, but we always called him "Schoenpants" I don't know just why. He specialized in music, actually, and later on moved uptown and became a music shop. Bender moved uptown, also, and had an art shop until he died.

On Fourth Avenue also was a well-known little man named Max Breslow. I think he was rather nice. He had a large shop, and he was quite literate, was interested in little magazines, and he had the corner shop at Ninth Street in the Bible House, which was a very, very large, rambling building, taking up the whole block from Fourth to Third Avenue, and from Eighth to Ninth Street, that is Eighth Street being Astor Place there. It was a very, very large shop, and Leon Kramer had some of his stock there sometimes. Argosy had his main big shop in the building on Fourth Avenue, at number 45, and also a place upstairs, where I met John Kohn first, which was the loft or storage room that Argosy kept. Argosy's shop there at number 45 was tremendous, and, when he moved away to Fifty-ninth Street to become a big man, he offered me the chance of taking over the shop. But I preferred to be away from Fourth Avenue and didn't take it. It was then taken over by an old socialist labor man, who kept the place open mostly as a propaganda thing for his Socialist Labor party, although he kept the stock that Argosy had left. He made some sort of living by staying open till ten or eleven at night also. He died later on, and also his hanger-on, Max Sparber, who was a scout and whom I knew quite well, used to hang out there.

Breslow employed one or two people, one of whom, Steve Seskin, had worked for Schulte. However, during the late 1930s Schulte's, which was a very successful shop, had a strike of its employees, and Steve was one of the movers in the movement. Three of the employees out of four joined the picket line and picketed for many, many weeks. But Mr. Pesky, who was then the owner of the shop, and his son Wilfred, and one employee who refused to go on strike kept the place going perfectly well. Nothing ever came of it, and the boys had to find jobs elsewhere. After Steve left Breslow, he went into business for himself downtown [Eureka Bookshop – M. M.], was unsuccessful, and later on was employed by Harry Gold, who I will mention later. But when he demanded part of Harry Gold's business, Harry Gold let him go, and he then went to work for Benny Bass at the Strand Bookstore, but he suddenly died at an early age (we would consider it an early age), three or four years ago of a

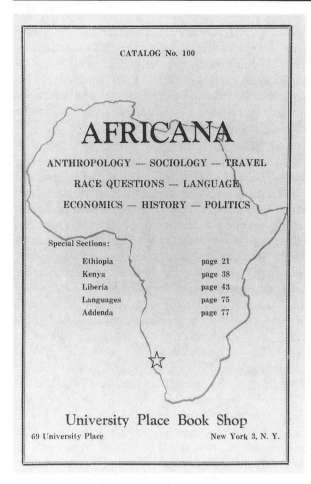

CATALOG No. 100

AFRICANA

ANTHROPOLOGY — SOCIOLOGY — TRAVEL

RACE QUESTIONS — LANGUAGE

ECONOMICS — HISTORY — POLITICS

Special Sections:

Ethiopia	page 21
Kenya	page 38
Liberia	page 43
Languages	page 75
Addenda	page 77

University Place Book Shop

69 University Place   New York 3, N. Y.

Front cover for Catalog No. 100 of Goldwater's University Place Book Shop

heart attack. He was probably in his early fifties. [Older, I believe. I worked with Seskin at Strand in mid 1960s. – M. M.]

Downtown there were two important and good bookshops. One of them was called Thoms and Eron at 89 Chambers Street, which was a very old shop, having started perhaps in the 1870s or 1880s, possibly later, but not too much later. The other shop on Anne Street was the shop established by Isaac Mendoza and later given over to his three sons. It still exists but is, in my opinion, quite moribund. The Thoms shop was the place that we would always go that Sugarman [Abe Sugarman, the uncle of Ethel Goldwater, Goldwater's first wife; he was Goldwater's first partner in the book business] first taught me about. "Always go to Thoms and Eron; they have very good volumes on their tables." It was a shop which was very big, with table after table of cheap books, ranging from ten cents up to thirty-five cents. There were always specials, so many for a dollar. There were always sec-

tions which were especially cheap, [Mayne] Reid's first editions were a dollar each. Besides that, Mr. Thoms was always ready to make a deal on any large quantity. I would go down there and listen to him and take his advice. I remember him judiciously saying, "If you don't buy, Walter, you can't sell." I've always remembered this great thing, and I guess we would have to say it was true enough. However, Mr. Thoms was not completely pure in the matter, because what he meant was, "If you don't buy these particular books that I am offering you, then you can't stay in business." That was not the case. Later on I found that, in spite of all his knowledge of the books, he had feet of clay, because Heinz [Heinz Maienthau, Goldwater's second partner in the book business] and I had not been in business more than two or three years when Heinz found a sleeper in a Dauber and Pine catalogue, the *Petit Plus*, which was a large atlas, a nineteenth-century atlas of the world, and particularly of the Arctic regions, which Dauber and Pine had in their catalogue for about $25. Heinz ran over early in the morning and bought it and sold it to Frank Walters, I think, for $175. Later I mentioned the book to Thoms, and he looked it up in the *Book Prices Current* and found it at an auction price of $25 and said, "I guess that's what it's worth." Of course, it isn't that I blame anybody for not knowing an individual book. It is simply that the question of looking up books and *Book Prices Current* from that moment to this has always seemed to me a matter which does not teach anybody much, unless he knows something about books in general. And, although it was sort of a well-known fact within the book business that the more bibliography you had the better bookseller you were, and, although it was also known that it was very important to have *Book Prices Current* from the beginning to the day that you were working, I have always found it a very unimportant part of my business, and I believe it should be an unimportant part of anybody's business. There are many good booksellers who don't agree with me. But I believe that I can hold my point and indicate that, throughout our career, the importance of having *Book Prices Current* on hand did not make an important difference in a dozen cases. And, in some of those cases, it made a negative difference.

There's no other reason why you should want it, except how much you should pay for a book and how much you can sell it for. If you will look at such things as *Uncle Tom's Cabin,* you will find with the same five-year period a difference between $25 and $500, and you cannot tell anything about that, unless two things: you see the book and you had experience. Nothing else will do, and it will simply not do you any good to know such a thing. There are, of course, cases of a book coming up three times and ranging from a $100 to $125. Then you might have some idea, but even that might not do.

What happened was that Thoms died, and the business came up for sale. By that time it was bought by Mr. [Benjamin] Rosenzweig, the auction [City Book Auction] man, who had decided to extend his tentacles throughout the city and to buy up every shop that was available. He also bought G. A. Baker and Company, which was Hartzof's shop uptown; at the time Edward Lazare, Jack Kebabian, and a colleague owned the place since Hartzof died. Rosenzweig would simply go to these places, realize that he could get such and such an amount out of the auction, and keep the rest. So what he did with Thoms was simply that. He bought the place for a price which we would now consider extremely low, made an auction gallery out of it, sold week after week at auction, and then had a bookshop besides. In the case of G. A. Baker and Company, he knew that he could sell the sets at auction for a certain price and the first editions for a certain price, and then would sell out the rest for something else. He continued to do that, but he was *so* active. He was a very fat [and diabetic – M. M.] but very hardworking man and simply died of a heart attack, right at the peak of his earning power [at fifty seven – M. M.].

INTERVIEWER: He had the auctions at the shops that he bought?

GOLDWATER: He had the auctions at the shop, but he also had auctions other places. He wanted them to be varied, depending on where he was. When he had a shop on Fourth Avenue, he had the auction shop on Fourth Avenue. But he did it at Thoms and then he did it at G. A. Baker. But he also had a place which was at Meadowville, just an auction house. He called it City Book Auction, and City Book Auction was the place at which I put up these incunables and had to buy them back or leave them and the place at which I had bought all those seventeenth-century things for fifty cents apiece. He was the person, also, who discovered that one of the important parts about having an auction was how many pieces you could get done within a given period of time. So he simply had the catalogue, a very brief cataloguing of them. But then, instead of naming the piece each time, he simply named the number and looked in the audience to see if there was a bid. If there was, he recorded it. If

there was not, he simply recorded what the mail order was and went on. This way, he was able sometimes to get through with a thousand pieces in one day, whereas the normal person wouldn't get through more than three hundred. Since he was getting paid by the piece by the people who put the things up, he always knew he was ahead. This idea was later on taken on by Swann, who became the only remaining medium-priced auction in the city, who charged so much for cataloguing and for extras that he simply made money whether or not he got any price on the book.

Isaac Mendoza had three sons, each one of them stupider than the one before, but the first one, Aaron, not too stupid. They kept the thing going. They specialized in Americana, particularly New Yorkiana, but had a general bookshop which was quite good.

It was a very good shop. We used to go down there, but these things were a little bit more expensive than they were at Thoms, but they weren't too expensive anyway. And they were always very friendly. I actually never knew Isaac; I only knew the three sons.

I was always able to buy. They knew something about books. They knew first editions, and they knew Americana very well. They cared about some things and didn't care about others.

To get back to Fourth Avenue, the Green Bookshop was started by Harry Carp in the thirties. He first was on [number 11] Astor Place and then came over to number 108 or 110 Fourth Avenue. After he died of cancer five or six years ago, Mrs. [Ruth – M. M.] Carp continued the shop and still is there. He specialized to some extent in fiction, particularly translations of fiction. He never knew anything about books, and she doesn't, either.

There was a book scout called Stanley Grant who used to go around buying and selling first editions. He was not very interesting and was not very honest. And then there was another Grant named Charlie Grant who was both a very good book scout and very honest and was very well known. They both died at a fairly early age.

I think I mentioned before what a scout was. A scout generally is a person who buys from one bookshop and sells to another bookshop. A scout is always a bookseller without a shop and usually goes from one bookshop to another. But sometimes he goes from a bookshop to a library, sometimes has a private clientele, and once in a while buys a book from a private person and sells to a private person. In general, however, the definition of a scout is that of a runner in England, which is a person who buys from one bookshop and sells to another bookshop.

Alfred Goldsmith is one of the people who is best known in the world as a bookseller. He had a tiny shop on Lexington Avenue and called it The Sign of the Sparrow, between Twenty-fourth and Twenty-fifth streets, in the basement. It was considered the locale for Christopher Morley's book *The Haunted Bookshop*, which is a terrible book, and was frequented by Christopher Morley, Carolyn Wells, and a few other of the other semi-intelligentsia of the period. He wrote a bibliography of Walt Whitman and another of Lewis Carroll. These were both people in whom he was mainly interested, and he was supposed to be an expert in both these subjects. I am willing to accept this as so. Although there were considerable errors in both the bibliographies, still they were the best thing up to the time.

He was personally a very nice person. He was the person I think I mentioned before who hated Heinz and who always referred to Heinz as "that horrible creature." He never referred to him as anything else except "that horrible creature" and beseeched me never to send Heinz up to him with books to sell but always, if I had them, to come to bring them myself. His wife was an Englishwoman who was Cerberus sitting at the door, hating everybody who came in and trying to keep them for fear they might bother her husband. I think she made the exception in the case of such people as Carolyn Wells, but she did not make the exception in my case or the case of any other book scout who went there. Most of us knew that, at some price or another, Goldsmith would buy a book. How in the world he could do it, since it didn't seem to us as though he ever sold anything and he certainly was very cheap in price, we never could understand. But he always would buy a book at some price or other. If we were broke during those early thirties, we would go to Goldsmith and be able to get fifty cents or a dollar, because he would buy. He was famous for having his great books in the back room. That was where the first editions of *Leaves of Grass, Alice in Wonderland,* and so on were all supposed to be. After he died, the back room became open, and it was discovered that there was no such great thing in the back room after all. The material turned up in auction at Swann's, went for nothing, and there were no good Carrolls at all, and the Walt Whitmans were of a medium sort, such as *Goodbye, My Fancy;* the third or fourth or fifth edition of *Leaves of Grass; After All, Not to Create Only,* another medium-priced thing. They were perfectly good and not too com-

mon, but they didn't amount to anything. *November Boughs* he would have four or five copies of, and so on. It was all right and, if they came up at auction nowadays, they would bring something. But at that time, they brought nothing at all. Even I, who was not at all a specialist, was able to buy a few lots. They sometimes put as many as four or five things in one lot, which went for a few dollars. She, later on, got a job at NYU and was there for many years. But I don't know what happened to her; she is probably dead by now. I remember Goldsmith and his illness. Goldsmith never sat down; he always stood behind his little counter and made cute remarks to people who came in, usually the kind of things where you'd have to say, "When you say that smile." He always did smile, so nobody took it quite to heart. In fact, even Heinz, knowing that he referred to him always as "that horrible creature" – and in fact when he went in there, he would say, "Oh, here's that horrible creature again" – even Heinz could never really believe that he really meant that he was a horrible creature, but he did. He said it in such a sweet way that nobody could really believe that he really meant these terrible things that he said. He was famous for having made a mot about the book business. He said that the book business is a very pleasant way of making a very little money. That was true of him, and it has been taken for granted up to this time. Actually, it was just that the way he was running it was a very pleasant way of running a business and a way of making very little money. Other people who were handling Whitmans or Carrolls even said that he would have made a rather good deal of money, but he did not. I remember that, later on, I would come there and find him grimacing in pain. I said, "What's the matter?" and he said, "That damn sciatica that I have." A few days later I came, and he wasn't there. They said he was in the hospital. A few days later after that he died. The sciatica which he had turned out to be cancer, and terminal. He had never been told, and he had never realized it.

He was a friendly soul, but he wasn't able to give really good advice. He was a bookman, and he had his catalogue which he would bring out once in a while. It was a kind of cute catalogue of first editions. In general, the downtown people, as I have mentioned, were general booksellers, and in general the uptown booksellers were first-editions people, not specialists. I'll mention a number of those to show what they were like.

Max Hartzof was the doyen of the uptown scoundrels. He had his office in what was called the Grand Central Terminal Building, or Grand Central Building, I've forgotten which it was, at Forty-sixth Street and Park Avenue. In the same building, was Frank Walters, who was a wonderful man and knew everything. Hartzof's office was called G. A. Baker Company; the G. A. Baker name was completely arbitrary. There had never been anybody named G. A. Baker. Hartzof employed there or gave office space to a great many booksellers who later on became something in the book business; the main people remembered are Edward Lazare and David Randall.

It was quite large, a long shop, beautifully arranged, and with a lot of sets, and so on. He sold furniture in that way, as sets, but he also was a very good first-editions man and also had his eye out for the main chance. He was a good general bookman. He knew a great deal, I assume, from what Edward Lazare says. He was very difficult to work for, difficult to work with, difficult to buy from, difficult to sell to, a difficult man altogether, and generally a scoundrel, I believe, and certainly dishonest. He was sort of, as I say, the doyen of the uptown scoundrels.

I knew that he was dishonest, that is dishonest in the sense that he would not hesitate to state a book to be right if it was not or to sell it for more than it was worth on the basis that it was something which it was not. Also, he certainly would simply pocket money and would lack reference to keeping any track of it or anything like that. Of course, that's not too uncommon in the book business, generally. I imagine that not too many people are completely pure in the book business, actually.

When he died, it was taken over by these three employees: Edward Lazare, John Kebabian, and a third person whose name I know but have forgotten who has now disappeared. They bought it and kept it going until they had to go into the army. The other man's name was Otto. Otto didn't have to go into the army. He was the one who was the bookkeeper, or something, and knew least. So, when Edward and Jack had to go into the army, they sold it out to Rosenzweig, and it went out of business. That would have been a good buy for anybody at that time. I was interested in it, but Rosenzweig was able to do a good deal more. It had moved to the place on Forty-sixth Street, over to 3 West Forty-sixth Street.

Lathrop Harper was the doyen of rare-book dealers. He was the only person in town who really knew anything about incunabula and was the great specialist in that field and had been for many years. His shop was a large and beautiful one, on the second or third floor of a building opposite the public

library on West Fortieth Street. He was helped there by several people who did know a great deal about incunabula. Harper was known to be the great incunabula man, but the fact was that he didn't really know much about them at all, strangely enough. He was a very wealthy man who had made his money in other fields, mainly real estate, and who liked rare books. He was not pompous about his knowledge or lack of knowledge, however. The fact that he did not know any foreign languages at all, while rather unusual for a European dealer, to learn about all the European dealings, being quite acquainted with at least four or five languages, and the incunabula dealers being usually acquainted with still more than that, Harper didn't know Latin or any language, in fact, except English. But when Harper came back from Europe with his usual quota of several hundred incunabula and people asked him how he got along without knowing any foreign languages, his answer was this: "I know how to say 'imperfect' in every language."

He was married to a woman who had a column in hundreds of American papers, called "Seeing Europe with Helen and Warren" or "Helen and Warren Visit Europe" or something like that. And she was a very wealthy woman in her own right. After Harper died, the firm came upon evil days. She sold it first to a Latin American man, who bought the shop and continued it for a while, bringing in [Otto H.] Ranschburg to assist Douglas C. Parsonage, who had been there for a long time. Miriam Lone, who had been Harper's right-hand woman and who, I think, was an aunt of Douglas Parsonage, by that time was dead. With the advent of Ranschburg, it had a new lease on life. However, when this Colombian man died, the whole thing was sold to Indiana University, or given to Indiana University, and they took all the good incunables, and, for a moment, it seemed as though the shop would not continue. However, shortly after that, somebody else put in some money, and so it continues on now.

David Randall took all the incunabula which he wanted for the Lilly Library at Indiana, which was practically everything, plus all the general books which he wanted. But he left most of the Latin Americana which was there. The Colombian man's name was Mendel; of course, he wasn't entirely Colombian.

Parsonage was really an Americana man, but he had learned something about incunabula from the period there. But Otto Ranschburg really is an incunabula man. It was Miriam Lone who knew the most things about incunabula, but Harper surrounded himself with people who knew something about things and always got along and put out perfectly wonderful catalogues, particularly a series in 1926 which remains a standard work with prices and with discussion of each book and the place and date. Harper was particularly interested in incunabula from the point of view of places published, and was very proud when he would find something from a little town, the only one published there, or he would say, "This is the first book printed in Traviso" or in some even smaller town than that. That would be a great thing. However, from the way prices are nowadays, we would consider his catalogue prices quite cheap, although in some cases it's surprising how little difference there is between the price in those days and today. It is true, however, that up until 1946 or even 1950 fully half of the books which were available in the 1926 catalogue were still present and were still available for the prices.

At the point of Harper's death, I think that Yale was permitted to buy anything that was in the catalogue at a substantial discount, I think one-third, and Yale did avail itself of this opportunity. If I had known it at the time, I would have bought a few, but I didn't know anything about it.

INTERVIEWER: Did you ever buy anything from him?

GOLDWATER: From Harper himself, I don't think I ever bought anything. I mentioned previously that Harper was my friend and very kind to me, and that in one catalogue of mine he did allow me to borrow from him two seventeenth-century American imprints, just to sweeten up the catalogue, but neither of them sold. Aside from that and his putting me in touch with [Chavional] in Paris, we didn't have too much contact. He sort of liked me, but we never had much to do with each other.

INTERVIEWER: What do you think about the future of that shop?

GOLDWATER: Well, I think the future of the shop ... it's a crazy business. They're paying twenty-two thousand dollars a year rent in the new place, something like that. It was something quite fantastic. The new place on East Fortieth Street is one of the most beautiful shops there is. It's simply beautiful, but it costs to make it beautiful.

INTERVIEWER: Do they put out any catalogues?

GOLDWATER: They put out one or two absolutely wonderful catalogues. But, unless they have a regular sale of things, they cannot possibly make a go of it. Neither Parsonage nor Ranschburg is a merchandiser. They are both rare-book people. And, if they are not, then obviously the employees are not going to be. However, they've got some new money in from people who apparently can afford to lose it, so I think it will go on until the death of one or both of them. Ranschburg is now well over seventy, and Parsonage is in his mid sixties. It seems unlikely that anything will go on with the place after they go.

They don't know anything about merchandising; they never cared about merchandising. They wanted to sell a beautiful book for a beautiful price. Of course, they have customers; but if they had real customers, they wouldn't be able to put out such beautiful catalogues, because the material would be sold before they put out the catalogue.

Over on Park Avenue were two people, both of whom were so similar that I always get them mixed them up. One of them was called Harry Stone, and one was called Harry F. Marks. They both made their primary living out of erotica and fine bindings. But both of them disappeared during the Depression, because their fine customers disappeared, also. One of them, I don't know which [Stone, I believe – M. M.], went down to Florida and had a shop there and disappeared. The shop of the other one continued for quite a while under somebody else's sponsorship. Not too long ago, although I guess it is a long time ago now, possibly ten years, the remains of the shop became available there before they lost their lease. I bought from them a vast number of Black Sun Press imprints. That must have been Harry Marks, not Harry Stone. Harry Marks apparently was the contact of Edward Titus and Caresse Crosby here [Marks was an agent for Black Sun Press – M. M.]. I bought this vast number of Hart Cranes, Henry Jameses, Archibald MacLeishes, and so on. It was a very shrewd maneuver on my part, as these things so often are. I went immediately to the Gotham Book Mart, Seven Gables, and other places, and sold them to them for a dollar or two profit each, including thirty copies of the Ezra Pound and a number of the Joyces. After a year I discovered that if there had been one mistake in my life, it was exactly selling these books which I had sold. I did make a very substantial profit within a few days at that time, and I thought I was very clever. But the only cleverness that I would have had in that time would have been to forget the whole thing for about three or four years or ten, at which time I would be now quite wealthy. I still have one copy of the Henry James letters to Walter Berry and perhaps one copy of something else, but that's the entire stock which remains to me. In the meantime these things have simply skyrocketed. My usual shrewd maneuver.

There were two Friedmans downtown who were fairly interesting – three Friedmans, really. One of them was Maurice Friedman on 147 East Twenty-second Street, who had a little shop there which was about as filthy and jammed as any shop in the city. I think that it compared favorably with any shop that I've had anything to do with in that one can simply go in there and only had to squeeze his way by piles of books and everything if he wanted to find anything. Mr. Friedman was interested in radical things, but it didn't matter much, because when you went in there, you couldn't find anything anyway. On Twenty-third Street, between Fifth and Sixth avenues on the South Side, was the shop of the brothers Friedman, Ira and Harry. They had been in business quite a while before I started and had a very good shop, a very big one, very deep. The two of them got along quite well, but they were very different, and specialized in Americana, also in remainders, but had a good general shop. They got along quite well until a quite extraneous matter turned up: the question of parking. At some point or other during the early fifties, it was decided that there should be no parking on Twenty-third Street. As soon as there was no parking on Twenty-third Street, they lost their entire clientele, shut up the shop, and Harry Friedman opened a shop in White Plains; and Ira Friedman went to Port Washington. Harry Friedman's shop in White Plains closed about three or four years ago, but he still does business from his home. He's a man now in his very late seventies. Ira Friedman died a few years ago but, before he died, left to his son-in-law his whole business. The son-in-law, realizing that he knew nothing about secondhand and out-of-print books, went into the publishing business and became the Kennikat Publishing Company, which has done very well, indeed, on Americana and other, particularly New Yorkiana, reprints. That still exists out in Port Washington, and it's partly called Ira Friedman and partly Kennikat Book Company.

I knew Merle Johnson only very slightly. Merle Johnson is, of course, best known as the author of *American First Editions* and other books, such as *You Know These Lines* and *High Spots in American Literature. You Know These Lines* was, of course, a book of quotations and which books they came from, I think entirely American.

Johnson was a bookseller as well as being an illustrator as well as being a bibliographer. He worked from his home, a little place in the East Twenties, and sold first editions, mostly similar to Whitman Bennett, mainly what Randall calls "sophisticated copies." He found out what the first issue of a thing was and then would either insert the page with that issue point on it, or sometimes have a facsimile of a title page made with a date very carefully inked in – something like that. He was involved in those days with Kelleher and with Jake Blanck, who were, of course, much younger than he. I didn't know him well; I just became acquainted with him through Sugarman, and then he died not too long after that, during the thirties.

Another man who only recently died but was very much involved with the sophistication of copies for all his life was George Van Nosdall. He was the man who was the member of the Fritz Kuhn's bund [Kuhn was head of the American Nazi Party before World War II – M. M.]. Some of his catalogues said on the top, "Buy American." He was very anti-Jewish, and this was not the thing to be much during those days. So he was not generally liked. However, he was involved with Gabriel Wells, who was one of the most Jewish people that there ever was. His original name, as we know, was not Wells but Weiss. Van Nosdall claims to have sold as many as 150 or 200 sets of Harriet Beecher Stowe's *Uncle Tom's Cabin* and many, many copies of the Melvilles and other things, which were rather plentiful around town.

Van Nosdall never really had a shop, as far as I know. When I got to know him, he had a place up in East 126 Street, and he sold from that. It was a filthy place and smelled terribly, and it was just full of first editions – all bad first editions, but first editions. He cared about first editions, and he always complained about how things used to be, and so on. He used to come down to the shop and buy some things from me, from which I learned that he would buy a real first edition. It didn't have to be a fake; he would just rather have a fake than nothing at all. Later on, he became interested in a few authors only: Gertrude Atherton, because she was the only right-wing author that we ever had in America; and, for some reason not explained, also Theodore Dreiser. But he was also interested in, among the English, Rider Haggard, Swinnerton, and he was interested in Mayne Reid; and then he was interested in Anthony Hope. The only reason I really got to like him was about the Anthony Hope: he was the only person who really cared about the first issue of *The Prisoner of Zenda*, which had to have seventeen titles on the first page of the advertisements instead of eighteen titles. He was the only person besides me who knew that, and the only person besides me who cared. Whenever I came back from England with a copy with the seventeen titles, he was always right there to get it from me; and he appreciated that.

INTERVIEWER: Then he sold to other dealers?

GOLDWATER: No, he didn't, because no other dealers generally would buy from him anyway. He still had this mailing list, and he would send out mimeographed lists. He did very badly, and he died with a vast number of books, probably a hundred thousand or more, many of which were in Wappinger's Falls, others which were in Queens, others which were on Twenty-second Street. Fortunately, or unfortunately, a lot of them were destroyed by fire and water. He had also given a large number of them, perhaps ten thousand, to Rosenzweig to auction. When Rosenzweig died, Mrs. Rosenzweig denied everything; and so he never got anything out of it at all. It was sort of a case of where everybody was pretty amused by this sort of go at woman, go at bear. Nobody cared, so long as they were quarreling with each other. Each one of them was crooked as the other one. He also claimed to be swindled by several other people, which was probably true, although if anybody could swindle him, we always felt good luck to him.

John [Kohn] always hated him the worst of all, but I never could really hate him enough because I couldn't take the Nazi business seriously. I did know that he liked books; he really cared about books and really cared about first editions.

This reminds us of Gabriel Wells, of whom I didn't know anything because I never met him. Stories of Gabriel Wells would have to be heard from somebody else who's been in it longer than I. He was, and is known, as the only competitor that Rosenbach ever had. The two of them used to bid things up at auction against each other during the period when nobody else was around, except a man named George D. Smith, whom I also didn't know, except that I was at his place once. I did not know Wells at all.

Captain [Louis H.] Cohen; Nobody really believed that he was a captain. In joke they would always say that he was captain of the horse marines. It is probably true, however, that he had become

some sort of a lieutenant, at least, in the army during the First World War. But he was connected with the French army at that time. Whether he was in the American army, nobody knew whether he was in the First World War, of course. He was a man who had waxed mustaches and was very old-boyish. He was really Colonel Blimp, our own Colonel Blimp.

Yes, and he was the one who cared about Hemingway and put out a bibliography of Hemingway in 1932. His wife was Margie, and she had to take at least second place whenever he was around. He would always say, "Shut up, Margie; Don't be snotty, Margie"; or, "Get out of here, Margie," when anybody else was around. Whether he did that when they were alone, we don't know; but he always did it when somebody else was there. And she always did shut up, or not be snotty, or get out, as told.

They were in the East Fifties; that was called the House of Books. And they had two or three different places there, but they were always within one or two blocks of each other. They were always up one flight and very fancy. He would buy first editions, but they had to be in mint condition, and she kept that standard after he died.

They got with private people of a fancy type. Also, they had some money; anyway, they were a very modest business up until he died. He apparently must have left a good deal of insurance, and she apparently has never lacked for money since and has always bought anything she wanted, even just for prestige. I think that, in the long run, she got to know a good deal more about the business than he did. At the time she was considered, I think, nothing at all. But now she certainly knows a good deal about her business, and she also knows how to do business, which I don't think he ever did. In general, he wasn't particularly liked, and he wouldn't attract people much.

He was a first-editions man, and they did the printing of these various limited editions, and so on, with Saroyans and other stuff. That was all done by him. He was all right in the main. He never was mean or anything. It was just that he was kind of obnoxious.

He would buy first editions. If it were in fine condition, he would buy; and he was not so bad. There were a few other people who were in the first-editions business in midtown at that time. One of them was called Ernest Dressel North, who had a large beard. Another one was called Barnet B. Byer. They were all very expensive first-edition people, and most of them disappeared at the end of the Depression. I don't know what happened to them all. Barnet B. Ryer's shop continued for quite a while later – after the war, in fact. John Kohn was called in to appraise it, and I think to liquidate it finally. But I never knew these people. They were quite out of my sphere.

George Kirk was a very nice man who had a shop called Chelsea Bookshop. It was first opened at 365 West Fifteenth Street in Chelsea but, just about the time I went into business, moved down to Eighth Street and had a very nice little shop on the south side of Eighth Street near Sixth Avenue [58 West Eighth Street]. He was there for many years. His wife worked; she was at *Parents* magazine. So he was able to keep the shop going, even when business wasn't terribly good. He had a circulating library, mainly, but he was also interested in first editions and remainders. His shop was taken over by somebody who could pay four times as much rent – that was in the days just when Eighth Street was starting to boom – either Marboro or some other kind of shop took over his place and paid some fantastic rent, which he could not possibly touch. So he had to go out of business. And it was just at that time when I put my brother into the auction business, and George became his partner. It was probably through George that Robert Wilbur came into that circle, because Robert Wilbur used to hang around in the shop too, as I did at that time.

Later on, after the business of the auction disappeared – apparently he drank a good deal, which I hadn't known – his wife continued with her job, and it became better and better. She was quite well-off with her job, and he got a job in a defense factory and continued that throughout the war. But he died either toward the end of the war or a little bit after that. She's still alive.

There was a man named Maurice Sloog, who was a French dealer, whom we got to know fairly well after a while because he became a member of our group. After he never paid either the dues in the group or anybody else that he ever bought any books from, eventually he sort of dropped out. He was a real scoundrel, but a very lovable one. People liked him very much, but he never paid for anything.

He had an office, I guess, on West Forty-eighth Street. He knew the French book business very well and early books quite well. I guess he was a pretty big shot. He certainly talked awfully big and was always looking for big things. But I didn't know him too well. I used to kid a lot with him, because we'd speak French and so on, but I always

The Biblo and Tannen Bookshop at Ninth Street and Fourth Avenue, New York City, in 1921

knew that he had the advantage of me in whatever we were doing.

On Sixth Avenue – I think between Tenth and Eleventh – [161 Sixth Avenue] there was a very large shop called Pratt's which had been there since at least the 1890s, possibly before. It was a wonderful shop to go into, if you didn't have to have anything to do with Mr. or Mrs. Pratt, who were rather horrid people. It was similar to [Weyman] Brothers in that it specialized in pamphlets or little paperback material on how to fix your house, or how to play chess, or something like that; and that was the main thing that they did business with. But he did have a complete shop of secondhand books of all kinds, and a very large cellar also piled up with stuff. It was there when first Mr. Pratt died and finally when Mrs. Pratt died that I bought some thousands, possibly as many as ten thousand, little magazines, that is the English ones called *Dome, Yellow Book*.

I found perhaps a thousand *Black Cats* there, for instance. *Black Cat* had been considered very rare. Suddenly here was this vast number of *Black Cats*. With all of that, I had a great deal of difficulty selling them, and *Black Cat* was the one that I tried to sell to Princeton, because he was very anxious to have them. When I asked him twenty-five cents, he said no; he wanted me to give them to him for fifteen cents. This was in the late forties or early fifties. Well, he was no good. And then there were vast numbers of the *Philistine* and the other thing which was similar to the *Philistine* . . .

Bibelot. There were a tremendous number of things. I bought them for one or two cents apiece at that time, but I never made much off them. I did all right with them, but I didn't make a great deal of money on them. I sold to Yale and the University of Connecticut, and some other people, and probably even sold to Princeton.

The Pratts didn't like anybody there much, so a book dealer didn't go. After they died, it was taken over by a man named Edward Weiss, who wasn't particularly likable but who liked to sell books. So, at that time, we did go over and buy a good deal from Eddie Weiss. He later on sold it again to an Englishman who wasn't particularly liked but who was interested in bicycles. If you'd go there and talk to him about bicycles, then you could buy some books at a low price sometimes. Eventually the shop disappeared, and the bookshop became an art-supply shop, which it now is.

In New Brunswick, New Jersey, there were a couple of shops at given times. The oldest one was run by a man named Perry Kaiser. Kaiser was an old anarchist who had been involved in the Stelten, New Jersey, experiment and in others. He got into trouble with stolen books and was actually put in jail for them.

It was a very long time ago. Later on, after he got out of jail, he ran a bookshop there for many, many years. I was always quite friendly with him; I liked him quite a good deal. And I would buy batches of books from him quite often at low prices.

It was a general shop. Eleanor [Goldwater] would buy Edgar Rice Burroughs and cookery and whatever she was interested in at the moment. After the war he got involved with a man named Rizick, and that was a great error on his part because Rizick was, of all the people we knew in the book business, probably the most crooked. He never did anything honest at all. If he had been able to make more money being honest than dishonest, he still wouldn't have done it. Because what he really cared about was doing something crooked. So, suddenly Kaiser found himself in a position where Rizick had done something wrong but Kaiser was responsible. And this was great trouble for Kaiser, because he already had this criminal record. I remember going in there when this was going on and Kaiser saying to me, "You know, Walter, I really admire that Jim. Listen to this." And then he told me the story about

how Rizick and he had gotten involved in this thing, which was doubtful, but how Rizick had carefully arranged it so that Kaiser would be responsible. He said, "You know, you really need to be smart to do that. I really admire that." And he was perfectly serious.

It wasn't the stuff from Lehigh, and it wasn't the stuff from this other place in Pennsylvania, and it wasn't all the money that he had gotten from those doctors and lawyers who didn't dare to say anything because they had kept them in a crooked way themselves, and it wasn't the question of the records which he had gotten on consignment and then suddenly went bankrupt. It wasn't any of those things. It was something quite else which he was involved with. Kaiser died after a while.

Fourth Avenue even now has as many as twenty bookshops right there or around the corner. But in that time it must have had thirty or forty. Right up from Eighth Street to Thirteenth Street, on both sides of the street (of course, on the West Side, it was only from Tenth Street up because Wannamaker took the whole block from Eighth to Tenth Street), it was all secondhand bookshops. I have mentioned already the Bible House, which was at Eighth Street to Ninth Street; I've mentioned Breslow and Argosy and Schoenpants and Leon Kramer up in the building. . . . On these blocks, some of them I remember and some of them I forget just where they were. Between Ninth and Tenth streets, there was a man who called himself the Astor Bookshop, and that was Abe Klein. He was always trying to maneuver, but later everything went bad with him. He sold out, and his place was eventually taken over by Biblo and Tannen. He became a salesman for Abraham and Strauss, and he may still be alive. He was never involved, as far as I knew, with the real crooked things which were going on on Fourth Avenue, which were mainly the activity of Charles Rohm, who was on the other side of the street, Ben Harris, and Harry Gold. These were the ones who were really involved with books being stolen from libraries, which was different from the sort of run-of-the-mill kind of things being stolen from new bookshops and sold on Fourth Avenue. Harry Gold went to jail, and I guess Rohm did also. And I guess Harris did also. The stuff that they stole, or had stolen for them, was so important and was so professional that the people wanted to make an example of them. Actually, stuff stolen from the New York Public Library, Edgar Allan Poes and things of that sort, was really big stuff.

There were many things stolen, and eventually Mr. [Bernquist] of the library and other people got the goods on these people and sent them to jail. Even after they came out of jail, they continued to traffic in stolen books, but only in a very minor way. They didn't certainly make a business of it; that is, they trafficked in it only in the same way, only to perhaps a larger extent than most of the other booksellers on Fourth Avenue; namely they would not inquire too deeply into the stolen books. Perhaps this is the time when I should mention my tale of Benny Bass, who at that time was a poor little thing and had this bad bookshop.

He's the one who has the Strand Bookshop, and it's a great success. At that time Benny Bass was a poor thing on Fourth Avenue trying to make a go of it. At one time during this period, I've forgotten the exact date, I was quite friendly with him. I used to lend him five dollars, which he would give me a check for, and the check wouldn't be any good. It was always that small a situation with him.

In the long run I would get paid or take books, or something like that. Whenever it was something like that, you knew you could always get books that were worth that much. If a check weren't good this time, why, it would be good the next time, or something like that. It didn't ever amount to anything.

One day he came to me and said that he had been indicted for the theft of a large collection of law books in new condition, which he had bought. If he hadn't sold them himself, he was accused of receiving these stolen goods. And would I come down to the court and testify to his good character. I said I would. Well, I went down, and, when the case came to trial, the city prosecutor produced the evidence, showed the books, and Ben said that he hadn't known that they were stolen. The city's case was that these books being new, and being in quantity of this sort, and being expensive, and being only published the year before, would normally have to be understood to have been stolen, and that a man of this sort should know that they were stolen. So I was put on the stand and, apparently, was there both to testify to his good character and also to be as a witness about this matter. The prosecutor, as it turned out, foolishly asked me did I not think that a person who had been in business as long as Mr. Bass would recognize these books as stolen books — to which I was able to say "no," because during that period books were remaindered very quickly, and a book a year old could very easily be a remainder, and the price he had bought them at was not zero but a price which would be a normal remainder price for that kind of thing. Therefore, it was perfectly possible that Mr. Bass

would not know that they were stolen but would think that they were remainders.

He was acquitted. It did not come to jury trial. The judge acquitted him at once after the witnesses had testified. He was supposed to return the books, but there was no turpitude involved. Bass was very pleased, of course, about all this, and the two of us came up on the subway together. We got to the subway, and he turned to me and said, "You were just wonderful. After you finished talking, I was almost convinced myself that I hadn't known that those were stolen."

In the same building, or the next building to Lathrop Harper on West Fortieth Street, was one of the most respected firms of rare books, particularly first editions, in the country, James F. Drake. Mr. Drake I never met; he was already quite old at that time. The two sons continued the business during my period, and I got to know them fairly well. They were pretty much stuffed shirt kind of persons, but they were both members of my book club, so I got to know them all right. Their names were James H., instead of James F., and Marston Drake. Marston was also called "the colonel" in the same way that Captain Cohen had been called "the captain." I imagine he had been a colonel somewhere at some time. They were both rather dull people, in the same sense that most of these booksellers were dull. Their stories were always about what book they had bought at such and such a price and sold at such and such. They were interested only, really, in first editions, and mainly in modern first editions. They didn't know anything about early books at all and, I don't think, too much about other things. But they were considered quite expert in their field and were great purveyors of Galsworthy, Kipling, Stevenson, and others. They apparently had some very good customers for Kipling, at least, and had sold some great collections of Kipling. After Marston died and James was pretty moribund, I used to go there fairly often and see the stuff. It looked like a pretty bad collection of stuff, but it was always supposed to be, as in the case of Goldsmith, that somewhere or other there were wonderful things. After they both died and the shop was liquidated — they moved first over to East Forty-first Street before liquidation — it was sold to University of Texas, having been appraised by Laurence Gomme. Laurence Gomme would never say how much he had appraised it for. Laurence Gomme is one of the doyens of the book business, and he's still alive at the age of eighty-eight, or something like that. He was with Fred Thoms for a long time and in business for himself. He is another man who is a good bookman but a terrible bookseller. And he was never able to make a go of it himself. He's one of the people that we always feel that . . . Eleanor always felt that he didn't know anything anyway. Actually, the only thing was that, since he had an English accent, which he had preserved for sixty years, that having the English accent and being old, people assumed that he knew something, when actually he didn't at all. I've never discovered whether it was true or not, never will discover it.

INTERVIEWER: What happened to Drake? Texas bought it?

GOLDWATER: Yes, Texas bought it. There was no possible point in Texas buying it, since there wasn't a single book in that whole thing that they didn't have. It was completely crazy. He did have one Gutenberg leaf that everybody wanted because it had either the Ten Commandments on it or the Sermon on the Mount, or something like that. It was one of the leaves which, if you wanted a particular leaf, that was the one you wanted. I offered him a thousand dollars for it and was rejected. I don't know eventually what he got for it. That was simply packed up as a whole. Boy, was that a bunch of junk! By the time they died, there was nothing left really. They hadn't been buying for many years, really. They had just been sort of living on it. The Galsworthys still remained, and the Kiplings still remained, and some of the Stevensons still remained. A few late Cathers, and that stuff, John Masefield . . . there were fifty John Masefields, and they had them on the shelf at a dollar and half. But nobody bought them, even at a dollar and a half. These were mint first editions in dust jackets. I think I did buy a batch of those. I think when he said I could have them for half price I did buy fifty of them, or something like that.

INTERVIEWER: Texas paid a lot of money for that shop. I don't know how much.

GOLDWATER: Well, we don't know. Unless we find out some day, we'll never know. But, whatever they paid, it was too much. It was just crazy. I don't think the stuff was worth five thousand dollars, except maybe for that leaf.

Schulte's Bookstore, number 80 Fourth Avenue, was one of the largest shops in the city, and also one of the older ones, started about in the 1890s or early 1900s. Theodore Schulte was a vestryman or member of the Grace Church, and the Grace Church owned the Schulte Building. It had a

very large basement, very, very large main floor, and balconies. It still does. It was generally a good secondhand bookshop. It's the kind of place where, if you were coming to New York and just had time to go to one place, this was the place you'd go, because the prices were reasonable, and the quantity of material was very large, indeed. Schulte died during the thirties, and the shop was taken over by his main employee, whose name was Phillip Pesky, who was a horrible man. Well, of course, that was very offensive to me, but nowadays I wouldn't mind that so much. It was just the way he was. Anyway, he was a fairly good bookseller and kept the thing going quite well. After he died it was taken over by his son Wilfred, who was one of the nicest people there ever was in the book business, but he didn't know anything about books at all. He was a very good salesman and was always able to convince people that, whichever *Britannica* he had, whether it was the eleventh, thirteenth, or fourteenth, was the very best *Britannica*. He never looked inside of them, but he did have the proper salesmanship approach. I think he may have gotten it from the original *Britannica* salesman himself. The shop continued for many years and is still there, but it went downhill after the older Pesky's death.

It was mainly that Wilfred didn't understand the question of cost accounting and didn't understand how much wasted effort he was putting into very small things, that every book that was sold didn't need to have any special record of that particular book, but simply that the book was sold for such and such a price. But his bookkeeping was meticulous. He had a full-time bookkeeper, just to keep record of each book that was sold, and made sure that, after a book was paid for, it still had its line underneath it, showing that particular account was finished.

If he didn't sell it or didn't have it or didn't have it on hand, he kept a record for everybody. This was really very good. Everybody liked him for this, and, at the beginning, most of us also did this because we felt that was the way the book business was. In a sense, as a social work, that was what the book business was for, namely to help somebody who wanted an out-of-print book find an out-of-print book. But, since we were buying these books for, say, fifty cents or a dollar and a half, and selling them for two and a half to five dollars, the amount of time which was involved in finding these things never at all compensated us. Most of us discovered this after a while and simply wouldn't do it. Wilfred never discovered it, to the day of his death. Even after I explained it to him a few years before his death, he simply said that it was impossible for him to change this. He just wouldn't and couldn't do it.

The way Wilfred was able to keep going during the 1940s and 1950s after his father's death and into the early sixties was by a very peculiar kind of bookkeeping, which showed that he was still perfectly solvent, when the fact was that he was bankrupt. He had very good contacts which had been built up by Schulte and his father with Ivita Van Doren as the reviewer for the *Herald Tribune,* and reviewers for other magazines, and with *Time* magazine, and so on, which was very good for him. He also had great contacts with large libraries with duplicates and many places. But, when it came to getting cash or having cash available, he would borrow from the Pesky estate, which was substantial, or from relatives, or from the bank, or from friends like myself.

We would be supposed to take our money out in buying books from him at half price, or something like that. Well, for a while, one would be able to do that; and, after a while, one wasn't, because there wasn't enough good stuff to do it. He would always have some big deal in the offing, which was going to pay for everything, and sometimes they would come through. Eventually, however, the way he was able to keep going was by simply not paying Ivita Van Doren and these other people, but simply owing it to them. Ivita Van Doren, fortunately for him, died about this time, and nothing ever happened about that. So he continued to think that he was solvent. When I got a chance to look at the books later on, when the estate was asking me to see if I would take it over, I discovered that the way the thing was solvent was that, although he owed forty-odd thousand dollars in actual debts for book purchases or for actual loans (in most cases loans) and only $125 in the bank, or even less. The way the situation was made to show solvency was that he had goodwill worth $20,000 and books on the shelf worth $30,000. Actually, the books on the shelf weren't worth more than $5,000 or $6,000, in my opinion, and the goodwill wasn't worth anything at all, since what goodwill means is ability to make money in the book business. And that wasn't proved. The money was also borrowed from his employees, who would either take part of the salary and be owed the rest – their whole salary wasn't very much; as a matter of fact, I don't think he ever paid anybody $100 a week, including himself – but sometimes he would actually borrow money from them which they had saved or gotten from other sources. He himself tried to take out $50 a week and was successful in doing that most of the time. But

sometimes he was unable to and simply lived on what his wife made as an employee of Stuyvesant Town.

This is in the late fifties and early sixties. The final situation with the Schulte business, or almost final, was that, still thinking he was perfectly solvent, he made his one and only trip to Europe in the early 1960s and bought a great deal on credit there, including a very large batch of bindings at about a dollar and a half apiece, which he was going to sell for two and a half to three dollars when he got back. He got back, and the books came. They weren't in such good condition as he had hoped. During the unpacking of the books, which took a considerable number of weeks, Wilfred suddenly died and left the problem of paying for these books to his successors.

The estate cast around to see what was going to happen to the shop and, among others, approached me to see if I would first buy it and later on take it over for nothing. Although I was tempted to do this, I, fortunately, with the aid of my wife, was able to reject it, because I saw that the whole thing was a losing proposition. I did gather some ideas about who else might take it over, such as Eugene Schwab, who was a great entrepreneur, or Argosy, or Haskell Gruberger, all of whom might have been able to put something over on libraries or something of that sort. But they all rejected the idea, and eventually it was taken over by the employees and lately bought by Dave Butler, one of them. Within the last few weeks, however, things have come to such a state that he is offering the shop for sale at $50,000 for the alleged 120,000 books, which I suppose is a true case, which is less than fifty cents apiece. But, in my opinion, they aren't worth more than five or ten cents apiece on an average. However, a library still might be able to buy them and make a good thing of it. Just a few days ago, Dave called me very urgently and asked me first to lend him $1,500, then a $1,000, both of which I rejected, and finally $700, which I foolishly, I think, lent him, with the understanding that I could take books that I wanted at half off marked prices. However, I went with great care with Bill yesterday, and we chose all the books in the shop that we could want at all. They only came to $133, so I still have a good deal of money to get out of this, and I don't know what the future holds.

They're paying $700 a month rent. Well, it's worth it for the space. It's just that they can't afford it. They've got these five employees, all of whom are getting paid almost nothing, but still something.

And then there are other expenses which they can't do, so the situation has not improved. It's simply going on in the same way as before. It is the only one which is still surviving in the same place that it started. It may have started just after 1900.

The people uptown were Ernest Gee and the Gannons, both of whom specialized in sporting books. Gee died in the late fifties, I think, but I never knew him. The main Gannon, Thomas Gannon, I didn't know; I knew the sons William and Ambrose. I don't know what eventually happened to them.

E. Byrne Hackett may have originally been uptown, but when I knew him, he was at 55 Fifth Avenue, the same building opposite Dauber and Pine's, which also housed Baker and Taylor Company. Byrne Hackett had been a very expensive and very high type of bookseller. He had started shops in Princeton and in New Haven, both of which failed. He was asked to leave one of the places or the other (I've forgotten which) because of his technique of getting the youngsters to buy expensive books and then suing the parents for payment. This apparently he made a good thing of at either Princeton or New Haven – I've forgotten which – but it was frowned upon by the authorities because apparently there was a good deal of high pressure involved. He was asked to leave, but I think, actually, he would have failed in either of those places anyway, and maybe did. He came to New York. He was a member of the Old Book Table, but that was before my day, and was considered one of the old scoundrels, along with Wells and Rosenbach. When I met him, it was during the Depression. I went up there and was astonished at what beautiful books he had. There may still have been employed there at that time Michael Papantonio and someone else, but I wouldn't have know them then.

INTERVIEWER: What was this place called?

GOLDWATER: The Brick Row Bookshop. I do remember going along the shelves and seeing among the Lewis Carrolls first a copy of *The Hunting of the Snark* for ten dollars, then a reprint of *Alice in Wonderland* for a dollar and a half, then the correct first edition of *Alice in Wonderland* for sixty-five thousand dollars, which he had bought at the Kern sale in 1929 and had paid so much for it that he was never able to dispose of it. That is what it was marked. I don't doubt that he would have taken less, but that was what it was marked. I think he had paid twenty-odd thousand dollars or more for it. I remember that quite well at that time. I always

remember that I was able actually to buy some books from him at that time – books on Haiti or Negro or something like that – because he had other books which were perfectly reasonable in price. His shop was taken over by somebody else, who simply moved it from New York down to Texas. His name is [Franklin] Gilliam.

A man that was quite nice was Gabriel Engel, who was really a violinist by profession. He was never a great violinist and eventually decided he would like to be in the book business instead. So he went into first editions very modestly and had an office on Union Square, up in the building there, with his wife, and made first-edition catalogues, always at low prices. His first editions were always honest, and he was completely honest about his materials. He was interested in the posters of the 1900s and 1910s period and was one of the main purchasers over at the Pratt store when Pratt went out of business, because Pratt had a lot of those things. Besides little magazines, he also had first editions of Harold Frederic and people of the 1890s and early 1900s, particularly these posters and all kinds of broadsides and throwaways for Stephen Crane and people like that of the period. Engel was very nice indeed, and we were all sorry when he died of a heart attack some years ago. His wife continued the business and may, for all I know, still have some of the books left. If she does, she works from her house instead.

Dauber and Pine – Sam Dauber and Nat Pine – started business a good many years before me, probably in the early 1920s. They may have been on Twenty-third Street earlier – I think that they had been somewhere else before they moved to Fifth Avenue – but the whole time I knew them, they were at number 66 Fifth Avenue, between Twelfth and Thirteenth streets. They had the rather nice shop which was small and a very large basement, which was well arranged, and they also for quite a period of time had another basement around on Thirteenth Street, which could be reached only by going around into the street. They had a very, very large stock, and they always knew their business quite well. They also knew something about it, which was to hire good people. So, for a very long time, they hired a man named Charles P. Everitt, who was, aside from Wright Howes, the best Americana man in the country, or was known to be. Also, sometimes along with Everitt, they had as a cataloguer a man named Sam Loveman, whose job was entirely that of cataloguing. He had a flair for description and for exaggeration and for inserting erotic overtones into almost any book, which was very, very successful. And their catalogues were notorious for this kind of description. Everybody would say, "Oh, that's a Dauber and Pine catalogue" or "That's Sam Loveman's descriptions."

It was a big business, and they are famous for the case of having found an Edgar Allan Poe *Tamerlane* and had given somebody a dollar for it, later on having sold it, I think, to Owen D. Young for seventeen thousand or twenty-seven thousand dollars, whereupon the man who sold it to them came around and complained. They told him to go chase himself, and he went and committed suicide. They are famous for this adventure. I'm not sure of the exact figures in these cases, but I'm not far off.

Dauber lived to a ripe age but died a few years ago. Pine is still alive and is running the shop, along with a woman who has been there practically forever. Dauber's son Murray, who didn't want to be in the book business, went over to the Spanish civil war, came back, and seems to be a little bit touched, but not much. There's something a little bit wrong, although it's a little hard to place it. I suppose you could possibly place it as shell shock or something like that. He's quite nice. He didn't want to be in the shop at all and, while his father still kept it, he went into business for himself and sold books by mail from an office in the Broadway Central Hotel down on Broadway. After his father died, he was persuaded to go back to the shop again. He had been down there even before his father died, doing cataloguing and staying out of the way of everybody. After his father died, he went back there and is now the full-time person in the basement.

Yes, their contacts were always very good. They got the Joel Spingarn library, and they got a lot of stuff that we would have said they had no business to get. I have been calling the place moribund for quite a while now, but it's the longest moribundity that I've ever seen. Every once in a while, there will be an infusion of a new library having been bought. They do have plenty of money, and they can buy stuff, and they do buy stuff.

Their catalogues are all right. I always think that this is the last gasp, but actually they are keeping going. There were many times when they didn't have any money, and at those times they were left first by Everitt and then by Loveman, each of whom went into business for himself – Everitt quite early, during the Depression actually.

Everitt continued for many years. He first had a shop of his own upstairs on Fifth Avenue and later a shop of his own upstairs on Fifty-ninth Street, above where Swann was having his first book auction. It was during that period that I got to know

him fairly well. I always liked him, and I would listen to what he had to say a great deal. One of the things which he had to say was, "My shop is in my head." People would know that he was a great Americana expert, would go to his shop, and would find 150 books, and would say, "Where's your stock?" He would point to his head and say, "Right here. I don't need a stock, because I know where to sell the books." It was due to this that I was always able to say, "All these books on the shelf are mistakes," because that's what he would have considered them. Only a mistake was on the shelf; every other book was sold.

He had a fabulous memory, and he also just knew where to sell everything and knew everything about everything. His book, *Adventures of a Treasure Hunter,* is not terribly interesting because, again, he tends to emphasize, "I bought a book for such-and-such a price and sold it for such and such." But, in general, that was the way he was. It was he who, during the 1930s, probably about 1937 or 1938, after he had left Dauber, had no money, actually no cash, and came to me, a poor, miserable creature; because somehow or other it was known that I did keep cash on hand. I always kept cash on hand, and he borrowed from me whatever I had, which couldn't have been very much, I suppose – two or three hundred dollars. While it was pretty astonishing – of course, not many people knew about it – but it was astonishing to anybody that Everitt would have to come to me for money. But yet he did, because he had no cash, and I did have cash.

It was slow paying, but he did pay me back. Later on I became very good friends with his employee. He had an employee a little later called Harry Alper, and it was from Harry Alper that I learned how to whistle trills using my epiglottis. He's the only person who ever knew about that, because I thought that you had to whistle a trill with your tongue. But he said no, if you can get to learn it, you'll be able to do it this way. He was able to do it beautifully, and after I had some practice, I was able to do it too. But I can only do it within a certain range. On the other hand, I can only do the other with a certain range too, so one of them had to supplement the other. But it was very good, and it opened up a new vista of whistling to me.

Everitt isn't still alive, but he didn't die too long ago. It was probably eight or ten years ago, I guess. But Loveman, of all people, is still alive. He is very old. I saw him just yesterday on Fourth Avenue, looking at the stands to see what he could pick up as a sleeper. He's still in business. He calls himself the Bodley Bookshop, and he has always called himself that when he was in business for himself. He continued the business of putting out catalogues with these descriptions which were sexy, but that sort of failed lately because he had to make a non-sex book sound like a sex book. Nowadays it wouldn't matter much. He's a homosexual, a very famous homosexual, and was always surrounded by these young boys. But, as he got older, they took advantage of him and did terrible things to him. They would steal everything from him and eventually took his name. There's a Bodley Gallery now which is run by some of his ex-boys. They've taken his name, and the little Negro boys would just steal from him right and left and take advantage of him. They would treat him terribly, simply kick him around and do any old thing.

Maybe eight or ten years ago he started a little shop on one of these streets – on Sullivan, I think it was – not McDougal, but one of the ones east of McDougal. They would simply steal him blind, he would simply not have anything. It was just terrible. He was a friend of Hart Crane's and wrote at least one book on Hart Crane. Then he had some letters of Hart Crane which were published. But he did all sorts of things. He was a swindler in many unusual, very amusing ways, and I was involved with him in some of these. I don't deserve any credit for my part in this, although, since they were more amusing than they were crooked . . . I'll tell at least one or two of these.

When I was in England in the late fifties, I bought a hornbook which was made of leather. It had a leather cover and sort of transparent horn over the piece of paper which had the hornbook material on it. It looked very old. But the man who had it, which was Mr. [Howes], wanted only three pounds for it. So I knew that it was not a real, original hornbook. I said, jokingly, "I assume this is original." And he said, "I'm not saying anyting about this at all, the price is three pounds." I brought it back to America and found out somehow or other later on that there was a man near Hastings who was making these. When Loveman came around, as he did very often, looking for material to put in his new catalogue, I showed him this hornbrook. I said, "Maybe you'd like to catalogue this." He correctly did not ask whether it was real or not. He simply said, "How much do you want for it?" And I said, "$75." He thought that was all right. He wouldn't buy it outright, of course. He only catalogued things and later on paid for them if he sold them. So he took it from me, and in due course I got his list in which he had catalogued it as "eighteenth-century American hornbook" for, I

think, $175 or $250. Well, in the first place, we didn't know what date it was. And, in the second place, we certainly had no idea that it was American. An American hornbook for that period would be worth not $150 or $175 but almost whatever you could get – for it might be worth in the thousands. In fact, I've never even heard of one. I don't doubt that they exist and that the New-York Historical might have one. So I said, "Gee, Sam, you say eighteenth century? You don't know what date it is." He said, "Well, it doesn't have any date on it, does it?" I said, "No." And he said, "Well, couldn't it be eighteenth century?" I said, "I suppose." He said, "Leather certainly could be eighteenth century." And I said, "Yeah, I suppose." He said, "That horn – you can't tell how old that is." I said, "No." He said, "And, after all, you didn't open it up to look at the paper, so you don't know how old." He said, "I don't know why it can't be eighteenth century." So I said, "All right, but American, Sam? I bought it in England." He said, "You mean it's not possible for a hornbook to have come from America to England?" So I said, "Yes, I suppose so." He said, "Well, then?" He sold it. I don't pretend any great virtue in this transaction, but I thought it was pretty amusing just the same.

Then there was one thing that I got from Thoms's employee Vanover when Vanover was getting very old. He sold me a lot of little odds and ends of things. His name was Charles Vanover. He was an employee of Thoms and Eron, but later on, after Thoms and Eron disappeared, he was a scout by himself. He still had a few of Thoms and Eron's customers; he became very broke toward the end. I bought up some of his stuff, and one of the things he had was a poem printed on toilet paper by Rudyard Kipling. There was an original poem written by Kipling and printed on toilet paper, and you couldn't be sure that this was not right. The only thing was that the chances were very little and, again, I gave that to him to catalogue.

There were some fancy things of that sort. There were a good many facsimiles of things which looked right. In one of the sets of Stevensons, for instance, there was a facsimile of one of the pamphlets he printed in Samoa. That is very scarce, and the facsimile is quite good. The only way you can tell it's a facsimile, I think, is not on account of the paper but on account of the fact that it has a place for stitching where they've stitched it to sew it into the book. So this sometimes is palmed off by Loveman and others as the original.

That's the kind of thing he does. Also, I think that he once came into possession of a great batch of

John Keats bookplates, or Shelley, I've forgotten which. And so, whenever he gets a book of that period, he always catalogues it and says either, "with the John Keats bookplate" or, more likely, "from John Keats's library." I've forgotten which he says, but he always does that. That's been going on for years. He's a good old scoundrel, and we all really like him a good deal.

Well, not too many more. Carol Cox was a man who was a very good merchandiser. His original shop was 125th Street. Later on he moved downtown and had a large place on Park Avenue at Thirtieth Street, between Thirtieth and Thirty-first streets. Then he had a big shop on Fifty-ninth Street, opposite Argosy. He was a man who also didn't like Jews very much, but he liked the Negroes even less and felt very unhappy about having to move from Harlem, which had been his home. He became a wholesaler and supplier to libraries, and I bought great quantities of books from him. He also had regular books, first editions. And, whenever he had a collection of fifty or a hundred cookery books, he would call Eleanor up and she would come and get them. After he moved out of Fifty-ninth Street, the building was pulled down. He moved to a loft at Twenty-fourth Street, which went all the way through on Twenty-fourth and Twenty-fifth streets, an absolutely tremendous place. But something happened to him both physically and financially, and his place was taken over by an idiot who, however, had a lot of money, and who continued to call himself Carol Cox Book Company. Carol died in hospital under circumstances which I don't know, and the man simply owned the business. I never knew what the circumstances were. He eventually sold a large proportion of them out and moved, first over to Ninth or Tenth Avenue and then eventually to Jersey. The Carol Cox business still exists, but it's a wholesaling business to libraries.

Arthur Swann had a bookshop, a high-class bookshop, in the mid fifties in the same building or nearby with Gabriel Wells and other people of that sort. I think I visited the shop once, but I don't remember for sure. Later on he went out of business, probably failed, and became the manager of the book department of Parke-Bernet, or at that time with the American Art Anderson Galleries. He was supposed to be a scoundrel. I never liked him, and he certainly must have been a scoundrel because of the cases that are known about his collusion with Rosenbach and so on in selling the famous *Tom Jones* to Owen D. Young.

It's a rather long story which is hard to make brief. This copy of *Tom Jones* was sold to Young for a very high price as being original boards, uncut, and so on. Young found out about it's being wrong and demanded his money back. Rosenbach wouldn't take it back; he never would do anything like that and always tried to put everybody else in the wrong. But the position of Rosenbach was such that either he was ignorant about the situation, which he would have denied with both hands, or he was crooked, which he would also deny with both hands. There was no third way out of it, because he had sold this thing as being perfect, although it was known where the book came from, exactly how it had been doctored, where the missing leaves had been put in, exactly where the boards came from. The whole story was known from beginning to end — whose set it had been, how much it had brought at auction, and so on. Swann was in collusion with Rosenbach in this matter, I believe. Other similar cases were known.

Arthur Swann died in harness at the Parke-Bernet Galleries, and then his material came up at sale later thereafter and brought a high price, strangely enough partly because it was called the Swann sale, even though everybody knew that he was the wrong guy. Still, it was known also that he cared about books and that, whenever he saw a copy of a book of which he already had one, he would always keep the better copy. This finally was the best copy which came up, and that was true. This was quite late — late fifties or early sixties. It was a quite recent sale.

Max Sparber was a book scout. He used to go along Fourth Avenue daily and pick up sleepers. He was interested in Judaica primarily but would buy everything, and was a great quoter in the *AB* or before the *AB,* the *Want List,* and before the *Want List, PW.* He had a club foot, and he never had a shave. He was sort of a fixture on Fourth Avenue, going along there day after day with his club foot and without a shave. He lived in Brooklyn with his mother. Nobody was ever invited to his house, and nobody ever saw his stock. Everybody resented very much the prices that he would quote things at. He would sometimes quote things as high as four or even five dollars when other people were quoting them at only a dollar or a dollar and a half. People would say, "Max, does anybody ever buy them?" And he'd say, "Well, not very often, but I always do feel that, if I sell one-fourth as many and charge this much, why, I'll be just as well off as anybody who sold four copies at a dollar." Well, he was right, but he was a little before his time. So he never really made much of a go of it. Later on he was in the hospital, and his sister didn't know what to do with him. I was then interested in getting some money from the Antiquarian Booksellers Benevolent Fund for him, but I was not shrewd because they came to the hospital – Haskell Gruberger, who was disliked by everyone, including by Sparber, but who persuaded Sparber to sell him his books in case he died. He did die, and Haskell Gruberger got his stock of books. We always felt rather bad about that. As a matter of fact, this Antiquarian Booksellers Benevolent Fund, which was mainly Mr. Wormser's brainchild, has been fed until it now has tens of thousands of dollars in it, and it is administered by some very high-class types like Mr. Walter Schatzki, Mr. Harold Graves, and Mr. Richard Wormser; but they administer it to such a degree that they never give out any money at all. I have gotten money from them [for destitute booksellers] about five times, so I shouldn't be the one to talk. But I believe that almost nobody except myself has ever gotten anything from it. I got money for Sparber, for Harry Carp, for Bill [Barnette] of New Brunswick who had been victimized by Mr. Rizick in some of Mr. Rizick's early days, for Max Besant of Haiti and of New York, and for one other person whom I don't remember just now. But I don't think that, outside of those people, the fund had given money to half a dozen other people in the whole twenty or more years of their existence. They keep on building up the fund, for some purpose as yet unannounced, hoping that someday there will be some holocaust in which they will be able to use it – maybe hoping that or maybe hoping not. The idea is simply to have a fund. I said that this is ridiculous, and so for the past years I haven't given anything to them, and I think anybody else is crazy to give it to them, too. They've been able, actually, even with my things and the other few things they've given, to live entirely on income and never touch the capital at all, which was not the original intention.

There were two Robertses in the book business – R. F. Roberts, who was John Kohn's first partner, except they weren't quite partners, when John had a shop at 37 West Forty-seventh Street, after he left Argosy, which he called The Collector's Bookshop. On the top of the letterhead there was "John S. Van E. Kohn." Then there was a line, and underneath the line there was "R. F. Roberts," so that you could see that there was quite a differentiation between the two partners. He was a very good bookman but a terrible bookseller. He was all right as an investigator and as a checker-up of things.

He would come down and look over those tens of thousands of playlets that I had, and he would finally pick out twenty-one as being of interest. Then he would take them up to 37 West Forty-seventh Street, and he would work on those. He would find that three were possibly by American authors. Then he would find out that one of them really was by an American author and who it was. This was very important, and, therefore, you could charge $17.50 for it instead of $3. It would have taken him maybe a week of time to get this, and it would be very much worthwhile, except in a business way. Later we tried to get him jobs at various places where this wouldn't make any difference. John got him a job at Scribners to work on the, I think, Hemingway or other material which was in the Scribners archives – the proofs and that sort of thing. I think he worked with Randall there, and that was fine because he didn't have to account for his time; it was all research, and the business aspect of it didn't matter. He was a real drinker. He was always in a fog. He was one of the people who had the greatest sense of humor of anybody we ever knew in the book business. He was very, very funny with sort of a dry, cynical humor, and about himself, as well, when he was in Riker's Island, whichever island he was kept in where he still probably is or is again. He would write amusing letters about himself. I think he's still there, if he's still alive, which I think he is. John sort of gave him up. John lets people go more than I do. He's more like Eleanor – what's the use of my being made unhappy? I think John tends to feel like this. When he gets a letter from Roberts, he doesn't really feel he has to go and see him, whereas I would feel, "My God, I'm involved; I've got to go and see him."

The other Roberts . . . I don't think his real name was Roberts, but he was always called Roberts. He always called himself "Nostradamus, Jr." He had a shop down on Canal Street, and he was one of the earliest ones to go into this silliness of horology and occult, foreseeing, and so on. He published an edition of Nostradamus and was always involved with language of the hand, phrenology, and so on. He had a big shop there, was very cheap, and it was good fun going down there. Eventually the thruway coming out of the Holland Tunnel kicked him out. I guess he died; I never heard from him later on.

Moe [Murray] Gottlieb originally worked for Dauber also. Dauber had a good many people working for him as cataloguers. He had a fellow named Joe Levine, also, who came and worked there. I guess Ben Swann also worked for him for a while. Gottlieb then went into business for himself at number 69 Fifth Avenue, which was between Thirteenth and Fourteenth streets, and had quite a good business there in Americana. He was a good bookman and a good bookseller. Later he discovered that he could make more money by being in the medical business. He never had any medical training whatever, but he simply discovered that nobody was doing early medical books. He went into it and made a great success of it.

Something should be said about Simon Gould and his son Raphael. Simon Gould was a man who never did anything honest in his life. He became quite wealthy during the early 1920s by being the one who promoted Coué with his "Day by day in every way I'm getting better and better." He published that and promoted it. He also was a vegetarian and ran for president on the Vegetarian party several elections. The American Library Service was so well known as being crooked that somebody going to Europe and coming from America would not be able to get any credit because of the name of the American Library Service. I had that experience more than once, somebody saying, "No, I cannot do any business with you, since the government itself does not pay its bills." Upon inquiring what this was about, I discovered that it was the American Library Service which had ordered material and simply not paid for it. Mr. Gould had more systems of not paying for something than anybody you can possibly imagine. I will give a few. He would order books and then not pay and, when being pressed, would simply not answer. If the amount was small, eventually the seller would give up. Sometimes he would do the same thing and would continue not to pay until he was sued. He then would still not do anything until the final moment came when he might have to pay, and in that case he did. He would order books from people and then, when they would ask for payment, he would say he had not received them. Since most people did not insure books, there was no proof of this, and he never had to pay in this way. He would send out books to people with a bill, even if they had not asked for them, and then dun them. A certain number of people would pay in this way. His rule was never pay until you have to. Something might happen. There might be, for instance, a world war which would take place. Or the person might die, or the person might lose his accounts, or the person might think that he was wrong. In this way, he was able to accumulate a vast stock, paying almost nothing for it. After he died, his son Raphael took over the business and still is in it. Raphael became a great power in the Ethical Culture Society, which we always thought

Page from Catalog No. 117, 1961–1962, of Goldwater's University Place Book Shop. Item 517 is a rare signed book by Phillis Wheatley.

was kind of amusing, and moved up to New City in New York, where he continues to run the business, but not in the same way his father did. Not long ago I was called up to New City to look at some material and found it was Raphael Gould's discards. But among this we found correspondence from his father's day verifying all the things I have just said.

One thing which infuriated Leon [Kramer] particularly, although it could have infuriated anybody else who had the same situation, was that one day one of Leon's customers called him up and said, "I've just received a very interesting list from American Library Service. It seems to be very similar to your material, although the prices are about three times as high." He read the things off to him over the phone, and Leon discovered that what Mr. Gould had done was to take Leon's catalogue and simply triple the prices in them and offer the books to this man as if they were his own stock. He had all sorts of things. He was a very imaginative person.

He would write to the various embassies and say that he had a collection of material on their country. He didn't have anything at all at the time, but, as soon as they answered, then he would go out and get them. This, of course, is a perfectly legitimate kind of thing. He would do legitimate things if that was the only way of managing, but he was very imaginative and quite successful indeed. Eventually, not having paid his bills at the *New York Times,* at the *Want List,* at the *Antiquarian Bookman,* at the *Publishers Weekly,* and so on, he was not able to advertise in any of the normal outlets and had to keep on finding new outlets – the *New Republic,* or the *Nation,* or the *Progressive,* and so on. Finally, I believe no single place would take his ads. Although he saved a great deal of money because he had been advertising them for some months and in some cases for years without paying, eventually he had no exact place to advertise which would reach any large audience.

In my early days I was introduced to [Guido Bruno] – I keep forgetting whether his name was Giovanni Bruno or Donald Bruno – anyway, he wasn't burned at the stake. He had a bookshop on Fourteenth Street, and he was one of the first introducers of the little magazine into the Village and was a typical Village character. When he died, his stuff came up for sale; that was the early 1930s, and it was one of the bases I had for building up my little magazine collection. A lot of the stuff which he published, which was done, for instance, by Djuna Barnes and others, is now very rare and expensive, but we don't find it around very much. He had a publication which was called *Bruno's Weekly* and then *Bruno's Magazine,* and then he also had a great many little monographs which were published there. One of them was a John Reed thing. He was one of the ones who did publish and be a bookseller at the same time. He was typical of Greenwich Village for that period.

Downtown there were a couple of bookshops which specialized in Judaica, Hebraica, usually in Yiddish, in Hebrew, and in Russian. Of these, the very largest was Max Meisel down on Grand Street, who had an incredibly vast stock and continued on for many years. I didn't have too much to do with him because I didn't speak Yiddish, and I wasn't really handling Russian books at that time. But Leon Kramer was down there all the time, and when he died, his stuff came on the market. It was mostly bought by a [Biederman] who was over on Second Avenue, and when Biederman went out of business, I bought a good part of the Russian material. This was a case where I found a great many Russian

pamphlets published in 1905 and 1917, which were just wonderful. I had three hundred of them in my car and left them overnight. When I came there in the morning, they were gone. They were things which were worth many thousands of dollars to the right person, who in this case was me – nothing at all to anybody else – and the person who took them probably was greatly disappointed when he found what he had. We scoured the trashbaskets in the neighborhood but couldn't find any, and they never appeared on the market, as far as I know. This was fairly late; this was only about ten years ago.

In midtown there were a couple of people who lasted for more or less a great length of time. One of them was named [Leitendorf], whom everybody called the Manados Bookshop, *manados* being the old Indian name for Manhattan. He specialized in first editions. He and I got on the outs for some reason which I don't remember, and we didn't speak to each other for several years, but eventually we made it up. Usually I got on the outs for something which some people wouldn't have considered very strong but which I was very bitter about. That was usually something like the one I got on the outs with Peter Smith of the National Bibliophile Service. I think that Manados did the same thing, and I think one other person did the same. Peter Smith phoned me and asked if I had a certain book in stock which was in my field, Negro. I did, and I said it was $7.50 and he could have 20 percent off, which was $6. So he thanked me, and he bought it from me. Then later I found that he had sold it to my customer at $6, having taken no profit for himself. I wrote an article about that in the *AB* under my pseudonym C. Emptor, in which I bitterly excoriated this kind of thing. I had already explained to him over the phone what the trouble was about this, namely that he takes my book, which I have given to him at $1.50 less than I would normally sell it for, and sold it to my customer at a price which I would not have sold it to him for at all, makes me out to be too high, makes himself out to be a great guy, and, at a cost of $1.50 to me, spoils my sale and makes himself fine. It is understood in the book business that, when you give a discount to a dealer, you give it to him so he can make a profit, and only so he can make a profit – not for any other reason. He didn't see this, so we were on the outs for a great many years, until finally he moved away to Gloucester. Since that time we've been on perfectly good terms, since I've never seen him again.

He's a reprinter. He was the first one who made a business of being in the out-of-print-want-list business. He'd send around his employees, usually employee, to every shop in town with his long list of wants, pick them up, and then ship them out. He advertised in all the papers, saying that he could get books. Now, of course, this is a very well-known kind of thing, although lately it's been going down somewhat because the profit isn't sufficient. He was the first one to really make a big thing out of that. He was a very good bookseller in that respect.

It was in the thirties; it would have been after the thirties. One of his employees, Jack [Weiss], became disaffected with him and came to work for me for a while and then went up to Syracuse or Rochester — I always get those mixed up — and has a bookshop there even now that he's had going there for almost thirty years.

Uptown also there was David Moss, who, with Martin Kamin and Martin Kamin's wife, ran a bookshop which mainly specialized in first editions and then in dance and later on became the Kamin Bookshop. David Moss was, I believe, a sweetheart of Miss [Frances] Steloff long, long ago and is supposed to have committed suicide by diving off something and hitting a rock. The reason I say supposed to be a suicide is that it seems like a strange way to commit suicide, and it may have been an accident. This, I don't think has ever been established. The Kamin Bookshop lasted for years and years after that, and Sally Kamin was the great dance expert until quite recently. All the people are dead now, but I think the shop still exists in some form or other as a mail-order business.

J. Ray Peck was a rather nice man who had a shop on East Fifty-first Street near the subway station, a beautiful shop. He cared about first editions, and he had two daughters, each of which was stupider than the other and each of which was nicer-looking than the other. After he died, the two daughters kept it going for a while, and then the one daughter. Eventually it petered out. There were a few places in midtown that you could go and find sleepers or first editions at low prices. I never quite found out how he made a living out of it, but most of these people had some small income besides which kept them going in some way.

The Staegers, father and son, had the shop called the Cadmus Bookshop. The older Staeger was a horrid man and very, very good Americana man. The Cadmus Bookshop dealt entirely in Americana. You could go into his shop, first in the Fifties and later on West Forty-sixth Street where they moved, and you'd find both father and son [Samuel] there. He always called his son "Son." The father would always have his hat, and usually his coat, on — no matter what the temperature outside, no matter what the conditions. The reason for this was a strange one. He had hurt himself at some time years before and had insurance on which he was collecting. It was for complete disability. The consequence was that he was not supposed to be working, but, actually, he was the one who was in charge of the shop. However, he always kept his hat, and usually his coat, on in case the insurance company should send an agent in and find him there, at which time he would always have just come in to visit the son. He did this, I should say, for fully twenty years that I remember, possibly even longer. He was always there and always had his hat and coat on. I don't think that the insurance company did ever catch him, because the place flourished for all this time, in spite of the fact that the son was a very horrible person also. It was about then, the story goes, after the older Staeger died, they went to the burial and said that they couldn't bury him until somebody said something good about him. Everybody stood around and stood around until finally a person was able to say that, compared to the young man, the old man was a lovely person, at which time they were allowed to bury him. The young man continued in business for quite a while, but he apparently drank a lot and eventually is supposed to have had to go to an institution and, for all I know, may be dead. The shop disappeared from Forty-sixth Street, having gone downhill little by little and stuff being sold at low prices until it simply petered out.

Whitman Bennett was the man who was a real expert in American first editions and wrote a book called *American Colorplate Books,* a bibliography. Strangely enough, he came from a good old American family and in a sense was very intelligent and very well read. He was quite illiterate as far as writing is concerned, but he managed to put this book out, which is about the only thing that's been done on it. He had two sons, Josiah and another whose name I don't remember, who used to work with him. It was both a bindery and a repair place and a first-editions place. He also made a great collection of aeronautics. The son Josiah went to work for Scribners later on and is now the second in command in the Lilly Library at Indiana University under David Randall. The other son, I think, disappeared. The father finally died at a very, very old age, just a few years ago, having been senile for quite a while, however. The bindery still exists, and I think it's called Bennett Book Bindery. If I didn't mention this before, Bennett is the one who used to joke with me about first editions which were in fine condition. Bennett is the one who got hold of me one day in an expansive mood and said, "These collectors want *Tom Sawyer* first issues in mint condition. There are no *Tom Sawyer* first issues in mint condition, yet these people want it. They are rich, they are my customers, they have a right to have them. Very well, then, I will give them *Tom Sawyer*s in mint condition." So he would take a fine copy of the second or third issue or a later edition, take the binding off it, put it on the insides of a first issue, and produce a mint copy of *Tom Sawyer* for them as they wanted. Some people felt this was reprehensible, and, in a sense, I do too. But I feel it's a very mild kind of reprehensibility, and I am perfectly willing to survive it.

INTERVIEWER: You could tell it had been rebacked.

GOLDWATER: If he did it well enough, it was terribly difficult, but not impossible. Usually the way you tell is that you can look at the binding on the inside and say to yourself, "This binding cannot have come with this, because how did this binding get into this condition when this page is foxed, is dog-eared?" and so on. However, if he was lucky and able to do it, very often you couldn't tell. I do not doubt for a minute that a dozen of these things are in libraries around the country, supposed to be first issues and first editions in fine condition, which are Bennett copies. In fact the words "Bennett copy" became a sort of well-known thing. John Kohn always used to use that – "That must be a Bennett copy" – sometimes just not "is" but "it must be," because it looks like that. Randall would call it a "sophisticated copy," but a "Bennett copy" had a better connotation.

Louie Scher, who just died only a couple of months ago, was a Frenchman who came over just after the First World War as a young man and started a book business on West Ninety-sixth Street, between Amsterdam and Broadway, which he called the French Bookman. He may not have started until the late twenties. Sugarman introduced me to him, because he was a good book scout and would buy books in English also – first editions and so on and particularly erotica. That was how Sugarman got to know him – partly because certain books at that time were called erotica, as I think I've mentioned before, which nowadays we wouldn't call that at all, particularly books from France entitled "Nu" or pictures of nudes. That kind of thing was not common in New York, but in France it was fairly common. People would use a book of nudes as an erotic book in those days. Scher imported a

good deal of material. I don't think he really knew just how to make a living in the French book business, although he learned fairly quickly. In any case, I remember quite well the day that he changed his style of work. It was quite early in the thirties; I don't remember just which year. The French franc, which had been at four cents (it had been at two cents in 1926 and 1927 and had gone up to four cents, where it was quite stable for a number of years. In 1933, after Roosevelt came in and closed the banks, the franc, as the pound did for a certain period of time, went up by about 60 percent to correspond to the drop in the American dollar. So the franc for a moment was worth about seven cents. At that time Scher suddenly found that the books which he had purchased at a rate of four cents had to be paid for at the rate of seven cents. Although, as we knew later on, it didn't last and, in fact, went back to four and then lower in the late thirties, Scher said to me one day, "I'm going to quit this whole importation business. You now have to be not a bookman but an international financier. Everything depends not on whether you can buy a book and sell it at a profit from what you bought but on whether you know how the franc is going to go. I can't do this any more; I'm not going to do it any more." I think he erred because he did know more about French books than anybody else did, and there was a large market here for them. In a way, it was too much for him, and also, of course, it wasn't too long from then that 1939 came and importation from France became impossible for six years. So perhaps he was lucky he was in something else. He then set himself up as The Seven Bookhunters and remained The Seven Bookhunters for thirty years until his death just a few months ago.

INTERVIEWER: Did he have seven book hunters?

GOLDWATER: He never had seven, but he did employ two or three people at various times.

INTERVIEWER: Were those French books he was importing erotica?

GOLDWATER: No, just books, just French books. He would import erotica when he could, but that wasn't his main business. He was sort of like Sugarman, that is, the way to make extra money is sell erotica. So when he was able to import erotica, he did, but it wasn't his main business. He had a regular bookshop. He later moved away from Ninety-sixth Street and took a large loft on West

Seventeenth Street, I think it is, where he was until just now. . . . At his death the books were sold to the library. He had several employees during this period. I mentioned already that Noy had come from Stammer's and that he had fired him abruptly because he found that he was stealing . . . . Scher later on had a man named [Jeltra] who stayed with him for a long time but who has now gone into another bookshop in Saint Thomas in the Virgin Islands.

George Preston was a lovely man who was a fine tennis player and a bibliographer of Thomas Wolfe. He was no good as a bookseller and never could make a go of it. He worked at odds and ends for people around wherever he could get a job or as a bibliographer wherever he could get a job. He may still be alive; I don't know. I've seen him once or twice since our famous tennis match. At a time when I was priding myself very much on my play – I don't know why – I found out that George played. We decided to play a match. It was one of those hundred-degree days, and our two wives went out to watch. We went out there, and we played 5–5, 6–6, 7–7, 8–8. At 12–12 both of us were really in a condition that nobody would have given a cent for our chances of living. Neither of us was giving up, however. Finally I looked at him and saw that he was green. I don't know what color I was, but my wife said that I was a color which could not be described. The two girls simply marched on the court and stood there so we couldn't play any more. I believe that was the last time he ever played tennis. He had heart trouble and various things, and his wife said she had to preserve him. So we never played again, and I don't think he ever did. I've spoken to him several times since, but I don't know if he's still alive or not. He was a lovely man.

The Rand Bookstore was a bookshop on the ground floor of the Rand School of Social Science on East Fifteenth Street. It was primarily a bookshop for socialist materials and was always run by some member of the Socialist Party, or later on the Socialist Democratic Federation. Among these was a man who later on ran the Bryant Bookshop up on West Forty-eighth Street. When he started in business, nobody was too surprised to find that his main stock-in-trade was material which had come from the Rand Bookstore. Most people felt that he had not paid for it. Later Charlie Salzman worked there for a long time and then went into business for himself. We also felt that the same thing was the case with Charlie. Charlie is now in business out on the coast, and the Bryant Bookshop has died. There was still a third man who worked there and who we believe did not steal anything, although we're not

sure, and then went into business as a book scout and then went into selling rugs, at which he presumably did much better. The shop had a lot of good material at the time, and then little by little it was stolen, either by the employees or by the customers. It went downhill until it disappeared altogether.

A strange thing has happened to Brooklyn, as I suppose it has to a great many places, particularly on the East Coast. It used to be a very good borough for books. The shops were mainly run by old American families, not by Jews. Of those, I remember three – Niel Morrow Ladd, Reed and Chappell, and [Somerbell]. There were also some further out – one run by the man that I already mentioned long ago as being the one who sold Freddie [Brandeis] his stock. Then there was an old German out on Franklin Avenue. All these shops were very good shops and had books at low, low prices. People who lived in Brooklyn, like Ike Brussel and Rosenzweig, would be in there all the time, picking up the sleepers and bringing them into New York to sell. We would go out there now and then. Sugarman introduced me to the section, and it was a pleasure to go there in most cases. Somerbell was an exception; he didn't like Jews at all. He particularly didn't like what he called "New York Jew booksellers." When I went there one day as a young man, he immediately told me about the New York Jew booksellers, because apparently he didn't realize that I was all those things. I sort of escaped as soon as I could, having said that not all New Yorkers were bad, or something of that sort. I believe he had a sign saying that New York Jew booksellers weren't welcome there; it was something quite specific, but I've forgotten the exact wording of it. I think it actually was "New York Jew booksellers stay out."

Niel Morrow Ladd eventually died, and I bought the contents of the shop. I don't remember how I engineered the thing. I guess I continued to have a sale there for a while and then brought the rest over to my shop. I remember at that time there were remainders of certain histories of Flatbush, which he was selling for ten cents and later on using for backing on shelves, which now bring $10 to $25 on the market. He had simply a vast number of them, perhaps hundreds. They were either published by him or published by some friend of his, and they were in great quantity. There were a number of things of that sort – histories of Brooklyn – which we didn't know anything about and didn't care about. In fact, they didn't have any market value at the time. There was a history of Harlem by Riker which he had in great quantity which is now

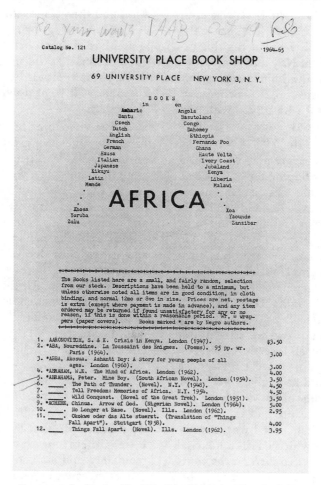

Front cover for Catalog No. 121 of the University Place Book Shop

desirable. But those were the old days, of course, and that's the typical thing that happened.

Reed and Chappell closed their larger shop, and Mrs. Chappell continued it for very many years on Flatbush Avenue. I used to go there quite often with Eleanor. Eleanor never liked to go there; she never found anything. I'd find something every time I went there, mostly first editions at low prices, also Negro material. She kept it as sort of a modest little shop. She was keeping it because she had some young man who was a protégé; I think you would call him a hippie nowadays. In those days he was simply a hanger-on. She kept that going until only a few years ago. In fact, I thought it was still on two years ago and went out there and found that it was finally gone. I always found things there – first editions, mild people like H. G. Wells or Kipling, or something would always be there for a dollar. Then the place out on Franklin Avenue also closed. That would have closed for a different reason; that would have closed because it became what is called a decaying neighborhood, and all his books would

have been stolen and he would have been broken into. There are at present just two bookshops in Brooklyn, both of which are much more recent and both in the Borough Hall area. One of them is run by an old Socialist; he is called the Boro Bookshop. Then there is Irving Binkin, who has been in it for quite a while. He's sort of a crazy guy and has a great big bookshop with a lot of stuff in it.

One of the Village characters was Bernard Gilbert Guerney, who was a translator of a book called *Yama the Pit*. He was also a translator of other books from Russia, including one anthology which he did for the Modern Library. He was a very intelligent and erudite man. He may still be alive. First he had Bernard Guerney's Bookshop and then he had the Blue Faun Bookshop in various places in the Village and on the East Side. He was a great talker and one of the ones who was very resentful about the way things were going: things always used to be better; people are now illiterate; he can't stand people coming in; they don't know anything, and so on. He was very difficult to do business with, but we got along quite well because we used to talk in Russian or talk about Russia. He was always glad to have somebody who knew something about his Kuprin book and other things which he had done. I sort of had some acquaintance with Russian literature, so I was able at least to make a pretense of knowing something about it, which was all that was necessary. I think he is still alive, but he must be quite old by now.

On East Fourteenth Street a little man had a shop down in the basement — Edward Lipton. It was the most modest bookshop of all in New York, really. It was between Second and Third avenues. You could hardly tell it was there at all, except that, as you went past, you would notice that he had a little stand outside with about twenty books on it. Then you could go down the flight and there you would find paperbacks and other things. He had, however, been a bookman for many, many years and would sell books at a reasonable price. I bought a lot of Negro stuff and radical things from him. Later on he moved to West Twenty-third Street and eventually moved to his home in Brooklyn, where he now operates from.

Further on West Twenty-third Street, Felix Cornell, who had been an able seaman, opened a shop which was primarily to be for the seamen who would come off the ships over on the West Side (he was near Ninth Avenue) and buy his books on seamanship and that kind of thing. Then he went into the publishing business. He published a great big book called *Encyclopedia of Knots,* which we thought was tremendously overpriced at ten dollars, but it was not overpriced. It sold well and is still a standard work. He eventually accumulated tremendous stock in the late thirties but then decided he didn't want to be in the book business anymore. It was his stock which my brother Harry, when he had his auction license, sold at auction. But after the first half of the day of auction took place and whole lots of twenty books were bringing only twenty-five to fifty cents, they called off the auction. Harry was paid his day's work but no commission, and the whole lot was sold to somebody else. I think that during late 1939 or early 1940, when this was, may have been the worst time of all for the book business. Simply nobody would buy anything at all. That was one of the reasons why Harry did go out of business; nobody was paying anything for books, and nobody knew, due to the war in Europe, what was going to happen. Cornell is still alive, but I don't know where he is.

On 125th Street, there were several bookshops at one time. One of those, Number One, was on 125th Street, just at the corner of Fifth Avenue. It was run by two brothers who called themselves the Ideal Bookshop. They stayed there for a while until the neighborhood condition deteriorated. Then they moved one flight up on Amsterdam Avenue and 114th Street, right near Columbia. They've been there ever since and still have a very good bookshop there. There was a man named Ben Shaw, a kind of schizophrenic, who went around as a book scout and used to make a miserable living. He didn't know anything about books and yet was a book scout, picking up books one place and going to another. I remember how modest his prices were from the fact that I bought from him for ten cents a first edition of Harold Frederic's *Damnation of Theron Ware,* inscribed by Willa Cather. It was true that he didn't know it was inscribed by Willa Cather. It was true he did not know it was a first edition. To have bought this book and sold it for ten cents and make a profit indicates what kind of a price he was paying for things. I will admit that at that time I probably sold it myself for two or three dollars, whereas now I would probably charge fifty, seventy-five, or even a hundred. Still it was the kind of thing he was selling and I was buying. Later he opened several shops and became a very big dealer in periodicals. Just after the war, with money from some relative of his, he had a tremendous storehouse near Twelfth Street and Broadway, filled with periodicals, a tremendous place. There was a large fire, and a great deal of material was destroyed. It was a very suspicious fire, and all of us who knew Ben felt that he had set it. The people who were the insurers, Dewitt Stern and Company, were the insurers for most of us around town, and we told Dewitt that this was very suspicious. Dewitt, who was not the insurer himself, of course, but just the agent, said it was up to the insurance company, not up to him, to make the point, and he wasn't going to do anything about it. Shaw received some tens of thousands of dollars, I believe, for this. But shortly afterward he decided to make a confession and made a statement that he had, indeed, set the fire. By this time it was too late for the insurance company to collect any money. All that happened was that we were able to say to Dewitt, "You see? We told you so." Nothing else ever happened to Shaw or about the matter, and he continued in business and continued to be a crook right to this very day. His crookedness was mostly in a different way from others. He simply gave bad checks wherever he went. Eventually people who dealt with him knew that they must not take a check or that they must meet and go to the bank and get it cashed while they were with him. Later he did buy some stuff from me, and we always demanded cash immediately and, in those cases, very often got it. He became quite big and at a given moment may always be big. It's just that at certain moments he's very small again. He doesn't have a shop, and he varies from California to New York, back and forth, and varies his name a good deal. But he has dealt with Kraus and particularly with Kamin, who was of the same type, and, of course, with the New Jersey fellow who's still out of jail for some reason – Rizick. He and Rizick were great pals.

On Eighth Street at that time there were several shops. It astonishes me to think of how many shops there were in the early 1930s. There was Joe Kling, who later moved to Greenwich Avenue and just died a year or so ago. He was also, like Bruno, a publisher of little magazines and a writer of poetry. He published *Pagan,* but he also published other things. He published his own poetry and was involved in all kinds of little magazine things. There was also Nat Kaplan, who had a shop just east of Fifth Avenue on Eighth Street, in the basement, which was sort of a hangout for the Sugarmans and the Brussells and the other people who dealt in erotica. He was kind of a nut and eventually died a couple of years ago in an institution. Then there was Tim Trace, who also dealt in erotica and was a scout. His idiosyncracy was his way of talking. It was rather a wonderful way; he repeated everything, sometimes two or three times, something like this. He would say, "Walter, Walter, I was down – Walter, I was down – I was downtown the other day. Walter, I was downtown the other day, and I tell you what, tell you what. Walter, I was downtown the other day, and I tell you what happened." We used to sit fascinated with this kind of thing. Eventually he married a girl he was going with whose name was Lorraine. They got along together for quite a while, but eventually there was a rupture in the household, and Lorraine married Robert Wilbur. Trace married a rather nice girl whose father was in the antiques business. They moved up to Westchester, had some children, and have been very successful in both the antiques business and in the art-book business ever since then. They're still in business.

The two Scheinbaum brothers both ran mail-order businesses, but they also had shops. The older one went into mostly remainders and new books up in the Forty-second Street area. The younger one, Al Scheinbaum, who now calls himself the Colonial Book Service, had a bookshop for a while in the Bible House. In fact, I think he took over the

Mosks' shop after Mosk died. Then he went into business, and he's on East Twenty-fourth Street now, running a very large and successful out-of-print business. The other brother also ran an out-of-print business for a long time, until quite recently. He had his ups and downs; sometimes he was very well-off, and sometimes he was very poor.

Harvey Brewer had a little shop on Eighth Street, also, at the corner of McDougal Street. He was a friend of George Kurtz and ran into the same business as he had, namely a circulating-library business, plus first editions, and so on. Later he gave up the shop there and worked for E. Weyhe and Company at Lexington Avenue and Sixty-second Street, the greatest art-book shop in the country. He worked there for many years. Eventually he claimed that he had a heart ailment, left Weyhe, and went into business for himself in Jersey, where he has now been for many years. Some people wonder how he managed to accumulate the stock which he got. We have no proof of how that happened, so we assume that everything is OK. He is a very shrewd guy, and we all feel that, although he is very nice, he's not the kind of person to get involved with in a business deal. Weyhe still exists at the age of almost ninety, I guess, and has been there ever since we remember. He has the greatest art books imaginable. What will happen when he dies, nobody quite knows, because his main assistant is also by now quite old. So it's not certain what the future of that shop is.

There was a shop first over on Bank Street and then on East Twelfth Street and now upstairs on Fourth Avenue called Orientiala, which specialized in books on the East. It was run by a man named Mr. Brown and a woman named Miss Pickering. As each one of the principals died, somebody else took it over, and it's still in business. It has just recently moved to a place on Fourth Avenue.

On East Tenth Street, just east of University Place, there's a large building which is now called Stechert-Haefer and Company. At that time it was called G. E. Steckert and Company. They are importers of German and French material, and had a parent body, presumably in Switzerland, although actually we think in Germany. They always denied their German parentage during the thirties and during the war. Although they never employed a Jew there at all; eventually they may have employed somebody who might have been Jewish, but in general the rule was no Jews.

There had been another company which was very similar to that called B. Westermann and Co. on [24 – M. M.] West Forty-eighth Street which imported material from Germany and during the war was shut down by the government. At that point Stechert claimed its Swiss ancestry and was let alone. Therefore, they became practically the only people that were importing material from Germany during the 1939–1940 period. It's a large building there, about ten stories, of which Stechert themselves occupied the first lowest five, later on six. Most people didn't know about this, but the fourth and fifth floors were entirely given over to used books. So, even though it was a comparatively small part of their business, it was one of the largest and best secondhand bookshops in New York. Since it was rather close to us, we were able to go there quite often and buy material. Their prices were usually reasonable. They had whole sections on any subject imaginable. Once in a while I would buy out the whole African section. Sometimes I would buy out the whole radical section, and so on, American Negro. As their prices went higher, I wasn't to do that any longer. This went on until quite recently. They kept on expanding and expanding and taking the building next door, and so on. Within the last year they finally were bought by Crowell-Collier or somebody and have gone out of the secondhand business altogether and generally out of the book business. Just what the future holds there, I don't know.

When I first started in, all the major publishers in the forties had their own bookshops, which were primarily new books but all of which had a rare books section. That included, I definitely remember, Putnam, Dutton, Brentano's (which, of course, was a publisher at that time, as well as a bookseller), and Scribners. Brentano's actually had a fine shop at the corner of Twenty-sixth Street and Fifth Avenue. That went out of business during the depression. There was a great sale there, at which everybody made a great deal of hay. Putnam's also went out of business. They were on West Forty-fifth Street, Dutton's on Park Avenue, and, as you know, Scribners' is the only one of these which still remains. Lou Cohen, who I mentioned before, had the shop at 45 Fourth Avenue in the Bible House, quit that large place, and went up to Fifty-ninth Street, becoming part of the Fifty-ninth Street complex, which at that time had about half a dozen shops. However, just about the time that he moved up there, all the other ones went out. Although Mr. Cox came from 125th Street down there for a while, eventually Lou Cohen remained the only one on street level. Mr. [David] Kirschenbaum's Carnegie Bookshop up one flight at a near corner . . . The Cohn shop has always been called Argosy. As you know, this has become one of the largest shops in the city and perhaps in the country, and very successful. He first only employed his family and friends, and he had a very large number in the family. Even now, I guess he still has the three daughters there and some various cousins. But he's gotten up to an employee group of perhaps thirty or forty by this time, and he is largely taken up, not only with books, but with prints, maps, and even paintings and has bought the building there. He is very wealthy by this time.

Frances Steloff you know about. She has always had a fine shop on Forty-seventh Street, but she did move once down a few doors from her former shop. She is still alive, as you know, and is in her eighties. The shop has recently been bought by a young man named Andreas Brown.

Of the booksellers who are still in business, I may not have mentioned Biblo and Tannen, who started business just before I did on East Fourteenth Street as poor little creatures and who have since then become quite large, substantial, and have bought their building on Fourth Avenue, and also are publishers. Mr. [Thomas J.] Gerald had a shop called the Friendly Bookstore, which was notorious for buying stolen books and who also specialized in music books. He moved away from Fourth Avenue for a while and now is back on Fourth Avenue again. . . . It's still called the Friendly Bookshop. Harry Gold, I may have mentioned, who was involved in the theft of very good books from the New York Public Library, including Edgar Allan Poe and other important works, having served his time in jail, came back to Fourth Avenue and later on became quite big again, mostly by the sale of his shop at the corner of Thirteenth Street and Fourth Avenue. He has just in the last month sold his shop on Fifth Avenue for a very high price, and his books, also, which went to Pennsylvania State University.

The brother of David Kirschenbaum of the Carnegie Bookshop is Louis Kirschenbaum, who is not on speaking terms with his brother and has not been for thirty or forty years. They were the sons of a former Kirschenbaum whom I did not know who was the original person in the book business. Louis Kirschenbaum had a small bookshop on Ninth Street for a long period of time, but he eventually went into the auction business, which he continued for a dozen years or more, but he never made a great success of. He did, however, continue to buy and sell sets and made a living of sorts. Even now, in semiretirement, he continues to do something of this sort.

Ben Swann originally worked, if I remember correctly, for Dauber and Pine for a while, then went into the Americana business for himself – I think in some other place first and then on Fifty-ninth Street in two places. He had two very fortunate fires – I think maybe only one very fortunate fire, but I certainly remember that one – which made him a great deal of money. Eventually he went into the auction business and is now the only other auction place in New York besides Parke-Bernet. He's been extremely successful, and he calls himself Swann Book Auction. His place, however, has moved a couple of times and is now on East Twenty-fifth Street.

The following people I have listed as being re-tired, semiretired, or not in the book business any longer, who were in the book business when I started: Laurence Gomme, now probably in his late eighties, who came over from England in about 1910, and worked sometimes for himself and some-times for Brentano's. He is considered the doyen of the old book trade and is now doing some appraisal work. He, in my opinion, has a reputation for knowledge which is not justified. I am not sure about this, and some people may know more about it than I do. . . . He specializes in first editions, and I don't think he knows much about them. Then what does he know about? Let's say he knows about En-glish literature, because I don't know anything else about that.

INTERVIEWER: I was just curious, because everybody seems to think so very, very highly of him. Is it just because he has survived longer?

GOLDWATER: I think it's because he's very nice. I don't really know this for a fact. I think that some of the other people might be able to tell more about it than I. As far as I can see, there's no proof that he does know anything, but I don't know.

Edward Lazare, of course, started very early and worked for G. A. Baker and Company, that is Mr. Hartzof, for a period of time. Then he went into business just before the war, after Hartzof's death, with two other employees of G. A. Baker. They ran the G. A. Baker business for a while and then an auction business, which was called G. A. Baker Company. But when the war came, they sold the thing out, as I mentioned before, to Mr. Rosenzweig of City Book Auction. One man, Mr. Otto, disappeared; I don't know what happened to him. Kebabian went to work for H. P. Kraus shortly after that. Lazare became the editor of *American Book Prices Current*, which was his sole job for some

twenty years. Recently he finally sold out his rights in the *American Book Prices Current* to somebody, pre-sumably Columbia University. Although he still has his hand in and he is doing some other work as well, he is now doing the editing of the big Streeter catalogue.

Jacob Blanck, as I mentioned before, I think, was a freelance scout for a while and was involved in more-or-less shady dealings with Merle Johnson and with Bill Kelleher. In due course, however, he got the job of editing the *Bibliography of American Lit-erature*, sponsored by Mr. Lilly and the Bibliograph-ical Society of America, and has made a lifetime job of that. I do believe he has done a very good job. He's not in good health now, but we hope that he'll be able to finish it. It is practically finished, I be-lieve.

Also, there was always a question with Merle Johnson of manufactured first editions and things of that sort. I mentioned in that respect William Kelleher who is still alive but very old. He lives in New Jersey and still has some Americana and things like that.

Ike Brussel liked to call himself LOGS – the last of the great scouts. That was a play on words because Buffalo Bill was supposed to be called the last of the great scouts. The great scouts, of course, in this case meant book scouts. He used to go to En-gland and buy things there. He considered that he was well up on all kinds of things. Actually, how-ever, I think he was mainly up on first editions. He wrote the bibliography of James Branch Cabell, which is quite good, as well as two books, one called *Anglo-American First Editions: East to West* and the other *Anglo-American First Editions: West to East*, which are books listing the English authors whose first printings were in America and American au-thors whose first printings were in England. The job has been better done since then, but he was a prime mover in the matter and did a good deal of work on it. I consider him quite a good man as far as this is concerned. He is very noisy!

His brother, Jack Brussel, has been in trouble with the police ever since his earliest days, either for erotica or for stolen books or something else. He has been in jail at least once, I think possibly twice. During the days when something perfectly mild, like *Lady Chatterley* or other things, was illegal – whenever there was anything illegal, he seemed to get into it. Later on he became quite successful, par-ticularly with his wife, who was a very active woman, and went into the reprinting of color prints and things of that sort. He is still around and still dabbles in these prints and other things. I believe he has a collection of *Aesop's Fables* which by this time should be quite good. Jack Brussel had a shop until very recently. He had a shop right next door here.

Meyer D. Wechsler, who was on Fourth Avenue for years and years and years and who called himself "Wex," Wechsler's Bookshop, a dozen years ago moved to Third Avenue because his rent was raised so high on Fourth. He was never liked by anybody and never liked anybody. People avoided going into his shop. Once in a while, however, a person could gain his way into his good graces for a short period of time and buy a few books. He mostly had a rather bad shop made up of fiction and textbooks. He was supposed to have good first editions in the back room, but, at a certain point when he announced that he was willing to sell out, I got into the back room and looked it over, and found that there was nothing decent in the back room either. He lasted until very, very recently. It hasn't been more than six or eight months now that he finally sold out the shop on Third Avenue. In general, I believe that the shop was supported by his wife Connie, who was a schoolteacher on maximum pension, and that he simply had the shop there to keep himself out of mischief. He also did have coins and stamps.

Dave Randall you know about. He worked first at Baker and Company, then for himself, then for Scribners, and then got the more-or-less sinecure out at the Lilly Library in Indiana. He has told his own story better than I could tell. John Kohn wanted to remind me about A. B. Schiffrin, who was one of the shops on Fifty-ninth Street, but I did not know him well.

The two Eberstadts are, of course, well known. The father, Edward Eberstadt, had started a very good Americana business on Madison Avenue long ago. It became the best-known Americana shop in the country. The two sons were called Lindley and Charles. I knew them slightly, but they generally dealt in material which was different from my own, although I had some connection with them during my period of interest in Haiti. I always found them too expensive to buy from and too cheap to sell to.

One of the shops on Fourth Avenue, when I first started out, was called the Astor Bookshop, which was run by Abe Klein. He went out of business quite early in my period, and I bought some stuff from him. That was the first time I recognized that, when a bookshop goes out of business, there are always little things to be found in the drawers and around which people have forgotten about. It was the ephemera which was interesting in his shop, just as it would be in my own case if I were to give up. Later he got a job as a salesman for Abraham and Strauss and then did freelance work. He's still around, doing something of this sort now. He was never particularly liked.

There was a man named William Pearce who was quite nice and worked for Barnes and Noble. He was the rare-book and old-book man there for many years. I think he probably started the department, because Barnes and Noble had only been a textbook place up to that time. I was always very envious of him because he had a beautiful girl working for him. I remember that, during the period when it wasn't considered proper, he went to Europe along with her. I've met him recently. He's quite old now. He told me that there actually never was anything between them, and that she was always sweet on a certain longshoreman whom she finally married. He's still alive, in his eighties, and lives in Delhi, New York, which is quite far up in the state.

INTERVIEWER: Did you know Kebabian very well?

GOLDWATER: Not terribly well. I knew him well enough, and I still know him fairly well. He's the one, you remember, that was a member of our book club for many, many years, long before I was. Eventually he resigned demonstratively because the person that he wanted to get into the club was not invited in. That was Lucien Goldschmidt. What happened was that there were two people in the club who didn't want Lucien, one particularly that didn't want him in. Whenever anybody is very strongly opposed to somebody, we usually don't get them in. That was Shatzki. In due course Shatzki said he didn't feel that way so strongly anymore. By that time we were perfectly willing to have Lucien in. Even though Kebabian was then approached and told that we would now do that, he was angry, and he wouldn't ever come back. So we never got him back, and we never got Lucien in. I don't think it matters too much.

One of the small people on Fourth Avenue whom I used to visit during my poorer days was Morris Pomarin. The reason I always visited him was that I was able to see directly somebody who was worse off than myself. So I used to go and visit him almost every day. He had a very small shop; the shop still exists here at number 116.

INTERVIEWER: He's still in business here?

GOLDWATER: No. He went later on to Morristown, New Jersey, and then finally back to Brooklyn, which was his original home, and is doing business from there. Sy Silverman, who was one of the Geffen boys, has become very wealthy and a great success. He calls himself, among other things, Humanities Press, Hillary House, and various other names, mostly publishing and taking over of English books. He has almost a thousand titles on his list.

Bernie Kraus started a shop called the Raven Bookshop here on Fourth Avenue and stayed in business for fifteen or twenty years. He was a partner with Larry Verry, who became the first and possibly the only Jew ever employed by Barnes and Noble. We all felt that Barnes employed him only because they didn't know he was a Jew, although most of us couldn't see how that was possible. Later on Verry got a lot of money from someone else to start in business for himself, went into business on Twenty-third Street, had a grandiose affair for a number of years, and went bankrupt, losing all the money of the other fellow. He, himself, however, seems to have done fairly well out of it and is now in business in Long Island, where he is an importer of English books and has some kind of publishing business. I'm not sure just what. . . . He's a rather shady character, in my opinion, but, in any case, we don't have very much to do with him. I mentioned that Kraus at the Raven Bookshop split up with Verry and later went into his own mail-order business, which he still has in a loft building on Broadway and Eighth Street. He specializes in English and American literature mainly.

Howard Mott, fresh out of Harvard, went into the rare-book and first-editions business on Fortieth Street, a rather high-class place right next to where Lathrop C. Harper had his shop. After struggling for a number of years, he finally became quite successful and then moved to Sheffield, Massachusetts, where he has now been for a dozen years or more.

Montague Hankin was a successful businessman, I think mainly in the oil business, in Summit, New Jersey, who became and has been for forty years or more a dealer mainly in Americana. He is generally liked, and I don't dislike him, but I've never been able to stand his advertisements which he had in the trade journal for twenty years or more, saying, "I sell only to dealers," because we knew very well that he does not sell only to dealers. We knew a great many of his private customers, and Rutgers University was probably his main customer, and Princeton his secondary customer. He's in Summit, New Jersey, and he specializes in sporting books, chiefly Derrydale Press, and in Americana, chiefly New Jersey and eastern Americana. But he is a good Americana man. He's now quite old, and we see him very seldom.

I don't know just where Peter Decker came from or how long he has been in business. We know it's been a long time, and he, himself, is quite old. However, I understand that he had been in some other business prior to this. He is known to be one of the most knowledgeable of the Americana men, particularly western Americana.

Jack Bartfield worked for a firm in the forties called Himebaugh and Browne. He tells me now that there was never any Himebaugh, that is, that Himebaugh was Mr. Browne's wife's maiden name. I knew Mr. Browne quite well. During the Depression the shop simply went out of business, as so many of them did. They catered to a fancy trade, and it simply didn't work. The only success that came out of that shop was Mr. Bartfield, who apparently got a number of customers and became a good bookman and was able to sell later on. Mr. Browne I remember chiefly as a seedy, poor thing, going around town, trying to pick up a few dollars here and there by being a scout. He disappeared altogether. I don't know what happened to him.

Leo Weitz was also mainly in the bindings and fine-looking books. He was a stupid man who had no knowledge of books whatever. He did, however, like, as he said, lovely things. He would fondle a binding as he would a woman's breast, saying, "Isn't this wonderful, Walter?" He was on Madison Avenue for a long time, and he is mainly known for two things: one, that he won the Irish Sweepstakes, I think a hundred thousand dollars; and the second, when many of the gangsters, possibly including Capone but certainly many others, were brought up to trial for evading income tax, Mr. Weitz was brought in to testify that he sold them large quantities of fine bindings and sets for their mansions. He's still alive, still loves nice things, like particularly Arthur Rackham's, which he tries to buy and then have rebound in full Levant morocco, gilt. He has office space in a shop on upper Lexington Avenue with a man named Feldman [Lov Applefeld], possibly the best chess player in the book business, who has been in the business also for about forty years . . . and who has one of the few shops in New York which still is a general secondhand shop and does not put out catalogues. He's up near the YMHA [Young Men's Hebrew Association] at Ninety-second Street.

[Louis] Schucman and Schwab graduated from library school about 1934 or 1935 and decided to go into the out-of-print book business. After a year or two, Schwab left and has since become extremely successful, having become part of the J. S. Canner organization, finally, I believe, superseding Canner as the owner of the organization in Boston. Canner was a very crooked man who was involved with Williams Company in Boston, which was possibly the most crooked place in the country, with the exception of the American Library Service.

He could almost be gotten on the same principle, only he was even worse. The Williams Company still exists there, but with Miss Williams, Williams's daughter, in charge. She has kept up her father's principles. Canner may still be involved in Canner and Company. Schwab, however, who sold the firm to some other large company for a price probably over a million dollars and reputed to be as much as two and a half million dollars, is still involved in certain other things . . . in Boston or the Boston neighborhood. He, himself, I understand, is in Israel at the moment with a nineteen-year-old girl. But he has various vicissitudes. I gathered this information from Schucman, who still keeps track of him.

Schucman himself had a number of shops, both upstairs and on the street level, after 1935. He never really made a success of it, but he got along all right, considering that his wife was the main breadwinner of the family. Only in this last week, as you know, finally he sold the whole contents of the shop to Penn State. However, at the moment he intends to go to work for somebody, but in the long run I have no doubt that he will go back into the book business again.

INTERVIEWER: What was the final price on that?

GOLDWATER: Thirty-five thousand dollars, out of which I'm to get a commission. . . . As a matter of fact, when he started to dig up the stuff, it turned out that he had not the twenty-two thousand books which he thought he had, nor the twenty-two thousand plus the four thousand paperbacks he had, nor the twenty-two thousand plus the four thousand paperbacks plus about four thousand other books that he had, but about thirty thousand books, plus about seven or eight thousand paperbacks, plus some ten thousand prints which he found there.

So the people are really getting a rather tremendous buy because, obviously, we're not in a position to say "you should pay more," although we might. Simply the idea was they were willing to buy

as it was, and we obviously wanted to sell it as it was. He wants the paperbacks because he proposes to have a room where the undergraduates can come. At this moment, he intends to have them check them out. But I suggested to him that he simply have them there, tell them that they should bring them back, but that nobody's going to check over on them. So the people who want to bring them back so somebody else can have them can do so, but, if anybody takes one and keeps it, he's paying absolutely nothing for them. Therefore, it's just a very good room altogether, and I think he's going to accept that idea, which I think is great.

At Stanford they must have actually bought them and bought them for some price. But here is a case where you're simply getting them for absolutely nothing, and there's no harm to be done for anything. I think it's just a wonderful idea. He doesn't have to do any cataloguing of them; they're simply there for this purpose.

Peter Lader started in business late in the thirties over on Fourth Street, just west of Sixth Avenue, right next door, or perhaps in the very same shop where Freddie Brandeis had the shop which he called the Bad Bookshop for a short period. Later on Freddie Brandeis sold it to a man named Richman. Richman died, and Lader took it over. Lader has been there ever since. He is a very nice man; everybody likes him. We believe that he does not know anything. He has always had a shop in which every book was a good book, so he can't be so terribly stupid.

He calls it Martin's Bookshop. It's the same now as it has been for the last ten, twenty, or thirty years. It is a small shop with not more than two to three thousand books in it, every one of which, however, is an out-of-print, good, scholarly book. He used to go scouting a great deal with Mr. Scher of The Seven Bookhunters; he used to go to the coast and back. His wife worked and works, but the main thing is that he has always lived on a very, very modest scale. He never bought anything and did anything which cost any money. And he's still there. He has a very lugubrious view. I've never seen him smile or laugh in my whole career with him, which is rather a strong thing to say. The world is always in terrible shape, and everything is always miserable and getting worse.

My friend Larry Maxwell, who, after being in the radical movement, decided to go into the book business on Fourth Avenue, had one of the shops here. That was possibly the one which was least successful of any of the shops on Fourth Avenue. He lived on almost nothing, although he came from a fairly wealthy family. He used to just get along on selling magazines for five cents apiece and so on. I would lend him money from time to time, and I would buy things from him when I could. He married a nice girl from Texas who had come into the shop one day. Her salary from the Girl Scouts kept them going for a long time, until the beginning of the war.

As soon as the war was over, he came back to New York. He then decided he wanted to be in the book business again, so he came to work for me for a while to get his hand in. Then, with a little money he had saved plus some money his wife had saved, he opened up a very nice little bookshop on Christopher Street, which was going exactly the way he wanted, namely, it was going to specialize in ballet, movies, theater, little magazines, and avant-garde literature. He was also going to have teas, and, besides that, a great many pretty girls were going to come to visit the shop. This all happened exactly as he had planned, and, possibly not as he had planned, his wife fell in love with one of his clients and went off and married him instead. But he had a plethora of beautiful girls who used to hang around his shop anyway. Everything went along perfectly smoothly, except for one thing, and that was that he couldn't meet his bills. He used to borrow money from me rather regularly for given moments, and eventually he stopped answering the phone because every phone call would be somebody asking for money. Finally somebody decided to put him into bankruptcy, which was rather unfortunate for everybody.

The Great Bibliographers Series

Dean H. Keller
Kent State University

In the early spring of 1970 Eric Moon, who was executive officer and soon to be president of the Scarecrow Press, wrote to his friend Norman Horrocks, then teaching in the School of Library Science at the University of Pittsburgh, about his desire to launch a series on great bibliographers. As Moon envisioned it, the series would reprint important articles by the bibliographers who were selected, along with a checklist of their writings. Moon suggested such figures as Alfred W. Pollard, Arundell Esdaile, Douglas C. McMurtrie, Ronald B. McKerrow, Axel Josephson, Daniel Berkeley Updike, and John Carter, and he asked Horrocks if he would be interested in editing the series. Horrocks agreed, and the first volume in the Great Bibliographers Series appeared in 1974, after Horrocks had moved to Halifax, Nova Scotia, to become director of the School of Library Service at Dalhousie University.

Ten volumes have appeared in the series during its existence, with two more in the development stage, and Norman Horrocks, now vice-president, editorial, at the Scarecrow Press, remains the series general editor. Three of the seven bibliographers mentioned by Eric Moon as possible subjects have found their way into the series. The format of the series remains very much as Moon planned it. Each volume begins with an original or reprinted biographical essay on the subject followed by a selection from the writings of the bibliographer which is intended to give the reader a good overview of the range and depth of the subject's work. Each volume concludes with a checklist of the subject's writings, and all but the volume on Thomas Dibdin have indexes.

It is appropriate that the first volume in the Great Bibliographers Series is on Ronald B. McKerrow (1872–1940), considered by many to be the father of twentieth-century descriptive bibliography. His *Introduction to Bibliography for Literary Students* (1927) is still a standard textbook, and his textual scholarship is demonstrated in his five-volume edition of the works of Thomas Nashe. He is also noted for his *Dictionary of Printers and Booksellers . . . , 1557–1640* (1910) and for his work on early English printers' and publishers' devices and title-page borders. He also edited the *Review of English Studies* and the *Library.*

In this collection editor John Phillip Immroth brings together some of McKerrow's more fugitive writings, representing most areas of his interest. There are four articles on the techniques of sixteenth-century printing, three on his concept of the Elizabethan printer, three reviews, and an article on Shakespeare's text. His last published work, "Form and Matter in the Publication of Research" (1940), is also reprinted. Twenty-three pages are devoted to W. W. Greg's biography, published originally in the *Proceedings of the British Academy* at the time of McKerrow's death in 1940, and the book concludes with a revised version of F. C. Francis's checklist of works by McKerrow that was originally published in the *Library* in 1941.

Over 125 of the 244 pages in Fred W. Roper's 1976 volume on Alfred William Pollard (1859–1944) contain a biographical study of Pollard by John Dover Wilson that was first published in 1945 in the *Proceedings of the British Academy,* an essay on Pollard's influence on contemporary bibliography that was derived from a master's thesis by Roger Leachman, and a checklist of his writings that numbers over five hundred entries. Nine of Pollard's essays, ranging in publication date from 1901 to 1933, were chosen to represent his principles and theories in the areas of bibliography and librarianship to the exclusion of his many contributions in the field of textual criticism. Because of space limitations and the difficulty of selecting truly representative works from Pollard's considerable output in the area of textual criticism, the editor chose to leave this material for another volume. Among the nine essays which are included are his exchange with James Duff Brown on the subject of "Practical Bibliography," which appeared in the *Library* in April 1903; the essay called "Some Points in Bibliographical Descriptions," which he wrote with Greg; and "The

Davis A. Randall

Regulation of the Book Trade in the Sixteenth Century," the Sandars Lecture that he delivered at Cambridge in 1915 that was reprinted in the *Library* the following year.

In a sense, Thomas Frognall Dibdin (1776–1847), the earliest bibliographer to appear in the series thus far, may have been the most difficult subject to excerpt. Although characterized by William A. Jackson as "one of the world's worst" bibliographers, Dibdin was nevertheless a great enthusiast for books and wrote effectively about them. He not only inspired the collecting of books and manuscripts, but he recorded events and provided descriptions of the collectors and book dealers of what was certainly a golden age of book collecting. Dibdin wrote at length on his chosen subjects, and Victor E. Neuburg, drawing on nearly thirty years of study of Dibdin's writings, managed to provide a balanced overview of the author in all of his variety. The first edition of *The Bibliomania* (1809), Dibdin's best-known work, and the little-known and never-before-reprinted *Bibliophobia* (1832) are printed in their entirety, and there are generous selections

from the second edition of *An Introduction to the Knowledge of Rare and Valuable Editions of the Greek and Roman Classics* (1804), *The Bibliographical Decameron* (1817), *The Library Companion* (1824), the second edition of *A Bibliographical, Antiquarian, and Picturesque Tour in France and Germany* (1829), and *Reminiscences of a Literary Life* (1836). *The Bibliographical Decameron* is considered to be the high point of Dibdin's writing, and its three sumptuous volumes, finely printed by William Bulmer, are impressive. To give the typographical flavor of the work, Neuburg reprinted in facsimile the fourteen-page prospectus which Bulmer printed to describe the book. Dibdin's life is outlined in Neuburg's introduction, and William Jerdan's lengthy contemporary account of Dibdin, from his *Men I Have Known* (1866), is reprinted in full as an appendix. A select list (29 entries) of Dibdin's bibliographical writings is provided but with reference to William A. Jackson's much lengthier bibliography (106 entries) which was published in 1965.

The first American bibliographer to be treated in the series, as number 4, is the remarkable Douglas C. McMurtrie (1888–1944). Scott Bruntjen and Melissa L. Young edited the volume devoted to this printer and type designer, historian of printing, and author of the monumental history *The Book* (1937). He was also the director of the American Imprints Inventory and a bibliographer. Given McMurtrie's diversity of interests and the fact that the checklist of his publications with which this book concludes contains 789 entries, one can understand the dilemma faced by the editors. It is difficult to select works from such an array that will demonstrate the depth and variety of McMurtrie's contribution to the field. From the third edition of *The Book* (1943), the editors chose the section called "Baskerville and His Disciples" as representative, and they also included a section from chapter 25 of volume two of *A History of Printing in the United States* (1936). Sections from his long essay on *Type Design* (1927) are reproduced in facsimile. Several of the selections are concerned with his work with the American Imprints Inventory, including "Locating the Printed Source Materials for United States History" (1944), a transcription of a 1938 radio interview called "A Nationwide Search for Early American Printing," and excerpts from the fifth edition of the inventory's *Manual of Procedure* (1939). Thirteen selections out of a possible 789 is a tantalizing taste. A twenty-three-page biographical sketch of McMurtrie by Herbert A. Kellar that first appeared in 1955 in the *Revista Interamericana de Bibliografía* precedes the selections.

The next two volumes in the series, numbers 5 and 6, on Michael Sadleir (1888–1957) and Henry Bradshaw (1831–1886) are by Roy B. Stokes, former director of the School of Librarianship at the University of British Columbia in Vancouver. Moon, who established the Great Bibliographers Series when he was president of the Scarecrow Press, was one of Stokes's students when he served as a visiting professor at Loughborough Technical College in England. Michael Sadleir wrote well and with enthusiasm. He was a popularizer, in the best sense, of the literature of bibliography. He was at once a publisher, a novelist, a biographer, a bibliographer, and a book collector, and this collection assembled by Stokes gives a view of Sadleir in all of these roles. Sadleir's interests as a bibliographer, writer, and collector were concentrated in the nineteenth century; he did much to popularize that period as an area for book collecting, and he was one of the pioneers in the study of bibliography of the Victorian era. Excerpts from his works on Lady Blessington-D'Orsay (1933), Edward Bulwer Lytton (1931), and Anthony Trollope (1927), as well as from more general works such as *Excursions in Victorian Bibliography* (1922), *XIX Century Fiction* (1951), and *Authors and Publishers* (1932), and from his novels are reprinted. The selection from the preface to *XIX Century Fiction* is especially interesting because it is the closest Sadleir ever came to writing an autobiography. Stokes provides a biographical introduction and a list of biographical and bibliographical references to Sadleir, and there is a checklist of Sadleir's writings based upon the work published by Simon Nowell-Smith in *The Transactions of the Bibliographical Society* in 1958.

Stokes's second volume in the series is on Henry Bradshaw, quite a different figure from Sadleir. Bradshaw was a scholar and librarian who spent most of his career at the Cambridge University Library. His main interest was in manuscripts and early printed books, and he gave special attention to Irish printing and to liturgical books. Stokes carefully outlines Bradshaw's life in his introductory "Commentary," giving special attention to his achievements as librarian, bibliographer, and book collector. Stokes also compiled the checklist of Bradshaw's writings, providing lengthy annotations for many of the works listed.

In 1889 Bradshaw's successor as librarian at Cambridge University, Francis Jenkinson, published the *Collected Papers of Henry Bradshaw*. Seven of the excerpts from Bradshaw's writings, arranged in chronological order by date of first appearance, are drawn from these *Collected Papers*. The rest appeared in a wide variety of publications, among them *Notes and Queries*, the *Academy*, *Hermes*, and other journals. Titles such as "Letter on the Codex Sinaiticus" (1863), "The Printer of the Historia S. Albani" (1868), "The Irish Monastic Missal at Oxford" (1878), and "Note on Mediaeval Service Books" (1881) indicate that subjects of special interest to Bradshaw are adequately represented.

Three essays about Montague Summers (1880–1948), the subject of number 7 in the series, make up part 1 of the book. Taken together they present a biographical and critical view of the most controversial individual to appear in the series thus far. Father Brocard Sewell, Summers's biographer, contributes a biographical essay which was first published in 1981; Robert Hume's essay is a reassessment of Summers's value and competence as a critic and editor of Restoration drama; and Devendra P. Varma discusses Summers's scholarship relating to the Gothic. Part 2 presents selections from Summers's writings, divided into three sections: "The Restoration Theatre," five selections including "The 'Nonesuch' Restoration Dramatists" from his autobiography, *The Galanty Show;* "Demonology and Witchcraft," four selections; and "The Gothic Novel," six selections including the preface to his *Gothic Bibliography* together with a specimen entry from that work. Part 3 of the book begins with a biographical chronology of Summers and concludes with a 326-item annotated bibliography of his work, based upon the article by Timothy d'Arch Smith, published in 1964 and revised in 1983, which is divided into five sections: "Gothic Studies and Horror Literature"; "Witchcraft, Demonology, Satanism, Vampirism, Lycanthropy, and Sadism, and Other Occult Subjects"; "Restoration Theatre and Other Dramatic Literature Including Shakespeare and Elizabethan Drama"; "Religious Mysticism, Hagiology, and Other Theological Subjects"; and "Miscellaneous Writings and Autobiographical Reflections."

With the publication in 1990 of number 8 in the series, *George Watson Cole, 1850–1939*, by Donald C. Dickinson, the format of the books changed, and the texts no longer were reproduced in typewritten copy.

Cole began a career as a lawyer but soon became interested in library work. He was a member of the first class to graduate from Melvil Dewey's School of Library Economy in New York in 1888. In 1901 he was hired to catalogue the library of Elihu D. Church, a seven-and-a-half-year project which resulted in the publication of *A Catalogue of Books Relating to the Discovery and Early History of North and South America*... (five volumes, 1907) and *A Catalogue of Books Consisting of English Literature*... (two volumes, 1909). In 1915 Cole became Henry E. Huntington's first librarian, overseeing the cataloguing of his massive collection and later supervising its transfer from New York City to San Marino, California. Cole's life is recounted in detail in part 1 of Dickinson's volume, and it is followed by fifteen essays by Cole, in chronological order, selected to demonstrate the "diversity of his interests and the range of his learning." Between "American Bibliography, General and Local" (1894), his first major paper, and the posthumously published "Do You Know Your Lowndes?" (1939) there is an impressive array of bibliographical studies, philosophical statements, historical works, the introductory pages for the church catalogue, along with some sample entries, and even his poetic spoof of the Harvard Classics called "The Five-Foot Shelf." The list of Cole's writings is based upon the list that appeared in the *Bulletin of Bibliography* in 1936 and 1937, and there is a checklist of writings about him to conclude the work.

At 479 pages, Francesco Cordasco's volume, *Theodore Besterman, Bibliographer and Editor: A Selection of Representative Texts* (1992), number 9 in the series, is nearly twice as long as the other volumes published thus far. Cordasco's lengthy introduction is followed by four essays on Besterman's life and work, including Sir Frank Francis's "A Bibliographical Appreciation" of 1967 which describes and annotates sixty-three of Besterman's major works. Then follow nineteen selections from Besterman's writings. A chapter from *The Mind of Annie Besant* represents his interest in theosophy and psychical research. There are nine pieces on bibliographical matters, including fifty-eight pages of introductory material from the second edition of the now-classic *Beginnings of Systematic Bibliography* and the introduction to *A World Bibliography of Bibliographies,* fourth edition; eight essays on Voltaire including "Voltaire Bibliography: The Impossible Dream," which was the first Ralph R. Shaw Memorial Lecture delivered in 1973; and his reminiscences of his long career called "Fifty Years a Bookman," also in 1973. Besterman's writings, numbering 258 items, are listed in chronological order at the end of the book, and there is a list of thirty "Related Titles of Interest," mostly biographical and critical articles on Besterman.

The two careers of David A. Randall (1905–1975) are described in the tenth and last volume to date in the Great Bibliographers Series, edited by

Dean H. Keller. From 1935 to 1956 Randall managed the rare book department for Charles Scribner's Sons in New York, and from 1956 until his death in 1975 he headed the Lilly Library at Indiana University. Part 1 is a biographical sketch of Randall, and it is followed by twenty-four selections from his writings. These range from bibliographical studies such as his discussion of American editions of Sir Walter Scott's novels, to recollections of great collectors such as J. K. Lilly and Michael Sadleir, to introductions to Lilly Library exhibition catalogues and a sampling of bibliographical notes and book reviews. The exhibition catalogues which he produced at the Lilly Library are described in the chronological list of his writings that makes up part 3 of the book. Part 4 is a checklist of works about Randall, and part 5 lists catalogues he produced as a book dealer.

The next volume in the series will be on Frederick James Furnival by Kirk Beetz, and Roy Stokes is working on a book on Montague Rhodes James.

Volumes in the Series:

Ronald Brunless McKerrow: A Selection of His Essays, compiled by John Phillip Immroth (Metuchen, N.J.: Scarecrow Press, 1974);

Alfred William Pollard: A Selection of His Essays, compiled by Fred W. Roper (Metuchen, N.J.: Scarecrow Press, 1976);

Thomas Frognall Dibdin: Selections, compiled and introduced by Victor E. Neuburg (Metuchen, N.J.: Scarecrow Press, 1978);

Douglas C. McMurtrie: Bibliographer and Historian of Printing, compiled by Scott Bruntjen and Melissa L. Young (Metuchen, N.J.: Scarecrow Press, 1979);

Roy B. Stokes, *Michael Sadleir, 1888–1957* (Metuchen, N.J.: Scarecrow Press, 1980);

Stokes, *Henry Bradshaw, 1831–1886* (Metuchen, N.J.: Scarecrow Press, 1984);

Frederick S. Frank, *Montague Summers: A Bibliographical Portrait* (Metuchen, N.J.: Scarecrow Press, 1988);

Donald C. Dickinson, *George Watson Cole, 1850–1939* (Metuchen, N.J.: Scarecrow Press, 1990);

Theodore Besterman, Bibliographer and Editor: A Selection of Representative Texts, edited by Francesco Cordasco, foreword by William A. Munford (Metuchen, N.J.: Scarecrow Press, 1992);

Dean H. Keller, *David Anton Randall, 1905–1975* (Metuchen, N.J.: Scarecrow Press, 1992).

Mencken and Nietzsche:
An Unpublished Excerpt from H. L. Mencken's
My Life as Author and Editor

Terry Teachout
New York Daily News

H. L. Mencken published what he expected to be his last column for the editorial page of the *Baltimore Sun* on 2 February 1941. He had written for the *Sun* since 1906; he served (and would continue to serve) on its board of directors. But Mencken was no longer willing to write for a paper that supported Franklin D. Roosevelt's foreign policy, and his by-line did not appear again in the *Sun* until 1948, three years after Roosevelt's death: "[T]he paper began supporting Roosevelt II's effort to horn into World War II in a frantic and highly unintelligent manner, and I withdrew from its editorial pages ... after having cavorted there more or less regularly for thirty-five years." Finding himself with time on his hands, Mencken spent the spring and summer of 1941 finishing up two books, *Newspaper Days* and *A New Dictionary of Quotations*. He then began work on a new book – one not intended for publication.

Thirty-Five Years of Newspaper Work, as Mencken eventually dubbed this book, is a detailed record of Mencken's association with the *Baltimore Sun*. He prepared it with an eye toward the possible writing of an informal, *Newspaper Days*–style memoir of his years at the *Sun*, as well as to supply future scholars (to whom he referred as "resurrection men") with an unexpurgated account of his post-1906 career as a newspaperman. *Thirty-Five Years* dealt only in passing with Mencken's personal life. "Once these notes are on paper," he explained in his diary, "I'll have a pretty complete and accurate record of my professional life, and if I ever decide to write and print a volume of serious reminiscences the material will be readily at hand, and I'll be saved the interruptions for investigation that often held up 'Happy Days' and 'Newspaper Days.' There will be very little about my private life, and next to nothing about women. Such things, it seems to me, are nobody's business – and I must always remember that what I write may be read by others after I am gone."

H. L. Mencken, 1913 (courtesy of Enoch Pratt Free Library, Baltimore, Maryland)

By the time Mencken completed the 1,687-page typescript in the summer of 1942, it was clear that his pro-German (though not pro-Hitler) views would make it impossible for him to write about public affairs for the duration of World War II, just as they had forced him into semiretirement during World War I. He therefore resolved to follow *Thirty-

Five Years of Newspaper Work with a similar volume devoted to his literary career. In August, he began work on *My Life as Author and Editor.* Unlike *Thirty-Five Years,* which was written in a continuous burst of effort, *My Life as Author and Editor* was interrupted twice, as a note on the title page of the typescript indicates: "Begun in 1942; halted in July, 1943, to make way for *The American Language, Supplement I;* resumed in July, 1945. Halted again at the end of 1945 to make way for *Supplement II;* resumed in 1948." It was halted permanently on 23 November 1948, when Mencken suffered a stroke that left him unable to read and write. The 1,025-page typescript breaks off in 1923, just as Mencken and George Jean Nathan were preparing to leave the *Smart Set* and start a new magazine, the *American Mercury.*

Prior to his death in 1956, Mencken presented the typescripts of *My Life* and *Thirty-Five Years,* together with the diary he kept between 1930 and 1948, to the Enoch Pratt Free Library in Baltimore. The typescripts were packed in wooden crates, sealed with steel bands, and stored in the basement of the library. The two memoirs were deposited "on the explicit and irrevocable understanding that [they were] not to be open to anyone, under any circumstances whatever, until either January 1, 1980, or thirty-five years after the death of the author, whichever may be the later"; the diary was placed under a similar embargo lasting for twenty-five years. The Pratt followed Mencken's instructions to the letter. Mencken's diary was opened on 29 January 1981 and subsequently published by Alfred A. Knopf in 1989 in a trade edition edited by Charles Fecher. *My Life as Author and Editor* and *Thirty-Five Years of Newspaper Work* were opened on 29 January 1991. *My Life* was published by Knopf in 1993 in a trade edition edited by Jonathan Yardley; *Thirty-Five Years* is currently being prepared for publication by Johns Hopkins University Press.

The publication of *The Diary of H. L. Mencken* caused a nationwide stir, partly because it contained unguarded remarks that struck many readers as racist and anti-Semitic and partly because Mencken wrote with unusual candor about his friends and colleagues — a few of whom lived long enough to find out what he really thought of them. It brought about a critical revaluation of Mencken as writer and thinker that continues; three new biographies of Mencken, all based in part on the sealed typescripts, are presently in press or under way. *My Life as Author and Editor,* which was even more candid than the diary, received equally contentious reviews. Controversy aside, both books have proved to be of the highest value to scholars, not only because of what they reveal about Mencken himself but because of their vivid accounts of Mencken's

friendships with many of America's leading literary figures. Especially in *My Life,* Mencken's personal and professional relations with Nathan, Knopf, Theodore Dreiser, Sinclair Lewis, and F. Scott Fitzgerald, among many others, are described in considerable detail.

Though both the diary and *My Life* were abridged with great care, some material of interest was necessarily left unpublished. Yardley's edition of *My Life,* for example, leaves out virtually all of Mencken's account of his literary apprenticeship, from which the present excerpt is drawn. In this excerpt Mencken describes the writing and reception of his third book, *The Philosophy of Friedrich Nietzsche* (1908). Harrison Hale Schaff, a partner in the Boston publishing firm of John W. Luce and Company, suggested in 1905 that Mencken write a book about the influence of Nietzsche on Bernard Shaw, Henrik Ibsen, Maurice Maeterlinck, and other European playwrights. (Mencken wrote the daily theatrical column for the *Baltimore Morning Herald* from 1902 to 1903, and his dramatic criticism had already attracted attention outside Baltimore.) Mencken's immediate interest was in Shaw, and his *George Bernard Shaw: His Plays* (1905), the first book written about Shaw, was the result. But Schaff still wanted a Nietzsche book, and Mencken ultimately agreed to write one.

In the process of writing *The Philosophy of Friedrich Nietzsche,* Mencken first made the acquaintance of the writer who did more than any other to shape his mature understanding of man's nature and destiny. It is impossible to understate the extent to which this fateful encounter influenced him, for better or worse. "Like Nietzsche," he wrote in a private memorandum in 1941, "I console myself with the hope that I am the man of the future, emancipated from the prevailing delusions and superstitions, and gone beyond nationalism." The sources of this extraordinary conviction can be glimpsed in this previously unpublished excerpt from *My Life as Author and Editor.*

An excerpt from *My Life as Author and Editor*

[Harrison Hale Schaff 's] first suggestion that I do a study of Nietzsche was made in his letter of March 14, 1905, hitherto quoted. I was not enthusiastic, for I knew next to nothing about Nietzsche, there was little intelligent writing about him in English, and my German was even rockier than it is now. When we met in New York — probably early in 1906 — he renewed his proposal, and in December of the same year, just before leaving on another trip to Europe, he began pressing it by mail. In a let-

H. L. Mencken at the Baltimore Sun, *1913 (courtesy of the Enoch Pratt Free Library, Baltimore, Maryland)*

ter dated December 19 he set it forth in some detail, as follows:

> The sort of a book I want to get together is in some respects not unlike your Shaw book. I should like a comprehensive review of his life followed by a statement in simple terms of his personal philosophic belief together with extracts from his books showing his method of stating or eliminating propositions. These extracts would in most cases be so blind that considerable explanation would have to go with them. Then I would like a portion of the work, presumably the last, to show the influence that Neitzsche [*sic*] is having in the literature and thought of the world....

I allowed myself to be persuaded, though with misgivings, and in a little while I was hard at work upon the MS. First I gathered together everything that I could find of or about Nietzsche in English — mainly magazine articles, but also including some books. Of Nietzsche's own works only five volumes of a projected translation in nineteen volumes had appeared, and of the large literature of commentary that has since appeared there was scarcely more than a trace. I gave hard study to everything I could find, but it was not much, and I thus had to tackle the original canon. A few volumes of it were in the

Pratt Library, Baltimore, but for most of it I had to go to the Library of Congress. What I found was written in a kind of German that I found extremely difficult, at least until I got used to it, but I kept at my exploration resolutely, and soon began to get something on paper. I recall that all the writing was done in a small third-floor hall bedroom that I then occupied in Hollins street. The room was so small that I had to move my cot every time I sat down to my typewriter, which stood on a small table at the window. I worked hard and late, and when I finished and was ready for bed I would pull back the cot. This made a noise, for the cot was a rickety iron one, and my mother, who slept in the room below, complained that it disturbed her. So did our nextdoor neighbor, William Deemer. After that I had to let the cot stand back from the window, which began to be uncomfortable as the Spring came on. But I stuck to the job until the full heat of Summer, and when it was done at last the book that I had produced was several times as large as my Shaw book. I delivered the last of the MS. to Schaff at the end of July, and on August 2 he wrote to me that it had gone to the printer. He said in this letter that he proposed to make its price $2, and that he would pay me 10% royalty. Unhappily, most of his letters to me after 1905 have been lost, and all of mine to him likewise, so that the details of our negotiations are only dim memories. I recall that I was somewhat uneasy about the effect of the book in the *Sun* office, for the proprietors of the paper, the Abells, were Catholics. I knew, of course, that no Abell ever read a book voluntarily, but I feared one of them might make an exception in favor of (and to the peril of) a member of the staff. However, nothing of the sort happened, and the *Sun* notice, printed on February 9, 1908, was very favorable. It ran to more than a column, and was written by Dr. S. Z. Ammen, an old-time editorial writer who hailed from Virginia and was an agnostic. I suspect that when he read the book Dr. Ammen was making his first acquaintance with Nietzsche's ideas. They plainly made a powerful impression on him, and so he undertook to state them at some length in his notice. Of me he said: "Vigor, lucidity vivacity and directness mark his style, converting a dry theme into a racy comment on modern life." The Abells, if they read the review, accepted it on trust, and no indication of disfavor came to me from the front office. On the contrary, my credit in the place, which had been rising since the appearance of my Shaw book, took another upward turn, and a little while later there was a notice on the bulletin-board saying that I had been made an editorial writer. I had been writing occasional editorials, as a matter of fact, since I joined the *Sun* staff in 1906, and after my annunciation I continued as Sunday editor, but to be raised formally to the status of an editorial writer on the old *Sunpaper* was to be admitted to the inner circle of dignitaries, and therein I basked until the Abells, who were of the third generation, lost control of their heritage in 1910, and I went over to the new *Evening Sun.* When, in April, 1908, I started off on my first trip to Europe, Walter W. Abell, the president of the company, called me to his office, handed me a check for $100, and said the directors had instructed him to offer it to me in recognition of the extra work I had been doing. I was then getting $40 a week. On December 30, 1908 I was raised to $43.

The Nietzsche also boosted my stock in other quarters, for it got a good many long notices, and most of them were favorable. The book, indeed, not only made me known but served an actual need, just as my Shaw had served one. Nietzsche in 1908, like Shaw in 1905, was widely discussed and almost as widely denounced, but most of those who wrote about him knew him only vaguely, and some knew him not at all. James Huneker had published a pioneer study of him in "Mezzotints in Modern Music" in 1899, and another and better one in "Overtones"

in 1904, and was to return to the subject at greater length in "Egoists" in 1909, but I can recall no other writer of the time, not a professional metaphysician, who had dealt with him in a manner even remotely describable as illuminating. . . .

Schaff had scheduled the Nietzsche for October, 1907, and it was listed in his Autumn catalogue for the year, but there were the usual delays in printing and binding, and it did not come out until January 20, 1908. Schaff had sent out advance notices describing me as a fellow of the Johns Hopkins specializing "in the study of contemporary continental dramatists" and saying that my "knowledge of European languages" enabled me to pursue my studies "in the original tongues of the writers." Whether this was an honest error or deliberate *blague* I did not know and never inquired, for the lie was very embarrassing to me, and I was eager to forget it. Fortunately, the notice was not printed in any Baltimore paper. The first reviews that I saw were somewhat discouraging, for the longest of them, in the New York *Globe* for February 6, was devoted wholly to my contention that Roosevelt I [Theodore Roosevelt] had borrowed many of his ideas from Nietzsche, and the second, in the New York *Evening Sun* of February 8, was tart and even scornful. "In spite of its occasional bad taste," said the *Evening Sun's* anonymous reviewer, and "its frequent indications of a lack of a sense of proportion, it may do for the vulgar what certain stupid treatises on Browning have done for the poet – that is to say, drive the fairly intelligent reader to consult the work of the man commented upon, in order to find out what the commentator means." But when the Philadelphia *North American* – then an important paper – of the same day called the book "an illuminating and eventful work, in which popularity is flouted and precedent is thrown to the dogs," I was bucked up somewhat, and when the New York *Sun* (the parent of the *Evening Sun*) and the New York *Times* came along before the end of February with very favorable notices I began to be serene and optimistic. The *Sun's* long review, as was its custom at that time, was mainly devoted to a summary of the book, with an incidental summary of Nietzsche's main ideas, but it also included the following: "Mr Mencken . . . provides us with a very readable and clear account of the philosophy and the philosopher. . . . He admires Nietzsche, we should say, but not always does he speak of him quite reverentially, and he appears to be amused by him now and then." As for the *Times,* it allowed that I had "a clear, forceful, even ardent style, a keen and thoroughgoing intellect, knowledge of men, and a sense of humor." Nearly all the other early reviews were equally favorable. . . .

In March I sailed for Liverpool in the Cunarder *Lucania* on my first trip abroad, so I did not see most of the other reviews until my return. They were, like the first ones, mainly friendly. . . . Even the *Nation,* then extremely conventional in its book reviews, permitted itself to say:

> His exposition of Nietzsche's philosophy is clear, simple and orderly, quite free from the cobwebs of metaphysics; if he shows bad taste in the details of writing this may be passed over as a mark of zeal in imitating his master. We can commend the exegesis, though we repudiate the conclusions.

This complaint of bad taste in my exposition appeared in various other reviews, and I must confess after 36 years that it was well founded. In my eagerness to make the book readable I often bulged over the line separating serious writing from mere journalism, and sometimes my journalism was of a pretty feeble sort. . . . Most of the downright denunciations that the book got — they were not many — were directed at Nietzsche rather than at me. "The enthusiasm for Nietzsche, like the enthusiasm for Ibsen," said the San Francisco *Argonaut,* "is among the saddening signs of the day." To which Mrs. Elia W. Peattie, literary editor of the Chicago *Tribune,* added the Rotarian complaint: "The great defect of Mr. Mencken's appraisement of Nietzsche is his inability to realize that Nietzsche is a destructive force." But as I have said, the majority of the reviews were amiable and some of them were very complimentary. "The book," said the Los Angeles *Times,* "is neither long nor diffuse, and on account of its calm, judicial and unprejudiced attitude (*sic!*) will probably be the standard English interpretation of Nietzsche for some time to come." To which the New York *Press* added: "In its 325 pages one will find not only a sufficient biography of the blasphemer to give an adequate idea of the man, but also his several works discussed in detail and expounded with commendable clarity. The author, we fear, will never acquire a reputation for learning. He is too little given to dragging in the technical terminology of philosophy for that. And he deserves a vote of thanks for this." And the Philadelphia *Public Ledger:* "He has the first qualifications of a successful biographer and expositor; that is, sympathy with his subject without blind acceptance of all the conclusions to which his prophet and philosopher led." But the review that pleased me most came out in the *Educational Review* for May, 1908, for I got word (from what source I forget) that it had been written

Dust jacket for the memoir that generated controversy because of its alleged anti-Semitism

by Nicholas Murray Butler, editor of the *Review* and president of Columbia University. It began as follows:

> Unfortunately, we do not know who Mr. Mencken is. Neither his title page, his introduction, not yet "Who's Who," gives any trace of him. Nevertheless, he has written one of the most interesting and instructive books that has come from the American press in many a long day. Mr. Mencken can write. In addition, he has something to write about. His own light touches are quite charming, and his editorial impertinences are often more delightful than Nietzsche's astonishing intellectual impudence.

I never met Butler until 1932, and then my exchanges with him were only casual. But when the American Mercury started in 1924 he became one of its most ardent readers, and not infrequently sent me contributions for its department of Americana. [Author's note]

When the English edition of the Nietzsche came out in London in September, 1908, it encountered a more hostile press. Most of the reviews made some reference, usually invidious, to my American English, and some of them searched the book, in the English fashion, for slips and blunders. The London *Standard,* in a column-long notice printed on October 13, found *jus gentian,* Liebnitz and Pythagorus, and flogged me deservedly for not knowing the meaning of *Pussta,* the name of the great Hungarian plain. Having thus done its duty by an American writer in the traditional English manner, it proceeded:

> But in spite of his defects, Mr. Mencken's book is rather good reading, and, in its way, it is extremely useful. It is a breezy account of a writer whose works have been making a considerable noise in the world during the past few years. If Mr. Mencken's general culture leaves something to seek, he has, at any rate, read up his Nietzsche with commendable care and industry. He knows the text of his master extremely well, and has all the most quotable passages at his fingers' ends.

The Edinburgh *Scotsman* and the *Athenaeum* also denounced my Americanisms, the latter in a lofty and patronizing manner. "The style," is said, "is racy with American idiom, but it would be unfair to a great country to make it responsible for the tone of exaggeration that at every turn offends the critical sense." The *Scotsman* said:

> Mr. Mencken reproduces the worst vituperative excesses of his author and gilds them with an American slang of his own. . . . Apart, however, from its crudities and its blind prejudice against whatever has been accepted by mankind in the way of religion or morality, the book gives a readable and intelligent account of Nietzsche and his ideas.

But there were also some dissents, even in Scotland. The Dundee *Advertiser,* for example, praised the book as "the best exposition of the Nietzschean philosophy in the English language," and even had compliments for my writing, thus:

> It is written in a style that carries the reader along from page to page. The language is direct and vigorous. An obscure sentence will not be found in the whole book.

But the friendliest of the English notices was that of W. L. Courtney in the London *Telegraph.* It ran to two columns, and was mainly made up, of course, of a discussion of Nietzsche, but there were also some kind words for me, and there were more in Courtney's book, "Rosemary's Letter-Book,"

published a little while later. I wrote to him thanking him for the *Telegraph* notice, and was enormously pleased when his book came out, for in it was the first mention of me that had appeared between covers. The publication of my book brought me into contact, destined to be long and friendly, with Dr. Oscar Levy, but not immediately. When, in 1909 or thereabout, he took over the English translation of Nietzsche that had been launched in 1896 by Dr. Alexander Tille, he began to send me the revised and additional volumes as they were issued, and in 1911 we started a correspondence that has continued ever since.

When, in 1912, Dr. Levy reached the index volume, he wrote to me offering to print in it an advertisement of my book, along with one of "Men vs. the Man," which I wrote in collaboration with Robert Rives LaMonte in 1910. "I propose," he wrote from London on January 7, 1912, "to give a whole page for these books and would ask you to draw up yourself a little advt. with, if you like, a few press notices. Do not mind blowing your own trumpet: we all do it, though sometimes with blushes. But 'who wants the end must want the means,' as Nietzsche says somewhere." I contented myself with a very modest announcement, chiefly made up of quotations from the Courtney and Butler reviews and those in the *Outlook* and the New York *Sun.* On my second trip to Europe, in May, 1912, I visited Dr. Levy at his house in London, and at later times, as the vicissitudes of war drove him from country to country, I met him elsewhere.

In July, 1932, my friend Philip Goodman of New York, happening to be in Weimar, called upon Frau Elisabeth Förster-Nietzsche, the philosopher's sister, who was then in charge of the Nietzsche-Archiv there. Goodman gave her a copy of my book, but added the characteristically buffoonish touch of inscribing it "To my sweetheart." She was then 86 years old, and her sight was failing, but she made some attempt to read it, and presently sent me (through Goodman) a postcard photograph of herself, inscribed in her own shaky handwriting: "Dr. h.c. Elisabeth Förster-Nietzsche sendet in aufrichtiger Dankbarkeit u. Verehrung Herrn H. L. Mencken die herzilichsten Grüsse. Nietzsche-Archiv, Juli, 1932." I dispatched a note of thanks for this souvenir, and she wrote to me at some length on September 24, 1932. "Es war immer mein lebhaftesten Wunsch," she said, "Sie persönlich kennen zu lernen and Ihnen zu sagen, wie innig dankbar ich es empfunden habe, dass Sie in Amerika, welches den Lehren Nietzsches so freud gegenüberstand, mit so warmer Wertschatzung geschrieben und gesprochen haben." This, of course, was only politeness. In a note to Goodman dated July 26 she had spoken of me as "Ihren von mir so verehrten Freund" and "unsern gemeinsamen Freund, der lange Jahre mir als her Einzige in Amerika ersehin, der Nietzsche wirklich tief ergriffen hatte und darüber so fortrefflish schrieben konnte," and added: "Ich glaube, dass es besonders seinem Einfluss zu danken ist, wenn allmählich in Amerika ein Verständnis für Nietzsche sich gezeicht hat." I never met the old lady, for I did not visit Germany again until 1938, and by that time she was dead. She told me in her letter of September 24 that the Nietzsche-Archiv had lost an endowment of 400,000 marks in the German inflation, and hinted that I should try to help replace it by raising funds in the United States, but I was never a hand for raising funds, so I did nothing about it.

My Nietzsche continued to get notices for several years after its publication. On March 28, 1909, there was a review in *L'Economiste* of Florence, Italy, saying 'tutto il lavoro del sig. Mencken e interesante,' and others kept on drifting in from near and far. Also, though Nietzsche continued to be anathema to the right-thinking, the book was bought by a number of public libraries, and the correspondence from readers that I have already mentioned gradually increased. For fully twenty-five years, in fact, I continued to hear from persons who liked it, and some of them liked it so well, despite its youthful gaucheries and the frequent appearance of other and better books on the subject, that they could almost be described as fanatics for it. . . . I was constantly besought to bring it up to date, but I always had too many other irons in the fire; moreover, Schaff was disinclined to do a revision that would involve a resetting, and by the time he sold the plates to Knopf World War II was raging and it was obvious that a book favorable to Nietzsche would have a hard row to hoe.

"The Philosophy of Friedrich Nietzsche" was signed Henry L. Mencken, and it was not until 1910 that I settled down to H. L., though I had used it in the cut head of my "Knocks and Jollies" column in the Baltimore *Morning Herald* so early as 1900. All of my short stories were signed either Henry L. or Henry Louis, and so were my poems in the magazines. But my contributions to the *Smart Set* after my first article in 1908 were signed H. L., and so was "The Artist," which I contributed to the *Bohemian Magazine,* then edited by Theodore Dreiser, for December, 1901. In 1913 Henry L. appeared on "The Gist of Nietzsche," but that was Schaff's doing, not mine. It took me a long while to establish H. L. The reporters and copyreaders of the Baltimore *Sunpapers* continued to make me Henry L. until 1935 or thereabout, when Paul Patterson issued a stringent order that I was to be H. L. To this day that order is sometimes violated, and when my time comes to die I assume almost as a matter of course that I will be Henry L. in the *Sun's* obituary.*

* [Not so. The headline read: "H. L. Mencken, Author Dies at 75."]

Rachel Maddux

(15 December 1912 – 19 November 1983)

Nancy A. Walker
Vanderbilt University

BOOKS: *The Green Kingdom* (New York: Simon & Schuster, 1957);

Abel's Daughter (New York: Harper & Row, 1960);

A Walk in the Spring Rain (Garden City, N.Y.: Doubleday, 1966);

The Orchard Children (New York: Harper & Row, 1977);

Communication: The Autobiography of Rachel Maddux (Knoxville: University of Tennessee Press, 1991);

The Way Things Are: The Stories of Rachel Maddux (Knoxville: University of Tennessee Press, 1992).

SELECTED PERIODICAL PUBLICATION – UNCOLLECTED: Weekly column as "Apple Annie," *Buffalo River Review,* Linden, Tennessee, 1 October 1982–19 October 1983.

In June 1937 a radio producer named Savington Crampton, on his way from Pennsylvania to California to take over production of the *Camel Caravan* program, made a detour to Kansas City, Missouri, to meet the author of the novella *Turnip's Blood,* which he had read in *Story* magazine the previous year. His companion, a writer named George Corey, was interested in collaborating with the author on a script based on the story. The meeting was the beginning of a lifelong friendship between Crampton and Rachel Maddux, who, then in her midtwenties, had recently dropped out of the University of Kansas Medical School and had begun to write fiction for the first time since she completed a novel at the age of nine. The meeting was also fortunate for literary history; not only did Crampton continually encourage Maddux's writing, but he also preserved for nearly fifty years the only known copy of *Communication* (originally subtitled "Being the Mental Autobiography of a Sturdy Quest"), the remarkable autobiography she wrote in 1941, at the age of twenty-eight. Shortly after Maddux's death in 1983, Crampton gave the manuscript to Susan

Rachel Maddux, early 1970s (photograph by Mary Ellen Breyer, courtesy of Nancy A. Walker)

Ford Wiltshire, who showed it to Nancy A. Walker in February 1990. The publication of *Communication* by the University of Tennessee Press in 1991, fifty years after it was written, inaugurated that press's Rachel Maddux series, which includes *The Way Things Are,* a volume of her short stories (most of them previously unpublished), which won the Dictionary of Literary Biography Yearbook Award for a Distinguished Volume of Short Stories Published in 1992.

This series of chance meetings and coincidences could have been written by Maddux herself. Her fiction is filled with life-changing encounters: the meeting of Penny Curtess and John Frazier in the title story of *The Ways Things Are,* the unlikely pairing of Libby Meredith and Will Workman in *A Walk in the Spring Rain* (1966), and the concert tour that introduces composer Justin Magnus to Erma Herrick in Maddux's first and most ambitious novel, *The Green Kingdom* (1957). Her characters, like her fiction, are by turns passionate and whimsical, capable of deep commitment and amused skepticism – qualities that seem to have characterized Maddux as well. Although much of her writing is notable for its concern with pressing social issues, she believed that the key to writing was staying in touch with the childhood self that draws no sharp lines between the real and the imaginary. No wonder, then, that she wrote both fantasy and social realism, sometimes combining both modes in the same work.

Maddux's fiction derives much of its richness of detail from her own life experiences, including the various places where she lived. Even *The Green Kingdom,* which borrows from the utopian tradition, can be seen as an imaginative response to the midwestern drought of the 1930s and a dream of a better life, engendered by the Depression. Maddux was born Juanita Rachel Maddux on 15 December 1912 in Wichita, Kansas, the third child of a city employee and a woman who had grown up in a sod house on the Kansas prairie. She attended Wichita State University from 1930 to 1933, when she transferred to the University of Kansas, from which she was graduated in 1934 with a bachelor's degree in zoology and where she started medical school the same year. When health problems forced her to withdraw from medical school in the spring of 1936, she began writing and publishing short stories, and she spent some time in Hollywood considering the possibility of writing film scripts, as so many other American writers were doing. Instead, she returned to Kansas City, working for a paint company and a real-estate agency while beginning her first novel. Several of the stories in *The Way Things Are,* including "No Smoking, No Spitting" and "They're Laughing," draw upon her experience of Depression-era Kansas City: twenty-five-cent meals at cheap diners and hoarding milk bottles to return for the deposit. Unlike John Steinbeck and John Dos Passos, however, Maddux's fiction of this period is marked by the high spirits of young people who take pride in surviving hard times.

By the late 1930s Maddux, whose career was off to a promising start with the publication of three stories ("Turnip's Blood," "Mother of a Child," and "We Are Each Other's Children") in *Story* magazine, was the center of a group of aspiring writers who met at her apartment at 16 West Forty-third

Street in Kansas City. One of them, Kansas City journalist Martin Quigley, recalls in *Mr. Blood's Last Night* (1980) that this gathering was "the only Bohemia in town," and he remembers Maddux as a "beautiful Junoesque young woman," a "reclusive mystic" who was "wise and gifted." Quigley's characterization of Maddux as gifted is borne out by the description in her autobiography of a difficult childhood in which her searching questions about the world around her were met with perfunctory answers.

Communication is a remarkable autobiography in several ways. Written in the form of a letter to a man whom Maddux had met in California, it is a candid account of her attempt since early childhood to find someone who could understand and accept her on her own terms – who could see, as she puts it, her "Rachelness." Convinced that every person and object had its own essence, yet that no one understood her own, she grew up in an isolation that was compounded by mysterious back problems and blackouts. By the age of ten she was certain that the latter (much later diagnosed as petit mal) were triggered by certain fears and were a sign of approaching insanity, and she set out systematically to eradicate all emotion from her life, to become pure intellect, and was so successful that by the time she realized that "in life, even as in literature, the *plot* is *not* the thing," she had to relearn how to experience feeling. Many of the themes and concerns in *Communication* are reflected in Maddux's later work, and indeed, despite its air of utter honesty, Maddux reminds one of the autobiographer's ability to shape rather than simply record a life when she writes at the outset, "It is my privilege to do myself justice." With the exception of *The Green Kingdom,* most of Maddux's fiction is highly autobiographical, and her commitment to honesty ("a mind that could not fool itself," as she put it), individuality, and creativity were hallmarks of her life as they are of her work.

Maddux completed *Communication* a few months before her marriage to King Baker in January of 1942. The manuscript of *The Green Kingdom* traveled with her as she embarked on the peripatetic life of a serviceman's wife before settling in southern California when Baker was sent overseas in 1944. Nearly twenty years elapsed between the time Maddux began *The Green Kingdom* and its publication in 1957; added to the sheer scope and complexity of the novel were the uncertainties of wartime, the need to support herself while Baker was overseas, and, when he returned, the couple's frustration at repeated denials of Baker's security clearance for a

Maddux in Kansas, August 1941

job in electronics during the McCarthy era. The plot of the novel brings together a well-known composer, Justin Magnus, and two young couples he meets while on a concert tour of the Midwest during the Depression. Eventually, following the suicide of Justin's wife and his own subsequent long illness, the five follow his grandfather's map to find a hidden world beneath a western mountain, to which access is allowed only every ten years. Here, as the only human beings in a world otherwise richly populated with strange plants and animals, they attempt to accommodate themselves to the environment and, less successfully, to living in close proximity to one another. Thus, in addition to working within the utopian tradition, Maddux also makes use of the ancient "ship of fools" device of isolating a group of people so that they must work through whatever conflicts their differing beliefs and personalities create.

The sole survivor of this experience is Erma Herrick (named for Maddux's older sister), who, to-

gether with Justin Magnus, represents the force of creativity in the novel. Though not a publicly recognized artist, Erma has a natural talent for drawing and sculpture; moreover, she is the figure of the nurturing female and is the character who adapts most readily to this strange green world, naming and taming its animals. Fittingly, at the end of the novel she chooses to remain in the Green Kingdom, pregnant with Justin's child. In addition to expressing Maddux's belief in the power of creativity and generativity to counter what by the early 1950s seemed an increasingly arid and hostile world, the novel affords some insights into her methods of writing. *The Green Kingdom* is in four parts which correspond to the four movements of a symphony by the same name that Justin Magnus is composing during the course of the novel. In fact, as Maddux explains in notes accompanying the manuscript, the music preceded the words of the novel; that is, for this as for others of her works (most notably *A Walk in the Spring Rain*) Maddux first heard a musical score (which she regretted lacking the skills to write down) and then wrote a narrative to represent the tone and mood of the music. Also Maddux's practice of keeping a detailed journal that she called the "Record" is reflected in the project in which Arthur Herrick and Joe Roberts are engaged early in the novel: creating a "Human Record" by encouraging ordinary people to write down the details of their daily lives.

Maddux's increasing reliance on her own journal to provide material for her published work gives her fiction after *The Green Kingdom* a decidedly autobiographical character, and her last book published during her lifetime, *The Orchard Children* (1977), was published as nonfiction. At the same time, she began to devote her work more and more to specific social issues about which she had deep convictions. Her second novel, *Abel's Daughter* (1960), is based closely on her actual experience of living in Occoquan, Virginia, while Baker was stationed at Fort Belvoir during the early 1940s, and this account of a friendship between a white woman and a black woman is an eloquent plea for racial tolerance.

As her autobiography attests, Maddux's belief in the inherent dignity of all individuals in spite of racial or other differences developed early in her life, as did her conviction that the written word could be a powerful instrument for social justice. While still a small child, she wrote to the governor of Kansas, asking him to pardon a man who had stolen chickens to feed his children; when the man was pardoned, she realized that "this writing . . . is a serious thing, and not to be fooled around with."

Maddux with Savington Crampton in Washington, D.C., February 1943 (courtesy of Nancy A. Walker)

Later, as a student in high school, she came to the defense of a friend who was being accused of being a homosexual, risking the ostracism of her peers. The young army wife whom Maddux names Molly Demerest in *Abel's Daughter* is similarly innocent of prejudice when she and her husband move to a sharply segregated southern town, and despite ample evidence that she is doing the "wrong" thing in the eyes of the white townspeople, Molly chooses to shop at the grocery story run by a black man, Abel Loftis. She also meets and befriends Abel's daughter, Serena, a divorced woman with two children. The relationship between Molly and Serena becomes an oasis of human caring amid stark reminders of racial prejudice, which is exemplified most memorably by Lee Carter Higgins, who prides himself on the restoration of his ancestral plantation, where slaves were bred for sale.

Yet despite its serious message *Abel's Daughter* is far from being a grim book, in part because Maddux is careful to depict the small but significant ways in which the black residents of the town maintain their self-esteem by retaliating against racial prejudice. It is Abel Loftis's custom, for example, to present his customers with gifts of canned goods when they pay their bills; to Molly, whom he admires, he gives fruit cocktail, but to a woman who is

openly haughty toward him he presents a can of kidney beans. And Molly and her husband understand only when they are leaving that their black friends have sought to protect them from ostracism by the white residents by deliberately failing to acknowledge their relationships in public. The novel also has flashes of the same kind of playful humor that characterizes many of Maddux's short stories. For instance, Molly and her husband name certain pieces of furniture after their landlord's descriptions of them, so that a desk is known as "Nothing Elaborate" and a dresser as "Halfway Decent."

At the time Maddux wrote *Abel's Daughter* in the mid 1950s, she and King Baker were living in the Los Angeles area, where they had settled after World War II; by the time it was published in 1960, they had made their final move — to one hundred acres of land in Houston County, Tennessee, where Baker fulfilled his dream of starting an apple orchard. The land was part of a five-hundred-acre tract that Maddux's friend from Kansas City days, Katherine Brown, and her husband George had bought a few years before and named "Green Kingdom Acres" in honor of Maddux's first novel. It was here that Wiltshire met Maddux in the late 1970s, unwittingly becoming an important link in

Maddux, King Baker, and their adopted daughter, Melissa, in King County, Tennessee, November 1967 (courtesy of Nancy A. Walker)

the chain of events that could eventually lead to the rediscovery of this remarkable author in the 1990s.

Although Maddux continued to write short stories (and had begun work on a play at the time of her death), the last entry published during her lifetime was "Clay Pigeon," which appeared in the *Toronto Star Weekly* in October of 1959. Relieved to have left behind the freeway traffic and professional rat race of Los Angeles, Maddux and Baker set about learning the features of their rural environment. As Baker established the orchard, Maddux began raising Nubian goats and wrote to friends about her delight in gathering watercress in a creek. These and other elements of the Tennessee hills found their way into Maddux's short, lyrical novel *A Walk in the Spring Rain,* which is set in West Virginia perhaps in part to mask the autobiographical elements that were causing gossip in Houston County. *A Walk in the Spring Rain* invites comparison with Robert James Waller's 1992 novel *The Bridges of Madison County.* Both novels tell of brief but trans-

formative relationships between people of radically different backgrounds; both authors avoid the sentimentality with which a less-skilled writer might infuse such a story.

Ingrid Bergman, who had admired Maddux's previous work as well, was eager to play the part of Libby Meredith when the novel was filmed in 1969; she, like the reviewers of the novel, was pleased that Maddux had so compellingly acknowledged a middle-aged woman's capacity for passionate involvement. In the film, which premiered in Knoxville, Tennessee, in the spring of 1970, Anthony Quinn played Will Workman, the backwoods handyman with whom Libby, the wife of a professor on sabbatical, falls in love. More than merely a love story, however, the novel depicts a sophisticated woman learning to appreciate the more straightforward amenities of rural life – which include Will Workman's gentle, unconditional love. Perhaps inevitably, Maddux was extremely disappointed in the film version of her novel, despite Bergman's sensitive portrayal of Libby and her own involvement as a consultant for the project. The adaptation from page to screen removed what Maddux regarded as the "music" of her narrative. As a film adaptation of a novel, however, *A Walk in the Spring Rain* became a case study with the publication of Neil D. Isaacs's *Fiction into Film* in 1970; the volume contains the text of the novel, the filmscript, and an account of the stages of production.

In the early 1960s, before either the publication or the filming of *A Walk in the Spring Rain*, Maddux and her husband had a series of experiences that became the basis for her book *The Orchard Children.* Whereas *Abel's Daughter* had been marketed as a novel despite its acknowledged basis in fact, *The Orchard Children,* though in some ways a more deliberately shaped narrative, was presented as nonfiction – and then, somewhat ironically, achieved the status of fiction when it was developed into a made-for-television movie titled *Who'll Save Our Children?* by CBS in 1978. In both forms the story is an indictment of a court system which, in adoption and custody cases, seems not to have the welfare of the child as its highest priority.

As Maddux's autobiography and her story "Mother of a Child" attest, she had since childhood wanted to have children, but a combination of circumstances (including her erratic health) had precluded motherhood, and there is no evidence that Maddux and Baker had actively pursued adoption before the 1960s. But when the grandmother of two young children prevailed upon them to take care of the children, whose parents were separated and showed little interest in their welfare, Maddux and Baker quickly became fond of the pair and wanted to provide them with the stable home that no one in their biological family seemed able or willing to provide. The court, however, refused to remove custody from the hastily – and temporarily – reunited parents, despite the opinion of social service agencies that the children would be better off living at the orchard.

It took Rachel Maddux a long time to write *The Orchard Children* for several reasons. One of these was the need to achieve some emotional distance from a painful experience. Another, happier reason was that shortly after the loss of what she would call the "orchard children," Maddux and Baker did adopt an infant girl whose mother had heard about their caring for these two, and she called to say that she could not keep her daughter. The third reason has to do with the fact that Maddux and Baker were considered outsiders whose liberal sociopolitical views did not endear them to some of their Houston County neighbors. Maddux, along with Katherine Brown, had worked with a black Girl Scout troop there and had suffered the same sorts of threats and hostility that she had depicted as resulting from racial interaction in Virginia twenty years earlier. It is difficult to know how much these attitudes had to do with the local court's decision about the "orchard children," but Maddux later told friends that she had to wait to write the book until she could decide which experiences of that period to leave out of it. The result is an account that is deeply poignant when it deals with the children but that portrays Maddux and Baker's lives in Tennessee in a generally positive manner.

Maddux's fiction has been compared to that of southern writers such as Eudora Welty and Truman Capote; other readers have noted that her work has a midwestern quality. While it is true that *Abel's Daughter* evokes the social attitudes of the South and *A Walk in the Spring Rain* reflects her residence in Tennessee, it is important to note that her central character in each of these works is a newcomer to the area rather than someone steeped in the region's habits and customs. She disliked the regional label, and the voice and consciousness in her work seems less tied to a place than to a philosophy involving awe at the mysteries of life and the need to survive its pains and losses – to be, in the words of Justin Magnus in *The Green Kingdom,* "grappling, rather than buffeted." In a talk on writing that Maddux once gave, she described great writing as that which is done "without compromise, without concession, without apology and without fear," and, in her commitment to her own vision and her own sense of human justice, she lived up to her own high standards.

References:

Nancy Bradford, "Nature Spawns Novel for Rachel," *Nashville Tennessean,* 23 January 1966, pp. 3A, 6A;

Mary Ann Gibson, "A Look at Rachel Maddux: A Talented and Successful Author," *Tennessee Magazine* (August 1980): 10–11;

Thomas D. Lane, "Rachel Maddux," in *Critical Survey of Short Fiction,* volume 7, edited by Frank N. Magill (Englewood Cliffs, N. J.: Salem Press, 1981), p. 2708.

Papers:

Rachel Maddux's papers are housed in the special collections department of the Mugar Memorial Library at Boston University. The fourteen boxes of material contain correspondence, manuscripts, portions of her journal, and miscellaneous papers.

The Seventy-fifth Anniversary of the Armistice: The Wilfred Owen Centenary and the Great War Exhibit at the University of Virginia

Wilfred Owen: A Centenary Celebration

Charles Stiles
Wilfred Owen Association

During 1993 there was extensive celebration of the centenary of Wilfred Owen's birth (18 March 1893) and commemoration of the seventy-fifth anniversary of his death (4 November 1914). One is left with a vast, kaleidoscopic impression of people, lectures, discussions, assessments, and reassessments of Owen's work, readings, places, events, and new work all confirming the widespread interest in – and continuing influence of – the life and work of Owen.

Given that there were about one hundred known events, it is inescapable that this account has to be selective. Much of what took place was a high quality reaffirmation of the intrinsic merit of Owen's work, its influence on other poets in content and technique, its political boldness and human compassion, its literary and social context, its prompting of conduct, and its inspiration to other artistic expression in drama, poetry, music, drawing, dance, and sculpture. In choosing what to include here, priority has been given to those things which can be regarded as adding to knowledge about Owen and his work, understanding of it, and new works it has inspired.

Celebration began early. International connections were evident from the start. At the Imperial War Museum on 17 March, Sir Stephen Spender, Jon Stallworthy, and Martin Jarvis, who has acted in Los Angeles and London, combined to give a stimulating portrait and evaluation. Of the many memorable features Jarvis's reading of "Anthem for Doomed Youth" remains strongest.

In Oswestry, at the Marches School some four hundred yards from Owen's birthplace, on the evening of 18 March, the biographer and poet Stallworthy, the critic and commentator Dominic Hibberd, the poetess Patricia Beer, the actress and author Susannah York, and Poet Laureate Ted Hughes spoke about and read Owen's works. Owen's ability to give such moving expression to the human suffering he witnessed and experienced was evidenced with intelligence and feeling, the readings by the poet laureate being especially dramatic.

The morning of 19 March saw the unveiling by Peter Owen, Wilfred's nephew, of the commemorative plaque in the Broadwalk at Oswestry. It celebrates Owen as poet and includes the whole of "Anthem for Doomed Youth" and "Futility," which were read by the poet laureate to an attentive crowd.

On the evening of the same day Saint Oswald's Church, where Owen's parents married and he was baptized, was the venue for Peter Florence's *The Pity of War*. The drama is an adaptation from Owen's correspondence of the war years and twenty-nine poems and fragments. Florence's performance was most affecting, moving some to tears. Characterized by apt diction throughout his rendering of "Exposure" chillingly conveyed the merciless, scything winds of early 1917.

The year also saw performances of Nigel Boden's *Dark Star* and Stephen McDonald's *Not About Heroes*. But there was new work as well. In June *A Field Half Sown,* by Kenneth Simcox, had its

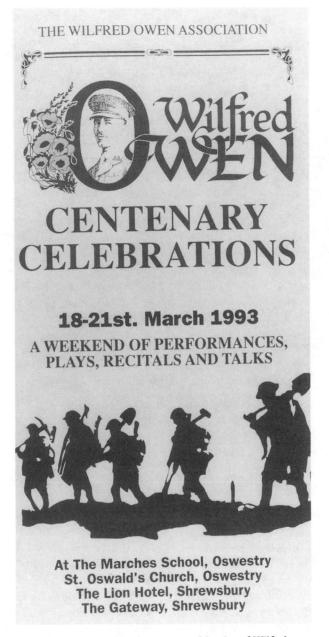

Program cover for the centenary celebration of Wilfred Owen's birth

first public performance in Saint Mary's Church, Shrewsbury.

Owen's fondness for music was recognized in the event at the Marches School. "On Wenlock Edge" (1896), A. E. Housman's words set to music by Ralph Vaughan Williams, was handsomely sung by Michael Bennett accompanied by a quintet from the Royal Northern College of Music. During the March weekend there was also an evening of English song of World War I. Stephen Banfield, Elgar Professor of Music at Birmingham University, accompanied the tenor John Potter. A range of emotion arose from the songs for soldiers, those written in a spirit of patriotism, and songs by those who died.

Throughout the year there were many performances of Benjamin Britten's *War Requiem* (1962), which incorporates nine of Owen's poems into the Latin requiem. But there were also new settings of Owen's work to music. David Grundy's setting of "The Parable of the Old Man and the Young" was performed in June at Saint Mary's Church, Shrewsbury, in June and again at the abbey in November. The English Song and Poetry Society held a competition in which composers were invited to set any of

Ted Hughes, British poet laureate, reading Owen's poetry at Oswestry, England, 18 March 1993 (photograph courtesy of Charles Stiles)

Owen's poems to music. Performances and adjudication in Birkenhead, where the Owens lived for some ten years, resulted in a setting of "Futility" being placed first.

There were many new pictures stimulated by Owen's work. Laurent Lourson's calligrams dramatically emphasize Owen's message, one of the strongest being "The Pity of War" with its tortured face and imprinted hand trapped by barbed wire. Woodcuts by Nicholas Parry reinforce the starkness of Owen's descriptions. Parry's representation of "The Soldier's Dream" is both powerful and haunting. A pencil drawing by Thelma Ayre merges the encumbered sleepers of "Strange Meeting" with the rock of its profound tunnel. As the dead soldier enters, it is a forlorn place without apparent exit.

"Symmetry," Paul de Monchaux's granite sculpture, is also informed by ideas from "Strange Meeting." Commissioned by the association and installed in the grounds of Shrewsbury Abbey, it bears the quotation, "I am the enemy you killed my friend." "Symmetry" presents many images. Some see it as a representation of a pontoon Owen may have used in his fatal attempt to cross the Sambre-Oise canal. Others consider it to reflect trenches and duckboards. Equally it can appear as parapets and bridges.

The common features of these perceptions are attempts at communication, efforts to reach through, over, and across the divisions of war. The very symmetry of the sculpture reminds one that the terror of war, its pains, agonies, and anguish are the same from whichever side they may be viewed. Yet the sculpture also serves as a bench offering literal as well as figurative support for those who pause to reflect.

Three new books on the life and work of Owen were published in 1993. In *Wilfred Owen Poet and Soldier* one of Helen McPhail's aims is to make it possible to follow Owen's movements in France with accuracy. McPhail's robust narrative is strong enough to carry the reader through the demanding and punishing terrain of wartime troop movement. Links are made between place, the details of military history, and Owen's experiences during its making. The merits of this kind of exploration are plain when it is shown that Lt. Hubert Gaukroger's death can not have been as Owen described it. Owen's mistaken account, it is suggested, could well reflect emerging confusion of mind.

The account of events on the Sambre-Oise canal, where Owen was fatally wounded, show similar attention to detail and a matter-of-fact approach yet are given successful, imaginative treatment, as in the prelude, which captures noise, confusion, tension, danger, and apprehension. The informed background of events and place, together with landscape description, enables a perspective which helps show Owen more clearly than accounts which rely only on generalizations about the front line.

Merryn Williams's *Wilfred Owen* (Seren) begins with a brief biography and moves quickly to poetry. A new suggestion is made about the origin of Owen's pararhyme. Attention is drawn to Kathleen E. Royds's book, *Elizabeth Barrett Browning and Her Poetry,* a copy of which was given to Owen at Christmas 1912 by Clyde Black. In that book there is a discussion of Browning's use of "peculiar rime," and mention is made of her "generous large souled championship of the down trodden and the injured." Using this and other evidence, Merryn Williams concludes that Browning was not only the source of Owen's pararhyme but that she also influenced him to "break with his old style of writing and to speak his mind about the war."

Of the elegant essays on many of the poems that on "The Send Off" anticipates some of the thinking in the book's last section, "Breaking Ranks." Here there is illumination of Owen's attitude toward women, which will need to be taken into account in any future discussion of Owen's sexual orientation. Owen's influences on poets and artists responding to later wars — World War II, Vietnam, the Falklands, and the Gulf War — are sensitively chronicled. One is left with an overall sense of freshness from this well-balanced, informed, and informative book, written with insight and understanding in prose which is easily accessible.

Douglas Kerr's *Wilfred Owen's Voices* (Clarendon Press) details the life of Owen's language. Taking as its starting points the four communities of family, church, army, and previous English poets, differences in the use of language by these communities — their discourses — are indicated. While the strands may be teased out, Kerr is firm in asserting that the interaction of the strands is as important as the strands themselves.

It is Kerr's view that Owen's writing is at its most interesting when two or more discourses are present. An outstanding and extensive illustration of this view is given in Kerr's discussion of the relationship between officers and other ranks. Conventionally, one sees much of Owen's poetry and correspondence as a plea and protest on behalf of sol-

diers who are unable or not allowed to speak for themselves. One example is "The Parable of the Old Man and the Young." But Kerr reminds one that subalterns were the immediate voice of authority to other ranks. They gave orders. They could order field punishments. These included the power to order offenders to be bound to fixed objects by straps, irons, or ropes, just as Abraham binds Isaac in the poem. The fact of being an officer inescapably casts Owen in the role of Abraham. Against this background Owen shares guilt with those he reproaches. Kerr sees in the parable not only plea and protest but also self-reproach. The "dark side of an officer's responsibility was guilt."

Here there is a combination of discourse which is military in several senses and religious at both a public and personal level as well as the voice of social protest. The tensions generated between authoritative discourse — the power to command and punish — in a military setting and the compassionate discourse of Christianity, again authoritative, create the unique language of the poem and extend the discourse into political and personal domains.

These books have different approaches. McPhail's particular emphasis is topographical. Williams explores the affective domain. Kerr's approach gives one a map of Owen's language and the communities from which it sprang. Together they combine to give an enlarged understanding of Owen's life and work. Each of these books has original aspects. That this can still be so is a measure of the complexity of Owen as an individual, the questions and issues he posed, and their continuing relevance.

There was much else besides in this anniversary year. There were commemorative services in Saint Oswald's Church, Oswestry; the abbey at Shrewsbury; and in Uffington Church. Explorations were made of Owen landscapes — at Broxton, where he said his poethood was born, and Haughmond Hill, with its commanding outlook across the Severn toward Shrewsbury — as well as a journey through those parts of Flanders in which Owen fought, culminating in a visit to Ors, where Owen is buried.

There is much that will endure. The new studies, the original expressions of some poems, and the fresh works in other art forms will continue to stimulate interest in the ideas Owen was so concerned to convey. But the anniversary year has confounded one of Owen's assertions. Concluding "Miners," he wrote despairingly

"But they will not dream of us poor lads,
Left in the ground."

That has proved to be mistaken. There has been much thought of those lost in the ground, especially

Owen and the still-challenging legacy of his thinking.

Anyone who would like to learn more about Wilfred Owen Association and how to join can write to Charles Stiles, Bodawel, Trefonen, Oswestry, Shropshire SY10 9DQ United Kingdom.

The Great War Exhibit
at the University of Virginia Library

Edmund Berkeley
Alderman Library, The University of Virginia

The University of Virginia Library observed the seventy-fifth anniversary of the end of World War I with a major exhibition entitled The Great War: An Exhibit Commemorating the Seventy-fifth Anniversary of the Armistice Ending World War I and Honoring the Joseph M. Bruccoli Great War Collection in Alderman Library's McGregor Room and Stettinius Gallery cases from 11 November 1993 through 28 February 1994.

The Joseph M. Bruccoli Great War Collection is the library's major collection of books, posters, sheet music, soldiers' letters, memorabilia, photographs, and other material about World War I. With the encouragement of John Cook Wyllie, then the university librarian, Dr. Matthew J. Bruccoli established the collection in 1965 to honor his father, a veteran of the war who participated in many of its major battles.

A 1968 exhibition of materials from the collection, on the fiftieth anniversary of the Armistice, displayed novels and books of poetry from World War I. The 1993 exhibition emphasized other areas of the Bruccoli Collection – and included material from the library's Special Collections Department's general collections – to demonstrate the breadth of the library's holdings relating to World War I. While much of the material shown in the exhibition reflected the United States and its people, the Joseph M. Bruccoli Great War Collection includes material from Great Britain, France, Australia, and other nations involved in the war, and some of these items were on display.

The Armistice ending the Great War occurred at 11:00 A.M. on the eleventh day of the eleventh

The cover for the catalogue of the University of Virginia exhibition reproduced the Joseph Pennell Liberty Bond poster.

month, 1918, and the exhibit concentrated on material about the end of the war and the work that went on in France and elsewhere to conclude America's involvement. Vast stores of ammunition, vehicles, weapons, and supplies had to be collected from the battlefields, storehouses, supply dumps, and the like, to be checked, cleaned, repaired, packed, and shipped home. The men and women of the military forces and support services had to be fed and kept busy until there were spaces on board ships for them to sail home.

The exhibition was divided into topics that emphasized strengths of the Bruccoli Collection. These included Newspapers Published by Military Units, Movies About the Great War, After the War, and Treasures – a section that included Joseph M. Bruccoli's campaign medal with eight bars, an essay about World War I written by James Dickey for the exhibition, and the Joseph Pennell Liberty Loan poster reproduced as the exhibition poster and catalogue cover. Other sections were Artists and Cartoonists, General Pershing, and Personal Accounts – which included samples from the Bruccoli Collection of its large number of published autobiographies and reminiscences by soldiers, sailors, and airmen of many countries about their experiences during the Great War. Some original material – letters, documents, and photographs – was shown.

Photography, both motion and still pictures, was extensive during World War I. The governments involved had crews on the battlefield taking both types, and still photographs were published in newspapers and magazines as well as in books. The department's regular collections include a good many books of photographs taken during the war, and the Joseph M. Bruccoli Great War Collection is especially rich in books of this type. These materials were represented in a section of the exhibition titled Pictorial Histories, and with stills from movies in the section called Movies About the Great War.

The moment of the Armistice was one that all who experienced it in the trenches and elsewhere never forgot. In the exhibition there was a section entitled The Armistice that included manuscript and printed items in which were recorded the feelings of persons in France at the hour of the Armistice. Also included was a recording from a recording machine that demonstrated graphically the silence that fell on the battlefield as the guns ceased firing.

A section of the exhibition called Memorabilia and Treasures included such items as war savings stamps; a set of cigarette cards bearing likenesses of winners of Great Britain's highest military award, the Victoria Cross; a set of children's alphabet blocks with patriotic drawings; and picture postcards, stereopticon views, lapel pins, and the like. The Bruccoli Collection's strength in the area of flight was shown in a section titled Aviation that included firsthand accounts by those who participated in this new type of warfare.

Unspeakable Practices II: The Festival of Vanguard Narrative at Brown University

by John Foley

What happens when avant-gardes collide?

A collision took place during 24–27 February 1993 at a Festival of Vanguard Narrative in Providence, Rhode Island, sponsored by Brown University's Program in Creative Writing. But collisions produce accelerations in new directions as well as wreckage, even (to raise this metaphor above the mechanical) transformations. The clash at the festival was chiefly between everyone there who writes with a pen or a typewriter and the new personal-computer technology called hypertext that threatens to make pen, paper, and book obsolete. (Typewriters are already obsolescent.)

Few of the attendees were prepared for this. Although the four-day agenda prominently featured hypertext show-and-tell sessions, it consisted mostly of familiar ingredients. Readings alternated with panel debates and mixed-media events, including films, electronic music, and an ongoing exhibit of paper art. Accent was on the radically new, especially, in keynote speaker Ronald Sukenick's words, "writing that does not make money." One small-press publisher of such writing, The Fiction Collective Two, was especially honored, and one current of the radically new was celebrated under the name *avant-pop*. With a bow toward the old new, the festival, called Unspeakable Practices II, also cast a backward glance at a 1988 festival named Unspeakable Practices. The earlier festival brought together such postmodern writers as John Hawkes, William Gaddis, William H. Gass, Stanley Elkin, Toby Olson, Jonathan Baumbach, and Donald Barthelme. Both festivals were organized by Robert Coover, author of *The Public Burning* (1977), *A Night at the Movies* (1987), and *Pinocchio in Venice* (1991), among other titles. He has also for many years taught literature and creative writing at Brown and other universities.

The news, however, was hinted by the first evening's "overture" speaker. Michael Joyce, author of a novel, *The War Outside Ireland* (1982), as well as the best-known and admired hypertext narrative *Afternoon* and the new hyperfiction *WOE*,

read from two sections of an essay entitled "A Feel for Prose: Interstitial Links and the Contours of Hypertext." The first "contour" spoke movingly of the sensual experience of turning and reading the pages of a book; the second of reading a hypertext narrative on the radiant screen of a personal computer. He left it at that, yielding the lectern to keynoters Sukenick and Kathy Acker; but next morning the first hypertext show-and-tell was packed.

Hypertext is a form of interactive writing composed for viewing on a personal computer screen. Whether narrative or discursive, it is characterized by blocks of text (usually no more than one screen long) which follow one another in no fixed sequence but are linked by embedded electronic commands (often working through word or phrase associations, or even sounds or graphics) which, at the reader's option, can be activated to improvise any order the reader wishes to follow. The author may create the texts and links and limit the network (or "web") of possible reading paths, but the reader creates, and may continually re-create, the structure. In some hyperfiction narratives and scholarly hypertext webs, the reader may also create or revise texts and links as well. In development for over thirty years, available during the last ten, and evolving by the month, hypertext is a classic instance of the impact of new technology on art.

It was at the first show and tell that Joyce announced flatly that the book is dead. The tyranny of the linear is broken. The hierarchical author-reader relationship is overthrown and revolutionized into something more than "democratic." This was a bit much for all the print writers present, otherwise ideologically predisposed in favor of revolution and overthrow. Avant-gardes, historically, have aligned themselves with revolutionary political movements (right-wing as well as left-wing). *Avant,* after all, means "out in front" on one wing or other of the conventional. Avant-gardes tend also, as Renato Poggioli observed, to push irrationally toward their own overthrow (or, more positively,

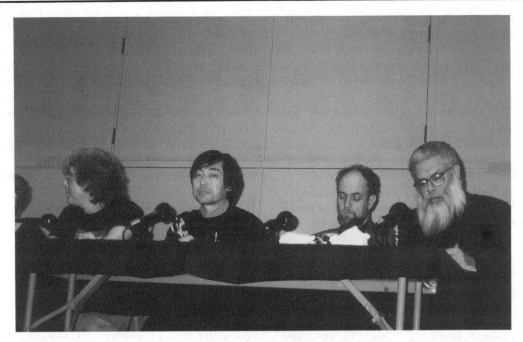

From left, Larry McCaffery, Takayuki Tatsumi, Michael Joyce, and Samuel Delany during the "Storming the Reality Studio" panel discussion (photograph courtesy of Takayuki Tatsumi)

self-transcendence), in part as a kind of sacrifice-offering to future avant-gardes.

But here was something else. The print writers present were not just being told they were old hat, obsolete, irrelevant (especially hard to take for the young ones hearing it), they were being told that even if they climbed back out of the dustbin, went into debt to acquire, say, a Macintosh and hypertext software, what they wrote would no longer be theirs alone. This, more than nonsequential structuring of *lexia* (blocks of text), was the heart of the change. Hypertext empowers the reader as much if not more than the writer. It creates a situation which not only lets the reader manipulate elements of the story the writer has written into different shapes the writer has not determined. Ultimately it lets the reader erase and rewrite (in hypertext lingo, *replace*) those elements and transform the writer's story utterly. It was this that brought howls of protest and scorn. It also brought everyone back, again and again, to pack the show-and-tells and learn more. Hands-on experience of hypertext was also provided at various personal computers in Brown's Center for Innovative Technology.

The key idea stressed by Joyce and his colleagues was network. In the most advanced hypertext environment, the familiar (one-way) author-reader dialogue of the book is replaced by a several-ways multiple dialogue (or "polylogue") of several readers with the author and with one another, each making his/her own "contour" of the narrative texts, even rewriting some or all of them (or changing the rules of the game encrypted in the electronic links between lexia), and communicating what they have done with electronic-mail messages flashed around a common network.

The show-and-tells were conducted in a kind of polylogue with the attendees by Joyce and his fellow hypertext authors Carolyn Guyer (*Quibbling*), Robert Arellano (*RABYD*), Alvin Lu (*Bobby Doubleday*), and John McDaid (*Uncle Buddy's Phantom Funhouse*), as well as Mark Bernstein of Eastgate Systems (Civilized Software, 134 Main Street, Watertown, Massachusetts, 02172). Bernstein is the publisher of *Afternoon, Quibbling,* and Stuart Moulthrop's *Victory Garden* ("the new bench mark in hyperfiction," according to Coover), as well as of the software, Storyspace, on which all these hypertext narratives have been composed. (Storyspace is currently available for Macintosh computers only, but will be available for IBM-compatible Windows by the end of 1994.) Another key participant was Prof. George Landow, author of the hypertext nonfiction *Dickens Web* and *"In Memoriam" Web,* as well as of *Hypertext: The Convergence of Contemporary Critical Theory and Technology* (1992).

As part of the effort to introduce hypertext to the uninitiated, Coover staged the first full evening of readings to simulate a hypertext environment for a large audience. In Brown's darkened Grant Recital Hall an overhead projector cast the texts of a computer screen on a large movie screen. Joyce actually did his own reading from the big screen as Coover clicked random lexia from *Afternoon*. Word-processed introductions to the other readers were similarly projected, as the order of readings, one after another, was also clicked at random. Ideally the print texts would have been projected, too, with the reading voices disembodied. Technical difficulties prevented this fuller experience, but audience attention bouncing back and forth from screen to spotlighted reader provided a rough analogy to the engagement and estrangement involved in reading hypertext.

(Coover, who has conducted hypertext fiction workshops, and is himself the author of such well-known proto-hypertext stories as "The Babysitter" and "Beginnings," has published in the *New York Times Book Review* the most lucid brief introduction to hypertext – "Hyperfiction: Novels for the Computer" – I have read to date, including thumbnail reviews of *Afternoon, Quibbling, Victory Garden,* and other hypertext fictions available to the public.)

Hypertext and all the questions it raised became the sensation of the festival, but it also highlighted the other big issues: what is new? and where does it get published? The exhibit of paper art curated by Pilar Coover provided a concrete symbolic link between the advent of hypertext and the ongoing evolutions of innovative fiction on the printed page. In the midst of the constructs and photographs of Johanna Drucker, David Baumbach, Florence Ormezzano, Dennis Ashbaugh, and others, the witty deconstructive artifacts of "Norman Conquest" (Derek Pell), and the Xerox pop-ups of Edin Velez was wheeled a dark metal box containing William Gibson's *Agrippa (A Book of the Dead)* (1993). This text, designed by Gibson and Dennis Ashbaugh, is truly post-Gutenberg, post-McLuhan, indeed postliterate. Under pages of letters making up DNA code combinations but no words and copper etchings and ancient advertisements whose ink comes off on the page turner's fingers there lies embedded a computer disk which, when retrieved on a personal computer, erases Gibson's story (about his father) as it scrolls, a little too quickly, past the reader's eyes. This "Book of the Dead" seems to anticipate not only the death of the book but the death of the computer as well. Elaborate prank that *Agrippa* is – celebratory and nihilistic at once – it signals the mutual penetration of the literary avant-garde and the cyberpunk movement of science fiction. Science fiction has always focused on the

human impact of advanced technology. Cyberpunk, which emerged in the early 1980s, crossed advanced computer technology with the subversive energy of punk rock and underground comic books, mixed in the familiar *Star Wars* motif pitting outlaw rebels against an Evil Empire, and sang it all in prose owing as much to William Burroughs, Dashiell Hammett, and Thomas Pynchon as to Isaac Asimov and Robert Heinlein. Gibson is author of the definitive cyberpunk trilogy: *Neuromancer* (1984), *Count Zero* (1986), and *Mona Lisa Overdrive* (1988).

Although he was unable to attend the festival, Gibson was invoked frequently enough to seem a distinct presence all the same. For good reason. The avant-garde group, or vector, that crystallized at the festival owes much to cyberpunk. Larry McCaffery, who named the vector, has written extensively about cyberpunk and postmodern fiction and edited a casebook on the two entitled *Storming the Reality Studio* (1991). A professor of English at San Diego State University, McCaffery has also edited a new anthology, *Avant-Pop: Fiction for a Daydream Nation* (Fiction Collective Two, 1993), from galleys of which several writers at the Festival performed readings. Avant-pop caught fire as a very sharp name for all the tendencies converging at Unspeakable Practices II.

The term *avant-pop* is not wholly new, having first appeared in a Lester Bowie jazz album. But McCaffery and Sukenick developed the concept from perception of a cultural phenomenon into a stance toward that phenomenon with a definite political edge. The cultural phenomenon, as McCaffery has written (with Takayuki Tatsumi), is "the growing popular acceptance of art whose radical formal features would previously have likely relegated it to the fringes of public awareness." Andy Warhol, Laurie Anderson, the Sex Pistols, cyberpunks, David Lynch, Burroughs, Sonic Youth, and Mark Leyner are all "artists of genuinely 'underground', or 'avant-garde', aesthetic sensibilities who during the 1980s were very much 'aboveground', in terms of popularity." Avant-pop artists, says McCaffery to Mark Amerika in a unpublished interview, "have nearly all grown up inside the Pop-Cultural realm of the Postmodern [and most] appreciate and even love many aspects of Pop Culture."

But not all of it. Pop culture also tends to "banalize and distort our relationship to the real" – MTV being the easy example. Blame is laid, in part, upon multinational corporate capital, seen to manipulate the explosive innovations in telecommunications technology to increase its own power at the expense of the people, while distracting them with electronic bread and circuses. McCaffery even speaks of pop culture as "colonizing" the unconscious as well as every day consciousness, especially sexual desires. Avant-pop marks a rebellion against these tendencies in pop culture, an active resistance attacking it on its own ground. This resistance demonstrates a strong thematic link with cyberpunk, whose rebel heroes appropriate and turn against the "Empire" the very tools it uses to suppress and dehumanize them. As Sukenick says in the *Nation*, avant-pop is a "new move to turn hypercapitalist mass culture against itself." In this respect, the writers of both avant-pop and of hypertext at Unspeakable Practices II share the concern about political control of the new technology.

How then (in McCaffery's appropriation of a Burroughs phrase) to "storm the reality studio and retake the universe?" The first step appears to be, for avant-pop artists, to retake from the pop imperialists their own imaginations. The *Avant-Pop* anthology collects early mixed-media dispatches from that combat zone. NB: sexual renunciation is not in the order of battle.

Sex and violence – from Eurudice's short film *f/32*, a visual tease from her novel of the same name (1990), to Acker's reading from *My Mother: Demonology* (1993) to Doug Rice's "Of Lightening and Disordered Souls" (a cut from the *Avant-Pop* anthology, which demonstrates just how weird, and weirdly funny, sex and violence can get) – the festival was full of them, and a bizarre sense of farce, too. They infected even the non-avant-pop crowd, writers as diverse as Paul Auster, Diane Williams, Curtis White, Patrick Comiskey, Elizabeth Searle, Elizabeth MacKiernan, David Matlin, Craig Padawer, Ben Marcus, Paul Di Filippio, Mary Caponegro, David Baumbach, and Siri Hustvedt. Which suggests that what Harold Jaffe likes to call the "sex guerillas" of avant-pop at the festival (among them Eurudice, Acker, Rice, Samuel R. Delany, Rob Hardin, Pell, Ben Marcus, Ricardo Cortez Cruz, and Amerika) were already winning hearts and minds.

Still, avant-pop describes not so much a self-conscious, self-elected group like the futurists, surrealists, or the Beat Generation, as a vector: a swarming of similar perceptions, a shock of mutual recognition, a thrusting, in response, in many different directions. It was McCaffery the editor, not the writers and artists themselves, who conferred the name on the pieces in the anthology, nor did he suggest they were exclusive or exhaustive. One big influence on the book, for instance, was David Blair's feature-length videographic "docudrama," *WAX; or, the Discovery of Television among the Bees,* an epic of twentieth-century war from the point of view of Mesopotamian bees, who happen to be the reincarnated souls of all the war dead from 1914 to 1991. Even before the book came out the concept of avant-pop was international, having won a good deal of attention in Japan in 1992, thanks to McCaffery's friend Tatsumi, critic and introducer of cyberpunk to that country. (Both Tatsumi and Blair attended Unspeakable Practices II, where *Wax* received its large-screen premiere.)

Notwithstanding avant-pop, there was much debate at the festival as to whether it is useful at all to speak of an avant-garde in the postpostmodern world. Marc Chénetier, a leading French postmodern critic, considered the whole notion out of date. What counts, in his view, is the quality of the work done, its mastery of language, regardless of subject, style, or writing technology. By choosing the less common, less flamboyant English "vanguard" to characterize the festival, Coover himself seemed to shun the glamor of the French term, to get to the heart of the matter: new kinds of writing. Sukenick preferred "innovative" not only because it was more precise but because it applied, not just to a particular movement but to anyone trying something new.

Sukenick – novelist [*Up* (1968), *Oat* (1973), *Blown Away* (1986)]; critic [*In Form: Digressions on the Act of Fiction* (1985)]; publisher [*American Book Review*]; and former chairman of the Coordinating Council of Literary Magazines – has written extensively about the problems of innovative writers in the American economy. His American Book Award–winning *Down and In: Life in the Underground* (1987) is a rich and lively chronicle-essay on the subject, covering four decades of literary bohemia.

Sukenick's keynote remarks at the festival, entitled "Unmaking It," expanded wryly on his observation that the avant-garde, once a poverty-electing adversary of bourgeois capitalism, has since the early 1960s become a vehicle to fame and fortune. He did not condemn this. "The sexiness of success seems almost to be replacing sex for contemporary writers, present company not always excepted." The point was to "make mental space once again for the acknowledgement of a non-profit zone, an underground, where it is allowed that the best work is often not the most popular, and like opera, museums, libraries, ballet and schools may never make money (grants agencies take note)." To make such space the avant-garde must "[alter] mainstream channels and [occupy] establishment niches, creating its own networks, using the apparatus instead of

Festival keynote speaker Ronald Sukenick (photograph courtesy of Takayuki Tatsumi)

indulging in the vendable narcissism of quixotic rebellion."

Nineteen years ago Sukenick and novelist Jonathan Baumbach (also at the festival) joined with several other writers to found such an apparatus-network, The Fiction Collective. They had all had critically acclaimed novels published by major houses but, before The Fiction Collective, could find no one to publish their new, much more experimental work. They have continued to publish with major houses as well as university presses, but their favorite work comes from the Collective: Jonathan Baumbach's *Reruns* (1974), *My Father, More or Less* (1982), and *The Life and Times of Major Fiction* (1986), as well as Sukenick's *98.6* (1975), *Long Talking Bad Conditions Blues* (1979), and *The Endless Short Story* (1986). It has also showcased a great deal of work by another lively presence at the festival, Raymond Federman, author of *Take It Or Leave It: An Exaggerated Second-hand Tale To Be Read Aloud Either Standing Or Sitting* (1976), *To Whom It May Concern* (1990), and *Double Or Nothing: A Real Fictitious Discourse* (1992). The Collective not only publishes "nonprofit" fiction but keeps in print over eighty-five titles.

Unspeakable Practices II honored The Fiction Collective for its two decades of commitment and used the occasion to feature its new venture to expand the market for "quality innovative fiction that doesn't sell." Recently reorganized and relocated from Brooklyn College to both the University of Colorado at Boulder and Illinois State University,

the Collective, rechristened Fiction Collective Two, has launched a series of mass-market–sized paperbacks at seven dollars each, called Black Ice Books. Heralding "a new generation of dissident writers in revolt," the first four titles include McCaffery's *Avant-Pop* anthology and three individual collections – Cris Mazza's *Revelation Countdown* (1993), John Shirley's *New Noir* (1993), and Amerika's *The Kafka Chronicles: A Novel* (1993) — that illustrate just how varied avant-pop can be. Sukenick's own contribution to the movement, *Doggy Bag*, is scheduled to appear as a Black Ice Book in 1994, along with Bayard Johnson's *Damned Right*, D. N. Stuefloten's *Ethiopian Exhibition*, and Delaney's legendary "unpublishable" porno/anti-porno novel *Hogg*.

Despite famous groupings, avant-garde writers are ordinarily as scattered and isolated as other writers. Unspeakable Practices II was convened, in part, to overcome isolation and introduce writers (students and visitors alike) to one another. In this, by all accounts, it was extraordinarily successful. From the formal opening, which featured the music of John Cage, through the planned events, a collective momentum gathered. Three days and four nights of provocative film and text performances, of informal symposia aided by quantities of Samuel Adams and Bass Ale, of sharply intensifying debate and keen listening and exchange, all climaxed in a festive "Last Night All-Night Unspeakable Circus." A grand finale of readings and language happenings, it was like Monday night in a comedy club with all comers (thirty to forty) taking turns at an open microphone for five minutes each. But the revels had to end and were closed appropriately by a student reading from William Shakespeare, whom he introduced as "the most innovative writer of all time."

Unspeakable Practices II did not pretend to represent all vanguard tendencies in the land, certainly not all the arts (dance and nonfilm performance arts were largley absent, not to mention architecture, for which the term *postmodern* was originally coined). It also remains to be seen how hypertext will affect avant-pop and how avant-pop will affect hypertext experimentation. But their collision should produce fascinating repurcussions.

References:

Robert Coover, "Hyperfiction: Novels for the Computer," *New York Times Book Review* (29 August 1983): 1, 8–12;

Michael Joyce, "A Feel for Prose: Interstitial Links and the Contours of Hypertext," *Writing On the Edge,* 4 (Fall 1992): 83–101;

Larry McCaffery and Takayuki Tatsumi, "Graffiti's Rainbow," *Science Fiction EYE,* no. 12 (September 1993): 43–49;

Renato Poggioli, *The Theory of the Avant-Garde*, translated by Gerald Fitzgerald (Cambridge, Mass.: Belknap Press, 1968);

Ronald Sukenick, "The N.E.A. and the Avant-Garde," *Nation* (11 October 1993): 400–401.

Guide to the Archives of Publishers, Journals, and Literary Agents in North American Libraries

Nan Bowman Albinski
Pennsylvania State University

The following guide to publishing archives was begun as an aid to my primary research into Australian literary manuscripts and letters in North American libraries. The need to establish the location of likely collections to be examined, and the absence of a comprehensive guide, gave the impetus to what was, for me, a new area of research. The list has taken considerable time to compile and has entailed some surprising discoveries. As an attempt to chart some hitherto uncharted waters, it is a beginning only; much more remains unlisted.

The guide is divided into three sections: publishers' archives, journal archives, and literary agents' archives. Of the first, the number of British archives in American repositories exceeded expectation, and acquisitions are continuing to add to their number. While these, and the archives of American publishers, are mostly held in the great research libraries on this continent, the holdings of many of the excellent smaller libraries augment them, and relevant collections are not restricted to one or two geographic areas.

Eclecticism is the hallmark of section 2, where the *New Review, Adventure Weekly,* and *Atlantic Monthly* are juxtaposed. Of such a group, the productions of Street and Smith's "fiction factory" might seem out of place. Yet these are the most ephemeral, and many a successful "literary" author began (and continued) a career of writing with them – if under an assumed name. Such journals as *Origin* or *Poetry* require no such special pleading.

The literary agents listed in section 3 are a treasure of publishing history. Their vast archives, the nexus of publisher-agent-writer relationships, are a rich field awaiting intensive research.

The following guide remains work in progress. The list as of June 1993 was made available electronically through SHARP-L, the bulletin board of the Society for the History of Authorship, Reading, and Publishing. The compilation published here represents a further six months of work. I will continue to extend and refine it; additions and corrections continue to be welcome. Ideally, the list would be maintained as a database at an institutional location, where it would be available for consultation and where additions would continue to be made. Until mid 1995 I will keep the list active, and through visits to collections to examine Australian manuscripts I hope to identify additional publishing history collections.

For each entry detailed information of location, size, period, and content of a collection have been supplied. The source of information is given in square brackets; a guide to the abbreviations used follows. The notation *[guide]* refers to a published guide to a specific library; the notation *[published index]* refers to an index for a specific archive (for example, Richard Bentley). All guides and indexes are listed in the concluding bibliography. Where materials are held in a collection under a name other than that of the heading (as is the case with many of the editors' papers), the collection name is given in parenthesis before the location. Where a single collection includes material of more than one publisher, this is indicated by a parenthetical note at the end of the entry.

I am especially indebted to Dr. Alexis Weedon, School of Media Arts, University of Luton. Many entries were identified first through access to her research on the location of British publishers' archives. Where a more readily accessible print or on-line source has been available, I have, of course, included it; only where one is absent have I identified her work (as *[HOBODS]*). Her forthcoming *Location Register* is listed in the bibliography.

My thanks to the many scholars of publishing history and manuscript librarians who contributed to the information listed – particularly, as always, the rare books and reference librarians at Pattee Library, Pennsylvania State University, who have shared their specialized knowledge with me.

SECTION ONE: PUBLISHERS' ARCHIVES

Albatross Verlag, Leipzig
HRC University of Texas: 1931–1954: a substantial collection of papers (also 2,000 volumes of Tauchnitz Editions) [guide] (also **Tauchnitz Editions**)

Alicat Bookshop, New York City
HRC, University of Texas: 1940s: correspondence [guide]

Allen & Unwin, London
(Graham Rawson, editorial adviser, drama): University of Georgia: 1913–1947: 8,199 items: correspondence, playscripts [NUCMC 84-2359]

American Book Co, New York City
Syracuse University: 1801–1964 (bulk 1900–1950): 522 linft: business records, illustrations, unpublished company history, print collection (textbooks): f/a [RLIN]

American Heritage Publishing Co, Boston
University of Oregon: 1954–1968: 3 ft: correspondence, founding and financing reports, business papers [NUCMC 76-1277]
(James Parton, publisher 1953–1970): Houghton Library, Harvard University: 1914–1986: 80 ft (206 boxes): business records, personal papers: f/a [NUCMC 74-342 / RLIN]

D. Appleton & Co, New York City
Columbia University: 1864–1933: 128 items: correspondence: f/a [NUCMC 64-1332 / RLIN]

Appleton-Century Co, Indianapolis
Indiana University: 1846–1962: 9 ft (6,249 items): author correspondence, contracts, royalty statements, galley/page proofs: f/a [NUCMC 78-294]

Ashendene Press, Bayford, Herts/London
Southern Methodist University: 1894–1935: 10 bound vols, 3 lge flat boxes, one Albion printing press: ledger books, account books, graphics, correspondence (*DLB* 112: 31, Colin Franklin, *The Ashendene Press* [1986])

Banyan Press, Pawlett, VT
Getty Library: 1946–1988: 5 linft (12 boxes): correspondence, typescripts, business records [RLIN]

W. E. Benjamin, New York City
Columbia University: 1917–1940: 14 linft (ca 4,000 items in 32 boxes & 4 vols): correspondence, mss, documents: f/a [RLIN]

Richard Bentley & Son, London
University of Illinois: 1806–1915: 29 cuft: correspondence, mss, files, ledgers [published index: Chadwyck-Healey mfm]
UCLA: 4 reels: correspondence, mss [published index: Chadwyck-Healey mfm]
Richard Bentley: Princeton University: 1794–1871: 2 folders: correspondence: f/a [guide]
The Berg Collection, NYPL: miscellaneous correspondence [published index: Chadwyck-Healey]
Houghton Library, Harvard University: 1836+: 1 bound vol: copyright agreements: name and title index bound in [guide]
(Richard Bentley 111): Temple University: 1883–1934: 113 items (1 box): correspondence (on publishing, international copyright) [RLIN]
Huntington Library: 1835–1863: 12 items: correspondence [guide]

Big Sky Press, Bolinas, CA
(Bill Berkson, publisher): University of Connecticut: ca 1960–1988: ca 30 linft: correspondence, mss, ephemera [RLIN]

Bird & Bull Press, North Hills, PA
Columbia University: 1958–1983: 1 ft (230 items & 2 boxes): correspondence, mss, proofs [RLIN]

Black Sparrow Press, Los Angeles
University of Alberta: 1966–1970: 25 ft: correspondence, manuscripts, artwork, suppressed issues, unpublished variants [ULMC]

Pennsylvania State University: 1971–1973: 18 linft: correspondence, mss, proofs: f/a [personal enquiry]

University of New Mexico: 1973–1975: 8 ft: f/a [Hinding 11,221]

(John Martin, editor): Brown University, John Hay archives: 1968–1980: 68 items: correspondence (with William Young, Sans Souci Press, Cambridge, MA): f/a [RLIN]

Black Sun Press, Paris

(Caresse Crosby, publisher): Southern Illinois University: 1912–1970: ca 27 cuft: correspondence, mss, business records (also material relating to Crosby's art gallery): f/a [NUCMC 82-252 / NIDS(US) 4.30.123]

Blanchard & Lea, Philadelphia
(see **Lea & Febiger**)

Blue Sky Press, Chicago

Newberry Library: 1900–1921: 160 items & 2 vol: correspondence, mss, sketches, business records: f/a [NUCMC 80-157]

Bobbs-Merrill, Indianapolis

Indiana University: 1885–1957: 131,056 items: correspondence (1903–1940), autobiographical questionnaires, responses to reader survey, promotional material, contracts, business records: f/a [Ash 1695 / *DLB Yearbook 1984*: 109–115]

(Angus Cameron, editor 1930s): Oral History, Columbia University: transcript, 640 leaves: [RLIN] (also **Little, Brown**)

Albert Boni Microprint

HRC, University of Texas: 1915+: archive documenting development of the microprint publishing industry [guide]

Boni & Liveright, New York City

University of Pennsylvania: 1918–1934: 566 folders (11 boxes): correspondence, mss: f/a [RLIN]

Book-of-the-Month Club

Library of Congress: 1939–1958: 23 ft: editorial and publishers' correspondence, readers' reports (mostly rejections): f/a [NUCMC 64-1558/Hinding 2,216/NIDS(US) 2.1.98]

(Robert K. Haas, cofounder): NYPL: 1911–1976: 3.6 linft: personal and professional correspondence, memorabilia: f/a [RLIN]

(Henry Scherman, cofounder): Columbia University: 1937–1969: 19,500 items: correspondence, photographs, personal papers: f/a [RLIN]

(Ralph Thompson, editor, 1951–1975): Columbia University: 1944–1956: ca 700 items (4 boxes): correspondence, readers' reports [RLIN]

(Amy Loveman, editor): Columbia University: 1935–1943: 28 items (1 box): literary correspondence: RLIN (also *Saturday Review of Literature*)

Book-of-the-Month-Club project: Columbia University: 1926–1955: transcripts, 1,099 leaves: interviews with founders, members of Selection Committee, executive and technical personnel: name/topic index available [RLIN]

Book Trades Collection

American Antiquarian Society: 1726–1939: 3 boxes, 1 folder: receipts, accounts, correspondence [RLIN]

Bookstore Press, Lenox, MA

University of Connecticut: 1967–1976: 1 file drawer: correspondence, mss, audiotapes of readings/interviews: f/a [RLIN]

R. R. Bowker & Co, New York City

Fred G. Melcher Library, company offices, 205 E 42nd St, NY, 10036: 80-drawer vertical file [Ash 1696]

(Richard Rogers Bowker): Library of Congress: 1831–1931: 2 ft: correspondence, mss: f/a [NUCMC 59-208]

(Richard Rogers Bowker): NYPL: 1856–1958: 61 linft (126 boxes): correspondence, mss, photographs, scrapbooks, family papers: part f/a [Hinding 12,395 / RLIN] (also *Harper's Magazine, Library Journal, Publishers' Weekly*)

Brentano's, New York City

(Lowell Brentano): University of Oregon: 1917–1952: 6 ft: f/a [Hinding 14,328]

Cadell & Davies, London

Duke University: 1775–1832: 87 items: business papers, correspondence [guide]

Beinecke Library, Yale University: correspondence [HOBODS]

NYPL: 1778–1831: 1 box: correspondence [guide]

Boston Public Library: 1791–1820: 27 items: correspondence: card index [HOBODS / personal enquiry]

Huntington Library: 1769–1832: 496 items: literary correspondence [guide]

Calder & Boyars, London
Indiana University: 1875–1950: 250,000 items [Ash 1695]

Capra Press, Santa Barbara
Indiana University: 1955–1983: 9,600 items: publishing records [*DLB Yearbook 1984*: 109–115]

Mathew Carey & Co, Carey & Hart, Carey & Lea, Carey, Lea & Blanchard, Philadelphia
(Mathew Carey, publisher): American Antiquarian Society: 1785–1859: 41 vol: business ledgers, invoices: f/a [RLIN] (part of collection available on mfm (3 reels) at the American Philosophical Society [RLIN])
(Edward Carey Gardiner, collector): Historical Society of Pennsylvania: 1632–1939: 32 linft: correspondence, record books, journals: f/a [RLIN] (part of collection, letterbooks 1788–1794, available on mfm [1 reel] at the American Philosophical Society)
(see **Lea & Febinger**)

Casanova Society, London
(John Rodker): HRC, University of Texas: 1923–1961: publication files, correspondence: [guide] (also *Imago,* **International Literary Agency, Pushkin Press**)

Cassell & Co, London
(see **Macmillan**)
(James A. Manson, editor): Duke University: 1897–1912: 17 items: correspondence, mss [guide]

Chatto & Windus, London
UCLA: 1861–1900: 877 items: correspondence: f/a [Ash 1695 / guide]
(F.A. Swinnerton, editor 1912–1926): University of Arkansas at Fayetteville: 1899–1964: 22 ft: correspondence, mss, clippings, scrapbooks: f/a (4 vols) [*DLB* 112: 172]

Chilmark Press, New York City
Columbia University: 1960–1976: 7 linft (ca 9,100 items in 16 boxes): correspondence, memoranda, mss, documents, photographs, illustrations: f/a [RLIN]

The Chiswick Press, London
NYPL: 1831–1933 (bulk 1870–1918): .8 linft: correspondence, financial papers, printing history,

photographs, and memorabilia: advance notice required: f/a [RLIN]

City Lights Books, San Francisco
(including the papers of Lawrence Ferlinghetti): University of California, Berkeley: 1953–1970: 13 boxes, 4 cartons: correspondence, editorial files, clippings: f/a [NUCMC 80-2249]

Colophon
(Elmer Adler, founder): Princeton University: 1651–1961 (bulk 1925–1955): 158 cuft (448 boxes, 75 vols): correspondence, business archives (Colophon, Pynson), documents, printed material: [RLIN] (also **New Colophon, Pynson Printers, Random House**)

Colt Press, San Francisco
Stanford University: 1920–1973: 3.5 linft: correspondence, business records: f/a [RLIN]

William B. Conkey Co, Chicago
(Rand McNally archive): Newberry Library: 1890s–1950: 8 boxes: correspondence, promotional materials, photographs [personal enquiry]

Constable & Co, London
Temple University: 1899–1959: 9.6 cuft (24 boxes): correspondence (10,000+), corrected proofs, typescripts, financial records: index to correspondence: [Ash 1696 / RLIN]
(Michael Sadleir, editor): Brigham Young University, Utah: 1915–1970: 1 carton (not available until processed) [RLIN]

Copeland and Day, Boston
American Antiquarian Society: 1880–1900: 2 boxes: correspondence: f/a [NUCMC 62-3209 / RLIN]
(F. Holland Day): Archives of American Art: 1858–1977: ca 1,500 items (2 mfm reels): correspondence (incl six letterpress books), photographs, Copeland and Day files, scrapbook of European travel clippings: (originals held at Norwood Historical Society, Norwood, MA) [RLIN]
(Joe Walker Kraus, historian): Princeton University: 1977–1983: 1.8 cuft: notes, photographs, correspondence [RLIN] (also **Way and Williams**)

Covici & Friede, New York City
(Donald Friede, publisher): Library of Congress: 1919–1980: 3 linft: correspondence, mss, diaries, reports, photographs: f/a [RLIN]

Coward-McCann, New York City
(Ernestine Evans, editor): Columbia University: 1939–1965: 600 items (1 box): correspondence, mss [NUCMC 70-112 / RLIN] (also **J. B. Lippincott**)

Coyote Press, San Francisco
(William D. Brown, editor): Columbia University: 1946–1968: 1 linft (165 items in 2 boxes): literary correspondence: f/a [RLIN]

T. Y. Crowell/Crowell-Collier Publishing Co, New York City
NYPL: 1931–1955: 806 ft: correspondence, readers' reports, proofs, typescripts, correspondence (mainly 1931–1950): f/a [RLIN] (also *Collier's, Woman's Home Companion*)
(M. J. Moses, reader): Duke University: 1789–1960: 22,079 items & 409 vols: correspondence, research notes: card index [NUCMC 75-1963] (also **Little, Brown**)

Cuala Press, Dublin
Adelphi University: 1908–1940: 17 items: correspondence, business cards, mailing lists: f/a [RLIN]
(Yeats family): Columbia University: 1896–1968: 79 items (2 boxes): correspondence, family photographs, clippings, Michael MacLiammoir television script and catalogue of Russell K. Alspach's Yeats collection: [RLIN]
(Wilde collection): Cornell University: .33 cuft: correspondence, publishing ephemera: f/a [RLIN] (also **Dun Emer Press, Thomas Bird Mosher**)

C. H. K. Curtis, Philadelphia
Historical Society of Pennsylvania: 1912–1938: 667 items: correspondence [NUCMC 60-3152 / RLIN] (also *Ladies' Home Journal*)

The Dalkey Archive Press, Elmwood Park, IL
Stanford University: 1980–1988: 30 linft: correspondence, mss, proofs, writer interviews [RLIN] (also *The Review of Contemporary Fiction*)

John Day Co, Inc, New York City
Princeton University: 1926–1968: 256.50 cuft (570 boxes): editorial files, correspondence: folder list [Hinding 11,166 / RLIN]

Dennis F. Dealy, Philadelphia
(C. Victor Dealy, collector): Historical Society of Pennsylvania: 1853–1887: a collection of diaries [RLIN]

Dent & Sons, London
University of North Carolina at Chapel Hill: 1880s–1980s: 121 linft (149,000 items): correspondence, readers' reports: mss, financial accounts: currently being processed: advance notice required (Rare Book Room holds ca 6,000 volumes of file and proof copies) [personal enquiry]

Derrydale Press, New York City
(Eugene V. Connett, founder): Princeton University: 1926–1960 (bulk 1928–1942): 69 cuft (106 boxes, 4 cartons): correspondence, business papers, scrapbooks, memorabilia [RLIN]

Andre Deutsch, London
University of Tulsa: 1950–1988: 300+ boxes: correspondence, editorial & business files: f/a [HOBODS]

Divers Press, Majorca, Spain
(Robert Creeley, publisher): Washington University, Saint Louis): 1951–1984: 50,000 items: mss, correspondence: f/a [guide] (also *Black Mountain Review*)

Dodd, Mead, New York City
American Antiquarian Society: 1836–1939 (bulk 1839–1900): 2 boxes: copyright certificates, contracts [RLIN]

Doubleday, New York City
(Frank N. Doubleday, Nelson Doubleday): Princeton University: 1885–1963 (bulk 1890s–1940s): 5 cuft (17 boxes): correspondence, mss: f/a [RLIN]
(Ellen McCarter Doubleday, director 1949–1965): Princeton University: 1930s–1978: 13 linft (6 boxes, 7 cartons): correspondence: some restrictions: f/a [RLIN]
(Daniel Longwell, editor): Columbia University: ca 1920–1974: 24,750 items (89 boxes, 3 oversize boxes, 43 vols): correspondence: f/a [RLIN] (also **Time-Life**)
(Margaret Cousins, editor): HRC, University of Texas: 1921–1973: 14.5 ft (35 boxes): correspondence, mss, photographs, memorabilia : f/a [RLIN]
(Ken McCormick, editor): Library of Congress: 1882–1992 (bulk 1910–1992): 67.8 linft (60,000 items): correspondence, mss, memoranda, legal and business records: f/a: advance notice required [NIDS(US) Newsletter / personal enquiry]

Dramatists Play Service, New York City
American Play Co: NYPL: 1940–50: 1 carton
[Hinding 12,372]

Dun Emer Press, Dublin
(see **Cuala Press**)

E. P. Dutton & Co, New York City
Syracuse University: 1852–1969: 89 linft: papers of founder Edward P. Dutton, business records, letter books, photographs, scrapbooks, diaries: f/a [RLIN]

Elizabeth Press, New Rochelle, NY
(James L. Weil): University of Connecticut: 1963–1980: 1 box: correspondence, mss [RLIN]

Ember Press, London
HRC, University of Texas: production files [guide] (also *Littack*)

Fantasy Press
Temple University: 1938–1981: 2.8 cuft (7 boxes): correspondence, mss: register/inventory [RLIN]

Farrand & Mallory, Boston
Baker Library, Harvard University: 1913–1908: 1 linft: vertical file on printing/publishing: material on bankruptcy of D. Mallory & Co. and Farrand & Mallory: advance notice required: f/a [RLIN]

Fields, Osgood
(see **Ticknor & Fields**)

S. Fischer Verlag
Indiana University: 1887–1965: 5,162 items: correspondence, mss [*DLB Yearbook 1984*: 109–115]

Friends' Book Association of Philadelphia
Swarthmore College: 1873–1909: ca 100 items: business records, some publication records: f/a [RLIN]

Galaxy Publishing Co, New York City
Syracuse University: 1960–1969: 33 linft: correspondence, mss, production records: f/a [RLIN] (also *Galaxy Magazine, International Science Fiction, Worlds of Fantasy, Worlds of If, Worlds of Tomorrow*)

Gay Publishing Co, Toronto
Cornell University: 1964–1965: 1.3 cuft: business records, correspondence: f/a [RLIN]

Giligia Press, Fresno, CA/Lyme Center, NH
University of Connecticut: ca 1966–1979: 3 record cartons, 1 file drawer, 1 flat bundle: correspondence, mss, photographs: f/a [RLIN]

Gilliss Press, New York City
(Walter Gilliss, printer): Grolier Club Library, New York City: [ca 1906–1925]: ca 1.3 cuft: invitations, catalogues, personalia, Grolier Club material: [RLIN]

Charles Gilpin, London
Duke University: 1832–1875: 239 items & 97 addl uncat: correspondence [HOBODS]

Ginn & Co, Boston
(George Plimpton, 1881–1931 [chair 1914–1931]): Columbia University: 1855–1936: 22 linft (ca 21,700 items): correspondence, accounts, notes for a history, personal papers: f/a [guide]
(Doris Gates, editor): University of Oregon: 1936–1985: 27 ft: literary correspondence, mss, personal papers: [RLIN / NIDS(US) 4.109.97]

Gnome Press
(David A. Kyle, cofounder): Syracuse University: n.d.: .5 ft: mss: f/a [RLIN]

David R. Godine, Boston
Getty Library: 1969–1987: 240 linft: mss, proofs, photographs, extensive correspondence: unprocessed: advance notice required: partial inventory [RLIN]

Golden Cockerel Press
(Christopher Sandford, editor): HRC, University of Texas: 1922–1960: mss, correspondence, page proofs, ca 900 hand-engraved woodblocks and copper plates [guide]

Goliard Press, London
Columbia University: 1961–1970: ca 500 items (8 boxes): correspondence, production/editorial files: f/a [NUCMC 77-94 / RLIN]
(Tom Raworth, publisher): University of Connecticut: ca 1960–1978: 1 box, 1 file drawer, 4 record cartons: mss, correspondence: f/a [RLIN] (also **Matrix Press,** *Outburst*)

Greenberg: Publisher, New York City
Columbia University: 1894–1976: 49,000 items (98 boxes, 462 vol): editorial, production, publicity files: f/a [RLIN]

Greenwillow Books (division of William Morrow & Co, New York City)

University of Oregon: 1974–1984: 72.5 ft. (448 v, 46 boxes): correspondence, production files, accepted and rejected mss: f/a [NUCMC 89-1521: NIDS(US) 4.109.101]

Greenwood Press, San Francisco

(Jack Stauffacher, editor): Archives of American Art: 51 items: correspondence [RLIN]

(Jack Stauffacher, editor): Archives of American Art (LA only): interview on 3 sound cassettes: advance notice required [RLIN] (also *Circle Magazine*)

The Grey Walls Press, London

(Charles W. Gardiner, publisher 1940–1954): Emory University, GA: 1942–1967: 232 items: correspondence, mss [RLIN]

(Charles W. Gardiner): Columbia University: 1918–1981: 3 linft (ca 250 items in 6 boxes): correspondence, mss, photographs: f/a RLIN

The Grolier Club, New York City

The Grolier Club: 1884–1984: 40 cuft: correspondence, publication records, publishers & dealers catalogues: [RLIN] (see **Gilliss Press**)

Grove Press, New York City

Syracuse University: 1953–1985: 775 linft: editorial files, literary correspondence, royalty statements, extensive legal records, book & film contracts: [RLIN] (also *Evergreen Review*)

E. Haldeman-Julius, publisher (Little-Blue Book, Big-Blue Book, People Pocket series)

Columbia University: 1919–1943: 2 linft (ca 600 items in 5 boxes): sample collection of publications [RLIN]

Hand & Flower Press, Kent

(Erica Marx, publisher): Washington University, Saint Louis: 1926–1966: 800 items: correspondence, business records: f/a [NUCMC 70-2063 / NIDS(US) 4.10.76]

(Erica Marx, publisher): SUNY, Buffalo: correspondence, mss [RLIN]

Harcourt Brace & Co, New York City

Houghton Library, Harvard University: miscellaneous correspondence [guide]

(Velma Varner, children's editor 1946–1953): Columbia University: 1946–1973: 250 items (3 boxes, 1 folder): contracts, ledger books, correspon-

dence, illustrations [RLIN]; (also **William Morrow, G. P. Putnam's Sons, Viking Press, World Publishing Co**)

Harcourt, Brace, Jovanovich, New York City

Company archive, 757 Third Avenue, New York City: editorial files [Ash 1696]

Harper, New York City

(Harper & Bros): Columbia University: 1817–1929: 53 linft (ca 13,275 items in 50 boxes, 2,890 volumes, 2 oversized folders): contract files, literary correspondence, financial records: f/a (1 vol) [Ash 1695 / RLIN / published index: Chadwyck-Healey mfm]

(Harper & Bros): Pierpont Morgan Library: ca 1850–1900: ca 300 items: correspondence: f/a [personal enquiry]

(Theodore Stanton, UK agent): Douglass College Library, Rutgers University: ca 1880–1925: ca 6,000 items: correspondence, literary mss: f/a [NUCMC 66-132] (also *North American Review*)

Princeton University: 1909–1960: 5.95 cuft (34 boxes): mss, book proposals, correspondence, business papers [NUCMC 61-969: RLIN]

(Harper & Bros/Harper & Row): HRC, University of Texas: 1928–1969: extensive correspondence [guide] (also *Harper's Magazine*)

(Harper & Row): Columbia University: 1935–1973: 23,750 items (69 boxes): correspondence files, mss: f/a [published index: Chadwyck-Healey mfm/guide]

Harper Square Press, Chicago

Brown University, John Hay archive: 1966–1979: 6 linft: mss, correspondence, business records [RLIN]

Leo Hart Printing Co, Rochester, NY

Rochester University: 1905–1975: 10 cuft, 26 vol, 19 items: plates, photographs, galleys/proofs: f/a [NUCMC 68-860 / RLIN]

D. C. Heath & Co, Boston

American Antiquarian Society: 1877–1899: 432 items: correspondence: f/a [Ash 1695 / RLIN]

Heritage Press, New York City

(G. J. Macy, publisher): Columbia University: 1900–1970: 13 linft: correspondence, financial/business papers, documents, photographs, awards [NUCMC 77-108 / RLIN] (also **Limited Editions Club, Nonesuch Press**)

(George Macy Companies): HRC, University of Texas: correspondence with illustrators, designers, binders and printing firms, original artwork [guide] (also **Limited Editions Club**)

Hogarth Press, London
(Virginia and Leonard Woolf, publishers): HRC, University of Texas: a near-complete collection of Hogarth Press books, 130 volumes from personal library [guide]
(John Lehmann, manager): Princeton University: 1800s-1980s: 60 linft: literary correspondence: unprocessed [RLIN] (also **John Lehmann Publishing,** *London Magazine, New Writing*)

Henry Holt & Co, New York City
Princeton University: 1859-1981 (bulk 1890-1943): 137 cuft (192 boxes, 297 letterbooks, 202 vols, 3 cartons, 2 packages, 1 file drawer): literary correspondence, ledgers, inventory books: f/a [NUCMC 61-831 / RLIN]
(Roland Holt, vice-president 1903-1924): University of North Carolina at Chapel Hill: 1883-1956: 3,000 items: correspondence, clippings, photographs [NUCMC 83-1744]

Houghton Mifflin, Boston/**Riverside Press,** Cambridge
Houghton Library, Harvard University: 1850-1958: 85,000 items: cost books, correspondence, business records: f/a [NUCMC 82-628]
(Horace Elisha Scudder, editor): Houghton Library, Harvard University: 1864-1906: 29 vols: literary correspondence: f/a [RLIN] (also *Atlantic Monthly*)
(see **Ticknor & Fields**)

Hours Press
(Nancy Cunard, publisher): HRC, University of Texas: 1929+: correspondence [guide]

Benjamin Huebsch, New York City
Library of Congress: 1893-1964: 17ft (10,515 items): correspondence, diaries, speeches, financial papers: f/a [NUCMC 66-1421: NIDS(US) 2.1.387]
Columbia University: 1876-1964: 59 items & 400 vols personal library (presentation copies) (also an oral history record, transcript 492 leaves, 1955, name index) [RLIN]

Imago, London
(see **Casanova Society**)

International Publishers, New York City
(Alexander Trachtenberg, publisher): State Historical Society, Wisconsin: 1870-1975: 1 cuft (3 archives boxes) & photographs: correspondence, mss, biographical material, subject files: f/a [RLIN]

William Isbister & Co, London
Princeton University: ca 1860-ca 1906: 1.80 cuft (4 boxes) correspondence [RLIN] (also *Good Words, The Sunday Magazine*)

Alfred A. Knopf Inc, New York City
(Alfred A. and Blanche Knopf archive): HRC, University of Texas: decades of personal and business correspondence (also the founders' 15,000-volume library) [guide]
NYPL: 1914-1961 (bulk 1930s-1950s): 68 linft (73 boxes): correspondence of Alfred Knopf, mss and readers' reports, mss rejection correspondence, children's dept rejection mss, records, clippings & reviews of Knopf books, t/s of Knopf publications: f/a: [NUCMC 69-891, 69-892/Hinding 12,537/RLIN]
(Alfred Knopf): Columbia University: Oral History Collection: transcript 325 leaves, name index [RLIN]
(Alfred Knopf): Huntington Library: 1913-1955: 72 items: correspondence [guide]
(Angus Cameron, senior editor) (see **Bobbs-Merrill**)

Kulchur Press, New York City
Columbia University: 1936-1983: ca 10,000 items (34 boxes & 10 o/sized folders): literary correspondence, manuscripts, photographs: f/a (14 pp) [RLIN] (also *Kulchur Magazine*)

John Lane, The Bodley Head, London
(John Lane archive): HRC, University of Texas: 1887-1921: voluminous collection of mss, readers' reports, correspondence, proofs, illustrations, business records [guide]

Lea & Blanchard, Lea & Febiger, Philadelphia
Historical Society of Pennsylvania: 100 linft: 1785-1941 (bulk 1788-1871): literary and business correspondence, contracts, account books: f/a [RLIN] (also **Blanchard & Lea, Mathew Carey & Co**)

Lee & Shepard, Boston
American Antiquarian Society: 1861-1942: 12 boxes: correspondence, book orders, receipts: calendar with collection [NUCMC 62-3059 / RLIN]

John Lehmann Publishing, London
(John Lehmann archive): HRC, University of Texas: mss, 4,700 items of correspondence [guide] (also *London Magazine,* (Penguin) New Writing)
(see **Hogarth Press**)

Limited Editions Club
(see **Heritage Press**)

J. B. Lippincott, Philadelphia
Trinity College, Hartford: 1860–1896: 65 items: correspondence [NUCMC 71-497]
Historical Society of Pennsylvania: 1853–1862: 1 vol (34 cm): personal ledger for real estate transactions [RLIN]
(Walter Lippincott, in Lippincott family papers): Historical Society of Pennsylvania: 1775–1950: 5,000 items: correspondence, mss, personal papers [NUCMC 65-829]
(Ernestine Evans, editor) (see **Coward-McCann**)

Little, Brown, Boston
(M. J. Moses, reader) (see **T. Y. Crowell**)
(Angus Cameron, editor) (see **Bobbs-Merrill**)
Houghton Library, Harvard University: 12 boxes, Roberts Bros.: cash books: uncatalogued

Long House Inc, New Canaan, CT
(John Howland Snow, publisher): University of Oregon: 1939–1974: 3 ft: correspondence, diary, publication list: f/a [RLIN / NIDS (US) 4.109.79#1]

Luna Bisonte Prods
(John M. Bennett, publisher): Washington University, Saint Louis: 1956–1985: ca 8,000 items: correspondence, art, poetry, notebooks, mss: f/a [RLIN / guide]

A. C. MacClurg & Co, Chicago
Newberry Library: 1878–1967: 5,100 items: correspondence, royalty statements, record books, scrapbooks: f/a [NUCMC 69-434]

MacGibbon & Kee, London
(Timothy O'Keefe, publisher): University of Tulsa: 1948–1962: 9 boxes: correspondence: f/a [personal enquiry] (also **Martin, Brian & O'Keefe**)

Macmillan (US), New York City
NYPL: 1889–1960: 91 ft: correspondence, author files, contracts, mss, photographs: f/a [RLIN] (also **Cassell & Co**) [*DLB* 106: 82]

(Granville Hicks, editor): Syracuse University: 1906–1980: 80 linft: correspondence: f/a [RLIN] (also *Masses, New Masses*)
(Charlotte Painter, editor): Stanford University: 1955–1992: 3.75 linft: correspondence, taped interviews: f/a: [RLIN]
(Louise Bechtel, editor, children's books 1919–1934): Vassar College: 1877–1980 (bulk 1913–1980): 8 cuft: correspondence, mss, illustrations, biographical material: f/a [RLIN] (also *Horn Book*)

D. Mallory & Co, Boston
(see **Farrand & Mallory**)

Manas Press, Rochester, NY
(Bragdon family papers): Rochester University: 1819–1973: 25 cuft: correspondence, diaries, mss: f/a [NUCMC 61-1364/RLIN]

Martin, Brian & O'Keefe, London
(see **MacGibbon & Kee**)

Matrix Press, London
(see **Goliard Press**)

S. S. McClure Publishing Co
Indiana University: 1865–1969: 21,000 items [RLIN]
Huntington Library: 1887–1908: 47 items: correspondence [guide]
(Alexander and Edith O'Dell Black, editors): Lawrence University, Canton, NY: 1884–1974: 1 linft: business and literary correspondence [RLIN] (also *Golden Book Magazine*)

Mercury Press
Syracuse University: 1956–1967: 40 boxes: manuscripts [personal enquiry] (also *Fantasy, Venture*)

G. & C. Merriam Co, Springfield, MA
American Antiquarian Association: 1818-1860: 3 boxes: business correspondence, account books: f/a [RLIN]

Merrymount Press, Boston
Huntington Library: 1893–1948: 214,729 items: correspondence, accounts: f/a [NUCMC 77-330]

Methuen & Co, London
Indiana University: 1892–1944: 12 v˜ stock ledgers [Ash 1695]

(E. V. Lucas, publisher): Columbia University: 1908–1931: 186 items (1 box): correspondence (much with Arnold Bennett), manuscripts [RLIN]

Modern American Library
(see **Random House**)

William Morrow Inc, New York City
(Velma V. Varner, children's editor 1955–1956) (see **Harcourt Brace**)
(see **Greenwillow Books**)

Thomas Bird Mosher, Portland, ME
Houghton Library, Harvard University: 1890–1939 (bulk 1895–1924): 3 linft (9 boxes/1,700 items): correspondence: f/a [RLIN / guide]
Huntington Library: 1894–1923: 152 items: correspondence: [guide]
(Wilde collection) (see **Cuala Press**)

Edward Moxon, London
Pierpont Morgan Library: ca 1830–1850: ca 100 items: correspondence: card index [*DLB* 106: 218 / personal enquiry]

F. A. Munsey
(William Dewart, collector): New-York Historical Society: 1902–1944: 433 items (3 boxes): correspondence [RLIN] (also *New York Sun*)
(see **Popular Publications**)

John Murray, London
University of North Carolina, Chapel Hill: Rare Book Room holds ca 8,000 volumes of file and working copies items, with dust jackets, inserts, and other loose material [personal enquiry]

Thomas Nelson & Sons (US), New York City
(Masnel Corporation): Temple University: 1870–1970: 4 ft (4 boxes, 20 ledgers): records: shelf list: poor condition [Ash 1696 / RLIN]

Thomas Nelson & Sons, London
(John Buchan, editor): Brown University: 1898–1976: 150 items: correspondence, literary mss, incl 60 letters as editor for Thomas Nelson, London: f/a [NUCMC 78-81]
(John Buchan, editor): Dartmouth College: 1898–1925: 313 items: mostly correspondence with literary agent J. B. Pinker: card catalogue [NUCMC 65-1845]

New American Library (Penguin, Signet, Mentor), New York City

New York University: 1943–1961: 100 linft: correspondence, galleys, contracts, photographs: advance notice required: f/a for major part of collection [personal enquiry]
(Victor Weybright, cofounder): University of Wyoming: 1920–1974: 8 ft: corporate papers (mostly dealing with 1960 merger), correspondence: f/a [NUCMC 75-2105]
(Kurt Enoch, cofounder): NYPL: 1960–1978: 12 linft: documents (much dealing with 1960 merger), correspondence, transcript of oral history: advance notice required: f/a [RLIN]

New Colophon
(see **Colophon**)

Nichols, Printers & Publishers, London
Beinecke Library, Yale University: 18th/19th-century correspondence [HOBODS]
Columbia University: 1713–1874: 1,064 items (11 boxes): correspondence, mss, documents, portraits [NUCMC 68-1122 / RLIN]

Nonesuch Press
(see **Heritage Press**)

W. W. Norton, New York City
Columbia University: 1923–1967: 165,000 items (453 boxes): correspondence, mss, proofs [NUCMC 70-135 / guide]

The Open Court Publishing Co, New York City
Southern Illinois University: 1886–1930: ca 30 cuft: correspondence (over 50,000 letters), mss [NIDS(US) 4.30.23/4.30.28]

James R. Osgood
(see **Ticknor & Fields**)

Overbrook Press, Stamford, CT
Columbia University: 1929–1978: 7,200 items (1 box, 337 folders): correspondence, memoranda, manuscripts, business records: f/a [RLIN]

Oyez (Press) Berkeley, CA
University of Connecticut: ca 1964–1987: 1 box, 11 file drawers & 4 record cartons: mss, business records, correspondence: f/a [RLIN]

Pantheon Books, New York City
Columbia University: 1944–1967: 12,500 items (27 boxes): editorial and production files: contents list [NUCMC 77-116 / RLIN]

Pierrepont Press, New York City
Washington University, Saint Louis: 1968–1969: 124 items: mss, galleys, correspondence: f/a [RLIN / guide]

Sir Isaac Pitman & Sons, London
(A. D. Power, editor): Princeton University: 1837–1946: 0.25 cuft (1 box): correspondence, photographs, memorabilia: contents list [RLIN] (also **W. H. Smith**)

Plain Wrapper Press, Quito/Rome/Alabama
(Richard-Gabriel Rummonds, founder): NYPL: 1948–1986: 21 linft: some restrictions: correspondence, proof sheets, galleys: f/a [RLIN]

Pomegranate Press, Cambridge, MA
Pennsylvania State University: 1970s: 1 linft, 5 woodblocks: correspondence, mss, broadsides: name index.

Popular Publications Inc., New York City
NYPL: 1910–1977 (bulk 1945–1960): 53 linft (80 boxes): correspondence (some on subjects of radio rights and syndication), author card files, personal papers of publisher Henry Steeger, illustrations, photographs, recordings: f/a [RLIN] (acquired properties of Frank A. Munsey in 1942)

Poets and Poets Press, Elmwood, CT
University of Connecticut: 1980+: 31 boxes: correspondence, mss: [RLIN]

Prairie Press, Iowa City
(Lawrence O. Cheever, editor): University of Iowa: 1931–1966: 619 items: correspondence, typescripts, illustrations [RLIN]

Pushkin Press, London
(see **Casanova Society**)

G. P. Putnam's Sons, New York City
(George Palmer Putnam): Princeton University: 1843-1869: 1,500 items (7 folio albums): correspondence: [RLIN / Greenspan]
(George Palmer Putnam): NYPL: 1843-1871: .2 linft: correspondence: requires advance notice [*DLB* 106: 257 / RLIN]
(George Haven Putnam): Columbia University: [ca 1900]–1930: 5 boxes, 1 vol: business correspondence [RLIN]
University of Illinois: 1891–1938: 6.5 cuft: London office business records, publishers agreements, ledger: f/a [guide]

Houghton Library, Harvard University: 1874–1924: correspondence [RLIN / guide]
(Velma V. Varner, children's editor 1953–1955) (see **Harcourt Brace**)

Pynson Printers, New York City
NYPL: 1927–1933: 10 linft: Elmer Adler's correspondence files, business records, sketches, examples of printed work [RLIN]
(see **Colophon**)

Rand McNally, Chicago
Newberry Library: 1870s– : 28 boxes & o/size material: cartographic material, job printing documents, railroad ephemera: f/a [personal enquiry] (also **William B. Conkey Co, Rolph-McNally**)

Rolph-McNally, Ontario
(Rand McNally archive): Newberry Library: 1957–1977: 2 boxes: company correspondence [personal enquiry]

Random House, New York City
Columbia University: 1925–1992: 691 linft (927,000 items in 1,657 boxes): correspondence, mss: f/a [NUCMC 78-667 / RLIN]
(Bennett Cerf, editor): Columbia University: 1898–1977: 53 linft (6,300 items in 63 boxes, 45 vols, 22 o/sized items): correspondence, mss, photographs, recordings: f/a [RLIN]
Saxe Commins (chief editor): Princeton University: 1933–1958: 6.05 cuft (17 boxes): author files, correspondence, typescripts, photographs: f/a [RLIN]
Elmer Adler (see **Colophon Press**)

Rapp & Carroll, London
Pennsylvania State University: 1967: 1 linft: correspondence files: card index [personal enquiry]

Renown Publications, New York City
University of Oregon: 1955–1972: 9 ft: correspondence, mss: f/a [NUCMC 72-1139] (also *The Girl from U.N.C.L.E. Magazine, Mike Shayne Mystery Magazine, Zane Grey Western Magazine*)

Grant Richards, London
University of Illinois: 1872–1936: 30.2 cuft (20,000 items): correspondence, incomplete typescripts, photographs, agreements [NUCMC 61-2210 / published index: Chadwyck-Healey mfm]
Georgetown University: 1872–1948: 2.5 linft: correspondence, mss: f/a [Ash 1695]

Princeton University: 1906-23: 1 box: correspondence [RLIN / guide]

(John Davidson, reader): Princeton University: 1890–1909: 1.60 cuft (4 boxes): 1 folder of readers' reports [guide]

HRC, University of Texas [HOBODS]

Roberts Bros, Boston
Columbia University: 1841–1932: 1,500 items (3 boxes): correspondence files [NUCMC 61-3355 / RLIN]

John Rodker, agent and publisher
(see **Casanova Society**)

Scorpion Press, London
University of Tulsa: 1958–1969: 14 boxes: correspondence, mss, ledgers, stockbooks: f/a [personal enquiry]

Charles Scribner's Sons, New York City
Princeton University: 1878–1960: 240 cuft (416 boxes, 26 cartons, 107 letterbooks, 2 files, 22 shelves of account books): mss, correspondence, business files: f/a [NUCMC 72-598 / guide]

Martin Secker, Ltd, London
(Martin Secker): Indiana University: 1930–1944: 200 items [Ash 1695]

University of Tulsa: the personal library of Martin Secker, with author inscriptions & letters [Ash 1696]

University of Illinois: 1910–1931: 2.8 cuft: correspondence, publishers' agreements: f/a [guide]

Simon & Schuster/Pocket Books, New York City
(Richard L. Simon, cofounder): Columbia University: 1915–1970: 14,000 items (51 boxes, 17 outsize folders): correspondence, mss, legal & financial papers, editorial files [NUCMC 84-624] / RLIN]

(Max L. Schuster, cofounder): Columbia University: [ca 1913]–1976: 110,150 items: personal and business correspondence, production files, editorial reports, photographs [NUCMC 73-102 / RLIN / guide]

Oral history, Lewis Freeman and Leon Shimkin: Columbia University: transcript, 63 leaves [RLIN]

Slow Loris Press, Pittsburgh, PA/Buffalo, NY

University of Connecticut: 1974–1984: 2 record cartons & 4 oversize bundles: [RLIN] (also *Rapport: A Journal of Contemporary Writing*)

W. H. Smith, London
(A. D. Power) (see **Sir Isaac Pitman & Sons**)

Smith, Elder & Co, London
(George Smith, founder): Princeton University: 1862-1891: .25 cuft (1 box): business correspondence, mostly relating to *Cornhill Magazine* [RLIN]

University of North Carolina at Chapel Hill: 1850–1923: 0.5 ft: correspondence, family papers: f/a (Rare Book Room holds ca 2,340 volumes of file and working copies) [personal enquiry]

Something Else Press
(Dick Higgins): Getty Library: 1960–1989: 28 cuft: correspondence, graphics: closed pending processing [RLIN]

Soft Press, Victoria, BC
(Robert Sward, publisher): Washington University, Saint Louis: 1951–1971: 13,000 items: correspondence, mss, journals: f/a [guide]

Stein and Day Publishers, New York City
Columbia University: 1963–1988: 28.75 linft (ca 34,500 items in 69 boxes): correspondence, manuscripts, documents, photographs [RLIN]

Herbert S. Stone & Co/Stone & Kimball Publ Co, Cambridge, Chicago, New York City
Newberry Library: ca 1889–1965: 25 boxes: mss, drawings, paintings, posters: f/a [NUCMC 80-162] (also *Chap-Book, House Beautiful*)

Story Press, New York City
Princeton University: 1931–1965: 69 cuft (168 boxes, 8 pkges, 7 cartons): business files, correspondence, artwork, photographs, scrapbooks, records [RLIN] (also *Story Magazine*)

Street & Smith
Syracuse University: 1855–1970: 407 linft: internal records, mss, scripts: cataloguing incomplete: f/a: partially restricted [RLIN] (also *Adventure Weekly, Ainslee's Magazine, Astounding Science Fiction, Astounding Stories, Detective Story Magazine, Fame and Fortune Weekly, Far West Stories, Good News, Gunter's Magazine, Mademoiselle, New Story Magazine, New York Weekly, Nick Carter Weekly, Pete Rice Magazine, People's Magazine, Popular Magazine, Sea Stories Magazine,*

The Shadow Magazine, Smith's Magazine, Sport Story Magazine, Starry Flag Weekly, Top-notch Magazine, Western Story Magazine, Wild West Weekly)

Tamarisk Press, Philadelphia
(Dennis Barone, editor): Temple University: 1971-1991: 2 cuft (4 boxes): mss, correspondence, contracts, several taped writer interviews: f/a [RLIN]

Tauchnitz Editions, Leipzig
(see **Albatross Verlag**)

Telephone Press, Guildford, CT
University of Connecticut: ca 1975-1983: 1 box, 3 record cartons, & 1 o/sized bundle: mss, correspondence [RLIN]

Ticknor & Fields, Boston
Houghton Library, Harvard University: 1832-1901: 120 vol: letter books (1848-1900), cost books (1832-1899) journals (including successors: **James R. Osgood; Fields Osgood & Co; Houghton Mifflin, & Co**): f/a [NUCMC 83-995]
(Ticknor family papers): Boston Public Library: 1859-1940: 20 items: chiefly correspondence with authors: f/a [NUCMC 73-33]
University of North Carolina at Chapel Hill, Rare Book Room: 1830s-1880s: publisher's working copies, [personal enquiry]
(James T. Fields/Annie Fields): Huntington Library: 1850-1914: 6,000 items: correspondence, mss (also *Atlantic Monthly*)
(Benjamin Ticknor, publisher): Library of Congress: 1805-1935: ca 6 ft (3,000 items): correspondence, mss, graphics [NUCMC 63-401]

Toothpaste Press, West Branch, IA
University of Iowa: 1970-1984: 16 ft: correspondence, financial records: f/a [NUCMC 89 1471 / RLIN]

Trigram Press, Ltd, London
Washington University, Saint Louis: 1965-1975: 1,750 items: correspondence, mss: f/a [guide]

Turret Press, London
University of Maryland: 1965-1975: 9 ft: correspondence, mss: f/a [personal enquiry]

Turtle Island Press, Philadelphia
Temple University: 1970-1979: 1.2 cuft (3 boxes): mss, graphics: f/a [RLIN]

Typophiles Society
(Paul A. Bennett, manager): NYPL: 1925-1966: 33 linft: personal and professional correspondence, typescripts, material relating to the Chap Book series: folder inventory: advance notice required [RLIN]

Frederick Ungar Publishing Co, New York City
SUNY, Albany: 1940-1988: 8 linft: correspondence, catalogues, dust covers [RLIN]

Universal Publishers Corp
Syracuse University: 1970: 1 linft: typescripts: [RLIN] (also *Galaxy Magazine, Worlds of Fantasy, Worlds of If, Worlds of Tomorrow*)

Untide Press, Waldport, CA
(Robert Everson, cofounder): Washington University, Saint Louis: 1942-1971: 199 items: correspondence, mss, corrected galleys: f/a [guide]

T. Fisher Unwin, London
Berg collection, NYPL: readers' reports [guide]

Vanguard Press, New York City
Columbia University: 1925-1985: 134 linft (ca 128,500 items in 260 boxes & 22 preservation cases): mss, correspondence, galley proofs, photographs: f/a [RLIN]

Viking Press, New York City
(Velma V. Varner, children's editor 1964-1972) (see **Harcourt Brace**)
(see **Benjamin Huebsch**)

James Vizetelly & Co, London
Getty Library: 1838-1854: ca 200 items (2 vol & 1 folder): correspondence received, mostly with reference to illustrated books [RLIN]

Walker, Wise & Co, Boston
(James P. Walker, publisher): Princeton University: 1850-1886: 2.18 cuft (6 boxes, 1 wrapped photograph): correspondence, mss, scrapbooks: f/a [guide]

Way & Williams, Chicago
(Chauncy Williams, publ): University of North Carolina at Greensboro: correspondence, scrapbooks [Ash 1696]
(see **Copeland and Day**)

Westgate Press, San Francisco
Columbia University: 1929–1931: 133 items
(1 box): correspondence, manuscripts, proofs: f/a
[RLIN]

Woman's Press, New York City

YWCA, National Board Archives, NY: 1917–
1955: 23 linft: administrative records, also printed
materials [RLIN]

World Publishing Co
(Velma V. Varner, children's editor 1956–
1964) (see **Harcourt Brace**)

SECTION TWO: JOURNAL ARCHIVES

13th Moon, New York City
NYPL: 1973–1982: 27 linft: (33 boxes, 5
sound recordings): correspondence, business records, project files, printed material, audio cassettes:
f/a [RLIN]

Accent, Urbana-Champaign
(Daniel Curley, editor): University of Illinois:
1941–1991: 17 linft: correspondence, mss, business
records: f/a [RLIN]

Adventure Weekly/Ainslee's Magazine
(see **Street & Smith**)

Ambit, London
Pennsylvania State University: 1961+: 38
linft: correspondence, mss, editorial files, Arts
Council correspondence: f/a [personal enquiry]
HRC, University of Texas: archival materials
[guide]

American Book Collector, Chicago
Brown University, John Hay archives: 1950–
1976: 24 linft: mss, proofs, correspondence, business records: advance notice required [RLIN]

American Heritage, New York City
(see **American Heritage Publishing Company**)

American Mercury, New York City
(George Jean Nathan, editor): Cornell Univer-
sity: 1913–1958: 14.7 linft: correspondence, mss:
[RLIN] (also *American Spectator, Smart Set*)

American Quarterly, Minneapolis
(W. V. O'Connor, editor): Syracuse Univer-
sity: 1943–1967: manuscripts, correspondence f/a
[NUCMC 68-1747, 70-715 / NIDS(US) 4.78.25]

American Review
University of Michigan, Bentley Historical Library: 1967–1977: 14 linft: correspondence, work-

ing files, administrative files: f/a [RLIN / NIDS (US)
4.61.28]

American Spectator, New York City
(see *American Mercury*)

Antipodes, Austin, TX
Pennsylvania State University: 1986+: 2 ft:
correspondence (also American Association for
Australian Literary Studies materials) [personal en-
quiry]

Antiquarian Bookman (later *AB Bookman's
Weekly*), Newark, NJ
Pennsylvania State University: 1954–1968: 24
ft: correspondence, account ledgers, business records [personal enquiry]

*Astounding Science Fiction/Astounding Sto-
ries*
(see **Street & Smith**)

Atlantic Monthly, Boston
Houghton Library, Harvard University:
1850–1958: 85,000 items: unbound correspondence
[NUCMC 82-628]
NYPL: 92 pieces, 2 boxes: typescripts,
authors' proofs [guide]
(Thomas B. Aldrich, editor): Houghton Library, Harvard University: 1855–1925: 5,400
items: correspondence, manuscripts: f/a [NUCMC
81-401]
(Thomas B. Aldrich, editor): Temple University: 1865–1904: .2 cuft (1 box): correspondence,
mss: shelf list [RLIN]
(James Russell Lowell, editor 1857-1861):
Houghton Library, Harvard University: 1835–
1919: 17 boxes: correspondence, manuscripts, commonplace books: [RLIN] (also *North American Review*)
(James T. Fields, editor 1861-1870) (see
Ticknor & Fields)

(Horace Elisha Scudder, editor 1890-1898) (see **Houghton Mifflin**)

(Bliss Perry, editor): Houghton Library, Harvard University: 1892–1942: 600 items: correspondence: f/a [NUCMC 82-658]

(Edward Weeks, editor): HRC, University of Texas: editorial materials [guide]

Aylesford Review
Indiana University: 1955–1968: publication files [*DLB Yearbook 1984:* 109-115]

Black Mountain Review, Black Mountain, NC
(Robert Creeley, editor): University of Connecticut: ca 1940–1974: 5 boxes: correspondence, mss [RLIN]
(see **Divers Press**)

Bookman, London
(Arthur Bartlett Maurice, editor 1899–1916): Princeton University: 1905–1945: 0.7 cuft (2 boxes): correspondence: f/a [guide]

(Flora May Holly, editor): NYPL: 1907–1960 (bulk 1930–1955): 7 linft (16 boxes, 1 mfm reel): literary, personal and business correspondence, photographs, memorabilia [RLIN] (also **Flora May Holly, literary agent**)

Botteghe Oscure, Rome
(Marguerite Caetani, Eugene Walter, editors): HRC, University of Texas: correspondence, mss [guide]

Briarcliff Quarterly, Briarcliff, NY
(Norman MacLeod, editor): (formerly *Maryland Quarterly*): Princeton University: .45 cuft: includes unpublished autobiography [RLIN]

Broom: An International Magazine of the Arts, Rome, Berlin, New York City
(Harold Loeb, editor): Princeton University: 1920–1956 (bulk 1921–1926): 2 boxes: correspondence files: f/a [guide]

Center Magazine, New York City
(Carol Berge, editor): Washington University, Saint Louis: 1970–1984: ca 24,750 items: correspondence, mss, drafts: f/a

Century Magazine, New York City (orig *Scribner's*)
NYPL: 1870–1924: 147 linft: correspondence, mss [[NUCMC 69-810/RLIN] (also *St Nicholas Magazine, Scribner's Magazine*)

AAA, Detroit: 15,000 items: correspondence, mss [RLIN]

Rutgers University: 1874–1909, 1 reel mfm (original in private hands) [RLIN]

(Richard Watson Gilder, editor): NYPL: 1855–1916: 22 linft: correspondence, diaries, contracts, scrapbooks: f/a [RLIN]

(Rodman Gilder, archivist): NYPL: 1895–1953: .7 linft (2 boxes): memoranda, financial records: catalogue of publications (1913), memorabilia/photograph of Richard Watson Gilder (father): [RLIN]

(Robert Underwood Johnson, editor): NYPL: 1875–1937: 4 linft: editorial correspondence, photographs, personal ephemera: f/a [RLIN]

Huntington Library: 1885–1914: 760 items [Hinding 1,410]

The Chap-Book, Chicago
(see **Herbert S. Stone & Co**)

Chicago Tribune–NY News Syndicate, Fiction Dept.
University of Oregon: 1919–1969: 78 ft (7,700 items): mss, literary correspondence: f/a [NUCMC 74-823]

The Chimera: A Literary Quarterly, New York City
Beinecke Library, Yale University: 1942–1951: 8 boxes: mss, correspondence, business papers: f/a [gopher]

Circle Magazine, San Francisco
(see **Greenwood Press**)

Collier's, New York City
NYPL: 1935+: typescripts [guide]
(see **T. Y. Crowell**)

Contact: A Quarterly Review
(Martin Kamin, founder): Syracuse University: 1789–1973: 18.5 linft: correspondence, photographs, printed material, also material 'related to Kamin Dance Bookshop, New York City: f/a [RLIN]

Contempo, Chapel Hill
(A. J. Buttitta, editor): HRC, University of Texas: 1931–1935: correspondence, 525 mss, business papers [guide]

Contemporary Poetry, Baltimore
(Mary Owings Miller, editor): University of Baltimore: 1918–1974: 2.5 ft correspondence, mss [RLIN / NIDS (US) 4.36.15]

Contemporary Verse, Philadelphia
(Henry Morton Robinson, editor): Columbia University: 1915–1965: ca 12,000 items (42 boxes): correspondence: f/a [RLIN] (also *Reader's Digest*)

Cornhill Magazine, London
(see **Smith, Elder**)

Coronet Magazine
Syracuse University: 1935–1961: 68 linft: correspondence, mss, dummies, editorial materials: f/a [RLIN]

The Delineator, New York City
(Marie Meloney, editor 1920–1926): Columbia University: 1915–1943: 4,730 items: f/a [Hinding 12,044]

Detective Story Magazine
(see **Street & Smith**)

The Dial, Chicago
(Scofield Thayer, editor): Beinecke Library, Yale University: 1879–1982: 49.75 linft (82 boxes): office correspondence, editorial files, mss, artwork, personal papers: f/a [gopher]
(Marianne Moore, editor 1925–1929): Rosenbach Museum: 1901–1972: 82 boxes: literary correspondence: f/a [RLIN / NIDS(US) 4.101.3]

Dublin Magazine, Dublin
(Rivers Carew, editor): Huntington Library: 1963–1972: ca 850 items: editorial correspondence, manuscripts [guide]

El Corno Emplumado, Mexico City
HRC, University of Texas: 1960–1968: correspondence, mss [guide]

Envoy: a review of literature and art, Dublin
Southern Illinois University: 1949–1951: 6 boxes: mss, correspondence, business papers: f/a [NIDS(US) 4.30.39]

Evergreen Review
(see **Grove Press**)

Exchanges: A Quarterly Review of Literature in English and in French, Paris
HRC, University of Texas: 1929–1932: correspondence [guide]

Fame and Fortune Weekly
(see **Street & Smith**)

Famous Story Magazine, New York City
(G. T. Delacorte, publisher): Columbia University: 1925–1927: .5 linft (26 items): literary correspondence [NUCMC 78-676 / RLIN]

Fantasy
(see **Mercury Press**)

Fantasy Magazine, Pittsburgh
Beinecke Library, Yale University: 1929–1979: 7 linft (10 boxes): correspondence, mss [gopher]

Far West Stories
(see **Street & Smith**)

Fiction House (pulp magazines)
(Malcolm Reiss, editor): University of Oregon: 1922–1975: 1.5 ft: correspondence, business records: f/a [NUCMC 89-1571: NIDS(US) 4.109.75, no. 2]

The Floating Bear
Indiana University: 1961–1969: publication files [*DLB Yearbook 1984:* 109–115]

Folder Magazine
(Daisy Aldan, editor): HRC, University of Texas: 1953–1959: production materials, correspondence [guide] (also *A New Folder*)

Fraser's Magazine, London
(William Allingham, editor): University of Illinois: 1846–1920: 2 cuft: correspondence, mss, notes, sketches [guide]

Free Lance, Saint Louis
Washington University, Saint Louis: ca 1964–1969: 845 items: mss, correspondence: f/a [guide]

Fuck You
(Ed Sanders, publisher): University of Connecticut: 1961–1978: 3 boxes & 8 record cartons [RLIN]

Furioso, Northfield, MN
(Howard Nemerov, editor 1946–1951): Washington University, Saint Louis: 1939–1985: ca 9,000 items: mss, correspondence: f/a [guide]

Galaxy, NYC (merged with *Atlantic Monthly* 1878)

(W. C. Church, coeditor): NYPL: 1863–1909 (bulk 1863-1878): 2.1 linft (7 boxes) [NUCMC 68-1124 / RLIN]

Galaxy Magazine
(see **Galaxy Publishing Co, Universal Publishers Corp**)

Genesis West
HRC, University of Texas: archival materials [guide]

The Girl from U.N.C.L.E. Magazine
(see **Renown Publications**)

Golden Book Magazine, New York City
(see **S. S. McClure Publishing Co**)

Good News
(see **Street & Smith**)

Good Words, London
(see **William Isbister**)

Grand Street Publications, Inc, New York City
Columbia University: 1981–1990: 24 linft (ca 5,500 items in 52 boxes): correspondence, mss, proofs: f/a [NUCMC 84-547 / guide]

Gunter's Magazine
(see **Street & Smith**)

Harper's Magazine, New York City
(see **R. R. Bowker** – English agent)
Library of Congress: 1869–1892, 1940+: 54 ft: editorial correspondence, mss (1952+): f/a [NUCMC 60-249]
(see **Harper**)

Harper's Monthly, New York City
(Edward S. Martin, editor): Houghton Library, Harvard University: 1874–1939: 14,000 items, 35 folders: correspondence: f/a (bMS Am 1863) [NUCMC 81-598]
(John Fischer, editor]: State Historical Scty of Wisconsin: 1945–1963: 3ft: f/a [NUCMC 64-1604]
Archives of American Art, Detroit: 1946–1965: 1150 items: illustrations, correspondence with artists/cartoonists, biographical material (mfm) [NUCMC 67-1070]

The Holy Door, Dublin
Southern Illinois University: 1965–1966: 3 boxes: correspondence, mss: f/a [NIDS(US) 4.30.37]

Horn Book, Boston
Simmons College: 1889–1986: 23.5 linft: [RLIN / NIDS(US) 4.108.12]
(Louise Bechtel, editor) (see **Macmillan**)

House Beautiful, Chicago
(see **Herbert S. Stone & Co**)

International Science Fiction
(see **Galaxy Press**)

Kenyon Review, Gambier, OH
Kenyon College: 1939+: correspondence, mss: name index [personal enquiry]

Kulchur Magazine
(see **Kulchur Press**)

La Nouvelle Revue Francaise, Paris
(Carlton Lake Collection) (Jean Paulhan, editor): HRC, University of Texas: correspondence [guide]

Ladies' Home Journal, New York City
(Christopher Morley, editor): Haverford College: 1900–1964: 28ft & 530 items: correspondence, manuscripts, family papers: f/a [NUCMC 89-663]
(Christopher Morley, editor): University of Virginia: 1915–1953: 160 items: correspondence: f/a [NUCMC 77-1239]
(See **C. H. K. Curtis**)

Liberty
(Benjamin R. Tucker, editor): NYPL: 1860s–1970s (bulk 1870s–1930s): 27 linft: correspondence, manuscripts, scrapbooks, photographs [RLIN] (also *Radical Review*)

Library Journal
(Paul Leicester Ford, editor): NYPL: 1869–1902 (bulk 1885–1895): 16.5 linft (42 boxes): correspondence, mss editorials and reviews, personalia: f/a [RLIN]
Pennsylvania State University: 1951–1968 (bulk 1958–1968): ca 2,000 items: author questionnaires, correspondence: [*DLB Yearbook 1987:* 52–53]
(see **R. R. Bowker & Co**)

Life Magazine, New York City
NYPL: 1892–1936 (bulk 1920–1936): 28 linft (30 boxes & 67 vols): records, mss, correspondence, art dept records: [RLIN]

Literary World, Boston
(Edward Abbott, editor): Bowdoin College, Maine: 1877–1903: 515 items, 4 vols: correspondence, manuscripts for special "tribute" issues: f/a [NUCMC 71-27]

Littack, London
(see **Ember Press**)

The Little Magazine, New York City
HRC, University of Texas: archival materials [guide]

Little Review, Chicago
University of Wisconsin – Milwaukee: 1914–1929: 2 cuft: f/a [Hinding 17,843 / Ash 1696]

London Magazine
(see **John Lehmann Publishing**)
(see **Hogarth Press**)

Mademoiselle
(see **Street & Smith**)

Masses, New York City
(Charles Humboldt, editor): Yale University: 1935–1963: 4 ft: correspondence: f/a [NUCMC 76-1433]
(see **Macmillan [US]**)

Merlin, Paris

(Alexander Trocchi, editor 1952–1955): Washington University, Saint Louis: 1947–1968: 355 items: f/a [guide] (also *Moving Times, Paris Quarterly*)

Mike Shayne Mystery Magazine
(see **Renown Publications**)

Micromegas
HRC, University of Texas: archival materials [guide]

Minotaure, Paris
(Carlton Lake Collection): HRC, University of Texas: archival materials [guide]

Modern Monthly, Modern Quarterly, London
(Victor Francis Calverton, founder): NYPL: 1915–1941: ca 35 linft: editorial correspondence, mss: f/a: advance notice required [RLIN]

Moving Times
(see *Merlin*)

Munsey's Magazine, New York City
(Robert H. Davis, fiction editor): NYPL: 1901–1942: 26 boxes: correspondence, mss [NUCMC 68-1681]
(see **Popular Publications Inc**)

Nation, New York City
NYPL: 1873–190?: 5 vol, 1 box [Hinding 12,572]
(Freda Kirchwey, editor/publisher): Schlesinger Library: 1910–1958: 9 cartons, 2.5 boxes, 1 o/size folder [Hinding 6,694]
(Wm. C. Brownell, editor): Amherst College: 1871–1928: 5.5ft [Hinding 5,861]
(Irita Van Doren, literary editor): Library of Congress: 1920–1966: 12 ft (ca 4,360 items): correspondence, manuscripts: f/a [NUCMC 69-2055: NIDS(US) 2.1.708]

New Directions, Norfolk, CT
Houghton Library, Harvard University: 1937–1974: 365 items: literary typescripts, galley & page proofs: f/a: some restrictions on use: [NUCMC 81-614]

A New Folder
(see *Folder Magazine*)

New Masses, New York City
(see *Masses*)

New Republic, New York City
(Willard Straight, editor): Cornell University: 1857–1922: 90 ft [Hinding 11,720] (also available on microform (12 reels) at Yale University [RLIN])
(Robert Littell, assistant editor): University of Oregon: 1901–1963: 8 ft: f/a [Hinding, 14,411]

New Review, Paris
(Sam Putnam, editor): Princeton University: 1927–1933: 1,500 items: mss: f/a [NUCMC 60-1397 / RLIN]
(Sam Putnam, editor): Southern Illinois University: 1892–1950: 12 cuft (40 boxes, 8 pkges): mss, correspondence (not indexed) [NIDS(US) 4.30.55]

New Story Magazine
(see **Street & Smith**)

New World Writing, New York City

Beinecke Library, Yale University: 21.75 linft: correspondence, mss, proofs, galleys: name index (correspondence) [gopher]

New Writing, London
(see **Hogarth Press**)
(see **John Lehmann Publishing**)

New York Evening Post
(John Thompson, literary editor 1868–1873): University of Virginia: 1842–1926: 2 ft: typescripts: f/a [NUCMC 65-1029]

New York Sun
(see **Frank A. Munsey**)

New York Weekly
(see **Street & Smith**)

New Yorker, New York City
NYPL: editorial files [personal enquiry]
(Katharine S. White, fiction editor): Bryn Mawr College: 1929–1976: 7 linft: correspondence: f/a [RLIN]

Nick Carter Weekly
(see **Street & Smith**)

Nimbus
HRC, University of Texas: archival material [guide]

North American Review, Cedar Falls, IA
(Theodore Stanton, UK agent) (see **Harper**)
University of Maryland: misc correspondence
(John Gorham Palfrey, editor): Houghton Library, Harvard University: 1836–1843: 626 items: manuscripts: f/a [guide]
(James Russell Lowell, editor 1864+) (see *Atlantic Monthly*)
(see *Golden Book Magazine*)

Origin, Boston
(Cid Corman, publisher): University of Connecticut: 1954–1989: 2 boxes: correspondence, mss: f/a [RLIN]
(Cid Corman, publisher): Washington University, Saint Louis: 1962–1964: 36 items: correspondence: f/a [guide]
(Cid Corman, publisher): HRC, University of Texas: correspondence [guide]
Indiana University: 1960–1962: publication files [*DLB Yearbook 1984:* 109–115]

Outburst, London
(see **Goliard Press**)

Pa'lante, New York City
Columbia University: 1959–1969: 600 items: correspondence, mss [NUCMC 73-98 / RLIN]

Palms, Washington/NYC/Grant, Michigan/Guadalajara, Mexico
(Idella Purnell Stone, editor): HRC, University of Texas: 1923–1930: correspondence, editorial files, mss [guide]

Paris Quarterly
(see *Merlin*)

People's Magazine
(see **Street & Smith**)

Perspective Magazine, Louisville/Saint Louis
Washington University, Saint Louis: 1947–1980: ca 3,600 items: business & editorial correspondence: f/a [guide]

Pete Rice Magazine
(see **Street & Smith**)

Poetry: A Magazine of Verse, Chicago
(Harriet Monroe, publisher): University of Chicago: 1912–1960: 32 ft: (ms before 1936), correspondence, business records: advance notice required: f/a [NUCMC 64-150]
(Augustine J. Bowe, collector): Newberry Library: 1903–1966: 5,000 items: correspondence: f/a [NUCMC 67-1958]
(Harriet Monroe Library of Modern Poetry): University of Chicago: 49 items: poetry manuscripts, correspondence: f/a [NUCMC 64-806]
(Isabella Gardner, editor): Washington University, Saint Louis: ca 1923–1968: ca 8,000 items: correspondence, mss: f/a [guide]
(Alice Corbin Henderson, editor): HRC, University of Texas: correspondence, mss [guide]
Indiana University: 1954+: publication files [*DLB Yearbook 1984:* 109–115]

Poetry London–New York
Columbia University: 1943–1968: 400 items: correspondence, poetry mss: f/a [NUCMC 84-605]

The Poetry Review, London
HRC, University of Texas: archival materials [guide]

Poets On, Chaplin CT/Mill Valley, CA
(Ruth Daigon, publisher): University of Connecticut: 1967–1983: 1 box & 2 file drawers: mss, editorial files: f/a: partially restricted: [RLIN]

Popular Magazine
(see **Street & Smith**)

Publishers Weekly, New York City
Princeton University: 1933–1945: 3.15 cuft (7 boxes): correspondence: unprocessed [RLIN]
(see **R. R. Bowker & Co**)

Putnam's Monthly Magazine, New York City
(Dix, Edwards & Co, publishers): Houghton Library, Harvard University: 1854–1859: 1 box: correspondence, partnership agreements: access may be restricted: f/a [RLIN]

Radical Review, New Bedford, MA
(see *Liberty*)

Rapport: A Journal of Contemporary Writing
(see **Slow Loris Press**)

Reader's Digest, Pleasantville, NY
(see *Contemporary Verse*)

Reality
(Raphael Soyer, editor): Cornell University: 1949–1954: 288 items: correspondence, minutes, illustrations [NUCMC 70-1128]

The Review of Contemporary Fiction
(see **Dalkey Archive Press**)

Rhythmus, New York City
(Ija Adler, collector): Washington University, Saint Louis: 1932–1967: 462 items: editorial files: f/a [guide]

Rocky Mountain Review, Iowa City
(Ray B. West, editor): Utah State University, Logan: 1920–1965: 30 linft (60 boxes): correspondence, mss: f/a [RLIN] (also *Western Review*)

Russell's Magazine
(Paul Hamilton Hayne, editor): Duke University: 1815–1944: 4,615 items: correspondence, mss: f/a [guide]

St Nicholas Magazine
(see *Century Magazine*)

San Fernando Poetry Journal
(Kent Publications): Brown University, John Hay archives: [ca 1980–1988]: ca 2,200 items: correspondence, typescripts [RLIN]

The Satirist or the Censor of the Times, London

(Bernard Gregory, editor): University of Illinois: 1828–1847: 4 cuft: correspondence [guide]

Saturday Evening Post, Philadelphia
(George Horace Lorimer, editor): Historical Society of Pennsylvania: 1900–1947: 3 ft: literary correspondence, photographs, personal papers; also the papers of Adelaide W. Neall, associate editor 1909–1942 [RLIN]

Saturday Review of Literature
(see **Book-of-the-Month Club**)

Scribner's Magazine, New York City
(Robert Bridges, editor 1887–1930): Dickinson College: 1865–1930: 1,200 items (8 boxes): mss, correspondence, biography, scrapbooks: f/a [NUCMC 66-464]
(Robert Bridges, editor): Princeton University: 1896–1939: 5.40 cuft (12 boxes): mss, correspondence, memoranda [RLIN / guide]
(J.G. Holland, editor 1864–1880): NYPL: 1943–1881: 1.8 linft: manuscripts, literary correspondence: advance notice required: f/a [RLIN]
(see *Century Magazine*)

Sea Stories Magazine
(see **Street & Smith**)

Sewanee Review, Sewanee, TN
(Andrew N. Lytle, editor): Joint University Libraries, TN: 1868–1966: 5ft: f/a [Hinding 15,934]

The Shadow Magazine
(see **Street & Smith**)

Shenandoah, Lexington, VA
Washington & Lee University: 1950–1979: 5.5 ft: mss, proofs of first 30 vols, editorial correspondence [NUCMC 89-2017]

Smart Set, New York City
(see *American Mercury*)

Smith's Magazine
(see **Street & Smith**)

Southern Humanities Review, Auburn, AL
(Eugene Current-Garcia, coeditor): Auburn University: 1934–1978: 3 ft: correspondence, personal papers, mss [NUCMC 83-136]

Sport Story Magazine/Starry Flag Weekly
(see **Street & Smith**)

Story Magazine
(see **Story Press**)

The Sunday Magazine, London
(see **William Isbister**)

Texas Quarterly
HRC, University of Texas: archival materials
[guide]

Time-Life, Inc
(Henry R. Luce, publisher): Library of Congress: 1917–1967: 35,000 items: correspondence, personal papers: partially restricted: f/a [NUCMC 77-1545: NIDS(US) 2.1.451]
(see **Doubleday**)

Top-notch Magazine
(see **Street & Smith**)

Transition, Paris
(Eugene & Maria Jolas, editors): Beinecke Library, Yale University: 1879–1979: 69 boxes: general office files: f/a [gopher]

Unmuzzled Ox, New York City
University of Tulsa: 1973–1985: 60 boxes, recordings: editorial correspondence: f/a [personal enquiry]

Venture
(see **Mercury Press**)

Western Review
(see *Rocky Mountain Review*)

Village Voice, New York City
(Joel Oppenheimer, poetry editor 1972–1984): University of Connecticut: ca 1953–1989: 3 boxes, 3 file drawers, 73 record cartons [RLIN]

Western Story Magazine
(see **Street & Smith**)

Westminster Review, London
(John Chapman, editor): Duke University: 1851–1867: 14 items: correspondence [guide]

Wild West Weekly
(see **Street & Smith**)

Woman's Home Companion
(see **T. Y. Crowell**)

Woman's Journal, Boston
(Mary Livermore, editor): Princeton University: 1846–1905: 7 boxes: f/a [Hinding, 11,167]

World Literature Today
University of Oklahoma: 1926–1983: 38.66 ft: correspondence, files regarding the exodus of writers from Nazi Germany and Spain, 1926–1951 [RLIN]

Worlds of Fantasy/Worlds of If/Worlds of Tomorrow
(see **Galaxy Press, Universal Publishers Corp**)

X: A Quarterly Review, London
Indiana University: 1959–1962: 334 items: correspondence, mss: f/a [NUCMC 83-1297]

Yankee Magazine, Dublin, NH
(Jean Burden, poetry editor): Syracuse University: 1931–1992: 11 ft: correspondence, mss, memorabilia [RLIN]

Yugen
Indiana University: 1958–1962: publication files [*DLB Yearbook 1984:* 109–115]

Zane Grey Western Magazine
(see **Renown Publications**)

SECTION THREE: LITERARY AGENTS

Authors Syndicate, London
(William Morris Colles): Columbia University: 1890–1928: 2.5 linft (ca 2,400 items in 6 boxes): editorial files, copyright and translation materials: f/a (5pp) [NUCMC 78-670 / RLIN]
(William Morris Colles): Rochester University: 1874+: 1 box: correspondence: f/a [NIDS(US) 4.21.58]

HRC, University of Texas: 2,000 items: correspondence [*Library Chronicle of the University of Texas at Austin,* 35: 60–87]

Lurton Blassingame
University of Oregon: 1965–1966: 5ft: correspondence files [NUCMC 70-1775]

Bolt & Watson, Ltd, London
(see **Harold Ober Associates**)

William Bradley Literary Agency (William A. and Jenny Serrys Bradley), Paris
HRC, University of Texas: 256,000 items: correspondence [guide]

Borchardt, Inc, Literary Agency (Ann and Georges Borchardt)
Columbia University: 1951–1986: 148 linft (ca 179,500 items in 363 boxes): literary correspondence, royalty statements, mss, contracts: f/a (37pp) [RLIN]

Brandt & Brandt, New York City
Princeton University: 1920–1970s: 6.3 cuft (14 boxes): A–P contract files: f/a [RLIN]

Collins-Knowlton-Wing
(see **Curtis Brown Ltd**)

Curtis Brown Ltd, New York City
Columbia University: 1914–1988: 794 linft (ca 1,000,000 items in 1,798 boxes & 132 bound volumes): correspondence, royalty statements, contract files: f/a: Curtis Brown permission required to examine: incorporating the literary agences of **Willis Kingsley Wing** and **Collins-Knowlton-Wing** [RLIN / guide]

James O. Brown Associates
Columbia University: 1927–1992: 231 linft (210,000 items, 503 boxes): correspondence: f/a (49pp) [Hinding 11,954 / RLIN / guide]

Maurice Crain, New York City
Columbia University: 1946–1970: 3,200 items: correspondence, financial records: partially restricted [NUCMC 73-71 / RLIN] (see also **Annie Laurie Williams**)

John Cushman Associates
Columbia University: 1965–1978: 61.5 linft (72,000 items) [RLIN]

Benjamin De Casseres
Brooklyn Public Library: 1900–1945: 521 items: literary correspondence: f/a [NUCMC 65-14]

Frieda Fishbein
NYPL: 1926–1931: 57 items: correspondence with actors, playwrights [NUCMC 72-1024]

Derek Gardner
HRC, University of Texas: 1960s: archival materials [guide]

Nathan Goldstone, (film agent)
University of Oregon: ?–1966: 1 box: screenplays, literary properties [NUCMC 72-378]

Greenburger Literary Agency (Sanford J. Greenburger)
University of Oregon: 1931–1961: 33 ft (incl 20,000 letters, 200 mss): correspondence, mss: f/a [NUCMC 78-1126] (also agent for **International Literary Agency**)

Blanche Gregory
Columbia University: 1963–1982: 355 items (2 boxes): correspondence: [RLIN]

David Higham Literary Agency London
HRC, University of Texas: 1951–1970: archival material [guide]
(see **Harold Ober Associates**)

Flora May Holly
(see *Bookman*)

Jeanette Hopkins
Vassar College: 1965–1980: 3 cuft: literary correspondence, contract summaries, production records [RLIN]

Hughes Massie, London
(see **Harold Ober Associates**)

International Literary Agency
(see **Casanova Society**)
(see **Greenburger Literary Agency**)

Lenniger Literary Agency, August Lenniger & Edith Margolis
University of Oregon: 1961–1966: 12 ft: correspondence, mss: f/a [NUCMC 69-996]

Harold Matson Co
Columbia University: 1937–1980: 75,000 items: correspondence, contract files 1937–1980 of McIntosh, McKee & Dodds, whom they acquired: [NUCMC 84-557]

Monica McCall
Boston University: 1936–1963: 3,000 items, 72 boxes: correspondence: f/a [NUCMC 70-49: Hinding 6,045]

Emma Mills
NYPL: 1920–1946: 3 boxes: literary & theatrical correspondence [guide]

Harold Ober Associates
Princeton University: 1927–1982 (bulk 1968–1982): 163 cuft (262 boxes, 14 cartons): correspondence, mss, contracts: f/a [RLIN / guide] (also **David Higham Associates, London** (1965–1972); **Hughes Massie Ltd, London** (1968–1972); **Bolt & Watson Ltd, London** (1971–1972)

P.E.N. International
University of Tulsa: 1940–1980: 100 boxes: correspondence: f/a [personal enquiry]
HRC, University of Texas: 1921–1972: correspondence, activity files [guide]

A. D. Peters Literary Agency
HRC, University of Texas: 1926–1963: archival materials [guide]

J. B. Pinker & Son
Huntington Library: 1903–1913: 600+ items: correspondence mainly with Ford Maddox Ford: f/a [NUCMC 81-76 / guide]
Houghton Library, Harvard: 1900+: 31 boxes, 143 items: correspondence [NUCMC 83-946]
Northwestern University: 1900–1934: 50,000 items: correspondence [NUCMC 60-2951]
Southern Illinois: 1929–1934: 200 items: correspondence, mainly with Richard Aldington: f/a [NUCMC 77-527]
HRC University of Texas: 1901–1939: archival materials [guide]
NYPL, Berg Collection: correspondence [guide]

Paul Revere Reynolds
Columbia University: 1899–1980: 139,720 items (280 boxes): correspondence [NUCMC 78-712 / RLIN]
Princeton University: 1895–1940: 11 folders: correspondence [guide]

Leah Salisbury
Columbia University: 1925–1975: 149 linft (185,000 items): correspondence with writers, actors [NUCMC 69-638 / RLIN]

John Schaffner
Columbia University: 1940–1989: 90 linft (108,650 items in 222 boxes): correspondence, financial papers [NUCMC 69-639 / RLIN]

Toni Strassman
Columbia University: 1937–1984: 30,000 items: correspondence, contracts, royalty statements, photographs [NUCMC 78-718 / RLIN]

Tillotson's Syndicate
(Philip Gibbs, editor): Temple University: 1900–1914: 1 box: accession list, correspondence, manuscripts [RLIN]

Louis Untermeyer
University of Delaware, Newark: 1906–1940: 4 ft (1194 items): correspondence: advance written request required: f/a [NUCMC 71-1647]
Huntington Library: 1917–1975: 70 items: correspondence [guide]

Watkins Loomis, Inc (formerly A. Watkins, Inc)
Columbia University: 1883–1987: 131,500 items (261 boxes, 42 vols, 27 card file drawers): correspondence, mss, business records: f/a [NUCMC 84-483 / RLIN]

Armitage Watkins
Columbia University: 1941–1948: 500 items: correspondence related to US Office of War Information [NUCMC 84-644]

A. P. Watt & Son
NYPL, Berg Collection: 1883–1924: letterbooks (not indexed), correspondence [guide]
University of North Carolina at Chapel Hill: 1888–1982: 213,400 items & 33 vols (an additional acquisition is currently being processed): correspondence, contracts, legal records: f/a: advance notice required [personal enquiry]

Annie Laurie Williams
Columbia University: 1922–1971: ca 35,000 items: correspondence, contracts, ledgers: restricted use [NUCMC 73-111] (also **Maurice Crain**)

Willis Kingsley Wing
(see **Curtis Brown Ltd**)

Abbreviations
NUCMC – National Union Catalogue of Manuscript Collections
NIDS(US) – National Inventory of Document Sources (US), microfiche series
RLIN – Research Libraries Information Network (on-line catalogue)
gopher – Internet library catalogue

ULMC – *Union List of Manuscripts in Canadian Repositories*

HOBODS – *Location register of British book publishers and printers archives 1830–1939*

Ash – *Subject Collections, a guide to special book collections*

Hinding – *Women's History Sources, a guide to archives and manuscript collections in the United States*

Works Cited

Catalogue of Manuscripts in the Houghton Library, Harvard University, 8 volumes (Alexandria, Virginia: Chadwyck-Healey, 1986–);

Catalogue of Manuscripts in the University of Oregon Library, compiled by Martin Schmitt (Eugene: University of Oregon Press, 1971);

Dictionary Catalogue of the Henry W. and Albert A. Berg Collection of English and American Literature, 5 volumes and supplement (Boston: G. K. Hall, 1969);

Dictionary Catalogue, Manuscript Division, New York Public Library, 2 volumes (Boston: G. K. Hall, 1967);

A Guide to the Harry Ransom Humanities Research Center (Austin: University of Texas at Austin, 1990);

Guide to Literary Manuscripts in the Huntington Library, compiled and edited by Sue Hodson and Mary L. Robertson (San Marino, Cal.: Huntington Library, 1979);

Guide to the Manuscript Collections in the Manuscript Department of the William R. Perkins Library, Duke University, edited by Richard C. Davis and Linda Angle Miller (Santa Barbara, Cal.: Clio Books, 1980);

A Guide to the Manuscript Collections in the Rare Book and Manuscript Library of Columbia University (Boston: G. K. Hall, 1992);

A Guide to the Modern Literary Manuscripts Collection in the Special Collections of the Washington University Libraries (Saint Louis: The Libraries, 1985);

A Guide to Modern Manuscripts in the Princeton University Library, edited by John M. Delaney (Boston: G. K. Hall, 1989);

Index to the Archives of Harper & Bros, 1817–1914, compiled by Christopher Feeney (Cambridge: Chadwyck-Healey, 1982);

Index to the Archives of Richard Bentley & Son, compiled by Alison Ingram (Cambridge: Chadwyck-Healey, 1977);

Index to the Archives of Grant Richards, 1897–1948, compiled by Ingram (Cambridge: Chadwyck-Healey, 1981);

Location Register of British Book Publishers and Printers Archives 1830–1939, compiled by Alexis Weedon, History of the Book on Demand Series (HOBODS) (Bristol & Oxford, forthcoming 1994).

Manuscripts Guide to Collections at the University of Illinois at Urbana-Champaign, edited by Maynard J. Brichford, Robert M. Sutton, and Dennis F. Walle (Urbana: University of Illinois Press, 1976);

Subject Collections, a Guide to Special Book Collections, compiled by Lee Ash and William G. Miller, sixth edition (New York: Bowker, 1985);

Union List of Manuscripts in Canadian Repositories, revised edition, edited by F. Grace Maurice (Ottawa: Public Archives, 1975);

Women's History Sources, a Guide to Archives and Manuscript Collections in the United States, edited by Andrea Hinding (New York: Bowker, in association with the University of Minnesota, 1979).

The American Library in Paris

Mary C. Grattan

The American Library in Paris (ALP), located at 10, rue du Général Camou in the Seventh Arrondissement of Paris, is a private, nonprofit, nongovernmental subscription library with holdings of 80,000 books and 450 periodical titles, largely in the areas of American literature, American history, and American culture and society. It has a membership of 2,356 (40 percent French, 40 percent American, 20 percent other) and is open to the public, each year serving an additional 2,000 readers and researchers who are not members but use the library for short-term projects. The American Library is important, not only for its collection but for its nearly seventy-five years as an American presence in Europe and for its role as a model of American library principles and service on the Continent.

When the Armistice was signed ending World War I, the American Library Association's (ALA) Library War Service collections for American soldiers were dismantled throughout the European theater. But the demand for English-language books remained even as the soldiers returned home. Thousands of American and British expatriates were living in France and sought an affordable means to stay abreast of English-language writing. Moreover, French readers in their postwar enthusiasm were eager for American books and magazines. Thus, the ALA decided to put the War Service books to a new use. The ALP was founded in 1920 as an independent nonprofit subscription institution through the cooperation of the ALA, the American and French governments, and many private citizens of both nationalities. The library was envisioned as a model of American librarianship, reflecting the democratic principles of open access and a strong public-service orientation.

Probably the single most instrumental person behind the conversion of the ALA's military libraries into the ALP was Burton Egbert Stevenson (1872–1962). From 1917 to 1920 Stevenson was European director of the ALA Library War Service, and when the war was over he remained long enough to help establish the new facility. Later, from 1925 to 1930, he served as director of the ALP. Except for these two stints in Paris, Stevenson devoted his career to being librarian at the Chillicothe (Ohio) Public Library and author of such noted reference books as *The Home Book of Verse*, *The Home Book of Quotations*, and *The Home Book of Shakespeare Quotations*. Although the library world remembers Stevenson mostly for his contributions to their reference shelves, his work in the war effort was met with high regard at the time, most dramatically in a letter he received from Gen. John J. Pershing, commander in chief of the American Expeditionary Forces, dated 18 April 1919, commending Stevenson and the ALA for their excellent work.

The American Library's first quarters were at 10, rue de l'Elysée, across from the gardens of the residency of the president of France, in the former residence of the papal nuncio to the French Republic who had left France thirteen years before. At this location some thirty thousand books were housed and made available to any readers who sought membership. The library's first official director was William N. C. Carlton, former head of the Newberry Library in Chicago.

The library was born out of a world war, but it was nurtured in these crucial early years by a French society hungry for American books and ideas and by an expatriate American community hungry for Parisian intellectual and artistic life. Numerous details from the ALP archives indicate that the opening of the facility was taken quite seriously by the French government. Among those Frenchmen who agreed to serve as members of an advisory council in support of the new library were former president Raymond Poincaré; Marshals Joffre, Foch, and Lyautey; M. René Viviani and Baron d'Estournelles de Constant; Henri-Louis Bergson, Paul Bourget, Emile Boutroux, M. Brieux, Gabriel Hanotaux, and Eugène-Marcel Prévost, all members of the French Academy; Alfred Croiset Lévy-Bruhl and Camille Saint-Saëns, members of the Institute of France; and André Tardieu, member of the Chamber of Deputies.

Among American standard-bearers of the library in these formative years were several who had ties with the American expatriate literary community. One was Charles L. Seeger, father of war poet Alan Seeger. Mr. and Mrs. Seeger had made the decision to travel to France in 1917 to be near

226

their son Alan, an American who had enlisted as a soldier in the French Foreign Legion. But before they arrived Alan Seeger was killed in action. The Seegers remained in France as residents for several years, becoming involved with the new library. In 1921, during Mr. Seeger's term as president of the Library Board, the couple presented the ALP with a commemorative tablet of names of American volunteers (including their own son Alan) killed in World War I. In addition, the Seegers designated that royalties from their son's poetry go to the ALP as a permanent fund for purchasing books of American poetry. Not only was this donation a much-needed boost to the resources of the fledgling library, but the Seeger collection's bookplates even today serve as an ongoing reminder to patrons, both American and French, of the haunting contribution to American poetry of this young soldier who wrote "I Have a Rendezvous with Death."

Also significant to the financial success of the library at this time were legacies from noted supporters such as author Mildred Aldrich, perhaps best known for her work on wartime France, *A Hilltop on the Marne* (1915). Aldrich was popular in France for her help in influencing Americans to be more sympathetic toward entering World War I and for her assistance to soldiers and refugees, for which she was awarded the French Legion of Honor in 1922.

Another literary figure who played a prominent role in the library's success during the early 1920s was Edith Wharton. Wharton, who had come to Paris as a permanent resident in 1912, gave her full support to the library by serving as a board member for several years beginning in 1921 and by becoming a life member in 1923. She contributed her prestige as one of the few widely revered American women writers of the period, and she contributed her books as well. There is no doubt that her presence enhanced the image of the institution among the literati, and in general among the French, who during World War I had already awarded Wharton the Cross of the Legion of Honor (1916) for her relief work in Paris.

One other figure from this era with ties to the literary world was Laurence Benét, uncle of Stephen Vincent and William Rose Benét. Laurence Benét was a member of the ALP board of trustees in 1920 and remained active in the library's administration for several years more. Stephen was later to become associated with the library, too. Stephen and his family moved to Paris in 1926 and stayed until 1929, and in this period he is reputed to have written much of *John Brown's Body* (1928) within the

The original seal of the ALP (courtesy of Mary C. Grattan)

halls of the ALP, feeling close ties to the library partly, no doubt, because of his uncle's deep involvement.

From 1923 to 1925 the library published a literary journal called *Ex Libris,* which though short-lived remains a valuable reflection of the interests and tastes of the American and French reading public of the day. Edited by W. Dawson Johnston, *Ex Libris* was a monthly publication containing features about authors, American arts, and other similar subjects, often with a French slant. Its features included such pieces as "Negro Art and America" by Albert C. Barnes, "Writings of the American Volunteers in the French Legion During the World War" by Paul Ayres Rockwell, "The Vogue of Shakespeare in France" by Comtesse de Chambrun, and "He and They, Hemingway: A Portrait" by Gertrude Stein. Stein's whimsical piece, published in December 1923, is of only minor interest as a sample of her writing, but it does show that she was willing to lend her prestige to the library in this way.

Besides the featured articles in *Ex Libris* were lists of new library acquisitions, reviews of current books, and advertisements purchased by commercial enterprises – ranging from bookstores like Brentano's, W. H. Smith and Son, and the Galignani Library, to the Typewriter Emporium ("All American makes sold, rented and repaired"), Walk-Over Shoes ("The latest American styles for men and women"), and even funeral director and embalmer Bernard J. Lane ("Direct shipment to all parts of the world"). All of these offer contemporary readers a glimpse of what life was like, especially for Americans, in the Paris of the 1920s. Among the many contributors of reviews were Stein and Ernest Hemingway, both of whom wrote pieces responding in March 1925 to Sherwood Anderson's *A Story Teller's Story* (1925), published a few months before. Legends of Stein's stage whispers to Alice B. Toklas in the ALP stacks and of Hemingway's forays into the library are part of the oral tradition, but the real evidence of their connection is in *Ex Libris*.

It is evident from the reviews that the library tried to keep abreast of current publishing, including works of Americans living in France. Besides Hemingway's and Stein's reviews of Anderson's books are reviews for Ezra Pound's *Indiscretions* (1923), Wharton's *The Mother's Recompense* (1925), Ford Madox Ford's *Joseph Conrad: A Personal Remembrance* (1924), and E. E. Cummings's *The Enormous Room* (1922).

The library discontinued the publication of *Ex Libris* after the July 1925 issue, presumably because of funding problems. There was no clue in the magazine itself that it was about to vanish. Perhaps its disappearance was simply one early sign of the financial difficulties that plagued the library even in the late 1920s, before the Depression really began. Yet despite the hard times, the library continued to attract important writers. In 1930 such authors as Joseph Wood Krutch, André Maurois, Ford, Allen Tate, and Hemingway were frequent visitors.

Less of a written record remains of library activities and patrons over the next few years, although Henry Miller was one noted habitué during this time; the library still has a copy of a 1938 letter from Miller requesting a book on Zen Buddhism. But library documents of the 1930s were mostly preoccupied with the sensation of financial plummeting. During the early 1930s staffing was reduced, salaries were cut, and finally the building was sold outright. The library had to move its headquarters in 1936 from 10, rue de l'Elysée to 9, rue de Téhéran, in an old building near the Parc Monceau. Thanks to sizable donations from the French government, from a group of local citizens, and in 1937 from the Carnegie corporation, the library was rescued from extinction. It was just about the time that the library found itself swamped with requests for Adolf Hitler's book *Mein Kampf* (1937). Things were about to change.

Or perhaps one should say that library history was about to repeat itself. On Monday, 3 September 1939, the day after France declared war on Germany, ALP director Dorothy Reeder founded the Soldiers Service and in doing so revived the library's original function of twelve years before as distributor of books to soldiers in wartime. In 1940 more than 21,000 books and magazines had already been collected, and 12,000 of these already distributed to French and British soldiers in France. But even as these books were flowing to the troops, the German authorities were suppressing certain authors at the ALP. All of the books censored by the Germans were in French, but among these were translations from English of American authors such as Hemingway, John Steinbeck, and William Shirer. Under duress the library crated the offending books and stored them in the cellar until the end of the war.

It was in such a repressive atmosphere that, against her will, Reeder was forced to leave France in May 1941. But the library remained open during the entire war through the efforts of the French staff under the direction of the countess de Chambrun (née Clara Longworth of Cincinnati, sister of Nicholas Longworth, the late Speaker of the U.S. House of Representatives). The countess, although not a librarian, had been associated with the American Library since its early days. A Shakespearean scholar, she had written several articles for *Ex Libris* and was an active member of the library throughout the 1920s and 1930s. Now, because she was an American married to a Frenchman, she was permitted by French and German authorities to operate the library. In fact, as the countess accepted the responsibility of directing the ALP, her husband, Count Jacques Adalbert de Chambrun, himself a descendant of Lafayette, took on the same task at the American Hospital in Neuilly. These American institutions seemed in safe hands.

Yet, even with the special permission to keep the library open, the countess de Chambrun faced serious problems. She continued to send books to British and French soldiers in German prison camps, but German cooperation was intermittent, as was mail service. In a practice begun while Reeder was still director, the countess and other staff members (all French nationals) voluntarily placed themselves at personal risk by regularly delivering books to Jewish borrowers who were forbidden by law to frequent such public establishments as libraries. And throughout the war she aided staff members and their families, among others, who were plagued by varying degrees of German harassment.

Original location of the library at 10, rue de l'Elysée (courtesy of Mary C. Grattan)

The present location of the library, 10, rue du Général Camou (courtesy of Mary C. Grattan)

Interior of the library at its second location, 9, rue de Téhéran (courtesy of Mary C. Grattan)

With the help of her staff she managed to keep the library doors open until the liberation in June 1944. But the battle was not yet over for the countess de Chambrun. Perhaps it was inevitable that the special status allowed the library during World War II would arouse some suspicion – especially when the count and countess were the parents of Count René de Chambrun, who in 1935 married Josée Laval, daughter of Vichy chief of government Pierre Laval. In September 1944 the countess de Chambrun and her husband were arrested in connection with reports of alleged collaboration with the Germans. They fervently denied such reports, and in the end no charges were proved against them. The countess wrote extensively of the war years and her role as the war administrator of the ALP in her book *Shadows Lengthen* (1949).

Despite her official exoneration, the library board of trustees decided to step in to make politic changes in the directorship of the institution. The minutes of the 9 November 1944 annual membership meeting reflected a decision to remove the library from any cloud by placing it temporarily under the control of Milton E. Lord of the Boston Public Library:

> The Countess de Chambrun (Clara Longworth) continues to direct the library activities and credit is due her for keeping the library going during the critical period. However, her connections have given rise to some hesitation on the part of the American military authorities to deal with her or the library and as a consequence it is not playing the role it should be playing in Army morale work under the Division of Special Services headed by Colonel Solbert, with whom I have discussed the problem. He and others are of the opinion that the situation would be materially relieved if the Countess could be retired to an honorary post in the immediate future and an American who has no associations with the occupation period appointed active director.

In the postwar years the library continued to experience financial difficulties, but it remained an active institution. An unpublished paper written by Campbell Kilduff characterizes the reading habits of the membership in the late 1940s: "The most popular fiction books, year in and year out are the Jalna series. [Louis] Bromfield holds a close second. At the moment top place on the non-fiction list is held by *The God That Failed*, three of whose authors, André Gide, Richard Wright, and Arthur Koestler have, at one time or another, used the library." He also emphasized the open-access policy of the library: "[It] has no forbidden book shelves. Occasionally though a book is put under the counter. This is not so much to protect impressionable readers as to protect the book itself. Henry Miller's *Tropic* series, which are presented regularly to the library by homeward-bound, law-abiding Americans, usually disappear rapidly."

In 1948, under the directorship of Dr. Ian Forbes Fraser, the library opened a Left Bank branch at 173, boulevard Saint-Germain. Of the opening-day celebration André Siegfried (historian and member of the Académie Française) wrote in *Le Figaro:* "[The American Library is] a valuable center, well known to all those who are interested in American civilization, and even more generally, the civilization of English-speaking peoples." The only protest appeared in the communist newspaper *L'Humanité,* which called the American Library "a menace to France . . . endangering the French book world . . . [and] spreading . . . its ideological propaganda into the very heart of the cultural center of Paris."

Such outright hostility from the communist front seems particularly ironic in light of events only five years later. In 1953 Roy Cohn and David Schine, two of Sen. Joseph McCarthy's assistants, visited the library in the hope of unearthing evidence of anti-Americanism. Then-director Fraser turned them away, explaining that the library was private. Thus, while Howard Fast's *Citizen Tom Paine* (1943) was banned from U.S. libraries, the ALP purchased six copies to meet the great demand from French readers. The library managed to withstand the censorship threats of the 1950s because it was an institution under the control of no government.

It is important to note that the membership of the American Library, even in the 1950s, was 60 percent French. Some of the postwar interest in America had cooled, but the French still craved English-language reading matter. Significantly, during Fraser's term as director, librarian Ruth C. McBirney assisted in the establishment of branch collections in Rouen, Le Havre, and Rheims in cooperation with local municipal libraries. McBirney was awarded the Palmes Académiques for her work in this area. The establishment of regional collections proved a far-sighted one. Although the sites have shifted with the times and the circumstances, the library has continued to support branch libraries around France to this day. In 1993 the library opened a new branch in Angers, and it maintains other branch collections in the cities of Grenoble, Montpellier, Nancy, and Toulouse. A library for the blind, created in 1955 as a part of the ALP, still functions as well but is currently in its own quarters and independent of the ALP. Long-range plans call for the possible reunion of the two library collections.

In the midst of all this outreach activity, the library moved in 1953 to new quarters, an old Second Empire mansion at 129, avenue des Champs-Elysées. It remained at this site for a decade, until for the first time in its history the library was fiscally strong enough to purchase its own building. In 1965 the ALP moved into its present location at 10, rue du Général Camou. Here, in the shadow of the Eiffel Tower, more changes came. During the directorship of Harry Goldberg, a donation from C. Douglas Dillon, former secretary of the treasury and ambassador to France, allowed the ALP to build a new wing, christened the Dillon Wing, to house the Center for American Studies, a special collection of mostly American literature and history resources. In the 1970s, during Paul McAdam's term as director, the library contracted with the American College (now University) of Paris to lease space and library access to the college's faculty and students. The American College established its own library adjacent to the ALP's collection so that its students would have easy access to both collections. During the early 1980s the library began its first major microfilm project. Since its early days the ALP has always owned the largest English-language periodicals collection on the Continent, but over time storage space has become a problem. When completed, the retrospective microfilm project, begun more than a decade ago and still in progress today, will not only help to free precious space, but will also make the contents of older, more fragile periodicals more freely accessible to members.

Over the years the American Library has benefited enormously from the donation of books from the personal collections of several important members and friends. Books from such notable persons as Stein, Sylvia Beach, Janet Flanner, and Nadia-Juliette Boulanger are thus sprinkled among the circulating collection or have been placed in the director's office for reference use by researchers. The Beach donation, which numbered over five thousand volumes, was the most substantial of the gifts. The most recent celebrity connection was the delivery in 1992 of Marlene Dietrich's personal book collection to the ALP by Dietrich's grandson Peter Riva. The Dietrich collection contains novels, poetry, nonfiction, and reference works but is composed mostly of books by and about figures of the worlds of stage and cinema. Some of the books are autographed dedications by the author to Dietrich, and others contain marginal annotations by

Library staff securing important documents after the German invasion of France in September 1939 (courtesy Mary C. Grattan)

Dietrich herself. The collection is an important addition to the library's growing sections on American popular culture, a subject of wide interest among French readers.

In 1986, when the library made the decision to automate its collection and administration, Robert Grattan III was appointed director. He served for the next seven and a half years, bringing the library into the technological age. Under his leadership the library converted from a card catalogue to an online public catalogue, and the departments of circulation, serials, acquisitions, cataloguing, and accounting were also automated. Several periodical indexes and other reference sources were introduced in CD-ROM format, and a circulating compact-disc collection was established to augment and update the phonograph and audiocassette holdings. From the start the ALP automation has been a joint venture with the American University of Paris, allowing cooperative online access to a total of 125,000 book titles and more than 700 periodical titles, with systems management and ownership at the ALP. The

Bookplate for books added to the ALP collection through the Alan Seeger Endowment (courtesy of Mary C. Grattan)

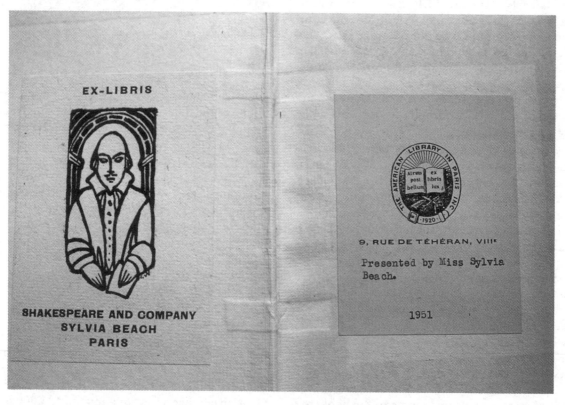

Bookplate for one of the several thousand volumes added to the ALP collection through a gift of Sylvia Beach (courtesy of Mary C. Grattan)

implications of automation are far-reaching. Before his departure from the library in mid 1993, Grattan laid the groundwork for automation of the library's branches and also for the inclusion of the ALP online catalogue to MINITEL, the nationwide telecommunications system in France. The library's periodical holdings are already accessible on MINITEL.

The periodicals collection, with its more than 450 titles, is undoubtedly the single most widely used resource of the ALP. In 1992 this collection was made much more easily available to the public through the construction of the new Research Center, which houses all the library's periodical indexes (in both book and CD-ROM formats), the microfilm holdings and equipment, and the most recent issues of more than 350 current periodicals. The Research Center is designed according to the principle of open access, strongly reflecting the democratic tradition of American library service. Open access is taken for granted by most American users, but the French readers – long inured to closed stacks and interminable waits for requested materials – are delighted with the self-service concept.

Today the American Library still draws writers and other researchers through its collection and through its monthly "Evenings with Authors." In recent years speakers in the series have included fiction writers Mary Gordon, Mavis Gallant, Michael Mewshaw, Hugh Nissenson, and Diane Johnson; nonfiction authors Mort Rosenblum, William Pfaff, and Axel Krause; drama critic Sheridan Morley; and jazz critic Mike Zwerin. In 1987 Samuel Beckett became interested in the library through correspondence with director Grattan, who had written to ask him if James Joyce might have ever used the ALP. In the last years of his life Beckett made several donations to the library.

With the library's seventy-fifth anniversary approaching, financial problems persist, as they have through most of the library's history. But the library remains both a significant center of research for American and French scholars and a haven for French university students. As it has from its beginnings, the library continues to assist students and other readers throughout France with its branches and serves a major role by supplying hundreds of photocopies of articles needed each year by those studying for national exams in American literature and social sciences. It also continues to serve the English-speaking expatriate community in much the same way as an American public library, by maintaining a children's collection and weekly story hour (inaugurated in 1923), the "Evenings with Authors" series, an ongoing variety of annotated reading lists, a members' newsletter, and the timely acquisition of best-sellers. As has always been true, today's collection is strongest in the fields of American history and society, American literature and criticism, and the American presence in France. And thanks to those who support it financially, it remains true to its original mission, serving as a vital center of research and a paradigm of American librarianship in the heart of Europe.

References:

"America in Paris," *Time,* 70 (23 September 1957): 70;

William N. C. Carlton, "The American Library in Paris, Inc.," *Library Journal,* 46 (15 October 1921): 831–834;

William K. Harrison III, "Paris Library Opens Branch," *Library Journal,* 73 (15 May 1948): 758.

The Center for the Book in the Library of Congress

John Y. Cole
Library of Congress

In 1977 the Library of Congress, under the leadership of Librarian of Congress Daniel J. Boorstin, established a new office: through the Center for the Book it began promoting books, reading, and book culture. The center started modestly with one staff member. Today it has four staff members and is the catalyst for projects and promotional activity in a national network of more than 25 state affiliates and 120 national organizations. One important factor has not changed, however; today, as in 1977, the Center for the Book depends on private contributions to support its program of symposia, publications, and projects. It is a successful partnership between the federal government and the private sector and one of the Library of Congress's most successful educational-outreach efforts.

The Center for the Book was founded in the belief that there is a "community of the book" that stretches from author to reader and that this community can be mobilized to keep books and reading central to individuals and to the life of America's knowledge-based democracy. The most important person in the community of the book is the individual reader. Boorstin emphasized this point when the center was founded:

> As the national library of a great free republic, the Library of Congress has a special duty and a special interest to see that books *do not* go unread, that they *are* read by people of all ages and conditions. . . . here we shape plans for a grand national effort to make all our people eager, avid, understanding, critical readers.

In *A Nation of Readers,* a talk presented and published in 1982, Boorstin asserted that, at least in the past, America has been a country of readers. America could be so again, he maintained, if its citizens and institutions made a new commitment to keeping "the culture of the book thriving." In this effort, which is the basic mission of the Center for the Book, technology is an ally: "We have a special duty to see that the book is the useful, illuminating servant of all technologies, and that all other technologies become the effective, illuminating acolytes of the book."

The promotion of book culture in the United States is not new. The story in recent decades is a mixture of solid accomplishments and periods of frustration. It reflects the tenuous nature of alliances among book-minded people, traditional American uncertainty about the proper role of government in culture, and, especially in recent years, uncertainty about the effect of new technologies on the world of books.

In 1950 a small group of leading American publishers, including Cass Canfield of Harper, Curtis McGraw from McGraw-Hill, Harold Guinzburg of Viking Press, and Douglas Black of Doubleday and Company, established the American Book Publishers Council (ABPC), a trade association that reached beyond traditional business concerns to promote books, reading, and libraries. The first discussions between the council's representatives and librarians took place at the 1950 annual conference of the American Library Association (ALA). Postal rates, book distribution, copyright, and reading promotion were early agenda items. The anthology *The Wonderful World of Books* (1952) was a result of the 1951 Conference on Rural Reading, sponsored by the ABPC, the U.S. Department of Agriculture, the ALA, and other organizations.

Censorship became a topic of mutual concern to publishers and librarians in the early 1950s, when private groups and public officials in various parts of the country attempted to remove books from sale, censor textbooks, and purge libraries. In response, in May 1953 the ALA and the ABPC sponsored a conference on the freedom to read. Librarian of Congress Luther H. Evans chaired the two-day meeting, which soon led to the Freedom to Read Declaration, which was adopted by both associations and soon thereafter by other book and educational associations.

John Y. Cole with state center coordinators Valerie Watt of Connecticut and Faye Glick of Pennsylvania during the annual state center meeting in April 1993 (photograph by Yusef El-Amin, Library of Congress)

The Freedom to Read Declaration and related intellectual-freedom issues united publishing and library leaders and their organizations and stimulated, in 1954, the creation of the National Book Committee. Declaring itself a citizen-oriented, public-interest voice on behalf of books, the book committee urged the "wider distribution and wider use" of books and encouraged greater use and support of libraries, the development of lifelong reading habits, improved access to books, and the freedom to read. Its approximately three hundred members worked together with the professional book community to "foster a general public understanding of the value of books to the individual and to a democratic society."

The American Book Publishers Council and the American Library Association, the primary sponsors of the National Book Committee, provided the committee with its small, paid professional staff and with office space. Most of its projects were supported by grants from foundations or by government funds. The Commission on the Freedom to Read was established in 1955. In 1958 the book committee launched National Library Week, a year-round promotion and media campaign that encouraged citizen support for libraries, and administered it in collaboration with the ALA for the next sixteen years.

In 1960 the committee began administering the National Book Awards, which honored American books of literary merit and their authors. For the next decade the committee initiated and cosponsored, with a wide variety of organizations, useful conferences on topics such as the development of lifetime reading habits, the role of U.S. books abroad, books in the schools, the need for books in both rural areas and inner cities, the need to strengthen school libraries, and the public library in the city. The book committee also guided development of *Reading Out Loud,* an educational television series, and sponsored the publication of enduring classics such as Nancy Larrick's *A Parent's Guide to Children's Reading* (1958) and G. Robert Carlsen's *Books and the Teen-Age Reader* (1967).

The National Book Committee's sponsorship of projects and publications about the role of American books overseas, particularly in Asia and Africa, reflected widespread recognition of the key role that books could play in economic and cultural development. American government officials, publishers, educators, and librarians established several important programs that stimulated book exports, foreign trade, and international exchange; encouraged publishing in developing countries; and promoted books, libraries, and reading around the world.

The major projects were the Informational Media Guaranty Program (IMG; 1948–1968), a program which borrowed funds from the U.S. Treasury to enable U.S. book publishers, as well as producers of other "informational media" such as films and recordings, to sell their materials in countries that were short of hard-currency foreign exchange; Franklin Book Programs (1952–1979), a nonprofit, private educational corporation established by the publishing community and supported by U.S. government information agencies and foundations to "assist developing countries in the creation, production, distribution, and use of books and other educational materials"; and the Government Advisory Committee on Book and Library Programs (1962–1977), a panel of publishers, booksellers, and librarians that met with government officials to provide advice about federal book and library programs.

The United Nations Educational, Scientific, and Cultural Organization (UNESCO) proclaimed the year 1972 as International Book Year in order to "focus the attention of the general public [and of] governments and international and domestic organizations on the role of books and related materials in the lives and affairs of the individual and society." The National Book Committee organized and supported U.S. participation in International Book Year. The year 1972 was a high-water mark in the United States for cooperative organizational efforts on behalf of books and reading.

Two years later the National Book Committee was disbanded, in 1977 the Government Advisory Committee on Book and Library Programs was abolished, and in 1979 Franklin Book Programs was formally liquidated, contributing its remaining cash balance and receivables, amounting to less than ten thousand dollars, to the nascent Center for the Book in the Library of Congress. Thus by 1982, when UNESCO sponsored the World Congress on Books to assess international progress in promoting books since 1972, the key U.S. organizations that had participated in International Book Year were gone.

What had happened to the programs that made the 1960s and early 1970s such a productive period of cooperation in the U.S. book community? The answers are many but include financial uncertainty, new government policies, leadership changes in publishing and librarianship, the divisiveness of the copyright issue, distrust heightened by the growth of publishing and communication conglomerates, and increasing specialization and fragmentation in the library profession. Writing in the April 1977 issue of *Scholarly Publishing,* Herbert S. Bailey, Jr., director of the Princeton University Press, lamented that although the book community "should be working together for the advancement of scholarship and for the good of society," it seemed instead to be separated "by a system that puts authors and publishers and booksellers and librarians and finally readers in opposition to each other."

A modest step on behalf of a more unified book community was taken in the autumn of 1977, when Congress, at the behest of Librarian of Congress Boorstin, established the Center for the Book. Boorstin, a historian who became librarian of Congress in 1975, was eager for the institution to play a more prominent role in the national culture. In an article in *Harper's* written in 1974, he had explained why "the book" was the best "do-it-yourself, energy-free communication device" ever invented. He reasoned that the development of a new national office at the Library of Congress for promoting books was a natural and logical way for the library to use its prestige and resources on a national level and for a broad educational purpose.

The Joint Committee on the Library sponsored the necessary legislation, and the center was established by Public Law 95-129, in which the U.S. Congress affirmed its belief in "the importance of the printed word and the book" and recognized the need for the continued study of the book and the written record as "central to our understanding of ourselves and our world." President Jimmy Carter approved the legislation on 13 October 1977, affirming his "commitment to scholarly research and the development of public interest in books and reading."

The new law authorized the Center for the Book to use private, tax-deductible contributions to support its program and publications. Thus the new organization was founded as a partnership between government and the private sector. Its initial planning meetings and programs were supported by contributions from two generous donors: McGraw-Hill and Mrs. Charles W. Engelhard. Over a dozen people who had been closely associated with the National Book Committee, the Government Advisory Committee on International Book and Library Programs, and Franklin Book Programs became valuable members of the Center for the Book's National

Center for the Book Project Specialist Michael Thompson addressing participants at a partners' idea exchange (photograph by Reid Baker, Library of Congress)

Advisory Board. Their previous experience helped shape the Center for the Book's program.

There are important differences, however, between the Center for the Book and its organizational predecessors, and perhaps these differences will help ensure a long life for the center. The creation of the Center for the Book was supported by the U.S. Congress and endorsed by the president. The center has the authority of a government agency and enjoys the prestige of being part of the Library of Congress, a unique and most appropriate home for such an endeavor. But it does not depend on government funding for its program; in fact more than half its total annual budget comes from private contributions from corporations, foundations, and individuals. The center serves as a catalyst, a source of ideas, and a forum but not an administrator of major programs or long-term projects. Its full-time staff has never exceeded four people. Thus while it is part of a large and prestigious government institution, that also happens to be the world's largest library, the Center for the Book itself is small and flexible, two desirable traits in the fragile and always-changing community of the book.

Today the Center for the Book is still pursuing the ambitious mission Boorstin advocated six-

teen years ago. It uses the prestige and resources of the Library of Congress to stimulate public interest in books, reading, and libraries and to encourage the study of books and print culture. "Books Give Us Wings" is its slogan, and expanding the audience for books and reading is its principal goal. Each year approximately thirty corporations and two hundred individuals make tax-deductible contributions to fund its projects and publications.

The activities of the Center for the Book are aimed both at the general public and at scholars interested in the history of books, reading, and print culture. Its program includes reading-promotion projects with three national television networks (CBS, ABC Children's Television, and the Arts and Entertainment Network), symposia, lectures, exhibitions, publications, multimedia projects, and special events that honor anniversaries or individual achievement in the world of books.

Since 1978 the center has sponsored publication of more than twenty-five books and fifty pamphlets. Most of its publications are the result of symposia, lectures, or projects. One of its major projects in the 1980s, for example, was "Books in Our Future," a three-year study and series of symposia that explored the changing role of books and reading in the electronic age. The results were published in *Books in Our Future: Perspectives and Proposals,* a 399-page book published by the Library of Congress in 1987. The range of the center's program is reflected in the titles of four of its 1993 publications: *Developing Lifetime Readers: A Report on a National Reading Promotion Campaign; Publishing and Readership in Revolutionary France and America* (published by Greenwood Press in cooperation with the center); *Donated Book Programs: A Dialogue of Partners Handbook;* and the third edition of *The Community of the Book: A Directory of Organizations and Programs.*

Since 1987 the Center for the Book has initiated national reading-promotion themes that have been used by organizations throughout America to promote books, reading, and libraries. First Lady Barbara Bush was the honorary chair of "1989 – The Year of the Young Reader," a campaign to stimulate the love of reading among young people, and of "1991 – The Year of the Lifetime Reader," which used all media to support family reading and literacy projects.

With the 1991 Lifetime Reader campaign the center inaugurated a partnership program with national organizations that agreed to publicize the theme, use the theme to develop their own projects with their members, or make a financial or in-kind contribution to the campaign. National partnership programs were important ingredients in "Explore New Worlds – READ!," the 1992 campaign. And more than 120 organizations are national reading-promotion partners for "Books Change Lives," the promotion theme for 1993–1994.

The affiliated state centers for the book also are important participants in each year's national reading-promotion campaign. Each state center is a voluntary, statewide coalition that has been created to work with the Center for the Book to promote books and reading and the state's literary heritage. State centers plan and fund their own projects, drawing on help from the state's "community of the book," from authors through readers, and from prominent citizens and public officials who serve as advisers. Most of the state centers are located in state libraries. When its application is approved, a state center is granted affiliate status for a period of three years. Renewals are for three-year periods.

State-center projects include annual book awards (Colorado, Minnesota, Oklahoma); book fairs and festivals (Kentucky, Nebraska, Pennsylvania); exhibits (California, Kansas, Texas); television programs (Arizona, Florida); radio programs (Connecticut, Washington); author recognition events (Indiana, Missouri); literary heritage events (Alaska, Illinois); and publications such as Iowa's *Iowa Literary Heritage Trail,* Virginia's reprint edition of *Virginia: A Guide to the Old Dominion* (1992, originally 1940), and Wisconsin's *The Wisconsin Community of the Book.* State centers also occasionally host traveling exhibitions from the Library of Congress. For example, from 1993 to 1995 sixteen of the centers are hosting "Language of the Land: Journeys into Literary America," an exhibition of literary maps, photographs, and quotations from authors funded by the Lila Wallace–Reader's Digest Fund.

The high visibility and the national partnership approach of the Center for the Book complement the plans of Librarian of Congress James H. Billington for the future development of the Library of Congress. In his inaugural address in 1987 Billington expressed his determination to move the Library of Congress "out more broadly," to see that its rich resources are shared more widely with the nation and the world. In order to increase the institution's usefulness and its public visibility, he has involved the library directly in discussions concerning contemporary issues such as education, literacy, economic competitiveness, and the future of Eastern Europe, Russia, and other newly independent areas. A parallel focus is on how to use new technologies to share the library's resources more broadly, nationally and internationally.

With congressional approval Billington has encouraged the Library of Congress to undertake a new educational role and established a development office to raise private funds for educational outreach projects. Thus the Center for the Book is a small pilot project in the library's effort to link itself more creatively and effectively to the nation's intellectual, educational, and cultural life. It is pointing the way to what might be possible through closer alliances among the library, other organizations, and the private sector.

The Center for the Book's role as a public advocate of books, reading, and libraries also focuses attention on the essential link between books, reading, and democracy. In a speech titled *Books and the World,* published by the Center for the Book in 1988, Billington vividly described this relationship and its importance:

> It is important to stress the central moral importance of the enterprise of reading itself for our kind of society. [It] arises first of all from the simple fact that our type of democracy has depended on knowledge and grown through books. By their very nature, books foster freedom with dignity. Books do not coerce, they convince. . . .

Historically books have been the companions of a responsible democracy citizenry. They provide keys to the dynamism of our past and perhaps to our national competitiveness in the future. Books link the record of yesterday with the possibilities of tomorrow.

References:

Herbert S. Bailey, Jr., "Economics of Publishing in the Humanities," *Scholarly Publishing,* 8 (April 1977): 223–224;

James H. Billington, *Books and the World* (Washington, D.C.: Library of Congress, 1988);

Daniel J. Boorstin, "A Design for an Anytime, Do-It-Yourself, Energy-Free Communication Device," *Harper's* (January 1974): 83–84;

Boorstin, *A Nation of Readers* (Washington, D.C.: Library of Congress, 1982);

John Y. Cole, *The Center for the Book in the Library of Congress: The Planning Year* (Washington, D.C.: Library of Congress, 1978), pp. 5–6;

Cole, "Is There a Community of the Book?," in *The Community of the Book: A Directory of Organizations and Programs,* edited by Cole (Washington, D.C.: Library of Congress, 1993);

Cole, "The U.S.'s Center for the Book: An Alliance Between Public and Private Interests," *Logos: The Professional Journal of the Book World,* 3, no. 1 (1992): 34–40;

Cole, ed., *The Library of Congress in Perspective* (New York: Bowker, 1978);

Joint Committee on the Library, Congress of the United States, *Books in Our Future: A Report from the Librarian of Congress to Congress* (Washington, D.C.: GPO, 1984).

New Literary Periodicals: A Report for 1993

Richard R. Centing
Ohio State University

The following report on new literary periodicals, the seventh in a series of annual reports appearing in the *Dictionary of Literary Biography Yearbook,* documents scholarly journals, annuals, newsletters, and reviews launched in 1993, along with some 1990, 1991, and 1992 titles that were not covered in previous reports. Any 1993 titles that are missed will be covered in *Yearbook: 1994.* These descriptions are not meant to be evaluative, although the importance of a few titles is stressed. By highlighting outstanding facets of each serial, our intention is to bring them to the attention of librarians and scholars for purposes of collection development and scholarly submission and to alert indexing services of the need for the inclusion of new titles in their core lists. Please contact the author with any comments on the report for 1993 or suggestions for inclusions in the 1994 report.

The Roman philosopher Boethius (circa 475–circa 525) is the concern of the International Boethius Society, whose journal, *Carmina Philosophiae* (University of Northern Iowa, Department of English, Cedar Falls, Iowa, 50614), was established as an annual in 1992. Edited by William Watts, Butler University, the journal studies the most famous work by Boethius, *On the Consolation of Philosophy,* and also includes two articles on the influence of Boethius's work on that of Geoffrey Chaucer. Christoph Houswitschka, Technische Universität of Dresden, examines the use of the concept of Fortune by medieval writers.

The *Arthurian Yearbook* (Garland Publishing, Inc., 1000A Sherman Avenue, Hamden, Connecticut, 06514), edited by Keith Busby, University of Oklahoma, is an annual devoted to Arthurian legend and literature of the Middle Ages. The first edition (1991) consists solely of eleven essays, and its "Preface" says that "The purpose of the *Arthurian Yearbook* is to provide a forum for scholarship on all aspects of Arthurian legends, literary, historical, art historical, and so forth." The essays treat such top-

Cover for the first issue of the journal devoted to the study of the Roman philosopher Boethius

ics as the artwork of the American illustrator and children's author Howard Pyle (1853–1911), Icelandic and Germanic versions of the romances, Sir Thomas Malory's *Tale of Gareth,* and the split-shield motif in the Old French *Lancelot.* Currently, Arthurian studies are the subject of *Quondam et Futurus: A Journal of Arthurian Interpretations* (1991) and the *Bib-*

liographical Bulletin of the International Arthurian Society (1949).

The semiannual *Medieval Folklore* (Edwin Mellen Press, P.O. Box 450, 415 Ridge Street, Lewiston, New York, 14092) is "an international, interdisciplinary journal dedicated to the study of all aspects of folklore in the Middle Ages and XVI century." For the first issue, in spring 1991, the editor, Francesca Canadé-Sautman, Hunter College and the Graduate Center of the City University of New York, provides an eight-page editorial titled "Medieval Folklore Today" that claims that "medieval folklore can be traced through a vast quantity of documents and disciplines." The field of hagiography, letters of pardon, manuscript decoration, and architectural motifs are all sources for medieval folklorists. There are four essays in the first issue: three are in French, and one is in English. The essay in English, "Literary Models and Folk Traditions: Ganfo the Fool in Giovanni Sercambi's *Novelliere*," is by Giuseppe Carlo Di Scipio, a member of the editorial board of *Medieval Folklore*. Bibliographic updates on the field are intended as a continuing feature, and the first issue includes "Selected Books on Medieval Folklore, 1985–1990" and "Medieval Folklore and Hagiography: Articles and Essays, 1985–1990." These bibliographies are international in scope and are multilingual.

Gary B. Goldstein is the founder, editor, and publisher of the independent *Elizabethan Review* (123-60 83rd Avenue, Kew Gardens, New York, 11415), a semiannual publication that began in spring 1993. An editorial statement says that the journal hopes to place the Elizabethan era (1558–1603) "within a multidisciplinary framework." The first issue treats questions relating to the William Shakespeare authorship debates. One article, "The Shakespeare Canon of Statutory Construction," is by John Paul Stevens, associate justice of the Supreme Court of the United States. Bette Talvacchia, associate professor of art history at the University of Connecticut, examines Shakespeare's knowledge of Italian art through an analysis of his reference in the *Winter's Tale,* to Giulio Romano the only artist whom Shakespeare ever mentioned by name. Goldstein offers a short note questioning whether Shakespeare was capable of reading Italian: Shakespearean lines echo Dante's *Divine Comedy,* yet Dante's work was not translated into English until 1802.

The *European Romantic Review* (Logos Press, P.O. Box 591402, San Francisco, California, 94159) is published semiannually in the summer and winter, and its first issue was Summer 1990. The review's cumulative index for volume three (1992) lists ten articles, a review essay, and nine book reviews. The scope of the review is defined as "the interdisciplinary study of history, philosophy, art and literature of the early nineteenth century." The articles cover such topics as William Blake and the French Revolution, George Gordon, Lord Byron's skepticism, aspects of William Wordsworth and Samuel Taylor Coleridge, Johann Wolfgang von Goethe's *Theory of Colours* (1810), irony in Heinrich von Kleist's works, Percy Bysshe Shelley's *Queen Mab* (1813), and the demise of mimesis. The "Review Essay" precedes the book-review section and is an extended review of Murray Krieger's *Ekphrasis: the Illusion of the Natural Sign* (1992). The signed book reviews are also quite lengthy, and most are review titles from American academic presses. The editor is Frederick Burwick, UCLA.

Approaches to the Spanish baroque is the theme of the inaugural Fall 1992 issue of the semiannual *Indiana Journal of Hispanic Literatures* (Indiana University, Department of Spanish and Portuguese, Ballantine Hall 875, Bloomington, Indiana, 47405). The continuing editor is Luis Beltrán, although this special issue was edited by Edward H. Friedman. The twenty-member editorial board is comprised of American academics. The scholarly interests of the journal are Spanish, Portuguese, and Catalan literature, linguistics, and language education. The eleven essays treat such subjects as the definition of *baroque,* the poems of Luis de Góngora y Argote, the structure of Miguel de Cervantes' *Don Quixote* (1615), the authorship of *Dineros son calidad* (usually attributed to Lope de Vega), Tirso de Molina, and the Devil as courtier in Pedro Calderón de la Barca's works. There are no miscellaneous materials such as book reviews.

Autumn 1992 was the date on the first issue of the *Journal of Hispanic Research* (Impart Publishing, 84 Dennett Road, Croydon, England CRO 3 JA), a journal devoted to the "languages, literatures, film, performing arts, and intellectual history of Spain and Spanish America." It is edited by Charles Davis, Queen Mary and Westfield College, University of London. Issued three times a year, the journal is comprised of contributions written in English, Spanish, or Catalan. Essays in English have covered such topics as the surrealism of Luis Buñuel, the asterisk in historical linguistics, the Spanish Middle Ages, and mystical poetry in the Spanish Golden Age. A section called "Open Forum" includes a historical overview of the teaching of comparative literature in North America.

A refereed journal dedicated to the French *nouveau roman,* the Hispanic *nueva novela,* and the Anglo-

Cover for the first issue of the new series of the journal devoted to the study of the life and work of novelist Lawrence Durrell

American new novel ("surfiction"), the *New Novel Review,* edited by Lynne Diamond-Nigh (Elmira College, Elmira, New York, 14901), is a semiannual that was first issued in October 1993. The journal publishes comparative and interdisciplinary essays in French, Spanish, and English. The English articles cover such topics as modern Latin American fiction and definitions of critical terms associated with the new novel. The book reviews discuss the French novelist Michel Butor and the Italian novelist Giose Rimanelli, whose novel *Benedetta in Guysterland* (1993) was written in English. The editor, Diamond-Nigh, is president and founder of the New Novel Association, which also issues an informal newsletter.

Travesia: Journal of Latin American Cultural Studies (King's College, Centre for Latin American Cultural Studies, Strand, London, England WC2R 2LS) began in 1992 and is published semiannually. The editors are Catherine Boyle, William Rowe,

and David Treece, King's College and John Kraniauskas, Birbeck College of the University of London. The first issue includes six essays plus a play and a short story. Boyle's "The Mirror to Nature? Latin American Theatre in London" focuses on Ariel Dorfman's play *Death and the Maiden* (1990) which received its first public reading in English as *Scars on the Moon* in November 1990 at the Institute of Contemporary Arts, London. Montserrat Ordóñez contributed a theoretical article, "Literature and Research," translated by Margaret Smallman. Democracy, the Gulf War, and the burden of the past in Brazil are other subjects explored.

The *Margaret Fuller Society Newsletter* (Texas A&M University, Department of English, College Station, Texas, 77843 is edited by Larry J. Reynolds. The society was organized in December 1992, and the initial six-page newsletter is dated Fall 1993. It includes short pieces about new books on Fuller, conference news, and announcements of papers accepted for publication in scholarly journals in 1994. Two issues a year are planned.

Emile Zola (1840–1902) and the naturalist school of fiction are the focus of *Excavatio: Nouvelle Revue Emile Zola et le Naturalisme Internationale* (460 Sandpiper Way, Chula Vista, California, 91910), edited by Monique E. Fol. The annual began in May 1992 and is bilingual in French and English. The English articles include "Birth Trauma, Infant Anality, and Castration Anxiety in *Germinal* and *The Sound and the Fury*," "Writing the Feminine in Zola," "Zola's Art of the Short Story," and "The View from Spain: Zola's First Trip Abroad." The journal is connected with the Association Internationale Emile Zola and Nouvelles Presses Universitaires Weslof, Berkeley, California. As the details of submission and subscription are fairly complex, it would be best to contact the editor, Fol, at the above address, which is new for 1993.

In 1992 the Powys Society published a valuable *Index* to the *Powys Review* covering the first twenty-six volumes (1977–1991). Compiled by Stephen Powys Marks, the *Index* is classified into useful sections, beginning with a list of the tables of contents for all of the issues, followed by sections devoted to John Cowper Powys (1872–1963), Theodore Francis Powys (1875–1953), and Llewelyn Powys (1884–1939); it concludes with a "General Index," a "Contributors Index," and a list of the books reviewed. An introduction to the *Index* called "Explanation" describes the transformation of the *Powys Review* (an independent publication edited by Belinda Humfrey and distributed by the Powys Society) into the *Powys Journal* (Powys Society,

Hamilton's Kilmersdon, near Bath, Somerset, England BA3 5TE), an annual controlled directly by the Powys Society. The first annual, edited by Peter J. Foss, is dated 1991. Around a dozen scholarly articles and four book reviews examine the life and work of this trio of literary brothers. The handsome format includes numerous illustrations. Original materials by the Powys family, such as letters and poems, are also published.

Dorothy Canfield Fisher (1879–1958), a once-popular American novelist, receives dutiful attention in the *DCF Newsletter* (Dorothy Canfield Fisher Society, Ida H. Washington, Secretary-Treasurer, RD 1, Box 66, Middlebury, Vermont, 05753), a semiannual that began December 1993. The editor is Joan G. Schroeter. The eight-page newsletter notes an increase in Fisher scholarship, to which it adds short articles on the Fisher papers at the University of Vermont, Fisher's letters, her relationship with the poet Sarah Norcliffe Cleghorn, and her lifelong friendship with Lucy Allen Smart.

The *Fannie Hurst Newsletter* (Gettysburg College, Department of English, Gettysburg, Pennsylvania, 17325) is edited by noted Hurst scholar Susan Koppelman, who founded the newsletter on 16 July 1991 as an informal vehicle for sharing information among a circle of Hurst's admirers. The newsletter became affiliated with Gettysburg College and the formalized Fannie Hurst Society with volume two, number 1 (Fall 1992). It is now published three times a year and executed by the managing editor, Temma Berg, due to Koppelman's chronic illness. Volume three, number 1 (Fall 1993), is a sixteen-page issue containing two articles on the film versions of Hurst's 1933 novel, *Imitation of Life,* along with short announcements and bibliographic developments.

The Irish novelist and playwright Samuel Beckett (1906–1989) has been studied in the *Beckett Circle,* the newsletter of the Samuel Beckett Society, since 1978. A bilingual newcomer to the family of periodicals devoted to Beckett is *Samuel Beckett Today/Aujord'hui* (Editions Rodopi, 233 Peachtree Street N.E., Suite 404, Atlanta, Georgia, 30303), an annual that was first issued in 1992. The first annual is a special number titled "Samuel Beckett 1970–1989" that is edited by Marius Buning, Sjef Houppermans, and Danièle de Ruyter. The papers published in the issue were given at a Beckett Symposium held at the University of Leiden in October 1991. Sixteen articles treat various aspects of Beckett's late work, including his film *Film,* a revival of *Waiting for Godot,* and catharsis in Beckett's late drama.

The major periodical devoted to Beckett is the revived *Journal of Beckett Studies* (Florida State University, Department of English, Tallahassee, Florida, 32306), edited by Beckett scholar S. E. Gontarski. The semiannual began in 1992 with a double number of 184 pages. The contents include the first publication of two poems by Beckett, short notes, book reviews, and illustrated play reviews. The bulk of the journal is devoted to nine scholarly articles that cover such subjects as Beckett's play *Ohio Impromptu,* totality and displacement in Beckett's fiction, and Beckett's use of the archetypal images of ashes and dust. Autumn 1992 and Spring 1993 are the two issues of volume two: the high quality of the contents continues with a special feature containing articles on Beckett by Irish writers and the publication of a revised text of the play *What Where*.

The British novelist and poet Lawrence Durrell (1912–1990) is given scholarly attention in the annual *Deus Loci: The Lawrence Durrell Journal* (SUNY Maritime College, Fort Schuyler, Bronx, New York, 10465), a new series that began in 1992. The old series ran from 1977 to 1984. The editor, Ian S. MacNiven, is a noted Durrell scholar whose biography of Durrell will be published in 1994. The first issue is a rich compilation of critical essays and appreciations, along with film and book reviews. A useful "Durrell Bibliography: 1983–1985" is included, updating the standard Durrell bibliography. The annual is associated with the International Lawrence Durrell Society.

The *Flannery O'Connor Society Newsletter* (Louisiana State University – Shreveport, Department of English, c/o Sura Rath, Shreveport, Louisiana, 71115), a four-page irregular newsletter first issued early in 1993, is edited by Virginia Wray, Arkansas College. O'Connor scholarship is also sustained in a major annual, the *Flannery O'Connor Bulletin,* issued since 1972 by Georgia College. The newsletter's purpose seems to be to announce new research projects, to promote forthcoming conferences, to provide short descriptions of archives, and, unfortunately for bibliographers, to launch a name contest to find a more exciting name for this publication than the "blandness of the appellation newsletter."

ALA Notes: Newsletter of the American Literature Association (Alfred Bendixen, California State University, Department of English, 5151 State University Drive, Los Angeles, California, 90032) is a four-page semiannual that was first issued in spring 1993 as volume one, number 1. It replaces the four-page irregular *Newsletter* that was first issued in December 1989 with no volume or issue numbering. The American Literature Association is "a coalition

Cover for the first issue of the journal devoted to advanced theoretical studies of techniques and forms of narrative

of societies devoted to the study of American authors." The new *ALA Notes* devotes most of its space to a valuable "List of the Societies Devoted to the Study of American Authors." The list contains the mailing address and annual dues for societies dedicated to thirty-nine American authors and nine societies oriented to general topics such as Western, Jewish, and American Indian literatures. It does not intend to publish scholarly articles or book reviews. Besides publishing *ALA Notes,* the association conducts an annual conference. The fourth annual meeting will be held in Baltimore in 1994.

Devoted to Celtic language and literature, the *Celtic Pen* (36 Fruithill Park, Béal Feirste, Ireland BT11 8GE) is a quarterly that began in autumn 1993. It is edited by Diarmuid Ó Breasláin. The articles in the first newsstand glossy issue cover the ancient Irish story of Da Derga's Hostel, Gaelic publishing in Perth, Manx Literature, the Welsh medieval poet Dafydd ap Gwilym, and the Gaelic writer Dòmhnall MacEacharn. The first issue also includes original poems by Nuala Ní Dhomhnaill and Gabriel Rosenstock. There are two book re-

views. Although this issue is entirely in English, future issues promise Irish short stories translated into Welsh and Breton stories translated into Scots Gaelic.

The independent *Arkansas Quarterly: A Journal of Criticism* (Epiphany Publications, 88 Dawn Hill Road, Siloam Spring, Arkansas, 72761) was first issued in January 1992. A "Welcome" from the editor, Dora Rainey, says that its purpose will be to "present literary scholarship dealing with 20th Century literature (mostly American), especially the latter half of the century." Each issue has five or six essays, short comments, and occasional book reviews, expressed in styles that range from amateur to academic complexity.

The semiannual *Creative Nonfiction* (The Creative Nonfiction Foundation, University of Pittsburgh, Department of English, Pittsburgh, Pennsylvania, 15260) was launched in 1993. It is devoted to essays or excerpts from books in progress that combine "strong elements of reportage" along with "fictional techniques," a genre that was once called "new journalism" when it was practiced by Tom Wolfe and Gay Talese. *New Yorker* writer John McPhee is profiled in the inaugural issue by Michael Pearson, a teacher of American literature and creative nonfiction at Old Dominion University. Natalia Rachel Singer contributes "Nonfiction in First Person, Without Apology," a version of a talk she gave at Saint Lawrence University. Eight other essays are included on a variety of subjects, such as a journey through Africa and growing up in Santa Barbara, California. The editor is Lee Gutkind.

Diversity: A Journal of Multicultural Issues (University of North Texas, Denton, Texas, 76203) is published twice yearly in the fall and spring. The first issue is dated Fall 1992 and includes six articles, a book review, and a short commentary. Literary topics dominate, although the journal is open to "any aspect of multiculturalism." Yoshinobu Hakutani, Kent State University, offers insights on the racial issues that pervade in Mark Twain's *Pudd'nhead Wilson.* Angela Chilton-Weger, a graduate student at Texas Woman's University, studies Zora Neale Hurston's *Seraph on the Suwanee* (1948) as a bildungsroman that has the unique perspective of an African-American novelist presenting a woman's development through a white protagonist. Mark William Rocha, California State University, Northridge, conducted an interview with the African-American playwright August Wilson on 24 January 1992 that he interweaves throughout his article on Wilson's "African sensibility." The book review is of Jill McCorkle's *Crash Diet: Stories* (1992).

The editors are Jocelyn Chadwick-Joshua and Kathryn Rosser Raign.

Fanfare: The Christopher-Gordon Children's Literature Annual (Christopher-Gordon Publishers, Inc., 480 Washington Street, Norwood, Massachusetts, 02062) first appeared in 1993. The editor, Joel Taxel, is a professor in the Department of English Education at the University of Georgia. The first annual is a special number on children's poetry, and a key essay in the collection is Myra Cohn Livingston's "Poetry and the Self," which uses examples of poetry in a discussion of teaching methods. Some essays provide historical overviews, such as Lee Bennett Hopkins's "American Poetry for Children: The Twentieth Century" and M. Jean Greenlaw's "A Retrospective of Outstanding Poetry for Youth: 1980–1992." Good reference bibliographies conclude the essays.

Futures Past: A Visual Guidebook to Science Fiction History (Futures Past, P.O. Box 610, Convoy, Ohio, 45832) is a heavily illustrated fanzine that devotes each issue to a particular year in science-fiction history. The premiere issue covers 1926, the second issue, 1927, and the third issue, 1928. The contents feature a chronology for each year, including non-science-fiction facts; an annotated list of books published in each featured year; remarks on the science-fiction films released; and reproductions of covers from magazines of the period (*Amazing Stories* was first published in 1926 as a "magazine of scientifiction," establishing 1926 as the birth year of the genre). There are profiles of important figures such as Hugo Gernsback, the founder of *Amazing Stories*. Each issue highlights some reference tools, describes collections in libraries, interviews authors, and provides information applicable to any time period. This unscholarly, irregular hodgepodge was first issued in 1992 and is edited by Jim Emerson.

Mediphors: A Literary Journal of the Health Professions (P.O. Box 327, Bloomsburg, Pennsylvania, 17815) is a semiannual first published spring 1993 as a market for short stories, poems, artwork, and essays on the theme of medicine and health. Dr. Eugene D. Radice is the editor. Citing the physician-poet William Carlos Williams, the journal calls for physicians, nurses, and technicians to contribute. A short story begins: "We are in the darkened Intensive Care Unit watching the heart monitors, the QRS configurations on the small screens rise to peaks then drop, valleys before us. Periodically, an aberrant PVC – a premature ventricular contraction – causes a quickening of our own hearts as we watch the deviant pattern." A patient's blood is described in one poem as "a galaxy of haloed white-cell planets and red-cell dust."

Murder is Academic: The Teaching and Criticism of Crime Fiction on Campus (Hunter College, Department of English, 695 Park Avenue, New York, New York, 10021) is an irregular, six-page newsletter that first appeared in May 1992. The editor, B. J. Rahn, hopes to establish a network of academic teachers and researchers of detective fiction. The goal is to share syllabi and teaching methods, announce meetings, document new books in the field, and provide lists of the most frequently taught authors (for example, the single most popular novel is Dashiell Hammett's *The Maltese Falcon* (1930), followed by works by Agatha Christie, and so forth).

The quarterly *Mystery Review* (C. von Hessert and Associates Ltd., P.O. Box 233, Colborne, Ontario, Canada, K0K 1S0) first appeared in fall 1992. Written primarily for Canadian fans of mystery and suspense, it features interviews, book reviews, lists of new releases, and even games and puzzles. Howard Engel, the author of the Benny Cooperman mysteries, is interviewed in the premiere issue. The editor of *Mystery Review* is Barbara Davey.

The Society for the Study of Narrative Literature, an international nonprofit association of scholars interested in the techniques and forms of narrative, sponsors *Narrative* (Ohio State University Press, 1070 Carmack Road, Columbus, Ohio, 43210), which appears three times a year. The first issue is dated January 1993. The journal is edited by Ohio State University professor of English James Phelan. The advanced theoretical articles in the first three issues cover such subjects as gossip in William Faulkner's *Light in August* (1932), sexual dynamics in Ernest Hemingway's *The Sun Also Rises* (1926), gender in Bram Stoker's *Dracula* (1897), issues of empire and domination in William Makepeace Thackeray's *Vanity Fair* (1848), and the relations of myth, history, and fiction in African narrative. There is a section, "Reply," in which scholars can respond to articles. Some of the articles are short position papers on topics such as the culture wars.

Prose Poem: An International Journal (Providence College, English Department, Providence, Rhode Island, 02918) is an annual that began in 1992. The editor, Peter Johnson, takes his definition of the prose poem from the *Princeton Encyclopedia of Poetry and Prose*. A major part of the definition says that the prose poem "differs from poetic prose in that it is short and compact, from free verse in that it has no line breaks, from a short prose passage in that it has, usually, more pronounced rhythm, sonorous effects, imagery, and density of expression." Some

Cover for the first issue of the journal featuring dada and surrealist literature

of the contributors are quite well known, such as Robert Bly and David Ignatow, while others are much less so. The pieces range from a few sentences to a full page in length and often have a narrative structure, appearing as epiphanies or extremely short stories. The pieces include translations from Greek, Spanish, and Hungarian.

Revival (Living Archives Company, P.O. Box 295, Amherst, Wisconsin, 54406), a quarterly founded in 1993, specializes in reprints of "carefully selected material from rare and long out-of-print publications on theatre history." The premiere issue is devoted to excerpts of the text and illustrations from *The Stage and Its Stars Past and Present: A Gallery of Dramatic Illustration and Critical Biographies of Distinguished English and American Actors from the Time of Shakespeare till to-day,* edited by Howard Paul and George Gebbie (1890). The editor, Robin Field, is a Broadway-based performer, director, composer, and lyricist.

Commedia dell'arte is the theme of the first annual *Theatre Symposium* (University of Alabama Press, P.O. Box 870380, Tuscaloosa, Alabama, 35487), a series begun in 1993 that publishes the papers presented at the Southeastern Theatre Confer-

ence. The editor is Philip G. Hill, Furman University. One contributor, Thomas F. Heck, Ohio State University, discusses music in commedia performance. Georgeann Murphy, Centre College, offers an overview of commedia in the classroom. Paul C. Castagno, University of Alabama, moderated a "Symposium Discussion" on the role of the scenario in commedia. Other articles show the influence of the commedia on the theater of the Spanish Golden Age and discuss the theatricality of the paintings of Antoine Watteau.

The biggest annual short-fiction prizes in the United Kingdom and Ireland, the Ian St. James Awards, were founded and funded in 1989 by British novelist Ian St. James. The prize fund for 1993 is thirty-two thousand pounds and will be divided among sixteen winners. The winners are published in an annual paperback. Because so many good stories did not reach the public as winners, it was decided to create a magazine devoted to publishing the short-listed stories. The result is the new fiction magazine, *Acclaim* (New Writers' Club, P.O. Box 101, Tunbridge Wells, Kent, England TN4 8YD), issued six times a year. The first issue, October/November 1992, includes nine stories. The editor is Barbara Large.

The *Amethyst Review* (Marcasite Press, 23 Riverside Avenue, Truro, Nova Scotia, Canada, B2N 4G2) publishes poetry and fiction by Canadian contributors. The independent semiannual's first issue is dated Winter 1993, and the second issue is dated Summer 1993. The editor is Penny L. Ferguson.

Arshile (96 Tears Press, P.O. Box 3749, Los Angeles, California, 90078) is an independent literary review featuring poetry, fiction, essays, and artwork. The semiannual began spring 1993 and is edited by Mark Salerno, a poet who contributed four poems to the first issue. The concluding essay, "Some Perplexed Ideas at the End of the Century," is by the distinguished art critic Dore Ashton. She offers a complicated overview of contemporary art theory and its relation to the failure of "postmodern relativism"; what is needed is a hierarchy of values. The artwork consists of a portfolio of excerpts from a series titled The Jungle Book by the abstract painter Leslie Diller Zollo, and the cover art is Roy Dowell's *Untitled # 581* (1992). "In or Out?," a fictional piece by John Laskey, concerns a man born with skin that is half-white and half-black. Robert Creeley, Gilbert Sorrentino, and Alice Notley are among the other poets represented.

Asylum Annual (Asylum Arts Publishing, P.O. Box 6203, Santa Maria, California, 93456) is a large, heavily illustrated anthology of poetry, prose, drama, reviews, and artwork that has its spiritual roots in dada and surrealism. Regular underground contributors such as Charles Bukowski, Richard Kostelanetz, and the late Edouard Roditi are included, along with newer names such as David Alpaugh, Rick Henry, and Maia Penfold. Harold Jaffe, the editor of *Fiction International,* and Jordon Jones, the editor of *Bakunin,* are also in the roster. There are many erotic undercurrents and political blasts in this irreverent and exciting gallery, where humor and serious questions coexist. Asylum Arts also publishes chapbooks, including translations of Gérard de Nerval. The annual is edited by Greg Boyd and was first issued in 1993.

A fellow at the MacDowell Colony, an English professor at Wheaton College, independent Bostonians, an Oklahoma geologist, an editor from Maine, a resident of Hong Kong who is a freelance photojournalist, and a poet and fiction writer from Albany, New York, are all contributors to *Atelier* (Bliss Publications, P.O. Box 580, Boston, Massachusetts, 02117), a quarterly collection of short fiction, poetry, and interviews whose first issue is dated Spring 1993. The first two interviews are with Artiom Soloveychik, a storyteller from Moscow, Russia, and the 1960s poet and rock musician Ed Sanders. A mixture of styles enlivens this literary review, with a slight emphasis on the Beat and the experimental. The coeditors are Sarah Jensen and Sheila Falcey.

The quarterly *Atlantean Press Review* (P.O. Box 361116, Milpitas, California, 95036), which began in fall 1993, is edited by Patricia LeChevalier. It contains one poem, "The Thinker," by Berton Braley, a reprint of a widely anthologized poem that is an apology for the businessman, " ... the Thinker, / The clear-eyed man who knows." There is one essay by Edward Cline, "The Wizards of Disambiguation: A Critique of Mystery Genre Criticism." Cline, a suspense and detective novelist, launches a neoconservative attack on "irrational and absurd" academic criticism that fails to understand the detective story. Ayn Rand is quoted as an authority on the genre. An excerpt from an unfinished manuscript, "The Survival Manifesto," is by John Stuart, an electronics engineer who died on 11 June 1993. A curious appendix, "Atlantean Favorites," recommends films, books, music, and painters.

Borderlands: Texas Poetry Review (P.O. Box 49818, Austin, Texas, 78765) is a semiannual that began in fall 1992. It places an emphasis on poetry, as the subtitle implies, but it also publishes essays and book reviews. Some of the poets are nationally known, such as William Stafford, Naomi Shihab Nye, Lyn Lifshin, and Stephen Dobyns, while others are unattached locals and professors from various western institutions. David Oliphant, editor of publications at the Harry Ransom Humanities Research Center, contributes an informal essay on the influence of Chilean poetry. Another essay examines the poetry of Alicia Ostriker. Several poems touch on multicultural themes, the environment, and the politics of everyday life and pay tribute to such significant figures as Pablo Neruda and Frida Kahlo. The editors change with each issue: Dorothy Barnett and Lynn Gilbert edited the first issue, and Pamela Cook and Lynn Gilbert edited the second issue. The Spring 1993 issue reproduced excellent photographs of southwestern views.

Break to Open (Last Generation Press, 2965 13th Street, Boulder, Colorado, 80304) is an irregular little magazine devoted to experimental "new writing." Number 1 appeared in 1992. The magazine is edited by Mark DuCharme "with help and advice from Rebecca Bush." A few short magazine and book reviews are also included of publications from small presses. The Last Generation Press also publishes chapbooks of poems and prose from such writers as Anne Waldman and Nico Vassilakis.

The monthly *Charlotte Poetry Review* (P.O. Box 36701, Charlotte, North Carolina, 28236) began in January 1992 with a credo of "poetry as a philosophical medium." While seeking to foster new talent in the Charlotte area, the poetry herald also includes non-Carolinians, such as the widely published Lyn Lifshin. Interviews with local poets are also included, along with poets from elsewhere now residing in Charlotte. A. A. Jillani is the editor.

The semiannual *Defined Providence* (Defined Providence, 59 Adams Street, No. 1, Somerville, Massachusetts, 02145) is a little all-poetry magazine. The contributors range from the established, such as David Citino, X. J. Kennedy, and Gary Soto, to the emerging, such as Michael R. Brown, James Files, Richard Cambridge, and Elinor Meiskey. The editor of this independent poetry host is Gary J. Whitehead.

Faultline (University of California, Irvine, California, 92716) is a semiannual literary review that was launched in fall 1992. It is not attached to a particular department, although its funding was partly supported by the Office of Academic Affairs, Office of Research and Graduate Studies, and the School of Humanities. It was printed by the University of California, San Diego, graphics department. The editor, Alyn Warren, expresses California's awareness of earthquakes in the journal's title and in his

"Editor's Note" concerning "the possibility that the earth may begin to shake, the ground open up beneath our feet, and that all that we have created can come tumbling down upon our heads." What tumbles out of the review is poetry, short prose works, and artwork.

Fall/Winter 1992 is the date of the first issue of the semiannual *Flying Island* (Writers' Center of Indianapolis, P.O. Box 88386, Indianapolis, Indiana, 46208), an outlet for short stories, poems, and book reviews by Indiana writers. The oversize tabloid contains about forty contributions in each heavily illustrated issue. It is edited by a collective that lists Bruce Gentry as editor in chief, Fall/Winter 1993. An interview is included with the African-American poet Etheridge Knight, who died in Indianapolis in 1991. Knight knocks M.F.A. creative-writing programs and talks about his youth as a shoe-shine boy in the South.

The premiere issue of the independent semiannual *Georgetown Review* (G & R Publishing, 400 East College Street, Box 227, Georgetown, Kentucky, 40324) is dated Spring 1993. The editor is Steven Carter. The contents consist solely of poetry and fiction from twenty-four contributors who are students, professors, translators, and editors of literary reviews. Known poets are included, such as Stuart Friebert, director of the writing program at Oberlin College, along with unknowns, such as Khaled Mattawa, a native of Benghazi, Libya.

The irregular, irreverent *Herman Review* (P.O. Box 48824, Los Angeles, California, 90048) was first issued late in 1993. The poetry review is edited by Rick Bursky. Forty-six poems are included, from contributors who have publications issued by small presses such as Graywolf and Bombshelter. Charles Simic offers five translations of the Yugoslavia poet Jovan Hristic.

Essays, fiction, drama, poetry, artwork, and reviews appear in the *International Quarterly* (P.O. Box 10521, Tallahassee, Florida, 32302), featuring writers from around the world in English originals or in translation. The quarterly first appeared summer 1993. An important segment includes Anna Akhmatova's "Poems and Fragments," translated from the Russian by Judith Hemschemeyer, containing poems that turned up after Hemschemeyer's translations in *Complete Poems of Anna Akhmatova* (1990). Several poems are translated from the Bulgarian. Edmund Keeley, director of the creative-writing program at Princeton University, contributes "Lunch on Thassos, A.D. 1939," an excerpt from a forthcoming novel. Aleš Debeljak's essay, "Expulsion From the Paradise of Dissent," concerns

his return to his native Slovenia. One of the book reviews discusses new poetry anthologies from Eastern Europe. The editor is Van K. Brock, professor of English at Florida State University.

Janus (New Jerusalem Books, P.O. Box 3346, Vancouver, British Columbia, Canada, V6B 3Y3) is an irregular poetry journal whose first issue appeared in 1992 and whose second issue appeared in 1993. John Hudson, the editor, says that his only criterion for selection is that a poem "be enjoyable." Six poems by the Yugoslavian poet Miodrag Pavlovic are included, translated by Bernard Johnson. Other poets include John Burnside, Norm Sibum, and C. H. Sisson.

Edited by Martin Lammon, Valerie Colander, and John King, *Kestrel: A Journal of Literature and Art in the New World* (Fairmont State College, 1201 Locust Avenue, Fairmont, West Virginia, 26554) is a semiannual that began spring 1993. It includes poetry, fiction, interviews, essays, and artwork. The most important inclusion is an interview with the distinguished American poet and writer Donald Hall, along with two poems, "Elbows" and "At the Spring Glen Grammar School," which are illustrated with reproductions of the five drafts of "Elbows." Also included are translations of four poems by the Italian poet Rosita Copioli along with the original Italian poems. The translator, Renata Treitel, prefaces the translations with an introduction, "On Translating Rosita Copioli." A portfolio of photographs taken in China in 1988 illustrates *Kestrel*.

Originally issued from 1947 to 1992 by the Caxton Press, the new series of *Landfall* (Oxford University Press, P.O. Box 11–149, Ellerslie, Auckland, New Zealand) was reborn April 1993 as volume one, number 1. The editor, Simon Cauchi, says that the next semiannual issue is scheduled for November 1993. *Landfall* is devoted to New Zealand arts and letters, publishing new poetry and prose along with interviews, artwork, criticism, and book reviews. The April 1993 issue is a special theme issue on "The Fifties." Several of the essays are memoirs of the intellectual scene in the 1950s when *Landfall* was the dominant New Zealand review. Peter Simpson, University of Auckland, Tamaki campus, contributes "Ways to the Museyroom: Poetry Anthologies in the Fifties," a deft analysis of anthologies devoted to New Zealand writers.

Edited by John Mella, the quarterly *Light* (Light, P.O. Box 7500, Chicago, Illinois, 60680) specializes in light verse and humorous pieces. Number 1 is dated Spring 1992. The contributors include such well-known names as John Updike, William Stafford, X. J. Kennedy, and W. D. Snodgrass along with lesser lights. Cartoons, offbeat crossword puzzles, and announcements of new books are also included. Many of the poems are short, and many feature rhyme. Each issue includes several poems by the "Featured Poet," with Tom Disch and Gavin Ewart featured in the first two issues.

Americans of Mexican descent are represented by *New Chicana/Chicano Writing* (University of Arizona Press, 1230 N. Park Avenue, Suite 102, Tucson, Arizona, 85719). The annual anthology began in 1992 and includes fiction and poetry by beginning and established writers. Ivan Argüelles, Pat Mora, and Gary Soto are included. The "Introduction" by the editor, Charles M. Tatum, draws interesting parallels between the position of Chicana/Chicano writers today and African-American writers of the 1940s and 1950s.

British writers Malcolm Bradbury – a novelist, television dramatist, literary critic, and part-time professor of American studies at the University of East Anglia – and Judy Cooke, a freelance editor who works in the literature department of the British Council, are the editors of the first annual anthology of *New Writing* (Minerva, Michelin House, 81 Fulham Road, London, England SW3 6RB). It first appeared in 1992 as a paperback featuring fiction, poetry, essays, and interviews. The fiction consists of short stories and extracts from novels in progress from such authors as Graham Swift, Alasdair Gray, Penelope Fitzgerald, and Marina Warner. The first anthology includes an interview with Martin Amis conducted by Christopher Bigsby and an interview with Angela Carter conducted by Lorna Sage. Well-established poets such as Ted Hughes and Dannie Abse are included, along with newer poets such as Wendy Cope. The novelist David Lodge offers an overview of "The Novelist Today: Still at the Crossroads?" The critic Peter Kemp surveys "British Fiction of the 1980s."

Since September 1992, the irregular *96 Inc* (Kenmore Writers Group, P.O. Box 15559, Boston, Massachusetts, 02215) has been edited by Vera Gold and Julia Phipps Anderson as an outlet for established and beginning writers in the genres of poetry, drama, and fiction.

The *North Carolina Literary Review* (East Carolina University, English Department, Greenville, North Carolina, 27858) has set a new standard of excellence for regional journals devoted to the literature of a single state. The first two issues of this beautifully produced semiannual total 424 pages.

Cover for the combined first and second issues of the journal devoted to poetry and fiction relating to the environment

Since its first issue of Summer 1992, it has reinterpreted the history of North Carolina literature and promoted contemporary writers, enlivening its showcase with photographs and drawings. The poet A. R. Ammons, a native of North Carolina, is featured in the first issue. The A. R. Ammons papers in the Southern Historical Collection at the University of North Carolina at Chapel Hill are described, and an interview is published. Fred Chappell is also well represented, with a description of his papers at Duke University along with his memoir of Randall Jarrell. The history of a little magazine of the 1930s, *Contempo,* is outlined. Other essays in this multifaceted review examine the murder of John Lawson by Tuscarora Indians in 1711, slave narratives, writers' conferences, North Carolina state-highway historical markers, and downtown movie theaters. Other continuing features are a "Dictionary of North Carolina Writers" and a "Directory of Small Magazines and Literary Journals in North Carolina." The journal is edited by Alex Albright.

Edited by John S. French, the irregular *Pacific Coast Journal* (French Bread Publications, P.O. Box 355, Campbell, California, 95009) is an independent compilation of language poetry and experimental prose. The contributors include professors of English and students from California. One of the essays is on the African-American image in Japan. The inaugural forty-eight-page issue is dated Summer 1992.

The quarterly *Quixotic Writer* (Quixotic Publications, 213 South Congress, Suite 321, Austin, Texas, 78701) began in spring 1993 with a twenty-eight-page issue containing three poems and four stories. No editor is listed for this anthology of beginning writers whose motto is: "Remember, it ain't no crime to be sublime."

The first number of the *Santa Barbara Review* (Shelly Lowenkopf, Editor, 104 La Vereda Lane, Santa Barbara, California, 93108) is dated Spring/Summer 1993. The semiannual includes fiction, essays, poetry, and artwork. The novelist Barnaby Conrad contributes a memoir of Sinclair Lewis, part of a forthcoming autobiography called *Name Dropping*. Marilyn Chandler, Mills College, provides an essay on doctors in literature. The poetry is from Anne F. Walker, Eleanor Vincent, Chris Stockton, and Stephen Ratcliffe. The fiction is from Dennis Lynds, Gayle Stone, and Beth Tjoflat.

Short Fiction by Women (Box 1276, Stuyvesant Station, New York, New York, 10009) publishes short fiction by women. Edited by Rachel Whalen, it is issued three times a year. The first issue is dated Fall 1991, while the fourth issue is simply dated 1993. The Fall 1991 issue includes thirteen stories in 121 pages.

Measuring 4 1/4 by 5 1/2 inches, the twenty-four pages of *Sticks* (Sticks Press, P.O. Box 399, Maplesville, Alabama, 36750) are indeed a little magazine. Devoted to poetry, it includes one poem each by X. J. Kennedy and Richard Kostelanetz and seven short poems by Charles Ghigna. The editor is Mary Veazey. This irregular first appeared in 1992.

Trafika (Modrá Musa Publishers, Janovského 14, 170 00 Prague 7, Czech Republic) is a quarterly literary review with an international reach that began in autumn 1993. It is edited by Michael Lee, Alfredo Sánchez, and Jeffrey Young. Along with works written originally in English, *Trafika* provides translations from Swedish, Czech, Polish, Spanish, and Romanian. Don DeLillo contributes a short story, "The Runner," and Stephen Dixon offers a prose poem, "Give and Take." The Czech writers, Arnost Lustig and Miroslav Holub, are jointly interviewed, and some of their work is translated. Other contributors are from Cuba, England, and the Philippines.

British students at colleges and universities are the sole contributors to *Cascando: the National Student Literary Magazine* (Cascando Press, P.O. Box 1499, London, England SW10 9TZ). Appearing three times a year in a slick, professional format, the first issue is dated Autumn 1992. The magazine is edited by Lisa Boardman and Emily Ormond. Included are poetry, essays, stories, and drama. The first issue also includes an interview with Toni Morrison, who was touring England to promote her novel *Jazz*. The British novelist Jeanette Winterson is profiled, as is another American, Sam Shepard. A useful appendix lists British literary magazines and author societies.

Publishing articles in either English or German, *Faultline* (Stanford University, Department of German Studies, Stanford, California, 94305) is an interdisciplinary annual of German studies founded by graduate students at Stanford University. First appearing in 1992, it is edited by Christa Johnson. The articles are rigorously intellectual, covering such subjects as the German film *Hitlerjunge Salomon* (*Europa, Europa*), syphilis and Jewish identity, fascist erotics, fiction in nineteenth-century German colonialism, and Weimar popular culture.

The *New England Intercollegiate Literary Journal* (Middlebury College, Middlebury, Vermont, 05753) publishes poems and fiction by students at the colleges of Amherst, Bowdoin, Colby, Connecticut, Dartmouth, Middlebury, and Williams and from Wesleyan University. The cooperative venture is edited by David C. Ferris and Cole F. Odell. Published semiannually, the first 125-page issue is dated Spring 1993.

Postscript: A Journal of Graduate Criticism & Theory (Memorial University of Newfoundland, Arts and Administration Building, A–3000, Saint John's, Newfoundland, Canada, A1C 5S7) is a semiannual published by graduate students in the Department of English, Memorial University of Newfoundland. The journal began in spring 1993, and each issue has around six essays on such subjects as Friedrich Nietzsche and postmodernism, the Canadian writer Mavis Gallant, Margaret Atwood's novel *The Handmaid's Tale,* and motherhood in Virgil and John Milton. The managing editors are Susan Drodge and Danine Farquharson.

The annual *Textshop* (Wilfrid Laurier University, Department of English, Waterloo, Ontario, Canada, N2L 3C5) first appeared in fall 1992. It publishes poems and short prose pieces by students and teachers from the Ontario area. Each original work receives an instant analysis in a section called "Reactions," in which the editor, Andrew Stubbs, along with other contributing editors, provides commentary on the entire contents.

Gaia: A Journal of Literary & Environmental Arts (Whistle Press, Inc., P.O. Box 709, Winterville, Georgia, 30683) is a quarterly that began with a double number, 1/2 (April/July 1993). It is dedicated to publishing original poems and short fiction that relate to the environment. More than thirty contributors appear in the first issue. The editor of *Gaia,* Robert S. King, edits publications for the University of Georgia Agricultural Experiment Stations.

Isle: Interdisciplinary Studies in Literature and Environment (Indiana University of Pennsylvania, Department of English, 110 Leonard Hall, Indiana, Pennsylvania, 15705) is a semiannual that began Spring 1993. It is edited by Patrick D. Murphy, Indiana University of Pennsylvania. Known for his work on Gary Snyder and environmental literature, he calls for "ecological criticism" that studies artistic depictions of nature, the human/nature dichotomy, and ecological theory. The 212-page first issue features essays on Henry David Thoreau from a feminist perspective, methods for teaching environmental writers, John McPhee's *Coming Into the Country,* the horticulturalist Lester Rowntree, and Aldo Leopold's *A Sand County Almanac.*

The monthly *Small Magazine Review* (Dustbooks, P.O. Box 100, Paradise, California, 95967) began in June 1993. It is published and edited by the king of alternative literary bibliography, Len Fulton, whose reference tools, such as the *International Directory of Little Magazines & Small Presses,* are widely held in libraries and writers' homes. This magazine about magazines is a spin-off of *Small Press Review,* another Dustbooks publication, which began in 1967 and which will continue as a book-reviewing monthly. While the emphasis in the *Small Magazine Review* will be on literary titles, it does embrace other fields such as environmental studies, fine arts, history, and education. The new service consists of signed reviews of recently released titles, such as the *Vinyl Elephant,* and titles that have been coming out for years, such as the *Nebraska Review.* Fulton's core reviewers, such as Robert Peters, Laurel Speer, and Hugh Fox, are well respected in the small press world. Short articles on small-press publishing are also included. The September 1993 issue had a checklist of sexually oriented magazines, including gay publications.

Taproot Reviews (Burning Press, P.O. Box 585, Lakewood, Ohio, 44107) is a quarterly tabloid that began December 1992. The editor, Luigi-Bob Drake, says that this reviewing service for books and magazines wants to represent the underground community, presses with a "do-it-yrself" attitude, and the "out-of-the-mainstream culture." A section devoted to "Zines" reviews around seventy magazines an issue. The reviews cover new as well as long-established titles. A section called "Chaps" reviews chapbooks and other small-press books, covering such presses as Post-Apollo, Meow, and Shattered Wig. Writers and bibliographers can also learn about alternative markets from the advertisements. Sometimes poems or other excerpts taken from the items under review are reprinted. The style of the reviews is informal, entertaining, and candid.

Synge Summer School:
J. M. Synge and the Irish Theater Rathdrum, County Wicklow, Ireland

Nicholas Grene
Trinity College, Dublin

"Go to the Aran Islands," W. B. Yeats commanded John Millington Synge magisterially at their famous first meeting in Paris in December 1896: "Live there as if you were one of the people themselves; express a life that has never found expression." That voyage of discovery to Aran and Synge's transformation by it into a great writer has been one of the key Yeatsian myths of the Irish Literary Revival, the myth of the return to Ireland as artistic subject, the myth of the primitive and simple life of the west of Ireland. But J. M. Synge (1871–1909), founder-director with Yeats and Isabella Augusta Lady Gregory of the Abbey Theatre and internationally famous as the author of *Riders to the Sea* (1904) and *The Playboy of the Western World* (1907), would have known the mountainous county of Wicklow on the east coast of Ireland far better than the Aran Islands. He came from a landowning Wicklow family and spent most of his summers in the county, walking and cycling its roads; it was in Wicklow in 1902 that he made his breakthrough as a dramatist, writing *In the Shadow of the Glen* (1903) and *Riders to the Sea;* it was in this area that he set four of his seven completed plays. One of the principal aims of the Synge Summer School, based in Rathdrum, county Wicklow, close to where those plays are set, is to resist the oversimplifying scheme of Yeats's grand "Go West, young man," and to claim Synge back for the East by an awareness of the importance for his work of his family background and of his intimate knowledge of the glens and mountains of Wicklow.

Synge was the first internationally known playwright of the Irish national theater movement, with plays already in his own brief lifetime translated and performed in Europe. But Ireland's extraordinary contribution to world theater, both before Synge (George Farquhar, Richard Brinsley Sheridan, Oliver Goldsmith, Oscar Wilde, Bernard Shaw) and since (Yeats, Sean O'Casey, Brendan Behan, Samuel Beckett, Brian Friel), is a striking phenomenon. The Synge Summer School's second aim has been to explore this continuing tradition of Irish drama, its origins, its characteristics, and its significance. And the school's concern has been with this tradition as a living continuum of performed theater, not just a collection of canonical literary texts. To this end, the school's speakers have always included theater professionals as well as academic authorities on Irish drama, and the program involves visits to major theater productions in Dublin for the students as well as an optional theater workshop. In sum, the Synge Summer School is intended to provide an opportunity to study the works of Synge in the context of the Wicklow locality and of the broader traditions of Irish theater from the eighteenth century to the contemporary period.

Established in 1991, at the suggestion of the Wicklow County Council, the Synge Summer School has been directed from the beginning by Nicholas Grene, who lives in the Rathdrum area and teaches in Trinity College, Dublin, with a main academic interest in drama. Like other Irish summer schools, it is a nonprofit enterprise with no institutional affiliations, offering a weeklong program of lectures, seminars, tours, and entertainments. Although the lectures are by recognized authorities and of a high level of originality, they are intended for students of widely different backgrounds and academic levels. The school has a policy of open access, does not offer academic credits, and aims to produce an atmosphere of informal, relaxed, and sociable learning. With relatively small numbers (thirty-nine students registered in 1993), there is plenty of opportunity for contact with the speakers outside the academic sessions. The course is residential, with the school organizing hostel, guesthouse, or hotel accommodations in the locality for the students and providing transport to and from all school events. Initial tours of places in the area associated with Synge's family and his work, which are given on the weekend of the students' arrival, are followed by three days of two lectures per morning and afternoon small-group seminars or theater workshops as well as trips to Dublin with evening theater visits on two other days. The students have been drawn from around the world – as many as thirteen countries were represented at the 1991 school session – including eastern Europe, Japan, Australia, the United States, Canada, Great Britain, and Ireland.

The 1991 inaugural school was opened by the school's patron, the distinguished actor Cyril Cusack, an embodiment of the Synge acting tradition (the fourth man to play the part of Christy Mahon in *The Playboy of the Western World*). Cusack died in October 1993. Outstanding events of the 1991 program were lectures by Ann Saddlemyer, editor of the definitive editions of Synge's plays and letters, on music in Synge; lectures by Katharine Worth on Beckett's voices; and a poetry reading by Seamus Heaney. The 1992 school highlighted the international standing of Synge's work with a message from the president of Hungary, Arpád Gncz, himself a Synge translator, read at the school's opening by the Hungarian ambassador to Ireland. Among the most memorable lectures of the 1992 program were a subtle analysis of the contrasting social and class background of Yeats and Synge by Roy Foster, professor of Irish history at Oxford, and a brilliant lecture by Angela Bourke of the Department of Irish, University College, Dublin, on the folk custom of keening the dead, so important to *Riders to the Sea,* and seen as itself a form of theater.

Such was the background and the established objectives for the 1993 Synge Summer School: the reinterpretation of the works of Synge; comparative readings of other major Irish playwrights along with Synge; the investigation and definition of theatrical traditions within Ireland; assessments of what is happening in Irish theater today.

The first vision of Synge at the 1993 school was offered by Thomas Kilroy, professor emeritus of English at University College, Galway, and himself a distinguished playwright. Speaking at the school's opening he commented on the quality of self-possession in Synge's work, which was in some sense a flight from self-expression. All of Synge's plays, according to Kilroy, make up a single self-contained world, witnessing to "the fierce individuality of the man, his sublime belief in the power of his own imagination." Such was the integrity of the work as a result, that it appeared complete in spite of Synge's early death, even in an unfinished play like *Deirdre of the Sorrows* (1910). This quality in Synge Kilroy associates with a now-

Ann Porter, left, the great-grandniece of John Millington Synge, at the 1993 Synge Summer School (photograph courtesy of the Irish Times *and the Synge Summer School)*

lost and underacknowledged strain within Anglo-Irish culture which Kilroy celebrated as an independence of mind, a cultivation of high and exacting artistic and intellectual standards.

The initial miscomprehension of Synge's vision in its original context was the starting point for Grene's lecture on "The Drama of *The Playboy.*" He pinpointed three sources of offense to the Abbey Theatre audiences in the notorious *Playboy* riots at the first production in 1907: obscenity, profanity, and misrepresentation. Nationalist audiences looked to their own national theater for reassuringly positive self-images to counter colonial caricatures. Synge's play, by its coarseness of language and its juxtaposition of sexuality and violence, by its disturbingly casual and indiscriminate oaths, and by its representation of an Irish wild west of anarchic peasants, appeared to collude with the very stage-Irish images which the Abbey was founded to combat. Grene concluded that these issues were not merely a matter of historical significance but that Synge's challenging treatment of sexuality, religion,

John Curley of the United States and Sandra Bursakova of the Czech Republic, students at the 1993 Synge Summer School (photograph courtesy of the Irish Times and the Synge Summer School)

and the representation of Irish life constitutes the continuing power of *The Playboy* as dramatic text.

The relation between national and nationalist drama in Ireland was recurrently addressed throughout the week of the school. Tom Paulin, well-known Irish poet and reader in poetry at the University of Nottingham, lectured on *Riders to the Sea* as a revisionist tragedy designed to counteract the avowedly nationalist *Cathleen ni Houlihan* (1902) of Yeats. Written in the year *Cathleen ni Houlihan* was produced, Synge's play with the same constituent elements – the country-cottage kitchen, the offstage action, the old-mother figure, the sacrificed sons – represents a re-writing of what Paulin excoriated as Yeats's "detestable piece of political pornography." Where Yeats's play had the kinetic aim of stimulating heroic action, Synge's vision was of a nonheroic tragedy of suffering. Analyzing the use of images of rope and ladder in *Riders,* which might have had subliminal associations with the theater of public executions, Paulin argued that the play found a means of representing the historic sufferings of the Irish people without turning them into political agit-prop. The difficulty of trying to stage the national life in all its multifariousness was brought out in a lecture on the Abbey Theatre after Synge by Philip Edwards, professor emeritus of English at the University of Liverpool. Looking at a group of lesser-known, largely realist plays written in the period from 1908 to 1912, Edwards brought out the problematic nature of the national idea in the context of the small-scale conflicts of family, class, sect and region which these plays dramatize. Edwards claimed that these plays – Lady Gregory's *The Image* (1909) with its skeptical satire on Irish hero worship, Conall O'Riordan's controversial *The Piper* (1908), which aroused audience hostility the year after *The Playboy,* Lennox Robinson's bitterly disillusioned *Patriots* (1912), T. C. Murray's bleak studies of rural culture in *Birthright* (1910) and *Maurice Harte* (1912), and St. John Ervine's troubled rendering of the Northern Irish Protestant working-classes in *John Ferguson* (1915) – in their range and diversity were a significant contribution to a national, if not a nationalist, drama.

The period of Synge's work, which was also that of an emerging Irish national self-consciousness, was the concern of many the school's speakers. Declan Kiberd, who lectures in Anglo-Irish literature at University College, Dublin, spoke on Wilde and the theater of subversion. Within the context of later Irish plays which could be categorized as a prefiguring of a subject people rehearsing the uprising, Kiberd argued for a view of Wilde as a first exponent of a decolonizing mission. The peculiarities of Wilde's family background, his position as Irish émigré writer in England, allowed him to develop a system of masks to subvert the opposed stabilities of nation and gender. As his dandyism at once flaunted and flouted the significance of clothing as social hieroglyphic, he undermined the idea of Englishness by exaggerated parody. In *The Importance of Being Earnest* (1895), which in its "celebration of multiple selfhood" was, among other things, "a parable of Anglo-Irish relations," the image of the double reveals the interlinked nature of self and other in the construction of national and sexual as well as individual identity. In their common celebration of the liberating power of fantasy, Kiberd bracketed Wilde with Synge as Utopian writers "less interested in writing social documentaries about the world they knew than in imagining a world yet to be."

Lectures by Terence Brown, associate professor of English at Trinity College, Dublin, and Bruce Arnold, literary editor of the *Irish Independent,* took the two Yeats brothers, poet and painter, as two other instances of the artistic expression of the national life in the period. Brown, now at work on a critical biography of W. B. Yeats, gave a rereading of the poem "Easter 1916" with the subtitle "revolution as theatre." He revealed a series of specific theatrical hinterlands for the poem's imaginative gestation: Yeats's work on *The Player Queen* (1919), a play which began as tragedy and was re-written as grotesque comedy; the complementary Renaissance textbook illustrations of the "tragic scene" and the "comic scene," of which Yeats was aware; the developing ideas of comedy and tragedy which Yeats had begun to articulate from the period of the death of Synge on. All of these conditioned the complex interweaving of images of comic and tragic form with their concomitant ideas of social life and historical destiny which underpin the structure and significance of the poem. Arnold, who is writing a biography of Jack Yeats, used letters between Synge and the painter to evoke their close and warm relationship. Beyond that personal bond, Arnold suggested a parallel track to the careers of Synge and Jack Yeats: a distancing period away from family and country before a dedicated return to Ireland as artistic subject, a common awareness of the need to find new imaginative forms to render the historical realities of post-famine rural

Ann Yeats, daughter of William Butler Yeats (photograph courtesy of the Irish Times *and the Synge Summer School)*

Ireland. Not only were they attracted to similar subjects – the country people, the tramps and tinkers of Irish roads – but, Arnold argued in a compositional analysis of Synge's plays and Yeats's paintings, they also had a similar concentration on a single decisive moment or movement caught against a background of continuing reality.

Many of the school's speakers used this strategy of comparison and contrast to redefine later Irish drama in a perspective that included Synge. Thus Christopher Murray, lecturer in English and director of studies of the Drama Centre, University College, Dublin, set up an opposition of "O'Casey v. Synge" not by way of contest between the two but in order to bring out their historical differentiation. In Synge's plays, he argued, written during the period before the Irish revolution, there remained an idea of community expressed through the poetic dialect. O'Casey's language, according to Murray, although possibly indebted to Synge as forerunner, "is a language of evasion because his characters do not inhabit a community in the sense in which we find a community in Synge, for good or ill, but discrete worlds of experience into which they are driven to invent roles to keep reality at bay." Murray read O'Casey's Dublin plays not as politically dispassionate realist reflections of city tenement life but as fractured and dislocated representations in the wake of revolution and world war. O'Casey's work was best when understood thus, in differentiating it from that of Synge, and, Murray judged, weaker in his later plays where he more nearly imitated Synge in an idea of communal life and a heightened poetic speech. It was affinities rather than differences that were stressed in Barry McGovern's talk on Synge and Beckett. McGovern, an Irish actor especially well known for his work in Beckett, including the one-man show *I'll Go On,* illustrated his perception of the similarities between the two writers with a series of readings from Beckett's fiction and Synge's poems as well as the plays of both. The talk/reading vividly evoked shared tastes for violence and the grotesque, a common preoccupation with aging and death, and the elaborated fantasias of black tragicomedy which were features of both writers.

Two of the lectures brought the issues of theater up to the present, bridging into other immediate events on the program. Riana O'Dwyer, who lectures in both the Department of English and the Women's Centre at University College, Galway, discussed the relationship between Synge and Tom Murphy, stressing their common concerns with the rituals of community and their comparable creation of an artificially native language which invariably sounds natural. On the evening of O'Dwyer's lecture Tom Murphy illustrated both the interest in myth and ritual and the heightened rhythmic dialogue in his own work with a fine reading from three of his plays, *The Morning after Optimism* (1971), *The Sanctuary Lamp* (1976), and *The Gigli Concert* (1983). Gerald Fitzgibbon, lecturer in English at University College, Cork, spoke on Friel the day after the school participants had seen Friel's latest play, *Wonderful Tennessee* (1993), which had opened at the Abbey two nights before. Fitzgibbon's lecture on "Interpreting Between Privacies: The Theatre of Brian Friel" analyzed the relationship between public and private selves in Friel's works, arguing that his characters had a problem not only of communicating with one another but of constructing inner selves, creating stories to support a sense of personal identity. This then flowed in to a discussion of the new play: whether *Wonderful Tennessee* represented an innovative departure after the enormous

success of *Dancing at Lughnasa* (1990) or whether Friel this time had failed to meld the naturalistic present-day plot of his six characters on a holiday outing to a deserted pier in Donegal with the deep structures of pagan myth.

It was theater all the way through the week of the Synge Summer School. A local amateur drama group presented *"Sunshine and the Moon's Delight": an evening with J. M. Synge.* Jennifer Johnston gave a moving reading of two of her dramatic monologues, the voices of women who are survivors/victims of the Northern Irish political crisis. On one of the outings to Dublin the school went to a revival of Frank McGuinness's first play, *The Factory Girls* (1982); on another the students had the opportunity of visiting the Abbey Theatre and questioning Garry Hynes, its current artistic director, about her work there. For those with practical interests in acting and production, there was a theater workshop on Synge's plays led by the veteran Abbey director Tomas MacAnna. The last talk of the week was given by Fiona Shaw, the Irish actress who has won such acclaim for her acting in British theater and who had come back to direct *The Hamlet Project,* a workshop touring production of *Hamlet,* for the Abbey. Her outside/inside perspective on Irish theater, often refreshingly critical and piercingly funny, stopped the school's view of the contemporary state of the art in Ireland from becoming too self-congratulatory.

The Synge Summer School was and is by design both focused and unfocused. In centering on the works of Synge in a local context it has a very specific subject, and an awareness of Synge provides a particular angle of approach to Irish drama. As a result there is a coherence of recurrent themes and issues: the historical and political context of Irish theater, the representation or alleged misrepresentation of Ireland, the creation of a specifically Irish dramatic language, and the relation between social surfaces and underlying mythic structures. All of these became the subject of running debate through the week of the 1993 school. But the program of the school is deliberately not shaped around a single theme nor tied to one critical approach. It is intended instead to use the extraordinary case of Synge's drama as a point of departure for the full range and complexity of the phenomenon which is Irish theater past and present.

The 1994 Synge Summer School will be held from 15 June to 2 July: contact Irene Parsons, Whaley Lodge, Ballinaclash, Rathdrum, County Wicklow, Telephone +353 404 46131, FAX: +353 404 46424.

The Book Trade History Group

Simon Eliot
Open University, Bristol, England

During a 1985 conference in Oxford on publishers' and printers' archives, Simon Eliot of the Open University and Michael Turner of the Bodleian Library found themselves discussing some of the problems of book history in the United Kingdom – in particular the fact that not one of the assembled academics was officially a book historian: they were literary scholars, social and economic historians, bibliographers, and academic librarians. They were scattered and isolated. This isolation meant that researchers ran the risk of duplicating others' work or of missing important information. Few book historians in the United Kingdom had any sort of interested and informed audience for their work. What was needed, they agreed, was a means of communication which would put scholars in touch with each other and coordinate information and advice. By improvements in communications, book history in the United Kingdom might gradually be turned into a more cooperative venture. No one wished to form yet another grand learned society; what was wanted was a workaday, loose-fit organization which would be dedicated to getting information to people quickly and informally and, when necessary, would be capable of giving new ideas a bit of a push.

Out of this conversation came the idea of a Book Trade History Group (BTHG). Near the end of the Oxford conference an informal meeting was called and the proposal put to the assembled scholars. The idea was endorsed, and Eliot and Turner were asked to set it up. What emerged in the next few months was a simple model of how the BTHG might work: its main function would be to circulate a newsletter three times a year free to all members. It would hold at least one meeting a year at which a major or pressing issue in book history would be discussed. If, as a result of these discussions, it was felt that the BTHG could contribute something to a particular aspect of the subject, then a small subgroup would be formed to work on it. Subscriptions were to be as low as possible, with special rates for postgraduate students; the money raised would be used to fund the newsletter, run the annual meeting, and, if necessary, support the subgroups in their activities.

The inaugural meeting of the BTHG was held at the British Library's Sheraton House on 11 November 1985. Ian Willison of the British Library was elected chairman, Eliot was elected secretary and editor of the *BTHG Newsletter*, and Annabel Jones of the publisher Longmans was elected treasurer and membership secretary. One of the main speakers at the meeting was Don McKenzie, professor of bibliography at Oxford University, and it was on this occasion that he proposed, for the first time in public, the idea of a multi-volume *History of the Book in Britain*. The debate that followed was vigorous and revealed tensions between the constituent parts of the book-history community. McKenzie's proposal, however, also seemed to strike a resonant chord with the majority of members, who resolved that, although the BTHG had a wider remit than any single project, its members would give the McKenzie proposal their full individual support. From that resolution the BTHG has had a close, albeit informal, link with the *History of the Book in Britain* project.

This link is most obvious in the case of shared personnel: BTHG chairman Willison is a general editor of the project, as is one of the subgroup chairs, David McKitterick of Trinity College Cambridge; the secretary, Eliot, is a volume editor, as is John Barnard (University of Leeds), who currently serves on the BTHG's committee. Most of the committee and many of the most active members of the BTHG are, or are likely to become, contributors to one or more of the seven volumes of the *History*. Many of the discussions initiated, and many of the projects launched, by the BTHG have direct relevance to the primary research work being undertaken in order to provide the *History* with a solid empirical foundation.

The second meeting of the BTHG was held in the archives department at the University of Reading on 30 May 1986 and focused on the problems of locating, preserving, and cataloguing book-history archives. It was clear that much work still needed to be done in this area and that, as yet, no organization had taken responsibility for it. The meeting proposed that the first subgroup of the BTHG should be formed with the express intention of developing "a coherent and practical policy on book trade archives."

Since 1985 the BTHG has met regularly once a year in London, usually in late November. On each occasion it has addressed a particular aspect or problem of the subject. In 1986 it discussed ways in which book history was being taught at undergraduate and postgraduate levels. In 1987 Frances Pinter, of Pinter Publishers, talked about the problems of establishing an independent publishing firm in the age of multinational conglomerates. In 1988 Gerry Davies addressed the meeting on the subject of writing a history of the Booksellers' Association. At the 1989 meeting Tim Rix discussed the establishment of the Centre for the Book in the British Library. In 1990 the BTHG considered the problems and pleasures of studying the history of textbooks. In 1991 the annual meeting turned its attention to the history of reading and heard papers from James Raven and Elizabeth Leedham Green. Pursuing its theme of improving communications, the 1992 meeting invited representatives from Cambridge University Press, Gale International, and Oxford University Press to discuss the business of book-publishing history. Last year attention was turned to British provincial publishers, and the group heard from Professor Peter Isaac a progress report on his British Book Trades Index (BBTI) project.

Following the Reading University meeting in 1986, David McKitterick was asked to chair the BTHG's first subgroup. Most of the subgroup's work has been concerned with creation of a location register of publishers' and printers' archives between 1830 and 1939. This has been a difficult process, but in cooperation with the National Register of Archives, the Business Archives Council, and Professor Trevor Howard Hill and many others, the subgroup has accumulated an impressive list of archives, some in the public domain, others still the private property of individual firms, but all of which offer significant quantities of primary material, much of it quantitative and financial, without which a rigorous and well-founded history of the book in the nineteenth and twentieth centuries cannot be written. The subgroup was most fortunate in having one of the Leverhulme fellows in book history, Dr. Alexis Weedon (now of Luton Univer-

sity), working on this very topic. Although her main task was the accumulation of production information from individual publishers, her initial job was to survey existing archives from the period. Weedon's work has formed the core of the BTHG's location register. The subgroup's work will reach a milestone with the production of an expanded and revised register in 1994.

In 1989, following a proposal by the secretary and discussion in the BTHG's committee, a second subgroup was established, this time to work on the problems of oral history as it applies to the history of the book. This subgroup was initially chaired by Dr. Michael Harris of London University and is now led by Robin Myers, honorary archivist of the Stationers' Company. The group is currently operating on two fronts. One is concerned with the development of a business plan, the purpose of which is to raise funds for a major academic project in oral book history. The other is more immediate and more pressing. The subgroup has identified what amounts to a "rescue archaeology" job to be done on printers who were working in the period from the 1930s to the 1970s before new technology began sweeping away many nineteenth-century practices which had survived until that time. If the oral history of this relatively inarticulate group (publishers of the same period are always much more forthcoming) is not recorded soon it will be lost forever. Members of the subgroup are currently being trained in interviewing techniques and have already made their first recordings. Two copies of each recording will be made: one will be deposited with the National Sound Archive in the United Kingdom, and the other will be deposited in the archives of the Stationers' Company. There is no doubt that this material will have a significant impact on the writing of volume seven (1914–present) of the *History of the Book in Britain*.

Although not formally associated with the BTHG, the Reading Experience Database (RED) is an example of a major project whose origins lie within the group. The 1991 meeting on the history of reading led the secretary to revive a proposal that he had made in an editorial in the *BTHG Newsletter* the year before. In the newsletter he had suggested that the new Centre for the Book, then being established at the British Library, should run a major project in the history of reading – in particular, that it should begin the creation of a database to record as many pieces of evidence as possible on the experience of reading in the past. This idea rumbled around for another year or so before the Centre for the Book was able to propose anything concrete.

However, by sur ... er 1992 Mike Crump (British Library) and Eliot were beginning to sketch out a project which became known in the next few months as RED, the aim of which was to collect documentary information about experiences of reading in the British Isles, and of reading by those born or normally resident in the British Isles, between 1450 and 1914. A steering committee was set up (Crump, Eliot [joint directors], Leedham Green, Raven, Weedon, Jonathan Rose), most of whom, needless to say, were members or close associates of the BTHG. A structure of record fields was devised and widely circulated (both in print and electronically) for comment and emendation, and a database was created on the Open University's Vaxcluster. The RED project will begin its long, but hopefully exciting, career with a formal launch in the spring of 1994.

Issue 1 of the *BTHG Newsletter* was published in February 1986, and the publication has continued to appear roughly three times a year ever since. Eliot edited the first twelve issues (February 1986–January 1991). Issues 13–20 (June 1991–November 1993) were edited by Lynette Hunter of Leeds University and Margaret Beetham of Manchester Metropolitan University. Since January 1994 (issue 21) the *Newsletter* has been published from Birmingham University under the editorship of Maureen Bell. Each editor has imparted something of his or her own personality to the publication, and that is as it should be. Unlike formal academic journals, newsletters have the freedom and informality to encourage the expression of individual style. Eliot tended to indulge himself by writing editorials which sometimes surveyed the state of a particular part of the subject, but more frequently and more controversially promoted a very particular view of what should be done. The tone of his editorials gradually became more strident, but, whatever he did, he never quite succeeded in his aim, which was to provoke a reader, any reader, into writing a letter disagreeing with him. Hunter and Beetham shifted the emphasis of the *Newsletter* and increased its coverage of the activities of other groups and societies.

Whatever the inclinations of its current editor, the *Newsletter* continues to perform its main function, which is to keep scholars in touch with each other by carrying announcements of conferences, reports of seminars, descriptions of current research topics, a notes and queries section, and reviews of relevant books. These provide the core of its coverage, and these on their own would justify publication. However, on top of this, the *Newsletter* has made a feature of printing "work in progress" on original bibliographical and historical research, and of information on the location and content of archives. Among the subjects of articles published are publishers' archives at Reading University (issue 2); Oxford University Press archives (issue 4); personal papers of Sir Victor Gollancz (issues 5 and 10); the Stationers' Company records (issue 6); the *Publishers' Circular* (issues 8 and 9); publishers' and printers' financial archives; a preliminary listing (issues 12 and 13); and a checklist of Victorian religious periodicals publishing verse, from 1850 to 1875 (issue 14).

It was publishing this sort of material that prompted Eliot and Turner to come up with the idea of the *History of the Book – On Demand Series* (*HOBODS*). The *BTHG Newsletter* had for some time been receiving material which, due to its length, could not be published within the modest covers of a twenty- or thirty-page newsletter. Much of this material was quantitative history, much of it works in progress and thus still subject to emendation; nevertheless it was a sufficient and pressing interest to be put into the public domain. For such material neither the learned journal nor the informal newsletter was quite right: the former would want something more finished, the latter something snappier. *HOBODS* would use a desktop-publishing system to produce short runs of, to quote from its prospectus:

> refereed material from a variety of sources: data that was used to write an article or monograph but which was itself never published in full; MA, M.Phil. and PhD theses or parts of theses which contain original and significant research; data from current research topics that, although subject to addition and emendation, is already of sufficient value to be made available in the public domain.

So far *HOBODS,* which was launched in 1992, has produced three titles:

1. Alexis Weedon, *Summary Statistics for George Bell & Sons and the Bohn Libraries 1865–1920* (1992);

2. Simon Eliot, *A Measure of Popularity. Public Library Holdings of Twenty-Four Popular Authors 1883–1912* (1992);

3. Rosemary Scott, *A Checklist of Religious Verse Publications 1851–1860* (1993).

Planned for 1994 is at least one and possibly two monographs derived from the production ledgers of the British publisher Chatto and Windus. These will deal with the production history (including lists of impressions, print runs, binding rates, and so forth) of novelists such as Mark Twain, Walter Besant, Wilkie Collins, and Robert Louis Stevenson. Also planned for 1994 is a revised and expanded version of a location register of publishers' and printers' archives, 1830–1939, the original version of which was published in issue 12 of the *BTHG Newsletter. HOBODS* is independent of the BTHG but, like RED, had its origins within it.

Despite its many successes there is one area in which the BTHG has not as yet been able to make much headway. In its second annual meeting, in 1986, members discussed the problem of teaching book history at the university level in general and to postgraduates in particular. Experiences were compared and grand statements made on the necessity, given that we were still such a small and scattered group of scholars, of cooperating on the writing and teaching of such courses. Sadly, it was felt that there was insufficient common ground to form a subgroup on the subject. In the years that followed we saw many separate projects rise, some flourishing, some not. The most recent proposal, initiated by BTHG members, for a taught M.A. in book history to be written and run by a consortium of universities became transformed into a London University proposal. There is a good chance that this may now run, and we should wish it well, but the goal of a cooperative degree program, drawing on the strengths of many widely scattered scholars, seems as far-off as ever.

When founded in 1985 the BTHG was designed to be a small, informal, gingery group with two main functions: to improve communications between book historians and to stimulate initiatives that would advance the subject. In 1994 the group remains small (despite the group's having members in Australia, Canada, France, Germany, New Zealand, and the United States, total membership is no more than 130). The *BTHG Newsletter* is consciously a product of a simple desktop-publishing system with a very flexible and open structure: this allows anything of relevance or interest to be published from the most combative editorial to the most meticulous listing of archives. The number and range of projects with which it is, directly or indirectly, involved suggests that the group's sparkiness, even after ten years, remains undimmed.

Kay Boyle

(19 February 1902 – 27 December 1992)

Elizabeth S. Bell
University of South Carolina – Aiken

See also the Boyle entries in *DLB 4: American Writers in Paris, 1920–1939; DLB 9: American Novelists, 1910–1945; DLB 48: American Poets, 1880–1945;* and *DLB 86: American Short-Story Writers, 1910–1945,* First Series.

BOOKS: *Short Stories* (Paris: Black Sun Press, 1929);
Wedding Day and Other Stories (New York: Cape & Smith, 1930; London: Pharos Editions, 1932);
Plagued by the Nightingale (New York: Cape & Smith, 1931; London & Toronto: Cape, 1931);
Landscape for Wyn Henderson (London: Curwen Press, 1931);
A Statement (New York: Modern Editions Press, 1932);
Year Before Last (London: Faber & Faber, 1932; New York: Harrison & Smith, 1932);
The First Lover and Other Stories (New York: Smith & Haas, 1933; London: Faber & Faber, 1937);
Gentlemen, I Address You Privately (New York: Smith & Haas, 1933; London: Faber & Faber, 1934);
My Next Bride (New York: Harcourt, Brace, 1934; London: Faber & Faber, 1935);
The White Horses of Vienna and Other Stories (New York: Harcourt, Brace, 1936; London: Faber & Faber, 1937);
Death of a Man (London: Faber & Faber, 1936; New York: Harcourt, Brace, 1936);
Monday Night (New York: Harcourt, Brace, 1938; London: Faber & Faber, 1938);
A Glad Day (Norfolk, Conn.: New Directions, 1938);
The Youngest Camel (Boston: Little, Brown, 1939; London: Faber & Faber, 1939);
The Crazy Hunter and Other Stories (London: Faber & Faber, 1940); republished as *The Crazy Hunter: Three Short Novels* (New York: Harcourt, Brace, 1940);
Primer For Combat (New York: Simon & Schuster, 1942; London: Faber & Faber, 1943);
Avalanche (New York: Simon & Schuster, 1944; London: Faber & Faber, 1944);

Kay Boyle

American Citizen Naturalized in Leadville, Colorado (New York: Simon & Schuster, 1944);
A Frenchman Must Die (New York: Simon & Schuster, 1946; London: Faber & Faber, 1946);
Thirty Stories (New York: Simon & Schuster, 1946; London: Faber & Faber, 1948);
1939 (New York: Simon & Schuster, 1948; London: Faber & Faber, 1948);
His Human Majesty (New York, London & Toronto: Whittlesey House/McGraw-Hill, 1949; London: Faber & Faber, 1950);

The Smoking Mountain: Stories of Postwar Germany (New York, London & Toronto: McGraw-Hill, 1951; London: Faber & Faber, 1952);

The Seagull on the Step (New York: Knopf, 1955; London: Faber & Faber, 1955);

The Short Novels (Boston: Beacon, 1958);

The Youngest Camel Reconsidered and Rewritten (New York: Harper, 1959; London: Faber & Faber, 1960);

Generation Without Farewell (New York: Knopf, 1960; London: Faber & Faber, 1960);

Collected Poems (New York: Knopf, 1962);

Breaking the Silence: Why a Mother Tells Her Son About The Nazi Era (New York: Institute of Human Relations Press, American Jewish Committee, 1962);

Nothing Ever Breaks Except the Heart (Garden City, N.Y.: Doubleday, 1966);

Pinky, the Cat Who Liked to Sleep (New York: Crowell-Collier / London: Collier-Macmillan, 1966);

Pinky in Persia (New York: Crowell-Collier, 1968);

Being Geniuses Together, 1920–1930, by Robert McAlmon, revised, with supplementary chapters, by Boyle (Garden City, N.Y.: Doubleday, 1968; London: M. Joseph, 1970);

Testament For My Students and Other Poems (Garden City, N.Y.: Doubleday, 1970);

The Long Walk at San Francisco State and Other Essays (New York: Grove, 1970);

The Underground Woman (Garden City, N.Y.: Doubleday, 1975);

Fifty Stories (Garden City, N.Y.: Doubleday, 1975);

Words That Must Somehow Be Said: The Selected Essays of Kay Boyle, 1927–1983 (Berkeley, Cal.: North Point Press, 1985);

This Is Not a Letter and Other Poems (Los Angeles: Sun & Moon Press, 1985).

TRANSLATIONS: Joseph Delteil, *Don Juan* (New York: Cape & Smith, 1931);

René Crevel, *Mr. Knife, Miss Fork* (Paris: Black Sun Press, 1931);

Raymond Radiquet, *The Devil in the Flesh* (Paris: Crosby Continental Editions / New York: Harrison & Smith, 1932; London: Grey Walls Press, 1949).

OTHER: Gladys Palmer Brooke, *Relations & Complications, Being the Recollections of H. H. The Dayang Muda of Sarawak,* ghostwritten by Boyle (London: John Lane/Bodley Head, 1929);

Ernest Walsh, *Poems and Sonnets,* anonymously edited by Boyle (New York: Harcourt, Brace, 1934);

365 Days, edited by Boyle, Laurence Vail, and Nina Conarain (London: Cape, 1936; New York: Harcourt, Brace, 1936);

Bettina Bedwell, *Yellow Dusk,* ghostwritten by Boyle (London: Hurst & Blackett, 1937);

Fourteen of Them, includes a memorial chapter of Anthony John Rizzi by Boyle (New York & Toronto: Farrar & Rinehart, 1944);

The Autobiography of Emanuel Carnevali, compiled, with a preface, by Boyle (New York: Horizon, 1967);

Enough of Dying! Voices of Peace, edited by Boyle and Justine Van Gundy, with an introduction and three selections by Boyle (New York: Laurel, 1972);

"Report from Lock-Up," in *Four Visions of America,* by Boyle, Erica Jong, Thomas Sanchez, and Henry Miller (Santa Barbara: Capra Press, 1977).

Kay Boyle's death on 27 December 1992 ended a literary life that spanned much of the twentieth century. Present at most of the important historical cruxes of our century, Boyle wrote with candor and understanding of the human repercussions of events played out in the impersonal international arena. First through her literary works and later through an unrelenting activism, she spoke for those who otherwise would have remained virtually silenced. Boyle saw all of her work as political, even though some of the early works were not recognized by critics as such, for she saw herself always presenting a case for human dignity and for the rights of the less fortunate. Indeed, her life was spent in the midst of such efforts, and her writing reflects the insight she brought to human concerns.

Born on 19 February 1902 in Saint Paul, Minnesota, Boyle delighted in later years in telling that until she applied for Social Security in the 1960s, she believed she had been born in 1903. Official biographical sketches to which she contributed prior to that date list the latter year as her birth date. Her father, Howard Peterson Boyle, at one time director of the Children's Homeopathic Hospital in Philadelphia, seems to have had little influence on Boyle's life. Certainly he seems to have been overshadowed by other members of the family — her paternal grandfather, her maternal grandmother, Eva Evans, and of course, her mother, Katherine Evans Boyle, for whom she was named — all extraordinary people who provided the young Kay with an atypical view of the world.

Her grandfather, Jesse Peyton Boyle, whom Boyle credited with providing stability to the fam-

Boyle (third from left) in 1929 with the countess of Polignac, Laurence Vail, Hart Crane, and Caresse Crosby

ily, headed a publishing company in Saint Paul. In various short stories, such as "Security," published in *The White Horses of Vienna and Other Stories* (1936), Boyle portrays him as a man of forceful personality who took an active interest in his young granddaughters' lives. His fortune largely sustained the family as well. Largely through his generosity the family traveled extensively in Europe during Boyle's early childhood, and he remained an influence as she grew older. Not all of her portraits of the grandfather are positive, however. In another story written at much the same time, "Black Boy," published in *The First Lover and Other Stories* (1933), she pictures the grandfather as a rigid, bigoted man who refuses to recognize viewpoints other than his own, even though his motives involve what he considers appropriate concern for his family. Probably all these elements of his personality coexisted, and certainly Boyle credited him with being a major influence in her life.

But it was the women of her family who had the most lasting influence on Boyle. She recalled that one of the first stories she ever wrote was about her maternal grandmother, who had married as a young woman and become a schoolteacher in Kansas. She left her husband, the superintendent of schools and an alcoholic, and took her two young daughters to Washington, D.C., long before such behavior was accepted for women. Her experiences became the subject of two of Boyle's stories. The first, "Episode in the Life of an Ancestor," published in *Wedding Day and Other Stories* (1930), is set on the Kansas prairie and features a young woman referred to only as "the grandmother." In the story she is seen as a person of independence and courage, observed by the father who loves her but cannot understand her. The second story, "The Man Who Died Young," published in *The First Lover and Other Stories,* chronicles the westward movement of the nation through the perceptions of a woman who records deeds and land grants for the government. As she marks the newly deeded land on her map, she sees the country expand. Boyle's fictional portraits of her grandmother, as well as her reminiscences of her, reveal the affection and the high esteem Boyle had for her.

Boyle's mother, herself an extraordinary woman, introduced young Kay to the world of avant-garde literature and art, refusing to allow the child to grow up in a restricted, provincial world. In

263

1913 she took Kay to the famous Armory Show in New York, which introduced American audiences to cubism and other modern art movements. In addition, she read Gertrude Stein and James Joyce to her children, as well as to family friends, ensuring that they knew of the experiments such writers were making with language and narrative. Boyle later mused that she had no idea how her mother came to know of these writers, but her insistence that Kay and her sister hear their cadences and listen to their themes influenced Boyle never to shy away from the experimental in her own work. In addition, Katherine Boyle was always active in civic affairs, supporting the Children's Crusade during World War I, for example, and later running for public office. Her influence encouraged Boyle to see artistic endeavor and political morality as closely and naturally related.

By the end of World War I, however, the family had suffered some financial reverses. They settled in Cincinnati, Ohio, where Boyle worked as secretary for her father's business. She briefly attended the Cincinnati Conservatory of Music and the Ohio Mechanics Institute but soon found she wanted a more active life than she could find in Cincinnati. In 1922 she moved to New York to work for fashion writer Margery Welles. During the summer of 1922 Boyle married Richard Brault, a French engineering student she had met in Cincinnati. From the beginning their marriage represented a clash of cultures, a theme she would develop in a variety of contexts throughout her literary career. In order to appease both their families, they were married in two ceremonies, one civil and the other Catholic. However, that period of time in New York proved significant for Boyle in ways far more noteworthy than in her personal life.

In November 1922 Boyle began working for Lola Ridge in the New York office of *Broom* magazine. There during the famous Thursday afternoon teas organized by Ridge, she met writers such as John Dos Passos, Marianne Moore, Glenway Wescott, Waldo Frank, Elinor Wylie, and William Carlos Williams, who with his wife Florence remained a valued friend to Boyle. Boyle absorbed the literary world in that basement office, talking with major writers engaged in the ferment taking place in twentieth-century writing. In the casual conversation of friends, they were reshaping the conceptions of what literature could do. Boyle published her first works, two poems, during this period: "Morning" in *Broom* (January 1923) and "Shore" in *Contact* (June 1923).

Meanwhile, Brault had been offered a job with the Michelin Tire Corporation in his native France, so in 1923 Boyle immigrated with him to his family home where they intended to live briefly with his traditional Catholic family. Boyle describes the experience of the next few years in the autobiographical chapters she added to her 1968 revision of Robert McAlmon's 1938 memoir, *Being Geniuses Together*. Boyle's American exuberance, as well as her taste in clothing and makeup, clashed immediately with the rather rigid conventions of Brault's family. After a few months, during which it became increasingly clear that Boyle would never win their approval, she and Brault moved to Le Havre.

Even as she lived with Brault's family, Boyle had been working seriously on her writing, and during a brief trip to Paris, she met McAlmon, who with Williams had founded *Contact* magazine in 1920. He was destined to be her professional mentor during her years in Europe, and she was to repay the favor after his death. In addition to revising and publishing his *Being Geniuses Together,* she also supported republication of his *A Hasty Bunch* (1922, 1977) and wrote the new afterword for that volume. She also met a young writer, Ernest Walsh, who with Ethel Moorhead edited *This Quarter,* one of the growing number of "little magazines" offering a forum for American and European writers experimenting with the forms and language of literature at the time. Boyle continued to publish poetry, with "Harbor Song" appearing in *Poetry* and "Summer" in *This Quarter* during 1924.

The Le Havre climate proved unhealthy for Boyle. At one time her doctors feared she had contracted tuberculosis, at that time virtually incurable, although her illness was later determined to be a severe case of bronchitis. They recommended she move further south to a gentler climate. Walsh, himself suffering from tuberculosis, urged her to join him in Grasse. In 1926 she left the marriage with Brault and joined Walsh on his travels through Europe during which she helped him with editorial correspondence connected to his magazine. On 16 October 1926 Walsh died of a massive hemorrhage; five months later Boyle gave birth to their daughter, Sharon.

After an unsuccessful and halfhearted attempt to reestablish her marriage with Brault, who had not told his family of Boyle's relationship with Walsh, Boyle and Brault separated for the final time. In 1928, she met Raymond Duncan, brother of Isadora, and joined his artists' commune, signing over custody of her child as an indication of her commitment to the group. While working in one of

Boyle with Laurence Vail, 1929 (Southern Illinois University, Special Collections/Morris Library)

the commune's craft stores, Boyle became acquainted with Harry and Caresse Crosby, founders of Black Sun Press, who became personal and professional friends. Ultimately disillusioned with Duncan's colony and with his lavish lifestyle at the expense of other colony members, Boyle, with the help of the Crosbys, kidnapped Sharon from the commune and escaped to the Crosbys' country home on 31 December 1928.

She had by this time met Laurence Vail, an expatriate writer, and in 1929 moved with him to Saint Aulde in the south of France. That same year, Black Sun Press published her first collection of stories, entitled *Short Stories,* which contained seven works, four of which had previously appeared in Eugene Jolas's *transition.* Boyle worked briefly as a secretary for Bettina Bedwell, fashion editor of the Paris *Tribune,* and she translated several novels from French for Black Sun Press. She published *Wedding Day and Other Stories,* which contained the seven stories she had previously published as *Short Stories* along with six others. This volume demonstrated Boyle's technical virtuosity and her narrative experimentation, and it proved to be a critical

success. Publication of this volume also began a period of astounding literary productivity for Boyle. Early in 1931 she published her first novel, *Plagued by the Nightingale,* which she had completed several years previously, a translation of Joseph Delteil's *Don Juan,* and in September her second novel, *Year Before Last,* which appeared as a limited edition from Black Sun Press. It was published again in 1932 in both a British edition by Faber and Faber and an American edition by Harrison and Smith. In addition, she and Vail married in April after her divorce from Brault was final. They began a life together that included friendships with Joyce, Samuel Beckett (who served as godfather to one of their children), and Marcel Duchamp (godfather to another of their children). They were active participants in the literary movements of the decade, expanding their own literary endeavors to include editing collections of experimental prose, as well as producing their own.

Boyle mined the substance of her relationship with the Braults in *Plagued by the Nightingale,* which took its title from Moore's poem, "Marriage" (1923), and it became an intimate, if fictionalized, portrait of her marriage to Brault. In this novel Boyle introduced what became one of her signature characters, the "American girl" who must fend for herself in a world vastly different from the one she values, alone in a Europe grown fusty and stale. In an interview years later, Boyle admitted that by the late 1930s she consciously tried to steer away from that character, but by that time their identification was too strong. In *Plagued by the Nightingale* Bridget, the female protagonist, becomes a hero figure who initiates both decision making and action within the novel. It is she who provides emotional support for her husband and protects him from the overpowering demands of his family. It is she who ultimately rescues the husband – who appears as a virtual "damsel in distress" throughout the events of the story – and brings about the resolution of the novel. But the book is more complex than a mere hero narrative.

Drawing on the sensitivity she developed for imagery as a poet, Boyle establishes a central metaphor which operates somewhat as a metaphysical conceit in the novel, for she uses a genetic disease passed from one generation of the novel's central family to its next generation. A disease that literally saps its victim's strength, it has weakened the family until most of the current generation are suffering from it. Bridget, the American outsider who serves as protagonist of the novel, must confront the family's insistence that one's major duty in life is to produce as many children as one's reproductive years will allow – thus perpetuating the incurable lethargy of the disease in future generations – with her own reluctance to bear a child and with her husband's reluctance to pass his own illness on to his children.

As the novel progresses, the family members urge Bridget and her husband to conform to the decisions that generations of the family have made, and ultimately they offer the couple a substantial amount of money to produce a first child. Fearing that they will be submerged by the family, Bridget and her husband realize that they must escape, but he is helpless to suggest a way of doing so. Ironically, Bridget recognizes that escape will be easy: she decides to have a child and use the money promised them by the family to take husband, child, and self far away. While this seems to be a self-explanatory story of escape, Boyle uses it to represent the ferment of ideas prevalent in post–World War I Europe. Her metaphor of energy-depleting illness places a vital America against a fading Europe, a younger generation against one bound by convention. Capturing the spirit of experimentation

rife among the artists and writers congregating in Europe, Boyle's novel places the new worldview taking shape in the midst of postwar disillusionment and shattered cultures in conflict with old, irrelevant, convention-bound ones trying to hold onto a world no longer possible. She clearly portrays change, embodied in the young and American Bridget, the origin of hope and freedom from spiritual lassitude.

In equally autobiographical and fictionalized form, Boyle's second novel, *Year Before Last,* portrays the months of her life with Walsh. Casting the novel with a trio of characters centered once again by the "American girl," this time called Hannah, and completed by the dying poet/editor Martin and his older mentor/financier Edith, Boyle again recreates the clash of old worldview, represented by the jealous and vindictive Edith, and the new, represented by the younger, life-preserving Hannah, as they vie for Martin's affections. In personal terms, the novel explores the currents and dimensions of love in its positive and negative guises. In metaphorical terms, the novel explores conflicting views over the course of twentieth-century literature, a conflict Boyle herself would engage throughout the late 1920s and the 1930s.

One of the most poignant elements of the novel is Boyle's graphic portrait of the ostracism the dying Martin must endure as his tuberculosis becomes recognized by landlord and store clerk alike. Fearing contagion and sure death for themselves, various versions of them refuse shelter or sustenance to Martin and Hannah. Rootless, looked at with suspicion, Martin and Hannah wander throughout southern Europe searching for a place to reside as the last weeks of Martin's life play out. Again, Hannah stands as his protector, and while her efforts at his salvation ultimately fail, it is she who provides him with whatever security he is to know within the novel.

During the next two years Boyle published a collection of short fiction, *The First Lover and Other Stories,* and two more novels: *Gentlemen, I Address You Privately* (1933), about the bohemian night world, and *My Next Bride* (1934), chronicling her stay in Duncan's colony. In April 1934 she received the first of two Guggenheim Fellowships she would be awarded during her lifetime (the second was awarded in 1961). Her reputation as writer was growing steadily, with several of her stories appearing in the O. Henry Award and the Edgar J. O'Brien Award collections. In 1935 she won the prestigious O. Henry Award for the year's best short story for "The White Horses of Vienna," published in the April issue of *Harper's Monthly*. She used that story as the title piece of another collection, *The White Horses of Vienna and Other Stories,* which contained eighteen stories not previously collected. This volume marks a change in Boyle's fiction, for the stories in it reflect much more specifically than any of her previous works the socioeconomic and political tensions that were growing in Europe. These stories combine her consistent concern for human relationships with an increasingly persistent discussion of explosive social and political movements around her.

"The White Horses of Vienna," one of her most widely anthologized stories, illustrates this shift very well. Divided into three parts, the story again uses a trio of characters, this time a pro-Nazi Tirolian doctor and his equally anti-Semitic wife against an apolitical young Jewish student doctor sent to help them during the older doctor's recovery from an injury. As the plot unfolds, the characters consistently fail to communicate with each other because the doctor and his wife interpret the young doctor's actions and opinions through the veil of their own negative stereotypes of Jewishness. For his part, the young doctor naively assumes the doctor and his wife view him as a friend. As an additional irony, the reader realizes that the older doctor had been injured setting swastika fires in a gesture of solidarity with the Nazi movement that had not at that time yet established itself in Austria. Boyle does not explain the significance of those fires to her reader. In fact, she merely suggests the political elements of the story through patterns of interaction among the three characters. Thus, through the device of a puppet show, ostensibly designed by the older doctor for his younger colleague's entertainment, the older doctor voices his support of Adolf Hitler, an allusion the younger doctor fails to understand. Ultimately the older doctor is sent to prison for his activism, but the younger doctor, still not comprehending the political issues, tries to help his colleague.

From a post–World War II perspective, the irony in this story becomes more moving. But at the time of its publication, it was a more subtle discussion of the artificial boundaries people erect in their dealings with others. In this story and others she was to write during this time period, Boyle expects her readers to be aware of the events taking place in Europe and of the forces building within countries battered by economic depression and national tensions. Against this background she explores the world she sees shaping itself through the lives of the people that inhabit it.

Boyle in 1932 (Southern Illinois University, Special Collections/Morris Library)

During the 1930s Boyle's literary work spanned the genres, including essays, a collection of poetry entitled *A Glad Day* (1938), a ghosted book for her friend and former employer Bettina Bedwell, translations, a children's book entitled *The Youngest Camel* (1939), and two more novels, *Death of a Man* (1936) and *Monday Night* (1938), which she later recalled as her favorite of all the novels she had written. It is noteworthy, for, unlike many of her other works, it contains a male as the central character. Yet, despite the variety of her works, her short stories gained the most critical acclaim, winning for Boyle a reputation as stylist and crafter of exquisite short fiction. Appearing regularly in prestigious American magazines such as *Harper's* and the *New Yorker,* her stories introduced Boyle to a reading public in the United States. They also provided Boyle with the opportunity to educate stateside readers about the turmoil waiting to erupt in Europe.

Her story "Anschluss" (*Harper's Monthly*, April 1939; collected in *Nothing Ever Breaks Except the Heart*, 1966) demonstrates the point. Appearing in both *Best Short Stories of 1940* and *0. Henry Memorial Award Prize Stories of 1939*, it deals with the dampening effect political events have on individual relationships, especially if the people involved belong to different sides of the political question. Again, her American protagonist, a young fashion writer from Paris, confronts her Tirolian lover, a young man infatuated with the Nazi promise of prosperity and jobs. After the Anschluss, during which his country is absorbed by the Nazis, he becomes a willing part of the militaristic atmosphere that drives the protagonist away.

But even as her literary career gained momentum, Boyle's personal life became more difficult. In a scenario that eerily mimicked the theme of "Anschluss," Boyle found herself growing further apart from Vail. He believed strongly that writers and artists had no business becoming embroiled in the political machinations of the decade. Boyle, on the other hand, felt strongly the writer's responsibility to speak for those otherwise disenfranchised; her position became more definitive as World War II approached and France fell to the Nazis. By the time Boyle and her family had to leave Europe in the summer of 1941, her marriage to Vail was over.

Boyle portrays the fall of France in another award-winning story from this period, "Defeat" (*New Yorker*, 17 May 1941; collected in *Thirty Stories*, 1946), which captured the O. Henry Award for the year's best short story in 1941. Told from the perspective of an ordinary citizen, a bus driver, the story reveals the human disillusionment of this character at the unexpected collaboration he sees between French citizens and the enemy. An escaped soldier, the bus driver journeys through the French countryside, assuring himself that France will never be defeated "as long as its women aren't," only to find on Bastille Day that the women of the village have joined a Nazi celebration. Using the convention of the journey for her motif, Boyle recreates the metaphorical journey of a nation from hope to despair.

She returned to war themes in her next novels. *Primer for Combat* (1942) explores the theme of political commitment versus compromise, in much the same terms she uses in "Anschluss," for her protagonist and her lover separate because he cannot accept the commitment to political morality. A pair of novels originally serialized in *Saturday Evening Post*, *Avalanche* (1944), which involves the French Resistance movement, and *A Frenchman Must Die* (1946), which concerns allegations of collaboration against a French woman later proved innocent, presented American readers with decidedly European concerns. So realistically did they portray the mood and tensions of Europe that *Avalanche* was used by the United States Armed Forces to train personnel on the way to France. After the war two more novels dealt with war concerns. *1939: A Novel* (1948), set deliberately in the prewar years in order to emphasize the importance of moral commitment, again returns to the themes of *Primer for Combat* and "Anschluss." *His Human Majesty* (1949) was the last of her novels to deal with war themes, this time more tangentially.

Boyle's fiction of this period, whether in short story or in novel, consistently explored the meanings of war in the lives of individuals caught in it. Ironically, she was now writing of the war from her home in Nyack, New York, which she shared with her four daughters. When her divorce from Vail became final in 1942, she married Joseph Franckenstein, an Austrian nobleman who had escaped from the Gestapo and entered the United States as a political exile. Boyle had helped to arrange for his U.S. visa, as she had for other exiles in the late 1930s and early 1940s. After the war, Boyle and Franckenstein returned to Europe, she working for the *Nation* and the *New Yorker*, he for the U.S. State Department.

Boyle's knowledge of the Europe that had existed before the war added to the power of her postwar articles and stories. She explored occupied Germany with a combination of sympathy for the survivors living now in destitution and of censure for the callousness with which they as a nation of individuals tolerated the horrors of the Holocaust. She presents the rise of Nazism as a moral as well as political problem within the German nation. Nevertheless, she saved some of her disapproval for the arrogance with which the United States treated the defeated Germans, especially as it showed up in daily commerce between the Germans and American-occupation military personnel and their families. Over and over in her articles and stories she portrays human miscommunication as the cause of pain and despair. Many of these stories and a report of the trial of Nazi Heinrich Babb, which Boyle covered for the *New Yorker*, were collected in *The Smoking Mountain: Stories of Postwar Germany* (1951). A later novel, *Generation Without Farewell* (1960), explores many of the same themes, with the American-woman protagonist trying to understand the tensions of occupied Germany.

In the early 1950s both Boyle and Franckenstein were called before the McCarthy Senate hearings on un-American activities. Against the advice of friends in Europe, they returned to the United States to defend themselves. Franckenstein was dismissed from the State Department, and Boyle found that virtually the only magazine that would publish her work was the *Nation,* which served as a forum for other writers persecuted by the McCarthy hearings. The next few years were extremely difficult ones, for the emotional strain of Boyle's family coexisted with a severe economic one. Both Boyle and Franckenstein taught in private schools, but Boyle was forced to sell some of her prized mementos, such as a letter to her from Joyce. They eventually succeeded in clearing their names and in 1957 received an official letter of apology from the United States government. Nevertheless, the momentum of their lives had been inexorably changed. In 1962 Franckenstein was reinstated to the State Department and sent to Tehran, Iran. Unfortunately, he died of lung cancer within a few months.

Boyle accepted a position as faculty member at San Francisco State University in 1963, where she taught until her retirement in 1979. During these years she became actively involved in many of the anti–Vietnam War protests and became a tireless crusader for many human-rights issues. She was arrested twice for her participation in nonviolent sit-ins at the Army Induction Center in Oakland, California, at one point sharing the experience with Joan Baez. Her collection of essays, *The Long Walk at San Francisco State and Other Essays* (1970) eloquently documents some of these experiences, while her novel *The Underground Woman* (1975) juxtaposes the experiences of her American woman, now a widowed professor protesting the Vietnam War, with that same American woman as a mother whose youngest daughter has joined a fanatical religious commune. As did many of her stories and essays from the 1950s on, this novel explores the societal tensions prevalent in the United States. A strong supporter of civil- and human-rights issues, Boyle felt compelled to turn the spotlight of her prose on matters close at hand.

In 1973, at the age of 71, Boyle cofounded the San Francisco chapter of Amnesty International and continued active support of the group until her death. The last two decades of her life marked a time of awards for Boyle, who was elected to the Henry James Chair of the American Academy of Arts and Letters in 1978 and awarded a National Arts Endowment fellowship in 1980, an American Book Award in 1983, and a Lannan Literary Award in 1989.

Boyle's writing followed the movements of her life. With unswerving courage in the face of adversity – be it economic, societal, political, or moral – she faced the challenges of a tumultuous century. Through her pen, history takes on human faces and records its passage in human concerns. While Boyle's contribution to literature has been extensive, her contribution to the human spirit stands as her most profound legacy.

References:

Elizabeth S. Bell, "Henry Miller and Kay Boyle: The Divided Stream in American Expatriate Literature, 1939-1940," Ph.D. dissertation, University of Louisville, 1979;

Bell, *Kay Boyle: A Study of the Short Fiction* (New York: Twayne, 1992);

Richard C. Carpenter, "Kay Boyle: The Figure in the Carpet," *Critique,* 7 (Winter 1964–1965): 65–78;

Frank Gado, "Kay Boyle: From the Aesthetics of Exile to the Polemics of Return," Ph.D. dissertation, Duke University, 1969;

Patricia Holt, "Kay Boyle," *Publishers Weekly,* 219 (17 October 1980): 8–9;

Byron K. Jackson, "The Achievement of Kay Boyle," Ph.D. dissertation, University of Florida, 1968;

"Kay Boyle," in *Talks with Authors,* edited by Charles F. Madden (Carbondale: Southern Illinois University Press, 1968), pp. 215–236;

Harry T. Moore, "Kay Boyle's Fiction," in *The Age of the Modern and Other Essays* (Carbondale: Southern Illinois University Press, 1968), pp. 32–36;

Sandra Whipple Spanier, *Kay Boyle: Artist and Activist* (Carbondale: Southern Illinois University Press, 1986);

Dan Tooker and Roger Hofheins, "Kay Boyle," in *Fiction! Interviews with Northern California Novelists* (New York & Los Altos, Cal.: Harcourt Brace Jovanovich/William Kaufman, 1976).

Papers:

The primary collection of Boyle's papers is held at the Morris Library, Southern Illinois University, Carbondale.

Albert Erskine

(18 April 1911 – 5 February 1993)

A TRIBUTE_____

from Peter De Vries

Albert was one of a kind. One of those unique spirits whose departure seems to leave a kind of hole in the world, or broken window in it that can never be refilled or repaired.

He had a razor-sharp mind combined with a mastery of English that served him well professionally as well as socially. Friends thought him easily the equal of the Random House stars, most of whom counted it lucky to have Albert for their editor. Faulkner rejoiced at this "find" who studied a manuscript line for line and even word for word as though with a jeweler's loupe. Red (Robert Penn) Warren said Albert will willingly spend as much time on anything as it takes. What, a new manuscript in the house, possibly in need of some surgery? Albert could adeptly undertake anything of that gravity. His writers were invited to dinner parties. He keenly enjoyed the role of host, seated opposite his beloved Marisa, giving and taking in the general crackle of conversations, Albert was in his element there.

Some found our dear Albert a bit disputatious, even when breaking bread with friends. He had his pet peeves, like all of us. One was the women's movement. "It's all a lot of bilge," he said, "we shouldn't even be talking about it here," gazing around the group with a kind of truculent hospitality. Now, there's an oxymoron for you, which Albert would have spotted, with pleasure.

Farewell, then, Albert.

We shall spend the rest of our lives mourning your departure. You lived life your way, to the hilt. You were so perfectly, so consummately yourself. We shall never see your like again.

A TRIBUTE_____

from Michael Mewshaw

In a fairer, more rational world this encomium to Albert Erskine would have been written by one of the dozens of celebrated authors whom he served

so loyally during a career that spanned more than half a century. William Faulkner, Robert Penn Warren, John O'Hara, Malcolm Lowry, Eudora Welty, Ralph Ellison, James A. Michener, Cormac McCarthy – the list of Albert's authors reads like the index to an anthology of twentieth-century American literature. While there's little doubt that these writers could have described far better than I the steady hand that shaped so many works of lasting merit, it falls to me – perhaps the least and apparently the last of the novelists Albert took onto his list – to speak a few words about a man who has been called the last, best editor of the old school.

The way that my first novel, *Man in Motion,* wound up in Albert's care and the kindness with which he treated this ill-favored premature baby reveal volumes about his honesty, industriousness, and professionalism. From the beginning he was blunt and said that although he saw signs of talent and a certain crude energy in my writing, he didn't believe he was the right editor for an embryonic author – I was twenty-five – whose sensibility seemed to be shaped by 1960s pop culture. But he promised to pass the book along to a young eager editor at Random House with whom, Albert felt, I'd be more comfortable.

Four months later, the young editor agreed to accept the novel. Apparently this decision took a lot out of the fellow; he went on sick leave, and I never heard from him again. Instead, Albert wrote to say the young editor had resigned, leaving behind a letter that suggested "Mewshaw be given his small advance and dropped." Because Albert believed I had been treated shabbily, he insisted that Random House honor its commitment to *Man in Motion* and he agreed to edit the manuscript.

Only somebody who has had no contact with contemporary publishing could fail to be struck by this extraordinary concatenation of events. These days it's a rare editor, especially one of Albert Erskine's stature – he was then a vice-president of Random House – who would deign to read a book that came in over the transom. It's even less likely that anybody would bother to pass along a manu-

Albert Erskine (left) with John O'Hara (center) and Bennett Cerf in the courtyard of the old Random House building, viewing O'Hara's Rolls-Royce

script to an editor who might be more receptive to it. As for rescuing a novel that had been cast adrift, that might happen in the case of a writer who had received a sizeable advance, but I had been promised a mere fifteen hundred dollars, and no contract had been signed.

The most amazing fact, however, was that Albert agreed to edit the manuscript. He invited me to his home in Westport and went over the novel line by line, word by word, suggesting stylistic improvements, unkinking the time scheme, testing each chapter for continuity, each character for consistency. This was the way he worked with all his writers, regardless of whether they were geniuses or best-sellers or callow fledgling authors.

Albert Erskine edited three more of my novels, and the process was always the same – days in Connecticut of hard work, of delicious meals prepared by his wife Marisa, and of delightful evenings when Peter De Vries, Donald Klopfer, Eleanor Clark, John Hersey, Cleanth Brooks, Robert Penn Warren, and Anatole Broyard came for dinner. Though I was too much in awe to take these experiences for granted, I started to assume that this was what it meant to be a novelist; this was what a writer could expect – an attentive editor, stimulat-

ing company, a spirit of collegiality from fellow writers.

Now, twenty-five years later, having published thirteen books and having worked with several dozen editors in countries around the world, I know better. I know I've never met Albert Erskine's equal, and much as I'd like to think I've lived up to the standards he set, I'm sure I've fallen short. Still, it's consoling to think back on my time with him and to realize that so much of what he stood for remains. Of the English architect Christopher Wren it has been said that anyone who cares to see his monuments has only to look around. Those who'd like to see Albert Erskine's monuments can step into a library or bookstore and look on almost any shelf.

A TRIBUTE

from James Wilcox

In 1971 John Palmer, the editor then of the *Yale Review* and dean of Silliman College, arranged for me to be interviewed for a job with his friend of many years, Albert Erskine. When I returned from Mr. Erskine's office in New York to New Haven, where I was finishing up my senior year at Yale, I was so keyed up by the possibility of working for

Oct 11, 1948

Dear Howard,

Here are the Notes promised in the note of a few days ago. Since Bennett has not yet arrived with the Ms, which I need for my specific trivia, I had best begin the General Remarks (the General Endorsement has already been tendered, by me and others, so forgive me if I more or less skip the amenities and compliments here and now in favor of minor carping — except for Driving Home this Point: that all the nagging to follow proceeds from, and is indeed founded upon, my Unbounded Admiration for the Book; and you are to understand that you are to leave or take, as you see fit, any suggestion, emendation, criticism that I might make. So; and I'll skip the Capital Letters too.).

Somehow I feel the need of (or note the lack of) some follow-up, no matter how brief, of Averist's selling-out to Hogan. He sets out (as you say) feeling like a Knight (even if unaccountably) and comes back a Traitor, having been bought very easily and quickly for very little. One wonders (this one anyhow) at this point (p. 190), What will he say to Susan when he makes his first report; or for that matter when he from time to time (presumably) sees her, how does he explain the defeat? I would suppose he would stall. But how would he feel, about her and about himself? I wouldn't care how you made him feel, or what you made him say; but my point is simply that an expectation is set up by the scene with Hogan and is never satisfied. Could you insert some reference to these questions somewhere nearer the end (perhaps in the scene beginning on 234)? I don't mean necessarily a scene between Averist and Susan; his recollection, in a few sentences, would do.

Similarly, but less importantly, there might be received in Boston some bulletin, some report of unprogress, from Virginia. For though the king is in exile he has not exactly abdicated; and Susan and Claire must wonder (and the reader too), is he coming back? — or think, he is not coming back. In other words, there is some continuing awareness of his existence (and Mrs Boyne's) and condition, if not from sentiment, at least from anxiety.

You will say perhaps that I am basing these (2) observations on a desire for a kind of verisimilitude that you are not interested in and not attempting. But you have in fact not thrown out v'tude altogether, not even nearly. I think these two things are needed to answer inevitable questions in the mind of the reader; and the questions are the logical consequence of the characters and events xx as you have arranged them. Perhaps what I want is already enough there, implied, but I don't think it would hurt to pin it down a little.

It would seem to me more seemly (on more than one level) if Hogan and Fosker had already been using the unusual situation for procuring on a small scale before they plan (on 283 and ff) the grand debacle. I seem to remember from that outline that you'd planned something like this, and maybe that is why I feel a lack, a slight twinge of disappointment. We wouldn't have to see this happening, but merely to be told that it had been and that they were not content, now, with

On this and the following four pages: letter to Howard Nemerov in which Erskine offers editorial suggestions for Nemerov's 1949 novel The Melodramatists *(Columbia University Library, by permission of Random House)*

2

such small game. I like the idea of both activities going on at the same time under the same roof, with the girls as principals in both, and the Church unaware, for a time, as well as implicated. I miss a little the ultimate conjunction of Leonora and Uncle Fred (which you once, I recall, had planned and which now seems to be faintly foreshadowed on p 67 and by the nature of the creatures themselves), but I suppose you decided, perhaps rightly, that that might be a little thick. But he could (couldn't he) take her home from the party —in the best avuncular fashion....

So much for that section of the Notes (which now go into page-and-line items, the t, c, and b meaning top center bottom):

1 (4b   The Caravaggio is later (I don't remember the page now) referred to as a fake. I take it your withholding of that information here is a strategy and not an oversight?

  (b   appropriate and even respectful / seems to me "respectful and even appropriate" wd make more sense here.

2 (t   Aunt Fred Seely /you ref to her this way until 14, where suddenly it is Aunt Emma. Might not an Emma be dropped in nearer the first ref?

3 (b   yr purpose in naming the soup escapes me

5 (b   Claire thought, the operatic moment / this sounds to me like a Susan thought Inevitably there is overlap in the way these ladies respond to things and
in the way they speak, but you have differentiated them as you go along. But this is a situation that Claire takes more seriously than Susan (whom C thinks disgracefully at ease (1b); so that this comparison with the opera and the one (7c) two pages later don't go with Claire as well as with Susan. On 58 (I must say, Susan remarked, etc) the remark seems one of Claire's to me. These are the only three instances I recall, and I didn't notice them until the third reading; so it may not matter at all.

9c   disinterested silence / sure you don't want uninterested?

16c   both because of his own tension and the fact that .../ I think this is what you would call (on a freshman theme) faulty parallelism. Because of both ... and.... or: both because of.... and because of.... Either of those would be right, but both sound awful. Maybe I'm wrong on the rules, but I think yours is wrong the way it is. Does it matter though?

34 (7   etc. /I had the feeling there were so many reappearances of this little dodge, that on rereading I noted down where they are. I hope you'll change most of them, or at least some of them, to something else. Some uses seem justified, as when you mean: and all the other gems which are usually
in this cluster; but sometimes it seems to be saying, in effect, to the reader,
Write your own sentence, I'm tired, and what I mean is clear. Especially if it occurs often enough that one becomes overaware of it. In dialogue it looks funny, so that I think it would be better to spell it out or say and so forth, und so weiter, or something. (Besides this page, see also 54, 62, 94, 106, 110, 118, 135, 148, 152, 156, 173, 175, 181, 196 — and I probably missed some.)

3

63 (5b   must inevitably have satisfied/ I question the choice of inevitably; it just seems the wrong word, I don't quite know why. Doesnt greatly matter of course. Inexact, though.

64 (2   If there was between the sisters/ you changed was to were, and I've changed it back to was. The rest of the sentence makes the subjunctive out of place.

67 (t   Even Uncle Fred would not, I believe, in 1941 said this about Russia; the intellectual priest who later in the book gives them just five weeks to hold out sounds more of the time. But hell....

70   The last sentence sounds beyond what Mrs B's imagination would conceive, even in the flights of sleep.

87c   that she do something — do something or.../ how about italics for the first do something ? Or perhaps do something (which is the way I used to hear it addressed to my sister). You had quotes and took them off, and it is now not too clear at first glance.

91   What is gained by announcing Mr B's going mad before we get to it? I think something vague and portentous would be better, but I am without strong conviction.

92 (4   how about sub Nicholas Boyne for the first he, esp if you do anything about the previous note? Wd be better anyway.

101 c   what is flyting ?   flitting, flying, or flyting?

107   Why bring in and explain Uncle James when you never use him? He simply makes a small loose end, and we already have Uncle Fred.

133   penis / marginal note to tone down. I'd suggest phallus as a better running mate for caduceus anyway, but I haven't checked to see if it is acceptable.(Crosier wd make make a nice image, but it is a little remote, I fear.)

149 b   why quote Conrad instead of making up something of your own here?

150 (b7 look up trophesial (in the big dic) Isnt trophic what you want, trophesy being a defect in the function trophic—or so it seemed to me when I looked it up, as I had to.

151   I hope youre accurate in yr spelling of all these weird woids from the orient. I wdnt know where to find them. And I hope all the Latin phrases are right to the last inflexion. Ive forgot the little I ever knew except for one rule about verbs to profit hurt favor trust assist spare command obey heal (mederi) marry (nubere) take the dative, or I think it was the dative.

155 4   remained pretty much as always previously/   this sounds as though you lifted it out of a freshman theme.

156 3b. look up dilection/.wdnt it be followed by of or for, rather than in? It is obsolete too. What about delectation in?

4

162   Holy Church herself/ on 172 it is Herself. Which is right? and does one not use the def article?

167   Not important, but food shortages and the bribing of suppliers was not part of the hist of 1941 in Boston.

168 9b   ...carefully studied out as this may have been/ ref of this not clear. Mus refer to script, in which case that wd be better. Seems to refer to this here now scr. (1 e yours), and if it does it seems not a good idea.

169 c the parentheses within paren seem unnecessary, as commas wd do.

170 t anchored equally/   I dont get the equally
                    (Our eye-beams twisted and did thread/ Our eyes upon one double str!

190 1st par   hiding place of money has already been specified (p 180), so that this vague ref sounds as though you'd forgotten.

206-09   All four other readers so far are unanimous that this aside should come out. Since I've been dubious though neutral from the first, I don't feel strongly enough to defend it in the face of such resistance. If that's the kind of response it calls forth, I think you'd do better to get rid ärik of it. If you feel strongly (and I gather from your note you don't), say so; but I don't think it is worth an argument.

214 c   Why not tropo- strato-   ionosphere, which is the order in which something would travel through them (I looked this up too)

218 manage / someone put a question mark by this (though it occurs elsewhere too) it is archaic as a noun, but it sounds rather nice.

234   (6   to his mind/ why not cut this phrase? I don't know why this seems to me important enough to note down, but it sounds so lame and unneeded.

249   (2   shdnt there be a new section number here? It is a new and entirely dif-ferent scene.

263   in line with getting the author the hell out of the book, this page seems to call for two adjustments:

          (deliberately primitive, I believe)
          ...too vast to be dealt with here.
The I believe could be changed to something meaning probably, or very likely; and the other sentence could end with something like ...a vast subject in itself...

277   and that seldom / this phrase, coming where it does, causes a reading difficulty how about altering it or using some substitute?

298 b the author with the truss seems lame and forced to me.

219 c "tone down" the semen   (which reminds me I forgot the same note on shit on 188

5

There. I'm exhausted. It occurs to me that it will be an exhausting job to reply to all this. You could simply reply to most of the little notes in one word or so in the margins of these pages and return them; or you can ignore any of them you like without hurting my feelings. I assume you have a carbon and can find the feferences; I hope I've been clear at least about what I meant.

I do want when you're here to have some conversation about what I think the book is about — partly because I can't quite fit the end into the scheme as I understand it. And since I'll have to be writing copy about it, I don't want to commit you to any meanings you don't intend, or to fail to credit anything that is there that I don't see.

In spite of all these words I still think it is a fine book. I'm too hungry now to say more than best to you both...

the man who had edited William Faulkner and John O'Hara that it was hard to get any sleep at all. A year or two later Mr. Erskine let me know, in an off-hand way, why he had decided to hire me as his editorial assistant at Random House. I had assumed that Dean Palmer and Robert Penn Warren, whom I had studied with at school, must have put in a good word for me. And the resumé I had turned in was chockfull of every single last honor and award I could dredge up, including my election as Most Popular Boy in eighth grade. The real reason I had got the job, Mr. Erskine said, was because when I showed up for my first interview, I didn't sit down before being asked. He considered this the sign of a gentleman. Of course, I didn't let on that I was simply too dazed to be there, in the corner office on the eleventh floor of the Random House building, to make any decision for myself.

Today the idea of being a gentleman is not only out of fashion, but is looked upon with suspicion, if not outright condemnation. Unfortunate associations of the term with sexism and racism have caused some people to throw the baby out with the bathwater. Albert Erskine was first and foremost a gentleman. So at home did he make me feel from the first day of work on that it only gradually dawned on me, several months later, that our political viewpoints were diametrically opposed. He never made a single comment about my vote for George McGovern, nor did he ever seem irked by my longish hair, sideburns, and moustache. In fact, the only mention of my general appearance cropped up one sultry August afternoon when I had taken the train to Westport, where he and I were going over Douglas Day's edition of *Flags in the Dust* using photocopies of Faulkner's typescript and manuscript for reference. Mr. Erskine advised me to let my knit shirt hang out since it would be cooler. But I kept it tucked in, afraid I would look too sloppy in front of his elegant wife. My vanity would have made her smile, I'm sure, for she couldn't have been a warmer, more congenial hostess.

Today, when editors' faces are gracing the pages of *Esquire, GQ*, and *Vanity Fair*, it is refreshing to remember how self-effacing Mr. Erskine was. A man who is often mentioned in the same breath with Maxwell Perkins, Albert Erskine shared Perkins's intense dislike of the limelight. Despite his working association with so many celebrated authors, he had little use for the notion of celebrity itself. One of my first duties as his assistant was to relieve him of the burden of going to an awards ceremony given by the Christophers. He was smart not to go, for as I tried to squeeze through to the

mobbed hors d'oeuvre table, I was elbowed aside by the lady who played the mother on *The Brady Bunch*. She was being honored along with Eudora Welty, who, like her editor, Mr. Erskine, knew when to stay home.

Although Random House was firmly ensconced in its sleek glass tower on Third Avenue and Fiftieth Street by the time I arrived on the scene, I heard enough about the glories of its former offices, the bishop's palace on Madison, to imagine how much more at home Mr. Erskine and his long-time assistant, Suzanne Beves, must have felt at the palace. There, in an elegant, haphazard warren of editorial offices, complete with a magnificent chandelier hanging above Suzanne's desk, publishing must have seemed more like the gentlemen's business it used to be, where the bottom line was not the be-all and end-all of an editor's worth. Courtesy and good will, dedication to the craft, the welfare of one's authors might have counted for more in such a setting. Suzanne made it clear to me time and again how much Bennett Cerf valued Mr. Erskine. It would have been inconceivable for Mr. Cerf to have hired an efficiency expert to interview his editors and their staff about speeding up production. Yet this is exactly what management at RCA did when I went to work for Mr. Erskine. Never one to lose his composure, my boss took it all in good humor, which lightened the burden for us all.

Anthony Trollope once wrote that Cicero "had not acquired that theoretic aversion to a lie that is the first feeling in the bosom of a modern gentleman." Albert Erskine had this first feeling. It was what made his unfailing courtesy resonate with such dignity, bringing out the very best in everyone he came in contact with.

A TRIBUTE

from P. M. Pasinetti

Around mid September of 1935 I came to the United States for the first time. It had all started several months earlier when my friend and adviser Mario Praz suggested that I apply for an "exchange scholarship" to the United States. On the American side the plan was administered by the Institute for International Education in New York (its secretary was Ed Murrow, then in his twenties). When the letter arrived to me in my hometown, Venice, announcing that I had won a scholarship and had been assigned to Louisiana State University in a town curiously called Baton Rouge, I rushed to a map to see precisely where Louisiana was. Soon, relatively speaking, I reached the place by steamer and bus.

On my second week after landing in New York, and on my second evening in Baton Rouge, I met Albert Erskine. Robert Penn Warren was our host, and I am sure another young man was there too – Cleanth Brooks. Whatever English I commanded had been learned in Great Britain; the English those young men spoke struck me as something friendlier, more leisurely and more simpatico. When Red Warren asked whether I preferred Scotch or Bourbon, I opted for the second, unknown to me. Another small discovery of the evening was the seersucker jacket. Light and durable, elegant and traditional, it fitted my first image of Albert Erskine perfectly; he was, and remained, as everyone knows, a nobly handsome gentleman, courteous and witty; his wit was intensely dry, hence of the most genuine quality. All his life, I think, he was very strict in excluding from his company the fools, the bores, the ill mannered, the pretentious. I asked him once whether anybody had ever addressed him as "Al." He came up, rather vaguely, with only one name – not of a friend anyway but of a passing acquaintance.

One of the important elements in my LSU experience was of course the *Southern Review,* a publication which is part of American literary history. I count it as an extraordinary piece of luck to have known, since the first days of my American life, the people who invented and edited it. It is easy to surmise that Albert, who from the beginning collaborated with the first editors Brooks and Warren, had there an early chance to practice his keen eye for the discovery of new talent, for separating the promising from the hopeless. He was a man with high standards of judgment; his taste was selective and definite – in prose and poetry, of course, and also, may I add, in matters like food and drink or like the proper look of the printed page. I remember him once asking for my opinion on some typographical change he wanted to make on the upper margin of the review's pages; it was a minutia but once realized you saw it made a difference. Albert had the rare virtue of combining intelligence with precision.

I may seem preposterously self-centered at this point to mention that my earliest printed stories appeared in the *Southern Review,* one of regular length, the other almost a novelette. As Red Warren's (first) wife was of Italian extraction and he didn't know very much Italian at the time, she read the short story to him, improvising an English translation as she went along. Red's reaction gave me one

of the most joyful moments in my life. Not to mention the pleasure of seeing the story in print a few months later, at Berkeley, where I spent my second academic year in the United States; the longer story I saw in print only after the war; while I was back in Europe it had appeared both in the review and in O'Brien's collection of the "best short stories of the year." Nevertheless – and this is my main point in the present context – Albert told me that he considered the first one a better story than the second; this verdict, not necessarily a pleasant one, oddly enough, or perhaps not oddly at all, made Albert's opinion of my work even more important to me. And it wasn't a question of shorter-is-better. In the future he was going to look with favor at incomparably longer specimens of my work.

During the war, the curse of difficult or impossible communications was somewhat alleviated when I was appointed Italian *lektor* at the University of Stockholm. It seemed like a dream: however slowly, cables could be exchanged, and letters; in them, one permanent theme was the eventuality, however distant, of my returning to America. Obviously for a long time it seemed hopeless. Then it all seemed to open up. The long, unforgettably generous help of my friends produced what had seemed unthinkable. Offer from a college. Contract from a publisher. So in December 1945 an intelligent U.S. consul put the permanent-immigration stamp on my Italian passport. It took seventeen days on a small cargo for the voyage from Göteborg to Philadelphia. On my second evening in New York I had dinner with Albert. He was then on his second marriage. One doesn't know much about Albert's rapport with his first two wives, so completely did the presence of the third one eventually supplant the images of the other two in quiet, permanent triumph.

Historical and private confusions and uncertainties, besides academic and journalistic writing, kept postponing for me the period of steady dedication to "the" novel. Off and on I must have worked on that project close to twenty years. At some point I sent Albert the draft of some sort of first chapter. I am sure that Red Warren, always immensely kind and generous in following my work, read the stuff too and that they both found it adequate. I have no doubt they were right. Being judged worthy of publication by the friends I had first met in Louisiana and who were now eminent in their careers became one of my major aims in life. It took me years to finish that first novel. A typescript of the original Italian was examined at Random House by readers conversant with the language, and their reports apparently were very favorable. The publisher took the gamble of giving me an advance with the proviso that I buy a tape recorder and on it do the English translation myself. I did so, and my professional work with Albert began after he had read my translation with minute attention.

Working with Albert was to me both instructive and entertaining. It was, in fact, an intellectual delight. We would work in his office at Random House or, preferably for both, in the Erskines's home in Connecticut. We would be well equipped with dictionaries and vocabularies. The idea of a "perfect" translation is of course nonsense. There were numberless cases when one *mot* would be replaced by another which sounded more *juste;* there were rearrangements of sentences, paragraphs, that would be chosen as the most effective, which may mean the most inventive, in translation. One learned a lot, and I feel Albert liked the idea of increasing his familiarity with his wife's native language. He was a literary expert who could himself handle language beautifully; and he was an involved reader with his likes and dislikes, his empathy or his impatience with characters and situations.

One example comes to mind, from the fourth and last of the novels of mine which he edited. I am now working (in Italian) on my eighth and I occasionally read half-forgotten pages from the early ones. In that fourth novel there is a very talkative young man, supposedly witty and likeable; however, each time he came on stage Albert would sigh, "Oh God, here he is again." The counterpart was a character I thought I had treated more or less as the caricature of an old dodo. Albert thought that if there was a character which made any sense in the book, it was the old fellow. On meeting the two again after so many years I very much tended to agree with Albert. The old man was the wiser and wittier one; the young man was a pretentious bore.

I saw Albert for the last time not long before his death, a paterfamilias surrounded by his wonderful wife, daughter, and son-in-law. He suffered physically, but his courage, his wit, were intact. He will remain a living presence to my last day. This sounds conventional, but it is the simplest truth. He would know. He could spot the phony a mile away.

A TRIBUTE

from Matthew J. Bruccoli

Albert Erskine was the best editor I ever worked with. I have worked with one better all-around publisher, and I have worked with one edi-

tor who has been accurately described as "the best friend a writer ever had." But Albert was the best editor word for word and line for line. By the time I became a member of his stable – an expression that irritated him – I was an experienced author; yet I was unprepared for the standards he applied to my work.

After I delivered the typescript of my first Random House book, *The O'Hara Concern,* to Albert in 1973, I was informed that we would be working at his house in Westport. At the Erskine residence I was received by his elegant and beautiful wife, who conveyed the impression that she had been waiting for me all of her life. Presently an extraordinary dinner appeared. The charming, unpretentious woman proved to be the best cook I have ever known. Over the years I ate scores of Marisa's meals, and they always materialized by some process of sorcery. The vegetables were grown by Albert. We were joined at the table by the Erskine's very amiable teenaged daughter Sylvia – the ultimate surprise in this perfect household. After dinner Albert and I engaged in some general talk about my TS, and I began to suspect that I had fallen into some sort of let's-pretend-we're-working situation. But that was okay with me as long as I was the beneficiary of the Erskine hospitality and that lovely woman was smiling.

The next morning work commenced in Albert's office. He had pages of notes on my work: he queried words; he identified clumsy sentences; he required me to recheck facts. When Albert challenged a detail he knew what he was talking about: he had a thorough knowledge of pre-1940 song lyrics; he had also memorized many English and American poems; he was well and widely read. The vetting sessions were punctuated with Albert's anecdotes about working with Faulkner, O'Hara, Welty, and Warren. I had been inducted into the most exclusive literary club in America. The editorial sessions on the typescript occupied as many days as needed; later there was another session for the galleys.

It is obligatory for me to acknowledge the gratifications of being a Random House author in the 1970s. Bennett Cerf and Donald Klopfer made writers feel valued. On one of my early visits to the building, Mr. Cerf made a point of coming to Albert's office and offering encouraging words. I doubt that Random House made any money on my books; but whenever I encountered Mr. Klopfer he expressed interest in my current work. They were classy publishers and real gents.

I did five books with Albert, all of which re-

Westport, Feb 20, 1963

Dear John,

I hope the trip was full of pleasure. If you kept to your schedule,
you missed a good day to miss yesterday.

Please don't be alarmed at the bulk of this packet, or the length of
my notes--mostly verbiage. Some of the items won't require anything more than a
properly curmudgeonly expression; only one seems to call for any rearranging or
rewriting (galley 30). A lesser man, or a tired one, might spend a half or even
a whole day on something like this, but you ought to be able to knock it off in
half an hour.

But please indicate everything on the galleys and rush them back,
leaving nothing hanging: yes or no or stet--obscenity will be construed as
negative.

The galley sheets, since they are part of your own set, have to be
returned even if you prefer to do this by phone, because they are destined to
be the property of Penn State, and I wouldn't want <u>them</u> to have anything of as
low value as an incomplete set of author's proofs.

I think I've covered everything, but I'm groggy with sleepiness.

The more I look at and think about this book the more I am aware of
how good it is.

All best,

PS Though I know you must be right, I still worry about R Norris Williams.
I'm only a year younger that Elizabeth Appleton, and I don't remember him among
my boyhood tennis heroes.

On this and the next three pages: letter to John O'Hara in which Erskine offers editorial suggestions for O'Hara's 1963 novel Elizabeth Appleton
(Bruccoli Collection)

Elizabeth Appleton

galley
number

3   This radio commercial is in the fall of 1950. Wouldn't it be advertising the

     brand new 1951 model, instead of the previous year's?

5   Since no one I've asked or authority I've consulted has been able to enlighten

     me on vici, I'm checking to be sure this is not a typo. (11th ed. of Encyc Brit

     has a town Vici on its map of Oklahoma, but they don't explain why.)

30   Betty Appleton was born in 1935; every other reference in book confirms this

     (esp several mentions of the fact that she is a year older than her brother, who

     was born June, 1934.) If you will examine the last paragraph on galley 30 and

     the passage above about Jarvis Webster's death, you will see why I couldn't simply

     change 1936 to 1935 without making hash of the context. Please rearrange.

45   All that was the old man.   This way in MS.   Did something get dropped? Or is

     it my fault I don't get it?   I think something went astray, and I don't think I'd

     be alone in this reaction.

49   This is a personal plea for the abolition of culturization, which barely exists
            if at all
     (outside/the yogurt industry, the sociology industry, and Madison Avenue--below

50th St, of course) anyway, and ought not in any case to be fathered or fostered by

     you, especially since cultivation would be what Spring Valley students would have

     in mind, whether they were achieving it or not.   I'm aware that you're probably

     implying a judgment of the curriculum by the use of that word, but I question

     whether the implication gets across.

     that
58   /she had never known with anyone else.   The ambiguity of this wording might be

     confusing, in spite of the information a few lines above (and later) that she'd

     never had any sexual partner besides John. The passage in question sounds like
     an evaluation
     a comparison of how it was with John in comparison with others. Worth fixing?

     It could be cut, simply.

galley

66   screwing every English dame~that~ he get his hands on.   I missed this one in Ms.

I started to make it <u>can get</u>, but then it occurred to me: <u>that</u> <u>he</u> <u>can</u> <u>get</u> <u>his</u>

<u>hands</u> <u>on</u>   doesn't sound like your kind of rendering of this kind of dialogue.

should it be: gets his hands on ?   Or what?   Please fix.

                English dame he gets his hands on

How's that?   "   "   he can get his hands on

67   She watched him as she undressed. Since they're both doing it, this could be

either way, but I want to be sure it wasn't meant to be <u>as he</u> <u>undressed</u>--because

of her comment. Please indicate.

72   Two sources give June 22, 1945, as end of Okinawa campaign (though neither says

anything about formal surrender ceremonies); July 16 was definitely the first

bomb explosion. If Okinawa ended "two weeks ago" this ~scene~ would be about July 6

and 10 days before bomb. Unless you have a better date than June 22 for Okinawa,

why not change "two weeks" to something longer? "a month" is hardly enough to

make "recently" satisfactory for the bomb. How about six weeks ago? That would

make today fall in first week of August. Please mark.

87   All right for O'Hara to invent <u>maternalistic</u>, by analogy with <u>paternalistic</u>; but

since the latter has nothing to do with the relations between parent and child, I

                  former
don't see why the ~latter~ should when it comes into use. Isn't she just trying not

to be too <u>maternal</u>?

87   Don't understand your substitution of <u>her</u> for <u>their</u>, which seems to be absolutely

correct in the context. Please look at it again.

95   respectablized   Mention this just to finalize my note on galley 49 (above);

        verb-wise I guess I've got to deconservativize myself

101, 102, 104 Warple, Marple. 2 of each. Please choose.

galley

114   In the alma mater you had added some quotes with pencil at the beginning of the

      first five lines, but you didn't continue on next page, where it carried over.

      You removed quotes from Be of good cheer.

      OK with you to open quote with first line, close with last, and eliminate others?

      And put single quotes around 'Be of good cheer' ?

       Not sure what you had in mind. Please mark.

115   I include this galley just to be sure the changes I made in ms are what is needed

      rather than something else. The three mentions of ten years were fifteen years,

      and the prediction for 1960 was 1965, which I changed to conform with the 10-year

      cycle. The 10 years is right, all right, and I don't see any reason why 1960

      won't do, unless what you wanted was to extend the prediction about Mildred Klein

      beyond now (1963)--in which case you'll have to contrive something. OK as is?

ceived his time-consuming attention. When I left Random House for a reason that had nothing to do with Albert, our friendship was unimpaired. I continued to visit Westport. Marisa's cooking aside, Albert's book talk was well worth a train ride. On what proved to be our last meeting he told me about his pleasure in rereading Yeats.

I was irritated at the memorial service because some of the attendees referred to Albert's eccentricity. He never seemed eccentric to me. Impatience with what he labeled "crap" is not eccentricity. Standards are not eccentric. Honesty is not eccentricity.

Albert's greatness as an editor was the result of his judgment and courage, as well as his capacity to respond to literature. (Many editors are literary ignoramuses.) Yet he resisted author egostroking; Albert was in charge of the editorial relationship; and he expected his authors to attend to his sound advice. At least twice to my knowledge he declined to edit leading Random House moneymakers because the writers ignored Albert's instructions about revising. At our penultimate meeting I tried to persuade him to write about his major authors, and he responded: "All writers are horses' asses." That was my friend and mentor Albert Erskine. He fostered some of the enduring literature of his time; but he regarded writers as a deplorable necessity in the publishing process. If they had sufficient good sense to pay attention, he would help them. Otherwise they could find somebody else to humor them. Albert did what he did because he was a man of letters whose gift took the form of editing. He was not a frustrated writer who wanted to collaborate with celebrated authors. He was secure in his work as the best literary editor of his time.

A TRIBUTE

from James Laughlin

It would have been around Christmas of 1939 that Delmore Schwartz and I and various campfollowers piled into my old Buick and drove down to Baton Rouge to attend the meeting of the Modern Language Association which was being held that year at Louisiana State University. (Delmore's myth of his hypothetical "sister," of whom I was supposed to be enamoured, had not yet materialized in his febrile brain.) The great attraction of the conference for me was meeting the legendary John Crowe Ransom, editor of the *Kenyon Review,* who had been revolutionizing literary criticism with his theories, later published by New Directions in 1941 as *The New Criticism,* studies of I. A. Richards, T. S. Eliot, Yvor Winters, and William Empson.

Ransom was giving a paper, but so was Schwartz, on Eliot, one of his idols, as I recall. Delmore had published his *In Dreams Begin Responsibilities* (the quote is from Yeats) the year before and became an instant star. No book of poems had had such universal praise from so many of the "right" people; he was the celebrity of the event. Riding on Delmore's back we received much hospitality. The welcome we liked best came from an affable, handsome young man named Albert Erskine, who seemed to be working jointly for the Louisiana State University Press and the *Southern Review.* But his immediate claim to fame was that he was married to a figure, yes, a literary figure, whom we all venerated, one of the great writers of Fiction of the period, Katherine Anne Porter (KAP). We were entertained several evenings at the Erskine-Porter cottage. There was something a bit odd. Albert was doing the cooking, and after the meal KAP would retire to her room to flog her typewriter all evening. "All is not well," Delmore said, "with this marriage." He was right. It was headed for breakup. I learned a few of the sad facts much later when Bob Phillips was researching for the Schwartz/Laughlin letters volume (Norton, 1993). There we find the note:

> At this time Porter had had four husbands: John Henry Koontz, Ernest Stock, Eugene Dove Pressly, and Albert Erskine. "It was not until their wedding in New Orleans that Erskine, then twenty-six, learned that Porter was nearly fifty." Joan Givner, *Katherine Anne Porter: A Life* (New York: Simon and Schuster, 1982)

Whatever his worries may have been, Albert gave us a good time. I suspect that all though his life he looked after people well and made them feel good. He had the charm and easy manners of a "Southern gentleman," but was never pompous. A nice wit he had, but he used it gently. And for a young man in his twenties he knew a lot about literature. I filed him in my mind as someone who might help me well if New Directions (ND) grew. And so it came about.

With faltering step, New Directions, urged on by Pound, who said I should "do something useful," began in 1936, when the first ND anthology, the one that was printed in Vermont by the printer who did the *Harvard Advocate,* and in which I forgot to number the pages, came out. In the first years I did everything myself. The "office" was my suitcase as I moved about. When there were more books than I could manage alone, I inveigled unemployed poets (first Kenneth and Mariam Patchem in Connecticut) into working for me; the wage scale, as I recall, was one dollar an hour, but that bought quite a bit in those days. Delmore and his first wife, Gertrude (she is now an editor in London) Buckman, later ran the office in one of the rooms of their apartment on Memorial Drive in Cambridge. Gertrude did most of the distribution work and accounts while Delmore read manuscripts and learned books, but he did take the packages to the post office in his jalopy . . . and he could be heroic. One night when the Charles River flooded, he carried a ton of books in cartons from the cellar up to the kitchen.

As the writers ND was publishing became known we needed more help. I though of Albert and was happy when he wrote that he might be interested in coming north, despite the fact that there was still no proper office and he would have to work out of his apartment. There was a problem with his draft board in Baton Rouge, but that was straightened out. There is a passage in his letter to me of 20 August 1940 which gives his state of mind:

> My interest in joining some "commercial" publisher is not as great as you seem to think; as a matter of fact, I prefer what I am doing now (or what you are doing): but I have begun to believe they will never pay me well here (they might if I threatened, but I cannot afford to take that chance at present). I don't care about getting a huge salary for doing things I don't like or don't think worth doing; but neither do I like getting paid like an office boy . . . not forever, in any case.

So Albert moved to Cambridge. He found an apartment big enough to provide a room for New Directions somewhere near the Radcliffe campus. What did he do? A little bit of everything except for the accounts and shipping orders with which the Schwartzes continued. Albert corresponded with authors, edited their scripts, did copyediting and proofs; dealt with paper dealers and printers and binders; wrote catalogs and copy for jackets . . . you name it, he did it, always with long-suffering good humour. The work was heavy at that time because I had started the Poets of the Month series (the lawyers of the Book-of-the-Month Club made us

change it to "Poets of the Year"). This was a series of thirty-two-page pamphlets each printed by a *different* fine printer. They sold for fifty cents each, or five dollars for a year's worth in a box. Albert got out forty-two numbers before exhaustion set in. Albert did have some help. A willowy graduate student appeared from time to time to do dull jobs. I think her name was Eleanor, but I'm not sure. I do remember Delmore saying that her eyes were too far apart in her face.

What was I doing? Flitting about. Much time was spent out in Utah where I was developing the Alta Ski Resort. My theory was that the resort would make money which would support the losses of highbrow publishing. Over the years this proved true. Or I was back in Rapallo getting a refresher course at the Ezuversity. But mail went back and forth to Cambridge every day. And Albert was so patient with my little scrawled "do this, do that notes." The man was a saint. Actually, he knew more about publishing than I did. He was the mentor, not I. His taste in poetry was excellent.

There is a curious mystery about Albert's folder in the New Directions archive. Only a few letters from him are there. Puzzling over this I now recall that one of Delmore's games was to carry on imaginary disputes which were always couched in an arch, Schwartzian way, usually very funny. Who weeded the file? It's a shame, those little missives were so comical.

The time came when New Directions grew to the point it had to have a New York base. George W. Stewart, a road salesman and small publisher, took it on, operating out of his office in Forty-fourth Street. The Schwartzes didn't want to leave Cambridge, and Albert wanted to be on his own. For a while he worked at the *Saturday Review* and Doubleday. Then for three years he was an editorial assistant at Reynal and Hitchcock. He came to Random House in 1947. There he became one of the greatest editors of the period, and one of the best-loved men in publishing. But that is a story for others to tell.

Daniel Fuchs

(25 June 1909 – 26 July 1993)

Gabriel Miller
Rutgers University

See also the Fuchs entries in *DLB 9: American Novelists, 1910–1945; DLB 26: American Screenwriters;* and *DLB 28: Twentieth-Century American-Jewish Fiction Writers.*

BOOKS: *Summer in Williamsburg* (New York: Vanguard, 1934; London: Constable, 1935);

Homage to Blenholt (New York: Vanguard, 1936; London: Constable, 1936);

Low Company (New York: Vanguard, 1937); republished as *Neptune Beach* (London: Constable, 1937);

Stories, by Fuchs and others (New York: Farrar, Straus & Cudahy, 1956); republished as *A Book of Stories* (London: Gollancz, 1957);

Three Novels by Daniel Fuchs (New York: Basic Books, 1961); republished as *The Williamsburg Trilogy* (New York: Avon, 1972) – includes *Summer in Williamsburg, Homage to Blenholt,* and *Low Company*;

West of the Rockies (New York: Knopf, 1971; London: Secker & Warburg, 1971);

The Apathetic Bookie Joint (New York: Methuen, 1979; London: Secker & Warburg, 1980).

SELECTED SCREENPLAYS: *The Big Shot,* by Fuchs, Bertram Millhauser, and Abem Finkel, Warner Bros., 1942;

The Hard Way, by Fuchs and Peter Viertel, Warner Bros., 1943;

Between Two Worlds, Warner Bros., 1944;

The Gangster, ABC–Allied Artists, 1947;

Hollow Triumph, Eagle Lion, 1948;

Criss Cross, Universal, 1949;

Panic in the Streets, adaptation, 20th Century–Fox, 1950;

Storm Warning, by Fuchs and Richard Brooks, Warner Bros., 1951;

Taxi, by Fuchs and D. M. Marshman, Jr., 20th Century–Fox, 1952;

Daniel Fuchs

The Human Jungle, by Fuchs and William Sackheim, ABC–Allied Artists, 1954;

Love Me or Leave Me, by Fuchs and Isobel Lennart, M-G-M, 1955;

Interlude, by Fuchs and Franklin Coen, Universal, 1957;

Jeane Eagels, by Fuchs, Sonya Levien, and John Fante, Columbia, 1957.

OTHER: "Pioneers! O Pioneers!," in *Story in America,* edited by Whit Burnett and Martha Foley (New York: Vanguard, 1934).

SELECTED PERIODICAL PUBLICATIONS – UNCOLLECTED: "Where Al Capone Grew Up," *New Republic* (9 September 1931);

"Dream City or the Drugged Lake," *Cinema Arts* (Summer 1937);

"My Sister Who Is Famous," *Collier's,* 100 (4 September 1937);

"Crap Game," *New Yorker* (25 December 1937);

"Last Fall," *Saturday Evening Post,* 210 (5 March 1938);

"Such a Nice Spring Day," *Collier's,* 102 (23 April 1938);

"Shun All Care," *Harper's Bazaar* (May 1938);

"Getaway Day," *Collier's,* 102 (10 September 1938);

"Lucky Loser," *Collier's,* 102 (15 October 1938);

"A Matter of Pride," *Collier's,* 102 (22 October 1938);

"Life Sentence," *Collier's,* 102 (19 November 1938);

"Give Hollywood a Chance," *Esquire* (December 1938);

"Fortune and Men's Eyes," *Saturday Evening Post,* 211 (10 December 1938);

"If a Man Answers, Hang Up," *Collier's,* 103 (22 April 1939);

"Crazy Over Pigeons," *Collier's,* 103 (29 April 1939);

"A Girl Like Cele," *Redbook* (April 1939);

"The Woman in Buffalo," *Esquire* (April 1939);

"Not to the Swift," *Collier's,* 103 (13 May 1939);

"Toilers of the Screen," *Collier's,* 104 (8 July 1939);

"The Hosiery Shop," *Harper's Bazaar* (1 September 1939);

"The Politician," *New Republic,* 100 (11 October 1939);

"A Mind Coat Each Morning," *Collier's,* 105 (27 January 1940);

"Pug in an Opera Hat," *Collier's,* 105 (23 March 1940);

"Daring Young Man," *Collier's,* 106 (24 August 1940);

"Racing Is a Business," *Collier's,* 106 (5 October 1940);

"The Fabulous Rubio," *Collier's,* 107 (4 January 1941);

"Strange Things Happen in Brooklyn," *Collier's,* 107 (1 February 1941);

"The Long Green," *Cosmopolitan* (February 1951);

"Writing for the Movies," *Commentary* (February 1962).

Daniel Fuchs was a writer's writer. John Updike recommended him for the National Academy of Arts and Letters and wrote an afterword to the paperback edition of his 1971 novel, *West of the Rockies.* Mordecai Richler wrote in the *New York Times Book Review:* "Whenever Jewish writers of my generation come together to celebrate those books that really mattered to us when we were young, the novels that shaped us . . . somebody will unfailingly ask, 'Do you remember the Williamsburg Trilogy?' " Irwin Shaw devoted an essay to Fuchs's second novel *Homage to Blenholt* (1936), James Farrell wrote glowingly about Fuchs in the *New Republic,* and Irving Howe contributed appreciative essays to *Commentary, Harpers,* and the *New York Review of Books.*

The three novels on which Fuchs's reputation primarily rests, *Summer in Williamsburg* (1934), *Homage to Blenholt,* and *Low Company* (1937), were initially received with a lethal combination of fine reviews and poor sales. Republished in one volume by Basic Books in 1961, they were issued in separate paperback editions by Berkeley Medallion in 1965. Avon Books then reissued them as *The Williamsburg Trilogy* in 1971. Carrol and Graf reprinted *Summer in Williamsburg* in 1983, while Omnigraphics reissued *Homage to Blenholt* in 1990 with an introduction by Fuchs that alone is worth the thirty-dollar price tag.

The poor sales and the reviews, which Fuchs labeled "scanty and immaterial," soured him, and he left for Hollywood in 1937. (RKO Radio had bought his short story "Crazy Over Pigeons," which was eventually made into *The Day the Bookies Wept,* starring Joe Penner.) Fuchs stayed on in Hollywood to become a successful screenwriter, winning an Academy Award for the original story of *Love Me or Leave Me* in 1955. The film's star James Cagney called the script the finest he had ever read. Other notable films include the cult classic *Criss Cross* (1949), *Panic in the Streets* (1950), and *Hollow Triumph* (1948).

Meanwhile, Fuchs published numerous short stories – many in the *New Yorker* and the *Saturday Evening Post* – as well as essays and reminiscences. The best of these were collected in *The Apathetic Bookie Joint* (1979), which also includes a masterful novella, "Triplicate," Fuchs's most openly autobiographical work and one of the most evocative stories ever written about Hollywood. He also wrote a Hollywood novel, *West of the Rockies.*

The forsaking of art for "commerce" was in part responsible for the poverty of Fuchs's reputa-

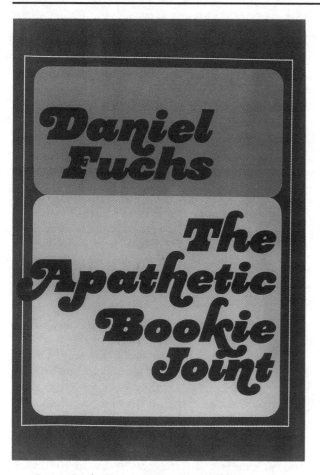

*Dust jacket for Fuchs's 1980 collection of fiction, essays,
and reminiscences*

tion. Ironically, Henry Roth, who also came of age in the 1930s and who until 1994 published only one novel, *Call it Sleep* (1934), has fared better among critics and intellectuals. (Fuchs was often amused at being confused with Roth by letter writers who wanted to know about his chicken farm in New Mexico.) Roth was romanticized by critics as a genius suffering from writer's block, an eccentric who exiled himself rather than compromise his art. Fuchs, in contrast, opted to make a living rather than struggle on as a permanent substitute in the New York City public school system while writing at night and during summer breaks.

Unfortunately, he made his choice during a decade when "commitment" was all, and *Hollywood* was a dirty word. His contemporary Clifford Odets might have agonized over the decision to "sell out" (and later write *The Big Knife* [1949] as an act of contrition), but Fuchs admitted no such qualms. In his autobiography, *A Margin of Hope* (1982), Irving Howe recalls being shamed by a letter from Fuchs, received after he had criticized Fuchs's move to

Hollywood in *Commentary.* Fuchs explained that he had simply wanted to make his living as a writer, but his fiction had not paid the bills. Should he have starved his young family for the sake of art?

Fuchs was bothered by the "Whatever happened to you?" queries. At times he protested too much, claiming that he had, after all, kept on writing. But in spite of the stories and essays he managed to produce, his film work clearly did keep him from the sustained artistry he might have achieved, the potential realized in "Triplicate," which appeared after he had stopped writing for the movies.

Unlike other easterners who went west, Fuchs considered writing for film difficult and said so. He never condescended to the movies as others did, but he respected its craft. Fuchs often wrote of the hard work and the grief that went into writing for the movies, the despair at not getting it right, "the mountains of failed screenplays on the shelf." He felt that it was the same with fiction writing: "You have the same record of misses, the bouts of wretchedness, the typed sheets of paper going flat in your hands." The central difference was that the studios paid you for unaccepted work, while publishers did not.

This is an attitude bred in the tenements, a law of Williamsburg, like the isolation and the claustrophobia. In all of Fuchs's novels one feels the oppression, the perception of imprisonment in an airless cell. This sense is both physical, enforced by the atmosphere, and psychic. Escaping it made the spaciousness of California seem positively magical to a young man who longed to breathe freely:

> The area is still undeveloped, so I am granted the boon of being in a new place, fresh and brimming and unawakened, at the beginning. There are masses of bougainvillea, Joshua trees and yucca on the hills, a light shining at the door, the scent of orange blossoms in the evening air, honeysuckle and jasmine. . . . Everything in this new land wonderfully solitary, burning and kind.

The final irony, as Fuchs himself appreciated, was a merging of the past's broken dreams with those of the future. The move from coast to coast finally would yield little, and even the capacity for wonder was to dissolve. His story "The Golden West" chronicles, in metaphoric terms, the disintegration of the studios and the end of dreams of the future. Fuchs's wealthy Californians still dream, but they now long only for eternal youth and beauty. Like characters in an Anton Chekhov play, they play out the string, talking, hoping, and failing. Yet they remain sympathetic: even the gangsters touch the reader, for their humanity outstrips their deeds.

If Fuchs could claim a central influence, it would be Chekhov. Like the Russian playwright, he was more interested in detail than in plot, preferring to build up the particulars, delineating atmosphere and character and trusting the confluence of all to reveal something significant. Like the young narrator of *Summer in Williamsburg,* Fuchs distrusted dramatic contrivances:

> These were people as God made them and as they were. They sat in the sunshine going through the stale operations of living, they were real, but a novelist did not write a book about them. No novel, no matter how seriously intentioned, was real. The progressive development, the delineated episodes, the artificial climax, the final conclusion . . . these were logical devices and they were false. People did not live in dramatic situations.

Of course Fuchs, like Chekhov, did have to resort to artifice, but much of his fiction is remarkably free of standard novelistic devices, eschewing even reliance on a hero. Reflecting in 1990 on his theory of composition he explained:

> Ideas [were] for me, at any rate, unsatisfactory, on the weak, insubstantial side. I used my theme, abandoned it, and devoted myself simply to the life in the hallways, the commotion at the dumbwaiters, the assortment of characters in the building, . . . their strivings and preoccupations, their troubles in the interplay of the sexes. There was always ferment, slums or no slums.

In a letter to Gabriel Miller in 1979 he wrote, "Maybe the whole idea of fiction is that it is a rebellion against the intellect. Fiction gives the actuality, the event, the image, the thing as it is. . . ."

Fuchs's three 1930s novels intersect the modernist and social-realist schools. Unlike the critically esteemed writers of that decade, he offered no call for revolt, nor did he articulate any political or social theories. Not only did he not seem committed to encouraging the rise of the working class, Fuchs, in fact, offered mankind no advice at all; perhaps it is not surprising that his novels never really caught on. Rejecting the esprit de corps of the decade, his work was marginalized in an era with little patience for individualistic writers of somber vision.

What Fuchs's novels do better than many of the better-known works of the time is to capture the eerie tenor of the Depression, the sense of living without a past or any hope for a future. His characters float idly in an emotional limbo, occasionally thrilling to an illusion of freedom or accomplishment, only to be dragged down to earth. Fuchs's ability to replicate the quixotic energy of life on the streets of New York in this age of futility is unmatched by any of his contemporaries.

Fuchs's novels also depict a profound and unrelieved spiritual vacuum at the heart of existence. Directly reflecting the moral bankruptcy of the modern age, his plots are full of gang wars waged by adults and children, murder, prostitution, and suicide. Fuchs's fictional universe, like that of many modern writers, operates without benefit of God or inherent spiritual value.

Howe once remarked that for Fuchs writing was as natural as catching a fly ball was for Willie Mays. (Fuchs claimed that the compliment made him nervous.) In another context Howe termed him a "true writer." Daniel Fuchs was indeed a natural; his work reflects experience more "truly" than that of many writers whose reputations eclipse his own. Of all the writers who came of age before the 1950s renaissance in Jewish letters, none rendered immigrant life more honestly. No other novels of the Depression evoke that decade more forcefully and more compassionately, and few novels of any age more vividly evoke the hollowness of modern-day America than his masterpiece *Low Company.*

Also, few American novelists can look so clinically at their characters, to see them for what they are and yet have the largeness of spirit to embrace and celebrate their humanity. This is nowhere more apparent than in his last major work of fiction, "Triplicate." In tone and theme Fuchs's novella resembles James Joyce's "The Dead," whose protagonist achieves spiritual awakening through a recognition of love and kinship with all of the dead. Fuchs, too, like Joyce's Gabriel Conroy, now partakes of this larger vision, and like Joyce he closes his novella with an eloquent meditation on death that, paradoxically, dwells fondly and gratefully on the small joys of living:

> The most vivid idea I have of what death is like is when I'm here, in California or New York, and think of London, the theaters, the parks, the greenery, the normal life of the city going on as it always goes on, except that you're not there, without you . . . The young girls in the late fall afternoons, the smell of snow in the air, the feel of winter coming on, the people getting out of cabs, bringing home packages, going to restaurants, the streetlamps lighting up, the bustle, the life – no more, no more, no more.

References:

Irving Howe, "Daniel Fuchs: Escape from Williamsburg," *Commentary* (6 July 1948): 29–34;

Gabriel Miller, *Daniel Fuchs* (Boston: Twayne, 1979).

William Haggard

(11 August 1907 – 27 October 1993)

Robin W. Winks
Yale University

BOOKS: *Slow Burner* (London: Cassell, 1958; Boston: Little, Brown, 1958);

The Telemann Touch (London: Cassell, 1958; Boston: Little, Brown, 1958);

Venetian Blind (London: Cassell, 1959; New York: Washburn, 1959);

Closed Circuit (London: Cassell, 1960; New York: Washburn, 1960);

The Arena (Harmondsworth, U.K.: Penguin, 1961; New York: Washburn, 1961);

The Unquiet Sleep (London: Cassell, 1962; New York: Washburn, 1962);

The High Wire (London: Cassell, 1963; New York: Washburn, 1963);

The Antagonists (London: Cassell, 1964; New York: Washburn, 1964);

The Hard Sell (London: Cassell, 1965; New York: Washburn, 1966);

The Powder Barrel (London: Cassell, 1965; New York: Washburn, 1965);

The Power House (London: Cassell, 1966; New York: Washburn, 1967);

The Conspirators (London: Cassell, 1967; New York: Washburn, 1968);

A Cool Day for Killing (London: Hodder & Stoughton, 1968; New York: Walker, 1968);

The Doubtful Disciple (London: Cassell, 1969);

The Hardliners (London: Cassell, 1970; New York: Walker, 1970);

The Bitter Harvest (London: Cassell, 1971), republished as *Too Many Enemies* (New York: Walker, 1972);

The Protectors (London: Cassell, 1972; New York: Walker, 1972);

The Little Rug Book (London: Cassell, 1972);

The Old Masters (London: Cassell, 1973); republished as *The Notch on the Knife* (New York: Walker, 1973);

The Kinsmen (London: Cassell, 1974; New York: Walker, 1974);

The Scorpion's Tale (London: Cassell, 1975; New York: Walker, 1975);

Yesterday's Enemy (London: Cassell, 1976; New York: Walker, 1976);

Visa to Limbo (London: Cassell, 1978; New York: Walker, 1979);

The Poison People (London: Cassell, 1978; New York: Walker, 1979);

The Median Line (London: Cassell, 1979; New York: Walker, 1985);

The Money Men (London: Hodder & Stoughton, 1981; New York: Walker, 1981);

The Mischief-Makers (London: Hodder & Stoughton, 1982; New York: Walker, 1982);

The Heirloom (London: Hodder & Stoughton, 1983; South Yarmouth, Mass.: Curley, 1985);

The Need to Know (London: Hodder & Stoughton, 1984; South Yarmouth, Mass.: Curley, 1986);

The Meritocrats (London: Hodder & Stoughton, 1985; South Yarmouth, Mass.: Curley, 1987);

The Martello Towers (London: Hodder & Stoughton, 1986; South Yarmouth, Mass.: Curley, 1987);

The Diplomatist (London: Hodder & Stoughton, 1987; South Yarmouth, Mass.: Curley, 1988);

The Expatriates (London: Hodder & Stoughton, 1989; South Yarmouth, Mass.: Curley, 1990);

The Vendettists (London: Hodder & Stoughton, 1990; Hampton, N.H.: Curley, 1992).

William Haggard most often is referred to as a writer of spy novels, but he was something considerably more than this, even though he properly takes his place somewhere between John le Carré and Len Deighton. He wrote political thrillers in which the world of spying plays the the dominant role, but his interest was in the British establishment and the uses of power. Haggard once called himself an "updated Trollope with a fair share of violent action": he was interested in how social machinery worked, in Britain and elsewhere, and in the relationship of class to what an older generation – his generation – would have called civilized men and correct behavior. This, quite incorrectly, led to his being labeled an elitist.

William Haggard

Haggard was a pseudonym. He was born Richard Henry Michael Clayton in Croyden, Surrey, 11 August 1907, and he died 27 October 1993, at age eighty-six. Educated at Lancing College, he studied history at Christ Church, Oxford, and in 1931 he joined the Indian Civil Service, serving as a magistrate and a sessions judge. In 1936 he married Barbara Myfanwy Sant, who predeceased him in 1989; they had one son and one daughter. At the outbreak of World War II Clayton joined the Mahratta Light Infantry, and after attending Staff College at Quetta, he was assigned to Special Operations in India and Burma. From 1947 until his retirement in 1969 he worked for the Board of Trade in London, first with the Department of Overseas Trade and then with the Enemy Property Department, of which he became controller. This work, together with his fluency in four languages, gave him insights into how class and property worked in many societies and close contacts with the financial community in London. As an intelligence officer in

southern Asia, and through his administration of his civil-service department, he learned much about banking and finance and the intelligence community's relationship to both.

Clayton wrote his first novel because he had, while traveling to London each day by train, exhausted all the fiction which suited his taste. Neither le Carré nor Deighton had published their first novels; Ian Fleming, on the other hand, had published five successful novels, the most recent, *From Russia, with Love* (1957), to considerable acclaim. Starting with *Slow Burner* in 1958, and taking the surname of his mother's distant kinsman, H. Rider Haggard, Clayton would produce virtually a book a year until shortly before his death. Nearly all of these, including the first, focused on Col. Charles Russell, the head of the Security Executive, a quasi-military organization within Whitehall which operated in the shadowland between the diplomatic service and the intelligence organizations, MI5 and MI6. Russell was markedly like Haggard in many ways: tall, intelligent, sophisticated and urbane, interested in oriental rugs – his only work of nonfiction, *The Little Rug Book*, published in 1972, is as good a primer as one could ask for – and decent wines. Russell was, it appears, born in 1905, and over half his adventures occur after his retirement from the Security Executive in 1965: thus Haggard and Russell were contemporaries.

Haggard enjoyed a substantial readership in Britain, though he never wrote a best-seller; in the United States he was not widely read, a circumstance that annoyed him but did not lead him to court a broader readership by changing his tone or approach. He was quintessentially British, wry, disillusioned with politicians, exceptionally allusive, and elliptical to American ears. No doubt he could have greatly increased his following had he chosen to follow more directly in the footsteps of James Bond, but for the most part he preferred his violence to take place offstage. The fact that he saw Russians as worthy opponents, clearly did not think Americans were up to the tasks being thrust upon them by the cold war, and had only scorn for "the most dangerous sort of man alive, a dedicated idealist off-centre" (*The Need to Know*, 1984), too many of whom were Americans, did not endear him to those readers who wanted their heroes unblemished. While Haggard introduced sex into his novels as publishing became more permissive, it was direct and almost incidental, never erotic; one student of the genre, John Atkins, described the sexual activity in *The Arena* (1961) as rather like "two old computers trying to get randy" (*The British Spy Novel*, 1984). Nor were Russell/Haggard's views fashionable about world affairs: patriots who understood patriots, they respected South African and Israeli intelligence and the ruthlessness with which both countries protected themselves; they thought that Britain was going soft; they had no interest in apportioning blame; they held much of the world – and all of the Looney Left, as Russell called it – in low regard; and their villains sometimes got off scot-free because they were, paradoxically, honorable men.

By the mid 1960s New American Library had launched a paperback promotional campaign in the United States, but despite high praise from critics, the alleged right-wing philosophy of the books and the air of erudition did not sell. In Britain a similar campaign by Penguin Books was quite successful. In the end, Haggard received no paperback publication in the United States at all, and after Little, Brown published his first two books, *Slow Burner* and *The Telemann Touch* (1958), Haggard was pub-

lished by Washburn and, from 1968, by Walker. His last books were not published in America at all.

This is unfortunate, for Haggard is a significant writer both in the history of the genre and for the clear talent and special flavor his work brings to the field. His sensitivity to hierarchy and to how levels of society in an ancient culture deal through nuance rather than the direct exercise of overt orders was unerring. He grasped the difference between the ambitious person and the incidentally ambitious. He explored layers of ruthlessness between classes, groups, and nations determined to survive, recognizing that each has its own code of conduct. Neither his heroes nor his villains are thick-eared heavies: in *The Heirloom* (1983) a central figure, due to meet with a high-level person from an organization very like the Mafia, takes four minutes off to visit the Redentore, in Venice, and to observe that he disagreed with John Ruskin's negative judgment on the church: "This was one of the world's most beautiful buildings." The reader is expected to know the church and who Ruskin was. Haggard spoke of tin-pot dictators in Latin America and of nations terrorized by "some ape in Africa," and he remained to the last both politically incorrect and unfashionable.

Perhaps the most appealing quality of Haggard's prose is its revelations of indirectness. Here is a typical exchange:

> Martin Dominy was a working operator but one day might be rather more. He was well worth sophisticating and Charles Russell began to do so. "Quite," he said finally. "Perfectly logical and it covers the facts as you know them." He was conscious this might sound pompous and pomposity he detested; he smiled, and added blandly: "Do you mind if I play at schoolmasters?" "I know I've a great deal to learn, sir!" The tone had been mild but Martin had moved up one: He could hit back gracefully and that was important. Russell said imperturbably: "I don't think I quite deserved that, but let's start at the beginning."

Only an attentive reader would be aware that this exchange was both authentic and important to the plot.

Or consider this scene, in which Russell is visited by the Chief Inspector who knows that Russell was the last person to see a distinguished, now retired, French civil servant alive before he apparently died while napping on a couch in their club. The Chief Inspector asks,

> "you were alone when you found him dead?" "I was." "So while you were asleep yourself another man could have come in without waking you?" "I only know that

men went out. There were six or seven there when we settled. When I found de Cox dead there was only myself." . . . It was Russell's turn to show sudden interest. "Surely you're not considering murder?" "We'd like to be sure of the negative, that it is not. If you'd said you'd seen a stranger come in – " "I should have assumed it was a member I didn't know." "But in any case you didn't?" "Confirmed. But if I may say so without offence this line of enquiry does surprise me." . . . "Did you know him well?" "Yes, pretty well. We dined together say once a month. His wife had learnt to cook French food and the wine on his table was always excellent. And talking of wine may I offer refreshment?"

With this question, Russell changes the relationship: he has now offered hospitality, and he may ask a question. This shift in power, and the reading of the Chief Inspector's club tie – which Russell knows has been worn precisely so that he will note that the Chief Inspector belongs to the same club as Russell's rising protégé at the Security Executive – alters the relationship, and with it, the story. Perhaps it is Jane Austen to whom Haggard should have compared himself, rather than to Anthony Trollope. The early Deighton could write by indirection; so too can Anthony Price; but there are very few authors who do so with such skillful purpose.

Haggard set his physical scenes as carefully as his social ones. *The High Wire* (1963), judged by Barzun and Taylor to be his best, concludes with a chilling confrontation in a funicular car high above Switzerland. *Venetian Blind* (1959) is a fine double pun, only part of which involves the Italian city outside which Haggard had a pied-à-terre: *The Scorpion's Tale* (1975) is equally fine on Spain; *The Powder Barrel* (1965) gets its unnamed oil-rich sheikhdom just right.

Though Haggard was always discreet, he was never unclear. In *The Power House* (1966) he drew a devastating portrait of the British prime minister: no one could not realize that it was Harold Wilson he had in mind. In *The Need to Know* Haggard depicted a genderless prime minister referred to as the Battle Tank and thus conveniently always "it" rather than "she," but no one could miss the admiration Haggard (and Russell) had for Margaret Thatcher. Yet this conservatism never moved toward the fascistic; violence was never for its own

sake. Britain had become a pawn in a Big Power game, and Haggard was not so much anti-American or anti-French, though he found enemies in both, as undeviatingly pro-British. The enemy was seldom a nation, or a people, but those individuals who were shown to be merely ambitious.

Haggard filled an important place in post–World War II thriller fiction. His work evolved through the cold war, flirted momentarily with science fiction when it dealt with world's early fears of atomic and hydrogen bombs, moved on to the "secret war" of the 1960s, opened up the Arab-Israeli conflict when few writers were interested, and took up industrial espionage well before other writers did so. Haggard posited a world based on détente, as Russell and his Russian counterpart worked together, the KGB usually portrayed as intelligent and even cultured operatives worthy of the club-land atmosphere in which Haggard so often drew his best portraits. The tone of a Haggard book remained *pukka sahib,* as he moved the genre toward the Right. All that was admirable, and all that angered some readers, appears in this dialogue from *The Scorpion's Tale*. British, Swedish, and American hippies, high on marijuana and LSD, have taken control of an island off Málaga. The Spanish owner is philosophical:

> "And on my island they're having a last blind orgy."
> "Singing I imagine."
> "Yes. May I ask how you knew?"
> " They always sing when they're certain they've had it. Its a song 'We Shall Not Be Moved.' When they've sung it twice they always are."
> "You're not sympathetic, then?"
> "Of couse not. But nor am I exactly hostile. I'm sorry for unfortunate children."
> "All very liberal. All very British."
> "Naturally. Since that's what I am."

Haggard was not an elitist as the term is normally understood, and certainly not a racist. Russell's most trusted, and independent-minded, successor is a West Indian. Rather, Haggard embraced the world of realpolitik without angst or undue complications, well apart from those better-known spymasters le Carré and Deighton, and perhaps more realistically.

William Ober

(15 May 1920 – 27 April 1993)

Hugh L'Etang

BOOKS: *Boswell's Clap and Other Essays: Medical Analyses of Literary Men's Afflictions* (Carbondale & Edwardsville: Southern Illinois University Press, 1979);

Bottoms Up! A Pathologist's Essays on Medicine and the Humanities (Carbondale & Edwardsville: Southern Illinois University Press, 1988).

OTHER: *Great Men of Guy's,* edited, with an introduction, by Ober (Metuchen, N.J.: Scarecrow Press, 1973).

I first heard of William Ober in the mid 1960s when I was working for an American pharmaceutical firm which was developing a new contraceptive pill. As a gynecological pathologist he had been invited to study any changes in the uterine and cervical cell lining resulting from use of the pill.

I nearly lost the opportunity to meet him because it was only by chance that I saw belatedly in November 1968 his contribution to the *New York State Journal of Medicine* written as far back as August 1967. Entitled "Conan Doyle's Dying Detective," the story describes how Doyle's fictional investigator, Sherlock Holmes, deceives and traps a murderer by simulating disease. In 1959 I had lectured to the Sherlock Holmes Society of London on the same story, and, as my talk had been reproduced in its journal, I sent Ober a copy. Fortunately, we had reached the same diagnosis of the disease faked by Holmes. His reply was the first of a series of friendly, amusing, helpful, and, above all, learned letters which continued for nearly twenty-five years.

Ober explained that his original title, "Conan Doyle's Dying Dick," was dismissed by the editor as being louche or suggestive but it quickly revealed his licentious sense of humor. We first met when he and his wife were in London in September 1969 on one of their regular trips when he visited his literary friends, bookshops, the British Museum library, his tailor, the theater, and unusual restaurants. He also displayed his instant generosity and thoughtfulness.

William Ober (courtesy of Mrs. William B. Ober)

The launch of my first book, *The Pathology of Leadership* (1969), coincided with this visit and, not only did he make constructive comments after rapid perusal of a copy bought at the publisher's office, but he wrote favorable reviews when the American edition appeared in 1970. Before this visit we had corresponded about another medical author, R. Austin Freeman, and his fictional detective, Dr. Thorndyke, as Ober was puzzled about the author's medical degrees.

William Bernard Ober was born on 15 May 1920. He was an unusual schoolboy because he later wrote how he was criticized when he was fourteen by a "Dickensian" teacher because he complained that *Nicholas Nickleby* (1839) was too long, too diffuse, and neither entirely logical nor realistic in terms of behavior. Aged sixteen, between school and college, he was a "newspaper man" who went to the scene, collected the facts, returned to the office, and wrote the story. In 1986, writing about Arthur Rimbaud, whose poems he studied as an undergraduate, he recalled the endless hours at college reading and translating them, as well as the poems of Charles Baudelaire, Paul Verlaine, Stéphane Mallarmé, and others. He would ask himself if it was all a waste of time and conclude that, though the enchantment had died down, some insights remained.

Ober's courses at Harvard included literature, history, and psychology, interspersed with music criticism. He confessed that his attempt to write fiction was a lamentable disaster. He did not decide on medicine as a career until his last year at Harvard, so, after graduating magna cum laude in 1941, he returned and took the minimum number of premedical science courses to permit entry into medical school. In 1946 he gained his medical degree from Boston University School of Medicine and completed his internship and residency at Beth Israel Hospital in Boston and the Boston Lying-in Hospital.

Despite his literary interests he never expressed regret about the demands of his medical career, and he adapted the microscope and the typewriter to a doubly creative life. His early medical papers on unusual tumors and their recurrence in the uterus and cervix, and also changes in the uterus associated with steroid contraceptives and intrauterine contraceptive devices, show how pathologists explore and discover the hitherto unrevealed. His critical faculties were extended by varied experiences at Howard University, the Armed Forces Institute of Pathology, the Department of Pathology at the Naval Medical School, Bethesda, and as an instructor at Harvard Medical School.

Two early incidents confirmed that, though he needed no reminder, there is life and death outside laboratory work confined to the study of cells and tissues. In May 1949 he assisted at the autopsy of James Forrestal, the first U.S. secretary of defense who, in a fit of depression, threw himself from the sixteenth floor of the Bethesda tower block. He could also counter the rumor that the pigmented mole removed from President Franklin Delano Roosevelt's left eyebrow in 1943 was malignant and had later spread to his brain. In 1949 Ober was shown the slide of the tissue removed from Roosevelt and confirmed that it was absolutely benign and not a malignant mole.

With a foot in both camps Ober was well qualified to provide medical analyses of literary men's afflictions. Some were included in his first book, *Boswell's Clap and Other Essays* (1979), with its revealing preface. He wrote that "medical information and insights can illuminate and perhaps resolve certain literary problems," although this did not imply "that every reader should read with a medical eye nor need any given writer be viewed as a 'case.' " Using the retrospectroscope rather than the microscope he went beyond tissues and cells and took into account his subject's personal history as well as the sequence of events. More important, to use his own words, must be the awareness that "each biographer is limited by his own psyche which determines his relationship to the subject."

When I first met Ober I had joined the editorial staff of the *Practitioner,* a medical journal established in 1868, and in December 1970 we published his clinico-pathological assessment of Beethoven although he admitted misgivings about the limitations of the retrospectroscope used nearly 150 years after the subject's death. In "Their Last Chords," five years later, he noted sudden deaths in musicians, including William Kapell and Guido Cantelli (aircraft accidents), Philip Heseltine (suicide), Wallingford Riegger (head injury after tripping over the leashes of two fighting dogs), Enrique Granados (drowned when his ship was sunk by a German U-Boat in 1916), and Charles Valentin Alkan (crushed by a falling bookcase). The next year he examined "Operatic 'Doctors,' " including those whose medical qualifications even onstage are dubious, such as Bartolo in the *Marriage of Figaro,* Malatesta in *Don Pasquale,* and Dulcamara in *L'Elisir d'Amore.* Part of Ober's literary skill was in linking trivial and unnoticed details and weaving them into an entertaining but scholarly story. In this manner he published in the *New York State Journal of Medicine* an account of the optical problems of Johann Sebastian Bach and George Frideric Handel together with their treatment or mistreatment by an itinerant English oculist named John Taylor who claimed to be both a chevalier and an Ophthalmiater.

The first two words of the title of his first book, *Boswell's Clap,* catch the eye as do the nineteen attacks of urethritis meticulously traced by Ober. But the more modest other essays contain the stimulating results of painstaking medical as well as literary research. He argues persuasively that Swinburne suffered at birth from anoxic brain damage but that his masochism and other abnormal behavior were due to psychological overlay. Minimal brain dysfunction could have been responsible, however, for Swinburne's increased activity; difficulty in writing, jerky, involuntary movements; and tics. Ober completes the clinical picture with other accounts of Swinburne jerking his legs, twisting his feet, flapping his hands, drumming on the ground with his feet, and tapping the table.

In a discomforting reminder, Ober points out that three British poets who used opium – George Crabbe, Francis Thompson, and John Keats – were also medically trained. Thompson's addiction released in his verse "not only the vivid imagery of hallucination but also the ill-formed, distorted attitudes of a weak, indecisive, withdrawn personality." Although Keats in the "Ode to a Nightingale" describes a trancelike state, Ober clears him of any criticism that the poem consciously attempts to re-create a narcotic experience, although the words suggest that Keats drew upon past experience.

Ober fixes a high-powered psychopathological lens when he writes in general about madness and poetry and in particular about William Collins, Christopher Smart, and William Cowper. As scholars in the future study and interpret these poems they may take into account Ober's conclusions that Collins had fits of depression which reduced both his output and emotional expression; that in the incomplete *Jubilate Agno* (finally published in 1939) Smart transcends the rational, physical world; and that Cowper wrote poetry as occupational therapy because of guilt and fears of eternal damnation.

While the general physician and surgeon have the satisfaction of treating, curing, or prolonging life in most of their patients, the pathologist is inevitably preoccupied with cadavers and death due to bizarre behavior. Ober ruthlessly explores the unspeakable in *Bottoms Up! A Pathologist's Essays on Medicine and the Humanities* (1988). Physicians would be fascinated by his iconography of leprosy, which includes a reproduction from a seventh-century Syriac Bible, although laymen could be disturbed by the illustrations of such a disfiguring disease. Both physicians and laymen could be disturbed, no doubt because of subconscious or suppressed emotions, by other iconographies in the book, namely "The Fine Arts and Flagellation" and another on " 'Fanny Hill' or 'How To Illustrate a Dirty Book'." "To Cast a Pox," later published in a journal, was another pictorial history with a revealing portrait of a young man with secondary syphilis, painted by Hans Holbein the Younger in 1523.

The inclusion in his second book of what he entitled "The Sticky End of Frantisek Koczwara, composer of *The Battle of Prague*" may have arisen from Ober's professional experience because, in his words, "autoerotic asphyxia is a problem in forensic rather than clinical medicine." He once wrote that it

was not a subject for dinner-table conversation but returned to the theme when his article " The Man in the Scarlet Cloak, The Mysterious Death of Peter Anthony Motteux" was appropriately published in the *American Journal of Forensic Medicine and Pathology*.

As a pathologist Ober can have had no illusions about his own arterial disease. It did not stop his active life, writing that must have been done out of office hours, love of food and drink, and, more serious, chain smoking. In 1970 he complained of the tiredness of being fifty. In our correspondence his first admission of cardiac pain was in December 1977 when he wrote that he was taking less nitroglycerine. When I told him a year later that my daughter was playing tennis during an English winter in a temperature of 40°C, he wrote that he never could and, with angina pectoris, exertion in cold weather called for nitroglycerine. Although his cardiac status was stable in 1986 with "no angina to speak of," pulse regular, and blood pressure normal, a special Doppler study showed severe disease in both carotid arteries. In December the left carotid was treated, and, although the right was also "reamed out" at the end of February 1987, he performed thirteen autopsies in the last week of March.

In September 1992 he gave sloth as a reason for failing to reply to two letters but that the last months had been fallow. Although his cardiac status remained stable and investigation disclosed no further carotid artery narrowing or plaques, his medications induced lassitude and even torpor. His last published article, "Obstetrical Events That Shaped Western European History," appeared around this time. Modestly describing it as based on after-dinner talks to OB/Gyn groups with ladies present, he assessed the possible brain damage sustained by Kaiser Wilhelm II at his birth in 1859, and its relation to his future conduct and its influence on world history.

He never mentioned the crippling effects of arterial disease which involved his legs. It was uncomfortably apparent to me on one of his last visits to London. After lunch we had to walk up the gentle slope of Saint James's Street. He could only avoid, and conceal, the pain by stopping regularly to look at the long-established sporting gun, fishing tackle, pipe and cigar, and wine shops that grace that part of London's Clubland.

He spent his last months writing clerihews, which he considered a subtler light verse than the limerick, as they enabled the writer to be bland, amusing, and scurrilous. Some could even be repeated in mixed company.

George Herbert Walker Bush
Did not know when to push
His record will always bear the stain
Of not having toppled Saddam Hussein.

Unfortunately he had not the mental or physical vitality to complete several projected articles such as "Soluble in Alcohol," a study of drinking among writers. Nor will one be published on the Reverend Harold Davidson, the notorious rector of Stiffkey, a village in Norfolk, who was unfrocked in 1932 for "disreputable association with women." Had it appeared it would have been entitled "The Vicar Was Quicker."

His last letter to me dated 19 January 1993 had an uncharacteristic conclusion which he had never written before: "Keep well." On 27 April 1993 he collapsed at a reception and dinner in Washington. He died four and a half hours later from rupture of an aneurysm in the abdominal aorta. Whether this could have added to the circulatory problems in his legs can only be a matter for conjecture.

Many will mourn the loss of a generous friend and stimulating teacher. His illustration on the jacket of his second book reveals that quizzical expression which preceded his unconventional but pertinent comments on life, learning, literature, and licentious behavior. He seemed particularly at home in his London club, the Savile, with its cultural associations and membership. There at one of the round tables, where strangers meet and conversation flows, only Bill Ober was able to eat strawberries and cream after a vast helping of the club's famous fish pie. He was never spared problems yet he enjoyed life and good company to the end.

A TRIBUTE

from Matthew J. Bruccoli

Literature did not supplement William Ober's life: it was integral to his life. Once after lunch at his London club Bill proposed that we go to Gough Square and pay our respects to Dr. Johnson because it was the proper thing for a couple of writers to do.

Wallace Stegner

(18 February 1909 – 13 April 1993)

Suzanne Ferguson
Case Western Reserve University

See also the Stegner entry in *DLB 9: American Novelists, 1910–1945,* 3 parts.

BOOKS: *Clarence Edward Dutton: An Appraisal* (Salt Lake City: University of Utah Press, 1935);

Remembering Laughter (Boston: Little, Brown, 1937; London: Heinemann, 1937);

The Potter's House (Muscatine, Iowa: Prairie Press, 1938);

On a Darkling Plain (New York: Harcourt, Brace, 1940);

Fire and Ice (New York: Duell, Sloan & Pearce, 1941);

Mormon Country (New York: Duell, Sloan & Pearce, 1942);

The Big Rock Candy Mountain (New York: Duell, Sloan & Pearce, 1943; London: Hammond, Hammond, 1950);

One Nation, by Stegner and the editors of *Look* (Boston: Houghton Mifflin, 1945);

Second Growth (Boston: Houghton Mifflin, 1947; London: Hammond, Hammond, 1948);

The Preacher and the Slave (Boston: Houghton Mifflin, 1950; London: Hammond, Hammond, 1951); republished as *Joe Hill: A Biographical Novel* (Garden City, N.Y.: Doubleday, 1969);

The Women on the Wall (Boston: Houghton Mifflin, 1950; London: Hammond, Hammond, 1952);

The Writer in America (Tokyo: Hokuseido Press, 1951; Folcroft, Pa.: Folcroft Press, 1969);

Beyond the Hundredth Meridian: John Wesley Powell and the Second Opening of the West (Boston: Houghton Mifflin, 1954);

The City of the Living, and Other Stories (Boston: Houghton Mifflin, 1956; London: Hammond, Hammond, 1957);

A Shooting Star (New York: Viking, 1961; London: Heinemann, 1961);

Wolf Willow: A History, a Story, and a Memory of the Last Plains Frontier (New York: Viking, 1962; London: Heinemann, 1963);

The Gathering of Zion: The Story of the Mormon Trail (New York: McGraw-Hill, 1964; London: Eyre & Spottiswoode, 1966);

Teaching the Short Story, Davis Publications in English, no. 2 (Davis: Department of English, University of California, Davis, 1966);

All the Little Live Things (New York: Viking, 1967; London: Heinemann, 1968);

The Sound of Mountain Water (Garden City, N.Y.: Doubleday, 1969);

Discovery! The Search for Arabian Oil (Beirut: Middle East Export Press, 1971);

Angle of Repose (Garden City, N.Y.: Doubleday, 1971; London: Heinemann, 1971);

Robert Frost and Bernard De Voto (Stanford, Cal.: Associates of the Stanford University Libraries, 1974);

The Uneasy Chair: A Biography of Bernard De Voto (Garden City, N.Y.: Doubleday, 1974);

The Spectator Bird (Garden City, N.Y.: Doubleday, 1976; London: Prior, 1978);

Recapitulation (Garden City, N.Y.: Doubleday, 1979);

American Places, with Eliot Porter and Page Stegner (New York: Dutton, 1981);

One Way to Spell Man (Garden City, N.Y.: Doubleday, 1982);

20-20 Vision: In Celebration of the Peninsula Hills (Palo Alto, Cal.: Green Foothills Foundation, 1982);

Conversations with Wallace Stegner on Western History and Literature, with Richard W. Etulain (Salt Lake City: University of Utah Press, 1983);

Crossing to Safety (New York: Random House, 1987);

The American West as Living Space (Ann Arbor: University of Michigan Press, 1987);

The Collected Stories of Wallace Stegner (New York: Random House, 1990);

Where the Bluebird Sings to the Lemonade Springs: Living and Writing in the West (New York: Random House, 1992).

The writing career of Wallace Stegner spanned over fifty years and the genres of short story, novella, novel, essay, biography, and history. His first novella was published as a result of a prize competition (by Little, Brown, in 1938), and he received such prizes as the 1972 Pulitzer Prize (for *Angle of Repose,* 1971), the 1977 National Book Award (for *The Spectator Bird,* 1976), three O. Henry First Prize awards for short stories (1942, 1950, 1954, and numerous inclusions in the O. Henry and Best Short Stories in America volumes). He held membership in the National Institute and Academy of Arts and Letters and the American Academy of Arts and Sciences; held Guggenheim (twice), Rockefeller, and National Endowment for the Humanities senior fellowships; was a fellow at the Center for Advanced Studies in the Behavioral Sciences in 1955–1956; was writer in residence at the American Academy in Rome in 1960; and received several honorary degrees and other awards. In 1992 he was selected for a National Medal of Arts from the National Endowment for the Arts but rejected it in protest of "political controls" over the agency in its director's denial of grants for peer-recommended projects, apparently because of their "offensive" content. Along with *Angle of Repose* and *The Spectator Bird,* at least two other books will be central to his lasting reputation as a novelist: *The Big Rock Candy Mountain* (1943) and *Crossing to Safety* (1987). Additionally, a substantial number of short stories, essays, and several of the longer nonfiction works — especially *Beyond the Hundredth Meridian* (1954) and *The Gathering of Zion* (1964) — will also remain important in the annals of American belles lettres and history.

Wallace Stegner was born at the Lake Mills, Iowa, home of his maternal grandparents on 18 February 1909, the second and last son of George and Hilda Paulson Stegner. His parents and older brother, Cecil, lived at the time in Grand Forks, North Dakota, where his mother had earlier gone to stay with a relative when her own widowed father chose to remarry one of his daughter's close friends. In Grand Forks she had met George Stegner, described in one instance by his son as "a boomer, a gambler, a rainbow-chaser, as footloose as a tumbleweed in a windstorm." His mother, on the other hand, "was always hopefully, hopelessly trying to nest." His family and its history are portrayed in detail in Stegner's first indubitable masterpiece, *The Big Rock Candy Mountain.* The young family followed in the wake of George Stegner's quest to "make a killing," as his son would characterize it: to Bellingham and Redmond, Washington (in the latter of

Wallace Stegner

which they lived in a tent and operated a café for loggers); Seattle (where the boys were apparently lodged for a time in an orphanage); and back to Lake Mills. From the ages of about six to twelve, Stegner lived with his family in East End, Saskatchewan (the "Whitemud" of *The Big Rock Candy Mountain* and various early short stories; spelled "Eastend" on contemporary maps and located near Saskatchewan's borders with Montana and Alberta), where his father engaged in a progressively disastrous venture into wheat farming. Stegner also wrote of the East End years in his memoir cum history, *Wolf Willow* (1962).

The inhospitable climate broke the farmer; the family house burned; they survived — barely — the flu epidemic of 1918; George Stegner turned to bootlegging; and the family moved on, first over the border to Great Falls, Montana, for about two years, then in 1921 to Salt Lake City. Even when they stayed in one town, they moved restlessly from house to house. Stegner has said that in the decade they spent in Salt Lake City, the family inhabited at least a dozen houses. In Salt Lake City, George Stegner turned to speculation in mining and grain futures, and he was for a time relatively successful. Wallace Stegner remained in Utah about fifteen years, entering the University of Utah in the fall of 1925 at the age of sixteen. He supported himself by selling rugs and linoleum, staying out of school one year simply to work. Following his parents briefly to Los Angeles, where they had moved, young Stegner enrolled at the University of California, Los Angeles, for a semester.

His freshman English teacher at Utah was the young novelist Vardis Fisher, who encouraged Stegner to think of himself as a writer and helped guide his budding career. In the fall of 1930 he enrolled as a graduate student at the University of Iowa. In Stegner's first year there his brother Cecil became suddenly ill with pneumonia and died. Shortly after, Hilda Stegner was discovered to have cancer. She now lived with her husband in Reno, Nevada, where he operated a casino, the Northern Club. In 1933, after an appallingly painful illness and having asked to move back to Salt Lake City for her last days, Hilda Stegner died. Stegner had completed his master's thesis, a group of short stories, at Iowa in 1932. The stress and disorder of his mother's illness interrupted his education (he had planned to continue at the University of California, Berkeley), but he reenrolled at Iowa in the spring of 1934, where he met and within a few months married another graduate student, Mary Stuart Page. The strength and stability of this marriage is hinted at in the dedication of his final book, the collection of essays, *Where the Bluebird Sings to the Lemonade Springs* (1992), which is "for Mary, who, like Dilsey, has seen the first and last, and been indispensable and inspiriting all the way." Stegner taught at Augustana College in Rock Island, Illinois, then at the University of Utah, while completing his Ph.D. His dissertation, under the direction of Norman Foerster, was a study of the American naturalist Clarence Edward Dutton, published by the University of Utah in 1935. Wallace and Mary's only child, Page, was born in 1937. George Stegner died broke and a suicide in 1940. Like his father Page Stegner became a writer and English professor, for many years at the University of California, Santa Cruz.

Responding to the announcement in the fall of 1936 of a prize contest by Little, Brown publishing house, Stegner wrote his first substantial piece of fiction, *Remembering Laughter*. Forrest G. and Margaret G. Robinson, in their Twayne study, *Wallace Stegner* (1977), describe it as being based on "a skeleton . . . from Mary's family closet" and report that it was written within eight weeks. It won the prize of twenty-five hundred dollars and earned nearly another two thousand dollars for publication in *Redbook* in 1937. In the fall of that year, Stegner accepted a position teaching freshman English at the University of Wisconsin and began to work out *The Big Rock Candy Mountain*. Before was finished, however, he wrote and had published several short sto-

ries and three more short novels: *The Potter's House* (1938); *On a Darkling Plain* (1940), and *Fire and Ice* (1941), along with his first study of the Mormons, *Mormon Country* (1942).

In the summer of 1938 Stegner began teaching at Bread Loaf Writers' Conference, and the Stegners purchased what would be the family's perennial summer home in Greensboro, Vermont. By the fall of 1939 he was on the composition staff of Harvard University, where he remained until 1946, when at the behest of one of his Breadloaf colleagues, Edith Mirrielees, he moved to Stanford to replace her as head of the creative-writing program. With time off for travel and guest appointments, he stayed at Stanford as Jackson Eli Reynolds Professor of the Humanities, until his early retirement in 1971. He and Mary Stegner continued to live in their custom-designed home in the Los Altos Hills, summering in Vermont, until his death on 13 April 1993 from complications following a 28 March automobile accident he had while he was in Santa Fe for a speaking engagement.

The early short novels, while competent and serious, gave but little hint of the magnitude and power of *The Big Rock Candy Mountain*. *Remembering Laughter* tells of the triangle that develops when a puritanical wife's younger and more lively sister comes from Scotland to live with the couple on their Iowa farm. The husband and sister have an affair, resulting in the birth of a son. Rather than break up the family, the wife forces the husband and her sister to live a life of cold, silent penance. The son is raised not knowing for sure who his parents are until after the father's death. He leaves to make his own life, and the two sisters, now in apparent amity, continue to live together, though the only delight of their lives is the "remember[ed] laughter" of their youth. Some of Stegner's recurrent themes appear here: the vigorous, somewhat irresponsible husband; the working out of a marital infidelity with a difficult truce and punishment within the family; the disaffected son's setting out on his own quest for adult identity. Although Stegner has reported that he did not read Edith Wharton's *Ethan Frome* (1911) until after writing *Remembering Laughter,* the melodrama of the situation recalls Wharton's short novel, though it is told from a different point of view. Another suggested influence is Vardis Fisher's *Dark Bridwell* (1931), which has a similar married couple as protagonists.

With his next novella, *The Potter's House*, Stegner strayed even further from what would be his true subject and gift. Here a deaf artisan whose wife is also handicapped allows himself to be talked into voluntary sterilization after having a series of deaf children (and one favored daughter who can hear and whom he encourages in music); sensing rejection, his wife is alienated and goes to the bad, and the family disintegrates. *On Darkling Plain,* with its title from Matthew Arnold's paean to disillusionment and social disaffection, "Dover Beach," takes place in Stegner's true "home country," the Saskatchewan prairie. Set just after World War I, it deals with a young and isolated veteran who lives as a recluse on the fringes of the town, believing that he can withdraw from human folly and evil. Repelled by the human destructiveness he has witnessed in the war, the hero, Edwin Vickers, begins to learn the positive values of social support and to fall in love with the innocent but enthusiastic daughter of one of his farmer neighbors. The influenza epidemic comes to the village, and the girl dies. Vickers is drawn into the service of burying the dead, and in the end he dies himself. Stegner's own memories of the epidemic and the landscape and people of East End give the work a kind of vitality lacking in *The Potter's House. On a Darkling Plain* pursues the typically Stegnerian motifs of individuality versus community and of the waste and destructiveness in which humans subvert their strength and virtue. Richard Simpson described its burden as "that brotherhood is achieved by grim and often costly struggle, not by vague idealism or empty political sloganeering, Marxist or otherwise."

The fourth of the short novels that preceded *The Big Rock Candy Mountain* again seemed a step backward in Stegner's development. Like *Remembering Laughter,* written in a period of a few weeks, *Fire and Ice* takes up the tribulations of a young Marxist, Paul Condon, who identifies with the Young Communist's League of Madison (whose meetings Stegner had briefly attended in his two years at the University of Wisconsin). Here Stegner chose his title from the sardonic, epigrammatic lyric by his Bread Loaf colleague and friend, Robert Frost, comparing the respective claims of the "fire" and the "ice" of human passion for ending the world. Though he pays lip service to the party line, Condon is at heart a renegade individualist who cannot discipline himself to put the party before his own desires and opinions. In a drunken escapade he tries to seduce, then to rape, a young, pretty, "capitalist" fellow student and wakes up in jail. Humiliated and putatively wiser, he leaves town, rejecting communism, which provided such easy and false answers to human problems. The Robinsons propose that Condon's difficulties are traceable in the novel to his own neurotic personality, thus undercutting his

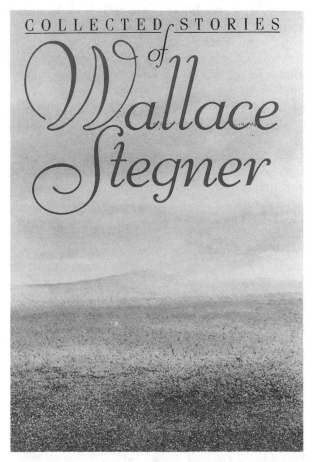

Dust jacket for the collection of Stegner's stories written from the late 1930s through the late 1980s

contention that it is the party which has led him astray. They write, "Because it tampers with the internal logic of its plot, *Fire and Ice* strikes us as a confused, and, therefore, as a weak argument."

It was with the completion and publication of *The Big Rock Candy Mountain* in 1943 – characterized by Joseph Flora and other critics as "panoramic" – that Stegner first fully realized his talent and his true subject matter: the character of the settlers of that last American frontier, the Canadian west. This book's title comes from a "hobo ballad" attributed to Harry McClintock in 1928 (that Stegner says he heard his father sing many years before) which captures the peculiar qualities of the American dream pursued by Stegner's father and others of his kind: "In the Big Rock Candy Mountains / There's a land that's fair and bright / Where the hand-outs grow on bushes / And you sleep out every night. . . . there's a lake of stew and of whiskey to . . ." and, of course, "the bluebird sings / To the lemonade springs." Stegner's passion to understand the lives of his parents, George and Hilda Stegner, by telling their story as the Bo and Elsa Mason of the novel and his wish to see himself (as Bruce Mason) in relation to his parents and brother (Chet Mason) through fiction's lens, along with the ever-powerful memories of the years in East End, allowed him to produce his first genuine masterpiece and one of the handful of books that makes him a major American novelist.

Stegner had published pieces of *The Big Rock Candy Mountain* as a series of short stories in the *Atlantic Monthly, Harper's,* the *Virginia Quarterly Review,* and the *Southwest Review* between 1938 and 1943. These stories – "Bugle Song," "Chip Off the Old Block," "The Colt," "Butcher Bird," "Goin' to Town," and "Two Rivers" – form illustrative and crucial "moments" – each one to some extent traumatic – of the novel and its characters. Stegner's habit of working up a novel from what originally took form as stories is not, of course, unusual, but it points to a characteristic quality of his practice: the tendency to return to a "story" – or the "story stuff," the life conflict or event – to probe it for further meaning or for a resolution to problems that were not satisfactorily solved by the original telling. Thus Stegner returns to the character of his alter ego Bruce Mason for additional exploration in his 1979 novel, *Recapitulation,* which itself began with another short story: "Maiden in a Tower," first published in *Harper's* in 1954. This recursiveness bespeaks not a lack of imagination, but rather the contrary – the ability to reimagine and rethink causes and motivations, to find the universal of these particulars.

Although Joseph Warren Beach found *The Big Rock Candy Mountain* (in the *New York Times Book Review*) lacking "an artistic individuality that speaks with authority," he nonetheless recognized the larger-than-life characterizations of Elsa and Bo Mason. The latter, he wrote, "is a fascinating figure, many-faceted and intensely human, interesting in himself, and doubly interesting as the typical man (or grown-up boy) . . . ." Beach also recognizes Stegner's aspiration to be the "voice" of the Northwest "as it was passing from the pioneer to the settled agricultural stage" and notes that he had "felt the spell of mountain and prairie, of drought, flood and blizzard." Many critics have pointed out the "once in a lifetime" nature of *The Big Rock Candy Mountain:* This was Stegner's personal history, and the effort of understanding it not simply as his own life but that of the closing frontier was extraordinary. Stegner admits in at least one interview that he wrote some of it "through tears." Yet there is little that one might see as sentimental in the book; all

three main characters – the unwittingly destructive Bo, the saintly Elsa, and the struggling child and adolescent Bruce – are drawn with a fine blend of sympathy and judgment. The narrative focus shifts among them, so that each is seen on his or her own terms at least part of the time. The omniscient author strives for neutrality; and indeed the actions speak much for themselves.

The effort of picking apart and recreating his past in *The Big Rock Candy Mountain* seems to have exhausted the novelist's energies for a time. The resettlement to California and the development of the Graduate Writing Program at Stanford into one of the top two or three in the nation doubtless took a good deal of his attention; and, of course, he kept on writing short stories. An undistinguished novel, *Second Growth,* appeared in 1947. Recounting the "second growth" of an old New Hampshire village as a summer resort, it draws upon Stegner's New England experiences as well as his effort to understand various contemporary social dislocations: a Jewish refugee couple's attempts to integrate themselves into the community are rebuffed; an educated "hometown" girl retreats into suicide after being drawn to an aggressive lesbian summer visitor; a sensitive young man decides to leave the town, rejecting the seductive pull of "the autumn woods and the mown meadows and the tarnished silver farms . . . the narrow security that it would be fatal to accept."

Stegner's interest in the history of his region had already been demonstrated in his dissertation and his first long essay on the Mormons, *Mormon Country.* As a youth in Salt Lake City he had become interested in the contrast between the highly socialized Mormons and their Gentile (that is, non-Mormon) neighbors – in general individualists, sometimes to the extreme, like his father. Forrest G. and Margaret G. Robinson have analyzed the interaction of personal experience and historical research in Stegner's work, his inability to write "pure" – that is, "objective" – history or even to write traditional narrative history. His habit of blending fiction with history and telling history with fictional techniques may have been regarded as weaknesses at first, but they have come to be appreciated as strengths both by historians and general readers. *Mormon Country* begins with a vignette of a rural teenage girl at a Mutual, a mixed social and religious meeting. Succeeding chapters of the first part of the book take up the various elements of the fictionalized meeting and, consequently, of Mormon culture. The antithesis of Mormon culture, "The Might of the Gentile," is explored in part

2: with a few exceptions – John Wesley Powell or paleontologist Earl Douglass, for examples – the Gentiles were not only a threat to the Mormons but to the land itself. These mountaineers, miners, railroaders, and cattlemen are portrayed as having come to loot the land, many times leaving it waste. Although there were "bad" Mormons as well, Stegner tends to see (or present) a basically positive picture of Mormon society, choosing to ignore its darker side. In 1964 Stegner published *The Gathering of Zion,* a more detailed, nuanced history, focused specifically on the migration of the pioneer Saints from the Mississippi River to the Great Salt Lake after their expulsion from Nauvoo, Illinois, in 1846; the history ends in 1869. Here Stegner's storytelling skills have full scope. The Robinsons judge *The Gathering of Zion* to be "informed, imaginative, dramatic to good effect, [and] superbly written."

Between the two studies of the Mormons, Stegner had turned his attention to two other "Westerners": the Wobbly songwriter and agitator Joe Hill and the self-made naturalist and public servant, John Wesley Powell, who among other enterprises led the exploration of the Grand Canyon in 1869, headed the U.S. Geographical and Geological Survey of the Rocky Mountain region, and produced several important ethnographic studies of the western Indians. Typically for Stegner, one study had turned into a novel, the other into a biography enlivened by a narrative approach having all the drama and characterization of excellent fiction. The Joe Hill book, called *The Preacher and the Slave* (1950), was republished in 1969 as *Joe Hill.* In some respects it was very much a precursor of Truman Capote's *In Cold Blood* (1966) as well as Stegner's own later documentary fiction, notably *Angle of Repose.* Stegner used documentary materials, especially of the trial; he walked Utah's death row in the footsteps of Hill (executed 19 November 1915); but he also invented appropriate incidents for the early part of the book, in which the historical record was sketchy or nonexistent. Ultimately siding with those who believed that Hill had in fact committed the murders for which he was executed, Stegner was rebuked by those who thought otherwise. In Hill, Stegner saw another incarnation of Bo Mason/George Stegner: the individualistic loner and dreamer, prone to violence and lawlessness.

Hill's opposite, though still handicapped by a certain individualistic arrogance, is Powell, whose career is set within the larger history of the settlement of the arid lands of the West. From naturalists as well as literary critics, the current consensus is that in *Beyond the Hundredth Meridian* Stegner not only wrote powerful, reliable history, but framed the terms in which continuing environmental concerns must be seen. T. H. Watkins, editor of *Wilderness Magazine,* has said "You cannot . . . understand the history of the American West without reading his biography of John Wesley Powell." At the same time, no novel could easily surpass the book's vitality of description or vigor of narrative.

By 1956 Stegner had two volumes of short stories out: *The Women on the Wall* (1950) and *The City of the Living* (1956), but this search for a novel to go beyond *The Big Rock Candy Mountain* was still largely stymied. In *A Shooting Star* (1961) he produced a "California" novel that does begin to open up the characters and themes that were to be more memorably realized in *All the Little Live Things, Angle of Repose,* and *The Spectator Bird:* the contemporary dilemma of the suburban westerner trying to live with and in the culture of greed and individualism that had lured Bo Mason to his destruction decades before. In a way *A Shooting Star* might be seen as a post–F. Scott Fitzgerald novel, in which one of the careless people tries to clean up her own mess. Having frittered away her youth in a sterile marriage, its well-to-do heroine, Sabrina Castro, is seen at the beginning of the novel revealing her adultery to her emotionally inept physician husband, a scion of native Californians of Hispanic descent. The affair soon ends, with Sabrina left pregnant. After a period of moral deterioration, she tries to recover or discover her own identity and to reestablish ties with her wealthy and isolated mother, the daughter of a highly placed New England family who was uprooted and transplanted to the West through her own marriage. Attempting to protect both her aged mother and parcel of land she and her mother own from her rapacious, financially successful brother (who believes his mother is mentally incompetent simply because she sees no point in making more money by developing her land), Sabrina is assisted in resolving her personal problems as well as taking up the environmental cause by the MacDonalds, Barbara and Leonard. They are a couple with several children and a baby on the way; Barbara was a friend in Sabrina's youth, and Leonard is a schoolteacher with a preachy temperament and a strong interest in the environment and community. Although the book sold well (it was a Literary Guild selection), it has not had the staying power of the novels that came after it, quite possibly because of a basic unattractiveness of the characters: those who are "bad" are not very interestingly bad, and those who are good seem priggish and unnatural.

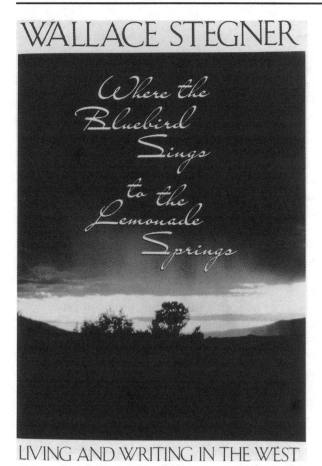

WALLACE STEGNER

Where the Bluebird Sings to the Lemonade Springs

LIVING AND WRITING IN THE WEST

Dust jacket for Stegner's collection of essays about western writing and living in the West

Coming at the virtual center of his fifty-year career, and culminating years of alternating history with fiction, Stegner's most experimental and likely most characteristic and original work is the 1962 *Wolf Willow,* subtitled "A History, a Story, and Memory of the Last Plains Frontier." Historian Merle Curti saw it as "fusing poetry, romance, realism and scholarship." The book begins and ends as Stegner's memoir of his own childhood experience of East End/"Whitemud," Saskatchewan. Drawing upon his personal memories, jogged and amplified by those of several of his old childhood friends and gathered on a pilgrimage/research expedition in 1953, Stegner re-creates that world of his youth in a provincial, unlovely, dirt-poor western Canadian village of the second decade of the twentieth century. He then sets out to tell the exemplary history of the region itself – of the Indians and settlers, the builders and the pillagers who passed through this forbidding, awe-inspiring landscape.

Supported by a grant from the Wenner Gren Foundation for Anthropological Research, Stegner had proposed to do a full-scale historical/ethnographic study of several small-town cultures in which he had a personal interest: East End; Greensboro, Vermont; and a Danish island in the Baltic Sea from which his ancestors had come. What emerged was both less than that and much more. Vermont and Denmark were set aside, and, in the memoir and fictional sections of *Wolf Willow,* the typical activities of everyday frontier life ground the historical record and analysis. Stegner explained the task of creating a history of a place that had never seen the need for one in several interviews, including Richard W. Etulain's *Conversations with Wallace Stegner on Western History and Literature* (1983). About two-thirds of the way through this narrative, however, he turns from both memoir and history to fiction ("Genesis") to tell what it was like to be a cowboy through a desperate winter storm from the point of view not of a "local" boy or a man remembering, but of a "tenderfoot" Englishman working with the cowboys. The next chapter is also a short story ("Carrion Spring"), which follows "Genesis" in fictional time, but it is told from a roving omniscient point of view. It traces how a young couple make the decision to stay in the brutal region and try again to succeed in farming, although their experience up to that point has been demoralizing and threatening to their relationship. Here Stegner's understanding of how fiction works to find the "truth" about experience is graphically juxtaposed to the historically truthful record, which gives the facts but cannot tell what it might have felt like to be a part of that history. (In an interview, Stegner claimed for his method the sanction of Robert Frost, who said "all an artist needs are samples" to get at the truth). Yet the most movingly truthful parts of *Wolf Willow* are in fact the memoirs, which use the techniques of fiction – the first-person narrator looking back to his youth, description, dialogue, "character" analysis, and sometimes even plot – to bring to vivid life the ugly, beautiful, arresting, bleak existence of this particular past.

In his next novel, *All the Little Live Things* (1967), Stegner was able to bring together several strands of his experience and feelings and to look at them through a lens that manages to embody and critique them at once: the first-person narrator of the long story "A Field Guide to the Western Birds" (1956) the irascible bird-watcher and person watcher, Joe Allston, who would return as narrator and protagonist of *The Spectator Bird. All the Little Live Things* revives the sweet, heroic woman character earlier portrayed in Elsa Mason and Barbara McDonald, here Marian Catlin, who loves "all the little live things," including gophers, poison oak, and all the other pests and weeds Joe tries vainly to extirpate from his garden. This character has not only a greater articulateness than her earlier avatars, but an almost unearthly vision of good in the contemporary universe. The novel's setting is indistinguishable from the Los Altos Hills site of Stegner's own residence. Like Ella, Marian Catlin is stricken with cancer while young. Her struggle to postpone death until her child can be born and Joe's struggle to understand why she is marked for suffering and death when the reprehensible developers and irresponsible hippie opportunists such as the scruffy, exploitative, careless Jim Peck seem to thrive are the twin themes that drive the plot. Peck, a dropout graduate student who is otherwise rather like the mature Bo Mason – promiscuous, contemptuous of authority, scruffy, arrogant – is a thoroughly unlikable figure, to Stegner as well as Joe, one senses.

All the various characters and plot threads come together in a horrendous accident as Joe tries to take Marian to the hospital where her baby is to be born (it dies) and she is to die, an accident left "waiting to happen" by Peck and the developers whom Joe has tried to fend off of the valuable real estate. The plot, characters, and style of *All the Little Live Things* are all polished and sure; and the Allston narrator allows Stegner to express his own feelings while revealing enough idiosyncrasy and limitation that Allston is distinct from the author. ("I gave him a lot of my prejudices and none of my profound thoughts," Stegner said to Suzanne Ferguson in an interview. If the book does not reach the level of achievement of *Angle of Repose,* it may be because it is too bound into its own historical moment and Stegner's never-resolved anger and pain from his mother's death or perhaps, as Granville Hicks complained in the *Saturday Review,* because the characters are not "people [but] embodiments of ideas."

In another of his revisitations of a complex character, Stegner revives Allston nearly a decade later to explore his own family drama in *The Spectator Bird.* This short novel won the National Book Award for 1977 and remains eminently readable. In it the now-seventy-year-old Allston (a retired literary agent) finds himself fairly miserable in his well-off, protected environment, angry at the daily news and angry at youth, at American society, and even at his long-patient wife, Ruth. Through a diary that he kept from a visit twenty years earlier to Denmark in search of his "roots" (similar to one the Stegners took while he was engaged in the anthropological research for the Wenner Gren Foundation grant) and to get away from grief over the perhaps accidental, perhaps suicidal surfing death of their only son at age thirty-seven, a diary read aloud at her insistence to Ruth, the reader learns that Joe was attracted at that time to an exotic and exciting friend – perhaps even a cousin – the countess Astrid Wredel-Krarup (based upon writer Isak Dinesen). The countess's family is racked with the results of experiments in genetic engineering via incest practiced by her father and apparently continued by her brother; and both she and Joe realize that they cannot pursue their attraction at Ruth's (albeit unknowing) expense. The revelations of the diary, however, cause an estrangement from Ruth that must be actively overcome. Meanwhile Joe is also working out his feelings toward his son, who was "nothing but anguish from the time he was breech-born." The reconciliation of Ruth and Joe, his recognition of what she has meant to his life, is moving as well as instructive. In this meditation on aging in late-twentieth-century America, Stegner tapped a streak of discontent and restitution that touched a sensitive chord for many readers.

Between these two excellent and characteristic novels came the book that most critics, if they had to pick, would likely designate as Stegner's "masterpiece," in which his inquiry into the themes of personal fulfillment and responsibility link up with his love and knowledge of western history, and the technique of the fallible narrator allows these explorations to achieve the resonance of rereading within the plot. There is an actual historical subject and quarry for *Angle of Repose,* the papers of author and illustrator Mary Hallock Foote (1847–1938), which had been in the Stanford library for years and in which Stegner had maintained an interest from the time they were first called to his attention by a graduate student. In the novel Foote becomes Susan Burling Ward, an imaginative and civilized woman brought west by her engineer husband, Oliver. Stegner's extensive use of Foote's own words in combination with a seeming desire to keep this use obscure provoked a challenge from Mary Ellen Williams Walsh, in her 1982 article, "*Angle of Repose* and the Writings of Mary Hallock Foote: A Source Study." Stegner defended both the use and the seeming lack of forthrightness by invoking the privacy rights of the family on the one hand and the quality of the writing on the other – to have paraphrased would not only have weakened the narrative, but would have been reprehensible in burying Foote's authentic voice. Here, as in the story of Joe Hill, Stegner has hewn close to his documentary sources: according to Walsh unjustifiably close and

Program cover for the memorial service held in honor of
Wallace Stegner

Stegner's old mentor, Norman Foerster, in his later life), having been left by his wife (who now wishes to return), Lyman is a more scholarly, more complex, more put-upon Joe Allston. In the course of his research with his grandmother's papers, Lyman discovers evidence that he believes points to her having had an affair which distracted her while her young daughter wandered off and drowned. Oliver, believing the worst of his wife and grieving for his daughter, had torn up a rose garden he planted in the wilderness for his wife. Yet they had stayed together, and Lyman now "rereads" his own youthful experience of his grandparents, who had seemed to the young boy a normal, peaceful older married couple. Reminiscent of *Remembering Laughter,* Lyman speculates a life of penitence and alienation for Susan and cool rectitude for Oliver. He recalls, now, that he has never seen them touch each other. He wonders, in the end, if he will "be man enough to be more of a man than [his] grandfather" and forgive his wife for her infidelity. But, as critic Audrey Peterson has suggested, the reader may well conclude differently, seeing in Oliver's having planted a new rose garden a new conjugal relationship that Lyman, in his own rigidity and pain, misses. Any brief summary must fail to do justice to *Angle of Repose,* a book rich in history, in family, in the exploration of how fiction can probe, illuminate, and restore life. Responding to its engagement with serious American themes, the Pulitzer Prize Committee awarded the book its 1972 prize for fiction. The novel was also the basis for an opera composed by Andrew Imbrie, with libretto by Oakley Hall, performed in San Francisco in 1976.

Between *Angle of Repose* and *The Spectator Bird,* Stegner again ventured into the biographical mode with *The Uneasy Chair* (1974), the life of his longtime friend Bernard De Voto, a Salt Lake native and staunch environmentalist who had for some thirty years occupied the "Easy Chair" editorial column for *Harper's Magazine* and who died in 1955 at the age of fifty-eight. This substantial book was also an opportunity for Stegner to review the literary and cultural history of his own era. After *The Uneasy Chair,* Stegner produced an edition of the *Letters of Bernard De Voto* (1976).

By then approaching his own seventieth year, Stegner was at work on the novel *Recapitulation,* noted above as the reexamination of his character Bruce Mason, from *The Big Rock Candy Mountain,* as well as reworking the situation of the short story "Maiden in a Tower" (1954). At the end of *The Big Rock Candy Mountain,* Bruce is leaving Salt Lake City, still grieving for his mother's early, painful

without the permission of some of Foote's heirs (though he had the assent of those most responsible for the papers). This ethical and political dilemma forms an interesting footnote to the novel. Rather than edit the papers or write a biography, as many feminist scholars would have done, Stegner judged Foote not worthy of a biography in her own right but an exemplary figure whose writing was an ideal basis for a fictional character that he would ultimately come to see and portray in a negative light.

Although certainly a good deal of the power and conviction of the novel comes from Foote's "voice," Stegner has set her story and those of her husband and her confidante, "Augusta Drake," within the narrative of Susan Burling Ward's grandson, Lyman Ward. Lyman's quest for his own identity is apparent in his researching and writing the history of his grandparents. Paralyzed, with one leg amputated (suffering infirmities borrowed from death, his older brother's shocking and sudden demise, and coming to grips with the suicide of his father, down and out for the last time in a cheap Reno motel. Returning years later to Salt Lake City to attend the funeral of an aunt, his father's sister, he finds that the funeral home was once an apartment house in which two of his early college girlfriends had lived. This realization provokes him to revisit that past in memory, probing the meaning of his youth from the vantage point of his celibate, isolated middle age. In addition to "Maiden in a Tower," Stegner drew upon two other stories for *Recapitulation:* "The Volunteer" (1956) and "The Blue-Winged Teal" (1950), the latter one of his finest works. This mining of works over twenty years old again confirms Stegner's relentless thoughtfulness, his persistence in using fiction's lens to reexamine life. As he grew older, he seems to have hoped newfound wisdom would shed further light on the human experiences of his own and America's past.

There was one more novel, almost another decade in coming: *Crossing to Safety.* For it Stegner returned to consider a friendship he and Mary had with another couple while they were young married colleagues, and then parents, in Madison, Wisconsin, in the 1930s. The book, first published in a limited edition by the Franklin Press for its subscribers, went into six printings from Random House as a hardcover book before being issued in paperback by Viking Penguin in 1988. A February 1992 appreciation in the *Washington Post* by David Streitfeld notes that it had "nearly 250,000 copies in print" by that time. Its theme is the difficulty of nurturing and maintaining friendship, even among the best intentioned, most civilized of peers. The narrator is a novelist called Larry Morgan; he muses on the nature of friendship: "There are no rules or obligations or bonds as in marriage or the family, it is held together by neither law nor property nor blood, there is no glue in it but mutual liking. It is therefore rare." And it requires forbearance, tolerance, and determination to survive the various vicissitudes of maturing and aging, success and failure, illness or idiosyncrasy. Through Morgan, Stegner is able to reflect in fiction rather than essay on what he has learned about human nature in his nearly eight decades of living, watching, and writing.

Larry Morgan and his wife Sally, who was stricken soon after the birth of their daughter, Lang, with polio that has left her ever after in braces and a wheelchair, look back at their own past and the joys and vicissitudes of their friends, Sid and Charity Lang, as they visit Charity shortly before her death of cancer. Some of Charity's grownup children urge Larry to tell their parents' story, so that it will become comprehensible to them. Undoubtedly voicing some of Stegner's own concerns about "using" real people in fiction, Larry says, "You can't write about your friends. . . . you've got the wrong idea of what writers do. They don't understand any more than other people. They invent only plots they can resolve. They ask the questions they can answer. Those aren't people that you see in books, those are constructs. Novels or biographies, it makes no difference. I couldn't reproduce the real Sid and Charity Lang, much less explain them; and if I invented them I'd be falsifying something I don't want to falsify." Conscious also – as Stegner stressed in interviews about the book – that there was nothing sensational in this narrative of the Langs and Morgans, Larry asks himself, "How do you make a book that anyone will read out of lives as quiet as these? . . . Where is the high life, the conspicuous waste, the violence, the kinky sex, the death wish? . . . Where are the hatreds, the political ambitions, the list for power? Where are speed, noise, ugliness, everything that makes us who we are and makes us recognize ourselves in fiction?" Yet precisely that ordinariness, and the mysteriousness of it, makes the Langs interesting to the reader. "They baffle their children because in spite of all they have and are, in spite of being to most eyes an ideal couple, they are remote, unreliable, even harsh. And they have missed something, and show it." The desires of the children to know the parents, to fathom their pain – and of the parents to know their children's lives – have been at the heart of Stegner's best work from the start.

In 1990 thirty-one short stories were reissued by Random House as the *Collected Stories of Wallace Stegner* – the complete contents of *The Women on the Wall* and *The City of the Living,* the two stories from *Wolf Willow,* and half a dozen others. A year later they were published in paperback by Penguin Books. In this new appearance and with a touching introduction by their author, they garnered extensive notice and praise in newspapers nationwide. The short story, the eighty-year-old Stegner wrote, "seems to me a young writer's form, made for discoveries and nuances and epiphanies and superbly adapted for trial syntheses." Though unwilling to call the stories his "autobiography," he admits that they "make a sort of personal record. I lived them, either as participant or spectator or auditor, before I made fictions of them."

Having surveyed all Stegner's novels and taken note of his nonfiction long works, there yet remain three significant books of essays that claim attention, mostly dealing with the West – its environment, its history, its residents, its writers. Of these three essay collections, the first, *The Sound of Mountain Water* (1969) and the last, *Where the Bluebird Sings to the Lemonade Springs,* are indispensable parts of the Stegner canon. In them reminiscence, history, and critical essays appear cheek by jowl, and their introductions are important reflective essays, as well. The famous "Wilderness Letter" Stegner wrote in 1960, originally to someone working on the Outdoor Recreation Resources Review Commission's report to Congress, a letter which was widely circulated by environmental groups, is reprinted in *The Sound of Mountain Water.* Here Stegner makes a powerful plea for the preservation of wilderness: "Something will have gone out of us as a people if we ever let the remaining wilderness be destroyed; if we permit the last virgin forests to be turned into comic books and plastic cigarette cases; if we drive the few remaining members of the wild species into zoos or to extinction; if we pollute the last clear air and dirty the last clean streams and push our paved roads through the last of the silence, so that never again will Americans be free in their own country from the noise, the exhausts, the stinks of human and automotive waste. And so that never again can we have the chance to see ourselves single, separate, vertical and individual in the world, part of the environment of trees and rocks and soil, brother to the other animals, part of the natural world and competent to belong in it. . . ." The letter ends with the phrase, "the geography of hope" – a moving metaphor for the wilderness that "can be a means of reassuring ourselves of our sanity as creatures" – which came to be a defining motto and goal of the American environmental movement.

Additional statements of Stegner's literary poetics (a pretentious word he would not have liked) appear in *One Way to Spell Man* (1982), including the 1951 lecture "Fiction: a Lens on Life." The essay summarizes Stegner's artistic credo, which among other things requires "putting a smear of culture on a slide for inspection under the microscope." He concludes, "a book which has profoundly and intensely moved us is a most intimate experience, perhaps more intimate than marriage and more revealing than fifty years of friendship. We can make closer contact in fiction than in reality; more surely than we know the secrets of our friends. . . . The work of art is not a gem, . . . but truly a lens. We look through it for the purified and honestly offered spirit of the artist." He never deviated from this vi-

sion of the value and power of fiction in nearly forty additional years of writing.

Wallace Stegner also published various and numerous miscellaneous projects and collections, notably including *American Places* (1981; written with his son, Page, to accompany the stunning color landscape photographs of Eliot Porter); the wise little pamphlet *Teaching the Short Story* (1966); and a book he edited, *This Is Dinosaur: Echo Part Country and Its Magic Rivers* (1955), reputed to have been instrumental in saving Dinosaur National Monument from private exploitation and in spurring the formulation of still-current legislation forbidding deleterious development in the national parks and monuments. For further information about Stegner's views on his own work as well as on history, society, and literature, there is a substantial body of interviews, including the book by Etulain noted above and a *Paris Review* interview by James R. Hepworth published in the summer of 1990. Nor are the writings and the interviews the whole public legacy of Wallace Stegner: there are the creative-writing students over the years, such as Wendell Berry, Ken Kesey, Larry McMurtry and a whole host of others; not to mention the literature students who benefited from the wisdom and scholarship of Stegner as well as his always-incisive, helpful comments on writing. There is, moreover, the public service – as a writer on the environment, as assistant to the secretary of the interior (Stewart Udall, 1961–1962), and a member of the National Parks Advisory Board (1962–1966).

Criticism of Stegner's work has been relatively slow in developing: there is to date only one full-length critical study, Margaret G. and Forrest G. Robinson's Twayne study of 1977. Merrill and Lorene Lewis's pamphlet in the Boise State College Western Writers Series (1972) is a judicious survey of the work to that point. The *Critical Essays on Wallace Stegner* volume edited by Anthony Arthur (1982) is a valuable collection of reprinted and original essays, as is the 1985 special edition of the *South Dakota Review* edited by John Milton. An authorized biography, by Jackson Benson, is reportedly in progress. In the latest criticism the established view of Stegner as a western regionalist is increasingly challenged by those who would see him as a national writer. Insofar as the West is a "synechdoche" for America, that argument is persuasive. Stegner's literary techniques and perceptions are strongly based in the realist/impressionist tradition of Henry James and Joseph Conrad. Willa Cather, not Ernest Hemingway or William Faulkner, showed him how to match a style to a subject matter. Eschewing modernist and postmodernist experimentation and reflexivity, Stegner joined the "great tradition" of writers who explore humanist themes through narratives representing the exemplary individuals and the society of their own eras. His bent was historical rather than philosophical or formalist, and the historical and geographical contexts of his fiction contribute powerfully to its authenticity and continuing relevance. A counterpart as well as contemporary of Robert Penn Warren, the southerner who explored the American experience from the vantage point of a major eastern university and continued to write and ponder the meaning of American history well into his eighties, Stegner moved to the outer edge of the West and looked back on American culture from his perch at a great western university: a "spectator bird" who made a difference in many American lives, both in person and as a writer whose thoughtfulness, integrity, and elegant style continue to win new readers.

Interviews:

John Milton, "Conversation with Wallace Stegner," *South Dakota Review*, 9 (Spring 1971): 45–57;

Suzanne Ferguson, "History, Fiction, and Propaganda: The Man of Letters and the American West, an Interview with Wallace Stegner," *Literature and the Visual Arts in Contemporary Society*, edited by Ferguson and Barbara Groseclose (Columbus: Ohio State University Press, 1985), pp. 3–22;

Kay Bonetti, "An Interview with Wallace Stegner," audiotape, American Audio Prose Library, 1987;

Richard W. Etulain, *Conversations with Wallace Stegner on Western History and Literature* (Salt Lake City: University of Utah Press, 1983; revised edition, 1990);

James R. Hepworth, "The Art of Fiction CXVIII: Wallace Stegner," *Paris Review*, 32 (Summer 1990): 59–90.

Bibliography:

Nancy Colberg, *Wallace Stegner*, with an introduction by James R. Hepworth (Lewiston, Idaho: Confluence Press, 1990).

References:

Kerry Ahearn, "Heroes vs. Women: Conflict and Duplicity in Stegner," *Western Humanities Review*, 31 (Spring 1977): 125–141;

Anthony Arthur, ed., *Critical Essays on Wallace Stegner* (Boston: G. K. Hall, 1982);

Chester E. Eisinger, "Twenty Years of Wallace Stegner," *College English*, 20 (December 1958): 10–16;

Joseph Flora, "Wallace Stegner," in *A Literary History of the American West* (Fort Worth: Texas Christian University Press, 1987), pp. 971–988;

Lorene Lewis and Merrill Lewis, *Wallace Stegner* (Boise, Idaho: Boise State College, 1972);

Forrest G. Robinson and Margaret G. Robinson, *Wallace Stegner* (Boston: Twayne, 1977);

Forrest G. Robinson, "Wallace Stegner's Family Saga: From *The Big Rock Candy Mountain* to *Recapitulation*," *Western American Literature*, 17 (August 1982): 102–116;

South Dakota Review, 23, special issue on Stegner (Winter 1985).

Papers:

According to Nancy Colberg, the manuscripts and special collections consist primarily of typescripts, as Stegner habitually wrote on a manual typewriter. Substantial collections of such manuscripts are held by the University of Iowa; Stanford University; the University of Utah; and, more recently, the University of Nevada, Reno.

Literary Awards and Honors Announced in 1993

ACADEMY OF AMERICAN POETS LAVAN YOUNGER POETS PRIZES

Thomas Bolt, David Clewell, Christopher Merrill.

AMERICAN ACADEMY AND INSTITUTE OF ARTS AND LETTERS

ACADEMY-INSTITUTE AWARDS IN LITERATURE

Ellen Akins, Richard Bausch, Vance Bourjaily, Debra Eisenberg, Rolf Fjelde, Tina Howe, Dennis Johnson, A. G. Majtabai.

AWARD OF MERIT FOR DRAMA

David Mamet.

MICHAEL BRAUDE AWARD FOR LIGHT VERSE

Turner Cassity.

WITTER BYNER PRIZE FOR POETRY

Patricia Storace.

E. M. FORSTER AWARD IN LITERATURE

Sean O'Brien.

GOLD MEDAL FOR BELLES LETTRES AND CRITICISM

Elizabeth Hardwick.

SUE KAUFMAN PRIZE FOR FIRST FICTION

Francisco Goldman, *The Long Night of White Chickens* (Atlantic Monthly Press).

MILDRED AND HAROLD STRAUSS LIVINGS AWARDS IN LITERATURE

John Casey, Joy Williams.

ROME FELLOWSHIP IN LITERATURE

Thomas Bolt.

RICHARD AND HILDA ROSENTHAL FOUNDATION AWARD IN LITERATURE

Robert Olen Bulter, *A Good Scent from a Strange Mountain* (Holt).

JEAN STEIN AWARD FOR NONFICTION

Stanley Crouch.

HAROLD D. VURSELL MEMORIAL AWARD IN LITERATURE

T. Coraghessan Boyle.

MORTON DAUWEN ZABEL AWARD IN FICTION

James Purdy.

BANCROFT PRIZES

Charles Capper, *Margaret Fuller: An American Romantic Life; Volume 1: The Private Years* (Oxford University Press).

Melvyn P. Leffler, *A Preponderance of Power: National Security, the Truman Administration, and the Cold War* (Stanford University Press).

IRMA S. AND JAMES H. BLACK AWARD

Katharine Patterson, *King's Equal* (HarperCollins).

BOOKER PRIZE

Roddy Doyle, *Paddy Clark Ha Ha Ha* (Secker & Warburg).

BOSTON GLOBE - HORN BOOK AWARDS

FICTION

James Berry, *Ajeemah and His Son* (HarperCollins).

NONFICTION

Patricia C. McKissack and Frederick McKissack, *Sojourner Truth: Ain't I A Woman?* (Scholastic).

PICTURE-ILLUSTRATION

Lloyd Alexander, *The Fortune-Tellers,* illustrated by Trina Schart-Hyman (Dutton).

JOHN BURROUGHS AWARD FOR NATURE WRITING

Vincent G. Dethier, *Crickets and Cicadas: Concerts and Solos* (Harvard University Press).

RANDOLPH CALDECOTT MEDAL

Emily Arnold McCully, *Mirette on the High Wire* (Putnam).

CHICAGO TRIBUNE LITERARY PRIZES

HEARTLAND PRIZE FOR FICTION
E. Annie Proulx, *The Shipping News* (Scribners).

HEARTLAND PRIZE FOR NONFICTION
Norman Maclean, *Young Men and Fire* (University of Chicago Press).

JAMES FENIMORE COOPER AWARD

Noah Gordon, *Shaman* (Penguin USA/Dutton).

JOHN DOS PASSOS AWARD

William Hoffman.

GOLDEN KITE AWARDS

FICTION
Mary E. Lyons, *Letters from a Slave Girl* (Scribners).

NONFICTION
Jim Murphy, *The Long Road to Gettysburg* (Clarion).

PICTURE
Patricia Polacco, *Chicken Sunday* (Filomel).

DRUE HEINZ LITERATURE PRIZE

Stewart O'Nan, *In the Walled City* (University of Pittsburgh Press).

INGERSOLL PRIZES

T. S. ELIOT AWARD FOR CREATIVE WRITING
Fred Chappell.

RICHARD M. WEAVER AWARD FOR SCHOLARLY LETTERS
Eugene Genovese.

HARRY LEVIN PRIZE

Mary Wack, *Love Sickness in the Middle Ages* (University of Pennsylvania Press).

RUTH LILLY POETRY PRIZE

Charles Wright.

LOS ANGELES TIMES BOOK PRIZES

BIOGRAPHY
John Mack Faragher, *Daniel Boone: The Life and Legend of an American Pioneer* (Holt).

CURRENT INTEREST
Peter Skerry, *Mexican Americans* (Free Press).

FICTION
Barbara Kingsolver, *Pigs in Heaven* (HarperCollins).

HISTORY
Anthony Grafton, *New Worlds, Ancient Texts: The Power of Tradition and the Shock of Discovery* (Harvard University Press).

ROBERT KIRSCH AWARD
Carolyn See.

POETRY
Mark Doty, *My Alexandria* (University of Illinois Press).

SCIENCE AND TECHNOLOGY
Daniel McNeill and Paul Freiberger, *Fuzzy Logic: The Discovery of a Revolutionary Computer Technology — and How It Is Changing Our World* (Simon & Schuster).

ART SEIDENBAUM AWARD FOR FIRST FICTION
Paul Kafka, *Love (Enter)* (Houghton Mifflin).

EDWARD MACDOWELL MEDAL

Harry Callahan.

NATIONAL BOOK AWARDS

FICTION
E. Annie Proulx, *The Shipping News* (Scribners).

NONFICTION
Gore Vidal, *The United States: Essays, 1952–1992* (Random House).

POETRY
A. R. Ammons, *Garbage* (Norton).

NATIONAL BOOK CRITICS CIRCLE AWARDS

BIOGRAPHY
Edmund White, *Genet* (Knopf).

CRITICISM
John Dizikes, *Opera in America* (Yale University Press).

FICTION
Ernest J. Gaines, *A Lesson Before Dying* (Knopf).

GENERAL NONFICTION
Alan Lomax, *The Land Where the Blues Began* (Pantheon).

POETRY
Mark Doty, "My Alexandria" (University of Illinois Press).

NATIONAL JEWISH BOOK AWARDS

MAURICE AMADO FOUNDATION AWARD FOR SEPHARDIC STUDIES
Jane S. Gerber, *The Jews of Spain: A History of the Sephardic Experience* (Free Press).

ARETE FOUNDATION AWARD FOR FICTION
A. B. Yehoshua, *Mr. Mani,* translated by Hillel Halkin (Doubleday).

GERRARD AND ELLA BERMAN AWARD FOR JEWISH HISTORY
Naomi W. Cohen, *Jews in Christian America* (Oxford University Press).

SANDRA BRAND AND ARIK WEINTRAUB AWARD FOR AUTOBIOGRAPHY AND MEMOIR
Norman Manea, *On Clowns: The Dictator and the Artist* (Grove Weidenfeld).

THE BARBARA COHEN MEMORIAL AWARD FOR CHILDREN'S LITERATURE
Karen Hesse, *Letters from Rifka* (Holt).

JEWISH THOUGHT
Susan Starr Sered, *Women as Ritual Experts: The Religious Lives of Elderly Jewish Women in Jerusalem* (Oxford University Press).

LEON JOLSON AWARD FOR BOOKS ON THE HOLOCAUST
Christopher R. Browning, *Ordinary Men: Reserve Police Battalion 101 and the Final Solution in Poland* (Aaron Asher Books/HarperCollins).

MORRIS J. AND BETTY KAPLUN AWARD FOR BOOKS ON ISRAEL
Anita Shapira, *Land and Power: The Zionist Resort to Force, 1881–1948* (Oxford University Press).

SARAH H. AND JULIUS KUSHNER MEMORIAL AWARD FOR SCHOLARSHIP
Ephraim Kanarfogel, *Jewish Education and Society in the High Middle Ages* (Wayne State University Press).

RONALD LAUDER FOUNDATION AWARD FOR BOOKS ON CONTEMPORARY JEWISH LIFE
William B. Helmreich, *Against All Odds: Holocaust Survivors and the Successful Lives They Made in America* (Simon & Schuster).

RAPHAEL PATAI AWARD FOR JEWISH FOLKLORE AND ANTHROPOLOGY
Jerome R. Mintz, *Hasidic People: A Place in the New World* (Harvard University Press).

MARCIA AND LOUIS POSNER AWARD FOR CHILDREN'S PICTURE BOOK
Michael J. Rosen, *Elijah's Angel,* illustrated by Aminah Brenda Lynn Robinson (Harcourt Brace Jovanovich).

VISUAL ARTS
The Jews: A Treasury of Arts and Literature, edited by Sharon R. Keller (Hugh Lauter Levin/Macmillan).

JOHN T. NEWBERY MEDAL

Cynthia Rylant, *Missing May* (Orchard).

NOBEL PRIZE FOR LITERATURE

Toni Morrison.

FRANCIS PARKMAN PRIZE

David McCullough, *Truman* (Simon & Schuster).

PEN AMERICAN CENTER AWARDS

PEN/MARTHA ALBRAND AWARD FOR NONFICTION
David G. Campbell, *The Crystal Desert: Summers in Antartica* (Houghton Mifflin).

PEN/BOOK-OF-THE-MONTH CLUB
TRANSLATION PRIZE
> Thomas Hoisington, *The Adventures of Mr. Nicholas* (Northwestern University Press).

PEN/JERARD FUND AWARD FOR
NONFICTION IN PROGRESS
> Patricia Foster, *A Female Education.*

PEN/NORMA KLEIN AWARD
> Graham Salisbury, *Blue Skin of the Sea* (Dell).

PEN/MALAMUD AWARD (1992)
> Eudora Welty.

PEN/SPIELVOGEL-DIAMONSTEIN AWARD
> Frederick Crews, *The Critics Bear It Away: American Fiction and the Academy* (Random House).

RENATO POGGIOLI ITALIAN
TRANSLATION AWARD FOR
WORK IN PROGRESS
> Ann Goldstein, *Journey to the Land of Flies.*

PHI BETA KAPPA AWARDS

RALPH WALDO EMERSON AWARD
> Theda Skocpol, *Protecting Soldiers and Mothers* (Harvard University Press).

CHRISTIAN GAUSS AWARD
> Eric Sundquist, *To Wake the Nation* (Harvard University Press).

SCIENCE
> Garrett Hardin, *Living Within Limits* (Oxford University Press).

EDGAR ALLAN POE AWARDS

BEST MYSTERY
> Michael Connelly, *The Black Echo* (Little, Brown).

JUVENILE
> Eve Bunting, *Coffin on a Case* (HarperCollins).

POET LAUREATE OF THE UNITED STATES

> Rita Dove.

POETRY MAGAZINE AWARDS

OSCAR BLUMENTHAL PRIZE
> Billy Collins.

FREDERICK BOCK PRIZE
> Jane Kenyon.

GEORGE BOGIN PRIZE
> Julie Suk.

KEMP PRIZE
> Allison Funk.

LEVINSON PRIZE
> May Sarton.

EUNICE TIETJENS PRIZE
> Joe-Anne McLaughlin Carruth.

UNION LEAGUE PRIZE
> William Matthews.

PULITZER PRIZES

BIOGRAPHY
> David McCullough, *Truman* (Simon & Schuster).

FICTION
> Robert Olen Butler, *A Good Scent From a Strange Mountain* (Holt).

GENERAL NONFICTION
> Garry Wills, *Lincoln at Gettysburg* (Simon & Schuster).

HISTORY
> Gordon S. Wood, *Radicalism of the American Revolution* (Knopf).

POETRY
> Louise Glück, *The Wild Iris* (Ecco).

QPB AWARDS

NEW VISIONS AWARD
> Melissa Faye Greene, *Praying for Sheetrock* (Caddison Wesley).

NEW VOICES AWARD
> Sandra Cisneros, *Woman Hollering Creek and Other Stories* (Random House).

REA AWARD FOR THE SHORT STORY

> Grace Paley.

TEXAS INSTITUTE OF LETTERS LITERARY AWARDS

BOOK PUBLISHERS OF TEXAS AWARD FOR BEST BOOK FOR CHILDREN OR YOUNG ADULTS

Sherry Garland, *Song of the Buffalo Boy* (Harcourt Brace Jovanovich).

BRAZOS BOOKSTORE AWARD FOR BEST SHORT STORY

William Cobb, "The Atmosphere of Venus" (*Literary Magazine*).

CARR P. COLLINS AWARD FOR NONFICTION

David Weber, *Spanish Frontier in North America* (Yale University Press).

SOEURETTE DIEHL FRASER AWARD FOR BEST BOOK OF TRANSLATION

Christopher Middleton and Letitia Garza-Falcon, *Andalusian Poems* (Taylor & Godine).

FRIENDS OF THE DALLAS PUBLIC LIBRARY AWARD FOR CONTRIBUTION FOR KNOWLEDGE

Joel Barna, *See Through Years: Creation and Destruction in Texas Architecture* (Rice University Press).

JESSE JONES AWARD FOR FICTION

Cormac McCarthy, *All the Pretty Horses* (Knopf).

NATALIE ORNISH AWARD FOR POETRY

Susan Wood, *Campo Santo* (Louisiana State University Press).

LON TINKLE AWARD

Vassar Miller.

KINGSLEY TUFTS POETRY AWARD

Susan Mitchell, *Rapture* (Harper Perennial).

WHITING AWARDS

Jeffrey Eugenides, Dagoberto Gilb, Kevin Kling, Mark Levine, Nathaniel Mackey, Dionisio D. Martinez, Sigrid Nunez, Janet Peery, Kathleen Peirce, Lisa Shea.

THORTON NIVEN WILDER PRIZE

Najaf Darycabandari, Lazlo Gy Horvath, Peter Magnus.

WILLIAM CARLOS WILLIAMS AWARD

Louise Glück, *The Wild Iris* (Ecco).

Checklist: Contributions to Literary History and Biography

This checklist is a selection of new books on various aspects of literary and cultural history, including biographies, memoirs, and correspondence of literary people and their associates.

Baker, Deborah. *In Extremis: The Life of Laura Riding.* New York: Grove, 1993.

Bannet, Eve Tavor. *Postcultural Theory: Critical Theory after the Marxist Paradigm.* New York: Paragon, 1993.

Beaumann, Nicola. *Morgan: A Biography of E. M. Forster.* London: Hodder & Stoughton, 1993.

Beckson, Karl. *London in the 1890s: A Cultural History.* London: Norton, 1993.

Bell, Ian. *Dreams of Exile: Robert Louis Stevenson: A Biography.* New York: Holt, 1993.

Benfy, Christopher. *The Double Life of Stephen Crane.* New York: Knopf, 1993.

Burns, Tom. *The Use of Memory: Publishing and Further Pursuits.* London: Sheed & Ward, 1993.

Coleridge, Nicholas. *Paper Tigers: The Latest, Greatest Newspaper Tycoons and How They Won the World.* London: Heinemann, 1993.

Costello, Peter. *James Joyce: The Years of Growth, 1882–1915.* New York: Pantheon, 1993.

Field, P. J. C. *The Life and Times of Sir Thomas Malory.* London: Boydell & Brewer, 1993.

Fitch, Noël Riley. *The Erotic Life of Anaïs Nin.* Boston: Little, Brown, 1993.

Fitzgerald, F. Scott. *The Love of the Last Tycoon: A Western,* edited by Matthew J. Bruccoli. Cambridge: Cambridge University Press, 1993.

Fountain, Charles. *Sportswriter: The Life and Times of Grantland Rice.* New York: Oxford University Press, 1993.

Gates, Norman T. *Richard Aldington: An Autobiography in Letters.* University Park: Pennsylvania State University Press, 1993.

Givner, Joan. *The Self-Portrait of a Literary Biographer.* Athens: University of Georgia Press, 1993.

Glendinning, Victoria. *Anthony Trollope.* New York: Knopf, 1993.

Gooch, Brad. *City Poet: The Life and Times of Frank O'Hara.* New York: Knopf, 1993.

Heath-Stubbs, John. *Hindsights: An Autobiography.* London: Hodder & Stoughton, 1993.

Judt, Tony. *Past Imperfect: French Intellectuals 1944–1956.* Berkeley: University of California Press, 1993.

Kavanaugh, Thomas M. *Enlightenment and the Shadows of Chance: The Novel and the Culture of Gambling in Eighteenth Century France.* Baltimore: Johns Hopkins University Press, 1993.

Krohn, Claus-Dieter. *Intellectuals in Exile: Refugee Scholars and the New School for Social Research.* Amherst: University of Massachusetts Press, 1993.

Leask, Nigel. *British Romantic Writers and the East: Anxieties of Empire.* London: Cambridge University Press, 1993.

Levi, Peter. *Tennyson.* New York: Macmillan, 1993.

McCormack, Jerusha Hull. *John Gray: Poet, Dandy, and Priest.* New York: Brandeis University Press, 1993.

McCormick, Donald. *17F: The Life of Ian Fleming.* London: Peter Owen, 1993.

McLynn, Frank. *Robert Louis Stevenson: A Biography.* London: Hutchinson, 1993.

Mehta, Ved. *Up at Oxford.* New York: Norton, 1993.

Meyers, Jeffrey. *Edgar Allan Poe: His Life and Legacy.* New York: Scribners, 1993.

O'Connor, Pat. *Don't Look Back: A Memoir.* New York: Moyer Bell, 1993.

O'Rourke, William. *Signs of the Literary Times: Essays, Reviews, Profiles, 1970–1992.* Ithaca, N.Y.: SUNY Press, 1993.

Ozick, Cynthia. *What Henry James Knew and Other Essays on Writers.* London: Cape, 1993.

Phillips, Robert, ed. *Delmore Schwartz and James Laughlin: Selected Letters.* New York: Norton, 1993.

Pocock, Tom. *Rider Haggard and the Lost Empire.* London: Weidenfeld & Nicolson, 1993.

Savigneau, Josyane. *Marguerite Yourcenar: Inventing a Life,* translated by Joan E. Howard. Chicago: University of Chicago Press, 1993.

Setterberg, Fred. *The Roads Taken: Travels Through America's Literary Landscapes.* Athens: University of Georgia Press, 1993.

Steele, Janet E. *The Sun Shines for All: Journalism and Ideology in the Life of Charles A. Dana.* Syracuse, N.Y.: Syracuse University Press, 1993.

Tribble, Evelyn B. *Margins and Marginality: The Printed Page in Early Modern England.* Charlottesville: University Press of Virginia, 1993.

Trilling, Diana. *The Beginning of the Journey: The Marriage of Diana and Lionel Trilling.* New York: Harcourt Brace, 1993.

Webster, Paul. *Antoine de Saint-Exupéry: The Life and Death of the Little Prince.* New York: Macmillan, 1993.

Whistler, Theresa. *Imagination of the Heart: The Life of Walter de la Mare.* London: Duckworth, 1993.

White, Edmund. *Genet: A Biography.* New York: Knopf, 1993.

Whitehead, Barbara. *Charlotte Brontë and Her 'dearest Nell': The Story of a Friendship.* London: Smith Settle, 1993.

Williams, Bernard. *Shame and Necessity*. Berkeley: University of California Press, 1993.

Wu, Duncan. *Wordsworth's Reading, 1770–1799*. Cambridge & New York: Cambridge University Press, 1993.

Zilboorg, Caroline. *Richard Aldington and H. D.: The Early Years in Letters*. Bloomington: Indiana University Press, 1993.

CATALOGUES

Roberts, Marion E., and Crosby, Everett U. *The Seventeenth-Century Restoration: Sir William Dugdale and His Circle*. Charlottesville: Department of Special Collections of the Library of the University of Virginia, 1993.

Silver, Joel. *J. K. Lilly Jr.: Bibliophile*. Bloomington: Lilly Library, Indiana University, 1993.

Necrology

Lauren Ackerman – 27 July 1993
Martin Ackerman – 2 August 1993
Wilmer Ames, Jr. – 16 February 1993
John Ashworth – 15 October 1993
Clarence Lewis Barnhart – 24 October 1993
Juan Benet – 5 January 1993
Nina Berberova – 26 September 1993
Margaret Van Doren Bevans – 14 July 1993
Clare Huchet Bishop – 11 March 1993
Wesdon Bishop – 25 May 1993
Jerome Blum – 7 May 1993
Carl Bode – 5 January 1993
Kenneth Boulding – 19 March 1993
Muriel Clara Bradbrook – 11 June 1993
Eugene Braun-Munk – 2 June 1993
William C. Brinkley – 22 November 1993
John Brooks – 27 July 1993
Chandler Brossard – 29 August 1993
Joseph Bryan III – 3 April 1993
Anthony Burgess – 25 November 1993
Kenneth Burke – 19 November 1993
Thomas Campbell – 11 July 1993
Gerald J. Carroll – 30 September 1993
Leslie Charteris – 15 April 1993
T. D. Clareson – 6 July 1993
Jerry Cohen – 8 May 1993
Elizabeth B. Coker – 1 September 1993
Louis O. Coxe – 25 May 1993
Robert Crichton – 23 March 1993
Martha Dalrymple – 1 March 1993
Mack David – 30 December 1993
Lillian de la Torre – 13 September 1993
Peter De Vries – 28 September 1993
Peggy Dennis – 25 September 1993
Joseph I. Dirwin – 4 July 1993
Tahar Djaout – 2 June 1993
Maurice Dolbier – 20 October 1993
W. J. Dorvillier – 5 May 1993
Arthur Dreifuss – 31 December 1993
William Pène du Bois – 5 February 1993
Andrea Boroff Eagan – 9 March 1993
Edwin Emery – 15 September 1993
Albert R. Erskine – 3 February 1993
Gordon W. Fawcett – 16 January 1993
Peter Fleischmann – 17 April 1993

Manuel da Forseca – 12 March 1993
Lacey Fosburgh – 11 January 1993
Frank Freidel – 25 January 1993
Kimon Friar – 25 May 1993
Daniel Fuchs – 26 July 1993
Yevgeny Gabrilovich – 6 December 1993
Christian Geelhaar – 31 December 1993
Penelope Gilliatt – 9 May 1993
William Golding – 19 June 1993
Charles Gosnell – 1 July 1993
Jean Gould – 8 February 1993
Nixon Griffis – 17 December 1993
Louis Grudin – 28 May 1993
Frederick Gutheim – 2 October 1993
Oliver Hailey – 23 January 1993
David Halvorsen – 29 September 1993
MacDonald Harris – 24 July 1993
Kiyoshi Hayakawa – 9 July 1993
Henry Hazlitt – 9 July 1993
William Randolph Hearst, Jr. – 14 May 1993
Maggie Hemingway – 9 May 1993
Charles Hepler – 24 May 1993
James Lee Herlihy – 21 October 1993
John Hersey – 24 March 1993
Eleanor Hibbert – 18 January 1993
Adamson Hoebel – 23 July 1993
Diana Holman-Hunt – 10 August 1993
Cy Howard – 29 April 1993
Irving Howe – 5 May 1993
Dorothy B. Hughes – 6 May 1993
Eliot Janeway – 8 February 1993
Hans Jonas – 5 February 1993
Aben Kandel – 28 January 1993
Abraham Kaplan – 19 June 1993
Jeremiah Kaplan – 10 August 1993
Patrick Kelly – 10 December 1993
Philip Klein – 15 February 1993
Fletcher Knebel – 26 February 1993
Julia Knickerbocker – 16 May 1993
Max Knight – 31 August 1993
Ruth Krauss – 10 July 1993
Ronald P. Kriss – 24 March 1993
Donald Kvares – 4 May 1993
Genevieve M. Landau – 29 June 1993
Margaret Landon – 4 December 1993

Irving Lazar – 30 December 1993
Richard Lederer – 28 January 1993
Eugenie Leontovich – 2 April 1993
Eleazar Lipsky – 14 February 1993
Coleman Lollar – 8 June 1993
Mary Luke – 24 November 1993
Roger MacDougall – 27 May 1993
Joseph L. Mankiewicz – 5 February 1993
Arthur Mann – 7 February 1993
Linda M. Martelli – 14 August 1993
May D. H. Martenet – 6 June 1993
Donald McAllister – 22 July 1993
Katharine McClinton – 27 January 1993
George McCorkle – 6 May 1993
William C. McNeil – 18 April 1993
Edith Meiser – 26 September 1993
Gerard P. Meyer – 23 February 1993
C. F. Mooney – 25 September 1993
Virginia Moore – 11 June 1993
Alice S. Morris – 24 September 1993
Terry Morris – 16 September 1993
Roger G. Morvan – 22 May 1993
Richard Murphy – 19 May 1993
John Murray VI – 22 July 1993
Frederick Nicklaus – 23 March 1993
Oodgeroo Noonuccal – 17 September 1993
Russel Nye – 2 September 1993
William Nygaard – 11 October 1993
William Ober – 27 April 1993
Monsignor J. M. Oesterreicher – 18 April 1993
David Paley – 4 July 1993
Saul Pett – 14 June 1993
Bruce Peyton – 25 December 1993
Eugene B. Power – 6 October 1993
Albert Prago – 27 July 1993
Gabriel Preil – 5 June 1993
Tom Prideaux – 8 May 1993
Joseph Pulitzer, Jr. – 26 May 1993
Peter Quennell – 27 October 1993
David Rattray – 22 March 1993
René Ray – 31 August 1993
Lester del Rey – 10 May 1993
Dorothy Roberts – 23 April 1993

Harold Rome – 26 October 1993
Richard Rosen – 13 July 1993
Arthur Roth – 5 March 1993
George Rudé – 8 January 1993
John Ryan – 15 April 1993
Otto R. Salassi – 10 February 1993
Harrison E. Salisbury – 5 July 1993
Leo Salkin – 13 October 1993
Penrod Scofield – 5 November 1993
Nelson Seitel – 14 July 1993
Julian Semyonov – 14 September 1993
Christopher Sergel – 7 May 1993
Louis Sheaffer – 7 August 1993
William L. Shirer – 28 December 1993
John Smart – 29 November 1993
Charles W. F. Smith – 18 July 1993
Kay Nolte Smith – 25 September 1993
Scott Sommer – 15 November 1993
Radcliffe Squires – 14 February 1993
William Edgar Stafford – 28 August 1993
Dame Freya Stark – 9 May 1993
Wallace Stegner – 13 April 1993
Chris Steinbrunner – 7 July 1993
James Stern – 22 November 1993
Samuel Steward – 31 December 1993
Harry A. Sylvester – 26 September 1993
Herbert Tarr – 18 November 1993
Harold Taylor – 9 February 1993
Walter Teller – 17 February 1993
John M. Todd – 9 June 1993
Edna Amadon Toney – 13 April 1993
James B. Townsend – 13 December 1993
Andrew Tully – 27 September 1993
Dorothy Van Doren – 21 February 1993
Barry K. Wader – 3 March 1993
John M. Wallace – 6 October 1993
Sam Wanamaker – 18 December 1993
Morris T. Weeks, Jr. – 22 July 1993
Robert Westall – 15 April 1993
Maxine Wood – 7 April 1993
Paul Zimmerman – 2 March 1993
Sam Zolotow – 21 October 1993
Lord Zuckerman – 1 April 1993

Contributors

Nan Bowman Albinski ....Pennsylvania State University
Elizabeth S. Bell ....University of South Carolina – Aiken
Edmund Berkeley.......................................Alderman Library, The University of Virginia
Richard R. Centing...Ohio State University
John Y. Cole ....Library of Congress
Simon Eliot ....Open University, Bristol, England
Amy Farmer ....University of Illinois – Urbana
Barry Faulk ....University of Illinois – Urbana
Suzanne Ferguson..Case Western Reserve University
John Foley..Silver Springs, Maryland
William Foltz...University of Hawaii
George Garrett...University of Virginia
Mary C. Grattan...Ashland, Virginia
Nicholas Grene ....Trinity College, Dublin
Caroline Hunt ....College of Charleston
Dean H. Keller...Kent State University
Howard Kissel...New York Daily News
Hugh L'Etang...London, England
Gabriel Miller..Rutgers University
Merritt Moseley ....University of North Carolina at Asheville
Pip Plummer..Shakespeare's Globe
David R. Slavitt ....University of Pennsylvania
Charles Stiles...Wilfred Owen Association
Ernest Suarez...The Catholic University of America
Terry Teachout ....New York Daily News
Kristin van Ogtrop..Vogue Magazine
Nancy A. Walker..Vanderbilt University
Robin W. Winks ....Yale University

Cumulative Index

Dictionary of Literary Biography, Volumes 1-139
Dictionary of Literary Biography Yearbook, 1980-1993
Dictionary of Literary Biography Documentary Series, Volumes 1-11

Cumulative Index

DLB before number: *Dictionary of Literary Biography*, Volumes 1-139
Y before number: *Dictionary of Literary Biography Yearbook*, 1980-1993
DS before number: *Dictionary of Literary Biography Documentary Series*, Volumes 1-11

Cumulative Index

Cumulative Index

C

E

K

Cumulative Index

ISBN 0-8103-5560-4

(Continued from front endsheets)

Documentary Series

Yearbooks